THE COBB GROUP

Word 5

Companion

THE COBB GROUP

Word 5
Companion

THE COBB GROUP

Gena B. Cobb
Allan McGuffey
Judy Mynhier
with Mark Nieker

Microsoft PRESS

PUBLISHED BY
Microsoft Press
A Division of Microsoft Corporation
One Microsoft Way
Redmond, Washington 98052-6399

Library of Congress Cataloging-in-Publication Data

Cobb, Gena B. (Gena Berg)
    Word 5 companion / Gena B. Cobb, Judy Mynhier, McGuffey, Allan
with Mark Nieker.
        p.   cm.
    Includes index.
    ISBN 1-55615-399-6
    1. Microsoft Word (Computer program)   2. Word processing--Computer
programs.   I. Mynhier, Judy.   II. McGuffey, Allan.   III. Title.
IV. Title: Word five companion.
Z52.5.M52C633   1991
652.5'536--dc20   91-31901
                                              CIP

Printed and bound in the United States of America.

    4 5 6 7 8 9   AGAG   7 6 5 4 3 2

Distributed to the book trade in Canada by Macmillan of Canada, a division of
Canada Publishing Corporation.

Distributed to the book trade outside the United States and Canada by Penguin Books Ltd.

Penguin Books Ltd., Harmondsworth, Middlesex, England
Penguin Books Australia Ltd., Ringwood, Victoria, Australia
Penguin Books N.Z. Ltd., 182-190 Wairau Road, Auckland 10, New Zealand

British Cataloging-in-Publication Data available.

Acquisitions Editor: Marjorie Schlaikjer
Project Editor: Casey D. Doyle
Editing and Technical Review: Online Press Inc.

Contents

SECTION ONE

The Preliminaries

1 Touring Microsoft Word   3

The Word screen ■ Windows ■ Telling Word what to do ■ The mouse pointer ■ The keyboard

2 Handling Files   23

Creating new documents ■ Opening existing documents ■ Saving your work ■ Closing documents and quitting Word

SECTION TWO

Word Basics

3 Working in Word   35

Entering text ■ Selecting the basic elements of a document ■ Navigating in your document ■ Editing basics ■ Copying and moving text ■ Canceling and repeating actions

4 Formatting Characters   69

Understanding the language of type ■ Formatting characters

5 Formatting Documents and Paragraphs   87

Applying top-down document design ■ Establishing basic page layout ■ Paragraph formatting ■ The Paragraph dialog box ■ Working with tabs ■ Working with borders ■ Applying shading to a paragraph

SECTION FOUR

Word-Processing Utilities

SECTION FIVE

Customizing Word

SECTION SIX

Appendixes

Acknowledgments

Although my name appears as an author of this book, many people have been involved in producing *Word 5 Companion*. I'd like to thank and acknowledge Gena B. Cobb, Allan McGuffey, and Judy Mynhier of the Cobb Group, for writing the best book on Word; Erin O'Connor, Mary DeJong, and Sally Brunsman, for guiding my own writing early on; and David Pearce, for providing beta support and assistance.

I'd also like to thank Joyce Cox, Jane Schulman, and Polly Fox Urban, who unified the old and new text, improving both considerably in the process; Pat Kervran, technical editor, who ensured the accuracy and clarity of the text and figures; and Ruth Pettis, Lisa Sandburg, and Peggy Herman, members of the production staff of Microsoft Press, who made sure that everything came together and looked exactly right.

Finally, I'm particularly indebted to Marjorie Schlaikjer, who provided me with the opportunity to write this book; and to Casey Doyle, who kept an amazing number of balls in the air during the project.

Introduction: Getting Started

Microsoft Word was the first word processor to take full advantage of the Apple Macintosh graphical user interface, and over the years the addition of proofing and layout capabilities and table and print preview features have ensured Word's position as the most powerful word processor available for this popular personal computer.

Word 5—the newest version of Microsoft Word—adds even more power and flexibility. Designed to be fully compatible with System 7, Word 5 makes the most of System 7's file and data sharing capabilities—enabling you to publish, subscribe, and link data between Word and other Macintosh programs. Other new features—including the ability to create and modify graphics, check and evaluate style and grammar, convert files created in other applications, and add voice annotations to Word documents—make Word 5 the application of choice for virtually all your word-processing needs.

Updates to existing features—including the addition of a ribbon that lets you apply character formatting directly, the introduction of drag-and-drop text editing, and the enhancement of Word's Find, Replace, and Print Merge commands—also enable you to create documents more easily and effectively than ever before. If you're already a Word 4 user, you'll find these new commands and features remarkable time-savers. If Word 5 is your first word processor, you'll be amazed at all that Word has to offer.

In this introduction, we give you an overview of the features that are new to Word 5. We also review the program's hardware and printer installation requirements and show you how to install the Word program software on your hard disk. At the end of the chapter, we discuss Word's balloon help feature and the Help command, which provide detailed quick-reference information about Word commands and options.

What's new in Word 5

If you're familiar with Word 4, you'll notice a change to Microsoft Word as soon as you begin installation. Word 5 is considerably larger than previous versions—in fact, the complete program requires about 7 megabytes (MB) of space. The Word program and its supporting files have been compressed to fit on the five installation disks. You need to use Word's installer program to decompress and install the files on your hard drive. We show you how to install Word in a few moments.

More than likely, you'll want to know something about Word's new features before you begin installation. The lists below introduce all that's new to Word 5. The items in the first list are an integral part of the new Word program—they are installed automatically, and you can use them immediately. The items in the second list are supplementary—you can install them optionally. Knowing the difference between the two when you install Word will enable you to control the amount of space that Word occupies on your hard drive. (If you choose not to install an optional item, you can always use the Installer program later to copy the item to your hard drive.) For detailed information about the items in the lists, refer to the chapter that follows each item's description.

A few new features—most notably Publish and Subscribe, which require System 7, and the voice annotation recording commands, which are operational only on a Macintosh equipped with a microphone—require software or hardware that might not be part of your Macintosh configuration.

New Word program features

These new features are an integral part of the Word 5 program. (You can take advantage of them even if you install only the Word program.)

- **New menus:** Word 5 has three new menus—View, Insert, and Tools—which replace the Document and Utilities menus on the Word 4 menu bar. Word 5 has no Full/Short Menus command; instead, the Word 5 menus have been reorganized to make it easy to locate the command you want. (Chapter 1 "Touring Microsoft Word.")

- **New commands, command names, and keystroke shortcuts:** Word 5 has several new commands. In addition, a few commands that could previously be chosen only by keystroke—Page Break and Section Break, for example—have been added to Word menus. Some command names and keystroke shortcuts have also changed slightly. If these improvements don't meet all your needs, you can easily customize Word menus and keystroke shortcuts. (We introduce Word commands and keystroke shortcuts throughout *The Word 5 Companion*. Chapter 18, "Customizing Word," describes customizing Word in detail.)

- **Drag-and-drop editing:** Word's new drag-and-drop editing feature enables you to cut and copy selected text or graphics using only the mouse. You simply highlight the selection, click it, drag the mouse to indicate the selection's new location, and then release the mouse button. Pressing the Command key as you drag puts a copy of the selection at the insertion-point location when you release the mouse button. (Chapter 3, "Working in Word.")

- **Ribbon:** In addition to the ruler, the top of the document window now displays an icon bar called the ribbon with which you can change the font and font size, apply character formatting, display Word's graphics window and formatting marks, and specify columns directly from the document window. (Chapter 4, "Formatting Characters.")

- **Change character case:** The Change Case command on the Format menu enables you to change the case of selected text. (Chapter 4, "Formatting Characters.")

- **Borders and shading:** The Borders command on the Format menu allows you to apply borders and shading to selected paragraphs and table cells. (Chapter 5, "Formatting Documents and Paragraphs.")

- **Frame positioning:** You can insert and position a new frame in your document in a single step by choosing Frame from the Insert menu. Frames are positioning tools that allow you to place text or graphics as blocks that text can flow around. (Chapter 10, "Creating Professional Documents.")

- **Document summary information:** The Summary Info command on the File menu lets you establish information about a Word document that you can specify later when locating the file with Word's Find File command. (Chapter 2, "Handling Files.")

- **Print Merge Helper bar:** The Print Merge Helper command on the View menu simplifies the creation of print merge documents. After you specify the print merge fields that will appear in your merge document, Word automatically inserts print merge field names—along with print merge instructions—in a Print Merge Helper bar at the top of your main document. Selecting field names from the Print Merge Helper bar ensures consistency and speedy completion of the main document. (Chapter 15, "Merging Documents.")

- **Publish and subscribe capability:** If you're using System 7, you can use the Create Publisher and Subscribe To commands on the Edit menu to establish dynamic links between Word documents and documents created by other applications. The Create Publisher command lets you make selected text and graphics available to other documents. The Subscribe To command lets you access information in another file and link it to the currently active Word document. You can use these commands to share information with any application that supports System 7. If you're not using System 7, these commands are dimmed on the Edit menu. However, you can use Word's Link commands to exchange information with applications that support linking. (Chapter 16, "Finding and Sharing Files.")

- **Object embedding:** The Object command on the Insert menu enables you to insert an object, such as text or a graphic, as well as the information used to create the object in the original application. Double-clicking the imported text or graphic automatically opens the originating application, where you can make changes immediately—without closing Word. You can also insert a complete document at the insertion point by choosing File from the Insert menu. (Chapter 16, "Finding and Sharing Files," and Chapter 13, "Using Word Tools.")

- **Additional features:** Word 5 has been changed in other helpful ways. Many commands—Find and Replace, for example—have been enhanced, and the appearance of many Word dialog boxes has been changed to better accommodate their new capabilities. In addition, the number of customizing options available in the Preferences dialog box has increased considerably in Word 5. (We introduce each Word command in detail throughout *The Word 5 Companion*. Chapter 18, "Customizing Word," discusses the Preferences command.)

New supplemental commands and features

In addition to the many commands that are automatically installed with the Word program, you can optionally install the following supplemental commands and features that are new to Word 5:

- **Supplemental glossaries:** The Standard Glossary accessed using the Glossary command on the Edit menu is now supplemented by a Date and Time Glossary, a Page Layout Glossary, and a Formula Glossary, each of which contains predefined entries that you can insert directly in your documents. (Chapter 13, "Using Word Tools.")

- **Spelling:** The Spelling command on the Tools menu now recognizes repeated words in your document. The appearance of custom dictionaries has changed, and you can now instruct Word not to offer suggested replacements for an unfamiliar word. (Chapter 7, "Editing and Proofing.")

- **Grammar:** The Grammar command on the Tools menu checks the style and grammar of a single text selection or of your entire document. You can use Word's recommended style and grammar rules or check only for the errors you consider important. When you finish proofing a document, Word evaluates your writing style and displays document statistics that tell you how easy your writing is to understand. (Chapter 7, "Editing and Proofing.")

- **Thesaurus:** The Thesaurus command on the Tools menu enables you to view the synonyms and antonyms of a selected word. When you find the word you're looking for, you can substitute it for the original word in your document. (Chapter 7, "Editing and Proofing.")

- **Picture:** The Picture command on the Insert menu enables you to create and edit pictures and graphics within Word. You can create simple illustrations, combine text with graphics, or import graphics created in other applications. Word inserts completed graphics in a frame that you can resize or position anywhere on the document page. (Chapter 6, "Creating Graphics.")

- **Find File:** The Find File command on the File menu lets you search for a file based on selection criteria that you specify. You can search for any file on any drive—you're not limited to Word files. When you find the file you're looking for, you can open, print, or preview its contents directly in the Find File dialog box. (Chapter 16, "Finding and Sharing Files.")

- **Symbol:** The Symbol command on the Insert menu lets you view and insert characters provided by a selected font. Installing this command enables you to display the Symbol window, where you can specify the font whose characters you want to view. You can then insert a character in a document simply by clicking it. (Chapter 13, "Using Word Tools.")

- **Equation Editor:** Word's ability to create simple mathematical formulas is now enhanced by the new stand-alone Equation Editor program, with which you can create, edit, and format mathematical equations that you can then insert in your Word documents as graphics. You can use this program by itself, or you can access it from within Word by choosing the Object command from the Insert menu. (Appendix D, "Using the Equation Editor Program.")

- **Voice Annotation:** The Voice Annotation command on the Insert menu enables you to add audio messages to your Word documents. Your Macintosh must be equipped with a microphone for you to create a voice annotation, but you can listen to a recorded message on any Macintosh that runs Word, by choosing Voice Annotations from the View menu. (Appendix E, "Voice Annotation.")

- **Microsoft Word stationery:** You can now save a Word document as a stationery file. Saving a document as stationery in the Save As dialog box lets you use the document as a template with which you can recreate often-used text, formats, or layouts automatically. (Chapter 16, "Finding and Sharing Files.")

- **Automatic file converters:** Installing Word's automatic file converters enables you to open files created in other Macintosh and PC-based programs in Word and lets you save Word documents in a format that can be interpreted by these programs. (Chapter 17, "Importing and Exporting Text and Graphics.")

- **Additional files:** Word 5 comes with a number of additional files, including practice documents, system resource files, and supplemental settings files.

Hardware and memory requirements

To run Word 5, you need a Macintosh Plus or a later Macintosh model with a hard disk and one floppy drive. You must be running Apple system software version 6.0 or later.

The Word program itself is approximately 850 kilobytes (KB). Full installation—including all Word files and commands—takes approximately 7 MB of disk space. To display the size of a supplemental file, click the Customize button in the Easy Install dialog box during installation, and then click each filename to display the amount of disk space that file requires. (We discuss installing Word in detail in a moment.)

The amount of random access memory (RAM) required for your system configuration depends on the system and the software you use. In addition to disk space, you should have at least 2 MB of RAM free to run Word. If you install the Grammar command, you must have at least 4 MB of RAM available. If you're not using System 7 or Multifinder, Word requires at least 1 MB of RAM and 2 MB is recommended. To use the Grammar command without System 7 or Multifinder, you need 2 MB of RAM.

You can change the amount of RAM available to Word by selecting the Microsoft Word icon at the Finder level, choosing Get Info, and then typing a new amount of memory in the Application Memory Size box at the bottom of the Get

Info dialog box. While working in Word, you can reduce the amount of RAM that Word needs by closing documents you're not using. And you can increase the amount of available memory by closing document windows and applications you're not using. (For more information about allocating memory and using the Get Info dialog box, see your system software documentation.)

Installing a printer

As you know, before you can use a printer to print the documents you create on your Macintosh, you must copy the resource file for that printer into the System folder on your hard disk. The printer resource files for most Apple printers and the instructions you'll need to copy the file that corresponds to your printer are part of your system software package. Your system software also includes a Print Monitor resource, which you must install in the System folder if you want to print in the background.

To install a printer, you must specify it in the Chooser dialog box. Display the dialog box by selecting the Chooser command from the Apple menu. As Chapter 8, "Printing," explains, the printer you specify significantly affects the layout of Word documents, so you should select the printer in the Chooser dialog box even if you don't plan to actually print your documents.

Chapter 8 discusses using Word with the ImageWriter and LaserWriter print-ers—the two most common Apple printers. We recommend that you use a Laser-Writer printer if you require high-quality printouts. For this book, we used a LaserWriter printer to produce our sample printouts because the ImageWriter's dot-matrix output doesn't lend itself to reproduction. If you're not using an Apple printer, you might experience some compatibility problems when you print. For example, you might find that some fonts can't be reproduced on your printer. Your printer might support only fixed-pitch fonts and be unable to handle the proportionally spaced fonts normally available with Word. See your printer's manual for more information about configuring the printer to communicate with the Macintosh. If you're deciding which printer to purchase, we suggest that you ask your local dealer about compatibility with your Macintosh and that you see a demonstration of the printer's performance.

Installing Word

The first step in installing Word is to make copies of the disks that come in the Word 5 software package. Word 5 is shipped on five disks: Install, Program, Con-verters, Proofing Tools, and Commands. The information stored on each disk has been compressed so that the Word program and its supporting files can be easily packaged. After you've made the copies, use Word's Installer program to install the Word files and utilities you select.

The Installer program is on the Install disk in your Word software package. Using Word's Installer ensures that the files are properly decompressed and arranged on your hard drive. If you have enough available memory and plan to use all Word's files and commands, you'll probably want to let Word install the files and commands automatically. You can then use Word for a while and decide which files you need and which you don't. You can also specify which supplementary commands and features you want to install in addition to the Word program to conserve the amount of storage space required by Word. During installation, you can specify the default font and the size for text in your Word documents.

To begin installation, first deactivate any virus-protection programs installed in your System folder. Next insert the Install disk in your Macintosh disk drive, and double-click the Installer icon shown in Figure I-1. After a moment, the Installer program displays a greeting. Click OK, and when an alert box appears—if you're sure all virus protection is completely turned off—click Continue to display the Easy Install dialog box shown in Figure I-2.

FIGURE I-1.
To begin installation, insert the Install disk in your Macintosh disk drive, and double-click the Installer icon.

FIGURE I-2.
Use the Easy Install dialog box to specify which files you want to install on which disk.

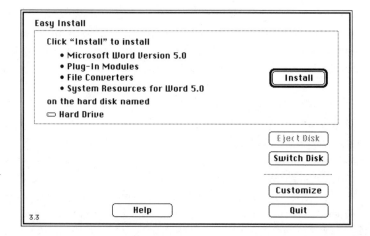

Installing the complete Word program

To install the complete Word 5 program—including all supplemental files and commands—click the Install button at the top of the Easy Install dialog box. Click the Help button to display additional information. Click Switch Disk to install Word on a different drive. Click Quit to close the dialog box without installing any Word files. (We'll discuss the Customize button later in this Introduction.)

When you click Install, the Installer first verifies that the specified disk has enough space to accommodate installation and then displays a dialog box that lets you specify where on the disk you want the Word program stored. Because the Installer creates several folders and files during installation, click New Folder to create a separate folder to contain these files and the Word program, and then specify a name for the folder. If you type *Word 5* in the Name Of New Folder Name edit bar and click Create, the dialog box looks like the one in Figure I-3. You can then click Install to begin installation.

FIGURE I-3.
*Click New Folder to
create a separate Word
folder, name the folder,
and then click Install.*

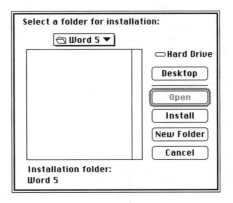

When you click the Install button, the Installer begins copying the files you'll need into the folder you've specified. As it copies, the Installer indicates the file it is currently transferring and the percentage of the total installation completed, as shown in Figure I-4 on the next page. Simply insert the remaining program disks as the Installer requests them.

After all the Word files are successfully copied to your hard drive, you'll see a message like the one in Figure I-5 on the next page. Click OK in the alert box to de-compress the Word 5 files. This process takes a few minutes. During this time, you'll see another dialog box that indicates the percentage of the file that has been decompressed.

FIGURE I-4.
As the Installer copies files to your hard drive, it indicates the current status of the Word installation.

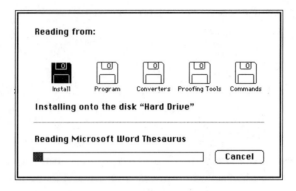

FIGURE I-5.
Click OK in this alert box to decompress the Word 5 files.

After the Word 5 files have been decompressed, you'll see the dialog box shown in Figure I-6, which enables you to select the font and size Word will apply by default to text in your documents. To accept Word's initial default settings— New York and 12 point—simply click OK. To specify different defaults, select a different font and size from the Font and Size lists. The sample in the middle of the dialog box shows you how the text will look when formatted with your selections.

FIGURE I-6.
In this dialog box, you can specify the font and size you want Word to use as the defaults for text.

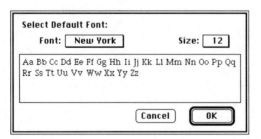

Throughout this book, our examples use Word's initial default settings: 12-point New York. If you're new to Word, we recommend that you retain these settings until you become familiar with the effect that different fonts and sizes have on your document's appearance. After you install Word, you can easily change the default font and size by choosing Default Font from the Font menu.

To finish installation, reinsert the Install disk when prompted. Word displays the dialog box shown in Figure I-7. Click the Restart button to close the Installer and restart your computer.

FIGURE I-7.
Word displays this
dialog box when
installation is
complete.

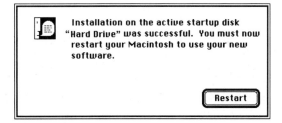

> **Installation on the active startup disk "Hard Drive" was successful. You must now restart your Macintosh to use your new software.**
>
> [**Restart**]

Customizing Word installation

Depending on your needs, you might not want to install all the files that come with the Word program. If you use Word primarily to compose letters or text documents at home, for example, you probably won't have much use for the file converters. Similarly, if you work alone on a Macintosh without a microphone, you probably won't make immediate use of Word's Voice Annotation feature. Installing these features in no way affects Word's basic operation—the Word program works exactly the same way no matter what supplemental features and commands you install. However, if space on your hard drive is limited, you can easily customize the list of files to be installed.

To specify a set of files for installation, click Customize instead of Install in the Easy Install dialog box shown earlier in Figure I-2. Word displays the dialog box shown in Figure I-8 on the next page, where you can select the files you want. Use the scroll arrows on the right side of the list box to view the files available for installation. Clicking an item from the list displays information about the item at the bottom of the dialog box. To install an item, select it, and then click Install. To select more than one item, hold down the Shift key as you make your selections.

When you begin installation, the Installer displays a dialog box like the one shown earlier in Figure I-3. If you've already installed the Word 5 program, select

FIGURE I-8.
*Clicking Customize
displays this dialog
box, where you can
specify the files you
want to install.*

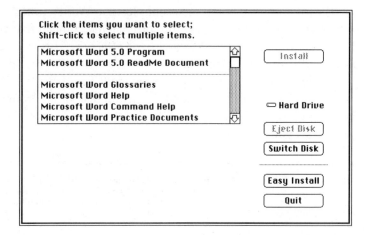

Click the items you want to select;
Shift-click to select multiple items.

Microsoft Word 5.0 Program
Microsoft Word 5.0 ReadMe Document

Microsoft Word Glossaries
Microsoft Word Help
Microsoft Word Command Help
Microsoft Word Practice Documents

Install

⊂⊃ Hard Drive

Eject Disk

Switch Disk

Easy Install

Quit

the folder in which this program is stored by using the Open button. If you're installing Word 5 for the first time, create a new folder by clicking New Folder.

When you click Install, the Installer copies the selected files to the specified
folder and asks you to insert additional installation disks as necessary. After de-
compressing the files, the Installer displays a dialog box with two buttons. (If
you're installing the Word program file, you'll also see the Default Font dialog
box shown in Figure I-6.) Click Continue to install additional files. Click Quit to
close the Installer and return to the Finder level. To begin using Word, simply
locate the folder that contains the Word 5 program, and then double-click the
Microsoft Word icon to launch the application.

Getting help

If you need more information about a Word command or if you're unsure of how
an option affects your document, you can get assistance by displaying Word's
"balloon help" or by choosing the Help command from the Window menu.
Word's balloon help feature displays an explanation of the function or purpose of
a command or option. Because this information is brief, you'll probably find it
most helpful if you're already familiar with a feature, but need a reminder to help
you along. Word's Help file gives more detailed quick-reference information
about all of Word's commands and options.

Displaying balloon help

If you're using System 7, you can display information about a Word command or
option simply by choosing Show Balloons from the Help menu at the right end of
the menu bar. (You must install Word's Command Help file during installation to
use this feature.) Then when you move the pointer over the Word document

window, you'll see small balloons that explain the function you are pointing to. For example, if you move your cursor over the word *Insert* in the middle of the Word menu bar you'll see the balloon shown in Figure I-9.

FIGURE I-9.
Choose Show Balloons
from the Help menu
and then move the
pointer to the Word
command or feature
you want to know
more about.

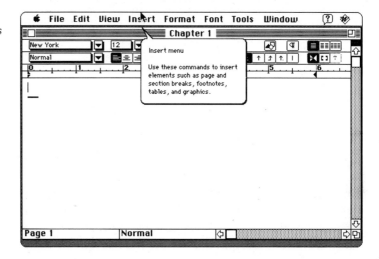

The balloon help feature comes in handy if you're new to Word or if a particular command or function isn't clear to you. As you become proficient in Word, however, you'll probably want to deactivate this feature so that you can work more quickly. (For more information about balloon help, see your System 7 software documentation.)

Displaying the Help dialog box

If you've installed the Word 5 Help file, you can display detailed information about a command or function in Word's Help dialog box. You can view help information in two ways: You can display the Help dialog box and then select the topic you want to learn more about; or because Word's Help feature is *context-sensitive*, you can directly access information that explains a particular command or feature.

To display Word's Help dialog box, choose Help from the Window menu. Word displays the dialog box shown in Figure I-10 on the next page, listing the available help topics. You can also display this dialog box by pressing Command-? twice, by pressing the Help button on the extended keyboard, or by choosing Microsoft Word Help from the Help menu.

FIGURE I-10.
*The Help dialog box
lets you select the
topic about which you
need information.*

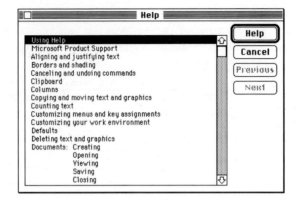

The list box on the left side of the Help dialog box serves as a table of contents to Word's quick-reference Help file. Scroll through the list box until the topic you're interested in comes into view, or type the first letter of the topic to move quickly to that part of the list. Then click the topic name, and click the Help button. For example, to select the topic *Finding and replacing text* from the topic list, type the letter *F*, scroll to that part of the list box. Then select the topic, and click Help to display the information shown in Figure I-11.

FIGURE I-11.
*Select a topic name
and click the Help
button to display
information about
a topic.*

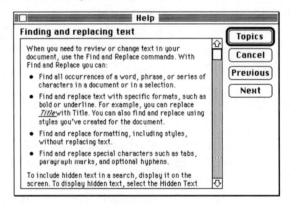

To return to the main list of topics shown in Figure I-10, click the Topics button. To move to the next topic in the list, click the Next button. To move to the previous topic, click the Previous button. To remove the Help window from your screen and return to your document window, click the Cancel button.

To go directly to the information that explains a particular command or option, press Command-?, and then choose the command or click the option or icon. Word displays the Help screen that corresponds to your selection. Similarly, you can get context-sensitive help about an open dialog box by pressing Command-? or the Help key. (You can't access the menu bar when a dialog box is open.)

For example, to learn more about the Character command on Word's Format menu, you can press Command-? and then choose the Character command instead of scrolling through the lists of general topics. Alternatively, you can open the Character dialog box and then press Command-?.

Now that you've installed Word and learned a bit about the program, you're ready to dive into the rest of the book and discover how to use this powerful program to create professional-looking documents with ease.

The Preliminaries

1

Touring Microsoft Word

*A*lthough many of its word-processing functions are quite sophisticated, Microsoft Word is remarkably easy to use, because you perform all operations in more or less the same way. After you display the Microsoft Word screen, you tell Word what you want to do by choosing the appropriate command from one of the menus at the top of the screen. In the document window below the menu bar, you enter and edit text, make it look the way you want, and view the results.

In this chapter, we introduce the menu bar and the methods of choosing commands in Word. We also discuss the document window and introduce the ribbon and the ruler—two Microsoft Word features that provide shortcuts for common commands. Finally, we discuss the pointer shapes that you see as you move the mouse across the Word screen, and we tell you how to use the keyboard to get the most out of Word.

If you're new to Microsoft Word, you'll want to read this chapter carefully. It lays the groundwork for the discussions in the rest of this book. But don't worry if you don't understand all that's presented here. We return to each concept in more detail in later chapters.

The Word screen

To help you design, create, and print your documents, Word offers four ways of viewing them. You create and edit documents in *Normal view*, which we discuss in this chapter. You can also display your document in *Outline view*, which lets you plan and rearrange longer documents; in *Page Layout view*, which lets you edit text while viewing how it will appear when printed; and in *Print Preview*, which displays the page layout of your document.

To open a new or existing document in Normal view, double-click the Microsoft Word icon on the Macintosh desktop. Word presents a screen containing four elements, like the one shown in Figure 1-1. At the top of the screen is the menu bar. The empty area that occupies the bulk of the screen is the document window, where you create, edit, and view your Word documents. At the top of the document window are the ribbon and the ruler, which enable you to make quick formatting changes to your document.

FIGURE 1-1.
When you load Word,
an empty document
window appears.

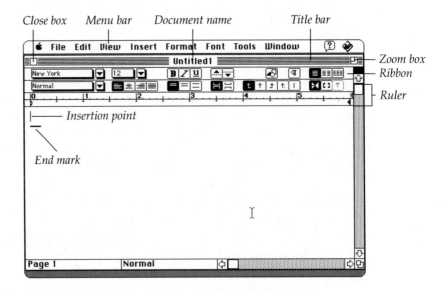

Windows

Word's document window enables you to view the contents of your document. Depending on the size of your monitor, you might not be able to view an entire document at one time. To compensate for any screen size limitations, Word allows you to manipulate the document window. You can resize the window to display more or less of your document, split the window to display different sections of the same document, and even create new windows to display duplicates of the document. Word also lets you display different documents in different windows.

In addition to letting you view your document, the document window also gives you direct access to formatting commands that change the appearance of characters and paragraphs in your text. You use the ribbon at the top of the document window to format characters, and you use the ruler, which appears below the ribbon, to format paragraphs. By default, Word displays the ribbon and ruler in each document window you open. You can tell Word not to include these elements in document windows by changing the ribbon and ruler settings in the dialog box that appears when you choose the Preferences command on the Tools menu. (We'll discuss the Preferences dialog box in Chapter 18, "Customizing Word.") You can change the ribbon and ruler display for a particular window by choosing the Ribbon and Ruler commands from the View menu.

When you open a new document, the document window contains only a horizontal line called the *end mark* and a blinking vertical bar called the *insertion point*. (You also see an I-beam pointer; we talk more about pointer shapes later in the chapter.) In a blank document, the end mark appears just below the first line in the document window, and the insertion point occupies the first character space in your document window. As you might guess, the end mark signals the end of the Word document. The insertion point indicates your current position in the document, moving one character space to the right each time you type a character. As you'll see in a minute, you can move the insertion point to indicate where you want to make changes to the document.

The title bar

At the top of the document window is the title bar. When you open a new document, Word assigns the generic name Untitled and an identifying number to the document. (We'll show you how to assign other names to your documents in Chapter 2, "Handling Files.") Notice the small boxes at either end of the title bar. Clicking the one on the left, which is called the *close box*, closes the window and removes your document from the screen. Clicking the one on the right, which is called the *zoom box*, resizes the window. As you'll see in Chapter 2, clicking in the close box is equivalent to choosing the Close command from the File menu.

The title bar does more than display the name of your document. It also indicates whether the document window is active—that is, whether you can currently work in the window. When a document window is active, Word displays dark horizontal lines on either side of the document name. As you'd expect, only one window can be active at a time. If you open another Word document, the new window becomes active, and Word removes the horizontal lines in the title bar of the old window to indicate that it is inactive. To reactivate the inactive window, click anywhere on it.

Resizing windows

When you open a document, Word initially displays it in a full-size window—that is, one that fills the screen. Word makes it easy to change the size of a document window, however. You can reduce the size in two ways: by clicking the zoom box at the right end of the title bar, or by dragging the size box located in the lower-right corner of the document window. Changing the dimensions of the document window changes only the view of your document; the document itself remains the same.

You might want to experiment with these two techniques to get a feel for when to use each. The zoom box enables you to change the size of your document window from full-screen to half-screen size. If you click in the zoom box, for example, your window looks like the one in Figure 1-2. To return the screen to full size, click the zoom box again. If you prefer, you can press Command-Option-] to zoom the window from the keyboard.

FIGURE 1-2.
*You can click in the
zoom box in the title
bar to reduce your
document window to
half-screen size.*

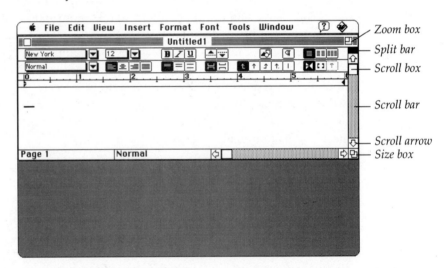

The size box allows you to change the height and width of your window. For example, if you drag the size box of a full-size window up and to the left, you can create a window like the one in Figure 1-3. After you've manually resized a window, you can use the zoom box to toggle between the full-size view and the size that you set manually. If you click in the zoom box in Figure 1-3, for example, your window looks like the one in Figure 1-1 again. If you click in the zoom box once more, your screen returns to the size that you set manually in Figure 1-3.

FIGURE 1-3.
To resize a window manually, drag its size box.

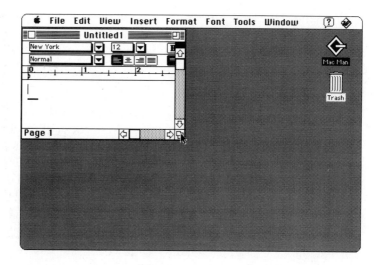

Using the split bar

You can split a window into panes to see two portions of your document at the same time. To split a window into panes, point to the black bar above the vertical scroll bar on the right side of the document window. Your pointer turns into a *split bar*. Drag this split bar downward on the vertical scroll bar to the position where you want to split the window. As you can see in Figure 1-4, Word now displays your document in two panes. The two sets of vertical scroll bars enable you to move through the two panes independently, making it easy to move, copy, or compare sections of your document that are far apart.

FIGURE 1-4.
To split a window into panes, drag the split bar toward the middle of the screen.

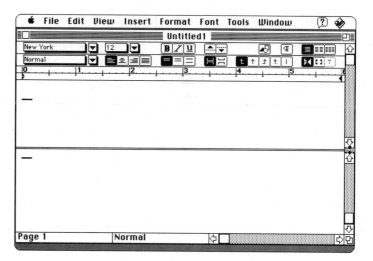

To remove the split pane from your window, point to the split bar again, and drag it past either end of the vertical scroll bar. You can also toggle the panes on and off by pressing Command-Option-S.

Opening new windows

In addition to splitting a single document window, you can create multiple windows to view different parts of a single document or even different documents. You can use each window to view a different part of the same document at the same time. You'll find this feature particularly convenient when you're working with a large document and you want to see several blocks of text simultaneously.

To create a new document window, choose the New Window command from the Window menu. If you choose New Window while the Untitled1 document is active, Word displays a new window called Untitled1:2. To avoid confusion, it also renames the original window Untitled1:1. The next window you open is called Untitled1:3, the next is Untitled1:4, and so on. Each window offers a separate view of the Untitled document. Any changes you make in one window affect the versions of the document in the other windows. You can also load different documents into different windows and view them simultaneously.

To remove a window from your screen, simply click its close box or press Command-W. Word renumbers the remaining document windows, if necessary. As we've already mentioned, if you click the close box of the only open document window, Word assumes that you want to close the document and asks if you want to save any changes before it removes the window from your screen. We'll talk more about closing and saving files in Chapter 2, "Handling Files."

Positioning multiple windows

If you're working with more than one Word document window, you'll probably want to resize or reposition the windows on your screen. You can reposition each window individually, or you can let Word do it for you. To reposition two open windows so that they don't overlap, click in the zoom box or double-click the title bar of the second open window. Word reduces the window whose zoom box you clicked to half size. The two windows then appear as shown in Figure 1-5.

If you open a third document window and click in its zoom box, Word reduces that window to quarter size, as shown in Figure 1-6. If you open more windows, clicking in the zoom box of each window after you open it, Word continues to resize and reposition the windows to make each one as easy as possible to view and access.

FIGURE 1-5.
*The second window
overlaps the bottom
half of the first
window.*

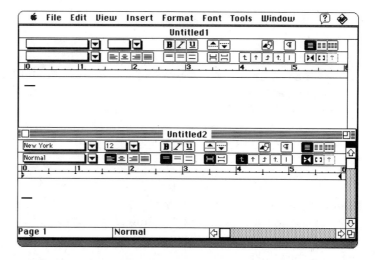

FIGURE 1-6.
*The third window
appears in quarter-
screen size.*

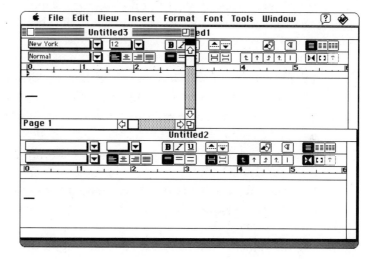

Although you can use the zoom box to display document windows one above
another, you must drag the windows to display them side by side. To reposition a
window manually, point anywhere on its title bar, except over the close or zoom
boxes, and drag.

To move an inactive document window around on the screen without deactivating the active window, hold down the Command key as you drag its title bar.
The inactive window "slides behind" the active window, rather than coming to
the top of the stack of windows. If you click anywhere except the title bar, or if
you click the title bar without holding down the Command key, Word activates
the window and brings it to the top of the stack. To reactivate the window you
were working in, select it from the Window menu or click it again.

Moving between windows

Moving between windows is much like shuffling a stack of playing cards. To move from one window to another, you can click the window you want, select the window name from the Window menu, or press Command-Option-W. When you press Command-Option-W, the next window in the stack comes into view and the previous window moves to the bottom of the stack.

Telling Word what to do

The menu bar at the top of the screen lists the menus from which you choose commands. In addition to the Apple menu, Word offers eight menus: File, Edit, View, Insert, Format, Font, Tools, and Window. If you select the Use Short Menu Name option in the View section of the Preferences dialog box, the Insert, Format, and Window menu names will be shortened to Ins, Fmt, and Wnd, respectively. (In Chapter 18, "Customizing Word," you'll also see a custom menu called Work, on which you can place your own Word commands and shortcuts.) Each menu contains a related set of commands. Together, these menus contain all the tools you'll need to write your documents. Here's an overview:

- The File menu contains document-handling and printing commands. You can open documents from this menu, and you can save and print them.

- The Edit menu contains commands for copying, moving, and replacing text, and commands that let you share text with other documents.

- The View-menu commands determine how Word presents your document on the screen. With these commands, you can display your document in Normal view, Outline view, or Page Layout view, and you can turn on and off the display of the document-window features such as the ribbon and ruler.

- The Insert menu commands let you add graphics and elements such as footnotes, a table of contents, or an index to your document.

- The Format and Font menus contain commands for controlling the appearance of the text.

- The Tools menu lets you check your grammar, spelling, and hyphenation; perform mathematical calculations; and sort your document.

- The Window-menu commands enable you to create new windows to view different parts of your document and move among different documents. You also use Window-menu commands to see the contents of the Clipboard and to access the Help feature.

Word can carry out many commands immediately. However, to execute some other commands, you will need to provide information to indicate exactly how you want the command to be carried out. Before you choose these Word commands, you first must select the part of your document you want the command to act on. For example, you can't choose the Copy command to copy text until you've selected the text you want to duplicate. As shown in Figure 1-7, Word dims these commands on the menu until you've indicated the part of your document you want to affect.

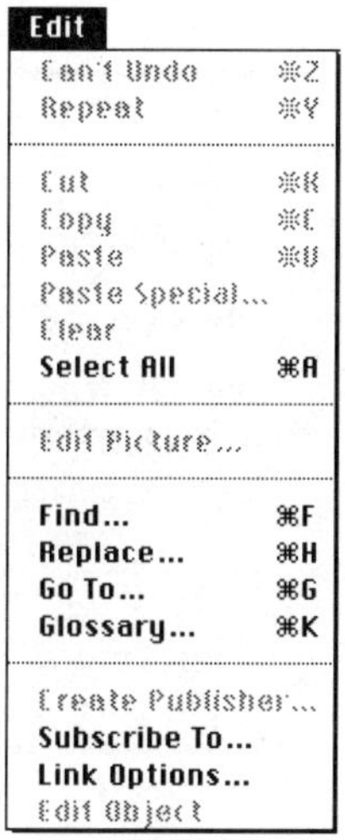

FIGURE 1-7.

The Copy command on the Edit menu is dimmed because no text is selected in the document window. The Find command is followed by an ellipsis to indicate that you must specify more information to carry out the command.

Edit

Can't Undo	⌘Z
Repeat	⌘Y
Cut	⌘X
Copy	⌘C
Paste	⌘V
Paste Special...	
Clear	
Select All	**⌘A**
Edit Picture...	
Find...	**⌘F**
Replace...	**⌘H**
Go To...	**⌘G**
Glossary...	**⌘K**
Create Publisher...	
Subscribe To...	
Link Options...	
Edit Object	

Other commands require that you specify a setting or select from a series of options to define exactly how the command should be carried out. Like the Find command in Figure 1-7, these commands have an ellipsis (...) following their names on the menu. When you choose a command with an ellipsis, Word displays a dialog box that lets you enter the additional information.

You can choose a command in Word in three ways. If you're a new Word user, you'll probably find it easiest to use the mouse to choose a command from a menu. Using this technique helps you become comfortable with Word, because you can visualize Word's command selection process. However, you can also give commands by using various key combinations on the keyboard, or by pressing keys on the numeric keypad.

Choosing commands from menus

To choose a command from a menu, move the pointer to the menu bar at the top of the document window until the pointer becomes an arrow. Position the arrow on the menu that contains the command you want to choose, and press the mouse button. When the list of commands available on that menu appears, hold down the mouse button, and drag downward until the command you want is highlighted. Release the mouse button to choose the highlighted command.

Using keystroke shortcuts

As you glance through the Word menus, notice the symbols and letters that appear to the right of many commands. This notation indicates that you can press the symbol and letter keys to give that command without using the mouse. For example, to save a document, you can press Command-S rather than choosing Save from the File menu. Table 1-1 lists the symbols used for the keystroke shortcuts on the menus.

Symbol	Key	Symbol	Key
⌘	COMMAND	⇥	TAB
⌥	OPTION	⌫	DELETE or (BACKSPACE)
⇧	SHIFT	▦	Key following symbol is on the numeric keypad
⌃	CONTROL		
↵	RETURN	⌧	ESC
⌤	ENTER	← → ↑ ↓	Arrow keys
␣	SPACEBAR		

TABLE 1-1.
Word displays these symbols on the menu to designate keystroke shortcuts.

You can also use keystroke shortcuts to perform actions not listed on the Word menus. You can, for example, use the Command key in combination with other keys to split windows into panes and to cancel any command or operation. Throughout this book, we'll introduce these keystroke shortcuts as we discuss the commands they perform.

Using the keypad

You can use the numeric keypad to browse through the menus without using a mouse. To pull down the desired menu, press the decimal-point key on the numeric keypad, and type the first letter of the menu whose contents you want to see. For example, to see the contents of the File menu, first press the decimal-point key. The menu bar appears in reverse video for about five seconds and then returns to normal if you don't select a menu. While the menu bar appears in reverse video, type *f*.

When you activate a menu from the numeric keypad, the menu remains open until you choose a command or click another area of the screen. You can also close a menu by pressing Delete (or Backspace on Macintosh Plus keyboards), Esc, or Command-period.

Another way to activate a menu is to press the decimal-point key on the numeric keypad and type a number from 0 through 9 that identifies the position on the menu bar of the menu you want to display: 0 for the Apple menu, 1 for the File menu, 2 for the Edit menu, and so on. (This technique is particularly handy because three of the menu names begin with *F* and because the Apple menu has no letter equivalent.)

In addition, you can press the decimal-point key, and then press the Right or Left direction keys to access the first or last item on the menu bar. The first menu is the Apple menu; the last menu can be either the Window menu or the Work menu (if you've created your own commands; see Chapter 18, "Customizing Word," for more information). After you've activated a menu, you can press the Right and Left direction keys to move from one menu to the next.

To choose a command from a menu you've displayed on the screen, use the Up and Down direction keys to move through the commands and highlight the one you want. After you highlight the command, press Return (or Enter) to choose it. You can also highlight a command by pressing its first letter. If more than one command on a menu begins with the same letter, successively pressing that key moves the highlight through the commands in order of their appearance. When Word reaches the last command on the menu, it cycles back to the first command on the menu that begins with the common letter.

The 4, 6, 8, and 2 keys on the numeric keypad serve the same functions as the Left, Right, Up, and Down direction keys, respectively, after you display a menu on the screen. (Before you can use the numeric keypad, Num Lock must be turned off. Pressing the Clear key turns it on and off.) Use the 4 and 6 keys to move from one menu to the next and the 8 and 2 keys to highlight commands in an open menu.

Dialog boxes

As we've mentioned, an ellipsis follows many of the command names on the Word menus, telling you that you must give Word more information before it can carry out that command. You provide this information in a special kind of window called a *dialog box*.

For example, when you choose the Character command from the Format menu, you see a dialog box like the one in Figure 1-8 on the next page. You can provide information in several ways from a dialog box like this one. Dialog boxes generally contain a combination of lists, buttons, and boxes in which you specify command options. Some dialog boxes also contain command buttons that you use to confirm or cancel your selections, and some may contain buttons that display additional dialog boxes. (Don't worry about what the options in the dialog box in Figure 1-8 do for now; instead, focus on the kinds of options that are available.)

FIGURE 1-8.
The Character dialog box appears when you choose the Character command from the Format menu.

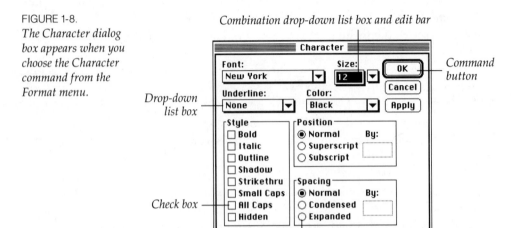

Combination drop-down list box and edit bar

Command button

Drop-down list box

Check box

Radio button

Check boxes

Check boxes, like the ones next to the Style options in Figure 1-8, represent options that can be activated simultaneously. To display text in bold and italic type, for example, you can click the Bold and Italic options in the Character dialog box. Word fills in the boxes next to the option names with an X. To deselect an option, you click the option again. For example, to change bold italic text so that it appears in small capital letters with an outline around each character, you must click the Bold and Italic options to deselect them, and then click the Small Caps and Outline options to assign your new formats.

Radio buttons

The small circles to the left of the Position and Spacing options are called *radio buttons*. To select an option, click the radio button next to the option you want, or on the option name, to fill in the circle and select that option. To assign the Superscript format to text in your document, for example, you can simply click the word *Superscript* or the radio button that appears next to the word.

Radio buttons represent mutually exclusive options—only one radio-button option can be turned on at a time. When you select the Superscript option, for example, Word fills in the circle next to the Superscript option and deselects the Normal option.

Drop-down list boxes

Some dialog boxes contain lists of options, called *drop-down list boxes*, like the Underline list box in the Character dialog box. When you click the arrow at the right end of the list box, a list of options appears, as shown in Figure 1-9. To select an option from the list, drag the highlight down to that option, and release the mouse button. The list box closes and the option's name appears in the box at the top of the list to indicate that it is selected.

FIGURE 1-9.
When you click the
arrow at the right end
of a drop-down list
box, a list of options
appears.

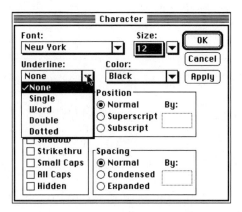

You can also click the name of the current option to display the other options. In addition, you can press Command and the first letter of the list box's name. For example, pressing Command-U while the Character dialog box is displayed on your screen causes the Underline list box to drop down.

In some instances, a drop-down list box "drops down" from an edit bar. For example, the Size list box in the Character dialog box is actually a combination of a drop-down list box and an edit bar and is called a *combination list box*. You can distinguish a combination list box from a true drop-down list box by the fact that the arrow and the box that displays the selected option are separate elements, with space between them. This combination feature gives you two ways to specify a setting: In this example, you can select an option from the drop-down list, or you can type a new font size in the edit bar.

List boxes

Some of Word's dialog boxes include list boxes whose contents reflect your actions. For example, Figure 1-10 on the next page shows the dialog box that appears when you choose Glossary from the Edit menu. This dialog box contains a list box of glossary terms. (If you're not familiar with the concept of a glossary, don't worry. We explain it in detail in Chapter 13, "Using Word Tools.") To view additional options on the list, you can click the scroll bar that appears on the right side of the list box. You can also drag the scroll box or click the scroll arrows. To select an option from the list box, simply click the option or use the Up or Down direction key to move through the options until you've highlighted the one you want.

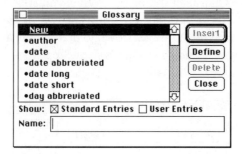

Command buttons

The large round-cornered rectangles in the upper-right corner of the Character dialog box are called *command buttons*. Generally, you click these buttons after you select options in the dialog box. For example, if you click the OK button in the Character dialog box, Word removes the dialog box from your screen and implements the character formats you've selected. If you click the Cancel button, Word removes the dialog box from your screen without implementing the formats. If the button you want is surrounded by a dark border, pressing Return has the same effect as clicking the button.

Navigational buttons

Navigational buttons resemble command buttons, but their names are followed by an ellipsis (...) which tells you that they provide direct access to another related command. Clicking one of these buttons displays another dialog box in which you can specify settings and select options, without having to first close the current dialog box. For example, Figure 1-11 shows the dialog box that is displayed when you choose the Paragraph command from the Format menu. This dialog box contains three navigational buttons: Tabs, Border, and Frame. Clicking these buttons opens the Tabs, Border, and Frame dialog boxes, respectively, just as if you had chosen the corresponding command from the Format menu.

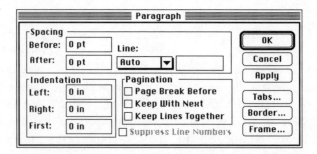

Dialog-box shortcuts

After you become accustomed to using dialog boxes, you'll want to know about several techniques for streamlining your work. We'll show you these dialog-box shortcuts as we introduce each command in the chapters that follow. In general, however, you can move from one group of options to the next by pressing the Command-Tab. When you "activate" a group of options, Word displays a flashing gray bar in that portion of the dialog box. You can then press Command-Spacebar or zero on the numeric keypad to select individual options from that group. For example, in the Character dialog box shown earlier in Figure 1-8 you might press Command-Tab to activate the flashing gray bar under the Subscript option.

If you press Command-Tab while the flashing gray bar appears under the last option in a group, Word moves to the first option in the next group. If you have a numeric keypad, you can also press the decimal-point key to move from the last option in one group to the first option in the next group. If you press Command-Shift-Tab while the flashing gray bar appears under the first option in a group, Word moves to the last option in the previous group. After an option you want is underlined with the flashing gray bar, you can press Command-Spacebar to select that item.

A similar shortcut allows you to undo selections before you close a dialog box. When radio buttons or check boxes are grouped under one option heading — as with the Style, Position, and Spacing options shown earlier in Figure 1-8 — you can often cancel your selections for that option by clicking on the heading itself. Suppose, for example, you've selected the Superscript, Expanded, Bold, and Italic options in the Character dialog box. To deselect the Superscript format, click the Position heading above that group of options to cancel your Position selection without altering the remaining selections in the dialog box. When you use this technique, Word reverts to the setting that was selected when you opened the dialog box — not necessarily to the default setting for that group of options.

Selecting dialog-box options might seem a bit confusing if you are new to Word, and having to remember shortcuts might add to the confusion. However, after you become proficient with the program, you'll find that these simple shortcuts can speed up your work considerably. We suggest that you take some time to experiment with these techniques as you create your documents to get a feel for the various keyboard shortcuts.

The ribbon

The ribbon, which appears below the document window's title bar, allows you to apply formatting directly to the text in your document without having to choose commands. (We'll show you how to format characters in your document in Chapter 4, "Formatting Characters.") If the ribbon doesn't appear when you open a document, you can display it by choosing the Ribbon command from the View menu or by pressing Command-Option-R.

The combination boxes at the left end of the ribbon specify the font and point size of the currently selected text. You can change the font and size; apply bold, italic, and underline formats; and make text superscript and subscript directly from the ribbon. Additional buttons let you position graphics; hide and display nonprinting characters that will help you format text; and print your document in one, two, or three columns. To apply the option represented by a particular button to selected text or to the insertion point, just click the button you want.

The ruler

You can specify paragraph formatting, such as line length, indentations, justification, line spacing, and tab settings, by using the ruler that appears below the ribbon instead of choosing commands. (We'll discuss paragraph formatting with rulers in detail in Chapter 5, "Formatting Documents and Paragraphs.") If the ruler is not displayed on your screen when you open a document, you can display it by choosing the Ruler command from the View menu or by pressing Command-R.

The ruler is both a row of buttons and a ruled scale. The buttons let you apply paragraph formats, and their current settings indicate the alignment, line and paragraph spacing, and tab alignment of the selected paragraph or the paragraph that contains the insertion point. You can change these settings by clicking on a new button. The set of buttons that appear at the right end of the row let you select one of three available ruler scales: indent, margin, and table.

The indent scale lets you determine the width of your document and apply tabs, margins, and indentations to selected paragraphs. The triangular markers that appear on the scale indicate the left and right margins specified for the selected paragraph. Although you can see only about 6½ inches of the scale on your screen at a time, the indent scale actually extends from –11 to 22 inches. You can display other parts of the scale by clicking on the right and left scroll arrows at the bottom of your screen. To see the negative values, press the Shift key, and then click the left scroll arrow. (We discuss the page scale in Chapter 5, "Formatting Documents and Paragraphs," and the table scale in Chapter 12, "Creating Tables.")

The mouse pointer

As you've no doubt noticed, the mouse pointer changes shape as it moves around the screen. The pointer's shape indicates the type of function you can currently perform in your document. Table 1-2 shows the pointer shapes you'll encounter most often as you work in Word. We'll discuss each of these pointer icons in detail at relevant points in the book, so we'll cover them only briefly here.

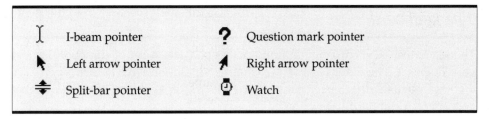

TABLE 1-2.
You'll see these pointer shapes most often in Word.

The I-beam pointer appears when you move the mouse pointer over the part of the window where the text of your document is displayed. (You'll notice the I-beam pointer becomes slanted when you move it over italicized text.) You'll use the I-beam pointer to select text and to move the insertion point around on your screen. The I-beam pointer is probably the pointer shape you'll see most often as you edit and format text, but don't confuse the I-beam pointer with the insertion point. You use the I-beam pointer to select an insertion point, but the selection does not go into effect until you actually click the mouse button to place the insertion point in your text. If you use the scroll bars to move through your document, the insertion point remains where it was and might end up in a part of the document that is not visible on your screen. Be sure the insertion point is in the correct spot before you begin typing or editing. (If the insertion point is not visible when you begin typing, Word moves the document to bring the location that contains the insertion point into view.)

The question-mark pointer appears when you press Command-? to access Word's Help utility.

The left-arrow pointer appears when you point to the menu bar, title bar, ribbon, ruler, or scroll bars. It also appears when you point to options in a Word dialog box. You'll use this arrow to choose commands and select options and to move through your document using the scroll bars.

The right-arrow pointer appears when you move the pointer to the left side of your window into an invisible selection bar. You know you're in the selection bar when your pointer takes on this shape. You can then use the pointer to select blocks of text quickly.

The split-bar pointer appears when you point to the split bar (the black bar) at the top of the vertical scroll bar. This pointer allows you to drag the split bar up or down the scroll bar.

The watch shape appears when Word is executing a command. While this watch is displayed, you cannot use the mouse to choose commands or select text. However, you can type text and use Command-key combinations to choose commands and select options. Word then catches up with you after it finishes the current task.

The keyboard

The Macintosh keyboard puts a numeric keypad and a set of direction keys at your disposal. These keys—and the Command, Option, and Return keys—are the most obvious differences between the Macintosh keyboard and the one that appears on a standard typewriter.

Although the numeric keypad is designed for quick numeric entry for spreadsheet and other business software users, Microsoft has turned it into a navigational tool for Word users. You must press the Clear key located in the upper-left corner of the numeric keypad to enter numbers from the keypad. If you don't press the Clear key, you can use the numeric keypad as a navigational tool to move quickly through a Word document. You can also use the Left, Right, Up, and Down direction keys.

Among other functions, the Return (and Enter) key lets you lock in dialog box selections and signal the beginning of a new paragraph in your Word documents. Don't confuse the Return key with the carriage return on a standard typewriter, however. You don't have to press the Return key at the end of a line to move to the beginning of the next line. Word automatically moves the insertion point from one line to the next as you type. Press Return only when you want to end one paragraph and start a new one.

As we've already mentioned, you use the Command and Option keys to choose commands and perform tasks without the aid of the mouse. Generally, you'll use these keys in conjunction with letter keys as handy shortcuts.

The Spacebar works just like the Spacebar on a standard typewriter. Use it to enter blank spaces in your document.

You use the Tab key to set up columnar tables of data and to control the positioning of text in your document.

The Shift key's primary purpose is to access uppercase characters. The Shift key also operates as a shortcut key when used in conjunction with the Command and Option keys.

The Caps Lock key on the Macintosh keyboard is similar to the Shift Lock key on a standard typewriter—it allows you to type in all uppercase letters without pressing the Shift key. Keep in mind that Caps Lock applies to letters only; it does not apply to the number keys along the top of your keyboard. To use the top-row characters such as !, @, and #, or punctuation marks such as :, ", and ?, press the Shift key.

The Delete key is primarily an editing key that lets you back up over typographical errors or delete blocks of text. On the Mac Plus and other computer keyboards, the Delete key functions like the Backspace key.

The extended keyboard also has a Del key above the direction keys. The Del key edits forward in your text. If the insertion point is to the left of the character you want to delete, you can use the Del key to delete forward without repositioning the insertion point.

Across the top of the Apple extended keyboard, you'll see an Esc key and a row of special function keys labeled F1, F2, and so on. The Esc key allows you to cancel commands and other actions, while the special function keys can be used to perform various other operations, which we explain later.

In addition to the special function keys, many of the standard typewriter keys also serve special functions. As we mentioned earlier, you can use the Command and Option keys in conjunction with some of the letter keys to choose Word commands and to perform other tasks. We'll introduce these functions and techniques as we discuss Word's features throughout the course of the book.

2

Handling Files

*B*efore you create a Word document, you should be familiar with the procedures for opening, closing, and saving document files. This chapter introduces six commands on Word's File menu: New, Open, Close, Save, Save As, and Quit. You use these commands to open a new or existing Word document, save and close a document file, and quit the Microsoft Word application. We also show you how to delete a document file from your hard drive or a disk.

Creating new documents

As we explained in the Introduction, you can create a new document by double-clicking the Microsoft Word icon at the Finder level. Your Macintosh then loads Word and displays the document window for a new blank document called Untitled1.

You can also create new documents by choosing the New command from the File menu within Word. (You can simply press F5 if you're using the extended keyboard.)

If you've already opened one untitled document, the next new document you create is called Untitled2. As you open new documents during a session, Word numbers the documents sequentially—Untitled3, Untitled4, and so on. Each new document window appears on top of any other open Word document windows.

Opening existing documents

You can use several methods to open existing document files. To start Word and simultaneously load a document, simply double-click the document icon on the Finder desktop. If Word is already loaded, the method you'll probably use most often is choosing the Open command from the File menu. When you choose this command, Word displays the Open dialog box so that you can specify the document you want to open. You can also retrieve any of the last four documents you've worked on by selecting the document name from the bottom of the File menu. (To use this method if you have a 9-inch monitor, you must first choose Preferences from the Tools menu, select the View icon, and then select the List Recently Opened Documents option in the Menus portion of the dialog box.)

As you begin working in Word, you'll find that these three methods are all you need to open existing documents quickly and easily. However, you can also open documents by using Word's Find File command. When we discuss this command in Chapter 16, "Finding and Sharing Files," you'll see that many of the Find File dialog box's features resemble those of the Open dialog box.

Using the Open dialog box

When you choose the Open command from the File menu (or press F6) to retrieve a stored document from disk, Word presents a dialog box like the one shown in Figure 2-1. The Open dialog box enables you to find and open any document accessible on your computer. You can move to any folder, display its contents, and select the document you want to open. Options available in the Open dialog box enable you to define the type of documents you want Word to list, access Word's Find File command, and instruct Word to prevent you from changing the document.

FIGURE 2-1.
*When you choose
the Open command,
Word presents a list of
folders and documents
on the active disk.*

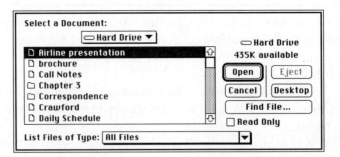

On the right side of the Open dialog box, Word displays the name of the active disk and the amount of space available on that disk. Also displayed are the Open, Eject, Cancel, and Desktop buttons. (If you're using a system other than

System 7, a button labeled Drive appears instead of Desktop.) To open a Word document, you must first display its name in the list box on the left side of the dialog box.

When you choose the Open command, the list box displays an alphabetical list of the items—both folders and documents—contained in the disk or folder whose name appears above the list box. (The name of the folder varies. The first time you use Word during a session, you'll see the disk or folder in which you've stored the Word program. If you move to another folder in the Open dialog box, Word remembers the folder and displays its name the next time you choose the Open command.) A small icon to the left of each item indicates whether the item is a folder or a document. You can open any listed Word document immediately. If the document is stored in another disk or folder, you must locate the document and display its name before you can open it.

If the Word document you want to open is located in the disk or folder whose name appears above the list box, you can open the document by first selecting its name and then clicking the Open button. You can also double-click the document name, or select the document and press Return, Enter, or Command-O. If the list box contains more than seven items, click the scroll arrows or the gray area of the scroll bar to bring additional names into view. You can also use the Up and Down direction keys to move through the list of document and folder names.

To open a document stored on another disk, click the Desktop (for Drive) button or press Command-D to display the disks currently available. Select the disk containing the document you want by double-clicking the disk name or by selecting its name and clicking the Open button. After you select the disk, Word displays the names of the folders and documents it contains in the list box.

To open a document stored in a folder, double-click the folder name, or highlight the name and then click the Open button (or press Command-Down direction key) to open the folder. You then see the names of the documents stored in that folder and any additional folders it contains. To close a folder and move up one "level" in the list box, point to the folder name that appears above the list box, hold down the mouse button, and drag downward. Release the mouse button when the folder or disk name you want to move to is highlighted. You can also press Command-Up direction key to move up to the next level.

In the file list, you can jump to the general vicinity of the document or folder you need by typing the first letter of its name. Word immediately scrolls the list and highlights the first item that begins with the letter you typed. If you type quickly, you can narrow your selection even further by typing the first two or three letters of the name.

When you've located the document you want, click the Open button to display the document in Word.

The List Files Of Type option

To make locating your documents in the Open dialog box easier, you can use the List Files Of Type option to restrict the documents that appear in the Open dialog box list box to one of fifteen document formats.

When Word Documents is selected, only Microsoft Word documents located in the current folder appear in the list box. If you select All Files, you can open files created in another application from the Open dialog box. Keep in mind that Word might not be able to read all the items whose names you can display in the list box, and that the more filenames you display, the more you'll have to scroll to find the document you want. For these reasons, you'll probably find that Word's default option generally meets your needs.

The Find File button

If you've forgotten where the document you want to open is stored, you can use the Find File button to display the Find File dialog box. The Find File dialog box gives you many ways to search for a file. Even if you can remember only the title, subject, author or just some text contained in the file, you can use Find File to locate it. You can also limit your search by file type, creation date, or last saved date. (We'll discuss Word's Find File feature in detail in Chapter 16, "Finding and Sharing Files.")

The Read Only option

If you want to view a document without making any changes to it, you can simply click the Read Only option before opening the document. You can then scan the document and even make changes to it, but you cannot save the document with its original name.

The Read Only option is designed primarily for Macintosh networks, where two or more users might have access to the same documents. To ensure that no one alters the master version of a document, you can use the Read Only option to guarantee that if you change the document, the altered version will be stored in a new file with a different name. If you choose the Save command to save a file that you opened with the Read Only option, Word displays the Save As dialog box so that you can give the document a different name. (We'll talk more about saving documents in the next section.) If you don't change the name, Word displays an alert box to tell you that you can't save the document under its original name. Although the Read Only option is hardly a foolproof security device, you might find it a convenient way to protect your documents from inadvertent changes.

Opening a recently used document

If the document you need is among the four you worked on most recently, you can open it again by selecting the document name from the File menu. Word even remembers the documents you opened in your previous Word session.

If you're using a large monitor, Word automatically displays the names of the last four documents you've opened in sequence at the bottom of the File menu. If you're using a 9-inch monitor, you must instruct Word to add the document names to the File menu, by selecting the List Recently Opened Documents option from the View section of the Preferences dialog box. (We'll discuss Word's Preferences command in detail in Chapter 18, "Customizing Word.")

To open a document on which you've recently worked, select the document name from the list at the bottom of the File menu. Word then displays the document just as it does when you use the Open command.

Saving your work

After you've opened a document and made changes to it, you'll generally want to save the document so that you can return to it later. You can choose either the Save or Save As command from the File menu to save a document. After you've assigned a name to the document, you can save any changes you make by choosing the Save command. To assign a different name to the current document so that you preserve a previously saved version, choose the Save As command. (To quickly choose the Save command from the keyboard, press Command-S or F7, and to quickly choose the Save As command from the keyboard, press Shift-F7.)

Saving new documents

When you save a document that you've created with the New command, whether you choose Save or Save As from the File menu, you'll see the Save As dialog box shown in Figure 2-2 on the next page. Like the Open dialog box, the Save As dialog box includes a list box that lists the folders and documents stored in the current folder on the active disk. Names of the documents already stored on the active disk are dimmed in the list box so that you can't select them. They appear only as a reminder of the names you've already used.

To save a new document, you must first select the folder in which you want to store the document in the list box that occupies the left side of the Save As dialog box. If necessary, use the Desktop button to access the disk you want and the Eject button to eject a disk from the external drive so that you can insert a new one. Then double-click the name of the folder you want to open. If you're using System 7, you can create a new folder from within Word to hold your document.

FIGURE 2-2.
The Save As dialog box appears when you choose the Save or Save As command to save a document for the first time.

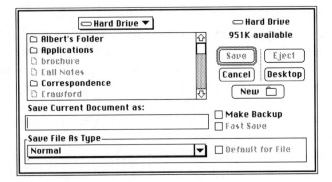

To create a new folder, click the New Folder command button located on the right side of the dialog box. (The button is labeled with the word New and a folder icon.) Word asks you to name the folder and then opens it so that you can store your document in the folder immediately. You'll see the new folder name above the list box. The list box itself will be empty, indicating that no document has been saved in the new folder.

When you've indicated where you want to store the document, you need to assign it a name. (The Save button remains dimmed until you provide a name.) When you're saving a document for the first time, the Save Current Document As edit bar is empty. You can enter up to 31 characters, including spaces, in this edit bar. (You can use any keyboard character except the colon in the edit bar.) To save the document and return to Word, click the Save button. When you exit Word and return to the Finder level, you'll see that Word has stored the document in the selected folder.

The Save File As Type drop-down list at the bottom of the Save As dialog box lets you specify the format in which your new document will be saved. When Normal (the default option) appears in the edit bar, the document is saved in Microsoft Word format. You can select from many other format options, including formats for earlier versions of Microsoft Word. These formats make it easy for you to transfer text to and open your Word documents in other applications. You can also save a document in Stationery format, which means that you can use it as a "template" or "form" document. We'll discuss document formatting options in Chapter 17, "Importing and Exporting Text and Graphics." For now, keep in mind that as long as you store a document using the Normal format, you can easily open it again in Word at any time.

You can save a document only if the active disk has enough free space to store it, so in addition to displaying the contents of the disk, Word also indicates the available disk space. The amount of available space is displayed under the disk icon in the upper-right corner of the Save As dialog box. As you work with Word documents, you'll soon get a feel for the amount of space required to store documents of various lengths and levels of complexity. As a general rule, a ten-page document requires about 30 KB of disk space.

If the active disk doesn't have enough free space to store your document, Word displays an alert box asking you to save the document on a different disk. At this point, you can save your document on another disk, or you can cancel the Save procedure and delete some of the documents on the disk. (We'll talk about the Delete command in a later section.)

The Summary Info dialog box

When you click the Save button to save a document for the first time, Word displays the Summary Info dialog box shown in Figure 2-3. You use the Summary Info dialog box to specify information that identifies the stored document. You can enter a title and a general description of the current document, identify yourself as the document's author, indicate the version of the document, and specify any keywords that you want to associate with the stored document.

FIGURE 2-3.
*The Summary Info
dialog box lets you
specify information
that identifies your
document.*

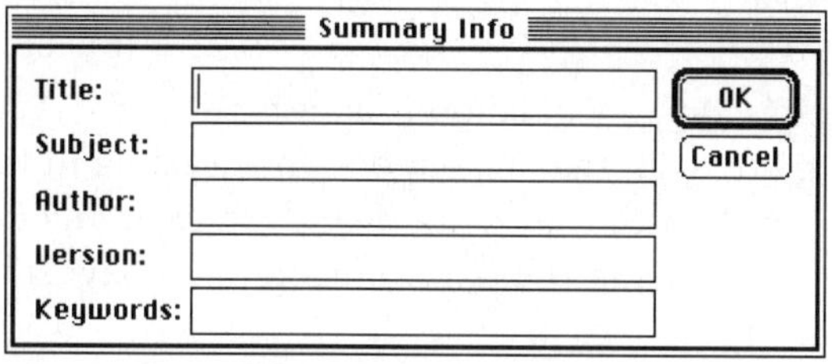

Summary Info	
Title:	OK
Subject:	Cancel
Author:	
Version:	
Keywords:	

You don't have to complete the Summary Info dialog box when you save your document. However, you'll find this feature helpful if you work on a network or share your work with others, or if you create a lot of documents. When you choose the Find File command, you can use this information in addition to the name of the document to specify the file you want to locate.

Even though you're not yet familiar with Word's Find File command, you'll probably want to specify summary information when you start saving documents. Entering this information for each document as you go means that you don't have to go back and add the information at a later time. You'll find this feature most helpful if you enter information that's useful and meaningful to you. For this reason, don't make your entries too elaborate.

To specify summary information, complete one or more of the edit boxes in the Summary Info dialog box. The categories Word provides in the Summary Info dialog box give you considerable flexibility. The Title and Subject edit boxes name and describe the document. The Version and Keywords edit boxes provide additional information — you can type something like *Version 1* or *Initial Draft* in the Version edit box for example, or specify in the Keyword edit box the names or account numbers of people to whom you've sent a letter. Word inserts the name you typed when you installed Word on your Macintosh in the Author edit box. You can change the author name stored with the current document by replacing the displayed name.

When you've completed the dialog box, click the OK button to record the information. If you select OK without filling in any information, Word stores your document without summary information. If you press the Cancel button without providing summary information, Word displays the Summary Info dialog box again the next time you save your document. If you want to add or amend the summary information you enter, you can choose the Summary Info command from the File menu to display the Summary Info dialog box. You can then make any necessary changes, clicking OK to record the new information.

Saving changes to existing documents

To save a document that is already stored on disk, you can choose either the Save As or Save command.

Using the Save As command

If you've saved the document before, choosing the Save As command displays the Save As dialog box with the current document name in the Save Current Document As edit bar. You can leave the name intact or enter a new name and then click the Save button (or press Command-S) to save the new version of the document.

If the name you entered in the Save Current Document As edit bar has already been used to name a document in the current folder, an alert box is displayed to prevent you from inadvertently replacing a stored document. The alert box asks if you want to replace the existing document with the document currently open on your screen. You can create documents with identical names on the same disk as long as those documents are in different folders, but we recommend that you avoid duplicate document names. Despite the alert box's warning, it's very easy to overwrite a document that you want to keep. If you click No when the alert box appears, Word redisplays the Save As dialog box so that you can enter a new document name in the Save Current Document As edit bar.

The Fast Save option

To make it easier to save changes to long documents, the Save As dialog box has a Fast Save option. Selecting Fast Save substantially shortens the amount of time it takes to save a currently open document because instead of completely rewriting the current document on the disk, Word appends your changes to the last saved version of the document. As a result, the document size increases each time you save your changes. To keep your document from getting too long, Word occasionally performs a full-fledged save procedure to consolidate your changes.

When you choose the Close or Quit command, Word rewrites the entire document to disk to save your changes.

The Default For File option

You use the Default For File option in the Save As dialog box to indicate a default format in which Word should save your document. When you select this option, Word "remembers" the format in which you want to save your document. Selecting the Default For File check box tells Word to continue saving the document in the format specified in the Save File As Type list box until you select a different format. This option isn't available when the document format is Normal (the default). If you've selected any other format, this option is available.

The Make Backup option

To create a backup of a previously saved Word document, you can select the Make Backup option in the Save As dialog box. When you select this option, Word duplicates the document stored on disk before it records your changes to the document. Word identifies the duplicate as a backup by adding the prefix *Backup of* to the document name. Word then records your changes in the document currently open. Each time you choose the Save command after selecting this option, Word creates a backup of the previously saved version of the document. You should note that the Make Backup and Fast Save options are mutually exclusive, even though they appear as check boxes.

Although the Make Backup option is a handy way to create backup copies of your documents, it won't help you if the disk on which your documents are stored becomes unreadable. As an added precaution, consider saving important documents on a separate backup disk. Regularly copying your documents to a separate disk decreases the chance of losing important work.

Using the Save command

You can choose the Save As command at any time during a Word session to save revisions to a document. If you want to replace an existing document with an updated version—that is, if you're absolutely sure you want to overwrite the stored document—you can choose the Save command instead of Save As.

When you choose the Save command to save a document that already has a name, Word assumes that you want to save the revised document under the existing name. Word replaces the version of the document stored on disk with the version of the document that appears on your screen.

We recommend that you save open documents at least every half hour to ensure that the changes you've made to those documents are recorded on disk. As you might have learned the hard way, a momentary power outage or an irreversible editing command can mean the loss of a lot of hard work. By saving your documents regularly, you ensure that you won't lose hours' worth of work. (You can also instruct Word to remind you to save your document. The Save Reminder option in the Open and Save section of the Preferences dialog box prompts you to save at an interval you specify. For information about customizing Word and using the Preferences dialog box, see Chapter 18, "Customizing Word.") If your document is especially important, consider saving it on more than one disk. That way, if a disk becomes corrupted or infected, you'll still retain a copy of your work.

Closing documents and quitting Word

You use Word's Close and Quit commands to close the active Word document and quit the Word program, respectively. As a safeguard, both commands offer you a final opportunity to save changes you've made to your document since the last time you chose the Save As or Save command.

If you choose the Close command after you've made changes to a document, you'll see an alert box like the one in Figure 2-4. If you click No, Word closes the document window without saving your changes. If you click Yes and you have previously saved the document, Word saves the document again under its current name. If you have not yet saved the document, Word displays the Save As dialog box to let you name and save the document.

FIGURE 2-4.
This alert box appears when you choose the Close command without first saving your changes.

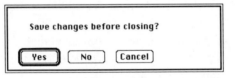

When you choose the Quit command after you've made changes to your document, you'll see an alert box like the one in Figure 2-5. Because the Quit command tells Word to close all open documents and return to the Finder level, Word presents the Save Changes alert box for any open document you've changed since you last saved it (including dictionary and glossary files, which we'll discuss in later chapters). You can then save or discard your changes to each file.

FIGURE 2-5.
Choosing Quit without saving your changes displays this alert box for each changed document.

Word Basics

3

Working in Word

*I*n this chapter, we show you how to enter text in Word, and we introduce the selection and navigation techniques that let you view, edit, and move text to suit your needs. If you haven't used Word before, you'll find this chapter especially helpful. It introduces the basic skills you need to get started. When you know how to select and move text and how to navigate in a Word document, you'll be ready for the Word formatting commands discussed in Chapter 4, "Formatting Characters" and Chapter 5, "Formatting Documents and Paragraphs."

On the following pages, you'll find dozens of shortcuts that allow you to execute Word commands directly from the keyboard. Practice using them. They'll help you work more efficiently in Word. For easy reference, Appendix A, "Keyboard and Mouse Techniques," summarizes these shortcuts.

Entering text

To illustrate some basic Word techniques, we'll enter the sample document shown in Figure 3-1 into a new Word document. To follow along with our example, load Word and open a new document by double-clicking the Microsoft Word program icon in the Finder. If you are already in Word and need to open a new blank document, choose the New command from Word's File menu. You then see a blank document window with a name such as Untitled1 or Untitled2.

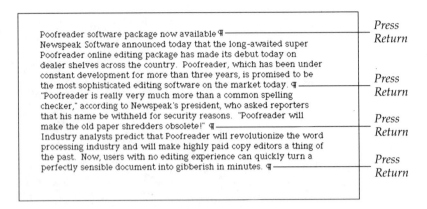

FIGURE 3-1.
We'll use this sample document to illustrate Word's selection, navigation, and editing features.

As you type the first line of text shown in Figure 3-1, keep an eye on the blinking insertion point, which moves one space to the right as you type each character, indicating your position in the document. If you make a mistake while typing, you can press the Delete key to move the insertion point a space to the left and remove text you've entered. If you notice an error after you've typed several more words, don't worry. We'll show you later how to correct those mistakes.

As you enter sample text, you'll quickly discover that Word lets you type a constant stream of characters without indicating the end of each line. If a word doesn't fit on the current line, Word automatically moves the word to the beginning of the next line. You don't need to press Return at the end of each line. In fact, the only time you need to press the Return key as you enter text is to begin a new paragraph. The symbol at the end of the first line and at the end of each paragraph in Figure 3-1 is a paragraph symbol. As you enter the sample text, press the Return key to begin a new paragraph only when you see one of the symbols shown in Figure 3-1. You can easily change the content, format, and layout of this text later if you let Word wrap text automatically for you now.

We used the Normal default type formats—12-point New York—to create the sample document in Figure 3-1. If you specified a different font or font size when you installed Word, your line breaks might be different from ours, or the text might take up more or less of the document window. Don't worry if text disappears from view as you type. In a moment, you'll learn how to use Word's scrolling features to bring that text back into view.

Displaying hidden symbols

Word displays text in the document window as it will appear when it's printed. This online display is whimsically called WYSIWYG (What You See Is What You

Get). You don't need to fill a document with hard-to-read codes to mark where you want to begin a new paragraph, change margin widths, or assign a special format to an element of your text.

Although you can't see them, Word does enter special coding instructions every time you create a new paragraph or change the format of your document. Word also inserts special symbols to indicate where paragraph breaks, line breaks, blank spaces, optional hyphens, and so on, occur in the document.

To see these symbols, choose Show ¶ from the View menu. Immediately, you see a series of ¶ and • characters, as shown in Figure 3-2. The ¶ symbol indicates the end of a paragraph. It stores the formatting you've assigned to your text and tells Word that you want to begin a new paragraph. The • symbols represent blank spaces. At first, you might not be able to distinguish these symbols from periods, but you'll see that the blank space symbols sit slightly higher than the periods do.

FIGURE 3-2.
The Show ¶ command displays special symbols on your screen.

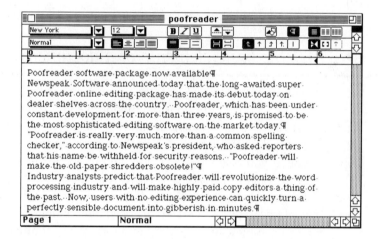

Table 3-1 on the next page shows some of the other symbols that Word displays on your screen when you use the Show ¶ command. We'll discuss these symbols in Chapter 5, "Formatting Documents and Paragraphs." For now, keep in mind that these symbols appear only on the screen; none appear in the printed document.

We show these symbols in our screens to help you interpret the content and design of the sample documents. As you begin editing and formatting text in Word, these symbols help you see the effects of changes in the document window. You can display or hide these symbols. When you choose Show ¶ from the View menu, Word replaces that command on the menu with Hide ¶. Choosing this command hides all special symbols. Move between the Show ¶ and Hide ¶ commands from the ribbon by clicking the ¶ button or from the keyboard by pressing Command-J.

Symbol	Name	To enter, press
¶	Paragraph symbol	Return or Enter
↵	End-of-line marker	Shift-Return
· · ·	Normal blank space	Spacebar
~ ~ ~	Nonbreaking space	⌘-Spacebar
→	Tab marker	Tab
●	End-of-cell marker	Option-8
≂ ≂ ≂	Nonbreaking hyphen	⌘-~
- - -	Optional hyphen	⌘-hyphen(-)

TABLE 3-1.
Word uses nonprinting symbols to mark paragraph breaks, spaces, tabs, and so on.

Selecting the basic elements of a document

Now that you've entered some text, let's examine the elements of a Word document. You type characters in your document one at a time, and groups of characters constitute words, sentences, and paragraphs. Word recognizes these elements a little differently than you might expect. Understanding this difference will help you as you begin to select, edit, and move text in a document.

When you select text in Word, the selected block is reverse highlighted: white type on a black background (rather than black type on a white background). The words *highlighted text* and *selected text* are used interchangeably to refer to such text.

When you complete many editing and formatting commands, you'll find that the text you selected remains highlighted. In fact, you don't have to reselect it to apply another editing or formatting command. When you've finished working with highlighted text, click anywhere in the document window. The insertion point appears at that location, and the text is no longer highlighted.

Most new Word users find it easiest to select text with the mouse, although you can also enter keyboard shortcuts to select text and move around in your document. Let's explore the standard mouse selection techniques and then review a keyboard shortcut for selecting text.

Selecting text with the mouse

The insertion point serves as the pivot or anchor point for one end of selected text. You can change the size and shape of your selection by clicking to position the insertion point, and, while holding down the mouse button, dragging the I-beam cursor around this anchor point. As you drag, the size of your highlighted selection changes, but the insertion point always marks one end of your selection.

To see this, click to the left of the word *much* in line 7 of our sample document, and then drag down and to the right of the word *president*. Your screen will then look like the one shown in Figure 3-3. If you click to the left of the word *much* and drag to the left of the word *is* in the same line without releasing the mouse button, your screen will look like the one in Figure 3-4.

FIGURE 3-3.
When you drag to the right or down, your insertion point marks the start of your selection.

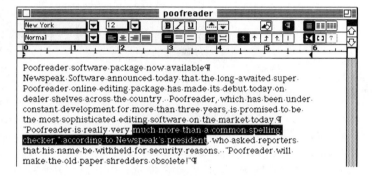

FIGURE 3-4.
When you drag to the left or up, your insertion point marks the end of your selection.

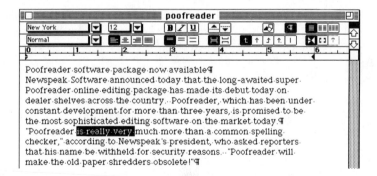

You've just performed the basic mouse selection technique: the click and drag method. As the name suggests, to select text you position the mouse at one end of the text, click the mouse button to fix the insertion point, and then drag the I-beam to the other end. When you reach the top or bottom of the window, the text will automatically scroll, allowing you to select large sections of text. But to make larger selections quickly, you can also click at one end of your selection, and then hold down the Shift key, and click again at the other end. This technique is called the Shift-click method. For example, to highlight all the text between, and including, the words *Industry analysts* and *gibberish in minutes*, first click to the left of *Industry*. Then hold the Shift key down as you click to the right of *minutes*. Figure 3-5 on the next page shows the results.

FIGURE 3-5.
You can select any
size block of text
by clicking at the
beginning of the block
and then holding the
Shift key down as you
click at the end of
the block.

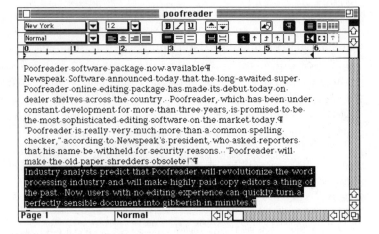

Selecting a character

A character is any single letter, number, punctuation mark, or special symbol that you enter. It can also be a blank space, which you enter to separate one group of characters from another. A character is the most basic element in your Word document. Words, sentences, and paragraphs contain combinations of the individual characters you enter. To select an individual character within a word, just click the insertion point to the left of the character, and drag over it. To select a character that is also a word, such as *a*, you can double-click it. This method also selects any trailing blank spaces after the character.

Selecting a word

A word is any group of letters or numbers or both set apart from other similar groups by blank spaces, by a punctuation mark, or by any one of the following characters:

!@#$%&*()−=+[]{};:",.<>\|/?«»

These characters mark the end of any preceding group of letters or numbers. Word also recognizes blank spaces at the end of a group of characters as marking the end of a word.

Some punctuation marks and symbols come in the middle of words, however. Word distinguishes these characters from those that mark the end of a word. For example, the apostrophe often appears within a word to indicate a contraction or the possessive form of a noun. Word treats the apostrophe and similar characters, like the ^, `, _, and ~ characters, as it does a letter or number; Word doesn't recognize these characters as marking the end of a word.

When the characters ?, +, =, −, and ! appear on their own after letters or numbers, they are interpreted as a "word," but when they are grouped with similar symbols or punctuation marks, the whole group is considered a "word." For example, Word interprets the characters +=− as one word, and considers the characters *abc+=−def* as three words: *abc*, +=−, and *def*.

With these definitions in mind, estimate how many words make up the quotation *"Poofreader will make the old paper shredders obsolete!"*? Did you guess eight? Because Word treats some characters as words, it recognizes ten distinct words in this sentence:

|"|Poofreader•|will•|make•|the•|old•|paper•|shredders•|obsolete|!"|

Word tries to keep characters in a word together. When a word is too long to fit at the end of a line, Word almost always places that word at the beginning of the next line. If a compound word contains a hyphen, Word treats the character group on each side of the hyphen separately. If the hyphenated word cannot fit on one line, the characters up to and including the hyphen appear at the end of the first line, and the remaining characters wrap to the beginning of the next line. You can control these breaks to some extent with Word's special hyphenation features, which we discuss in Chapter 7, "Editing and Proofing." The only other time Word doesn't keep all the characters in a word together is when a word is too long to fit on a single line; for example, when you are working with very narrow columns. In these cases, Word includes as many characters in the first line as possible and allows remaining characters to flow to successive lines as necessary.

You can select an entire word by double-clicking anywhere on that word. Word highlights the entire word, as well as any blank spaces that appear directly to its right. This function simplifies deleting and copying text; Word automatically deletes or copies blank spaces after a word.

When you double-click a word that is followed by a punctuation mark or formatting symbol, Word highlights only that word. For example, if you double-click the word *country* in the fourth line of our sample document, Word highlights *country*, but not the period or the two blank spaces that appear after that word. Instead, Word treats these trailing characters as a separate word. If you double-click immediately to the right of the word *country*, Word highlights the period and the blank spaces that mark the end of that word and sentence.

Selecting a sentence

A sentence is a group of characters and words ended by a period, exclamation point, or question mark. Formatting symbols such as a ¶ symbol also mark the end of a sentence as far as Word is concerned. Any character that marks the end of a sentence also marks the end of the last word in that sentence.

To select an entire sentence, press the Command key, and click anywhere on the sentence. Word highlights the entire sentence, as well as any period, exclamation point, or question mark, and trailing blank spaces. If a sentence falls at the end of a paragraph, Word doesn't highlight the ¶ symbol. In this case, the ¶ symbol is treated separately, like a period or blank space in word selection.

Selecting lines and paragraphs

A paragraph is any combination of characters, words, and symbols ended by a ¶ symbol. Word treats this hidden symbol as an individual word that marks the end of the last word in a paragraph. As a result, Word considers the ¶ symbol at the end of a paragraph to be a part of that paragraph.

To select an entire line or paragraph in Word, you can use the invisible selection bar on the left side of your document window. Although you can't see this selection bar, you know the mouse pointer is there when it changes from an I-beam to a right-arrow shape.

To select an entire line in the document window, as opposed to a sentence, move the pointer to the left edge of the screen until it changes to a right arrow, point to the line of text you want to select, and click. If you click in the selection bar to the left of the line that begins *Newspeak Software announced today* in the second paragraph of our sample document, your screen will look like the one in Figure 3-6. Notice that the blank space at the end of the line is also selected. If the line you select is the last line of a paragraph, the ¶ symbol is also selected.

FIGURE 3-6.
To select an entire line,
click next to that line
in the selection bar.

To select an entire paragraph, move your pointer to the selection bar, and double-click anywhere to the left of the paragraph. Figure 3-7 shows the screen with the entire second paragraph of the document selected. As you can see, because the ¶ symbol at the end of the paragraph is part of the paragraph, it's also highlighted.

FIGURE 3-7.
Double-click in the
selection bar to select
a paragraph of text.

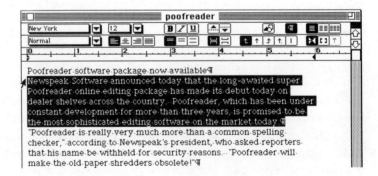

Selecting the complete document

To select the entire document in the document window, move the pointer to the selection bar, press the Command key, and click. All document text becomes highlighted. This technique is useful for making a global change to your document, such as changing the font or indentations for all your text. You can also select the complete document by choosing the Select All command from the Edit menu, or by pressing the keyboard shortcut for this command, Command-A.

Keep in mind that these selection methods select only the text that appears in the active document window. To select all of a header or footer, you must first choose the appropriate header or footer window from the View menu, and then choose the Select All command. You'll learn more about headers and footers in Chapter 10, "Creating Professional Documents."

Selecting blocks of text

With block selection, you select text by highlighting its position within the document, without regard for word, sentence, or paragraph breaks. This technique is convenient for working with tabular data.

To make a block selection, hold down the Option key, and drag the cursor through the characters you want to select. In Figure 3-8, we pressed the Option key, clicked to the left of the word *package* in the first line of the document, and then dragged down and to the right to select the highlighted text.

FIGURE 3-8.
To make a block
selection, press the
Option key, and then
drag through the
desired text.

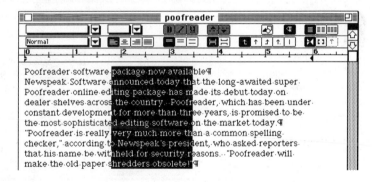

Some characters may be only partially highlighted when you use this technique. Word treats any character more than one-half highlighted as part of the selection.

Repeating selection modes

One of Word's most helpful features is its ability to remember the selection technique you've chosen whenever you use the mouse to select text. For example, when you double-click a word, you in effect enter the "word selection mode." If you drag to the right or left through additional text, Word highlights the next entire word that your pointer touches, even if you drag up or down through several lines, until you release the mouse button. In the same way, if you press the Command key and click a sentence, you can also select adjacent sentences by dragging until you release the mouse button.

Selecting text with the numeric keypad

From the numeric keypad, you can use the minus key to extend a selection from the insertion point to the next instance of a single character in your document. Whenever you press the minus key on the numeric keypad, the prompt *Extend To* appears in the status box at the lower-left corner of your screen. This prompt, shown in Figure 3-9, reminds you to type a single character to be the last character of some selected text. When you type the next character, Word highlights everything from the insertion point to the right of that character's next occurrence. In Figure 3-9, we placed the pointer to the left of the character *P* in *Poofreader*. When we pressed the minus key on the numeric keypad and then pressed the period key, Word highlighted the complete sentence, from the *P* in *Poofreader* to the period at the end of the sentence.

FIGURE 3-9.
You can select a block of text by clicking at the beginning of the block, pressing the minus key on the numeric keypad, and then typing the character through which you want to extend your selection.

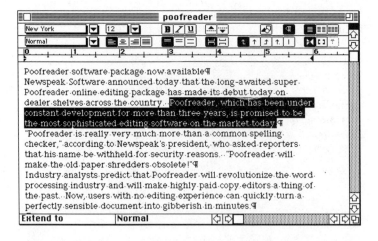

The *Extend To* command remains active until you choose another command or click somewhere on your screen. After typing one character to extend your selection, you can type another character to select beyond the currently highlighted text. In our example, if we next type the letter *g* while the *Extend To* prompt still appears, Word extends our selection from the original insertion point through the next occurrence of the letter *g* in the word *spelling* in the seventh line.

Navigating in your document

Although your Word document can be thousands of lines, the amount of text you can view on the screen at one time is determined by the size of your document window. Word offers several techniques for viewing the document. You can move forward and backward in your document a line or a screen at a time, and easily go from one section of your document to another. Many of these navigational operations are best performed with the mouse. Others can be executed from the keyboard. Let's first look at the standard mouse techniques, and then we'll review some keyboard navigational commands.

Navigating with the mouse

You can easily navigate in your document by using the vertical and horizontal scroll bars. As you learned in Chapter 1, "Touring Microsoft Word," the white squares within the scroll bars are called scroll boxes, and the white arrows at either end of each scroll bar are called scroll arrows. The vertical scroll bar on the right side of the document window displays the text that precedes and follows the text currently displayed on your screen. The horizontal scroll bar at the bottom of the window moves you to the right or left of the displayed text.

Using the scroll bars to view different areas of your document on the screen is called scrolling. Scrolling is the simplest way to change the display of text in your window. Although scrolling changes the display on the screen, it does not affect the text itself. In fact, because you must move the mouse outside the text area of your document, the insertion point within the text doesn't move at all when you scroll.

Using the vertical scroll bar

By using the mouse and the vertical scroll bar, you can move forward and backward through your document one line at a time, or through the length of your entire document.

To scroll one line at a time, use the scroll arrows at the top or bottom of the vertical scroll bar. Click the bottom arrow once to move ahead one line. The line of text at the top of your window disappears, and the remaining text moves up, displaying a new line of text at the bottom. Similarly, click the top arrow once to move back one line. The text line displayed at the bottom of your window disappears to make room for a line of text that now appears at the top of your window. You can hold the mouse button down on a scroll arrow to scroll continuously.

To scroll a full screen at a time, click once in the gray area of the scroll bar. Click above the scroll box to display a screenful of the text that directly precedes the text you just viewed. Click below the scroll box to display a screenful of the text that immediately follows that text. You can hold the mouse button down to scroll continuously. To help you keep your bearings, Word places a line from the previous screen at either the top or the bottom of the second screen.

To travel quickly through your document, you can also drag the white scroll box to the desired position in the scroll bar. Because the length of the scroll bar represents the length of your document, locations on the scroll bar are roughly equivalent to locations in your document. In a very short document such as our sample text, dragging the scroll box to the middle of the scroll bar advances you to the third or fourth paragraph. Dragging the scroll box to the middle of the scroll bar in a 50-page document moves you to about page 25.

The beginning and end of a document are always the same on the scroll bar. Drag the scroll box to the top of the scroll bar to display the first screenful of text (the beginning of your document). Drag the scroll box to the bottom of the bar to display the last screenful of text (the end of your document).

In a long document, you generally want to drag the scroll box to the position on the scroll bar that roughly corresponds to the location in the document you want to view. Word helps you zero in on the page you want by displaying the current page number in the status bar of your window. Once you've reached that page, you can easily click in the scroll bar or on the scroll arrows to fine-tune your position.

But remember, your insertion point has stayed exactly where you left it. Before you can edit or enter text in the window, be sure to click your cursor in its new location to move the insertion point. Otherwise, when you try to type, your screen moves back to the text located around the insertion point.

Using the horizontal scroll bar

If you're working with a document that is too wide to be displayed in one screenful—for example, a document with wide margins or in a narrow window—you can use the scroll arrows at either end of the horizontal scroll bar to move right and left through your document.

Horizontal scrolling is much like vertical scrolling. Use the scroll arrows to move short distances in your document, or click in the scroll bar to move a new screenful of information into view. You can also drag the scroll box to reposition the window horizontally. Unlike vertical scrolling, you can only drag the scroll box in the horizontal scroll bar 22 inches, the maximum width of the Word screen. Dragging the scroll box to the right end moves you to that location on the ruler, while dragging the scroll box to the middle of the scroll bar moves you to about 10 inches on the ruler. If you wish, you can also scroll left, up to 11 inches to the left of the zero point on the ruler. To access this section, press the Shift key as you click the left scroll arrow. The values become negative numbers when you scroll past 0 on the ruler.

Scrolling and selecting text

You often need to select more than one screenful of text. To select text that continues below the edge of the current screen, first click at the beginning of the text you want to highlight. Then, to display the next screen of text, keep the mouse button down, and drag the pointer past the horizontal scroll bar at the bottom of the document window. New text scrolls into view one line at a time, and the text at the top of the window scrolls out of view until you move the pointer back within the document window or until you release the mouse button.

If you click and drag the mouse above the title bar at the top of the document window, Word highlights text that appears earlier in the document. You can also click and drag to the left or right edge of the document window to scroll horizontally as you highlight text.

You can use the scroll bars with the Shift-click technique to quickly select larger text sections. Click at the beginning of your selection, and then use the scroll box in the vertical scroll bar to move to the end of the block you want to highlight. Hold down the Shift key as you click at the end of the block.

Navigating with the keyboard

In addition to the scroll bars, you can use the keyboard to move quickly through your Word document. Generally, keyboard techniques have one important difference from mouse navigation techniques: When you use the keyboard to change your location in a document, the insertion point travels with you; it does not remain at the point in the text where you began, as it does when you navigate with the mouse.

Using the Go To command

Word's Go To command allows you to display a specific page or location in your document. If you know the number of the page you want to view, you can use the Go To command to go directly to the top of that page—even if that page is in a different section of your document. (We'll talk about creating sections in your document in Chapter 10, "Creating Professional Documents.") You can also move an absolute number of pages from the current insertion point location.

Before you can use the Go To command, you must paginate your document. If you've selected the Background Repagination option in the General section of the Preferences dialog box, Word paginates automatically for you. If you've changed this default option, choose the Repaginate Now command from the Tools menu, or perform some other action that paginates your document, such as printing, before choosing the Go To command.

When you choose Go To from the Edit menu, you see a dialog box like the one in Figure 3-10 on the next page. To access this dialog box quickly, you can also press Command-G, or double-click in the status bar.

FIGURE 3-10.
The Go To command
lets you move quickly
to the page you
specify.

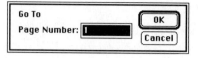

When the Go To dialog box is displayed, the number 1 appears in the Page Number edit bar. To indicate the page you want to view, type the page number in the Page Number edit bar, then click OK or press Return. Word displays the requested page on your screen and places the insertion point at the beginning of the first line. Word also displays the page number of your new location in the status box at the bottom of the window.

If you want, you can type the letter *p* before the page number. If you type *p* without a page number, you move to the top of the document. To go to the beginning of a section, type the letter *s* and the section number in the Page Number edit bar. To specify a page within a section, enter *p* and the page number, and then enter *s* and the section number. For example, type *p2s4* in the Page Number edit bar to go to the second page of the fourth section in your document.

Moving the insertion point to its previous location

As its many navigation uses indicate, the Go To command is an excellent way to move through large documents quickly and accurately. When you're editing a document, however, you'll often find yourself skipping from one spot to another. Word's Go Back command can help streamline this process. You can return to your previous insertion point location by pressing Command-Option-Z, or, if you have a numeric keypad, you can turn off Num Lock and press the 0 key. This technique is particularly convenient for moving between remote areas of your document when you need to compare two sets of text.

In fact, Word can remember more than the insertion point of only your last location. It remembers the last three insertion points prior to your current location. For example, suppose you've made editing changes in the four locations marked in the sample screen in Figure 3-11. If you press Command-Option-Z or 0 on the numeric keypad after making your change at insertion point 4, Word moves you back to insertion point 3. Pressing Command-Option-Z or 0 again takes you back to insertion point 2, then back to insertion point 1. If you press Command-Option-Z or 0 a fourth time, Word cycles back to insertion point 4.

FIGURE 3-11.
*Word remembers your
last three insertion
point locations.*

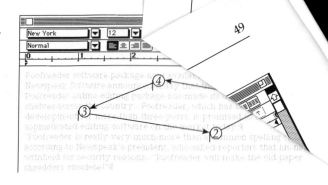

Using the direction keys

You'll find the Up, Down, Left, and Right direction keys convenient for moving short distances. Use these keys within text currently displayed to move the insertion point quickly from line to line. If you press these keys when the insertion point is at the top or bottom line of the window, you can also scroll through the document a line at a time.

Pressing the Left and Right direction keys moves the insertion point one space to the left or right. When you press the Left direction key with the insertion point at the beginning of a line, the insertion point moves to the end of the previous line. When you press the Right direction key at the end of a line, the insertion point jumps to the beginning of the next line. When working with very small font sizes or italicized text, these direction keys make it easy to get to the exact location you need.

To move through your document even more quickly, you can press the Command key as you press the Up, Down, Left, and Right direction keys. The Command-Up direction key combination lets you jump to the beginning of the current paragraph. If your insertion point is already at the beginning of a paragraph, Command-Up direction key takes you to the beginning of the previous paragraph. Similarly, the Command-Down direction key combination takes you to the beginning of the next paragraph.

The Command-Left direction key combination moves one word to the left, while the Command-Right direction key combination moves one word to the right. In either case, the insertion point lands immediately to the left of the next word. If your insertion point is in the middle of a word when you press Command-Left direction key, Word jumps to the beginning of that word. If you press Command-Right direction key while the insertion point is in the middle of a word, Word moves to the beginning of the next word.

...*he numeric keypad*

...keypad, you can simulate the action of the Up, Down, Left, and ... keys by using the 8, 2, 4, and 6 keys. Num Lock must be off for this ... you will simply enter the numbers. You'll find these navigational keys ...remember if you visualize the 8, 2, 4, and 6 keys as a diamond shape sur-...ing the 5 key at the center of the keypad. The highlighted keys in Figure 3-12 ...k exactly as their corresponding direction keys do, including the use of the ...Command key in conjunction with the 8, 2, 4, and 6 keys on your keypad to move up and down one paragraph at a time and left and right one word at a time.

FIGURE 3-12.
The 8, 2, 4, and 6 keys let you move the insertion point up, down, left, and right.

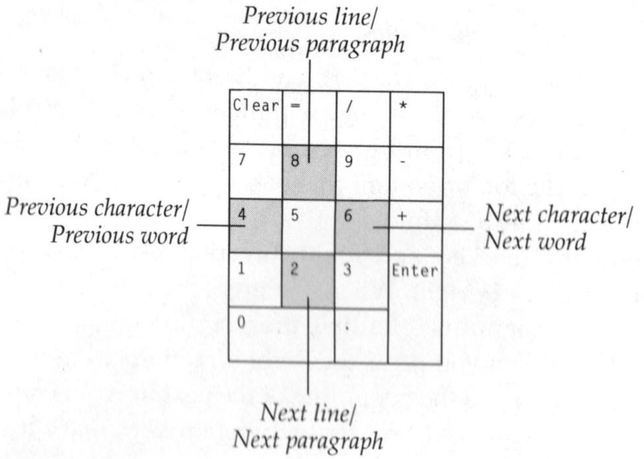

You can also navigate with the 7, 1, 3, and 9 keys—these keys form a box around the 5 key.

Press the 7 key on your numeric keypad to move to the beginning of the current line, and press the 1 key to move to the end of the current line. (Word does not move the insertion point to the right of the blank space at the end of the line. Instead, it places the insertion point before the last space on the line). If the insertion point is already at the beginning of a line, pressing the 7 key moves it to the beginning of the preceding line. If the insertion point is already at the end of a line, pressing 1 moves it to the end of the next line.

You can use the Command key in combination with the 1 and 7 keys to move through your document one sentence at a time. Press Command-1 to move to the beginning of the next sentence, and press Command-7 to move to the beginning of the preceding sentence. If you press Command-1 while your insertion point is in the final sentence of a paragraph, the insertion point moves to the left of the ¶ symbol. If your insertion point is in the middle of a sentence, press Command-7 to move it to the beginning of that sentence. If your insertion point is already at the beginning of a sentence when you press Command-7, the insertion point moves to the beginning of the preceding sentence.

The 3 and 9 keys move you through your document one screen at a time, as if you had clicked on the vertical scroll bar. To move down one screen, press 3 on the keypad; to move up one screen, press 9. When you press either key, Word places your insertion point at relatively the same window position in the new screenful of text. If your insertion point is in the last line of text on your screen when you press 9, for example, the insertion point appears in the last line of text in the new screenful of information.

You can also use the Command key in conjunction with the 9 and 3 keys to move the insertion point to the beginning or end of your document. No matter where it is currently located, pressing Command-9 places the insertion point at the very first character space in your document. Pressing Command-3 moves the insertion point to the very last character space in your document.

You can also use the 5 key to navigate within the lines displayed in the document window. Press Command-5 to move the insertion point to the upper-left corner of your Word screen. Figure 3-13 summarizes the functions of the 7, 9, 1, 3, and 5 keys.

FIGURE 3-13.
You can also use the 7, 9, 1, 3, and 5 keys to navigate in Word.

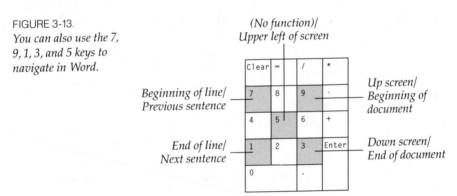

Selecting text with the Shift key

The keyboard shortcuts we've explored so far can also be used to select text by pressing the Shift key together with any of the direction or numeric pad keys described.

For example, you know that you can press Command-7 to move to the beginning of the current sentence. If you press Command-Shift-7, Word highlights everything from the current insertion point to the beginning of the current sentence. If you press Command-Shift-7 again, while this partial sentence is highlighted, Word extends your selection through the beginning of the preceding sentence. Similarly, press Command-Shift-Right direction key to select words or Command-Shift-Down direction key to select entire paragraphs. In fact, all the navigational keyboard shortcuts we've discussed in this section double as selection shortcuts when you add the Shift key to the original key combination.

Editing basics

The simplest way to edit text in your Word document is to insert new characters, delete existing characters, or overwrite the characters you want to change. These three procedures are among Word's most basic editing techniques. Each relates closely to the selection and navigation techniques we've just explored.

As we mentioned earlier, Word automatically reflows your text whenever you make editing or formatting changes—that is why we cautioned you against pressing the Return key at the ends of lines. As we describe insertion, deletion, and overwriting in the next few pages, notice how Word reflows your text to adjust for your changes. This is one of the features that makes electronic word processing so popular; editing text becomes much easier.

Inserting new text

Inserting text in your document is as easy as typing. To insert new text into an existing document, simply click the insertion point where you want to insert the text, and begin typing. Be sure that you have not highlighted any characters before you begin typing. Word overwrites such characters.

For example, suppose you want to change the phrase *users with no editing experience* in line 13 of our sample document to read *users with no proofreading or editing experience*. Begin by clicking immediately to the right of the space after *no*, and type *proofreading or*, followed by a space.

As you can see in Figure 3-14, when you type the new characters, Word pushes the remaining characters to the right to make room for your insertion. Word automatically repositions the words at the end of the line to the beginning of the next line, reflowing your existing text all the way to the end of the document if necessary.

FIGURE 3-14.
As you insert new text, Word reflows your text to make room for your changes.

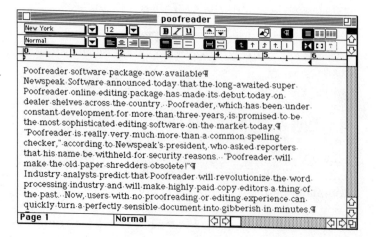

Inserting a paragraph symbol

Word provides two ways to insert a paragraph break into text. When you press Command-Option-Return to begin a new paragraph before you begin typing, Word inserts a new ¶ symbol (visible only if the Show ¶ command has been activated) and moves the text to the right of the insertion point into a new paragraph. Of course, you can also press the Return key to insert a new ¶ symbol. When you press Return, your insertion point moves down to the beginning of the next paragraph. When you press Command-Option-Return, however, your insertion point remains in place so that you can continue to insert text in the current paragraph.

When you've finished entering the text you want to add to your document, it's easy to recombine the two paragraphs. Just press Command-Option-F to delete the ¶ symbol. Command-Option-F lets you delete the character immediately to the right of the insertion point. (The Apple extended keyboard has a Del key that also deletes the character to the right of the insertion point.)

Deleting text

The easiest way to delete individual characters is to click to the right of each character you want to delete and press the Delete key. Word removes the character immediately to the left of the insertion point and automatically pulls the text to the right of the insertion point one character space to the left.

To delete several characters at once, highlight the unwanted block, and then press the Delete key to delete the entire selection. For example, suppose you want to delete the words *proofreading or* in line 13 in Figure 3-14. Select the words *proofreading or* and the blank space following *or*, then press the Delete key. If you double-click one or more words and press the Delete key, Word similarly deletes the selected characters and any trailing spaces. Word erases the selected words and pulls the remaining characters up and to the left to fill the gap.

Keep in mind that the Delete key deletes the character located immediately to the left of the insertion point, no matter where the insertion point is located. If you press the Delete key while the insertion point is at the beginning of a paragraph, Word deletes the ¶ symbol at the end of the previous paragraph and combines the two paragraphs—as long as your paragraphs are formatted in the same style.

If you try to combine two paragraphs with different formats, Word beeps to alert you to this situation. If you're sure you want to combine the two paragraphs, highlight the ¶ symbol at the end of the first paragraph, and then press the Delete key. The combined paragraph takes on the style characteristics of the second paragraph—the paragraph whose ¶ symbol remains.

Deleting with keyboard shortcuts

Word also offers special keyboard shortcuts that let you delete whole words or single characters on either side of the insertion point.

Press Command-Option-Delete to delete an entire word immediately to the left of the insertion point. To also delete the space to the right of that word (if you don't want to insert another word or phrase in that spot), click to the right of that space before you press Command-Option-Delete.

For example, to change the phrase *users with no proofreading or editing experience can* to *users with no editing experience can*, click to the right of the blank space after the word *or*, and press Command-Option-Delete. Word deletes the word *or* and the blank space after it. Repeat this process to delete the word *proofreading* and the blank space after it.

Click in the middle of a word, and press Command-Option-Delete to delete all the characters to the left of the insertion point up to, but not including, the blank space.

For example, to change the word *withheld* to *held* in the third paragraph of our sample document, click between the two *h*'s in the word *withheld*, and press Command-Option-Delete to delete the characters *with*. The space to the right of the word *be* remains intact.

Two additional keyboard shortcuts let you delete text to the right of the insertion point. Press Command-Option-G to delete an entire word. To also delete the blank space before that word, click to the left of the space before you press Command-Option-G. To delete a single character to the right of the insertion point, press Command-Option-F.

Deleting with the Clear command

You can also delete selected text by choosing Clear from the Edit menu. Word clears the highlighted text from your document and reflows the remaining text automatically.

Overwriting text

When you delete a block of text, you often insert new text to replace it. You don't have to delete text before you insert the new characters, however. The overwriting technique combines these steps.

You can overwrite text by highlighting the characters you want to replace and then typing your new text. Word automatically deletes the highlighted characters and replaces them with the new text. You don't need to press Delete.

This technique works well when you want to delete only text characters in your document, while keeping paragraphs and format styles. You can't overwrite a ¶ symbol accidentally by selecting it and typing. Instead, you must select the ¶ symbol, press the Delete key, and then type the new text. Word combines the current paragraph with the paragraph below, and because the first paragraph symbol has been deleted, the text adopts the format of the second paragraph.

Selecting and then overwriting text simplifies the most common editing procedures. A little more clarification about Word's overwriting function will help you to get the most out of this feature.

As you know, when you double-click a word to select it, Word automatically highlights any trailing blank spaces. Pressing the Delete key to delete that word removes these trailing spaces as well. If you double-click a word and then overwrite it, however, Word does not delete the trailing spaces. Instead, it leaves them in place so that you can insert another word easily without retyping any of the blank spaces.

This is true even when you select several words at a time. As long as you enter the word selection mode by double-clicking a word, if you then drag through additional words, Word leaves the last set of blank spaces intact.

Word handles ¶ symbols in the same way. When you double-click in the invisible selection bar to highlight an entire paragraph and then press the Delete key to delete the paragraph, the ¶ symbol disappears as well. If you overwrite the paragraph, the ¶ symbol remains. Again, Word functions this way whenever you enter the paragraph selection mode by double-clicking in the selection bar, no matter how many paragraphs you select.

Keep in mind that although Word operates this way with words and paragraphs, it does delete the blank spaces at the end of entire sentences when you delete or overwrite them. Because sentences are self-contained, you rarely replace a sentence with just a word.

Copying and moving text

Word's Cut, Copy, and Paste commands are the scissors and glue that make editing on line much faster than editing on paper. With a few clicks or keystrokes, you can easily reorganize your document or recreate a block of text. You can also copy items from one Word document to another, or even from one Macintosh program to another. When you finish, Word automatically reflows your entire document. We'll cover copying and moving text within Word now. Later, in Chapter 17, "Importing and Exporting Text and Graphics," we'll show you how to share information with other Macintosh programs.

Copying or moving text in Word is a two-step process. First, you select the text you want to copy or move, and then you select the spot where you want to paste that text. In this section, we introduce Word's basic Copy, Cut, and Paste commands. Next, we show you how to use the drag-and-drop editing feature to copy and move a selection using only the mouse. Finally, we look at two keyboard techniques that also let you copy and move text in your document.

Copying text

Instead of typing a word or text block again and again, use the Copy and Paste commands to copy and insert selected text in several locations. The Copy command is a great time-saver when you need to duplicate a word, a paragraph, or even an entire document in another location.

To copy a block of text, first highlight the text, and then choose the Copy command from the Edit menu. Next, move the insertion point to the location where you want the copied block to appear. Then choose Paste from the Edit menu. A copy of the selected text is inserted to the left of the insertion point. If you're pasting a large block of text, Word automatically scrolls the end of the pasted block into view. The block of text you copied remains unchanged at its original position.

Suppose you want to insert the word *online* to the left of the word *editing* in the sixth line of the sample document shown earlier in Figure 3-1. Instead of retyping the word, simply double-click *online* in the third line of the document, choose Copy, click to the left of *editing* in the sixth line, and then choose Paste. As you can see in Figure 3-15, a duplicate of the copied word and any trailing blank spaces appear to the left of the word *editing*.

FIGURE 3-15.
*When you choose the
Paste command, Word
inserts the copied
block to the left of the
insertion point.*

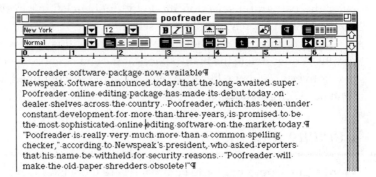

As with most Word commands, you can also execute the Copy and Paste commands from the keyboard. Press Command-C to copy a selected block of text, and then—after you've moved the insertion point—press Command-V to paste the selection into that location. If you have an Apple extended keyboard, you can also press F3 to copy and F4 to paste.

Replacing as you paste

If you want to paste a copied block over an existing block of text, select the text you want to overwrite after you copy, and then paste the text. For example, double-click the word *package* in the third line, and choose Copy. Then double-click *software* in the sixth line, and choose Paste. Word automatically over-writes the selected text with the pasted text.

Moving text

Moving text is much like copying text, except that the original selection is deleted and pasted into another place. Select the characters you want to move, and then choose Cut from the Edit menu. Place the insertion point where you want the text to appear, and choose Paste from the Edit menu.

To illustrate, let's move the sentence in the fourth paragraph of Figure 3-1 that begins *Industry analysts* to precede the sentence that begins *Poofreader, which has been* at the end of second paragraph. First, press the Command key and click the sentence that begins *Industry analysts*. Choose the Cut command from the Edit menu, click to the left of the sentence that begins *Poofreader, which has been*, and choose Paste. Figure 3-16 shows the results.

FIGURE 3-16.
Use the Cut and Paste commands to move a block of text.

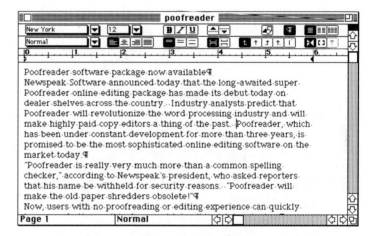

When you paste a block of text, Word inserts the text to the left of the insertion point. This leaves the insertion point at the end of the pasted block. Word automatically reflows both the cut and pasted areas of the text. You can also press Command-X or F2 to cut a selection, and Command-V or F4 to paste it into another location.

Replacing as you paste

As with the copy and paste procedures, when you choose the Paste command, Word deletes any highlighted text and pastes the cut selection in its place. For example, to move the sentence that begins *Poofreader, which has been* to the first line in the document, press the Command key and click that sentence, and then choose Cut to remove that sentence. Next, highlight the sentence in the first line, and choose Paste. Word replaces the sentence that begins *Poofreader software* with the cut selection.

Pasting text into other Word documents

In addition to copying or moving text within a Word document, you can also copy or move text from one Word document to another. Simply open both documents, copy or cut the text you want to paste, and then place the insertion point in the other document where you want the text to appear, and paste.

You can use Word's File and Window menu commands to open new documents, retrieve existing documents, or activate an open document window before you paste. Word remembers your copy block until you cut or copy additional text, or until you quit the program.

Using the Clipboard

When you copy or cut, Word places the text you have selected on the Clipboard. The Clipboard is a temporary storage place where Word stores the last copied or cut text. The Clipboard can accommodate any size selection you copy or cut (memory permitting). You can paste a copied or cut selection as many times as you like, as long as you don't overwrite the contents of the Clipboard by copying or cutting again. You can even open and edit new documents without losing the contents of your Clipboard. However, if you copy or cut another block of text before pasting the first block, the first text block will be lost. The Clipboard contents remain intact when you quit Word, but are lost when you turn off your Macintosh.

To avoid accidentally overwriting the contents of the Clipboard, use the Clear command on the Edit menu to remove highlighted text without placing it on the Clipboard. Or use the Delete key to remove text. If you're storing text for pasting to various parts of your document, these techniques will not disturb that text.

You can view the contents of the Clipboard. If you're ever in doubt about the last selection you have copied or cut, choose the Show Clipboard command from the Window menu. Figure 3-17 shows the Clipboard window, which contains the sentence we copied when we created Figure 3-16.

FIGURE 3-17.
The Clipboard window
displays the last
selection you copied
or cut.

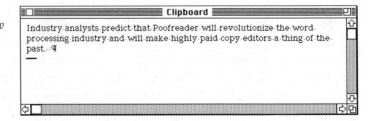

Using the Scrapbook

The Scrapbook, which is located on the Apple menu, can store data from almost all Macintosh applications. For this reason, it's a great place to collect text, graphics, and other data you want to share between Macintosh programs. (In Chapter 17, "Importing and Exporting Text and Graphics," you'll learn how to transfer information from one application to another.) Unlike the Clipboard, which can temporarily save only one item at a time, the Scrapbook can permanently hold as many items as you can accommodate on your hard disk. Pasting text in the Scrapbook lets you freely copy and cut other blocks of text without losing the first block.

Adding a selection

To place a selection in the Scrapbook, select the text and copy or cut it, and then choose Scrapbook from the Apple menu. (If you've added selections to the Scrapbook during this session, the last selection you added appears in the Scrapbook window. Otherwise, you see one of the items that was already present.) Then choose Paste to place your selection in the Scrapbook. In Figure 3-18, we've added a sentence from our sample document to the Scrapbook.

FIGURE 3-18.
Your pasted block appears in the Scrapbook window.

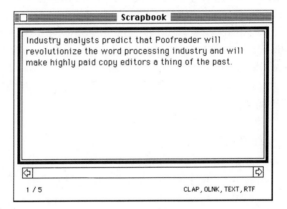

Industry analysts predict that Poofreader will revolutionize the word processing industry and will make highly paid copy editors a thing of the past.

1 / 5   CLAP, OLNK, TEXT, RTF

Viewing Scrapbook selections

Don't worry if your entire selection does not appear in the Scrapbook window. Although this window displays only about 11 lines of text, you'll be able to retrieve the entire selection. If you've assigned special formats to the selection, those formats are also retained, even though they do not display in the Scrapbook window. The contents of the Scrapbook window always appear in the 12-point Geneva font.

Pasting a new item in the Scrapbook updates the status message at the bottom of the Scrapbook window. When you paste the item, the notation 1/x (where x is the total number of Scrapbook items) in the lower-left corner indicates that the entry is the first of a total of several items in the Scrapbook. When you add another item, the new item will be labeled 1/x, and the previous item will become 2/x. Your most recent additions always appear at the beginning of the list. Use the scroll bar to move from one item to another.

In Figure 3-18, the words *CLAP*, *OLNK*, *TEXT*, and *RTF* appear in the lower-right corner of the Scrapbook window. This message indicates that the selection is a text block pasted from Word. You can also use the Scrapbook to store any graphics you create in Word.

To paste a selection from the Scrapbook, choose Scrapbook from the Apple menu (or click the Scrapbook window if it's already open), and scroll to the selection you want to use. Copy or cut the selection to place it on the Clipboard. There is no way to edit or partially select a Scrapbook item; instead, you must copy or cut the entire selection as it is. You can then paste it into your Word document. If you copy the selection, it remains in the Scrapbook, available for use later. If you cut the selection, it is removed from the Scrapbook, and the remaining selections are renumbered to reflect this action. The contents of the Scrapbook remain on your disk after you quit Word and restart your Mac.

To close the Scrapbook window and resume working in your Word document, click the close box in the upper-left corner of the Scrapbook window. You can also leave the Scrapbook window open. Click in one of your document windows to begin working again in Word. The Scrapbook will remain open and accessible until you exit from Word.

Drag-and-drop editing

In addition to using the commands on the Edit menu, you can copy and cut selected text using only the mouse. Word's drag-and-drop text editing feature lets you reproduce or move a selection by dragging it to a new location. After highlighting the selection, you simply click it, hold down the Command key, and then drag the mouse to indicate where you want the selection to appear. When you release the mouse button, Word inserts a copy of the selected text at the current insertion point. If you don't press the Command key as you drag, Word deletes the original selection and moves it to the current insertion point.

Drag-and-drop editing lets you quickly edit the text in the document window. If you want to place bullets at the beginning of items in a bulleted list, for example, you can copy and insert the character more quickly using this technique than if you use the Copy and Paste commands on the Edit menu. However, you can't use this technique to replace text or to copy and paste a selection into another document. In fact, after you've selected the text you can't release the mouse button without completing the operation, so you can't choose other commands or use the scroll box to move great distances in your document.

Unlike the Copy and Cut commands, drag-and-drop editing copies and moves text without placing the selection on the Clipboard. To return a selection to its original location, choose Undo Edit from the Edit menu, or press Command-Z immediately.

Dragging and copying

Suppose, for example, that you want to copy the word *online* in the third line of the sample document in Figure 3-16 and insert it before the word *software* in the first line. To copy and paste this word using only the mouse, double-click the word *online* to select the word and the space after it, and then point to the highlighted text, press the Command key, and hold down the mouse button. As you hold down the mouse button, notice that a dimmed border appears at the bottom of the left-arrow pointer. We've magnified the selected text in Figure 3-19 so that you can see this border clearly.

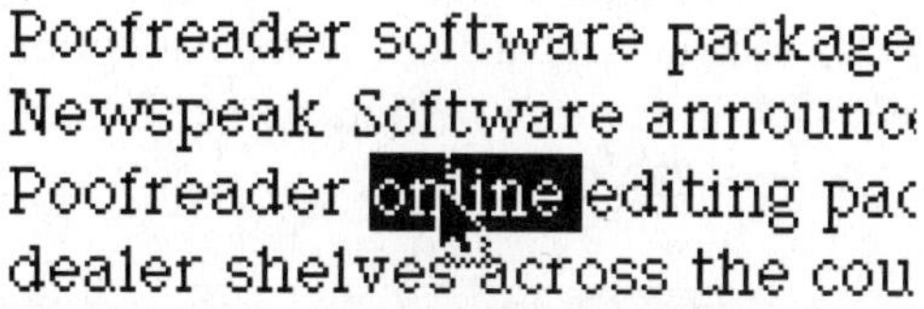

FIGURE 3-19.
*The dimmed border
at the bottom of the
left-arrow pointer
indicates that you can
drag and drop the text.*

Poofreader software package
Newspeak Software announc
Poofreader online editing pac
dealer shelves across the cou

The dimmed border that appears beneath the pointer indicates that you can drag the current selection to another location in your document. This border appears as long as you hold down the mouse button. To copy the selected text in the third line, drag the pointer without releasing the mouse button. As you move, a dimmed insertion point marks your current position in the document window. Figure 3-20 shows the document from Figure 3-19 after we "dragged" this insertion point to just before the word *software* in the first line. Figure 3-21 shows the sample document after we released the mouse button to insert a copy of the selected text.

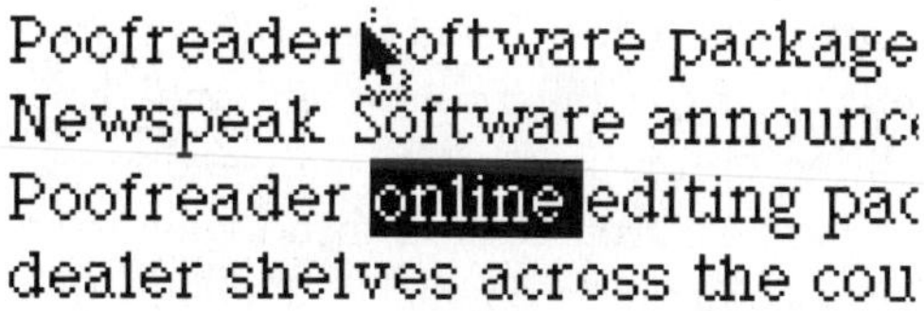

FIGURE 3-20.
*As you move the
mouse, a dimmed
insertion point marks
your current position
in the document
window.*

Poofreader software package
Newspeak Software announc
Poofreader online editing pac
dealer shelves across the cou

FIGURE 3-21.
Releasing the mouse
button inserts a copy
of the selection at the
insertion point.

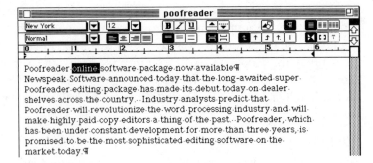

Dragging and cutting

Performing the drag-and-drop operation without pressing the Command key deletes the selection from its original location and moves it to the place in the document marked by the insertion point.

For example, to cut the word *online* from the third line and paste it before the word *software* in the first line, simply highlight the word as shown in Figure 3-19, and then drag the insertion point to the location in the first line where you want the word to appear. Dragging the insertion point before the word *software*, as shown in Figure 3-20, and then releasing the mouse button deletes the text from the third line and pastes it at the insertion point. The document window then looks as shown in Figure 3-22.

FIGURE 3-22.
If you don't hold down
the Command key as
you drag, Word cuts
the selection from its
original location and
pastes it at the
insertion point.

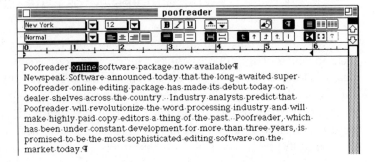

Deactivating drag-and-drop editing

You can use the drag-and-drop editing feature to copy and move graphics as well as text. If for some reason you don't want to use this feature, you can deactivate it by choosing Preferences from the Tools menu and then deselecting the Drag-And-Drop Text Editing option in the General section of the Preferences dialog box. Deactivating drag-and-drop editing in no way affects the operation of the Copy, Cut, and Paste commands on the Edit menu. (For detailed information about specifying preferences, see Chapter 18, "Customizing Word.")

Keyboard techniques

In addition to the keyboard shortcuts you can use to copy, cut, and paste text, Word offers two other keyboard techniques: The Copy From/Copy To and the Move From/Move To keystroke commands.

Copy From/Copy To

Instead of using separate Copy and Paste commands to move text in your document, Word's Command-Option-C or Shift-F3 technique reduces this process to one step. It works two ways, depending on whether you've selected any text before you choose the command. If you have selected a block of text, that highlighted text becomes your copy block and Word asks you where you want to paste the selection (Copy To). If you haven't selected a block of text, Word assumes that you want to paste text at the insertion point, and asks you to select a copy block (Copy From).

For example, suppose you are typing the sample document shown in Figure 3-1 and you want to insert the word *software* after the word *Poofreader* at the end of the third paragraph. Instead of typing this word, you can copy it from the first paragraph.

To use the Copy From technique, first place the insertion point where you want the copied text to appear—after the blank space following the word *Poofreader* at the end of the third paragraph. Then press Command-Option-C or Shift-F3. The prompt *Copy From* appears in the status box in the lower-left corner of your screen. Next, drag through the word *software* and the space following it in the second paragraph. Word displays a dotted line beneath the selected copy block, as shown in Figure 3-23. When you press the Return key, the copy selection appears to the left of the insertion point.

FIGURE 3-23.
Word displays the prompt Copy From in the status box and underlines your copy selection.

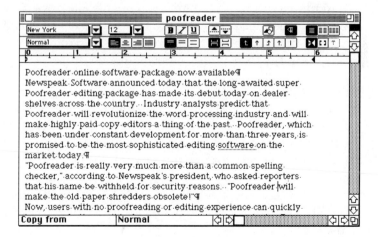

Use the Copy To technique to move already highlighted text to a new insertion point. For example, to copy the name *Newspeak Software* from the second paragraph, select the phrase, and then press Command-Option-C or Shift-F3. You'll see the prompt *Copy To* in the status box in the lower-left corner of your screen. If you click a new location, Word displays a vertical gray bar at the paste location. If you drag through text, Word displays a dotted line under your selection to indicate that those characters will be overwritten when you press Return, as shown in Figure 3-24.

This technique can also be used to copy text from one document to another. Be sure both documents are open and in view. When you move from the source document to the destination document, the *Copy From* or *Copy To* prompt appears in that window's status box.

FIGURE 3-24.
Word displays the
prompt Copy To
in the status box
and indicates your
paste selection with
a dotted line.

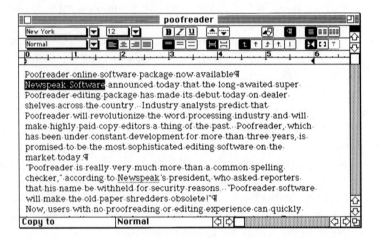

Word cancels this procedure if you use the File or Window menus to open or activate another document. Be sure that both the source and destination documents are open and visible before you use Copy From or Copy To. To cancel this procedure at any time, press Command-period or the Esc key.

Move From/Move To

Instead of copying a selection, you can remove a selection and paste it in another location. Select a block of text, press Command-Option-X or Shift-F2, and you'll see the prompt *Move To* in the status box. Click a new location, press Return, and Word deletes the selected text from its current location and places it in the new location.

If you drag through a block of text rather than clicking an insertion point, Word displays a dotted line under that text and overwrites it when you press the Return key.

If you don't select text before pressing Command-Option-X or Shift-F2, Word assumes that you want to move a block of text to the current insertion point and displays the prompt *Move From*. Simply drag through the text you want to move, and press Return.

As with the Copy procedure, you can drag, resize, or activate document windows while you're performing a Move From or Move To operation, but if you try to use the File or Window menu commands to access another window, Word cancels the Move procedure. You can cancel the procedure at any time by pressing Command-period or the Esc key.

The copy and move techniques and the Clipboard

When you use the copy or move techniques, Word does not place a copy of your text on the Clipboard. If you've previously placed a block of text on your Clipboard, that text remains undisturbed while you carry out a Command-Option key procedure. These procedures let you perform intermediate copies and moves without losing your last Clipboard selection.

Canceling and repeating actions

When you change your document or choose a command, Word remembers that action until you perform another one. The Undo command on the Edit menu allows you to change your mind about almost any action or series of keystrokes you perform while working in a Word document. The Repeat command, also on the Edit menu, lets you replay your last action or series of keystrokes. You'll find that these functions save time, both by undoing mistakes and by automating editing and formatting. Let's explore the Undo command, and then look at how to repeat a command or a series of keystrokes.

The Undo command

The Undo command is one of Word's most important features because it gives you a second chance when you make a mistake. This command can be a real lifesaver when you inadvertently alter a critical passage in a document.

Undo is a context-sensitive command; that is, it changes to reflect your last action. If you've inserted new text or overwritten some existing text, you'll see the command Undo Typing at the top of the Edit menu. If you have applied formatting, such as italic, to some characters, you'll see the command Undo Formatting. The Undo command has two keyboard shortcuts: Command-Z, and, if you have an Apple extended keyboard, F1.

Because Word remembers your last action, you can even undo an Undo command. When you choose Undo, or press Command-Z or F1, Word changes that command to Redo. If you cut a block of text and choose Undo Cut, you can then choose Redo Cut to delete the text again. Remember, the Undo command remains in effect only until you choose another command or begin typing new text. As soon as you perform another action, Word changes the Undo command to reflect your new activity.

In addition to the editing procedures in this chapter, many other Word procedures can be undone. If a command or action cannot be undone, *Can't Undo* appears in dimmed characters at the top of the Edit menu.

Because they do not affect elements inside a Word document, none of the commands on the Apple menu, File menu, or Window menu can be reversed with the Undo command. Table 3-2 summarizes the Word actions and commands that can be undone.

Menu	Command	Can undo
Edit	Undo	✓
	Repeat	✓
	Cut	✓
	Copy	✓
	Paste	✓
	Paste Special	✓
	Clear	✓
	Select All	
	Edit Picture	
	Find	
	Replace	
	Go To	
	Glossary	✓ Insert option only
	Create Publisher	
	Subscribe To	
	Publisher/Link Options	
	Edit Object	
View	Normal	
	Outline	
	Page Layout	
	Ribbon	
	Ruler	
	Print Merge Helper	

TABLE 3-2.   *(continued)*
You can use the Undo/Redo command to reverse those actions marked by a ✓ character in this table.

TABLE 3-2. *Continued*

Menu	Command	Can undo
	Show ¶	
	Header	✓ Only with Header window open
	Footer	✓ Only with Footer window open
	Footnotes	✓ Only affects footnote text
Insert	Page Break	✓
	Section Break	✓
	Table	✓ Insert option only
	Footnote	✓ Insert option only
	Date	✓
	Symbol	✓
	Index Entry	✓
	Index TOC Entry	✓
	Table Of Contents	✓
	Frame	
	File	✓
Picture	Object	✓
Format	Character	✓
	Paragraph	✓
	Section	✓
	Document	
	Border	✓
	Table Cells	✓
	Table Layout	✓
	Frame	
	Style	✓
	Revert To Style	✓
	Change Case	✓
	Plain Text	✓
	Bold	✓
	Italic	✓
	Underline	✓
Font	(Font Sizes)	✓
	Up	✓

(continued)

TABLE 3-2. *Continued*

Menu	Command	Can undo
	Down	✓
	Other	✓
	Default Font	
	(Font Names)	✓
Tools	Spelling	
	Grammar	
	Thesaurus	
	Hyphenate	✓
	Word Count	
	Renumber	✓
	Sort	✓
	Calculate	
	Repaginate Now	
	Preferences	
	Commands	

We'll talk more about these commands later. For now, keep in mind that you can undo most Word commands if you act immediately.

You should exercise caution when handling files. If you use the Delete command to erase a file, or if you accidentally overwrite a file with the Save As command, you won't be able to reverse those actions.

The Repeat command

Because Word remembers the last action you performed, you can repeat an action or a series of keystrokes automatically. To repeat an action, choose the Repeat command from the Edit menu or press Command-Y.

For example, if you insert text at one place that you need to insert immediately in another location, just click in the second location and press Command-Y to repeat your keystrokes. You can use this command to repeat just about any action or series of keystrokes. This shortcut is particularly helpful when you want to reapply complex formatting instructions in several areas of the document.

4

Formatting Characters

Selecting the right font and text style from Word's variety of text styles and options can substantially enhance your document's appearance. This chapter shows you how to choose and apply character formatting commands from the Font and Format menus, from the Character dialog box, from the ribbon, and from the keyboard. You can define how individual characters in your document will look, the font you'll use, and the size of the characters. You can also apply formatting features like boldfacing, italics, underlining, and hidden text, and specify the type case, the amount of space between characters, and the position of those characters in relation to each other.

We examine Word's other two formatting levels—document and paragraph formatting—in Chapter 5, "Formatting Documents and Paragraphs." Chapter 9, "Creating Style Sheets," discusses style sheets, one of Word's most powerful formatting tools, and shows how you can use styles to apply character formatting commands to your text quickly and consistently.

Understanding the language of type

Before you begin to format characters, you should be familiar with a few typographical terms. This section explains the concepts of fonts, font sizes, font styles, and type case.

Fonts

Generally, your first character formatting decision is choosing the font style. As far as Word is concerned, a *font* is a collection of type whose characters share a common design. For instance, all the characters in the font New York share characteristics that distinguish them from the font named Helvetica. (The Macintosh comes with several fonts, which you install in your System file.) Choosing a font in Word is a separate decision from choosing other formatting elements such as font size, style, or case.

Font sizes

After choosing the font, you need to specify the character size. Font sizes are measured in *points*, a printer's unit of measurement of the height of a letter. There are 6 picas in an inch and 12 points in a pica, which means that an inch equals 72 (6 x 12) points. Fonts, however, are never quite as large as their measure, and they can vary considerably in the way in which their sizes compare with others. If you select a block of text and tell Word to display it in 72-point type, the characters you selected will be approximately 1 inch high. If you specify 36 points, the type will be approximately half an inch high; if you specify 18 points, the type will be approximately a quarter inch high, and so on.

Of course, not every letter in the alphabet is the same height. The letter *h* is almost twice as high as the letter *e*. To understand how point sizes relate to the height of a character in your text, you need to consider three terms: *x-height*, *ascender*, and *descender*. As Figure 4-1 illustrates, the x-height represents the height of the "body" of the letter. Ascenders and descenders extend above and below the x-height.

FIGURE 4-1.
Type size is measured from the top of the ascender to the bottom of the descender.

In typography, the height of an individual character is determined approximately by the distance from the bottom of the lowest descender to the top of the highest ascender. As a result, the height of any individual character depends on whether that character has an ascender or descender. Even when you specify 36 points for your type, a given letter with no ascenders or descenders might be only

30 points high. The remaining height is dedicated to the ascending and descending strokes of the letters that have them. Consider the height of the letter x—actually referred to as the *x-height*—as the average character height. The x-height is equal to the distance between the mean line and the baseline, the two lines that appear above and below the bodies of the characters in Figure 4-1. In different fonts, the x-height of a letter of the same type size can vary significantly.

Font styles and type case

In Word, you can specify a *font style* and the *type case* in which you want your selected text to appear. Font style refers to the text's appearance. Unless you change the font style, text in your document appears in the Plain Text font style. If you haven't changed the default font in the Preferences dialog box, the Plain Text font style is the font and size you specified as the default font when you installed Word, with no formatting. To draw attention to the characters, you can also specify one or all of several additional font styles. Choose Bold, Italic, and Underline styles directly from the Format menu or the ribbon. These font styles, plus others, can be selected from the Character dialog box.

Type case refers to the combination of uppercase and lowercase characters in your text. You can apply the All Caps or Small Caps options to characters in your text, or any of five other options: Upper Case, Lower Case, Sentence Case, Title Case, and Toggle Case.

Formatting characters

Usually you select the text you want to work with before you apply your character formats. The text block you format can be as small as a single character or as large as your entire document.

Generally, any new text you enter takes on the format of the text immediately preceding it. For example, if you move the insertion point to the middle of a line of text that is formatted in 18-point bold type, any new characters you type there also appear in 18-point bold. If you highlight text and then apply character formats, Word applies the formats only to the selected text.

You can also change formats without selecting any text. Word applies the formats you choose to the insertion point. When you begin typing again, the text appears with the new formatting characteristics you've chosen. Those characteristics don't change until you apply new formats.

To take full advantage of character formatting options, Word allows you to choose formatting commands from the Font or Format menu or from the Character dialog box. You can also select the font, size, and style formatting options from the ribbon at the top of the document window. In the next paragraphs, we discuss in turn the formatting options available from each location. At the end of this chapter is an introduction to the shortcuts that let you apply character formatting from the keyboard.

The Font and Format menus

The Font menu allows you to apply a font and a point size to highlighted text or to the text at the insertion point. When you choose a font, Word displays a check mark next to the option you've chosen. You can also apply the three most often-used font styles to characters, remove formatting from selected text, and establish a default font and point size from the Font and Format menus.

Applying a font

The name of each font installed in your System file is displayed at the bottom of the Font menu. When you apply a font by choosing it from the menu, Word places a check mark next to that name on the Font menu and formats your text using that font.

Applying a point size

Choose a point size for your text or specify a nonstandard font size from the Other command on the Font menu.

The top of the Font menu contains the point sizes you'll most often need for your documents. If you're using System 7, the standard point sizes are 7, 9, 10, 12, 14, 18, 24, 36, 48, 60, and 72. (After 72, additional standard sizes are available in increments of 10: 82, 92, and so on.) If you're using an earlier system version, the standard point sizes are 9, 10, 12, 14, 18, and 24. Some or all of these point sizes appear outlined on the Font menu, depending on the font selected. An outlined point size indicates you've installed that size of the font in your System file, and Word can display or print those sizes easily.

If you choose a point size not outlined on the Font menu (or if you specify a custom size), the resulting font might not have good resolution on your screen; however, it usually looks fine when printed. If you use an ImageWriter printer, you may notice a few jagged edges or some "muddy" characters on your printed document. If you use a LaserWriter, you'll find that almost any type size between 4 and 127 points looks fine.

You can specify a point size immediately larger or smaller than the current size by choosing Up or Down from the menu, or by pressing the keyboard equivalents for these commands, Command-] and Command-[, respectively. You can also move up to the next standard point size, one on the Font menu, by pressing Command-Shift-period, or down one standard point size by pressing Command-Shift-comma.

If a block of highlighted text is currently formatted in a 12-point font, for example, choose Up from the Font menu, or press Command-], to change the font size to 13 point. Choose Down from the Font menu or press Command-[to change to 11 point. Press Command-Shift-period to change the font size to the next standard size, 14 point. Press Command-Shift-comma to move the font size down one standard size to 10 point.

To change the text size more dramatically, choose Other from the Font menu to display the Character dialog box, where you can specify any point size from 4 to 16,383. We discuss the Character dialog box in detail in a few pages.

Applying a font style

In addition to specifying a new font or point size, you can apply the three most common font formatting styles directly from the Format menu: Bold, Italic, and Underline. Word displays a check mark next to the Plain Text command as the default option. You can change the appearance of the characters in your document by selecting any or all of the other three font style commands.

As you'll see in a few pages, you can combine these font styles and even add other font styles from the Character dialog box to dramatically change the appearance of characters in your document.

Formatting sample text

We'll use the sample document we created in Chapter 3, "Working in Word," to illustrate how to apply character formats from the Font and Format menus. Figure 4-2 shows part of that document, which currently appears in unformatted 12-point New York type. We'll create a headline in 18-point Geneva Bold and change the body of the text to Times.

To display the first line of the sample document (the title) in 18-point Geneva Bold, first select the text. Next, choose the font Geneva and the size 18 Point from

FIGURE 4-2.
This sample document currently appears in unformatted 12-point New York type.

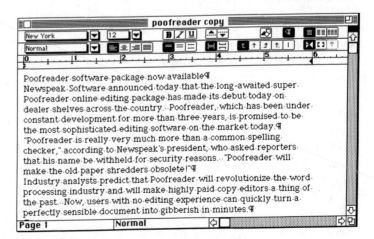

the Font menu. Finally, choose Bold from the Format menu. Notice that each new format you apply changes the appearance of the selected text. Change the body of the document, already in 12-point New York, to appear in 12-point Times by selecting all the text below the title and choosing Times from the Font menu.

Figure 4-3 shows the results of these formatting changes. Notice that within the body of the text, the line breaks have changed with the new font. Because our characters are now a different size, Word automatically reflows the text within our document margins.

FIGURE 4-3.
The title of the document now appears in 18-point Geneva Bold. The body now appears in 12-point Times.

You can't apply more than one font or point size to a character, but you can apply more than one style. If you first select the title and then choose Italic from the Format menu, when you open this menu again you'll see a check mark next to both the Italic and the Bold options. To remove the Italic formatting, highlight the first line, and then choose Italic from the menu again. The check mark disappears, and the text appears only in bold.

Using the Plain Text and Revert To Style options

To remove unwanted formatting quickly from selected text, choose either Plain Text or Revert To Style from the Format menu. You can also choose Revert To Style by pressing Command-Shift-Spacebar.

When you select text and then choose Plain Text, Word removes all character formatting from that text except the font, size, position (superscripting or subscripting), and spacing (condensed or expanded) attributes. (We talk about these other formats in a moment.) Formats such as italics, underlining, and color are stripped away.

Revert To Style does even more. This command removes all manual character formatting and resets the selection or the next text you type to the style formats specified for the paragraph.

For example, if a paragraph style specifies 9-point Helvetica Italic, but you've selected a word in this paragraph, changed its font to Times, and added boldfacing, you can select the word again and choose Revert To Style. Word returns the font to Helvetica and removes the boldfacing. Word does not change the italic formatting, however, because this formatting is part of the style definition for the current paragraph. Because the style applied to this paragraph specifies 9-point Helvetica Italic, any new text you type in this paragraph will also appear in this style. (We discuss styles in Chapter 9, "Creating Style Sheets.")

Changing character case

The Change Case command on the Format menu allows you to change the case of selected text. Unlike most character formatting options, you can't use this command to change the text that appears when you resume typing at the insertion point. You must highlight the text whose case you want to change.

The Change Case command alters the font style of the selected text. If you use Change Case to change a character's case and later change the paragraph style, the character retains the format applied with Change Case. To undo the effects of Change Case, choose Undo Change Case from the Edit menu, or press Command-Z, its keyboard equivalent, before you choose another command. You can't undo Change Case by selecting Revert To Style.

Figure 4-4 shows the Change Case dialog box. The appearance of each of its five options indicates the option's effect on selected text. Upper Case changes all the selected text to capital letters; Lower Case changes text to lowercase. Title Case capitalizes the first letter of each word in the selection. Sentence Case capitalizes only the first letter in a sentence. Toggle Case changes all uppercase text in the selection to lowercase and all lowercase text to uppercase. To apply a new case, simply select the option you want, and then click OK. Click Cancel to close the Change Case dialog box without applying the currently selected option.

FIGURE 4-4.
The Change Case dialog box lets you change the case of selected text.

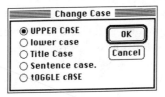

Using the Default Font command

The Default Font command on the Font menu lets you change the font and point size of the default style.

When you choose Default Font from the Font menu, Word displays the Default Font section of the Preferences dialog box, which contains drop-down font and size list boxes that display your installed fonts and point sizes. To change a font or point size from the default options of New York and 12-point, choose a new selection from the appropriate list box, and then click the close box in the upper-left corner of the Preferences dialog box.

Understanding the Character dialog box

The Font and Format menus provide the fastest and easiest way to change a character's font, point size, or style. Other character formatting options are not available directly from these menus. The Character dialog box enables you to specify the position, spacing, and color of selected text.

To display the Character dialog box shown in Figure 4-5, choose Character from the Format menu, or press Command-D or F14. In Figure 4-5, for example, the dialog box displays the format settings for the title of the sample document shown earlier in Figure 4-3. If a selection includes characters whose formats vary, the check boxes in the dialog box appear dimmed, and the other edit bars next to the options remain blank.

FIGURE 4-5.
The Character dialog box also lets you apply character formatting.

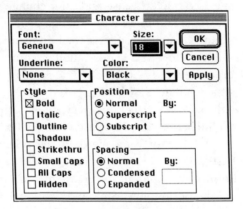

The Font drop-down list box at the top of the Character dialog box allows you to choose any installed font. The Size list box lets you select a point size. You can also specify the style, position, spacing, and color of selected text from the Character dialog box. We'll look at each of these options in turn, beginning with the drop-down Font and Size list boxes.

Font and Size

When you open the Character dialog box, the font applied to the current text selection appears at the top of the Font drop-down list box. (If your selection includes a variety of fonts or sizes, no font name appears.) To apply a font to the current selection, select its name from the list.

The Size drop-down list box displays the installed type sizes for the currently selected font. You can either select one of the standard options displayed or enter a custom size in the edit bar at the top of the Size list box. You can enter any size from 4 through 16,383; Word doesn't accept decimal values like 10.5 in the Size edit bar.

Type styles

In addition to the Bold, Italic, and Underline options on the Format menu, the Character dialog box offers Outline, Shadow, Strikethru, Small Caps, All Caps, and Hidden styles, and additional Underline options. You can apply almost any combination of character formats to text in your document. Notice that there is no Plain Text option. To revert to plain text, deselect all the character format options, and select the None option in the Underline drop-down list box.

Click the check boxes to select the desired combination of character formats. You can apply several character formats and also add an Underline option. The Underline drop-down list box gives you five mutually exclusive options: None, Single, Word, Double, and Dotted. Among the Style options, however, only the All Caps and Small Caps options are mutually exclusive.

Figure 4-6 illustrates several character format option combinations. All the characters in this figure appear in 14-point Times.

Plain

Bold

Italic

Bold Italic

<u>Single Underline</u>

<u>Word Underline</u>

<u>Double Underline</u>

Dotted Underline

~~Strikethru~~

Outline

Bold Outline

Shadow

Bold Shadow

Outline Shadow

Bold Outline Shadow

Bold Outline Shadow Italic

<u>**Bold Outline Shadow Underline**</u>

FIGURE 4-6.   *(continued)*
You can combine Word's style options to create different typographical effects.

FIGURE 4-6. *Continued*

SMALL CAPS

BOLD SMALL CAPS

ALL CAPS

BOLD ITALIC ALL CAPS

BOLD OUTLINE SHADOW ALL CAPS

All Caps and Small Caps

The All Caps and Small Caps options in the Style section of the Character dialog box change only the appearance of the case of the characters in your document. Importantly, Word still considers them to be lowercase. (As you'll see in Chapter 7, the distinction between uppercase and lowercase letters becomes significant when you choose Word's Spelling and Hyphenate commands.)

As Figure 4-7 indicates, when you use All Caps, Word displays the selected text in uppercase letters. When you use the Small Caps option, Word displays your text in capital letters, but reduces the size of the characters entered in lower-case to the immediately lower standard point size. If you use Small Caps to format 24-point characters, for example, Word displays the lowercase letters in 18-point capital letters.

FIGURE 4-7.
The All Caps and Small Caps options change the appearance of characters in your document.

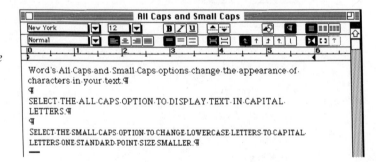

Hidden text

Although the Hidden option is found in the Character dialog box, this feature is really in a category by itself. The Hidden format enables you to suppress the display of text on your screen and in your printed documents. Use the Hidden format to flag special items like PostScript commands and index notations, or to enter notes and questions that you want to hide from view. You can easily control whether Word displays hidden text in the document window and whether Word prints hidden text when it prints your document.

Word displays a gray underline to indicate that the text is hidden. As Figure 4-8 shows, if we assign the Hidden format to the third paragraph in our sample document, Word displays a dotted underline beneath the text in that paragraph. This underline resembles the underline that Word displays when you assign the Dotted Underline format to your text. If you're using both formats, be careful not to confuse the two.

FIGURE 4-8.
Word displays a dotted underline beneath hidden text in your document.

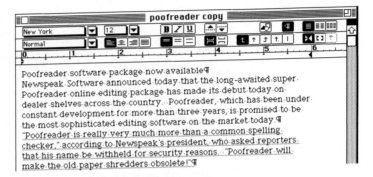

By default, Word displays text to which you've applied the hidden format. To hide this text in the document window, deactivate the Show Hidden Text option in the View section of the Preferences dialog box. You have the option of printing or not printing hidden text. You can display hidden text on your screen without printing it, or print hidden text without displaying it. To print hidden text, select Print Hidden Text in either the Print dialog box on the File menu or the Document dialog box on the Format menu. (Chapter 18, "Customizing Word," describes the Preferences dialog box. We discuss the Print dialog box in Chapter 8, "Printing.")

Position

You can also format your text to appear in superscript or subscript positions by selecting one of the Position options on the right side of the Character dialog box. The Normal option is the default. The Superscript and Subscript options are used to format mathematical notations like exponents and fractions, but you might also find more creative applications for superscripting and subscripting.

To understand the function of Superscript and Subscript, visualize all the text in your document sitting on a baseline like the one in Figure 4-1 that we used to illustrate type size. The Superscript and Subscript options tell Word to shift the selected characters above or below this baseline.

When you select Superscript in the Character dialog box, Word displays a default value of 3 points in the By edit bar. The default Subscript setting is also 3 points. You can change these values to control the distance between the baseline of the superscript or subscript character and the baseline of the rest of the text on the line. Word accepts any value between 0 and 63, but generally rounds the setting to the nearest half-point.

The first paragraph of sample text in Figure 4-9 contains a mathematical expression that is difficult to read because the base and exponent values are the same as the rest of the text. To correct this problem, we can select the desired characters one at a time, choose Character from the Format menu, and then select Superscript or Subscript. The second paragraph in Figure 4-9 displays the mathematical expression formatted with Word's default Superscript and Subscript settings.

FIGURE 4-9.
Superscripting and subscripting change the position of characters in your text.

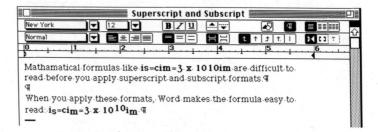

You can apply the default values of the Superscript and Subscript options directly from the keyboard. Press Command-Shift-plus to apply the 3-point Superscript default to selected text. Press Command-Shift-minus to apply the 3-point Subscript default.

Word might have to adjust your line spacing to prevent the superscript and subscript characters from overlapping preceding or succeeding lines. Adding a 3-point superscript to a line of text can have the same effect as using a type size three points larger than the rest of the text on the line. You might be able to avoid this problem by reducing the size of the superscript or subscript characters.

Spacing

The Character dialog box also lets you control the spacing between characters with three Spacing options: Normal, Condensed, and Expanded. These options are particularly helpful if you are working with a monospaced font, such as Monaco or Courier, for which characters are spaced evenly on the screen. When you specify very large or small font sizes, you can adjust large or small gaps between characters easily. Word always adds or subtracts space after a character. Normal spacing is the default. When you select Expanded or Condensed, the default setting for the Expanded or Condensed formats is 1.5 points.

You can specify your own spacing setting in the edit bar. Word accepts any value from 0 to 1.75 points for the Condensed option and up to 14 points for the Expanded option. You can enter decimal values, but Word rounds them down to the nearest 0.25 increment. For printing, Word rounds all decimal values down to 0. If you enter a point setting of 1.65, for example, Word rounds this value to 1.5 when you open the Character dialog box again, and uses a setting of 1 point for printing.

Figure 4-10 illustrates the relationship between the Normal, Condensed, and Expanded spacing. Each line of text is set in unformatted 14-point Times. The effect varies with different font styles.

FIGURE 4-10.
The Normal,
Condensed, and
Expanded Spacing
options control the
spacing between
characters.

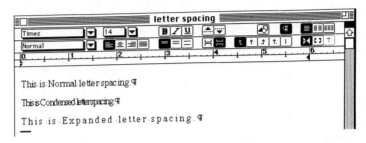

Color

The Character dialog box allows you to apply any of eight colors to a text selection. The default Color choice is Black. You can use different colors throughout a document to emphasize sections of text or individual words or phrases. The colors display only if you view your document on a color monitor or print it with a color printer.

To change the color of selected text, pull down the Color list in the Character dialog box, and select the color you want to use: Black, Blue, Cyan, Green, Magenta, Red, Yellow, or White. When you click OK or Apply, Word changes the color of the text to the one you've selected.

The ribbon

The ribbon at the top of the document window (see Figure 4-11 on the next page) has drop-down list boxes and buttons that let you apply fonts, point sizes, style formatting, and superscripting or subscripting. You can also insert a graphic, show the formatting marks in your document, and format columns directly from the ribbon. Although the ribbon can't control all the character formatting options that Word makes available, this feature does let you apply the formatting options you use most often.

The drop-down list boxes on the left side of the ribbon display the current font and point size and let you choose a new font and point size without leaving the document window. Simply click the arrow to the right of each list box to view the available font and point size options. To apply a new font or point size to your text, select the option from the list. In the appropriate edit bar, you can also type the name of the font or point size you want to apply. The font name must exactly match an option in the drop-down list, and the point size must match one of the available point sizes in the drop-down list.

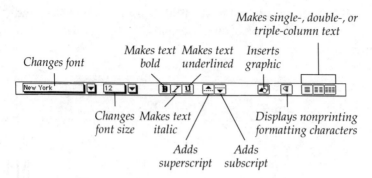

FIGURE 4-11.
The ribbon lets you apply many character formatting commands.

The first set of buttons on the ribbon apply Bold, Italic, and Underline formats. Select the text you want to format, and click the appropriate ribbon button. The button is highlighted to indicate that the format is applied to the current text.

The next set of buttons on the ribbon apply the default value of Word's Superscript and Subscript options. Word highlights the Superscript and Subscript buttons to indicate that they've been applied to the current text. Click the buttons again to deselect either formatting option.

The Insert Picture button and the Show ¶ button enable you to choose these commands directly from the ribbon. Chapter 6, "Creating Graphics," discusses creating and importing graphics in Word. Chapter 3, "Working in Word," introduces the Show ¶ command. You can use the last set of buttons on the ribbon to select the number of columns you want to appear in your printed document. As the graphics on the buttons indicate, you can specify one-, two-, or three-column formats. Chapter 10, "Creating Professional Documents," discusses multicolumn formats.

Keyboard commands

Word offers a number of keyboard shortcuts for formatting characters. Word also enables you to apply a new font and duplicate the format of selected text directly from the keyboard.

Formatting commands

Table 4-1 summarizes the Command-Shift-key shortcuts you can use to format characters in Word. You can also deselect most of these options with the same keyboard command. If you highlight text when you use a Command-Shift-key combination to apply a format, Word assigns that format to the selected text. Similarly, to begin typing in a new format, place your insertion point at the desired location, and use one of the key sequences to specify the new format.

Format	Command-Shift-key	Toggle
All Caps	K	✓
Bold	B	✓
Change Font	E (plus font name)	
Increase Size	Period	
Dotted Underline	\	✓
Double Underline	[	✓
Hidden	X	✓
Decrease Size	Comma	
Italic	I	✓
Outline	D	✓
Plain Text	Spacebar	
Shadow	W	✓
Small Caps	H	✓
Strikethru	/	✓
Subscript 3 points (reduces text one font size)	Minus	
Superscript 3 points (reduces text one font size)	Plus	
Underline	U	✓
Word Underline	]	✓

TABLE 4-1.
You can press the Command and Shift keys in combination with other keys to apply character formatting.

You can toggle many keyboard formatting options on or off by repeating the keystroke. For example, if while typing a sentence you want to underline the next several words, press Command-Shift-U to begin underlining with the next character. When you have finished typing the text you want to underline, press Command-Shift-U again. The next characters you type appear in the format you were using before you applied the underline format.

Although some formatting options shown in Table 4-1 can't be toggled on and off, you can always deactivate a selected option by pressing Command-Shift-Spacebar, which reverts any selected text to the Plain Text format.

Changing a font from the keyboard

You can also apply a new font to highlighted text or to the text that appears after the insertion point from the keyboard. To apply a new font, type the font name after pressing Command-Shift-E.

Suppose that you're currently using the New York font. To switch to Geneva, select the text you want to reformat, or click in the spot where you want to begin using the Geneva type, and press Command-Shift-E to signal a font change. Word displays the prompt *Font* in the status box at the lower-left corner of your screen, as shown in Figure 4-12. To change the font, type the new font name, or enough of the name to uniquely identify the font you want, and then press Return.

FIGURE 4-12.
When you press
Command-Shift-E to
signal a font change,
Word prompts you for
a font name.

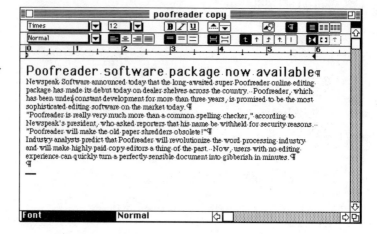

If you decide not to change fonts, press Command-period or click anywhere in the document window to cancel the change.

Format From and Format To

In addition to the keyboard shortcuts that enable you to apply a new formatting option, Word also allows you to copy both the character and the paragraph formats from one block of text to another by pressing Command-Option-V or Shift-F4. The effect of this shortcut depends on whether you've selected text before pressing these key combinations. If you've selected a block of text, Word assumes that you want to copy the formats of the current selection to another part of your document; if you have not selected any text, Word assumes that you want to copy the formats of another text block to your current insertion point.

For example, you can use this technique to apply the format applied to the heading at the top of the screen in Figure 4-12 to the quote in the third paragraph of that document. Rather than reformatting the text manually, select one or more characters from the first headline, and then press Command-Option-V or Shift-F4. Word displays the prompt *Format To* in the status box. Next, select the characters you want to format. As you can see in Figure 4-13, Word displays a dotted line under your *Format* selection. When you press Return to confirm your selection, Word changes the character formatting of the selection to match the original selection.

FIGURE 4-13.

When you press Command-Option-V or Shift-F4, Word prompts you to select the text block to which you want to copy your formats and then displays a dotted line under the Format To selection.

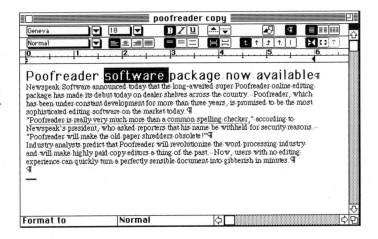

To copy character or paragraph formats, first highlight the characters whose format you want to reproduce, or double-click in the selection bar to select the entire source paragraph. Then press Command-Option-V or Shift-F4. Word displays the prompt *Format To* in the status box. If you highlighted text, reproduce that text's format by selecting your target text. If you selected an entire paragraph, double-click in the selection bar to select your target paragraph. When you press Return, Word transfers the character or paragraph formats as appropriate. (We discuss paragraph formatting in detail in Chapter 5, "Formatting Documents and Paragraphs.")

To copy both character and paragraph formats, you must perform this operation twice—once with the desired characters selected and once with the entire paragraph selected.

You can also change the formatting of characters as you type by pressing Command-Option-V or Shift-F4 without making a selection. When Word displays the prompt *Format From* in the status box, click or drag through a character or block of text in your document that carries the character formats you want to use, and press Return. Any new text that you type at the current insertion point appears in the selected format.

5

Formatting Documents and Paragraphs

Word's formatting capabilities are among the most sophisticated and easy to use of any word-processing program. Formatting in Word is easy because the screen shows exactly how your document will look when it is printed. You can see the effect of your document's page layout specifications and formatting effects such as margins, indentations, tabs, and borders. Word's Format menus show many options to help you lay out and design your document. You can also use the ruler to control your document's margin settings, line and paragraph spacing, and tab settings.

This chapter introduces Word's document and paragraph formatting techniques. We show you how to establish page layout by setting margins and specifying your paper size, page orientation, and page breaks. We also show you how to format paragraphs by using the ruler and the Paragraph dialog box. Finally we show you how to apply tabs, borders, and shading to selected text.

Because Word offers so many options for controlling the appearance of your documents—and because these options often interact—formatting is a vast and complex topic. But don't be intimidated. The majority of your formatting needs can be met using only a few basic techniques. Section Three of this book, "Advanced Formatting Techniques," addresses the more advanced formatting techniques not presented in this chapter. Chapter 10, "Creating Professional Documents," describes techniques for numbering lines and paragraphs, applying frames, and creating multiple columns and sections. Chapter 11, "Adding a Table of Contents, an Index, and Footnotes," shows you how to add a table of contents, an index, and footnotes to your document.

Applying top-down document design

Formatting a document occurs on four levels: the document level, the section level, the paragraph level, and the character level. Any changes you make at one level can affect the formatting characteristics of subsequent levels. For example, if you change a document's margins (a document-level formatting change), you affect every paragraph in your text.

Because the levels are interrelated, you should format your document by moving from the general to the specific. First, decide on the most general components of your document layout, like paper size and margins, and then fine-tune elements of paragraph and character formats. Designing "from the top down" simplifies the document design process and eliminates a lot of backtracking.

The formatting levels that most determine the general appearance of your document are document and paragraph formatting. In Chapter 4, "Formatting Characters," we discussed character formatting, which changes the appearance of the characters in your text. Section-level formatting is covered in Chapter 10, "Creating Professional Documents." Generally, you use multiple sections when you need to change characteristics—such as the number of columns on a page or the header or footer text—from one part of a document to another.

Establishing basic page layout

The first step in document formatting is to establish your overall page layout. In a simple document, margin settings, paper size, and page orientation affect page layout. In a more complex document, you might also consider factors such as multiple columns, mirror margins (different margins on the right and left pages, as you often see in bound documents), headers, and footers. Each of these topics is discussed in detail in Chapter 10, "Creating Professional Documents."

Let's consider how margin settings, paper size, and page orientation work together to determine page layout. Figure 5-1 shows a sketch of Word's default page layout characteristics. The default setting for both the left and right margins is 1.25 inches, and 1 inch for the top and bottom margins. These margin settings indicate the amount of white space between the edge of your paper and the edge of your text area. Word assumes that you're using the familiar "portrait" or "tall" orientation—that is, a document is taller than it is wide—and that the paper size is 8.5 inches wide by 11 inches tall (US Letter size).

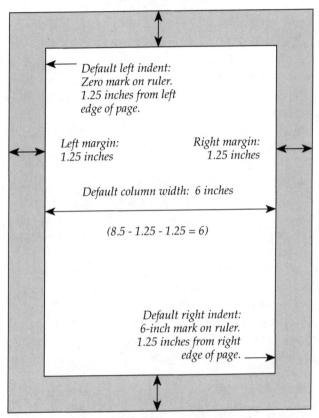

Top margin: 1 inch

Default left indent:
Zero mark on ruler.
1.25 inches from left
edge of page.

Left margin: *Right margin:*
1.25 inches   *1.25 inches*

Default column width: 6 inches

(8.5 - 1.25 - 1.25 = 6)

Default right indent:
6-inch mark on ruler.
1.25 inches from right
edge of page.

Bottom margin: 1 inch

FIGURE 5-1.
This layout sketch displays Word's default page layout settings.

Understanding text area size

As Figure 5-1 illustrates, your margins, paper size, and orientation work together to determine the document's text area. The width of the text area is determined by subtracting the left and right margins from the width of the paper. The height of the text area is determined by subtracting the top and bottom margins from the height of the paper. You can change Word's default settings whenever you wish. When you use Word's default settings, however, the text area on each page is 6 inches wide (8.5 − 1.25 − 1.25) and 9 inches high (11 − 1 − 1).

The size of your text area affects the appearance of each paragraph within the document. You should establish your margin settings, page size, and print orientation before you do any other formatting. This can save you time later; changing the text area size may require you to readjust section or paragraph formatting throughout the document.

Using the ruler

The ruler at the top of your document window lets you view and change many of the page layout specifications. If the ruler doesn't appear in your document window, you can display it by selecting Ruler from the View menu or by pressing Command-R. If you have more than one document window open, you can choose to view the ruler in some windows and not in others. As you can see from the tick marks that appear along the ruler line, Word divides the ruler into ⅛-inch increments.

The ruler can display three different scales: the indent scale (the default display), the margin scale, and the table scale. In the indent scale, the ruler shows you the width of the text column. The margin scale shows your left and right margin settings relative to the width of the paper. The table scale shows text boundaries when you're working in a table. We'll discuss the table scale in Chapter 12, "Creating Tables," when we cover tabular text. Now, let's see how your margin and page settings affect the appearance of the ruler in the first two scales.

The indent scale The ruler in the indent scale looks like the one in Figure 5-2 if you're using Word's default settings and if you've selected a LaserWriter in the Chooser. The ruler scale appears proportionally larger if you specify an Image-Writer, or if you don't specify any printer, in the Chooser.

FIGURE 5-2.

The ruler appears in indent scale when you use Word's default page and margin settings.

In the indent scale, the left edge of your text column is always indicated by the zero point on the ruler—regardless of your left margin setting, the paper size, or the orientation you're using. For example, with Word's default left margin setting of 1.25, the zero point on the ruler represents a position 1.25 inches from the left edge of the paper. If you change your left margin setting to 3, the zero point represents a position 3 inches from the left edge of the paper.

Word marks the right edge of your text by a dotted vertical line in the ruler. When you're using Word's default page and margin settings, the dotted vertical line appears at the 6-inch position on the ruler, as in Figure 5-2.

Below the dotted line is the right indent marker. In the default setting, this triangular marker aligns with the dotted vertical line that marks the right text edge. At the zero point, the first-line and left indent markers together make up a triangle the same size as the one that marks the right indent. We'll talk more about these indent markers later in this chapter. For now, remember that when the ruler is in indent scale these indent markers show only the width of your text column, not the absolute position of the left and right margins. You can drag an indent marker—without changing your overall document margins (indicated by the zero point and the dotted line)—to change the left or right boundary of one or more paragraphs.

The margin scale You can use the margin scale to change your document margins by dragging its margin markers. To change from the indent scale to the margin scale, click the middle button in the set of three scale buttons at the right end of the ruler, as shown in Figure 5-3.

FIGURE 5-3.
The ruler's margin scale shows your left and right document margins relative to the edges of the paper.

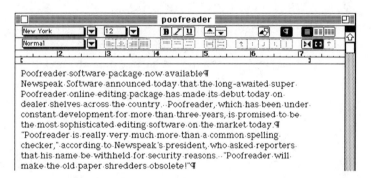

The main difference between the indent scale and the margin scale is the orientation of the numbers on the ruler. In the indent scale, the zero point represents the left edge of your text column. However, in the margin scale, the zero point represents the left edge of the paper. The length of the ruler in the indent scale is determined by the Paper option you select in the Page Setup dialog box, which we discuss later in this chapter.

The margin scale ruler shows two margin markers that correspond to your left and right margin settings in the Document dialog box. When you're using Word's default settings, the left margin marker appears at the 1.25-inch mark on the ruler. The right margin marker appears at the 7.25-inch mark.

Changing margins from the ruler

The easiest way to change the left and right margins of a document is to switch to the margin scale on the ruler and then drag the margin markers to the appropriate positions.

Suppose, for example, that you want to create a document with text lines 4.5 inches wide and left and right margins of equal width. To change the margin settings to fit these specifications, subtract the desired text width from the width of the paper. Assuming you're using paper that is 8.5 inches wide, use the formula:

$$8.5 - 4.5 = 4.0$$

The result, 4.0, is your total margin area. If you want your left and right margins to be equal, next divide the total margin area by 2. In this case, the left and right margins are each 2 inches.

To change the margin settings on the ruler, first click the Margin Scale button. When the margin scale appears, drag the left margin marker to the 2-inch point on the ruler, and then drag the right margin marker to the 6.5-inch point, 2 inches from the right edge of the paper. As you drag, Word displays the width of the margin in the status box at the lower-left corner of your window.

Using the Document dialog box

You can also change your margins by using the Document dialog box shown in Figure 5-4. Choose Document from the Format menu, or press Command-F14. Enter the margins you calculated earlier in both the Left and Right edit bars. In this case, enter 2 in each edit bar.

FIGURE 5-4.
You can use the
Document dialog
box to change your
margin settings.

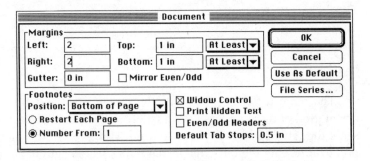

When you enter margin settings in the Document dialog box, you can specify your measurements in inches, centimeters, points, or picas. Use the abbreviations *in, cm, pt,* or *pi* to indicate the unit you're using. When you use the default unit of measure (inches, unless you've specified a different default with the Preferences command on the Tools menu), you don't need to type a unit abbreviation.

Figure 5-5 shows the sample document from Figure 5-3, with new margin settings displayed on the indent scale of the ruler. As you can see, Word reflows the text of the original document to reflect the new margin settings. Word also moves both the right indent marker and the dotted text area marker to the 4.5-inch position on the ruler.

FIGURE 5-5.
*The indent scale on
the ruler indicates
that the new margin
settings reduce the
width of the text area
to 4.5 inches.*

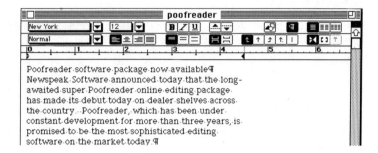

Word doesn't confine you to margins of equal width. If you want your left margin to be 1.5 inches but want to leave your overall text width at 4.5 inches, change your left margin setting to 1.5 and your right margin setting to 2.5.

Because you have changed only the margins, and not the text width, Word will not reflow the text on your screen, and you won't see any change on the indent scale of the ruler. The left edge of your text still begins at the zero point, and the dotted vertical line marking the right edge still appears at the 4.5-inch mark. If you switch to the margin scale, however, you'll see that the left margin is now narrower than the right margin, indicating that the text has been shifted left on the page. In this case, you haven't changed the width of your text area — only its position on the page.

Changing top and bottom margins

To change the top or bottom margin in a document, you must open the Document dialog box — you can't change these margins using the ruler. First, specify the distance from the top and bottom of your paper at which you want text to appear, and then tell Word how you want it to maintain these margins. When you increase the size of the top and/or bottom margin, you decrease the size of your text area, and consequently, the number of lines that can fit on each page. Decreasing either margin increases the size of your text area.

To increase the top margin of a document to 1.5 inches and increase the bottom margin to 2 inches, for example, first choose Document from the Format menu. When the Document dialog box is displayed, select the default *1 in* that appears in the Top edit bar, and replace it by typing *1.5*. Then select the *1 in* that appears in the Bottom edit bar and replace it with *2*. Changing your margins by these measurements reduces the height of your text area to 7.5 inches (11 − 2 − 1.5).

Use the drop-down list boxes at the right of each edit bar to tell Word how to maintain this margin. If you select the At Least option, Word maintains at least the margin measurement you specify. If you select the Exactly option, Word maintains this measurement in all cases.

Specifying paper size

Use the Page Setup dialog box to specify paper size. Although Word's default paper size setting is 8.5 by 11 inches (US Letter), you can easily select another. Table 5-1 lists the dimensions of some of the Paper options that are available in the LaserWriter and ImageWriter Page Setup dialog boxes. The appearance of the Page Setup dialog box depends on the printer and the version of the printer driver software you're using. Figure 5-6 shows a LaserWriter version of this dialog box, and Figure 5-7 shows the ImageWriter version. Keep in mind that changing paper size affects your document margins.

Paper option	Dimensions
US Letter	8.5 by 11 inches
	216 by 279 millimeters
US Legal	8.5 by 14 inches
	216 by 356 millimeters
A4 Letter	8.25 by 11.667 inches
	210 by 297 millimeters
B5 Letter	6.9 by 10.8 inches
	176 by 250 millimeters
Tabloid	11 by 17 inches
	279 by 432 millimeters
International Fanfold	8.25 by 12 inches
	210 by 305 millimeters
Computer Paper	14 by 11 inches
	355 by 279 millimeters
Custom	Paper size specified in the Preferences dialog box

TABLE 5-1.
You can select these dimensions in the LaserWriter or ImageWriter Page Setup dialog box.

The Paper options displayed in your Page Setup dialog box are determined by the printer you've installed and selected in the Chooser. (For more on installing and selecting a printer, see Chapter 8, "Printing.") If you're using an ImageWriter or another printer that can accept custom paper sizes, you can specify the

FIGURE 5-6.
*The Page Setup
dialog box for the
LaserWriter printer
allows you to alter
your page size and
orientation.*

```
LaserWriter Page Setup                          7.0        ( OK )
Paper: ⦿ US Letter  ○ A4 Letter
       ○ US Legal   ○ B5 Letter   ○ [ Tabloid      ▼ ]     ( Cancel )
Reduce or [100]%        Printer Effects:                    ( Options )
Enlarge:                ⊠ Font Substitution?
Orientation             ⊠ Text Smoothing?
                        ⊠ Graphics Smoothing?
                        ⊠ Faster Bitmap Printing?
( Document... )   ⊠ Fractional Widths   □ Print PostScript Over Text
                  □ Use As Default
```

FIGURE 5-7.
*This is the Page Setup
dialog box for an
ImageWriter printer.*

```
ImageWriter                                     7.0        ( OK )
Paper:   ⦿ US Letter          ○ A4 Letter
         ○ US Legal           ○ International Fanfold       ( Cancel )
         ○ Computer Paper
Orientation    Special Effects:   □ Tall Adjusted
                                  □ 50 % Reduction
                                  □ No Gaps Between Pages

( Document... )
               □ Use As Default
```

dimensions of your custom paper using the Preferences command located on the Tools menu. That custom paper size then appears as a Page Setup option.

If you select a Paper option with a width other than 8.5 inches, Word reflects this change on the ruler and in any text you've entered by decreasing or increasing the width of the text area. For example, Figures 5-3 and 5-5 show text entered using Word's default US Letter option. If you change the Paper option to A4 Letter (8.25 inches wide) and click OK to close the dialog box and lock in the new setting, the document window changes to look like the one shown in Figure 5-8.

By decreasing the paper width, we also decreased the width of the text area from 6 inches to 5.75 inches. Word still uses the default left and right margin settings of 1.25 inches, but these margins are now being subtracted from a narrower

FIGURE 5-8.
*Word adjusts text to
fit a new paper size
specified in the Page
Setup dialog box.*

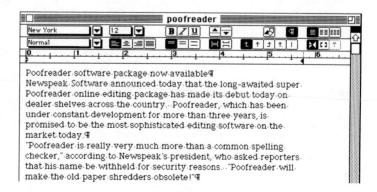

page width, resulting in a narrower text area. If you display the margin scale on the ruler, you'll see that the right margin marker now appears at the 7-inch mark. If you scroll to the right, you'll see that the ruler is now only 8.25 inches long, reflecting the new paper width.

Changing print orientation

The Page Setup dialog box has two Orientation options, as shown in Figures 5-6 and 5-7. The "tall" icon (on the left) tells Word to print your document across the width of the page. The "wide" icon (on the right) tells Word to print your document down the length of the page. Tall and wide orientations are also referred to as "portrait" and "landscape," respectively.

The tall orientation, shown in the layout in Figure 5-1, is Word's default setting and is the one most commonly used. Figure 5-9 shows a layout sketch of a page with a wide orientation using Word's default margin and paper settings. Notice that Word rotates the margins as well as the text. The top and bottom margin settings affect the long sides of the paper, while the left and right margins appear on the short sides.

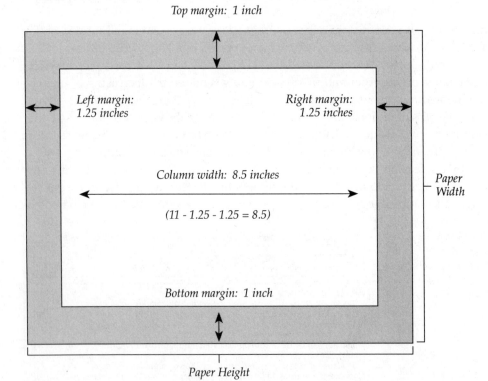

FIGURE 5-9.
When you select the wide orientation, Word rotates your page 90 degrees.

Figure 5-10 shows the document from Figure 5-3 after we changed the orientation from tall to wide. Changing to wide orientation made the text area so wide that you can't view the end of some lines without scrolling horizontally. In fact, if you're using the indent scale on the ruler and you click the horizontal scroll bar, you'll see that the dotted vertical line now appears at the 8.5-inch position on the ruler. Word calculates this new text width by subtracting the left and right margin settings from the width of the paper.

FIGURE 5-10.
After the orientation setting is changed to wide, the right edge of the document cannot be seen without scrolling.

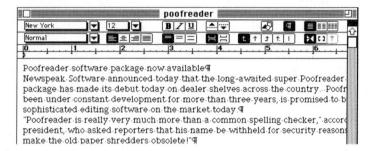

Controlling page breaks

As we've illustrated, the size of the text area on each page of your document determines how long individual lines of text can be and how many lines can fit on a page. Word also offers options that allow you to control more precisely where your page breaks occur. You can specify a page break automatically or manually and easily specify a line break. In addition, you can tell Word how you want to treat the single lines of text, called *widows*, that appear at the top or bottom of a page when you paginate your document.

Using automatic page breaks

You can instruct Word to calculate automatically where page breaks should occur in your document. Specify automatic pagination either by choosing Repaginate Now from the Tools menu as you compose your document or by selecting Background Repagination in the Preferences dialog box. These commands tell Word to mark page breaks on your screen based on the document's page setup specifications. Automatic page breaks are often called *soft page breaks* because their location varies as you make changes to your text. Word indicates an automatic page break on the screen with a dotted horizontal line across the window, marking where a new page begins.

Word doesn't display automatic page breaks on your screen until it has calculated at least once where they should occur. When you start a new document, you can instruct Word to calculate page breaks automatically. Select Background Repagination in the Preferences dialog box to calculate page breaks automatically as you enter and edit text. If you activate this option, depending on the length of your document and your computer's available memory, you might notice a slight slowdown in processing.

You can also instruct Word to determine your page breaks by choosing Repaginate Now from the Tools menu. If you choose Repaginate Now before you have made changes that affect your document's page breaks, Word will not repaginate. In this case, you can force repagination by pressing the Shift key and choosing Full Repaginate Now from the Tools menu. (This command replaces Repaginate Now on the Tools menu when the Shift key is down.)

Word also repaginates your document automatically when you preview it with the Print Preview command, when you print it, or when you choose Page Layout from the View menu. However, when you choose Page Layout, Word repaginates only from the beginning of the document through the current page.

You can determine if your document's pagination is current by checking the page number that appears in the status box in the lower-left corner of the document window. If Word hasn't repaginated since you last entered text or made changes to the text that affect your document's page breaks, the page number appears dim. After you choose Repaginate Now, the page number again appears black, indicating that the location is current. The page number displayed is the page at the top of your document window.

Using manual page breaks

Occasionally you need to force a page break at a particular location in your document. Word lets you insert a page break in your text manually wherever you need one. A manual page break is called a *hard page break* because its position in the document doesn't change when you repaginate or make changes to your text.

Like automatic page breaks, manual page breaks appear on the screen as a single dotted line. You can easily distinguish between these two page breaks, however. As Figure 5-11 shows, a manual page break looks slightly heavier than an automatic page break.

FIGURE 5-11.
Manual page break markers are slightly heavier than Word's automatic page break markers.

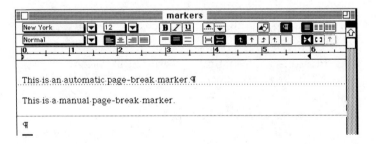

To insert a manual page break in your document, click at the spot where you want the new page to begin, choose Page Break from the Insert menu, or press Shift-Enter. Word inserts a page break before the insertion point. You can delete a manual page break by selecting it or clicking in front of the character that appears directly after it and pressing the Delete key.

Although the manual page-break function can be invaluable, use it sparingly. The position of manual page breaks within the document changes each time you add or delete text. These page breaks can cause unwanted gaps and awkward breaks in your printed document if you edit or reformat your document.

Controlling line breaks

Word automatically breaks lines of text at the right margin of your document, but you can also create your own line breaks. You can press the Return key to start a new paragraph. (If you're displaying paragraph symbols on your screen, you'll see the ¶ symbol at the point where you press Return.) You can also start a new line without beginning a new paragraph by pressing Shift-Return. Word marks the line break on your screen with a ↵ symbol, and considers the new line part of the same paragraph as the line just above it.

Controlling widows

In Word, the term *widow* refers to those straggling single lines of text that appear at the top or bottom of a printed page. Generally, it's considered poor style to allow the first or last line of a paragraph to stand alone on a page. If there isn't room for at least two lines of a paragraph at the bottom of a page, you should push the entire paragraph to the beginning of the next page. Similarly, if there's room at the bottom of a page for all but the last line of a paragraph—causing that last line of the paragraph to stand alone at the top of the next page—you should pull a line from the bottom of the first page to the top of the second page.

You can control widows by selecting the Widow Control option in the Document dialog box. To display the Document dialog box, choose the Document command from the Format menu. The Widow Control option ensures that no single line of text in a paragraph with more than one line appears alone on a page. If you use this option, Word automatically adjusts your page breaks to ensure that at least two lines of a paragraph appear on a page. In some instances, this means that Word won't print the maximum number of lines on a page. As a result, the bottom margin on those pages is slightly larger.

Other considerations

Later chapters of this book discuss other document elements that can affect page breaks. In Chapter 10, "Creating Professional Documents," we'll look at multisection documents. If you specify that each new section begins on a new page, this affects the location of any page breaks that occur after the start of the new section. We'll also consider headers and footers—text that appears at the top or bottom of each printed page. As you'll see, Word can automatically adjust your top or bottom margins to make room for multiline headers and footers. In Chapter 11, "Adding a Table of Contents, an Index, and Footnotes," we'll discuss footnotes, which change the location of page breaks when you place them at the bottom of a page.

Paragraph formatting

After you've established the page layout of a document, you're ready to format individual paragraphs. In many simple documents, your paragraphs might all conform to one or two formats. Other documents might need a variety of paragraph formats. A document with several subheading levels, for example, might require different formatting for each.

Word's paragraph formatting commands always apply to entire paragraphs. To format a paragraph, either place the insertion point anywhere in that paragraph or select some or all of the text in the paragraph before choosing commands. To format two or more paragraphs at once, select any portion of the text spanning both paragraphs.

In this section, we'll show you how to apply Word's paragraph formatting features using both the ruler and the Paragraph dialog box. We'll cover nearly every paragraph formatting option, saving the most advanced formatting options for Chapter 10, "Creating Professional Documents," where we'll cover topics such as applying a frame and positioning an object within a paragraph.

Word's default paragraph settings

You should be familiar with Word's default paragraph settings. Unless you change these settings, Word formats paragraphs in your document flush-left, single-spaced, with no first-line, left, or right indents.

The term *flush-left* refers to how the text is aligned—with an even left and ragged right margin. As you'll see in a moment, you can also format paragraphs to appear with centered, flush-right, or justified alignment.

Single-spacing refers to the amount of leading, or space, between lines of text. Word automatically adds a small amount of space between lines of text to create buffers between the ascenders and descenders of characters on adjacent lines. The amount of space varies, depending on the font and point size you've selected. You can increase or decrease this line spacing to suit your needs.

Word's default paragraph formatting calls for no indents. This means that all the text is aligned within the text column set by your document's margins. You can easily increase or decrease the width of one or more paragraphs, however, by dragging the ruler indent markers. For example, to set a quotation off from the rest of the text in your document, move the left and right indent markers to decrease the width of that paragraph. You can also instruct Word to indent only the first line of text in a paragraph.

Using the ruler buttons

You can use the ruler in the indent scale to apply most paragraph formatting features and to view those features in effect for any individual paragraph. When the ruler appears in the indent scale, you see buttons above and below the ruler line that allow you to control paragraph alignment, line spacing, paragraph spacing, and tabs, as shown in Figure 5-12. On the left, the ruler also displays a drop-down list box that can be used to apply a style to a paragraph. We'll show you how to use this list box in our discussion of style sheets in Chapter 9, "Creating Style Sheets."

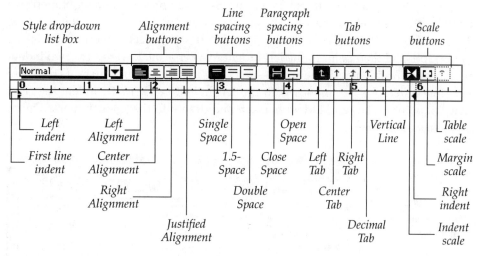

FIGURE 5-12.
You can use the ruler buttons to control paragraph formatting.

The ruler offers an excellent visual summary of the formatting features currently applied to the paragraph containing the insertion point. The ruler buttons, indent markers, and tab markers indicate how that paragraph is formatted. Word highlights the appropriate buttons and displays the tabs and indent markers at their current positions.

The ruler in Figure 5-12, for example, shows that the current paragraph contains all of Word's default formatting features. If you select two or more paragraphs with different formatting, Word dims the buttons and shades the area below the ruler line where the tab and indent markers appear to indicate that no one set of formats applies to the selected text.

Indenting whole paragraphs

When you know how to recognize a paragraph's formatting settings on the ruler, you can use the ruler's indent markers to change a paragraph's format. Using default settings, Word aligns the left and first-line indent markers with the left edge of your text column, and the right indent marker with the right edge. While the left and right margin settings indicate the margins throughout an entire document, the indent markers can control the margins or text width of an individual paragraph.

To change the width of a paragraph, first be sure that your ruler appears in the indent scale by clicking on the Indent Scale button at the left end of the set of scale buttons. Then place the insertion point anywhere in that paragraph, and drag the left and right indent markers on the ruler. For example, if the third paragraph in the sample document in Figure 5-10 was an extended quotation, we could use the indent markers to set this quotation apart from the rest of the text. To indent the left margin of the paragraph, click or select some portion of the paragraph, and then point to the left indent marker—the lower of the two indent markers on the left side of the ruler—and drag it to the 0.5-inch mark. (The upper first-line indent marker moves with the left indent marker.) To indent the right margin, point to the right indent marker, and drag it to the 5.5-inch mark. Figure 5-13 shows the results.

FIGURE 5-13.
Drag the indent markers on the ruler to indent the left and right edges of a paragraph.

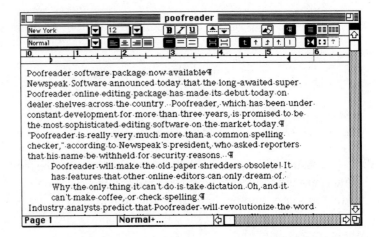

As you move the indent markers, keep in mind that the resulting paragraph indents are relative to the margin settings you've specified either in the Document dialog box or on the margin scale of the ruler.

Nesting paragraphs

Word offers a keyboard shortcut that moves the left indent of a paragraph the width of a default tab stop. (We discuss tab stops later in this chapter. Word's default tab stops are located every half inch along the ruler.) When you press Command-Shift-N, Word *nests* the current paragraph. That is, Word moves its left indent to the right by a half inch. Each time you press Command-Shift-N, Word nests the paragraph another half inch (or the width of a default tab stop). To unnest a paragraph—that is, to move its left indent to the left by a half inch—press Command-Shift-M.

Indenting the first line in a paragraph

Often, you want to indent only the first line of a paragraph to make it easier to distinguish paragraph breaks. You can do this easily by repositioning the top half of the indent marker on the left edge of the ruler. The upper half of the indent marker, called the first-line indent marker, lets you format only the first line of a paragraph. To change your first-line indentation setting, drag the top marker away from the left margin. You can also press Command-Shift-F to move the first-line indent marker to the first default tab stop on the ruler.

Figure 5-14 shows our sample document with a half-inch first-line indentation added to each paragraph. As you can see on the ruler, the first-line indent marker for the first, second, and third paragraphs now appears at the half-inch mark, while the left indent marker remains at zero. Because we changed the indentation in the quotation paragraph, the left indent marker is at the half-inch point and the first-line indent marker is at the 1-inch point.

FIGURE 5-14.
You can move the first-line indent marker to indent the first lines of paragraphs.

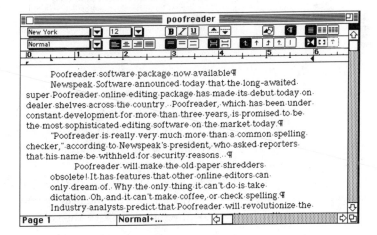

When you split the first-line indent and left indent markers, you can still move both markers simultaneously by dragging the lower, left indent marker. As long as you drag only the lower marker, the distance between the two markers remains unchanged. To shift the quotation in the sample document an additional half inch to the right, for example, point to the left indent marker and drag it to the 1-inch mark on the ruler. When you move the left indent marker, Word moves the first-line indent marker as well, so that it's set at 1.5 inches.

To move the left indent marker without changing the first-line indent, press the Shift key as you drag the marker; it will move independently.

Creating hanging indents

Sometimes, you need to format a paragraph so that the first line starts to the left of the left indentation—to create a numbered or bulleted list of items in which numbers or bullets hang outside the main list, for example. This effect is called a *hanging indent* or *outjustified text*, because the first line of the paragraph "hangs" outside the left margin of the paragraph.

To create the paragraph formatting shown in Figure 5-15, for example, we moved the left indent marker to the half-inch position and kept the first-line indent at the zero position. To create a hanging indent quickly, press Command-Shift-T. Word automatically moves the left indent marker to the first default tab stop on the ruler.

FIGURE 5-15.
To create a hanging indent, drag the ruler's left indent marker to the right of the first-line indent marker.

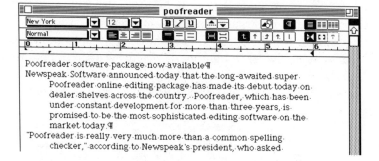

Placing text in the margins

Generally, you use the left, right, and first-line indent markers to decrease the width of a selected paragraph. Word also lets you increase the width of a selected paragraph—in effect, placing text in the margin areas of your printed page. You can use this technique to create headlines that extend beyond your text, or to place text or special symbols in the margin.

To increase the width of a selected paragraph, simply extend the paragraph's margins. The ruler (in the indent scale) extends far beyond the 6.5 inches or so visible in a standard document window. In fact, the ruler extends from –11 inches to 22 inches. To extend the margins, first click the paragraph whose text width you want to increase. Then move the left and first-line indent markers on the ruler to specify the new text width.

To place the first paragraph in Figure 5-15 in the margin, for example, first we placed the insertion point on the title paragraph. Then we scrolled the negative ruler values into view by holding down the Shift key and clicking the left arrow on the horizontal scroll bar. Next, we moved the left and first-line indent markers to the left of the zero point on the ruler. You can see the result in Figure 5-16.

FIGURE 5-16.
*To place text in the
left margin of your
document, move the
left and first-line
indent markers to the
left of the zero point
on the ruler.*

Keep in mind that text entered in the left margin may not be visible after you scroll the document window to the right. Also, when you close a document and then reopen it, Word automatically positions the window with the zero point at the left edge of the window (with the margin text out of view). To scroll to the left of the zero point, press the Shift key as you click the left scroll arrow on the horizontal scroll bar.

Aligning paragraphs

Word's default paragraph formatting aligns all the text in a document evenly with the left indent marker. You can easily change this default alignment, however, by placing the insertion point in the paragraph whose alignment you want to change (or by selecting some text in all the paragraphs you want to format) and clicking on one of the ruler's alignment buttons. The alignment buttons are the leftmost set of buttons on the ruler.

The image on each button indicates its effect: The Left Alignment button aligns the selected text with the left indent marker, creating a ragged right margin. The Center Alignment button centers each line of the selected text between the left and right indent markers. The Right Alignment button aligns the text with the right indent marker, creating a ragged left margin. The Justified Alignment button aligns both edges of the text evenly with the left and right indent markers. When you select justified alignment, Word often increases the width of the blank spaces in your text to keep the left and right edges even.

You can also use keyboard shortcuts to change a paragraph's alignment. Press Command-Shift-L to create left alignment, Command-Shift-C to center a paragraph, Command-Shift-R to create right alignment, and Command-Shift-J to create justified alignment.

Word always aligns text relative to the indent markers on the ruler, not to the page margins you've set up. This can have important implications for how your text is positioned on the page. If you want to center text on the page, for example, be sure that your left and right margins are of equal width before you apply the center alignment.

Figure 5-17 illustrates Word's alignment features. To format the first two lines of the sample page, we selected the title lines and clicked the Center Alignment button on the ruler. To format text in the center of the page, we clicked that text and placed the left and right indent markers at the 1-inch and 5-inch marks, respectively. Then we clicked the Justified Alignment button. To format the last few lines of text, we selected those lines and clicked the Right Alignment button. We also moved the left and first-line indent markers to the 2.5-inch position on the ruler.

FIGURE 5-17.
*Varying paragraph
alignment can dress
up a page design.*

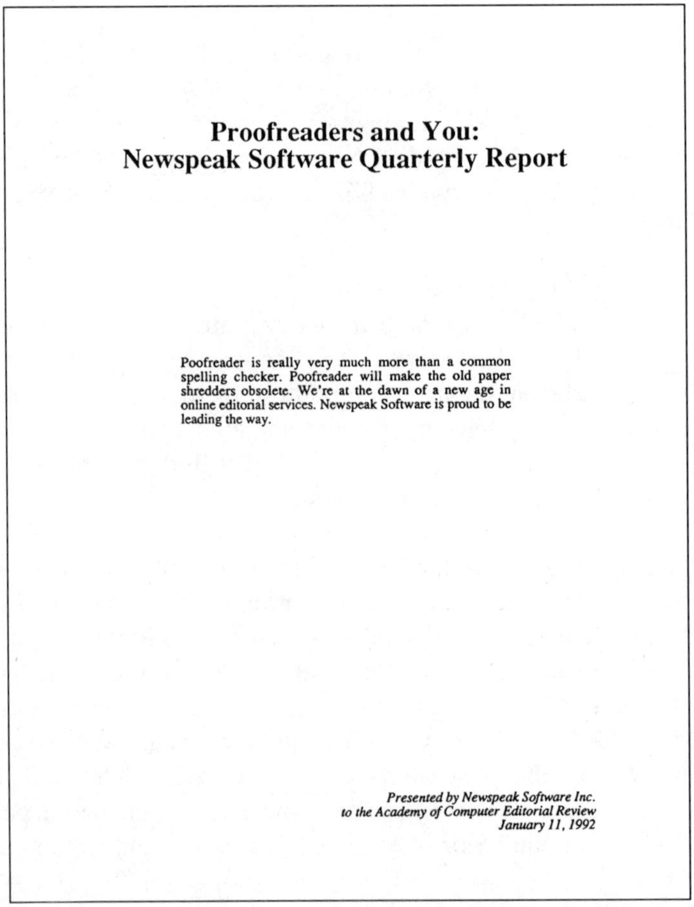

**Proofreaders and You:
Newspeak Software Quarterly Report**

Poofreader is really very much more than a common spelling checker. Poofreader will make the old paper shredders obsolete. We're at the dawn of a new age in online editorial services. Newspeak Software is proud to be leading the way.

*Presented by Newspeak Software Inc.
to the Academy of Computer Editorial Review
January 11, 1992*

Adjusting line spacing

The line spacing buttons on your ruler let you change the amount of space between lines of text in a paragraph. Word automatically adds a small amount of leading, or spacing, between lines of text. This amount varies, depending on the font and point size you've chosen. In the point sizes typically used for the body text of a document (10 and 12), Word generally allows one or two points of space between the tallest ascenders on one line and the lowest descenders on the line immediately above. For example, if you're using 12-point Helvetica type, Word allows 13 points from the bottom of one line to the bottom of the next line, creating a 1-point separator space between lines. When you increase your font size, Word increases the leading proportionally. (We discussed point sizes in detail in Chapter 4, "Formatting Characters.")

In addition to single-spaced lines, you can create 1.5-spaced and double-spaced lines of text. The three spacing buttons are the second group of buttons on the ruler. To apply the single-space, 1.5-space, and double-space line settings, select or place the insertion point in the paragraph you want to format, and then click the appropriate ruler button. The space between the horizontal lines on each button indicates the relative spacing that results.

Although the exact amount of space between lines varies with the font and size, when you use 1.5-line spacing, Word increases the line spacing to allow at least 18 points of space. When you use double-spacing, Word inserts at least 24 points of space above each line. Figure 5-18 shows examples of single-spacing, 1.5-spacing, and double-spacing.

FIGURE 5-18.
Using the ruler buttons, you can create single-spacing, 1.5-spacing, and double-spacing.

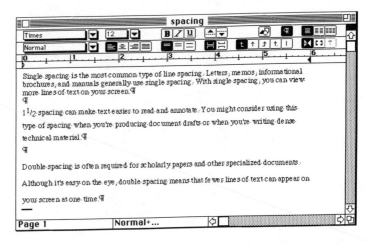

When you use larger type sizes, you may find that Word is unable to create 1.5-spacing or double-spacing. We'll show you how to overcome this problem in a few pages when we discuss the Line setting in the Paragraph dialog box. The

Paragraph dialog box also lets you create more precise line spacing than that
allowed by the ruler buttons.

Adjusting paragraph spacing

Paragraph spacing is similar to line spacing except that the spacing is applied
only above the first line of the selected paragraph. The paragraph spacing buttons
are the third set of buttons on the ruler. Word offers two standard paragraph
spacing options: open and closed. Closed paragraph spacing is Word's default
format. In closed spacing, Word inserts no additional line spacing between
paragraphs. When you use the open setting, Word adds 12 points of space before
the first line of text in each selected paragraph, in addition to any space specified
by the paragraph's Line setting or by the line spacing buttons on the ruler.

To apply an open or closed paragraph setting, select or click the paragraph
you want to format, and then click the appropriate ruler button. The button on the
left specifies closed spacing; the button on the right specifies open spacing. You
can also press Command-Shift-O to toggle between these two options. This keystroke inserts 12 points of space above a paragraph with closed spacing or removes 12 points of space above a paragraph with open spacing. Figure 5-19 shows
an example of a document in which the paragraphs are assigned open spacing.

FIGURE 5-19.
Use open spacing to
create extra space
between paragraphs.

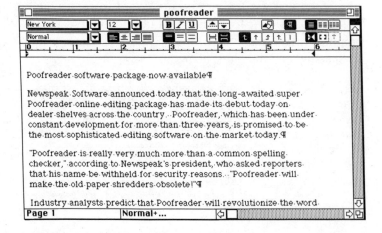

You can also insert space before and after a paragraph by using the Before
and After settings in the Paragraph dialog box. These settings allow you to
specify precisely how much space you want to insert, rather than Word's default
spacing of 12 points. We'll talk more about the Before and After settings when we
discuss the Paragraph dialog box.

A paragraph spacing tip

Although you might be inclined to create blank spaces between paragraphs by pressing the Return key, using the Open Space button or the Before and After settings in the Paragraph dialog box is more effective. When you press Return to create a blank paragraph, that paragraph will most likely carry the same formats as the paragraph immediately above it. As a result, the size of your blank lines may not be consistent throughout a document.

Using the Open Space button or the Before and After settings makes your blank lines the same size. To easily change or remove the spacing around multiple paragraphs, select those paragraphs, and then select the Closed Space button on the ruler, or change the Before or After settings in the Paragraph dialog box. Word reformats all the selected paragraphs in one step.

The Paragraph dialog box

Although the ruler usually offers the quickest and easiest way to format paragraphs, the Paragraph dialog box presents formatting options not available on the ruler, and lets you specify some format settings—such as the position of indents and the space between paragraphs—with greater precision than you can get from the ruler. The Paragraph dialog box also allows you to access dialog boxes that let you apply tabs, borders and shading, and a frame to a selected paragraph.

We'll talk about the setting options available in the Paragraph dialog box next, and then we'll discuss applying tabs, borders, and shading to paragraphs in your document. We'll save our discussion of the Frame command for Chapter 10, "Creating Professional Documents," where we introduce Word's other advanced formatting features.

To open the Paragraph dialog box, choose Paragraph from the Format menu or press Command-M or Shift-F14. Word displays the dialog box shown in Figure 5-20. You can also open the dialog box by double-clicking above the scale line on the ruler. As it opens the Paragraph dialog box, Word indicates the settings applied to the current paragraph and displays the ruler if it is not already in view.

FIGURE 5-20.

The Paragraph dialog box displays the format settings for the current paragraph.

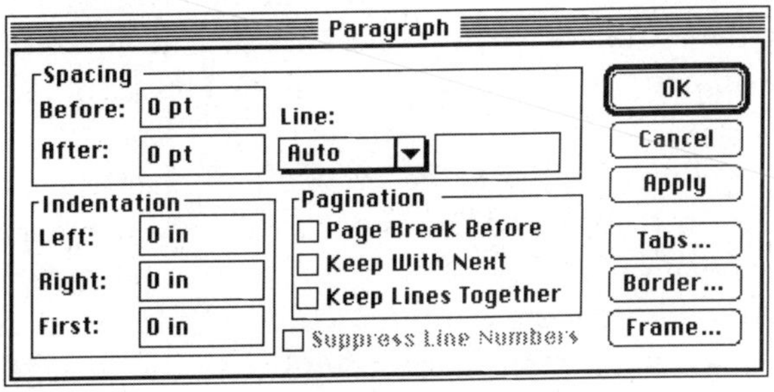

To change settings in the Paragraph dialog box, specify the new settings, and close the dialog box by clicking OK. If you want to apply some settings to the current paragraph(s) without closing the dialog box, click Apply. To close the dialog box without implementing any changes, click Cancel.

Spacing and indentation settings

The spacing and indentation settings in the Paragraph dialog box should look familiar to you. They resemble the formatting options available on the ruler. The Spacing settings allow you to indicate the amount of space you want to appear before and after a paragraph, as well as the line spacing within the paragraph. The Indentation settings let you specify exactly how far you want the selected paragraph to indent from the document margins.

Paragraph spacing

The Before setting, like the Open Space button on the ruler, specifies the amount of space you want to insert before the first line of a paragraph. The After setting inserts space after the last line in a paragraph.

When you enter a Spacing setting, you can use points, inches, picas, centimeters, or lines as your unit of measure. Type a number followed by *pt, in, ", pi, cm*, or *li*. Don't include a period after the unit's abbreviation, however. Word will be unable to interpret your entry and will display an error message. You need not include a space between the number you type and the unit of measure.

If you don't specify a unit of measure, Word assumes that the unit of measure is points. If you specify lines, inches, picas, or centimeters, Word then converts the unit into points. If you enter a Before setting of *0.25 in* and then close the Paragraph dialog box, for example, you'll see *18 pt* in the Before edit bar the next time you open the Paragraph dialog box.

Line spacing

The Paragraph dialog box allows you to create even more precise line spacing than do the ruler buttons. The Line setting establishes the total amount of space you want to allow for each line in the paragraph.

The Line edit bar specifies the amount of space allowed from the bottom of one line to the bottom of the next line. For example, if you enter *18* in the Line edit bar, Word allows 18 points of space from the bottom of one line to the bottom of the next line.

The drop-down list box to the left of the edit bar lets you select when to apply the spacing you've indicated. The default value, Auto, instructs Word to apply the spacing automatically to each line in the selected paragraph. When you select At Least, Word considers the figure in the edit bar to be a minimum line spacing value. This setting is particularly useful when the selected paragraph contains text of varying font sizes; Word automatically increases the spacing between lines to accommodate any unusually large character. If, as in Figure 5-21, a line in the selected paragraph contains a word in a font larger than the surrounding text, Word increases the spacing for this line to prevent the text from overlapping in the line above.

FIGURE 5-21.
When you select the
At Least spacing
option, Word increases
line spacing to
accommodate
unusually large
characters.

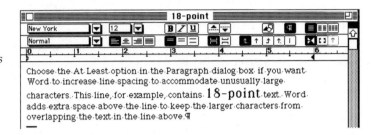

When you select Exactly, the spacing is set to be absolute, even if some characters will overlap. With this setting, some characters might appear truncated on the screen, but they appear in their entirety when you print.

Indentation

You can specify indentation settings in the Paragraph dialog box in the three Indentation edit bars: Left, Right, and First. Entering a value in one of these edit bars lets you specify the position of an indentation to two decimal places of precision.

You can specify your indent positions in inches, points, picas, or centimeters by typing *in*, *"*, *pt*, *pi*, or *cm* after the number in the edit bar. If you don't specify a unit, Word assumes inches (or whatever unit you're using on the ruler).

After you make an entry in one of the Indentation edit bars and close the dialog box, Word automatically moves the appropriate indent marker to reflect the specified setting. When you specify the first-line indent, keep in mind that you must specify the measurement in the First edit bar relative to the left-indent setting. To create a hanging indent of half an inch—that is, to create a paragraph whose first line extends half an inch beyond the left margin of the rest of the paragraph—type *−0.5* in the First edit bar. Word extends the first line half an inch to the left of the paragraph margin no matter what value you type in the Left edit bar.

Pagination settings

The Paragraph dialog box contains three check box options that help you to control page breaks in your document: Page Break Before, Keep With Next, and Keep Lines Together.

When you apply one of these settings to a paragraph, Word displays a small black box called a *paragraph properties mark* in the left margin, next to the first line of that paragraph on your screen. This mark informs you that a formatting option has been applied that doesn't change the appearance of the paragraph on your screen or change the markers and buttons on the ruler. The paragraph properties mark doesn't appear in your printed document.

The Page Break Before option

The Page Break Before option allows you to force a page break before a paragraph. This option is useful when you want a particular paragraph—such as a subheading—to always appear at the top of a page.

The Page Break Before option works like a manual page break before a paragraph with two exceptions: When you select Page Break Before, you won't see a line marking the page break on your screen until you repaginate the document. (If you've selected the Background Repagination option in the Preferences dialog box, the line may appear a few seconds after you assign Page Break Before.) More importantly, if you copy or move the paragraph, you copy the Page Break Before format as well.

The Keep With Next option

The Keep With Next option tells Word to print the selected paragraph on the same page as the following paragraph. If there isn't room for both paragraphs on the same page, Word pushes both paragraphs to the next page.

The Keep With Next option often comes in handy. If your document contains subheadings, assign the Keep With Next format to each subheading to prevent Word from printing a subheading at the bottom of a page and the following text at the top of the next page. When you create a list, use Keep With Next to keep related items together. If you want to keep more than two paragraphs on the same page, assign Keep With Next to all but the last paragraph.

Keep With Next doesn't guarantee that all the lines in each paragraph will remain on the same page. Word ensures that at least one line from each paragraph appears on the same page as the adjacent paragraph. The Widow Control option in the Document dialog box makes certain that at least two lines from each paragraph appear together on a page. If you want two paragraphs to appear together on the same page in their entirety, assign the Keep With Next format to the first paragraph and also assign the Keep Lines Together format to both paragraphs.

The Keep Lines Together option

The Keep Lines Together option tells Word you don't want to split the selected paragraph between pages. If the formatted paragraph falls at the bottom of a page, and Word doesn't have room to print it in its entirety, Word pushes the complete paragraph to the beginning of the next page.

Other options

In addition to letting you identify spacing and indentation settings and establish how Word paginates your document, the Paragraph dialog box enables you to suppress line numbers within a selected paragraph. We talk more about this feature in Chapter 10, "Creating Professional Documents," when we discuss line numbering.

Working with tabs

If you've used a typewriter or another word-processing program, you're probably familiar with tab stops. Tab stops are positions you set within the margins of a document to create columns of text, such as tables and charts. In Word, you might use tab stops to create simple tables such as a table of contents, or to format documents that contain lists. More complex documents should take advantage of Word's table feature, which does such things as wrapping text within individual columns of a table. We'll look at the table feature in Chapter 12, "Creating Tables."

Setting tab stops in Word is a two-step process. First specify the tab settings on the ruler, and then press the Tab key to position text according to these settings. Each time you press the Tab key, Word moves the insertion point to the next tab stop, creating a tab space. Word marks each tab space on your screen with a right-pointing arrow ($\rightarrow$), and stores the setting for the tab stops with the selected paragraph's other formatting information in the paragraph symbol at the end of the paragraph.

Word's default tab stops

If you press the Tab key without first specifying tab stops on the ruler, Word uses its default tab settings: left-aligned tab stops at every half-inch mark along the ruler. Word displays these default settings as inverted T marks that hang below the ruler line ($\perp$). You can easily change Word's default tab stops by changing the default tab settings in the Document dialog box.

To change Word's default tab settings, choose Document from the Format menu. In the edit bar labeled *Default Tab Stops*, enter a new tab interval that is less than the measurement of the right edge of your text, and click OK. To set default tab stops at every inch along the ruler, for example, enter 1 in the Default Tab Stops edit bar. To specify this setting for future documents as well as for the current document, click the Use As Default button, and then click the OK button.

Using tab stops

Although Word's default tab stops are often just what you need, you can also set tabs at uneven intervals, by creating your own tab stops. Word allows you to create up to 50 tab stops within a single paragraph. You can place tab stops beyond the right indent marker and the dotted line that marks the right edge of the text on your page. You also can place tabs to the left of the zero point on the ruler (in the indent scale).

When you create a tab stop, Word also allows you to specify how the text at that tab stop will be aligned. Table 5-2 shows the four tab alignment buttons that appear on your ruler. These buttons align numbers to the left or right of the tab stop, center text around the tab stop, or position numbers in a column that treats the tab stop as the decimal point location. Figure 5-22 on the next page displays the effects of the four types of tab stops.

Button	Name
↳	Left Tab Button
↑	Center Tab Button
↱	Right Tab Button
↑.	Decimal Tab Button
I	Vertical Line Button

TABLE 5-2.
The four tab buttons on the ruler allow you to select different tab alignments, and the Vertical Line button lets you create vertical lines.

To specify a new tab stop, first select the paragraph you want to format with tabs, or press Return to start a new paragraph. Next, highlight the tab alignment button you want by clicking that button, and then click below the ruler line where you want the tab to appear. When you insert a tab on the ruler, Word clears all default tabs that appear to the left of the new tab.

For example, to place a left-aligned tab at the 2-inch mark on your ruler, click the Left Tab button, and then click below the 2-inch mark. Word deletes the default tab stops at the 0.5-inch, 1-inch, and 1.5-inch positions on the ruler.

Word readjusts any existing spaces according to the new tab stop(s) you've established. Suppose that before you created the custom tab stop at the 2-inch position, you had pressed the Tab key to move the text at the beginning of the current line to the first default tab stop at the half-inch position. When you establish the custom tab stop, Word increases the tab space, moving the beginning of the line to the 2-inch position.

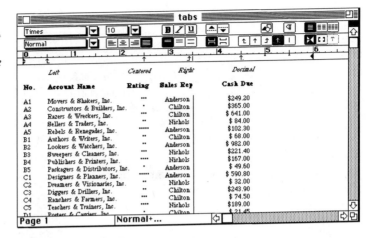

FIGURE 5-22.
*You can align text
with any of four
different tab stops. The
vertical line next to
the Sales Rep column
was created with the
Vertical Line tab stop.*

To reposition a tab, point to the tab marker on the ruler and drag. If you press the Shift key as you drag the tab stop, Word moves not only that tab marker, but also all tab markers that appear to the right of that marker.

To clear a tab stop, click the tab symbol with the pointer, and drag it up or down off the ruler. When you move or delete tab stops, Word automatically reformats the text of the current paragraph.

Adding vertical lines

Beside the tab buttons on your ruler, Word displays a Vertical Line button. You can select this button to create vertical lines in a paragraph. Because you often use this button to separate columns you create with tabs, it is grouped with the tab buttons. To insert a vertical line in a paragraph, click the button to select it, and then click the ruler to specify the position of the line. The example in Figure 5-22 shows how you can apply vertical lines to distinguish columns in your document.

Using the Tabs dialog box

You can also use the Tabs dialog box, shown in Figure 5-23, to set, move, and clear tab stops. Access this dialog box by choosing Tabs from the Paragraph dialog box, or by double-clicking a tab button or the Vertical Line button on the ruler.

FIGURE 5-23.
You can set, move, and
clear tabs with the
Tabs dialog box.

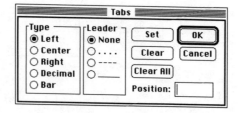

In most cases, it's more convenient to set, move, and clear tabs directly on the ruler. The Tabs dialog box offers some features not available on the ruler, however. You can position tab stops more precisely using the Tabs dialog box, and quickly clear all the tabs currently set on the ruler.

Setting tab stops

To set a tab stop using the Tabs dialog box, type in the Position edit bar the position along the ruler where you want to place the tab, specify the tab's alignment Type option, and then click the Set button. Word adds the type of tab you specified to the ruler. You can add only one tab in this manner. If you enter a new position in the Position edit bar, Word moves the currently active tab.

You can also use the Tabs dialog box to change the position of a tab or vertical line. With the Tabs dialog box open, select its marker on the ruler. Word displays the current position of the tab or vertical line in the Position edit bar. Change this position by typing a new one and choosing Set. Like the Indentation settings in the Paragraph dialog box, the position can be expressed in inches (*in*), centimeters (*cm*), points (*pt*), or picas (*pi*). If you don't specify a unit of measure, Word uses the unit of measure specified on the ruler.

Changing tab alignment

To change a tab's alignment in the Tabs dialog box, click the tab marker on the ruler. Select a different alignment by clicking another Type option.

Clearing a tab

To clear a tab using the Tabs dialog box, click the tab marker on the ruler (or type its position in the Position edit bar), and then click the Clear button. You can remove all tab stops in the currently selected paragraph—except the defaults—by choosing the Clear All button and then clicking OK in the Tabs dialog box.

Tab leader characters

The Tabs dialog box also enables you to create tab leader characters quickly and easily. A *tab leader* is a character that's repeated on a line to fill in the space between columns of text. Tab leaders are often used to connect items in a table, guiding the reader's eye from one column to the next. Word offers three kinds of tab leaders: periods, hyphens, and underline characters. Figure 5-24 shows a sample document that uses tab leaders. The periods guide the reader's eye from the chapter names in the second column to the page numbers in the third column, and underline characters separate the sections of the table. You can specify leaders before you enter text or add leaders to text that you've already formatted.

FIGURE 5-24.

The period characters help guide the reader's eye from the chapter title column to the correct page number.

Contents

Section 1		
Chapter 1	Worksheet Basics	3
Chapter 2	Formatting the Worksheet	25
Chapter 3	Editing the Worksheet	76
Chapter 4	Working with Windows	103
Section 2		
Chapter 5	Built-in Functions	137
Chapter 6	Date and Time	163
Chapter 7	Other Worksheet Topics	200
Chapter 8	Printing the Worksheet	254
Section 3		
Chapter 9	Basic Graphic Techniques	311
Chapter 10	Chart Formatting	349
Chapter 11	Advanced Charting Features	398

To add a tab leader, open the Tabs dialog box, and click the tab marker on the ruler to which you want the leader to extend. Then click one of the Leader options, and select Set. To delete a tab leader, select the tab marker that has a leader, and then select None from the Leader options.

As Figure 5-24 illustrates, you can also use a tab leader to create a horizontal line. To create the line that appears next to each section name, we placed the insertion point on a section name and inserted a left-aligned tab where the chapter names begin. Then we inserted a right-aligned tab at the 6-inch position, where the page numbers appear. The first tab marks the start of the line where the leader characters will begin, and the second tab marks the end of the line. We next opened the Tabs dialog box and clicked the tab marker at the 6-inch position on the ruler. Then we clicked the fourth Leader option (____) and selected Set.

When you create a horizontal line in this way, the line doesn't appear in your document until you press the Tab key. With the insertion point positioned just after the section name, we pressed the Tab key twice. The first time, Word moved the insertion point to the first tab stop, which has no leader. The second time, Word moved the insertion point to the second tab stop at the 6-inch position and filled in the space between the first and second tabs with underline characters. A similar line in your document may print as a solid line or a dashed line, depending on the printer you use.

Working with borders

Word's Border command lets you apply either a preset border box or a border of your own design to a selected paragraph or group of paragraphs. You can also apply shadowing and shading to a selected paragraph. We discuss adding borders to graphics in Chapter 6, "Creating Graphics," and to tables in Chapter 12, "Creating Tables."

To create a paragraph border, first place the insertion point in the paragraph (or paragraphs) where you want the border to appear. Then either open the Paragraph dialog box and click the Border button, or choose Border from the Format menu. The Border dialog box appears as shown in Figure 5-25.

The Border dialog box offers preset border formats, line style options, and a border guide that indicates how the selected paragraph will look with the options you've selected. Select a line style, and then click the sides of the model where you want the borderlines to appear on your paragraph.

When you apply a border, it becomes part of the paragraph's formatting. As a result, the width of horizontal borders is determined by the margin settings for the selected paragraph; the length of vertical borders is determined by the length of the selection. Because the border is part of the paragraph style, you can delete or add information to a selected paragraph without reapplying its border.

FIGURE 5-25.
Use the Border command to apply a border to a selected paragraph.

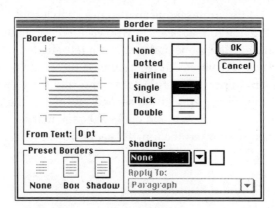

Selecting a preset border

The Preset Borders option in the lower-left corner of the Border dialog box lets you automatically apply either a box or a shadowed box to a selected paragraph. The Box option surrounds the selection with lines of even width; the Shadow option surrounds a paragraph with a border that gives the impression of depth. To apply either preset option, click the option. Word indicates how your paragraph will look in the border guide that appears above the preset options.

Select the line style you want by clicking a Line option: None, Dotted, Hairline, Single, Thick, or Double. None removes a selected border; Dotted applies a broken line; Hairline applies a half-point line that you can see only on a LaserWriter or equivalent PostScript printer (this style appears as a single line on your screen); Single applies a 1-point border; Thick applies a 2-point border; and Double applies two 1-point borders separated by 2 points of space.

When you select either preset border, the line style you choose applies to the entire paragraph border. Word indicates how the border will look by applying the line style to the border guide. If you select the Shadow Box with a double line, for example, Word displays the border in the border box as shown in Figure 5-26.

FIGURE 5-26.
*Word displays a
diagram of the
specified border in
the Border box.*

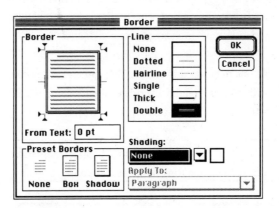

To apply the border selection to a paragraph, click OK in the Border dialog box to confirm your choices. (If you accessed the Border dialog box from the Paragraph dialog box, click OK or Apply in the Paragraph dialog box. If you click Cancel, Word doesn't apply the border you specified.) Figure 5-27 shows some printed examples of Word's preset borders with different line styles.

A Box border with a Single line looks like this. Word aligns the right and left edges of the border box with the right and left edges of the text area.

This is a Box border with a Thick line. Word aligns the right and left edges of the border box with the right and left edges of the text area.

A Box border with a Double line looks like this. Word aligns the right and left edges of the border box with the right and left edges of the text area.

We used the Dotted line border style and the Box option to create this border.

This border displays the Hairline style. You must have a PostScript printer in order to print a hairline border.

You can create a border on just the left side of your paragraph by clicking on the left side of the model in the Border dialog box. This border is formatted with the Thick line style. Bar borders help to mark new or changed text in a document.

We used a Double line to create this border. You can create a border on just the left side of your paragraph by clicking on the left side of the model in the Border dialog box. Bar borders help to mark new or changed text in a document.

You can use the Shadow Box border option to jazz up a document's title. This Shadow Box border was created with the Single line border style.

We used the Double line style to create this Shadow Box border. You might use the Shadow Box border option to jazz up a document's title.

FIGURE 5-27.
These are some of Word's standard border types.

Creating a custom border

You can use the Border dialog box to design your own border. Unlike a preset border, a custom border need not surround the selected paragraph on all four sides, and each side can have a different line style.

Creating a custom border is easy. First select a line style, and then click between the border guides on the border diagram to indicate where you want a line to appear. The border guides mark five border positions: above, below, left, right, and between paragraphs. Each time you click between two guides, a borderline in the currently selected style appears on the border diagram. Clicking a horizontal part of a border guide applies a horizontal border, and clicking a vertical part of a guide applies a vertical border. Double-clicking the border diagram applies a border on all four sides.

For example, to place a double line above and below a paragraph and a thick line on the left side of the same paragraph, first select or click the paragraph, and then open the Borders dialog box. Click Double in the Line options. Next, click between the top guides on the Border model to place the double-line above the paragraph, and then click between the bottom guides to place another double-line below the paragraph. Next, click the left side of the model. The double line border is applied. Change it to the thick border by clicking Thick in the Line options. The Border dialog box should look like Figure 5-28.

FIGURE 5-28.
Format different
border guides to create
a custom border.

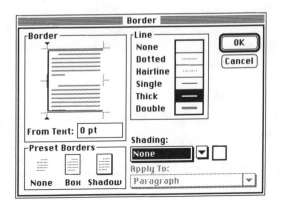

Removing a border

To remove a borderline, click it with the None line style selected. For example, suppose that you specified the border shown in Figure 5-28, then you decided that you want only the top borderline. If you select None and then click again on the left and bottom border guides in the border diagram, Word applies this style—in effect removing these lines.

If you're unsure about which style you've applied to a borderline, press the Option key, and then click the border guide section. Word highlights the border style applied to that section. This technique is useful mainly for distinguishing between a single line and a hairline border section. As we've mentioned, Word displays hairline borders the same as single lines on your screen.

Controlling border spacing

Word maintains at least two points of space between a border and the contents of a selected paragraph. Often, adding space to a border makes the paragraph much more attractive. To increase the amount of space between the border and a paragraph's text, use the From Text edit bar. In the From Text edit bar, enter the amount of space (in points) you want to add between the border and the paragraph text. Word adds the space you specify to the default 2-point space. For example, if you enter 4 in the From Text edit bar, Word inserts a total of 6 points of space between every borderline and the paragraph text.

Because Word adds space between a selection and a left and right border, borders extend at least two points outside a paragraph's margins. If you add space in the From Text edit bar, borders extend even farther. Word doesn't allow you to enter a negative number in this edit bar to decrease the amount of space between the border and the paragraph text.

To align borders with the rest of your margins, use the Paragraph dialog box to indent the paragraph by the same amount of space as between the selection and the border. You cannot make such fine adjustments from the ruler. If you're using the default 2-point space, for example, indent the paragraph 2 points. Its border then appears the same distance from the margin as the rest of your document. If you've specified 4 points in the From Text edit bar, indent the paragraph 6 points—2 points to compensate for Word's default spacing, plus the additional 4 points. If you've applied the Thick or Double line style to the border, you might need to increase this distance by one or two additional points to accommodate these larger line styles.

Placing borders around more than one paragraph

To place a single border around two or more paragraphs, select text from each paragraph before you open the Border dialog box. When you select either preset border option, Word places the appropriate border box around all the selected paragraphs, but does not place borderlines between each paragraph in the selection.

If you want a horizontal borderline to appear between each paragraph in the selection, click between the center border guides. Figure 5-29 on the next page shows a document with no indentation and a borderline between paragraphs.

Remember that the width of horizontal borders you apply to a selection is determined by the indents you've established for the selection. If, for example, you

FIGURE 5-29.
Clicking between the center border guides on the diagram places a horizontal borderline between paragraphs.

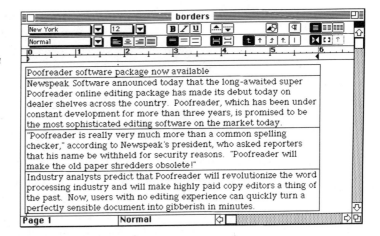

want to place several paragraphs within a single box border, be sure that all paragraphs share the same indent settings. If you try to apply a single border to selected paragraphs with separate indentation settings, Word places each paragraph in a separate border to accommodate the different widths, as shown in Figure 5-30.

FIGURE 5-30.
Word places adjoining paragraphs of different widths within their own borders.

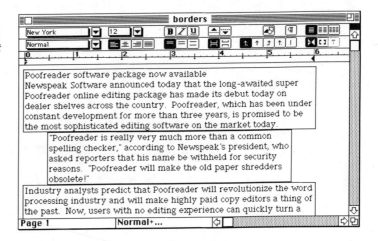

If you've used the Paragraph dialog box's Before and After settings to insert space before or after a paragraph, Word applies a 2-point space between the border and the paragraph, but maintains Before and After settings between paragraphs not immediately adjoining the border.

To separate the border boxes of adjacent paragraphs with some space, move the insertion point to the beginning of the lower paragraph, and press Return to insert a blank paragraph between the two paragraphs. Then remove the border from this blank paragraph.

Placing borders around different elements

If you select a paragraph or group of paragraphs with different elements — for example, if your selection contains text and a graphic or a table — Word monitors the elements in your selection and displays them in the Apply To list box. Use this list box to specify the element to which you want to apply a border.

If you want to apply a border to the entire paragraph or group of paragraphs you've selected, for example, specify Paragraph before closing the Border dialog box. To apply a border to a table within a paragraph, select the appropriate list box option. (We discuss creating and placing graphics in Chapter 6, "Creating Graphics." Chapter 12, "Creating Tables," introduces Word's table features.)

Applying shading to a paragraph

The Border dialog box also lets you shade the background of a paragraph. The shading you apply becomes part of the paragraph format, and it extends between the margins you've set for the paragraph, as shown in Figure 5-31. You can add, delete, and edit text in the shaded paragraph just like any other text. (You can also apply shading to cells in a table. We'll show you how to do this in Chapter 12, "Creating Tables.")

FIGURE 5-31.
You can also apply shading to a selected paragraph by specifying a shading percentage in the Border dialog box.

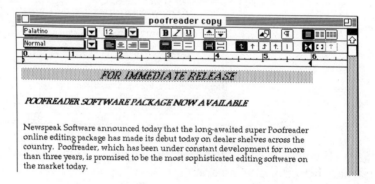

To apply shading to a paragraph, select the paragraph and display the Border dialog box. Then select the shading percentage you want to apply. You indicate the pattern of shade you want in the Shading drop-down list box, in the lower-right section of the Border dialog box. The Shading list box presents 17 shading percentages. The higher the percentage, the darker the tone that Word applies to your selection. When you select a pattern from the Shading list box, the shading percentage appears in the box at the top of the list and a sample of your selection appears in a box to the right. Click OK to confirm your selection and close the Border dialog box.

When you return to your document, you'll see that, like a border, the shading extends just beyond the paragraph margins. Just as you can adjust the paragraph margins when applying a border, you can adjust them when applying shading, to get the exact shading effect you want. As is the case when you apply a border, space that you've added before or after a paragraph generally isn't shaded; however, Word shades the spacing between shaded paragraphs.

The appearance of shading in your printed document depends on the resolution of your printer. The higher your printer's resolution, the finer the shading. Generally, you can use any shading pattern with a high-quality laser printer. If you're using a dot-matrix printer, shading percentages divisible by 12.5 (12.5, 25, 37.5, and so on) look best in your printed document.

6

Creating Graphics

*I*n this chapter, we show you how to use Word's Picture window to create graphics and add them to your document. If you're familiar with any of the drawing programs available for the Macintosh, the steps you follow to create graphics in the Picture window will already be familiar to you. If you've never used a drawing program, you'll find that drawing in Word is remarkably easy.

To draw a graphic like a line, rectangle, or circle, open the Picture window, and select the appropriate drawing tool. Then simply click and drag in the Picture window to specify the graphic's beginning and end points. You can easily change the width, pattern, and color of the lines that compose the graphic. If the graphic has multiple sides, you can also fill it with one of 36 fill patterns and with one of eight colors.

We discuss these procedures in this chapter. We also show you how to add text to a graphic and how to duplicate and modify Picture window elements. At the end of this chapter, we show you how to crop or scale a finished graphic and how to apply a border to a graphic to set it off from surrounding document text.

Displaying the Picture window

To create a new graphic, place the insertion point where you want the graphic to appear in your document, and then choose Picture from the Insert menu. Word displays the Picture dialog box, shown in Figure 6-1 on the next page.

FIGURE 6-1.
Word displays this
dialog box when you
choose the Picture
command from the
Insert menu.

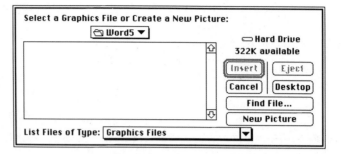

Click the New Picture button in the lower-right corner to create a new graphic. Word then displays the Picture window, shown in Figure 6-2. The words *Insert Picture* in the title bar indicate that when you close the window, Word will insert the graphic at the insertion point. You can also click the Picture tool on the ribbon to display a new Picture window immediately at the insertion point.

FIGURE 6-2.
Display the Picture
window by clicking
the New Picture
button in the Picture
dialog box, or by
clicking the Picture
button on the ribbon.

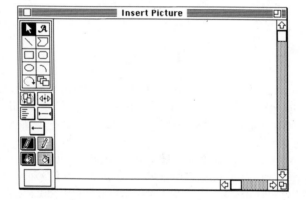

You can also use the Picture dialog box to open a graphics file created in another application. (Chapter 17, "Importing and Exporting Text and Graphics," explains how to import text and graphics into Word documents.) You can press the Find File button to display Word's Find File dialog box. If you know the file's location, select the type of file you want to import in the drop-down list box at the bottom of the Picture dialog box. Then to insert the graphics file, display and select the file's name in the list box, and then click the Insert button. Word inserts the contents of the file at the insertion point in your document.

The Picture window has a vertical scroll bar on the right and a horizontal scroll bar along the bottom. You can resize the window by dragging the size box in the lower-right corner. The status bar at the bottom of the window indicates the size of the graphic you're currently drawing or resizing, or the degree of rotation when you rotate a graphic. Close the Picture window by clicking the close box in the upper-left corner, by choosing the Close command from the File menu, or by pressing Command-W. When you close the Picture window, Word inserts its contents in your document, even if the window is empty.

Figure 6-3 shows a document that contains a graphic we created in the Picture window. When you close the Picture window, Word places the graphic at the insertion point and puts a frame around the graphic to distinguish it within your document. This frame appears only if you have chosen the Show ¶ command. We'll show you how to reposition the contents of a graphic frame at the end of this chapter.

FIGURE 6-3.
Double-click anywhere within the graphic frame to display the graphic in the Picture window.

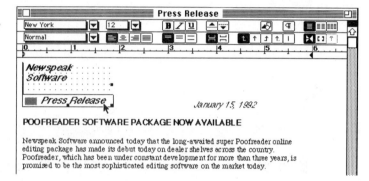

Although you can reposition the frame, you cannot change a graphic directly within the document window. To change an existing graphic, open the Picture window by double-clicking the graphic. Word places the graphic in the upper-left corner of the Picture window, and the words *Edit Picture* appear in the title bar. When you close the Picture window, Word replaces the old graphic with the contents of the Picture window.

To delete a graphic from your document, click the frame once to select the graphic, and then press the Delete key.

Using menu commands

You can open only one Picture window at a time. Only the Close command is available on the File menu while the Picture window is open, but you can use many other Word menu commands and their keyboard shortcuts in the Picture window. You can, for example, choose Select All to select all the elements in the Picture window, or you can choose Cut from the Edit menu to delete a selected graphic element. You can also use the formatting commands on the Format and Font menus to define the format of graphic text. The names of inaccessible commands appear dimmed when you pull down Word menus while the Picture window is open.

Selecting a tool from the Tool palette

You can select any drawing tool from the row of icons, called the *Tool palette*, on the left side of the Picture window. Each icon indicates the type of graphic or part of a graphic you can draw when you click it.

Table 6-1 summarizes the tools available on the Tool palette. To select a tool, simply click the corresponding icon once. Word highlights the icon to indicate that it is currently selected. The sample box in the lower-left corner of the Picture window shows the colors and patterns selected for the next element you draw.

With this tool	You can
Selection tool	Select, move, and resize graphics and text.
Text tool	Type text.
Line tool	Draw lines.
Polygon tool	Draw triangles and multisided figures.
Rectangle tool	Draw rectangles and squares.
Rounded-Rectangle tool	Draw rectangles and squares with rounded corners.
Ellipse tool	Draw ellipses and circles.
Arc tool	Draw arcs.
Rotation tool	Rotate an element.
Duplication tool	Duplicate an element.
Stack order tool	Move an element to the front or back of a stack of elements.
Flip tool	Flip a selected element horizontally or vertically.
Text alignment tool	Specify left, right, or center text alignment.

TABLE 6-1.   *(continued)*
Use the tools on the Tool palette to draw and modify graphic elements.

TABLE 6-1. *Continued*

With this tool	You can
Line width tool	Specify line width.
Arrowhead tool	Apply an arrowhead to a selected line.
Line Color palette	Apply a color to a selected line.
Line Pattern palette	Apply a pattern to a selected line.
Fill Color palette	Apply a color to the fill of a selected graphic.
Fill Pattern palette	Apply a pattern to the fill of a selected graphic.

Drawing lines and shapes

To draw a line or shape, select the appropriate line or shape tool from the Tool palette. When you move the pointer back to the Picture window, the left-arrow pointer changes to a cross-hair pointer. To set the beginning point of the line or shape, click once in the Picture window. Then drag the pointer to create the element.

Word places handles on the completed element so that you can easily move or modify the element with the Selection tool. To move the element, click anywhere with the Selection tool on the line or shape, and then drag. To change the line or shape, drag its handles to the desired positions. As you move or modify a selected element, Word displays its outline on the screen so that you can reposition it accurately.

Remember to select the appropriate tool each time you want to perform a new action, and remember to take your time. If you make a mistake, immediately choose Undo from the Edit menu, or press Command-Z. If you haven't selected another tool from the Tool palette, you can then simply click a new beginning point and try again. To delete a line or shape, you can select the Selection tool from the Tool palette, select the element, and then press the Delete key. (You'll know that the element is selected when you see its handles.)

Using the Selection tool

Of all the tools on the Tool palette, you'll probably use the Selection tool most often. You use the Selection tool to select, move, or change an element in the Picture window. Word highlights this tool when it first displays the Picture window.

After you select the Selection tool, Word continues to display the left-arrow pointer when you move the cursor to the Picture window. While this pointer is displayed, you can select an element by clicking it or select a group of elements by clicking and dragging the mouse. To select more than one element in the Picture window, you can also press the Shift key as you select each element. You can move a completed graphic or a block of text by dragging it to a new location and modify it by repositioning its handles.

Drawing lines and arcs

Use the Line and Arc tools to draw individual line and curve segments. First select the corresponding tool from the Tool palette. Then click the beginning point of the segment, and, without releasing the mouse button, drag the pointer until the line or arc is the length you want it to be. As you drag, Word draws the line or arc. The status bar at the bottom of the Picture window displays the length of the line or the width and height of the arc, as shown in Figure 6-4.

FIGURE 6-4.
The status bar indicates the size of the segment you're drawing when you select the Line or Arc tool.

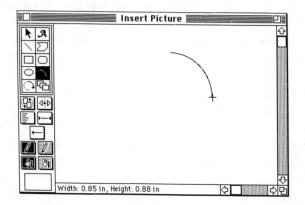

To draw a horizontal or vertical line, select the Line tool, and hold down the Shift key as you drag the mouse. To draw a perfect quarter-circle arc, simply select the Arc tool, and hold down the Shift key as you drag the mouse.

When you release the mouse button, Word places handles at both ends of the element you've just completed. If you've drawn an arc, Word surrounds the arc with handles, as shown in Figure 6-5.

FIGURE 6-5.
Word displays handles when you've finished drawing an element.

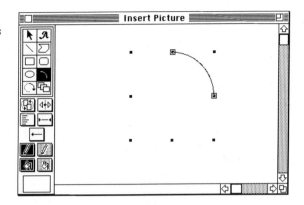

The handles make it easy to identify a new line in a crowded graphic. When you select the Selection tool, they also let you change the length of the line segment by selecting a handle at an end point and dragging.

You can also change the position of the segment by moving a selected handle to a new location. Word displays a broken line from the end point to indicate the length and path of the new line, as shown in Figure 6-6. In this figure, the dark line on the left is the existing line. Until you release the mouse button, the light, broken line that extends from the end point indicates the location and appearance of the new line.

FIGURE 6-6.
Word displays a broken line from the end point to indicate the length and path of the new line.

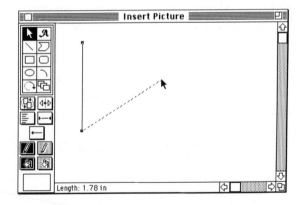

Figure 6-7 on the next page shows the broken line indicating the location and path of the new arc. Selecting and moving the handle placed above the middle of the original arc changes the arc's length and position, although the handle itself remains in its original position until the new shape is completed.

FIGURE 6-7.
Word displays a
broken line to indicate
the location and path
of the new arc.

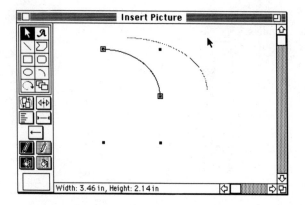

You can change the look of a selected line, or the appearance of lines that you draw with the Line tool, by clicking the Arrowhead tool and then selecting one of the arrow options that appears to the right of the Tool palette. Use the Arrowhead tool to draw right-facing or left-facing arrows, or to create lines with arrows at each end point.

Drawing rectangles and ellipses

Use the Rectangle tool, the Rounded-Rectangle tool, and the Ellipse tool to draw complete graphic objects in a single step. After you select the appropriate tool, click and drag the mouse to complete the graphic object. Word draws the sides of the object automatically, increasing its size as you move the pointer from the beginning point.

When you use either of the Rectangle tools, Word begins the rectangle where you clicked the mouse, and you can drag the mouse in any direction from this beginning point. Word displays the object's width and height in the status bar, as shown in Figure 6-8.

FIGURE 6-8.
As you draw a new
rectangle, Word
displays its size in
the status bar.

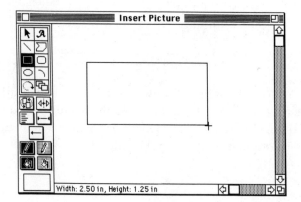

To draw a square, select the appropriate Rectangle tool and hold down the Shift key as you drag the mouse to create a rectangle with equal sides. The Rectangle tool creates rectangles and squares with square corners, and the Rounded-Rectangle tool creates rectangles and squares with rounded corners.

To draw an ellipse, select the Ellipse tool from the Tool palette, and then click anywhere in the Picture window. Word considers that location the corner of an imaginary rectangle that contains the ellipse. You can drag the mouse in any direction from this beginning point to create the ellipse. Again, Word displays the object's width and height in the status bar.

To draw a circle, hold down the Shift key as you drag the mouse. Word creates an ellipse whose radius is equal in every direction.

Modifying rectangles and ellipses

When you release the mouse button, Word places handles along the side and at the end points of the object you've just completed, as shown in Figure 6-9. To change the size of a rectangle or an ellipse, select the Selection tool from the Tool palette, select a handle, and drag. The side attached to the handle you've selected moves as you move the mouse. The other sides stay in place.

FIGURE 6-9.
Drag the handles that appear when you complete a figure to extend or shorten it.

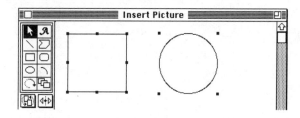

To increase or decrease a figure's height, select a handle along one of the horizontal sides. To change a figure's width, select a handle along one of the vertical sides. To change the size both horizontally and vertically, select and drag one of the corner handles.

When you use the Selection tool to modify an existing figure, a broken line indicates the shape of the new figure, as shown in Figure 6-10.

FIGURE 6-10.
Word displays a broken line to indicate the shape of the new figure.

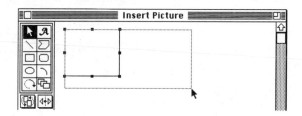

Drawing polygons

To create a multisided figure, select the Polygon tool from the Tool palette. Click in the Picture window to set the beginning point of the figure. When you move the pointer, you create a line. Click once to end that line. When you move the pointer again, you create another line whose beginning point is the end point of the previous polygon side.

You can continue to add sides to the polygon by moving the pointer and then clicking to specify the end point of the current line. To close the polygon, double-click to place the last point, or click the beginning point of the first line in the figure. Word automatically closes the shape you've created by drawing a line between the last point you specified and the point at which you began the polygon.

For example, Figure 6-11 shows a triangle that we made using the Polygon tool. We clicked at the highest point on the object, and then clicked again at a lower-left point, to create a line between these points that serves as the triangle's left side. Double-clicking to the right of this line created two lines: the bottom line, which forms the base of the triangle, and the right side, which closes the triangle.

FIGURE 6-11.
*Complete a polygon by
double-clicking or by
clicking the beginning
point of the first line
in the set.*

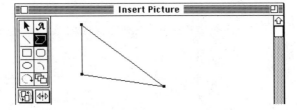

To move a completed polygon, select the Selection tool, click one of the polygon's sides, and then drag it to another location in the Picture window. You can also change the shape of a completed polygon by choosing the Selection tool and then repositioning the figure's handles.

To reposition the corners of the triangle shown in Figure 6-11, for example, we first chose the Selection tool and then selected the handle at the top of the triangle. As Figure 6-12 shows, dragging the handle moves the end point and changes the triangle's shape. Until you release the mouse button, Word indicates the shape of the new figure with broken lines.

FIGURE 6-12.
*You can change the
shape of a completed
polygon by dragging
its handles.*

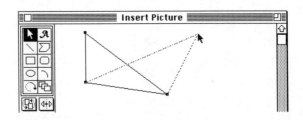

You can use the Polygon tool to create irregular figures composed of more than three sides. You can even overlap lines. Figure 6-13 shows some simple polygons drawn with the Polygon tool.

FIGURE 6-13.
You can draw a polygon of any shape or size with the Polygon tool.

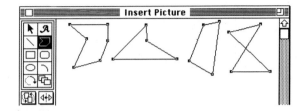

Changing line width

You can change the width of a single line or the width of the lines that compose an entire figure by selecting the elements you want with the Selection tool and then using the Line Width tool to select a different width. When you select the Line Width tool, Word displays a list of line width options on the right side of the Tool palette. Simply select the width you want from this list. Word applies the new line width to the elements currently selected in the Picture window.

Changing the pattern and color of lines and fills

Unless you select another pattern or color, Word draws black lines and does not fill in the objects you draw. You can change the look of a finished graphic in the Picture window by applying patterns and colors.

Change the pattern applied to a line segment or to the lines that compose a graphic by choosing the Line Pattern palette. Apply a pattern to the inside area of a graphic element by choosing the Fill Pattern palette. You can also select a line color from the Line Color palette and a fill color from the Fill Color palette. Word indicates the current line and fill selection in the sample box located in the lower-left corner of the screen.

Changing line and fill patterns

You can display the 36 fill patterns by clicking the Line Pattern or Fill Pattern icons on the Tool palette. Both palettes display the same set of pattern options, which are shown in Figure 6-14 on the next page, on the right side of the Tool palette.

The default line pattern is solid. The default fill pattern is no fill, which results in transparent objects. To change the pattern, select a new pattern from the corresponding palette. Word applies the new pattern to the line or fill, as shown in Figure 6-15 on the next page. The new pattern remains selected until you select another pattern or until you close the Picture window.

FIGURE 6-14.
*You can apply one of
32 patterns from the
Fill Pattern palette.*

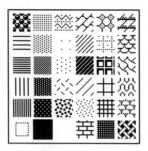

FIGURE 6-15.
*We used the
Line Pattern and Fill
Pattern palettes to
change the appearance
of these graphics.*

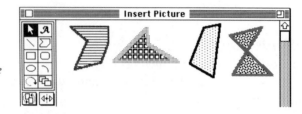

Changing line and fill colors

You can display the eight line and fill colors by clicking the Line Color or Fill
Color icons on the Tool palette. Word displays a list of eight colors next to the
icons. A check mark next to a color name indicates the currently selected color.

To change the color applied to a line or a fill pattern, select the graphic if it's
not already selected, and then select the new color from the options displayed. If
you're not working on a color monitor or if you print from a noncolor printer, you
won't be able to see the selected color, which appears as either black or gray on
the screen and when printed. (For more information, see Chapter 8, ''Printing.'')
The color you select remains in effect until you select another color from the palette or until you close the Picture window.

Adding text to a graphic

You can add text to a graphic by using the Text tool. Selecting the Text tool from
the Tool palette changes the pointer to an I-beam. To begin typing, position the
I-beam within the Picture window, and click to place an insertion point. If you
want to specify the exact size of the text block, drag the pointer away from the insertion point. The box you specify determines the left and right margins that
Word uses to wrap your text. After you move the insertion point from the text
block, the text boundaries snap in to fit around the text you've entered.

You can move the text block to another location by placing the selection tool pointer between the handles and dragging the block. You can also change the font, point size, formatting, and alignment applied to the selected text.

Formatting text in the Picture window

After you enter text, you can easily change the font and point size applied to the text, by choosing a new font name or point size from the Font menu. You can also apply formatting styles from the Format menu and use any of the character-formatting keyboard commands we introduced in Chapter 4, "Formatting Characters." However, you can't mix the style, font, or point size applied to individual characters within a single text block. The fonts and formats that you apply to text in the Picture window do not affect the fonts and formats in the document window.

Changing text layout

You can change the layout of a selected text block in two ways: by changing text alignment and by changing the size of the text block.

If the text takes up more than one line and if the text block is large enough for changes in text alignment to have a visible effect, you can realign the text. To change the alignment of text within a text block, select the Text Alignment tool from the Tool palette, and then select from three options that appear to the right of the Tool palette: Align Left (the default option), Align Center, and Align Right. If the text block contains more than one line of text, changing the alignment changes the appearance of the text within the graphic, as shown in Figure 6-16.

FIGURE 6-16.
We used the Text
Alignment tool to
position the text in
these text blocks.

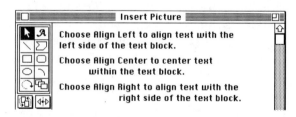

If you don't press Return to end a line, text within a text block wraps to the next line when it reaches the end of the block or the right edge of the Picture window. You can resize the text block to affect the way the text within it wraps. Use the Selection tool to drag the handles of a selected text block, repositioning its boundaries and the text within it. You can even resize the text block so that it is too small to display all the text on the screen. The text remains in the text block until you delete it, even if it's hidden from view. To display all the text, simply enlarge the block.

Figure 6-17 shows a text block that we duplicated and then resized twice. Notice that in the block on the lower right, the word *repositioning* has been wrapped in a way that makes it almost unrecognizable. When you resize a text block, you need to check that Word doesn't cut off a word or break a word in an abnormal way as it wraps the text.

FIGURE 6-17.
You can change the alignment of text within a text block by repositioning the block's handles.

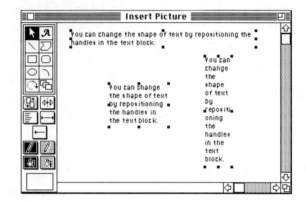

Changing graphic text

You can't edit a graphic element, including text, from the document window. To add or change text within a graphic inserted into your document, double-click anywhere in the graphic frame to display the Picture window, and then make changes as necessary. When you close the Picture window, Word inserts the modified graphic back into your document.

You can also paste text from your Word document into the Picture window. This technique allows you to use character and paragraph formatting options not available in the Picture window, and lets you use Word features such as the spell-checker to proof the text before you add it to a graphic. After you've formatted the text, you can copy it and paste it in the Picture window to create professional-quality graphics, such as logos and letterheads.

To copy selected document text into the Picture window, press Command-Option-D to choose the Copy As Picture command, and then paste the selection as you would any item you had cut or copied to the Clipboard. When you use the Copy As Picture command, Word considers the copied text to be a graphic element. In fact, if the Show ¶ option is selected, Word even copies special characters, such as paragraph symbols and tab marks. (The Copy As Picture command does not appear on any of Word's menus by default. If you plan to use this command often, you can easily add it to a Word menu by following the steps outlined in Chapter 18, "Customizing Word.")

To create the logo shown in Figure 6-18, for example, we first typed the text *BOB'S BAR AND GRILL* on two separate lines in the document window. Next, we applied 14-point Helvetica Bold and Italic to *BOB'S* and 12-point Helvetica Bold to *BAR AND GRILL*. We selected both lines of text, displayed the Paragraph dialog box, and specified 0 in the Before Spacing and After Spacing edit bars. Then we chose the Copy As Picture command by pressing Command-Option-D to copy the text to the Clipboard as a graphic. We then opened the Picture window and pasted. Each line of text was pasted as a separate graphic. Next, we created the background. Then we used the Stack Order tool to move the text on top of the background, and finally, we positioned the figure. (We'll discuss the Stack Order tool shortly.)

FIGURE 6-18.
We created the text for this logo in the document window and then used the Copy As Picture command to paste it in the Picture window.

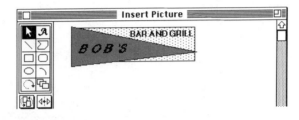

Modifying graphic elements

After you've drawn a graphic in the Picture window, you can select tools from the Tool palette to manipulate it quickly and consistently. You can duplicate an element by selecting the Duplication tool and rotate or flip an element vertically or horizontally by selecting the Rotation or Flip tools. To change the position of a stacked element in a graphic, you first select the element, and then move it to the front or back of other elements in the window with the Stack Order tool.

Duplicating an element

You duplicate a selected element simply by selecting the Duplication tool. Word places the copy on top of the original, just below and to the right of it. If you select the tool repeatedly to create additional copies, Word stacks each new copy just below and to the right of the previous copy, as shown in Figure 6-19.

FIGURE 6-19.
When you copy a selected element using the Duplication tool, each copy is stacked below and to the right of the original.

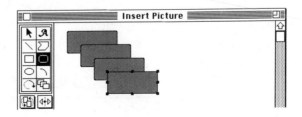

Rotating an element

You can rotate any selected element, including text, by selecting the Rotation tool and then repositioning the element in the Picture window. When you select the Rotation tool, Word changes the pointer to a circled X. Click a corner handle of the selected element, and then drag. Word rotates the element around the center of its enclosing box and displays the degree of rotation in the status bar at the bottom of the Picture window, as shown in Figure 6-20.

FIGURE 6-20.
Rotate a selected
element by choosing
the Rotation tool
and then dragging a
corner handle.

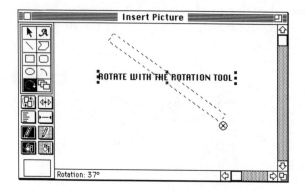

Flipping an element

You can flip a selected element in the Picture window by using the Selection tool to select the element and then clicking the Flip tool. On the right side of the Tool palette, Word displays commands that let you flip the selected element horizontally or vertically. The Undo All Flips And Rotations command returns the element to its original position.

Figure 6-21 shows text that we've flipped horizontally. Choosing the same command twice in succession flips the selected element back into its previous position.

FIGURE 6-21.
We flipped this figure
by selecting each
element and then
selecting the Flip tool
from the Tool palette.

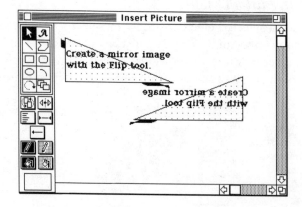

Switching the order of stacked elements

Word stacks elements on top of one another in the order in which they are drawn in the Picture window. If you first create a shaded rectangle, and then a shaded circle, and finally a black square, Word stacks these figures as shown in Figure 6-22. The whole rectangle and circle still remain in the window, but they are covered by the parts of the other elements that overlap them.

FIGURE 6-22.
In this figure, the first elements drawn are partially obscured by new, overlapping elements.

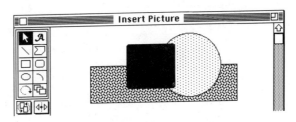

Using the Stack Order tool, you can change the order of elements in a stack. First, select the element you want to move, and then select the Stack Order tool. Word displays the Bring To Front and Send To Back commands on the right side of the Tool palette. The Bring To Front command moves the selected element to the top of the stack of elements, and the Send To Back command moves the selected element to the bottom of the stack, behind the other elements.

With a little planning, you can use this option to change the appearance of elements in the Picture window. Simply continue moving elements forward and backward until you have the arrangement you want. Figure 6-23 shows the elements from Figure 6-22 after we used the Stack Order tool to change their order.

FIGURE 6-23.
We changed the order of the elements stacked in this window with the Stack Order tool.

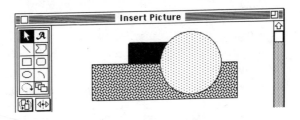

Modifying graphics in your document

Closing the Picture window encloses the graphic in a frame and inserts the graphic at the location of the insertion point in your document. You can click anywhere within the frame to select the graphic and display its handles, as shown in Figure 6-24 on the next page. You can drag the handles to change the dimensions of the frame within the document and to hide portions of the graphic that you don't want to display. Pressing the Shift key as you drag a frame handle resizes the entire graphic within the frame. You can also apply a border or reposition the frame to distinguish it from surrounding document text.

FIGURE 6-24.
Click anywhere within the frame to select the graphic and display its handles.

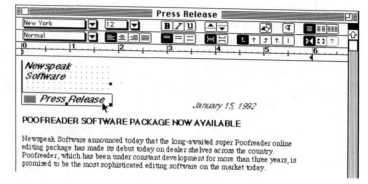

Cropping a graphic

Obscuring parts of a graphic is referred to as *cropping*. You crop a graphic to remove elements or blank space along the graphic's edges that you don't want to display. The complete graphic remains, however, and you can easily redisplay the cropped areas of the graphic by moving the frame back to its original position.

To crop a graphic in the document window, first click the graphic to select it and display its handles. As you saw in Figure 6-24, the graphic frame has three handles: one in the middle of the frame's right edge, one in the middle of the frame's bottom edge, and one at the intersection of these edges at the lower-right corner of the frame. Dragging the bottom handle changes the frame's height. Dragging the right handle changes the frame's width. Dragging the corner handle changes the frame's length and width simultaneously.

Suppose, for example, that you want to hide the small shaded box and the words *Press Release* in Figure 6-24. First select the graphic frame, and then move the bottom handle up until these elements are out of view. Figure 6-25 shows the result. As you can see, changing the length or width of the frame also changes the

FIGURE 6-25.
Changing the length or width of the frame changes the graphic's appearance.

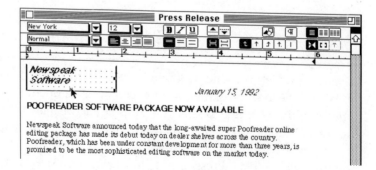

graphic's appearance. Word moves the surrounding text to maintain its distance from the frame. Bring the hidden parts of the graphic back into view by dragging the handles back from the center of the graphic.

You can add blank space to the edges of the graphic by dragging the frame beyond its original position. Word centers the graphic within the new frame, as shown in Figure 6-26. As a result, the graphic stands out more from the text that surrounds it. (For more information about positioning frames within a document, see Chapter 10, "Creating Professional Documents.")

FIGURE 6-26.
When you enlarge a frame in a document, Word automatically centers the graphic within it.

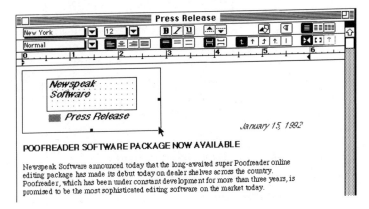

Scaling a graphic

You change the size of a graphic image by pressing Shift as you drag the edges of the frame. Hold down the Shift key, and drag the bottom handle to increase or decrease a graphic's height. Hold down the Shift key, and drag the right handle to increase or decrease a graphic's width. You can change the height and width in equal proportion by pressing Shift and dragging the corner handle. As long as you move the frame edges while holding down the Shift key, Word scales the graphic to fit within the frame. Figures 6-27 below and 6-28 on the next page indicate the results.

FIGURE 6-27.
Hold down the Shift key, and drag the right or bottom handle of the frame to change the shape of the graphic horizontally or vertically.

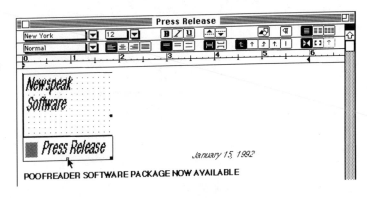

FIGURE 6-28.
Hold down the Shift
key, and drag the
corner handle to
rescale the graphic.

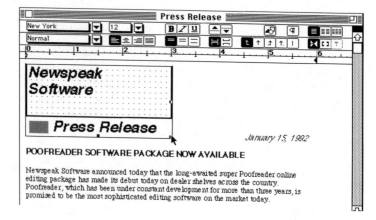

To return the graphic to its original scale, drag the corner handle slightly without holding down the Shift key, and then release the mouse button. Word restores the original graphic.

Putting a border around a graphic

You can set off a graphic from the text in your document by putting a border around it. Choose Border from the Format menu, and then specify the border you want. You can apply a single or thick line width border to a box or shadow box when a graphic is selected. Click OK in the Border dialog box to apply the specified border to the graphic. If you later reposition or resize the frame, the border adjusts automatically. Figure 6-29 shows the graphic shown earlier in Figure 6-24 with a Shadow border. (Chapter 5, ''Formatting Documents and Paragraphs,'' discusses the Border command in detail.)

FIGURE 6-29.
Applying a border to a
frame distinguishes
the graphic from
document text.

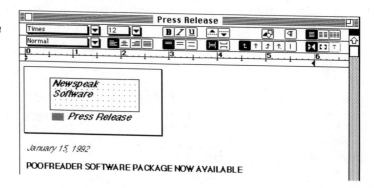

Repositioning graphics in your document

To reposition a graphic in your document, click the graphic, and drag it to a new location using Word's drag-and-drop feature. You can also reposition your graphic easily by choosing the Frame command from the Insert menu. Word then displays the Print Preview window, in which you can select the graphic frame and indicate the location on the page where you want the graphic to appear. Text wraps around the graphic when you reposition it. (For more information about drag-and-drop techniques, see Chapter 3, "Working in Word." For more information about the Frame command, see Chapter 10, "Creating Professional Documents.")

Printing graphics

In general, a printer's ability to print a graphic exactly as it appears on your screen corresponds to its ability to reproduce on-screen text accurately. If you print a graphic on an ImageWriter, the lines often remain jagged in the printed document. If you print the same graphic on a LaserWriter, however, the lines appear smooth. If your document contains many graphics, you might want to print each page that contains a graphic separately to verify that it looks the way you want it to.

Depending on the printer you're using, you might also want to specify print options in the Page Setup or Print dialog boxes to enhance the appearance of printed graphics. For more information about these options, see Chapter 8, "Printing."

7

Editing and Proofing

After you've created your document, you can choose commands from Word's Edit and Tools menus to edit and proofread your text before you print.

Word's Find and Replace commands make it easy to locate and change text in your document. Find searches for occurrences of a specific word or a series of characters. Replace locates a specific word or series of characters and replaces it with another. Both commands can also locate formats and special characters, such as tabs and paragraph symbols.

If you're not sure of the exact word you want to use in your document, choose Thesaurus to see synonyms and antonyms for a selected word. Word's Spelling command checks for spelling, case, punctuation errors, and repeated words in your text. You can create custom dictionaries for technical terms and proper nouns not found in Word's English Main Dictionary. The Hyphenate command lets you insert optional hyphens that determine where Word breaks the end of a line in your document. Word's Grammar command evaluates how easy your writing is for others to understand.

If you used the Installer to set up Word, all the necessary files to use the Thesaurus, Spelling, Grammar and Hyphenation commands were automatically placed in the appropriate folders. If you chose not to install these commands, their names appear dimmed on Word's Tools menu. For details on installing these commands, see the Introduction.

Finding text

Word lets you search through your document to find occurrences of a specified word or series of characters. Typically, you search for a single word or phrase, but you can search for a single letter or several sentences. You can search for whole-word instances or instances that match the capitalization as well as the characters of the text specified.

Word's Find command lets you do more than look for characters. You can narrow your search by specifying the format or style of the text you want to locate. You can even search for the next occurrence of a format or style—without specifying the characters to which the format is applied. In addition, Word lets you search for special characters such as tabs and paragraph symbols. Specifying document text and special characters lets you identify even more precisely the text you want to locate.

Specifying find text

You locate a word or character string in your document by first choosing Find from the Edit menu to display the Find dialog box shown in Figure 7-1, or by pressing Command-F.

FIGURE 7-1.
Specify the text you want to locate using the Find dialog box.

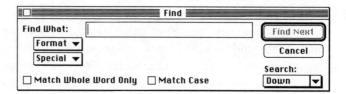

You enter the series of characters—the *find text*—that you want to locate in the Find What edit bar at the top of the Find dialog box. You can either type the find text in the Find What edit bar, or you can select and copy the text from your document and then paste it into the Find What edit bar.

The Find What edit bar can accept up to 255 find text characters. If characters in the edit bar scroll out of view, you can display them again by dragging to the left or right in the Find What edit bar.

The Search list box in the lower-right corner of the Find dialog box lets you specify the direction of your search. The default Down option begins the search at the insertion point's current location and searches forward to the end of the document. Select Up to search from the insertion point backward to the beginning of your document, or All to begin the search at the start of the document. You can also limit your search by highlighting the document text in which you want to perform the search before you choose Find. When you highlight text before you display the Find dialog box, you see the Selection option in the Search list box.

Because most searches take place from the insertion point location forward, Word resets the Search option to Down each time you choose Find, unless you have highlighted a selection.

Finding document text

When you're ready to search for the find text, click the Find Next button in the upper-right corner of the Find dialog box, or press Return. As Word scans your document looking for the find text, it scrolls the text on your screen as necessary to bring the next occurrence of the find text into view. When it locates the first occurrence, Word pauses and highlights the text in your document so that you can edit or modify the text. In Figure 7-2, for example, Word has found an occurrence of the word *silver* in our sample document.

FIGURE 7-2.
Word highlights an occurrence of the find text in your document.

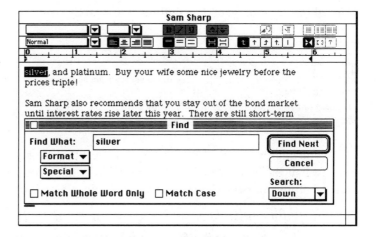

Although Word highlights the text it finds, you can't edit the text while the Find dialog box is active. To make changes to your document, click anywhere in the document window to activate it. The Find dialog box remains open but moves behind the document window.

Keep in mind that Word can't locate occurrences of your find text that are hidden from view. To locate every occurrence of your find text, activate the Show Hidden Text option in the Preferences dialog box before you begin your search.

To locate the next occurrence of the find text, choose Find from the Edit menu, and then click Find Next again to continue the search.

Stopping a search

To stop a search currently in progress, press Command-period or the Esc key. Word scrolls your document to display the insertion point, which indicates the point where the search ended. To stop searching entirely, click Cancel or click the close box in the Find dialog box. Word saves the find text in the dialog box until you replace it. When you display the Find dialog box again, you can click the Find Next button to search for the same find text or make a new entry in the Find What edit bar.

Reaching the end of the document

If you begin a search at the beginning or end of your document, Word completes the search and displays the message *End of document reached* when it comes to the opposite end of the document. If you begin a search elsewhere, when Word reaches the end of the document it displays an alert box like the one shown in Figure 7-3. (If you've chosen the Up Search option, Word displays a similar alert box asking if you want to continue the search from the end of the current document.)

FIGURE 7-3.
To search from the top of your document, click Yes in this alert box.

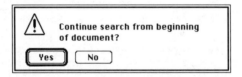

If you click Yes in the Continue Search alert box, Word finishes searching the text. To halt the Find procedure, click the No button. You can then specify a different find text or click Cancel to close the Find dialog box.

Searching for multiple occurrences of the same text

If you find yourself moving frequently between the document window and the Find dialog box, resize the document window so that part of the dialog box is visible when the document window is active. This way, you can switch quickly between the Find dialog box and your document by clicking one or the other.

If you need to search repeatedly for the same find text, use the Find Again command. Find Again lets you search for the current find text without displaying the Find dialog box; simply press Command-Option-A. You can also press equal on the numeric keypad to choose the Find Again command.

Find dialog box options

Four Find dialog box options let you define more precisely the text you want to find. Match Whole Word Only identifies only whole words that match the find text. Match Case looks for text that matches the find text's exact capitalization.

The Format drop-down list box lets you specify the format of the find text. The Special drop-down list box lets you find special characters, such as tabs and paragraph symbols, and lets you use wildcard characters instead of specific characters in the find text.

The Match Whole Word Only option

Use the Match Whole Word Only option when you want to locate a short word, such as *the* or *for*, that can be part of longer words. If you type *for* in the Find What edit bar, for example, Word highlights occurrences of this text in such words as *forecast* and *platform* unless you select Match Whole Word Only before you begin the search.

 You can also use Match Whole Word Only to find only singular nouns or the present tense of a verb. Selecting Match Whole Word Only before you begin searching for the word *book*, for example, lets you avoid finding the plural form of the word, *books*, or the past tense verb, *booked*.

The Match Case option

The Match Case option finds only those occurrences of the find text whose capitalization exactly matches the capitalization of your find text. Entering *Microsoft* as your find text without selecting the Match Case option, for example, results in Word highlighting such occurrences as *microsoft*, *MicroSoft*, and *MICROSOFT*.

The Format options

To narrow your search further, Word lets you specify the exact formatting applied to the text you want to find. Using the Format drop-down list box, you can display the Character, Paragraph, and Style dialog boxes directly from the Find dialog box.

 For example, if you select Character from the Format drop-down list box, Word displays the Character dialog box. Select the formatting you want to find, and then close the Character dialog box. Word confirms your selection by displaying the format you've specified beneath the Find What edit bar. As Figure 7-4 shows, Word adds any settings you specify in these dialog boxes to the criteria it uses when searching for the find text.

FIGURE 7-4.
*Word displays
formatting criteria for
the find text below the
Find What edit bar.*

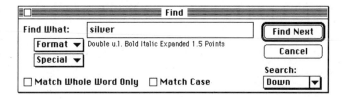

You are not limited to one category of formatting. You can combine character, paragraph, and style formatting by choosing one option at a time from the Format list box and completing the appropriate dialog box. Word adds each format you specify beneath the Find What edit bar and, when you begin the search, scans your document for text that matches all the specified criteria.

Word can also locate the next occurrence of the formatting you specify, no matter what text it's applied to. For example, you can search for italicized text in your document by selecting the Italic style option in the Character dialog box with no text in the Find What edit bar. Clicking Find Next begins the search. Word then highlights the first occurrence of italicized text.

The Special options

The Special drop-down list box lets you locate special characters such as tabs, end-of-line marks, and paragraph symbols. You can also insert wildcard characters that take the place of characters in the find text. You can search for special and wildcard characters in combination with text to specify exactly the part of your document you want to find.

The Special drop-down list box displays a list of the special characters for which you can search. When you select an option from the Special list box, Word inserts a two-character code in the Find What edit bar to indicate the character. This code is composed of a caret symbol (^) and another letter or symbol. You can also type the characters in the edit bar manually. Remember that special characters exist in your text even when they're not visible on the screen. When you select a special character from the Special list box, Word finds that character even when the Show ¶ command is not selected.

You insert wildcard characters into the find text in the same way you insert special characters. Word even enables you to distinguish between character and numeric wildcards in the find text: You can select from Unspecified Letter, Unspecified Digit, and Formula Character.

Table 7-1 summarizes the Special options available and the corresponding codes that Word inserts in the Find What edit bar.

You can narrow your search by combining special characters with find text. For example, to find every instance of a paragraph that begins with the word *For*, type *^pFor* as your find text. Word highlights the paragraph symbol at the end of the previous paragraph as well as the word *For* at the beginning of the next paragraph.

In addition to the characters listed in Table 7-1, you can search for any ASCII character by entering a caret followed by the character's three-digit ASCII code. For example, if you enter *^097*—the ASCII code for the lowercase character *a*—as

Select	To insert	And find all occurrences of
Tab Mark	^t	Tab marks and the space up to the next tab mark (→)
End Of Line Mark	^n	End-of-line marks (↵)
Paragraph Mark	^p	Paragraph symbols (¶)
Page Break	^d	Section-break marks (::::::::) and manual page-break marks (⋯⋯)
Nonbreaking Space	^s	Nonbreaking spaces (˜)
Optional Hyphen	^-	Optional hyphens (-)
Question Mark	^?	Question marks (?)
Footnote Mark	^5	Footnote reference marks
Graphic	^1	Graphics and empty graphic frames
White Space	^w	Any number and combination of spaces, including normal and nonbreaking spaces, tab marks, paragraph symbols, end-of-line marks, section-break marks, and manually inserted page-break marks.
Unspecified Letter	^*	Any single character. For example, type ba^*e to locate occurrences of *bale*, *base*, *bane*, and *bake*.
Unspecified Digit	^#	Any single number. For example, type 8^# to find all numbers in which the number 8 precedes another number. Type 8^# and select the Match Whole Word Only option to find numbers 80 through 89.
Caret	^^	Carets
Formula Character	^\	Formula characters. Word can find a formula that is part of a complete Word formula only when the Show ¶ command is active.
Any Character	?	Any single letter, digit, or formatting character. For example, type ?D to locate occurances of *3D* and *add* and to locate a paragraph that begins with the letter *D*.

TABLE 7-1.

You can use these codes to specify special and wildcard characters in the Find dialog box.

your find text, Word finds every occurrence of the letter *a*, both capital and lower-case. You can narrow the search by selecting Match Case. (We'll discuss working with ASCII codes in Chapter 13, "Using Word Tools." In addition, Appendix B, "ASCII Codes," lists the Macintosh character set and each character's corresponding ASCII code.

Navigating with the Find command

The Find command offers a quick way to move from one part of your document to another. Suppose you want to edit a section of your document, for example, under the heading *Part II*. To move to this section without scrolling, choose Find, and type *Part II* as your find text. Click Find Next, and Word brings the *Part II* heading into view.

To move from one heading to another, you can specify the style applied to the headings by selecting Style from the Format list box, selecting the style, and beginning your search.

To take real advantage of Word's Find feature, consider inserting hidden "bookmarks" into long documents to help you find key sections quickly. Use short, easy-to-remember symbols or codes to mark selected areas, and apply the Hidden format to this text. Then specify the bookmark as your find text to move quickly to that location.

Finding formats by example

Word provides another way to find formats without specifying a particular character or characters. If you often search for formats, consider adding the Find Formats command to a Word menu or assigning a keyboard shortcut to this command. (Chapter 18, "Customizing Word," describes how to assign keystrokes to commands and add commands to menus.) Then you can simply highlight a character or paragraph in your document and choose Find Formats to locate the next occurrence of the format applied to the selected text.

To use Find Formats effectively, you need to be aware that Word examines the highlighted selection one character format at a time. First, Word looks for character formats that you can turn on and off such as the Bold, Italic, and Hidden formats. Next, Word looks for Underline, Superscript and Subscript, Expanded and Condensed, and Color formatting in sequence. And finally, Word determines the font of the selection. When Word determines that one of these character formats has been applied to the selection, it stops and uses that character format as the criterion for its search.

As a result, Word might not always find exact matches to the format you've highlighted. If you select text formatted in both Italic and an Underline style, for example, Word uses only the Italic format as its search criterion. When you choose Find Formats, Word locates the first occurrence of italicized text, no matter what other formats are applied to the text it locates.

Replacing text

The Replace command on Word's Edit menu lets you locate specified text and replace it with different text. You can replace all the occurrences at once or consider each occurrence individually.

The Replace command is closely related to the Find command. You can use all the Find options to specify both the find text and the replacement text.

Specifying replacement text

When you choose Replace from the Edit menu, Word displays the Replace dialog box shown in Figure 7-5. You can also display the Replace dialog box by pressing Command-H. The Replace dialog box looks and functions much like the Find dialog box. In fact, when you enter text in the Find What edit bar of the Find dialog box, the text also appears in the Find What edit bar of the Replace dialog box.

FIGURE 7-5.
The Replace dialog box resembles the Find dialog box.

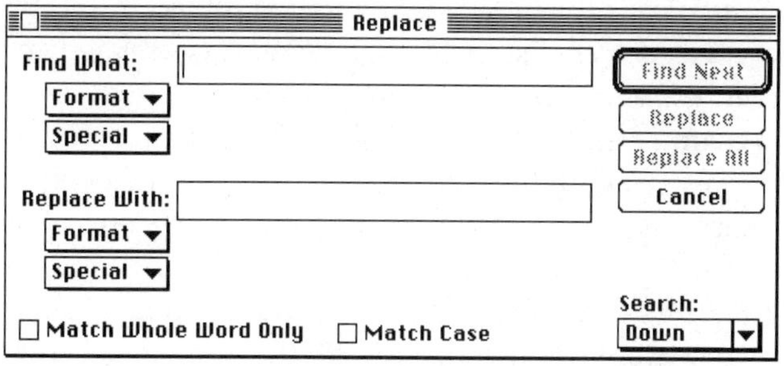

Enter the text you want to find in the Find What edit bar. Then press the Tab key to move the insertion point to the Replace With edit bar (or click anywhere on that edit bar), and enter the replacement text. You can type up to 255 characters of replacement text directly in the Replace With edit bar, though only about 25 characters are visible at a time. If you want to replace the find text with more than 255 characters, with text in a different format, or with a graphic, first copy the replacement text or graphic to the Clipboard. Then type ^c in the Replace With edit bar to specify the contents of the Clipboard as your replacement text. If you don't specify a format for replacement text, text pasted into your document assumes the

same format as the find text it replaces. However, the replacement text you provide from the Clipboard retains its original format.

The Search list box in the lower-right corner of the Replace dialog box lets
you specify the direction of your search. The default Down option begins the
search at the insertion point's current location and searches forward to the end
of the document. Select Up to search from the insertion point backward to the
beginning of your document, or All to start at the beginning of the document. You
can also limit your search by highlighting the document text in which you want to
perform the search before you choose Replace. When you highlight text before
the Replace dialog box appears, you see the Selection option in the Search list box.

Because most searches are done from the insertion point forward, Word automatically resets the Search option to Down each time you choose Replace, unless
you have highlighted a selection.

Replacing document text

After you've indicated the find and replacement text, you're ready to search your
document. Using the Replace All and Find Next buttons on the right side of the
Replace dialog box, you can replace every occurrence of the find text at once or
examine each occurrence in turn.

To replace every occurrence of the find text, click Replace All. Beginning at
the current insertion point, Word moves to the end of the document, substituting
each occurrence of your find text with the replacement text. As Word searches, it
displays the percentage of your document completed in the status box in the
lower-left corner of the document window.

To examine each occurrence of the find text in turn, click Find Next, or press
Return. Word highlights the first occurrence of the find text and brings this
occurrence into view. Move the Replace dialog box if you can't see the highlighted text.

In Figure 7-6, for example, Word has found an occurrence of the word *silver*
using the Replace command. To leave the highlighted text unchanged, click Find
Next to continue the search. Click Replace to replace the highlighted text with the
replacement text and to continue the search.

Like the Find command, the Replace command affects only text that appears
on your screen. If you have hidden text in your document, Word ignores this text
when it executes the Replace command. If you want to replace hidden text, be
sure to activate the Show Hidden Text option in the View section of the Preferences dialog box before you begin a Replace procedure.

FIGURE 7-6.
*When you use the
Replace command,
Word highlights an
occurrence of the find
text in your document
so that you can replace
it with the replacement
text.*

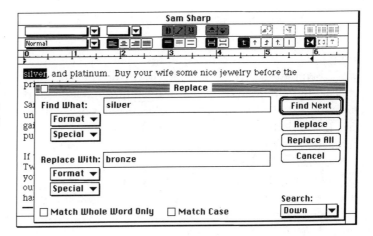

Stopping a search

To stop a search currently in progress, press Command-period or the Esc key. Word scrolls your document to display the insertion point, which indicates the point where your search ended. To stop searching entirely, click the Cancel button or click the close box in the Replace dialog box. When you close the Replace dialog box, Word saves the current find text and replacement text. Word also saves the find text in the Find What edit bar of the Find dialog box so that you can easily search again for the same text string.

Reaching the end of the document

If you begin a search at the beginning or end of your document, Word completes the search and displays the message *End of document reached* when it reaches the opposite end of the document. If you begin the search elsewhere, when it reaches the end of the document Word displays an alert box like the one shown earlier in Figure 7-3. To continue the search, click Yes in the alert box.

Replace dialog box options

The Match Whole Word Only and the Match Case options in the Replace dialog box function as they do in the Find dialog box. The Format and Special drop-down list boxes directly beneath the Find What and Replace With edit bars function like the corresponding list boxes in the Find dialog box, with one exception: The Special list box for the replacement text doesn't contain options for footnotes, white space, carets, formula characters, wildcard characters, unspecified letters or digits, or graphics.

The Match Whole Word Only option

The Match Whole Word Only option works just as it does in the Find dialog box; it replaces only whole-word find text matches. This option is likely to be important when the find text is a single short word or when the word you're replacing appears in more than one tense or form throughout your document. For example, suppose you want to replace every occurrence of the word *top* with the word *bottom*. If you don't activate the Match Whole Word Only option, Word replaces the characters *top* in such words as *topic* and *stop*. Your document might end up with nonsensical "words" like *bottomic* and *sbottom*.

Similarly, if you replace every occurrence of the word *boy* with *child* and your document contains the word *boys*, Word changes *boys* to *childs*. To avoid this problem, you can use the Match Whole Word Only option to perform separate Replace procedures for each form of a word.

The Match Case option

Use the Match Case option to specify the exact case in which replacement text will appear in your document. For example, select this option to replace *appletalk* with *AppleTalk*. If you don't select Match Case, Word matches the case of your replacement text with the case of the find text. For example, if you replace *lawyers* with *doctors*, Word replaces *Lawyers* at the beginning of a sentence with *Doctors*.

The Format options

If you don't specify a format for your replacement text, Word matches the format of the find text that it replaces. The replacement text could, for example, assume the format of its surrounding text and become 14-point Helvetica Bold in one case and plain 12-point Times in another. Word works exactly the way you want it to in most cases; you don't want to have to reformat text each time you use the Replace command.

Word also lets you specify the format of replacement text, enabling you to change the format of all instances of a foreign word from Plain to Italic, for example. Place formatted replacement text into your document either by storing the replacement text on the Clipboard, or by using the Format drop-down list box.

To use the Clipboard, first type and format your replacement text in a document window. Then select the text and use either Cut or Copy from the Edit menu to store it on the Clipboard. This replacement text can be any size. Next, choose Replace. Specify the find text in the Find What edit bar, but instead of typing the replacement text in the Replace With edit bar, type ^c or choose Clipboard Contents from the Special drop-down list box to instruct Word to use the contents of the Clipboard as the replacement text.

To use the Format list box to specify a replacement text format, select the Character, Paragraph, or Styles options to display their dialog boxes. You can combine character, paragraph, and style formatting by selecting the options one at a time from the Format list box and then completing the appropriate dialog box. Word confirms each format you specify by displaying the formatting options beneath the Find What and Replace With edit bars.

The Special options

When we introduced the Special drop-down list box earlier, we explained how to specify special and wildcard characters and insert the corresponding codes for these characters in your find text. To insert a paragraph symbol (¶) in your find text, for example, you select Paragraph Mark from the Special list box. Word then enters ^p, the code for this character, in the Find What edit bar.

Table 7-1 shown earlier summarizes the special and wildcard characters you can specify in your find text. Figure 7-7 displays the options available in the replacement text's Special list box. As you can see, Word removes elements such as wildcards, footnote markers, and graphics from the list of options.

FIGURE 7-7.
The Special drop-down list box in the Replace dialog box contains only replacement options.

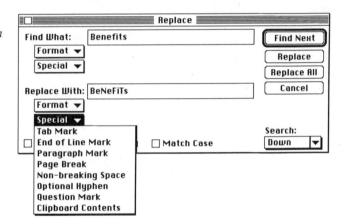

To specify a special character as replacement text, select it from the Special list box. You can combine special characters and add them to other characters. For example, to indent every paragraph that begins with the word *Step*, type *^pStep* as the find text and *^p^tStep* as the replacement text.

Your replacement text can also consist of a ^ followed by the three-digit ASCII code for a character. For example, if you enter *^097* as your replacement text, Word replaces the find text with a lowercase *a* if the selected occurrence of the find text is also lowercase and with an uppercase *A* if the selected occurrence is uppercase. (Chapter 13, "Using Word Tools," discusses ASCII codes in detail. Appendix B, "ASCII Codes," lists the Macintosh character set and each character's corresponding ASCII code.)

Deleting text using the Replace command

You can use the Replace command to remove spaces or characters from your document. For example, to ensure that your document doesn't contain sentences with an extra space between the last word in a sentence and the period, complete the Find What and Replace With edit bars as shown in Figure 7-8. In this figure, the find text contains a single space before the period, and the replacement text contains only a period. When you click the Replace All button, Word replaces the find text with the replacement text, thereby deleting spaces before periods.

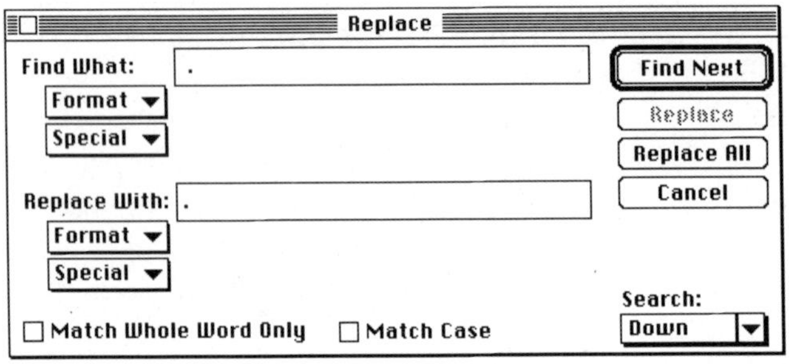

FIGURE 7-8.
Specify find text and replacement text like this to delete extra spaces before periods at the end of sentences.

	Replace	
Find What: `.`		**Find Next**
Format ▼		Replace
Special ▼		**Replace All**
Replace With: `.`		Cancel
Format ▼		
Special ▼		Search:
☐ Match Whole Word Only ☐ Match Case		Down ▼

To remove groups of several spaces, like those that often result when you convert an ASCII file to Word, begin with five spaces as the find text and one space as the replacement text. (You won't see the spaces in the Find What and Replace With edit bars, but the insertion point will move as you add each space.) Continue replacing this find text until Word no longer finds five spaces in your document. Repeat this process using four spaces, then three spaces, and then two spaces, until your document contains only single spaces between words.

When you import a file from another program into Word, some of the characters might appear on your screen as rectangular boxes. If the document you've imported contains many such characters, you can use the Replace command to remove these characters quickly. First, copy one of the boxes from the document, and then paste it in the Find What edit bar. Leave the Replace With edit bar empty, and press the Replace All button.

Using the Thesaurus

Word's Thesaurus lets you add variety and precision to your writing. Use the Thesaurus command on the Tools menu to display synonyms for a selected word. If the selected word has several meanings, you can select the meaning you want and then view a list of synonyms. When you find the right synonym, you can replace the word in your text immediately or look up synonyms for this new word. Word's Thesaurus also locates antonyms and words that are strongly related to a selected word.

Looking up a word

To look up a word in Word's Thesaurus, first highlight the word in your text. (If you don't highlight a word, Word looks up the word closest to the insertion point.) Then choose Thesaurus from the Tools menu. Word displays the Thesaurus dialog box, shown in Figure 7-9.

FIGURE 7-9.

The Thesaurus dialog box displays the synonyms of a selected word.

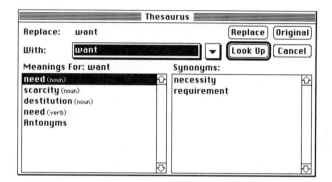

At the top of the Thesaurus dialog box, the word you've highlighted appears next to Replace and in the With edit bar. If the word you've selected has more than one meaning, all the meanings appear in the Meanings For list box. You can select a word from this list to specify the exact meaning you want. The Synonyms list box displays the synonyms for the word selected in the Meanings For list box. If Word doesn't recognize the word you highlight in the document, it displays an alphabetical list of similarly spelled words.

Each time you select a new word in the Meanings For list, the contents of the With edit bar change to reflect the latest selection. To replace the highlighted word in your document with the word in the With edit bar, click Replace. To display the word you originally highlighted in the With edit bar, click Original.

Selecting a synonym

To find a synonym for the word in the With edit bar, click Look Up, or press Return. If the word has only one meaning, you'll see only the word in the Meanings For list box, and you can simply select a synonym for this word from the Synonyms list box.

Selecting a synonym puts that word in the With edit bar. Insert this word in your text by clicking Replace. For example, in Figure 7-9, to insert the word *requirement* in your document, click this word in the Synonyms list box and then click Replace.

If the word in the With edit bar has more than one meaning, select the meaning you want from the list displayed in the Meanings For list box. In Figure 7-9, for example, Word displays four meanings for the word *want* and also indicates

whether the word is a noun or verb. Selecting a meaning from the Meanings For
list box inserts that word in the With edit bar. Click Look Up to see additional
meanings and synonyms for that word.

If you select *scarcity* from the Meanings For box shown in Figure 7-9, the
Thesaurus dialog box looks like the one in Figure 7-10. Word places *scarcity* in
the With edit bar and displays synonyms for *scarcity* in the Synonyms list box.

FIGURE 7-10.
When you select a
different meaning
from the Meanings For
list box, Word displays
new synonyms in the
Synonyms list box.

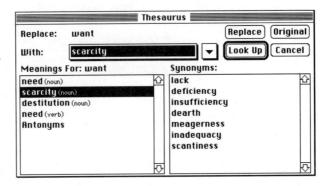

Selecting an antonym

If the Thesaurus contains an antonym for the word in the With edit bar, you'll see
the word *Antonyms* at the bottom of the list in the Meanings For list box, as shown
in Figure 7-10. Click this word to display a list of antonyms on the right side of the
Thesaurus dialog box. The first word in the antonym list then appears in the With
edit bar. Insert the antonym into your document by clicking Replace. You can display related words, and optional meanings, if they apply, on the left side of the
Thesaurus dialog box by clicking Look Up.

Formatting the new word

When Word replaces a highlighted word in your text with a synonym or antonym
from the Thesaurus dialog box, the new word maintains the capitalization and
formatting of the word it replaces. For example, if you replace the word *Want* at
the beginning of a sentence, Word inserts the word *Scarcity*, capitalizing the first
letter of the word.

Choosing a related word

In addition to displaying synonyms and antonyms, Word can also display *related*
words—words that share the same root, for example. In Figure 7-11, we've looked
up *scarcity* and then selected the Related Word(s) option from the Meanings For
list box. As you can see, the Related Word(s) list box replaces the Synonyms list
box, and the word *scarce*, which shares a common root with *scarcity*, appears both
in this list box and in the With edit bar.

FIGURE 7-11.
Click the Related Word(s) option in the Meanings For list box to display words related to the word in the With edit bar.

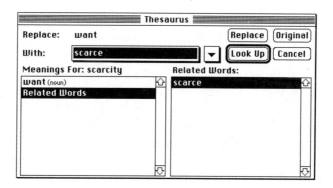

Selecting a different word

If the word you've highlighted in your document isn't in Word's Thesaurus, Word displays a list of words with similar spelling. After you've chosen a new word or spelling, look up synonyms or antonyms for the word by clicking the Look Up button.

Displaying previous selections

You can keep track of the words you look up by clicking the arrow on the right side of the With edit bar, as shown in Figure 7-12. Select a word from the list, and click Look Up to redisplay the synonyms for the word.

FIGURE 7-12.
Click the arrow to the right of the With edit bar to display the words you've previously selected in the Thesaurus dialog box.

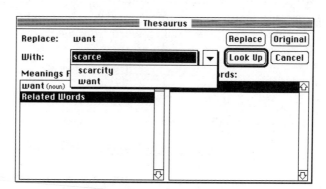

Canceling and undoing actions

Close the Thesaurus at any time by clicking the Cancel button in the upper-right corner of the dialog box. The selected text in your document window remains highlighted until you click somewhere else in your document.

If you insert a word in your document from the Thesaurus and then want to undo the insertion, immediately choose Undo Thesaurus from the Edit menu, or press Command-Z.

Checking spelling

As you prepare your document for printing, you'll find the Spelling command on the Tools menu indispensable. Word's Spelling command lets you check your document for spelling and punctuation errors and repeated words. Word's dictionary contains more than 80,000 words. Use the Spelling command to check your entire document, the words in a text selection, or a single word.

You can also create your own custom dictionaries to locate and correct technical terms and proper nouns not found in Word's dictionary. Adding words to a custom dictionary is easy. You can create as many separate custom dictionaries as you need. For example, one custom dictionary might contain only technical words and another only the names and addresses of friends and business associates.

Spell-checking your document

Word checks the spelling in your document beginning with the word in which the insertion point is positioned (or the word immediately to the right of the insertion point). When Word finds a word that is not in its dictionary or a custom dictionary, it highlights the word in your document and displays it next to Not In Dictionary in the upper-left corner of the Spelling dialog box, as shown in Figure 7-13. Word also offers a list of words in its dictionary that closely resemble the unknown word and inserts the closest match in the Change To edit bar. You can leave the text as it is in your document, type your own replacement in the Change To edit bar, or replace the text with a word from the Suggestions list box.

FIGURE 7-13.
Word highlights a word it doesn't recognize in your document and displays it at the top of the Spelling dialog box.

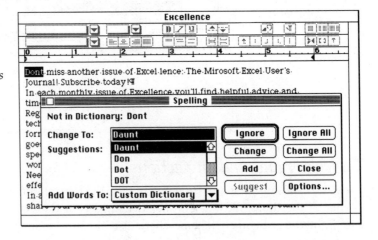

As we consider each option in the following paragraphs, we assume that you are checking the entire document. When we discuss checking only a selection and checking a single word, you'll see that these processes are very similar.

Leaving the word unchanged

If you want to leave an unrecognized word unchanged, click the Ignore button on the right side of the Spelling dialog box to continue the spell-checking operation.

If you want to leave the word unchanged and also want Word to ignore all subsequent occurrences of the text in your document, click Ignore All. Word ignores any further occurrences of the text until you close the Spelling dialog box.

If the unrecognized word is a typographical error or spacing problem that you can't correct directly in the Change To edit bar, click the document window and edit the word. The Spelling dialog box remains open but moves behind the document window. After you've made your change, choose Spelling again to continue spell-checking.

In Figure 7-14, for example, the Spelling dialog box displays the unrecognized word *lence* and suggests *lance* as a replacement. If you look at the document window, you'll see that the correct word is really *Excellence*, but because of the blank space in the middle of the word, Word treats it as two words. To correct this error, you must click the document window, and manually erase the blank space.

FIGURE 7-14.
You might have to correct some spelling errors manually.

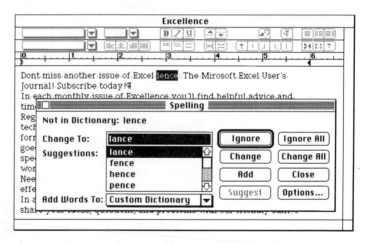

Typing a new word in the Change To edit bar

If you want to change a word that Word doesn't recognize, you can type a different word in the Change To edit bar. Click the Change button to replace the unrecognized word in your document with the one you've typed and to resume checking for more unrecognized words.

You can also click the unrecognized word to display it in the Change To edit bar and modify it there. Then click Change to insert the word in your document and continue spell-checking.

If you type a new word in the Change To edit bar, you can check its spelling by highlighting the word and clicking Suggest. Word displays the word at the top of the Spelling dialog box and then displays either the word or suggestions based on its current spelling. When you're confident that the word in the Change To edit bar is spelled correctly, click Change to correct your document.

You're not limited to typing a single word when you edit the contents of the Change To edit bar. The edit bar can display only about 19 characters at a time, but you can type a sentence or more and insert this text with the Change button. You can check only single-word entries in the Change To edit bar, however. If you check an entry composed of several words, Word verifies the spelling of only the first word.

Using a suggested word

You'll often be able to select one of Word's suggestions to change a misspelled word in your document. When Word locates an unfamiliar word, it displays alternatives that closely resemble the word, as shown in Figure 7-15.

FIGURE 7-15.
The Suggestions list box displays a list of alternatives to the unfamiliar word.

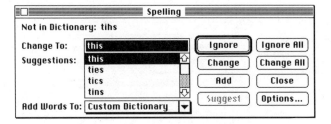

Notice that the first word in the list also appears in the Change To edit bar. To substitute this word for the misspelled word in your document, click Change. Word makes the substitution and continues checking your document.

To use a different word from the Suggestions list box as your replacement, simply click that word, and then click Change. For example, to use *ties* instead of *this*, click *ties* in the Suggestions list box to display that word in the Change To edit bar. When you click Change, Word substitutes the word *ties* for the unrecognized word and continues checking your document.

Word displays the message *(End of Suggestions)* at the bottom of the list of suggested replacements. Occasionally, you'll see the message *(No Suggestions)* when Word is unable to suggest an alternative to an unrecognized word. In this case, you can either keep the word in your document or type a new one in the Change To edit bar. You'll probably also need to correct the word yourself when the first letter of the unrecognized word is incorrect. For example, if you misspelled the word *during* as *suring,* Word assumes that the first letter is as you want it and displays alternatives that resemble the misspelled word more than they do the word you intended.

Using the Change All command

If you want to change all occurrences of the unrecognized word in your document to the word in the Change To edit bar, click Change All on the right side of the Spelling dialog box. Because you won't see the changes as they occur, Word displays the alert box shown in Figure 7-16, asking you to confirm the Change All command.

FIGURE 7-16.
This alert box lets you confirm that you want to change all occurrences of the unrecognized word in your document.

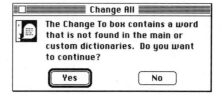

If you click OK in the alert box, Word doesn't change all the occurrences of the word at once. Instead, Word replaces the unrecognized word only as it encounters the word during the spell-check. If you cancel the spell-check procedure in the middle of the document, instances of the word in the parts of the document that you haven't yet spell-checked are not changed.

If you close the Spelling dialog box before the document is completely spell-checked, choose the Replace command from the Edit menu to change any remaining instances of the unrecognized word. Type the misspelled text in the Find What edit bar and the correct spelling in the Replace With edit bar. Click Replace All to change all occurrences of the find text.

Ending the spell-check

When Word has checked every word from the insertion point to the end of your document, you'll see an alert box that asks *Continue checking from beginning of document?* Click OK to continue checking from the beginning of the document. When Word reaches the point where you started the search, you'll see the message *End of document reached.* Click Cancel to end the spell-check and remove the Spelling dialog box from your screen.

If you click anywhere in the document window while the Spelling dialog box is open, Word activates the document window but doesn't close the Spelling dialog box. To reactivate the Spelling dialog box, click anywhere in this box if it is visible, or choose Spelling from the Tools menu, or type Command-L.

Spell-checking a selected portion of the document

To check for spelling errors in only part of a document, highlight the part you want to check, and then choose the Spelling command. Word scans the selected text and flags any unrecognized words, just as it does when searching an entire document. To leave an unrecognized word unchanged, click Ignore or Ignore All. To change an unrecognized word, type the correction in the Change To edit bar or select one of the suggested words. Word inserts the new word in your document and continues checking the selection.

When Word has scanned the entire selection, it displays the alert box shown in Figure 7-17. Click OK to close the Spelling dialog box and return to your document. Click Continue Checking to continue to check your document beyond the selected text.

FIGURE 7-17.
Word displays this alert box to notify you that it has finished checking a selection.

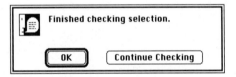

Spell-checking a single word

To check the spelling of a single word, highlight the word, and choose the Spelling command. Word checks the highlighted word against the entries in all open dictionaries.

If Word doesn't recognize the highlighted word, the word appears at the top of the Spelling dialog box. Click Ignore to leave the word as it appears in your document. To change the word, type a new word or select a suggestion and press the Change button. Word then displays an alert box that tells you the word is spelled correctly. Click OK in the alert box to close the Spelling dialog box and end the spell-check. Click Continue Checking to continue spell-checking your document.

Understanding dictionary conventions

You'll be able to use Word's Spelling feature most effectively if you're aware of how Word treats duplicate words and words with nonstandard case. In addition to handling these problems, Word spell-checks hidden text and elements like headers, footers, and footnotes that appear in separate document windows. Word also remembers how you've changed misspellings encountered during the current Word session.

Repeated text

Word alerts you to the presence of duplicate words in your document, such as *and and* by highlighting the repeated word in your document and displaying it at the top of the Spelling dialog box.

Nonstandard case

The Spelling command finds words in your document that have unusual patterns of uppercase and lowercase letters. For example, Word flags such occurrences as *BOok*, *boOk*, and *BooK*. Word generally suggests the same word, using standard case, in the Change To edit bar.

When an unrecognized word follows standard patterns of capitalization, Word's suggestions match the case of the unrecognized word. As a result, you generally don't need to be concerned with the case of the replacement text when you use one of Word's suggestions. For example, if the unrecognized word in your document begins with an uppercase letter, the alternatives in the Suggestions list box also appear in this form. Similarly, if the unrecognized text in your document appears in all uppercase letters, the suggested alternatives appear in all uppercase letters.

Checking hidden text

If you've assigned the Hidden format to text in your document, Word checks the spelling of that text only when the text is displayed in the document window. You should consider checking your final draft with text unhidden to catch errors in elements such as notes, index, or table of content entries.

Checking headers, footers, and footnotes

When Word reaches the end of the document text during a spell-check, it continues checking other elements, such as header, footer, and footnote text, that don't appear in the document window. You can thus verify correct spelling throughout your document. (We'll cover headers and footers in detail in Chapter 10, "Creating Professional Documents," and footnotes in Chapter 11, "Adding a Table of Contents, an Index, and Footnotes.")

Tracking repeated misspellings

Word keeps track of the way you change misspelled text. As long as the Spelling dialog box remains open, Word remembers the last editing change you made to an unrecognized word and suggests your correction as the replacement text the next time it encounters the misspelling.

For example, suppose you commonly transpose the letters *a* and *h* in the word *that*. The first time Word highlights *taht*, you correct it to *that* in the Change To edit bar and then click Change. The next time Word encounters *taht* in your document, it automatically enters the word *that* in the Change To edit bar. Simply click Change to accept Word's suggestion.

Dictionary preferences

You can control how Word checks spelling in your document by selecting three options in the Spelling section of the Preferences dialog box, shown in Figure 7-18. Display the Spelling section directly from the Spelling dialog box by clicking Options. Or display this dialog box by first choosing the Preferences command from the Tools menu and then clicking the Spelling icon.

FIGURE 7-18.
*The Spelling section of
the Preferences dialog
box lets you select
spelling options.*

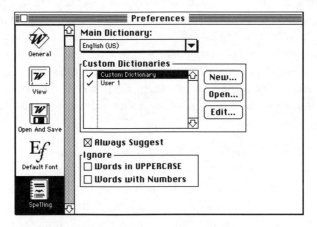

The Spelling area of the Preferences dialog box has three sections. The Main Dictionary drop-down list box lets you select a foreign-language dictionary as your main dictionary if such a dictionary exists in your Word Commands folder. (You can purchase foreign-language dictionaries separately.) The middle section lets you create and open custom dictionaries. (We'll discuss custom dictionaries in a few pages.) The bottom section lets you control whether Word offers suggestions each time it doesn't recognize a word and whether Word ignores uppercase letters and combinations of numbers and letters that it would otherwise flag.

The Always Suggest option

The Always Suggest option lets you control whether Word displays suggestions in the Spelling dialog box when it doesn't recognize a word. If you don't change this option, Word displays words that closely resemble the spelling of the unrecognized word in the Suggestions list box. If you're working with a document that contains many words you know aren't in the Word dictionary—for example, if you're spell-checking a letter that contains many personal names—you can deactivate this option to save time.

The Words In UPPERCASE option

Word's spelling feature generally flags instances of nonstandard case, which can be time-consuming if your document includes many words that are all uppercase. Selecting the Words In UPPERCASE option tells Word to ignore such words as it scans your document. Word continues to check the spelling of words formatted with the All Caps or Small Caps style.

Use this option sparingly, because it can cause Word to ignore words you want it to check.

The Words With Numbers option

Word always ignores combinations of numbers and one letter, such as *401k*, *24k* or *2b*, as it spell-checks your document. Selecting the Words With Numbers option in the Spelling section of the Preferences dialog box tells Word to also ignore words that contain a number and two or more alphabetic characters, such as *ex402*, *TV12*, and *400a30b*.

Custom dictionaries

To use Word's Spelling command efficiently, you'll want to create at least one custom dictionary that contains the names of clients or business associates, technical terms, abbreviations, and similar kinds of words not in the English Main Dictionary.

After you create a custom dictionary, you can add new terms during a spell-checking operation. You can also add proper names by typing them directly in the Spelling dialog box. You can easily delete words stored in a custom dictionary by displaying the Edit Custom Dictionary dialog box from the Spelling section of the Preferences dialog box.

Creating a custom dictionary

To create a new custom dictionary, display the Spelling section of the Preferences dialog box either by choosing the Preferences command from the Tools menu and then selecting the Spelling icon, or by clicking Options in the Spelling dialog box. The Custom Dictionaries list box displays the names of the custom dictionaries you've created. Initially, Word provides an empty custom dictionary for you. To create a new custom dictionary, click New to the right of the list box. Word then displays the Save New Custom Dictionary As dialog box shown in Figure 7-19 so that you can save and name a new dictionary file.

FIGURE 7-19.
Create a new custom
dictionary in Word by
naming and saving the
dictionary file in the
Save New Custom
Dictionary As
dialog box.

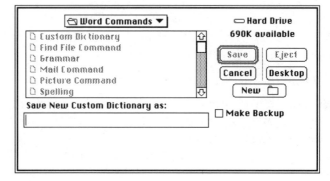

In the Save New Custom Dictionary As edit bar, type the name of the dictionary using up to 32 characters, including spaces. So that Word can locate the custom dictionary, store it in the folder that contains the English Main Dictionary. Click Save to add the dictionary name to the Preferences dialog box, as shown in Figure 7-20. The check mark indicates that this custom dictionary is now open and will open automatically each time you start a spell-checking session.

FIGURE 7-20.
Word displays the
names of custom
dictionaries in the
Preferences dialog box.

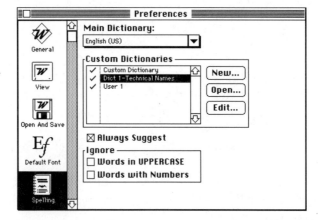

Opening and closing a custom dictionary

You open and close custom dictionaries by adding and removing the check mark beside the dictionary name in the Custom Dictionaries list box. To have Word consult a custom dictionary, be sure that the dictionary is open before choosing the Spelling command. However, spell-checking is faster if you close custom dictionaries you don't need for the current document. You can deactivate custom dictionaries by clicking the checkmark next to the dictionary name in the custom dictionaries list. The name of the custom dictionary will remain in the list, but will not be used until you click again to redisplay the check mark.

To open a custom dictionary stored in another folder or on another drive, display the Spelling section of the Preferences dialog box, and click Open. Word displays an Open dialog box that lets you locate the dictionary. When you select the dictionary and click the Open button in the Open dialog box, Word adds the custom dictionary to the Custom Dictionary list and places a check mark next to its name.

After you change the custom dictionary preferences, you see the results the next time you choose Spelling. Open dictionaries appear in the Add Words To list box at the bottom of the Spelling dialog box, as shown in Figure 7-21.

FIGURE 7-21.
Word adds the names
of open custom
dictionaries to the Add
Words To list box.

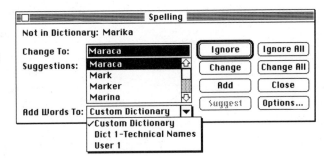

Adding new words to a custom dictionary

As you spell-check a document, you can easily add words not contained in the Main Dictionary to an open custom dictionary. First, move the pointer to Not In Dictionary in the upper-left corner of the spelling dialog box. When the pointer changes to a down-pointing arrow, click once to display the word in the Change To edit bar. Then click the arrow beside the Add Words To drop-down list box, and select the dictionary you want. Finally, click Add to add the word to the custom dictionary.

Another way to add a word to a custom dictionary is to open the Spelling dialog box, type the word in the Change To edit bar, select the name of the dictionary in the Add Words To list box, and then click Add.

To add many words to a custom dictionary—for example, the names and addresses of clients on a mailing list—first create a document that contains only the words you want to add. Next, in the Spelling section of the Preferences dialog box, open the custom dictionary or dictionaries to which you want to add these words. Then choose the Spelling command, and add each word to the custom dictionary by clicking Add when Word flags it as an unrecognized word.

Specifying capitalization

When you add a word to a custom dictionary, the word is entered exactly as it appears in your document. If the word is formatted in all lowercase, Word recognizes occurrences of the word formatted in other cases. If you add a word that contains uppercase letters, however, Word recognizes this word only when the same letters are uppercase. For example, if you add the name *MacArthur* to a user dictionary, during a spelling check, Word flags any occurrence of this name where the *M* and the *A* are not capitalized. Thus, *Macarthur*, *macarthur*, and *macArthur* are all unrecognized words.

Similarly, if you add a word that contains all uppercase letters to a custom dictionary, Word won't recognize lowercase or mixed-case occurrences of the word. Table 7-2 summarizes the way that Word recognizes words you've added to a custom dictionary.

Add	Word questions	Word recognizes
microsoft	miCRosoft	microsoft, Microsoft, MICROSOFT
Microsoft	microsoft	Microsoft, MICROSOFT
MICROSOFT	Microsoft, microsoft	MICROSOFT
MicroSoft	microsoft, MICROSOFT	MicroSoft

TABLE 7-2.
When you add a word capitalized like the examples in the first column, you can expect the results shown in the second and third columns.

Deleting a word from a custom dictionary

If you no longer want Word to recognize a word in a custom dictionary, you can delete the word. Word will then flag the word if it appears in your document. To delete a word stored in a custom dictionary, first display the Spelling section of the Preferences dialog box. Next, in the Custom Dictionaries list box, click the name of the dictionary that contains the word, and then click Edit. Word displays an Edit Custom Dictionary dialog box like the one shown in Figure 7-22.

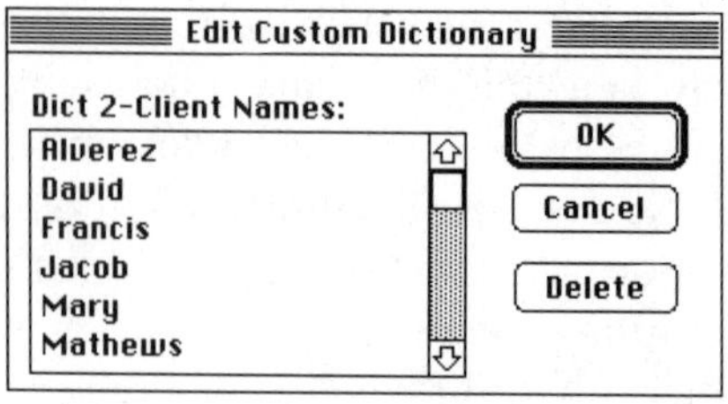

FIGURE 7-22.
The Edit Custom Dictionary dialog box enables you to delete words you've added to a custom dictionary.

Edit Custom Dictionary

Dict 2-Client Names:
Alverez
David
Francis
Jacob
Mary
Mathews

OK
Cancel
Delete

The Edit Custom Dictionary dialog box displays the name of the dictionary and presents each word it currently contains in alphabetical order. To delete a word from the list, simply select it, and then click Delete. You can delete all the words from the dictionary in this manner, but you can remove only one word at a time. When the dictionary contains only the words you want, click OK to close the dialog box. Click Cancel to close the dialog box without changing the dictionary.

Hyphenating text

Word doesn't automatically hyphenate words as you enter text in your document. However, you can hyphenate words at line breaks in existing text by using the Hyphenate command on the Tools menu. Hyphenating text improves your document's appearance by reducing the raggedness of the right margin, especially when you're creating narrow columns of text. By hyphenating selected words, you can also avoid the unsightly extra spaces that Word occasionally inserts to achieve a justified right margin.

The Hyphenate command allows you to hyphenate an entire document or only a selection. Your selection can be as small as a single word, but you'll probably want to select at least a paragraph or more. When you choose Hyphenate, Word scans your document beginning at the insertion point. If the first word in each line of text can be hyphenated, Word inserts a special hyphen, called an *optional hyphen*, and moves the first part of the word to the preceding line.

Before we discuss the Hyphenate command, we introduce the different hyphens that Word offers. After this discussion, we show you how to use the Hyphen dialog box to apply optional hyphens to your document or to a document selection after you've written it, and how to apply hyphens as you go.

Hyphen choices

Word treats a regular hyphen, which you enter by pressing the Hyphen key, like any other character in your document. If the hyphenated word falls at the end of a line, Word might split the word between two lines. All the characters to the left of the hyphen and the hyphen itself appear on the first line. Characters to the right of the hyphen wrap to the beginning of the next line.

Occasionally, you won't want to split a hyphenated word between two lines. At other times, words you normally wouldn't hyphenate might need to be split to balance lines of text. Word offers two special characters to help you handle these situations: optional hyphens and nonbreaking hyphens.

Optional hyphens

An optional hyphen appears only when the hyphenated word is broken at the end of the line. Word inserts optional hyphens when you choose Hyphenate from the Tools menu. You can also insert an optional hyphen in your document by pressing Command-hyphen. Use an optional hyphen whenever you hyphenate a word to break it at the end of a line. If the word later appears somewhere else in the line as a result of revisions you've made, Word hides the hyphen.

When an optional hyphen occurs at a line break, it looks like a regular hyphen and always appears on the screen, even when Show ¶ is not active. You won't see this character between parts of a word in the middle of a line, however, unless you activate the Show ¶ command. When you choose this command, Word displays the optional hyphen as ⌐ to distinguish it from the regular hyphen.

Nonbreaking hyphens

A nonbreaking hyphen is similar to a nonbreaking space; Word doesn't break a word that contains this kind of hyphen—even when the word appears at the end of a line.

For example, suppose you're writing about the software program Lotus 1-2-3. To prevent Word from breaking 1-2-3 at the end of a line, insert nonbreaking hyphens between the numbers by pressing Command-~. Nonbreaking hyphens are always visible on the screen. They look like regular hyphens when the Show ¶ command is not selected. When you activate the Show ¶ command, Word distinguishes these characters by the ≈ symbol.

Other hyphens

You can also use the hyphen key to create dashes in your document—for example, to introduce a pause in a sentence or set apart an explanatory phrase. Word lets you create both long dashes and short dashes. Type Shift-Option-hyphen to insert a long dash at the insertion point. Type Option-hyphen to create a short dash. Word treats the long and short dashes in your document just as it does normal hyphens.

Using the Hyphenate command

To hyphenate a document, choose Hyphenate from the Tools menu, or press Shift-F15. Word displays the Hyphenation dialog box, shown in Figure 7-23. Click

Hyphenate All if you want Word to scan through the entire document and automatically hyphenate words at line breaks where possible. If you want Word to pause each time it locates a word to hyphenate, click Start Hyphenation.

FIGURE 7-23.
The Hyphenate dialog
box lets you apply
optional hyphens.

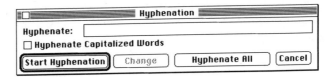

Whether you use automatic or confirming hyphenation, you have the choice of ignoring or hyphenating capitalized words. If you want to hyphenate words that begin with an uppercase letter, simply click the Hyphenate Capitalized Words option to activate it.

Hyphenating the complete document

If you click Hyphenate All, Word decides which words to break between lines and how to break each word. Word considers all the text between the insertion point and the end of the selection or the document. If you are hyphenating an entire document and you choose Hyphenate when the insertion point is anywhere other than the beginning of the document, you see the alert box shown in Figure 7-24 when Word reaches the end of the document.

FIGURE 7-24.
You see this alert box
when Word has
hyphenated from the
insertion point to the
end of your document.

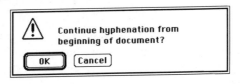

Click OK to continue hyphenating from the beginning of your document. When Word completes the hyphenation operation, you see the message *End of document reached*. Click Cancel to stop hyphenation and close the Hyphenate dialog box. After you've started the hyphenation process, you can cancel it at any time by pressing Command-period.

The Hyphenate All option can lead to some problems. For example, Word might hyphenate words at the end of two or more consecutive lines in your document and make the document difficult to read. Word might also hyphenate words that are already hyphenated, such as *long-suffering*. And keep in mind that Word's syllable breaks might occasionally be different from what you want. For important documents, we recommend that you use Start Hyphenation, which lets you consider each word to which Word wants to apply a hyphen.

Confirming hyphenation

When you select Start Hyphenation in the Hyphenation dialog box, Word scans
your selection or document from the insertion point for the first possible word to
hyphenate, displays the word in the Hyphenate edit bar, and highlights the portion of the suggested word break. Figure 7-25 shows how the Hyphenation dialog
box looks when Word finds a word to hyphenate.

FIGURE 7-25.
*Word suggests a word
break when it locates
a candidate for
hyphenation.*

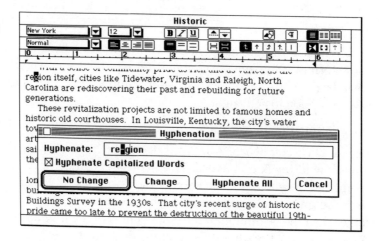

Generally, when a word contains two or more syllables, Word displays all the
syllable breaks in the Hyphenate edit bar and highlights the place where it plans
to hyphenate the word. To accept Word's suggested hyphenation, click Change,
or leave the word unbroken by clicking No Change. (No Change replaces the
Start Hyphenation button when a word appears in the Hyphenate edit bar.) Word
then looks for the next word to hyphenate and displays it in the edit bar.

If you want to place the hyphen break elsewhere in the word, click the Hyphenate edit bar between the letters where you want the hyphen to occur. In
Figure 7-26, Word suggests breaking *Carolina* between *Car* and *olina*, as shown by
the highlighted *o* in the document text. To break between *Caroli* and *na* instead,
click between *i* and *n* in the Hyphenate edit bar. Word highlights that syllable
break in the edit bar. Click Change to implement the syllable break.

If you click somewhere other than on a syllable break in the edit bar, Word
displays a vertical bar at that location. A dotted vertical line indicates how many
of the word's characters will fit on the current line. You can hyphenate the word
between any two letters located on the left side of this dotted line. (Inserting a
hyphen after the vertical line puts more characters to the left of the hyphen than
will fit on the line in your document. As a result, you can't break the word
beyond the dotted vertical line.)

FIGURE 7-26.
You can highlight the syllable break where you want Word to insert a hyphen.

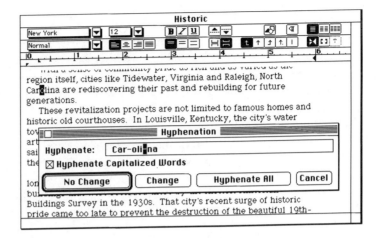

Hyphenating and editing

You might recall that some dialog box procedures, such as Find and Replace, let you click your document window and edit text without closing the dialog box. With Hyphenate, however, you must close the dialog box before you can access your document text.

If you make substantial changes to a document after you've used the Hyphenate command, some hyphenated words might move to the middle of lines, and others might move to the end of lines and need to be hyphenated. You can solve these problems by choosing the Hyphenate command again. However, remember that optional hyphens don't affect the appearance of your printed document; Word does not print optional hyphens unless they appear at line breaks.

To avoid having to use the Hyphenate command repeatedly, we recommend that you hyphenate your document after you've performed other proofing actions such as spell-checking and grammar-checking.

Undoing hyphenation

After you've hyphenated, you have the option of using Undo to delete all the hyphens, but you must choose Undo Hyphenate from the Edit menu immediately after you complete the hyphenation process.

You can also undo the effects of hyphenation by using the Replace command, which we introduced earlier in this chapter. First, choose Replace from the Edit menu, and enter a caret followed by a hyphen (^-) in the Find What edit bar, or choose Optional Hyphen from the Special drop-down list. Then delete the contents of the Replace With edit bar. Choose Replace All to delete every optional hyphen in your document, beginning at the insertion point. Choose Find Next if you want to confirm each deletion.

Checking grammar

Word's Grammar command lets you identify sentences in your document that contain common grammatical errors and that present your ideas in a confusing way. In many cases, Word suggests ways to correct or improve such sentences. You can apply the correction that Word offers to your document, or you can change your document manually. Because you might want to adhere to different grammar and style rules from one document to another, the grammar-checker also lets you select the rules you want Word to observe as it checks your document. When Word finishes proofing your document's grammar and style, you can also display document statistics that evaluate how easily a reader can understand your writing.

Using the Grammar command

You can check a complete document or the contents of a highlighted section using the Grammar command. When you choose the Grammar command from the Tools menu, Word displays the Grammar dialog box and then begins proofing your document from the insertion point forward. Word first verifies the spelling of the words in each sentence and then scans for text that violates the grammar and style rules selected in the Grammar section of the Preferences dialog box. (We'll explain in a moment how you can modify the list of rules that Word uses as a guideline.)

When Word locates a sentence that appears to violate a style or grammar rule, it presents the sentence in the Sentence list box at the top of the Grammar dialog box and highlights the relevant text. In the Suggestions list box, Word offers a suggestion for correcting the sentence, as shown in Figure 7-27.

FIGURE 7-27.
When Word encounters a sentence that contains questionable grammar or style, it displays the complete sentence in the Grammar dialog box and indicates the problem.

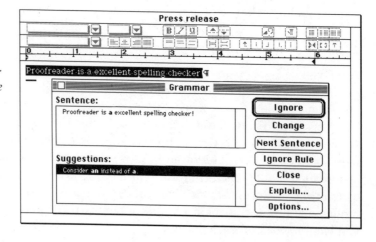

Spell-checking

As Word scans document text, it first searches each sentence for spelling errors. You don't see the Spelling dialog box unless Word does not recognize a word, at which point Word displays the Spelling dialog box, as shown in Figure 7-28.

FIGURE 7-28.
*Word spell-checks
each sentence when
you choose the
Grammar command.*

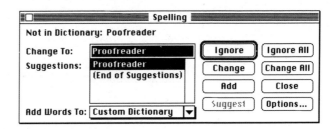

You can view spelling suggestions, add unrecognized words to custom dictionaries, and replace unrecognized words in your document from this dialog box, just as if you had chosen the Spelling command. However, because Word accesses the Spelling command through the Grammar command, you'll find that spell-checking is considerably slower than when you choose the Spelling command. (For more information about Word's Spelling command, see "Checking Spelling" earlier in this chapter.)

Viewing suspected errors

After checking for unrecognized words, Word searches for sentences that appear to violate the grammar and style rules selected in the Preferences dialog box. Word displays any such sentences one at a time in the Sentence section of the Grammar dialog box, as shown earlier in Figure 7-27. Word describes the problem in the Suggestions list box.

When Word displays a sentence in the Grammar dialog box, you can view a corrected version of the sentence, view more information about the error, ignore this occurrence of the error, or ignore all such occurrences. Click the corresponding button to perform the action and instruct Word to continue proofing your document. You can also move to the next sentence in the document or close the Grammar dialog box by clicking Next Sentence or Close.

Correcting the sentence

In many cases, Word is able to suggest an alternative to a sentence's current construction. To view a corrected version of the sentence, click the text that appears in the Suggestions list box once, and hold down the mouse button. Word displays a corrected version of the sentence in the Sentence list box and highlights the changes it has made. If you click the sentence shown in Figure 7-27, for example, Word displays the corrected sentence shown in Figure 7-29 on the next page.

FIGURE 7-29.
*Click the sentence
displayed in the
Sentence list box to
view Word's suggested
correction.*

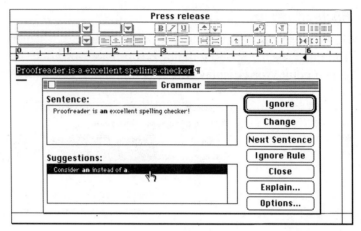

To replace the text in your document with the suggested correction, click the Correct button, or double-click the sentence in the Suggestions list box. Word replaces the sentence in the document and then continues checking your text.

Word doesn't offer an alternative in every case. For example, Word generally doesn't suggest alternatives that would require rearranging existing words or punctuation. In such cases, Word displays the message *No correction available* in the Sentence box.

To type your own correction, simply click the document window to make it active, and then edit the sentence as necessary. Choose the Grammar command again to resume checking the document from the insertion point.

Getting more information

The best way to write clearly and correctly is to learn and follow the rules of grammar and style, and the Explain button in the Grammar dialog box can help you. Click this button to display the Grammar Explanation dialog box, which describes the grammar or style rule that the selected sentence appears to violate. The Grammar Explanation dialog box shown in Figure 7-30, for example, explains why Word selected the sentence shown in the Sentence list box. After reading the explanation, click the close box in the Grammar Explanation dialog box to return to the Grammar dialog box.

FIGURE 7-30.
*The Grammar
Explanation dialog
box explains the rule
the selected sentence
appears to violate.*

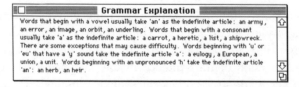

Ignoring occurrences

If you use Word's grammar-checker often, you'll discover that occasionally it flags sentences whose construction appears to violate a style or grammar rule even though the sentence is perfectly correct. Word doesn't read and understand your text. It simply looks for strings of text whose construction usually denotes faulty style or grammar.

If you don't want to follow Word's suggestion, click either the Ignore, Ignore Rule, or Next Sentence button to leave the text unchanged in your document. Clicking Ignore moves past the current problem in the sentence. Word continues to check this sentence against other rules and then proceeds through the document. Clicking Ignore Rule instructs Word to ignore any other apparent violations of this rule during the current grammar-check. Clicking the Next Sentence button tells Word to move to the next sentence in the document. Word continues to flag sentences that appear to violate the rule, beginning with the next sentence.

Understanding readability statistics

When Word reaches the end of your document, you'll see the alert message *End of document reached*. If the Show Document Statistics option in the Grammar section of the Preferences dialog box has been selected, Word then evaluates your document—or the selection it has just scanned—to determine how easy it is for a reader to understand your writing.

Figure 7-31 shows a sample Document Statistics dialog box. As you can see, Word groups information about the text it has proofed into three categories: Counts, Averages, and Readability. Each category builds upon the previous one to tell you more about your document's general readability.

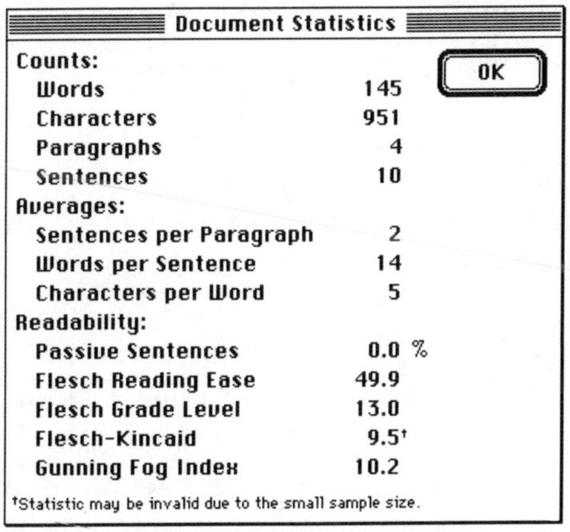

FIGURE 7-31.
*The Document
Statistics dialog box
indicates a document's
general readability.*

Document Statistics		
Counts:		OK
Words	145	
Characters	951	
Paragraphs	4	
Sentences	10	
Averages:		
Sentences per Paragraph	2	
Words per Sentence	14	
Characters per Word	5	
Readability:		
Passive Sentences	0.0 %	
Flesch Reading Ease	49.9	
Flesch Grade Level	13.0	
Flesch-Kincaid	9.5†	
Gunning Fog Index	10.2	

†Statistic may be invalid due to the small sample size.

To determine your document's readability, Word first counts the characters, words, sentences, and paragraphs it has scanned since you opened the Grammar dialog box. It displays this information, as well as the relationship between these elements, in the Document Statistics dialog box when the grammar check is completed.

Counts, the first category of data, indicates the number of words, characters, paragraphs, and sentences encountered during the grammar check. Averages, the second category, defines the average statistical relationship between these elements. Although such a method isn't foolproof, the ratio between these elements gives a good indication of the word, sentence, and paragraph length. The longer the words, sentences, and paragraphs are, the more difficult Word considers your text to be.

Word analyzes this data and presents the results in the Readability section of the dialog box. Word determines the percentage of sentences that contain passive voice and indicates how the text fares on four different indexes based on the average relationship between textual elements.

After you've reviewed the statistics for the current document or selection, click the OK button to close the Document Statistics dialog box and return to your document.

Passive voice

Sentences such as *The case is judged based on its merits* or *Your check has been lost in the mail* are examples of passive voice. The construction of these sentences makes it impossible to know who or what is responsible for the action being described.

Because passive voice can obscure meaning, Word flags instances of passive voice as it scans your document and indicates in the Document Statistics dialog box the percentage of sentences in the document or the highlighted selection that contain passive rather than active construction. A high percentage of passive voice occurrences probably indicates that your writing isn't as precise as it could be.

Flesch Reading Ease and Grade Level

The Flesch Reading Ease and Flesch Grade Level indexes help you evaluate how easily an average adult reader can understand your writing. These indexes are based on the average number of syllables per 100 words and the average number of words per sentence.

With these indexes, "standard" writing is considered to average 17 words per sentence and 147 syllables per 100 words. As Table 7-3 indicates, a score between 60 and 70 reflects writing that attains this standard. A higher score indicates that your writing is easier to read; a lower score indicates that the writing is comparatively more difficult. The score is also linked to the grade level at which a reader might be expected to understand your writing's grammar and content without too much difficulty.

Flesch Reading Ease score	Relative reading ease	Flesch Grade Level
90–100	Very easy	Grade 4
80–90	Easy	Grade 5
70–80	Fairly easy	Grade 6
60–70	Standard	Grades 6 and 7
50–60	Fairly difficult	Grade 8 through secondary school
30–50	Difficult	Secondary school, some higher education
0–30	Very difficult	Higher education

TABLE 7-3.
The Flesch Reading Ease and Grade Level indexes indicate how easily an average reader can understand your writing.

Flesch-Kincaid index

The Flesch-Kincaid index also correlates grade level and your writing. An index of 6–7 corresponds to the "standard" Reading Ease score.

Gunning Fog index

The Gunning Fog index is another way to measure sentence difficulty. This index ranks your writing on a scale from 1 to 100. The higher the Gunning Fog index, the more words with multiple syllables in your text.

Selecting grammar rule preferences

Because you might want to adhere to different grammar and style rules from one document to another, Word lets you select the rules you want Word to adhere to as it scans your document. You can also indicate the frequency with which you'll permit the occurrence of constructions that can make your writing difficult to understand.

Specifying grammar and style preferences

To change the current grammar and style rules, display the Grammar section of the Preferences dialog box by clicking the Options button in the Grammar dialog box or by choosing the Preferences command from the Tools menu and then clicking the Grammar icon. Word displays the dialog box shown in Figure 7-32 on the next page.

FIGURE 7-32.
*Specify the various
grammar and style
rules you want Word
to adhere to during the
grammar-check in the
Spelling section of
the Preferences
dialog box.*

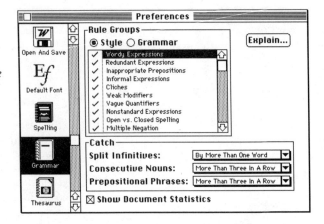

The rules that Word uses to check grammar and style in your document appear in two groups in the Grammar section of the Preferences dialog box. As Figure 7-32 indicates, when you first display this dialog box, Word presents the style rules in the Rule Groups list box. A check mark appears next to each rule that Word follows as it scans your document. Click the Grammar radio button at the top of the list box to view the grammar rules that Word follows. As shown in Figure 7-33, check marks next to these options indicate that they're all active.

FIGURE 7-33.
*Click the Grammar
radio button to view
the grammar rules
Word follows during a
grammar-checking
operation.*

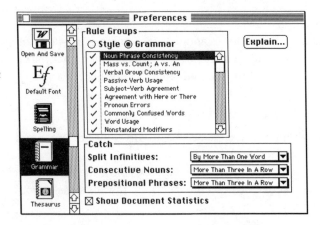

If you're unfamiliar with a grammar or style rule or unsure how Word applies it during a grammar-check, highlight the rule, and then click the Explain button to display an explanation of the rule. You can then choose to keep this rule active or remove it from the list of rules that Word considers as it scans your document.

To remove a grammar or style rule, first select the group to which the rule belongs in the Preferences dialog box. Then click the check mark to the left of the rule to remove the mark and make the rule inactive. When you quit the application, Word stores the currently selected grammar and style rules in the Word Settings (5) file. They remain in effect until you change them—even from one Word session to another.

Selecting Catch options

In addition to the grammar and style rules that appear in the list box, three categories in the Catch section of the Preferences dialog box let you determine how Word considers common grammar-related occurrences in your text. The drop-down edit bars to the right of the Split Infinitives, Consecutive Nouns, and Prepositional Phrases options let you specify the frequency with which you'll permit each occurrence in document sentences. The default settings for these options are used unless you change them by selecting a new option, as shown in Figure 7-34.

FIGURE 7-34.
*Select the frequency
with which you'll
permit the Catch
options in your
text from the
corresponding drop-
down list box.*

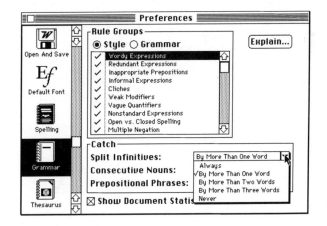

Split Infinitives One rule of grammar is to avoid split infinitives in your writing. An infinitive is the verb form in which the verb is preceded by the word *to*. *To eat*, for example, is the infinitive form of the verb *eat*. Splitting an infinitive means placing a word between the word *to* and the verb that follows. *To greedily eat*, for example, is a split infinitive. You can control the number of words that Word permits between *to* and a verb by selecting an option from the Split Infinitive list box. As Figure 7-34 indicates, By More Than One Word is the default for this option.

Consecutive Nouns Generally, using consecutive nouns makes it difficult for readers to understand the subject of the sentence in which they appear. Select the number of consecutive nouns you'll permit in a sentence in the Consecutive Nouns list box. For example, selecting More Than Two In A Row allows no more than one noun to modify another noun and causes Word to question *Action Item Committee*, but not *Action Committee*.

Prepositional Phrases Consecutive prepositional phrases also make it difficult to understand the information presented in a sentence. A preposition explains the relationship between two words. Generally, the more prepositions that appear in a sentence, the more difficult it is to see the relationship. Select the number of consecutive prepositions you'll permit in a sentence in the Prepositional Phrases list box. For example, selecting More Than Two In A Row limits the number of prepositional phrases permitted in a sentence to two and causes Word to permit *Chairman of the Joint Chiefs of Staff*, but question *vacation of the Chairman of the Joint Chiefs of Staff.*

Displaying the Readability dialog box

If you don't want Word to display the Document Statistics dialog box when it finishes checking your document, deselect the Show Document Statistics option at the bottom of the Grammar section of the Preferences dialog box. Word then returns to your text when it reaches the end of the document or selection.

8

Printing

When you've created, formatted, and edited a document, you're ready to print. After you install and select a printer from the Chooser, you can use the Print command from the File menu and Word's default Print and Page Setup settings to print a document in a single step.

To take full advantage of Word's printing features, you can select options in the Print and Page Setup dialog boxes to specify the number of copies, the specific pages of a document you want to print, and the method of feeding the paper into the printer. Depending on your printer, you can also select additional Print and Page Setup dialog box options that enable you to print in color and let you manipulate and change the printed image.

In this chapter, we explore Word's printing settings, and we show you how to print Word documents. We also introduce two features that let you view document pages as they'll appear when printed: Page Layout and Print Preview. As you'll see, Word offers all that you'll need to layout and print your documents easily.

Selecting a printer

Before you can print any Macintosh file, you must install the appropriate printer driver or printer resource file on your startup disk. You will find the Apple printer driver files stored on the disks that came with your printer. The documentation that came with your Macintosh system software explains the installation procedure. After you've installed the driver or printer resource file in your System folder, you must restart your computer and use the Chooser desk accessory to specify the type of printer you want to use.

Using the Chooser

To display a list of available printers, choose the Chooser desk accessory from the Apple menu. If you are using System 7, you can also double-click the Chooser icon to open it. You select the printer you'll use to print your document in the Chooser dialog box, shown in Figure 8-1. The printer you select in the Chooser determines how Word displays text on the screen and how Word prints this text. For example, the scale on the ruler at the top of the document window varies depending on the printer you select in the Chooser. The width of printed text characters also differs slightly. As a result, the appearance of text and the location of automatic line and page breaks in your document can change depending upon your printer choice.

FIGURE 8-1.
The Chooser dialog box allows you to select a printer.

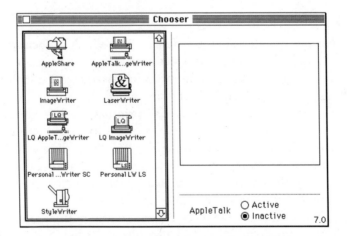

In this chapter, we show you how to install and print from ImageWriter and LaserWriter printers. The installation procedure for most printers generally matches the steps we describe. If you want to install a different printer, be sure to read your printer owner's manual before you begin. If you have trouble completing the steps outlined in the manual, contact your local hardware dealer.

Selecting an ImageWriter

To select an ImageWriter printer, click the ImageWriter icon in the Chooser dialog box. Two icons then appear, as shown in Figure 8-2, to let you indicate the port you want to use. The Printer icon represents the printer port on your Macintosh. The Telephone icon represents the communications or modem port. Generally, you attach an ImageWriter to the printer port. Do *not* select the communications port if you've attached a hard disk to that port or your hard disk might be erased!

FIGURE 8-2.
When you select the ImageWriter printer icon, Word asks you to indicate the port you plan to use.

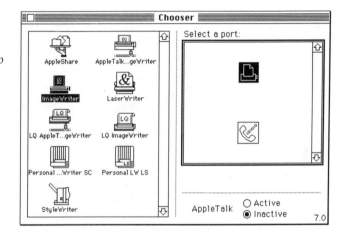

If you select the printer port while the AppleTalk setting is active, you'll see the message *ImageWriter cannot be used on the Printer port while AppleTalk is active. Do you want to make AppleTalk inactive? Access to current network services will have to be reestablished.* Click OK in this alert box. When you see the message *Please make sure that the AppleTalk Personal Network is disconnected*, click OK. You'll see an alert box telling you to confirm Page Setup settings so that your applications can format documents correctly for the ImageWriter. Click OK in this alert box. Then close the Chooser dialog box.

Selecting a LaserWriter

To select a LaserWriter printer, first click the AppleTalk Active option to indicate that you're hooked into the AppleTalk network. You'll then see the message *Please make sure that you are connected to an AppleTalk network.* Click OK in this alert box, and then click the LaserWriter icon. (If you select the LaserWriter icon while the Inactive AppleTalk option is selected, you'll see the alert message *LaserWriter requires AppleTalk. Please make sure that you are connected to an AppleTalk network.*)

When you click the LaserWriter icon, the names of the printers connected to the AppleTalk network are displayed on the right side of the dialog box. You'll also see the On/Off options for Background Printing, as shown in Figure 8-3. If the PrintMonitor file is not in your System folder, the Background Printing options appear dimmed. (We talk about background printing in a few pages.) If your Macintosh is connected to only one printer, the printer's name appears on the right side of the Chooser dialog box. If more than one printer name appears, click the name of the printer you want to use.

FIGURE 8-3.
When you select the
LaserWriter printer
icon, Word displays
the available printers.

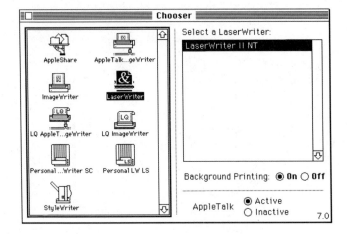

After completing these steps, close the Chooser dialog box to confirm your selections. You'll see a message that reminds you to confirm page setup settings in the Page Setup dialog box.

Using the Print command

After you've installed and chosen your printer, use the Print command on the File menu to print an open document. Choosing Print displays the Print dialog box. Figures 8-4 and 8-5 show the Print dialog boxes for the ImageWriter and the LaserWriter printers. As you can see, the dialog box varies slightly, depending on the printer you've selected.

FIGURE 8-4.
This is the Print
dialog box for the
ImageWriter printer.

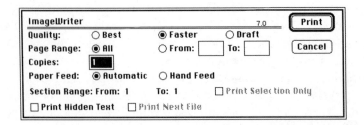

FIGURE 8-5.
*This is the Print
dialog box for the
LaserWriter printer.*

LaserWriter "LaserWriter" 7.0	**Print**
Copies: 1 **Pages:** ● All ○ From: To:	Cancel

Cover Page: ● No ○ First Page ○ Last Page
Paper Source: ● Paper Cassette ○ Manual Feed
Print: ● Black & White   ○ Color/Grayscale
Destination: ● Printer   ○ PostScript® File
Section Range: From: 1   **To:** 1   ☐ Print Selection Only
☐ **Print Hidden Text**   ☐ Print Next File   ☐ **Print Back To Front**

Make your selections, and then click OK to begin printing. As each page of your document is processed, you see the page number in the status box in the lower-left corner of the document window. You can cancel the print procedure by pressing Command-period.

The Print dialog box always offers two sets of printing options. The first group lets you specify how you want to print the current document. For example, you can indicate exactly which pages and the number of copies you want to produce. A smaller group of printing options lets you do things like print hidden text or link text files for printing.

We look first at the dialog box options that specify a printing range and the number of copies, and then at the more general printing options. Most of these options are common to both ImageWriter and LaserWriter printers. Some, however, are printer specific.

Specifying a print range

When you choose Print, you can print your entire document, only selected text, or only a range of pages. If you've recently made changes to your document, hold down the Shift key, and choose the Full Repaginate Now command from the Tools menu to repaginate your text. Then, in the Print dialog box, enter the pages you want to print. In Chapter 10, "Creating Professional Documents," we explain the Section Range settings when we discuss multisection documents.

Printing a text selection

The Print Selection Only option allows you to print currently highlighted text. Word makes this option available if you highlight as little as a single character in your document before you choose Print. (If you haven't selected text, this option appears dimmed.) Choosing this option is the easiest way to print a few lines or paragraphs of text.

Print Selection Only works best when you want a copy of your text for proofreading or editing and you're not concerned with final document formatting. When you select this option, Word prints only the currently highlighted text, beginning at the top of the printed page. Because you are printing the selected text out of context, page numbers, headers, or footers do not appear in the printed document.

Printing a range of pages

The Print dialog box also lets you print a specified range of pages. The radio button next to the All setting is the default page-range setting. To print the complete document, you don't need to change this setting. To print a specified range of pages, enter the starting page number in the From edit bar and the ending page number in the To edit bar. You must use Arabic numerals in these edit bars, even if you've used letters or Roman numerals to number pages in your document.

If you've numbered pages beginning with a number other than 1, be sure that the page numbers you enter in the From and To edit bars correspond to the page numbers as they appear in your document, and not to the pages' absolute positions. For example, suppose the starting page number in your document is 3. To print pages 4 and 5 (which are actually the second and third pages of the document), enter 4 in the From edit bar and 5 in the To edit bar. (Press the Tab key to move quickly from the From edit bar to the To edit bar.) If you enter 2 and 3 in these edit bars instead, Word prints only the first page of the document—the page on which the number 3 appears.

You can specify a range of pages for printing even if you have not numbered your document pages. To print pages 5 through 11 of a 25-page document, for example, click the From edit bar, type the value 5, and then type the value 11 in the To edit bar.

To print a single page of a document, enter the same number in the From and To edit bars. For example, to print page 3, enter 3 in both edit bars. To print from the beginning of your document to a specific page—for example, to print the first nine pages of a document—leave the From edit bar blank, and type the number of the last page you want to print in the To edit bar. Similarly, to print from a specified page to the end of your document, type the first page you want to print in the From edit bar and leave the To edit bar blank. Word provides this option as a convenience; you can, of course, fill in both boxes.

Specifying the number of copies

When you choose Print, Word automatically displays 1, the default number, in the Copies edit bar of the Print dialog box. To print more than one copy at a time, type the number of copies you want in the Copies edit bar. You can order up to 99 copies to be printed in a single print session.

On an ImageWriter, Word prints the complete selection for each copy. On a LaserWriter, however, it first prints all the copies of page 1, then all the copies of page 2, then page 3, and so on, to minimize the time required to convert each page into a LaserWriter format. Although this method of printing multiple copies is faster, you might prefer printing each copy of a long document individually. As we explain in Chapter 10, "Creating Professional Documents," you can use the File Series dialog box to connect a document to itself. After you've created this link, Word prints complete single copies of the active document until you cancel the printing, or until it prints the number of copies you've indicated. To display the File Series dialog box, choose Document from the Format menu, and click the File Series button.

Printing hidden text

If you want to print text that has been assigned the Hidden format, you can select the Print Hidden Text option to print this text along with the rest of your document. Word then prints any hidden text within the print selection, even if the text is not currently visible on your screen. (The Show Hidden Text option in the Preferences dialog box and the Print Hidden Text option are separate options; you don't need to select Show Hidden Text to print hidden text.)

Printing linked documents

The Print Next File option prints documents that you've linked to the current document. To print two or more documents consecutively, you must first link the documents. Choose Document from the Format menu, click the Files Series button, and click the Next File button in the File Series dialog box. Then select the next document you want to print. When the current document is linked to other documents, the Print Next File option in the Print dialog box is selected by default. Printing the current document with the option selected automatically prints the linked files. Be sure to deactivate the option when you want to print only the current document.

We'll talk more about linking files in Chapter 10, "Creating Professional Documents," when we discuss techniques for working with long documents.

ImageWriter options

If you use an ImageWriter, you'll find three Quality options in the Print dialog box: Best, Faster, and Draft. The Best option produces dark and dense characters and requires more time to print than do the other options, because the ImageWriter prints each character twice. The Faster option prints your document more quickly, but the printed text doesn't appear as dark. The Draft option prints your document very quickly but ignores almost all font and character formatting.

Figure 8-6 on the next page shows the difference between the Best, Faster, and Draft Quality options. All three text samples are formatted in 12-point Geneva, with the first line plain, the second line bold, and the third line italic. As you can

FIGURE 8-6.
You can select from
three Quality options
when you print from
the ImageWriter.

PLAIN   This text was printed with the Best quality option
             selected.

BOLD   **This text was printed with the Best quality**
             option selected.

ITALIC   *This text was printed with the Best quality option*
             selected.

PLAIN   This text was printed with the Faster quality
             option selected.

BOLD   **This text was printed with the Faster**
             quality option selected.

ITALIC   *This text was printed with the Faster quality*
             option selected.

PLAIN   This text was printed with the Draft quality option
             selected.

BOLD   This text was printed with the Draft quality
             option   selected.

ITALIC   This text was printed with the Draft quality option
             selected.

see, Word ignores font and character formatting (except for bold) when you select
the Draft Quality option.

LaserWriter options

The LaserWriter's Print dialog box offers six sets of options not available with the
ImageWriter. You can change your printer's paper source, print a cover page,
specify color printing, and print your document from back to front. In addition,
you can send PostScript instructions about the currently active document by
clicking the PostScript File Destination option. We discuss creating Word files
that contain PostScript commands in Appendix C, "Using PostScript Commands
in Word." If you've installed the PrintMonitor file in your System folder, you can
also take advantage of background printing and file spooling.

The Paper Source option

Word's default Paper Source option, Paper Cassette, feeds paper into the Laser-Writer automatically from a paper tray. To print on a few sheets of special paper or on envelopes that you feed into the printer by hand, select Manual Feed. Then your LaserWriter prints a page only when you insert a sheet of paper. After printing one page, the red Paper Out light on your printer flashes, indicating that the printer is ready for another sheet. If you don't feed paper into the printer within about a minute, Word automatically cancels the print job.

The Cover Page options

The LaserWriter's Cover Page options enable you to print the date and time that you printed a document on a cover page and also indicates the user from whose Macintosh the document was printed.

To print a cover page, indicate in the Print dialog box whether you want the page printed as either the first or last page of the current print job. When you select the First Page or Last Page option, Word prints a sheet like the one shown in Figure 8-7 on the next page. As you can see, the cover page sheet lists the application from which the document was printed, the document name, the date and time of printing, and the printer name.

The Cover Page options are particularly helpful when several users share a common printer. If your printer is hooked up to only one Macintosh, you probably won't use this feature often. In this case, leave the No radio button in the Print dialog box selected.

The Color/Grayscale option

If you're using a color printer, select the Color/Grayscale option to print color graphics or text in the colors selected in the Character dialog box. On a black-and-white printer, Word prints text only in black or gray, depending on the color assigned to the text.

The Print Back To Front option

Selecting the Print Back To Front option prints the pages of your document in reverse order. Whether you select this option depends on the type of LaserWriter you're using.

Some versions of the LaserWriter output pages with the printed side facing up. As a result, these printers stack printed pages in reverse order. To stack pages sequentially, select Print Back To Front so that Word will print the pages in reverse order, from the last page to the first. You'll then find the pages in sequential order when you retrieve the printed document from the paper tray.

FIGURE 8-7.
*When you select a
Cover Page option,
Word produces a sheet
like this one.*

User: Pat

Application: Microsoft Word 5

Document: CD Newsletter

Date: Friday, August 30, 1991

Time: 10:57:22 AM

Printer: LaserWriter II NT

FIGURE 8-7.
*When you select a
Cover Page option,
Word produces a sheet
like this one.*

If you're using a LaserWriter II NT or a similar printer, you don't need to activate the Print Back To Front option. These printers stack printed pages face down in sequential order. To have one of these printers stack the pages in reverse order, you can activate the Print Back To Front option.

Background printing

If you're using a LaserWriter, you can take advantage of two features designed to save you time. Background printing and file spooling enable you to print documents "in the background" while you work in Word, and to queue up multiple files for printing immediately or at a later time. Always save all open documents before using these features.

To take advantage of these options, you must first install the PrintMonitor file in the Extensions folder inside the System folder on your startup disk. (You can find a copy of PrintMonitor on the disk called "Printing" that comes with your Macintosh. Your Mac installs this file in the System folder automatically when you load System 7 using Apple's System 7 Easy Install option. If you're using Multifinder with a System version other than System 7, you can also take advantage of background printing.)

To specify background printing, open the Chooser desk accessory from the Apple menu, select the LaserWriter icon and the name of the printer in the Select A LaserWriter list, and then click the On option for Background Printing in the Chooser dialog box. When you're ready to print, choose Print from the File menu. When you click OK, the PrintMonitor program first saves your document in a special file on your startup disk and then sends the file to the printer. You can continue to work in Word while your document prints.

Background printing uses your computer's memory. If you don't have enough memory to load the PrintMonitor program, you can tell the PrintMonitor to reconfigure itself to consume less memory. If you still do not have enough memory to print, however, when you choose Print you'll see a message telling you that PrintMonitor can't print. You'll then have to abandon background printing by turning off the Background Printing option in the Chooser dialog box before choosing the Print command again.

When background printing begins, PrintMonitor opens automatically, and its name and icon appear in the Application menu at the right end of the menu bar. Choose PrintMonitor from the Application menu to cancel a printing job, to check printing status, or to print files at a later time. Again, your ability to use this feature can be limited by the amount of RAM installed in your Macintosh. We recommend that you save all open documents before you attempt to queue up documents for printing. For more information on using PrintMonitor, see the *Macintosh Reference Guide* that comes with your system software.

Printing from the Finder

When you choose Print from within Word, Word prints only the active document. If you want to print several Word documents, you can save time by printing them from the Finder.

At the Finder level, select each Word document you want to print (either by dragging across the document's icon or by pressing the Shift key and clicking each icon in turn), and then choose Print from the File menu. If the Word program isn't open when you choose Print, it loads automatically. Word then opens the first document and displays the Print dialog box. Word applies the settings you specify for this document to all selected documents and prints the documents in the order that they appear on the desktop—from left to right and from top to bottom in icon view, and in the order they appear in the window in other views.

Using the Page Setup command

The Page Setup dialog box lets you define settings that control your document's overall appearance. In Chapter 5, "Formatting Documents and Paragraphs," we explained how your choice of paper and print orientation affect the layout of your individual pages. Because the other Page Setup options also affect document appearance, after you specify the Page Setup options you want to use, you probably won't change them unless you decide to make a significant change to your document design.

To open the Page Setup dialog box, choose Page Setup from the File menu, or press Shift-F8. Figures 8-8 and 8-9 show the Page Setup dialog box for the Image-Writer and the LaserWriter printers, respectively.

FIGURE 8-8.
This is the Page Setup dialog box for the ImageWriter printer.

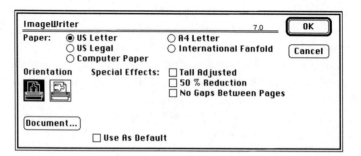

FIGURE 8-9.
This is the Page Setup dialog box for the LaserWriter printer.

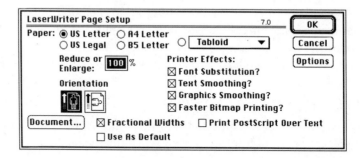

Word saves any settings you specify in the Page Setup dialog box with your document. Changes you make don't affect other Word documents already saved to disk, but changes do apply to new documents you create during the current Word session. To apply the selected settings to all future documents, select the Use As Default option at the bottom of the dialog box.

Clicking the Document button displays the Document dialog box, where you can also define your document's margins, page gutter width, and related page layout settings.

ImageWriter Page Setup options

If you're using an ImageWriter, you can change the appearance of your printed text by selecting the Tall Adjusted, the 50% Reduction, and the No Gaps Between Pages options in the Page Setup dialog box.

The Tall Adjusted option

The Tall Adjusted option primarily enhances the appearance of graphics that you've imported into a Word document. The difference between the horizontal resolutions of the Macintosh screen (72 dots per inch) and the ImageWriter (80 dots per inch) causes graphics in Word to appear stretched horizontally. When you select this option, the ImageWriter compensates by slightly stretching the graphic vertically.

The number of characters that fit on each line decreases when you use this option, and this in turn alters the way your lines of text wrap. If you're preparing your document on a Macintosh with an ImageWriter selected in the Chooser but plan to print on a LaserWriter, select Tall Adjusted to view line and page breaks as they'll appear when they're printed.

The 50% Reduction option

The 50% Reduction option reduces your text to half its original size, printing more text on each line and more information on each page. The 50% Reduction option is generally used with large text, such as for overheads or handouts. Text in 12-point type or smaller becomes virtually unreadable when printed with this option selected.

To indicate the 50 percent reduction on your screen, Word doubles the measurements that appear on the ruler and in Print Preview and Page Layout view. A right margin set at the 6-inch mark on the ruler, for example, appears at the 12-inch mark when you select the 50% Reduction option. Use the scroll arrows to display text that currently doesn't appear in the document window.

The No Gaps Between Pages option

The No Gaps Between Pages option works with the Top and Bottom margin settings to print your document as a continuous stream of text. After you select this option, click the Document button, and set your Top and Bottom margins to 0. Word then treats the paper that's being fed into your printer as though it were one long sheet.

Use this option to print a long table or graphic that won't fit on a single page or to squeeze as much information as possible onto each page. You can also use this option to print continuous forms, such as mailing labels.

LaserWriter Page Setup options

Many more Page Setup options exist for LaserWriters than for ImageWriters. The number of options you see in the Page Setup dialog box, shown earlier in Figure 8-9, depends on the LaserWriter printer driver version you're using. If you're using Version 7.0, you'll see options that let you adjust the print image, specify printer effects, and print PostScript on top of document text. The Options button on the right side of the LaserWriter Page Setup dialog box opens a dialog box that lets you select six additional printing options.

The Reduce Or Enlarge option

To reduce or enlarge the printed image on the LaserWriter, type the reduction or enlargement percentage you want to use in the Reduce Or Enlarge edit bar. You can specify any setting from 25 percent to 400 percent—that is, from one-quarter to four times the original image size.

A setting of less than 100 reduces the size of your text and fits more characters on a line and more lines on a page. A setting greater than 100 has the opposite effect; Word fits fewer characters on each line and fewer lines on each page.

To indicate the location of line and page breaks in the printed document, Word moves the right margin indicator on the ruler to make the page area between the margins proportionally larger or smaller when you adjust the print image. The actual margin sizes on the printed page remain unchanged.

The Font Substitution option

Although you can print documents using any fonts installed in your System file, for the best quality and performance, select fonts designed for your printer. ImageWriter fonts such as Geneva and New York don't give the finished appearance that Helvetica and Times do when you print them with a LaserWriter. Bitmapped fonts, including New York, Monaco, and Geneva, are designed for the ImageWriter. Fonts like Helvetica, Times, and Courier are designed specifically for the LaserWriter.

The Font Substitution option in the LaserWriter Page Setup dialog box converts ImageWriter fonts used in your document to corresponding LaserWriter fonts. Table 8-1 indicates some font substitutions that take place when you select the Font Substitution option. If you use only LaserWriter fonts in your document, Font Substitution has no effect.

If your document contains	The LaserWriter prints
Boston	Boston
Chicago	Chicago
Dover	Dover
Dover PS	Dover PS
Geneva	Helvetica
Monaco	Courier
New York	Times
Venice	Venice

TABLE 8-1.
The LaserWriter makes these font substitutions when you activate the Font Substitution option.

You must print your document to see the result of font substitution; the new fonts don't appear on your screen. If you've used Word's default New York font to format text, Word converts the text to the Times font for printing. The Laser-Writer offers no substitutes for the Boston, Chicago, Dover, Dover PS, or Venice fonts. When these fonts appear in your document, the LaserWriter must create a bitmap of the font characters to print them.

Font Substitution can significantly increase your printing time and can produce unsightly gaps between letters and words in your printed document. For a mock-up or "proof copy" of a document that will later be typeset or reprinted, you might find Font Substitution acceptable, but not for a finished document.

If you deselect the Font Substitution option, the LaserWriter prints fonts without converting them. Because the LaserWriter must produce a bitmap of the characters formatted with the ImageWriter fonts in order to print them, printing will be slow. In addition, although the LaserWriter can reproduce any font shown on your screen using this procedure, you'll probably find that the quality of the non-LaserWriter fonts is unacceptable for finished documents. (You can improve the quality slightly by turning on the Text Smoothing option.)

The Text Smoothing and Graphics Smoothing options

The LaserWriter's Text Smoothing and Graphics Smoothing options smooth out the rough edges of bitmapped fonts and graphics in your documents. Text Smoothing smooths out bitmapped fonts, and Graphics Smoothing smooths a graphic's jagged edges. However, these options can blur LaserWriter fonts and graphics and slow down printer operation. Don't select these options if your document doesn't contain bitmapped fonts.

The Faster Bitmap Printing option

The Faster Bitmap Printing option speeds up the printing of documents that contain bitmapped characters and graphics by accessing some of the LaserWriter's built-in memory. Although this option can decrease printing time substantially, using too much of your printer's memory can cause the current page to fail to print. If your printer runs out of memory, deselect the Faster Bitmap Printing option before printing again.

The Fractional Widths option

The Fractional Widths option achieves more accurate character and word placement by taking advantage of the LaserWriter's ability to work in fractional pixel widths. Selecting this option improves the appearance of most fonts in a printed document. With nonproportional fonts, this option simulates proportionally spaced fonts, such as Times, Helvetica, and Chicago, which assign horizontal spacing to a letter based on the width of the letter. Nonproportional fonts, such as Courier, assign the same space to every letter.

Although this option improves the appearance of most fonts in a printed document, text can sometimes appear distorted on the screen, and alignment problems may appear only in your printed document. If alignment problems occur, deselect the option before printing again.

The Print PostScript Over Text option

If you've inserted PostScript code into your document to create graphics or special effects, you may want your PostScript images to be printed "on top of" the Word text or on top of any other graphics inserted into your document. As the option's name implies, when you select Print PostScript Over Text, the LaserWriter prints your text and any inserted graphics first and then prints any PostScript images on top of them.

For more information on working with PostScript and text, see Appendix C, "Using PostScript Commands in Word."

Other options

The LaserWriter's Page Setup dialog box also includes an Options button. When you click this button, Word makes six additional options available, as shown in Figure 8-10. Each time you click an option, Word redraws the image shown on the left side of the Options dialog box to indicate how that option affects your printed document.

FIGURE 8-10.
*Clicking the Options
button in the
LaserWriter's Page
Setup dialog box
displays six additional
printing options.*

LaserWriter Options   7.0   OK

Cancel

☐ **Flip Horizontal**
☐ **Flip Vertical**
☐ **Invert Image**
☐ **Precision Bitmap Alignment (4% reduction)**
☐ **Larger Print Area (Fewer Downloadable Fonts)**
☐ **Unlimited Downloadable Fonts in a Document**

Flip Horizontal The Flip Horizontal option creates a mirror image of your document pages, with the lines of text in your printed document running from right to left across the page, instead of left to right, and with each letter printed backward. For example, Figure 8-11 shows some normal text, while Figure 8-12 shows the same text printed with the Flip Horizontal option activated.

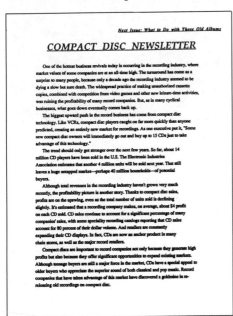

FIGURE 8-11.
This text was printed with no special printing options selected.

FIGURE 8-12.
The Flip Horizontal option prints a mirror image of the page.

Flip Vertical The Flip Vertical option prints an upside-down mirror image of your document. Figure 8-13 on the next page shows the text from Figure 8-11 printed with the Flip Vertical option selected.

Invert Image The Invert Image option prints white text on a black background, making a negative image of the page. Figure 8-14 on the next page shows the text from Figure 8-11 printed with the Invert Image option activated. Notice that the black background doesn't extend all the way to the edge of the page. Word prints the inverted image only to the edge of the LaserWriter's "no print" zone.

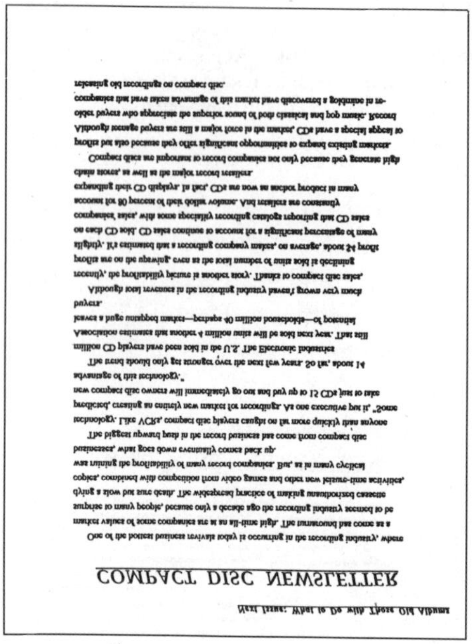

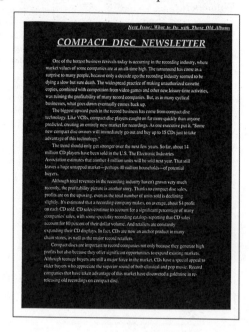

FIGURE 8-13.
The Flip Vertical option prints an upside-down mirror image of the page.

FIGURE 8-14.
The Invert Image option prints white text on a black background.

Precision Bitmap Alignment The Precision Bitmap Alignment option reduces the size of your text and graphics by 4 percent and, in some cases, gives a slightly cleaner appearance. It can also speed up the printing of bitmapped fonts and graphics. Selecting this option sometimes enhances the appearance of bitmapped fonts and printed graphics, but doesn't always result in a noticeable improvement in your printed text and graphics.

Larger Print Area The LaserWriter usually doesn't print any closer than about ⅜ inch from the edge of the paper. Any text or graphics that extend into this "no print" zone don't appear on the printed page. When you activate the Larger Print Area (Fewer Downloadable Fonts) option, you reduce this zone to approximately ¼ inch, increasing the area that does print.

Increasing the size of the print area consumes some of the LaserWriter's memory, allowing fewer downloadable fonts. Because different fonts require different amounts of memory, it's impossible to anticipate how many fonts can be downloaded when you activate this option.

Unlimited Downloadable Fonts In A Document The Unlimited Downloadable Fonts In A Document option allows you to use any number of downloadable fonts in a document, by using more of the LaserWriter's memory for downloadable fonts. It downloads one set of fonts, creates a partial page image, clears its memory, and then repeats the procedure. Switching downloadable fonts in and out of memory makes printing much slower, however.

Previewing your printed document

Word's Page Layout and Print Preview views let you check your document's appearance before you print. The Page Layout command on the View menu displays a full-size preview of your printed document. You can make text and formatting changes in this view and see immediately how they affect your document. The Print Preview command on the File menu displays entire page layouts at a reduced size on the screen. You can add page numbers to document sections; reposition margins, page breaks, headers, and footers; and move positioned text and graphics. We look first at the Page Layout command and then introduce Word's Print Preview feature.

Using Page Layout

Word's Page Layout view displays each page of your document in full size, just as it will appear when printed—with headers, page numbers, footnotes, and other special elements in place. This view lets you verify your formatting and page layout decisions and helps you avoid trial-and-error printing. Paging buttons at the bottom of the Page Layout window and special key commands let you navigate through your document quickly. You can use any of Word's selection, editing, or formatting commands in Page Layout view.

To switch the active window to Page Layout view, choose Page Layout from the View menu, or press Command-Option-P. While Page Layout view is active, a check mark appears next to its name on the menu. Word removes the check mark when you choose another view.

Word runs significantly slower when Page Layout view is active. Therefore, we recommend that you stay with the Normal view as you create your document and use Page Layout view to check document layout before printing. You can take advantage of Normal view's speed by splitting the document window and displaying Normal view and Page Layout view at the same time. Text you type in one window appears instantly in the other window, and you can see immediately how editing changes modify your document's appearance. We discuss how to use Word's window features in Chapter 1, "Touring Microsoft Word."

Let's use Page Layout view to take another look at the sample document shown earlier in Figure 8-11. If you choose Page Layout from the View menu when this document is active, Word displays the Page Layout view shown in Figure 8-15.

Page Layout view displays the main text area of the current page at the top of the screen. To bring other parts of the page into view, click the vertical or horizontal scroll bar. To see a different page, drag the scroll boxes or click the Page Back and Page Forward arrow icons at the bottom of the Page Layout view window.

FIGURE 8-15.
Word displays the main text area of the current page at the top of the screen when you switch to the Page Layout view.

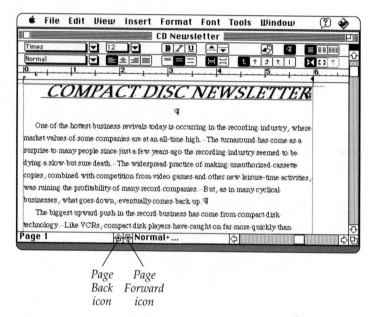

Page   Page
Back   Forward
icon   icon

Instead of marking page breaks with a horizontal line, Word displays the edges of the page when you scroll in Page Layout view. Figure 8-16, for example, shows the page from Figure 8-15 after we scrolled the upper-right corner into view. Notice that the shaded background helps distinguish the page area and that you now can see the margin at the top of the page. If you continue scrolling up from anywhere in the document except page 1, Word brings the bottom of the previous page into view.

FIGURE 8-16.
*You can scroll the
edges of a page into
view in Word's Page
Layout view.*

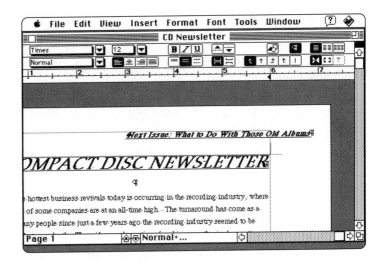

Text area boundaries

When you view your document in Normal view, you see only the single column of text that is bounded by your left, right, top, and bottom margins. In Page Layout view, Word also displays document elements, such as margins, headers, and footers. To identify each element's area on a page, Word displays *boundaries*, or dotted lines, around them and treats them as distinct text areas. Word offers several keyboard shortcuts for moving from one text area to another.

Whenever the Show ¶ option is selected, Word displays boundaries in Page Layout view. Turning boundaries off and on is as easy as choosing Show ¶ or Hide ¶ from the View menu. You can also display boundaries in Page Layout view by opening the View section of the Preferences dialog box and then choosing the Text Boundaries In Page Layout View option.

Figure 8-16 displays two types of boundaries. The vertical and horizontal lines that intersect in the upper-right corner of the page are the margin boundaries. Above the line that marks the top margin, you'll see the header boundary about a half inch from the top edge of the page (the distance specified as the From Top setting in the Section dialog box). If a page contains a footer, Word marks the bottom boundary of the footer with a similar line.

If your page is laid out in two or more snaking columns, Word surrounds each column with a boundary. Any object to which you have assigned a position using the Frame command appears within its own boundary. Boundaries also appear around tables created with the Table command and around the table cells.

Navigating in Page Layout view

To move quickly through a large document in Page Layout view, drag the scroll boxes or choose the Go To command from the Edit menu, and specify the page number you want to see.

To move smaller distances, use the Page Back and Page Forward icons at the bottom of the window. Clicking the Page Back icon brings the top of the previous page into view. Clicking the Page Forward icon brings the top of the next page onto your screen. In both cases, Word moves the insertion point to the beginning of the new page.

A number of keyboard shortcuts allow you to move quickly from one text area to another on a single page. Table 8-2 summarizes these keyboard shortcuts, which use the Command and Option keys in combination with the keys on the numeric keypad.

This key combination	Moves the insertion point to	Example
Command-Option-7	First text area	Move to header or first character space on page
Command-Option-1	Last text area	Move to footer
Command-Option-8	Text area immediately above	Move from main text area to header or from footer to main text area
Command-Option-2	Text area immediately below	Move from header to main text area or from main text area to footer
Command-Option-4	Text area immediately to the left	Move from right column to left column in a two-column layout
Command-Option-6	Text area immediately to the right	Move from left column to right column in a two-column layout
Tab key or Command-Option-3	Next text area on page	Move from first column to top of second column
Shift-Tab or Command-Option-9	Preceding text area on page	Move from second column to top of first column

TABLE 8-2.
With the numeric keypad, you can use these keyboard shortcuts to move from one text area to another on a page.

Selecting text

You can select text in Page Layout view using the same methods as in Normal view. To make text selection even easier, each text area in the Page Layout view has its own selection bar. When the pointer moves over the selection bar for a text area, the pointer changes to a right arrow. Select text on adjoining pages by dragging the selection beyond the top or bottom border of the window.

To select all the text in a document, move the pointer to any selection bar except those for headers and footers, and either press the Command key as you click the mouse button or triple-click the selection bar.

Editing and formatting

Any editing or formatting change that can be made in Normal view can also be made in Page Layout view. You can cut, copy, or paste text and graphics; find and replace text; and change style definitions. You can also insert page and section breaks; use the Tools menu; and change Character, Paragraph, Section, and Document dialog box settings.

To open the Document dialog box quickly in Page Layout view, double-click the corner of a page, where the lines that mark your side and top or bottom margins intersect.

Working with headers, footers, and footnotes

As illustrated earlier in Figure 8-16, Page Layout view shows headers (and footers) in position on each page. Altering a header or footer is as easy as clicking the text and making the change. Word applies the change to all headers (or footers) in the current section. (Chapter 10, "Creating Professional Documents," explains sectional headers and footers in detail.)

To add a header or footer in Page Layout view, choose the Header or Footer command from the View menu. Word moves the insertion point to the first character in the header or footer text area of that page so that you can enter and format the header or footer text.

The Even/Odd Headers option in the Document dialog box lets you create a header that appears only on even or odd pages.

Choosing Footnote from the Insert menu inserts a footnote reference mark and then moves the insertion point to the area in your document where the footnote is printed—the end of the document, the bottom of the page, or the end of the section. (Chapter 11, "Adding a Table of Contents, an Index, and Footnotes," discusses creating document footnotes in Word.)

Using background pagination

Word generally repaginates your document automatically only if you've selected Background Repagination in the Preferences dialog box. However, when you make an editing or formatting change that causes text to flow from one page to the next, Word repaginates to ensure that the page you're viewing reflects your current document layout. Changing document margins also causes Word to repaginate.

When you choose the Page Layout view, Word immediately repaginates your document from the first page through the page on which the insertion point is located. If you're working with a long document, you might have to wait several seconds before Page Layout view appears. If you move forward to another page in the document while in Page Layout view, Word repaginates through that page.

Of course, you can always choose Repaginate Now from the Tools menu. In Page Layout view, this command causes Word to repaginate only through the current page.

Page Layout view limitations

Page Layout view doesn't always represent exactly what will appear on the page when you print your document. If Show Hidden Text is activated, hidden text appears in Page Layout view, but it won't print unless you select the Print Hidden Text option in the Print dialog box. Line numbers in a document don't appear in Page Layout view. (They do appear in Print Preview.) If you've embedded a Post-Script code in a document, Word doesn't interpret the code until you print.

The results of many Page Setup options also don't appear in Page Layout view, because these options are implemented by your printer. For example, if you reduce or enlarge your document in the Page Setup dialog box, Word displays the text in normal size in Page Layout view. Although Word rewraps the text in shorter or longer lines, you must print your document to see the new text size.

Using Print Preview

Print Preview lets you see how your document will look when printed. When you choose Print Preview from the File menu, Word presents a window like the one in Figure 8-17, which displays a representation of two printed document pages. You can also display the Print Preview window by pressing Command-Option-I. Then you can view your document one or two pages at a time and see printable elements like headers, footers, and page numbers that don't appear in Normal view.

You can view a single page at a time by clicking the One-Page icon (the fourth icon on the left side of the screen). When you click this icon, Word displays only the first page of the two-page spread, as shown in Figure 8-18. The other icons let you magnify parts of a page; add page numbers to the document; change the position of page elements (such as margins, page breaks, and headers and footers); and print your document.

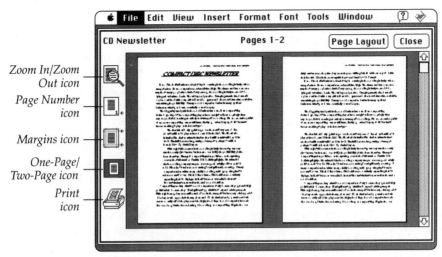

FIGURE 8-17.
The Print Preview command lets you view and alter your page layout.

FIGURE 8-18.
To preview a single page, simply click the One-Page icon.

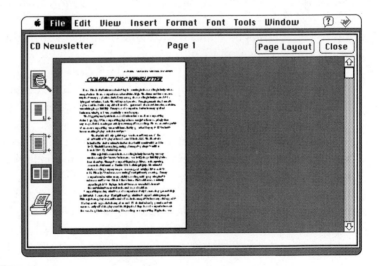

To close the Print Preview window, click either the Page Layout or Close button in the upper-right corner of the screen, or press Command-W. The Page Layout button displays your document in Page Layout view. The Close button returns your document to the view (Normal, Page Layout, or Outline) active at the time you chose Print Preview.

Navigating in the Print Preview window

When you choose Print Preview, Word repaginates your document through the page on your screen and displays a preview of that page and the following page. The number of the page (or pages) being previewed is displayed above the page layout. In Figure 8-17, for example, the notation *Pages 1–2* appears at the top of the window.

Click the scroll arrows or the gray area of the scroll bar to move through the document one page at a time. You can also press plus or 2 on the numeric keypad to move forward one page and press * or 8 to move back one page.

If you're viewing a two-page spread, moving forward causes the page on the right side of your preview screen to move to the left, and the new page comes into view on the right side. When you move back one page, the page on the left side of your screen shifts to the right, and the new page comes into view on the left side.

If you've activated either the Mirror Even/Odd or the Even/Odd Headers option, or if you've specified a Gutter setting in the Document dialog box, Word displays the document in two-page spreads, as though you were turning the pages of a book. As you move forward or backward, Word displays the next (or previous) two pages in the document in order to maintain this even/odd layout. If you're viewing pages 4 and 5 on the screen and you press plus, for example, Word brings pages 6 and 7 into view.

To move through several pages at a time, drag the scroll box. The page numbers at the top of the screen indicate what your new location will be when you stop scrolling. Release the scroll box when the number of the page you want to preview is displayed.

Word doesn't let you edit your document or change its character and paragraph formatting in Print Preview. If you want to make these kinds of changes while you are viewing a page, click the Page Layout or Close buttons in the upper-right corner of the screen to go quickly to that page in your document and make the change. When you close Print Preview, Word displays the text currently visible on the preview screen in your document window. After you make your editing or formatting change, you can again preview your efforts.

Magnifying the page

The Zoom In icon (the first icon on the left) lets you magnify a section of a page. You can scroll to see different parts of the current page. However, you can't move to another page in your document while the document is magnified.

To magnify the current page in Print Preview, click the Zoom In icon. The right-arrow pointer changes to a magnifying glass. Move the magnifier pointer to the part of the page you want to see, and click to enlarge that part of the page. Double-clicking the Zoom In icon displays an enlarged view of the upper-left corner of the current page.

Word toggles between the Print Preview display and the magnified display when you double-click the currently displayed page. To return to the standard Print Preview display, double-click the magnified image or click Zoom Out.

Adding and positioning page numbers

You can use the Page Number icon (the second icon) to add page numbers to your document or to reposition existing page numbers. Using this icon has the same effect as specifying in the Section dialog box that you want to use page numbers and typing page number positions in the From Top and From Right edit bars. Changes you make to the page number positions on the preview screen apply only to the current section.

To position a page number in its default location, double-click Page Number. Word inserts the page number a half inch from the upper-right corner of the page.

To add page numbers in any other location, click the Page Number icon once. When your pointer takes on the shape of the number 1, click where you want the page number to appear. Coordinates displayed at the top of the screen correspond to the From Right and From Top entries in the Section dialog box, and let you know exactly where the page number will be positioned. The coordinates *(1.00, 4.50)*, for example, tell you that the page number is positioned 1 inch from the right edge of the page and 4.5 inches from the top of the page.

You can reposition a page number by clicking the Margins icon (the third icon) and then clicking the number and dragging it to the desired position. You can also reposition page numbers at any time by clicking the Page Number icon and then clicking a new spot on the page.

If the Even/Odd Headers option in the Document dialog box is active, Word automatically reverses the position of your page numbers on facing pages. If you place the page number 1 inch from the right edge of an odd page, for example, that number appears 1 inch from the left edge of even pages.

To remove page numbers, click the Margins icon to display boundaries around the page number. Then point to the page number, and drag it off the page. When you click outside the page in the background of the window, Word updates the Print Preview display.

Changing margins

In Chapter 5, "Formatting Documents and Paragraphs," we showed how you can set and change margins by entering Top, Bottom, Left, and Right margin settings in the Document dialog box. You can also set and change margins for your entire document in the Print Preview window. Click the Margins icon. Word displays dotted lines that indicate your current margin positions, as well as header, footer, frame, and page-break positions, as shown in Figure 8-19 on the next page. If you're viewing two pages, click either page.

FIGURE 8-19.
When you click the
Margins icon, Word
displays dotted lines
that indicate the
current page layout
settings.

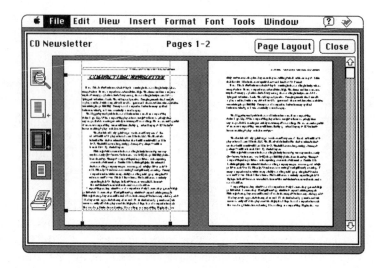

Notice the black squares, or *handles*, that appear at the edge of the bottom and left or right margin markers in Figure 8-19. To change a margin setting, click the appropriate handle, and drag it to the new margin position. When you move your pointer to a handle, the pointer assumes a cross-hair shape. Click the handle once, and at the top of the screen the margin's location appears and changes as you drag the margin marker. When you release the mouse button, Word transfers the value displayed to the appropriate margin edit bar in the Document dialog box.

To increase the Left and Right margin settings for the sample document shown in Figure 8-19 to 1.75 inches each, click the Margins icon. Then click the handle at the bottom of the left margin boundary, and drag it to the right. Release the mouse button when you see the value *1.75* at the top of the preview screen. To adjust the right margin, click the handle at the bottom of the right margin boundary, and drag it to the left. Again, release the mouse button when you see the value *1.75*.

After you've positioned the margins, click the Margins icon or click anywhere outside the page to see the effects of your changes. Word repaginates the document and redraws the pages on the screen to reflect the new margins. These margin settings apply to your entire document, not just to the page or section you're currently viewing.

Changing page breaks

When you select the Margins icon, the page-break line often appears just above the line marking the bottom margin. You can insert manual page breaks into your document by dragging the page-break line. This line appears between your left and right boundaries; unlike the top and bottom margin boundaries, however, it doesn't extend all the way to the edge of the page. You can also distinguish a page-break line because this type of line doesn't have a handle—you can point to any part of the page-break line to drag it.

To insert a manual page break, drag the page-break line to a new location. When you release the mouse button, Word inserts a manual page break at that spot and immediately repaginates the document. If you drag the page-break line up, any text that appears below the line moves to the top of the next page. If you drag the page-break line down, Word pulls text from the top of the next page down to the bottom of the current page. If the Widow Control option in the Document dialog box is active, Word will not allow only one line of text at the bottom or top of a page.

You cannot use the page-break line to flow text past the bottom margin boundary. However, to remove a manual page break that appears above the margin, you can drag the page-break line past the bottom boundary. Word then reflows your document to fill the current page.

Repositioning headers and footers

When you click the Margins icon in Print Preview, Word displays a dotted border around headers and footers. To reposition a header or footer within a section, click anywhere within this border, and drag the header or footer up or down. This action changes the value in the From Top or From Bottom edit bar in the Section dialog box. As you drag the header or footer, Word displays the distance between the header or footer and the edge of the page at the top of the preview screen. After you drag the header or footer, click the Margins icon or click in the gray area of the Print Preview screen to redraw the screen and display the header or footer in its new position.

You can't drag a header or footer past the top or bottom margin boundary. If your headers and footers require more than the space currently available in the top and bottom margin areas, you must reposition your top and bottom margin boundaries before you move the headers and footers.

To drag a header or footer past the current top or bottom margin so that it will print within the text area, press the Shift key as you drag the header or footer. Dragging this text area works just like typing a minus before an absolute Top or Bottom margin setting in the Document dialog box. (Chapter 10, "Creating Professional Documents," discusses creating headers and footers in detail.)

Printing from the Print Preview window

You use the Printer icon (the bottom icon) to print directly from the Print Preview window. When you click this icon, Word opens the Print dialog box to allow you to print your document immediately. You can change Print settings or click OK to print the document with the existing settings. The Print Preview window remains open after printing is completed.

Advanced Formatting Techniques

9

Creating Style Sheets

*I*n Word, a *style* is a named set of instructions for formatting a paragraph. These instructions specify character format options such as font and point size, and paragraph format options such as indentation and line spacing. A powerful feature of Word is the ability to group a document's styles into a *style sheet*.

Typically, you create a style to specify formatting instructions that you'll apply to many paragraphs throughout a document. Recording these instructions as a style in a style sheet frees you from having to repeat the same formatting process for all the paragraphs. Instead, you can simply apply the style from the style sheet.

Style sheets also make it easy to modify the formatting of an entire document. After you've applied a style to several paragraphs, you can alter the format of each paragraph to which the style is applied simply by changing the style's formatting instructions.

In this chapter, we show you how to get the most out of Word styles and style sheets. First, we discuss style basics: how to identify the standard styles that Word provides for new documents, as well as how to create custom styles and how to modify styles. At the end of this chapter, we show you how to apply styles and work with document style sheets. Style sheets save you time and ensure that your document is formatted consistently. At first, style sheets might seem complex, but they greatly reduce the time and tedium involved in creating and formatting documents.

Style basics

Each new Word document contains a default style sheet that determines paragraph formatting. The style sheet is part of the document file—it's permanently linked to the document. You can add new styles, modify existing styles, delete styles, and even borrow styles from other documents to change the content of a document's style sheet. When you save the document, Word also saves the current style sheet.

You can use a style to format any paragraph, and you can apply a style to as many paragraphs as you want. However, you generally can't use a style to format less than a full paragraph. For example, you can use a style to format headings, but you can't use that style to format only one word in a heading.

With a style, you can control the following characteristics:

- Font
- Point size
- Character formats (bold, italic, underline, and so on)
- Character spacing (normal, condensed, or expanded)
- Character position (superscript, subscript, or normal)
- Character color
- Paragraph alignment (flush-left, centered, flush-right, or justified)
- Line spacing within a paragraph
- Spacing above and below a paragraph
- Left, right, and first-line indents
- Other paragraph formats (such as Page Break Before and Keep With Next ¶)
- Paragraph borders
- Fixed positioning
- Tab placement
- Tab type (centered, right-justified, left-justified, or decimal)
- Tab leaders
- Vertical-line placement

Word offers two kinds of styles: standard and custom. Word provides standard styles for new documents, including the Normal style (Word's default text format) and styles for headings, the table of contents, and the index. You create and name custom styles. These styles store your formatting instructions for a particular kind of paragraph and let you automate and standardize the appearance of your document.

In this first section, we introduce standard and custom styles. As we discuss these style types, we show you how to assign style names and specify formatting information, and how to create a new style in the Style dialog box.

Standard styles

Standard styles are predefined to format common elements of a document, such as headings, footnotes, headers, and footers. Word comes with a built-in library of 33 standard styles.

The Normal style, which Word always places in the default style sheet, is the standard style you'll probably use most often. Word's other standard styles don't initially appear in a document's style sheet; Word adds them to the style sheet as you add the corresponding element to your document. For example, if you add a header, Word automatically adds a standard header style to the document's style sheet.

The Normal style

When you create a new document, Word uses the Normal style to format its body text. Think of Normal as the default style for the document. The paragraphs are formatted in Normal style until you apply a different style.

Figure 9-1 shows text formatted with the default Normal style, 12-point New York. Word uses the current default style—either the font and size you specified as the Normal style when you installed Word, or a new font and size specified in the Font section of the Preferences dialog box—along with flush-left paragraph alignment.

FIGURE 9-1.
This screen shows how Word's Normal style formats text.

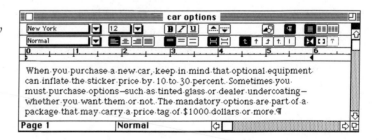

In Chapter 1, "Touring Microsoft Word," we selected New York as the default font and 12-point as the default point size. Throughout this chapter, we use a Normal style based on these formatting instructions. If you're using different defaults, changing the default font and point size to 12-point New York now will help you understand the Word features presented in this chapter. The section "Modifying the Normal Style" at the end of this chapter describes in detail how to change the default font and point size using the Default Font command.

Unless you select another style, Word assigns the Normal style to each body text paragraph in the document. In Figure 9-1, Word displays in the status box at the bottom of the screen the name of the style applied to the text at the insertion point. A plus and an ellipsis after the style name in the status box (see Figure 9-2) tell you that, in addition to the style applied to the current paragraph, the paragraph's format is also determined by manual formatting changes you've made.

FIGURE 9-2.
The status box shows
the style used to
format the current
paragraph.

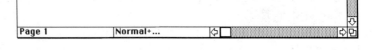

Displaying the available styles

You can quickly display all the styles available on the current style sheet by clicking the arrow to the right of the Style drop-down list box on the ruler. Figure 9-3 shows the Style drop-down list box as it appears for a new document. The check mark next to Word's default Normal style indicates that this style is currently applied to text containing the insertion point.

FIGURE 9-3.
When you first create
a new document, only
the Normal style
appears in the Style
list box on the ruler.

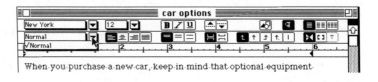

You can display Word's standard styles by holding down the Shift key and then clicking the arrow to the right of the Style drop-down list box on the ruler, as shown in Figure 9-4. Word can't display all the standard styles at one time on a 9-inch screen, but you can scroll through the list as needed. Table 9-1 summarizes the name and purpose of each standard style.

FIGURE 9-4.
You can display
Word's standard
styles by holding down
the Shift key while
clicking the arrow to
the right of the Style
drop-down list box on
the ruler.

Style name	Use to format
footer	Text in a footer window
footnote reference	The number or symbol that designates a footnote
footnote text	Text in a footnote window
header	Text in a header window
heading 1, heading 2, ... heading 9	Heading levels
index 1, index 2, ... index 7	Levels of entries in an index
line number	Line numbers
Normal	All text that has not been assigned another style
page number	Page numbers
PostScript	PostScript commands embedded in document text
toc 1, toc 2, ... toc 9	Levels of entry in the table of contents text

TABLE 9-1.
You can use Word's standard styles to format common document elements.

You can also display your document's style sheet by choosing Style from the Format menu or pressing Command-T. The list box at the top of the Style dialog box shows the styles in the current style sheet, and the title bar of the dialog box indicates the name of the document whose style sheet you're viewing. When you first display the Style dialog box, the radio button next to the Show Document Styles option is selected, as shown in Figure 9-5, indicating that the list box contains only the names of the custom styles currently defined for your document. To view the names of the custom styles and the standard styles, click Show All Styles. (We discuss each Style dialog box option in detail later in this chapter.)

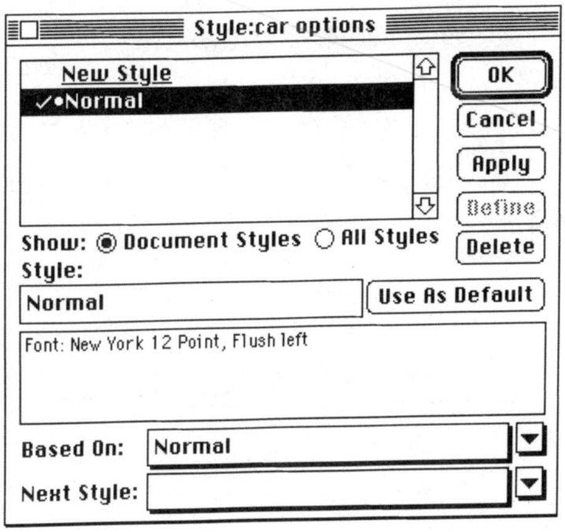

FIGURE 9-5.
In a new document, Word's default style sheet contains only the Normal style.

Viewing a style's formatting instructions

In Figure 9-5, the Normal style name appears in the list box. The formatting instructions for this style—Font: New York 12 Point, Flush left—appear in the middle of the dialog box. Text formatted with the Normal style also has single line spacing and no indentations. As you may remember from Chapter 4, "Formatting Characters," and Chapter 5, "Formatting Documents and Paragraphs," these are Word's default paragraph and character formats. However, except for font, point size, and paragraph alignment, default formatting characteristics don't appear in the middle of the dialog box.

To view the formatting instructions for any style, choose Style from the Format menu, and click the style name. If the style sheet contains many styles, you can scroll to the style you're interested in. After you click a style, the formatting instructions for the selected style appear in the middle of the Style dialog box.

Occasionally, a style's formatting instructions are too long to be displayed completely in the Style dialog box. In this case, you can examine the settings on the ribbon and the ruler and in the Character and Paragraph dialog boxes to see all the style's characteristics.

In many cases, a style's formatting instructions are more complicated than those in Figure 9-5. Figure 9-6, for example, displays the formatting instructions for the standard style footnote text, which we displayed by clicking footnote text in the Style drop-down list box. Notice that a bullet (•) appears next to this style name, indicating that this is a standard style. This symbol helps you distinguish standard styles from custom styles. No check mark appears next to the style name because we haven't applied this style to the document text containing the insertion point.

FIGURE 9-6.
Click the Show All Styles radio button to display the standard styles Word applies to your document. Word precedes each standard style with a bullet.

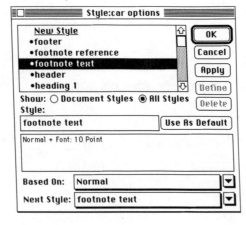

Standard styles and the Normal style

All of Word's standard styles are based on the Normal style and are similar to Normal. For example, the formatting instructions for the standard style header are shown in Figure 9-7. You can interpret these instructions as *Use all the formatting characteristics of the Normal style and add two tab stops, one centered at the 3-inch ruler position and one flush-right at the 6-inch ruler position.* If the Normal style specifies 12-point New York, then Word also formats the text in a document's header with 12-point New York font. Elements you add to a document, such as footers, page numbers, subheadings, and so on, will similarly use the New York font, or the font you've specified in the formatting instructions for the Normal style.

Any change you make to the Normal style affects the other standard styles. For example, if you change the Normal style's font from New York to Helvetica, all the other standard styles change to Helvetica as well to help you maintain consistency of appearance among the different parts of a document.

FIGURE 9-7.
This dialog box shows the default formatting instructions for the standard header style.

Adding a standard style to a document style sheet

Word adds a standard style to a document's style sheet automatically when you add the corresponding elements to the document. For example, if you use Footnote on the Insert menu to add a footnote, Word adds two styles: footnote reference, which formats the reference mark in the main body of your document, and footnote text, which formats the footnote itself.

Applying a standard style to a selected paragraph, such as a heading, automatically adds the style to the document style sheet. After a style has been added to the style sheet, that style remains—even if you delete the text to which you applied the style—until you delete the style from the style sheet.

To apply a style to a selected paragraph, select the style's name from the Style dialog box or from the list that appears when you press the Shift key and display the ruler's Style drop-down list box.

To add a style using the Style dialog box, first select the text to be formatted, and then choose Style from the Format menu. Be sure that all of Word's standard styles appear in the list box by clicking the Show All Styles radio button. Select the style you want, and then click OK or Apply. The Apply button adds the style to the style sheet and, at the same time, applies the style to the current paragraph. The OK button performs both of these actions and also closes the Style dialog box.

To add a style from the ruler, select the paragraph you want to format, and then display Word's standard styles by pressing the Shift key as you click the arrow to the right of the Style drop-down list box. Word adds the style to the style sheet and applies the style to the selected paragraph.

Using standard heading styles to produce a table of contents

Word adds standard styles to a document style sheet automatically, with the exception of the heading styles. If you use Word's built-in Outline feature to outline a document, Word formats the headings as heading 1, heading 2, and so on, depending on the outline level, and adds the heading styles to the style sheet. If you don't use the Outline feature, however, Word has no way to distinguish a heading from the rest of the document text, and you must manually apply heading styles to format your headings and add the styles to the style sheet. (Chapter 14, "Outlining," discusses the link between Word's Outline feature and the standard heading styles.)

After Word's standard heading styles have been applied to your document's headings, you can use them to create a table of contents for your document. Simply choose Table Of Contents from the Insert menu, click Start or press Return, and Word collects the headings and compiles the table of contents. If you format document headings manually or with custom styles, rather than using Word's standard styles, you must individually mark the headings you want to appear in the table of contents. (Chapter 11, "Adding a Table of Contents, an Index, and Footnotes," describes in detail how to create a table of contents using Word's standard heading styles.)

Custom styles

In this section, we show you how to define styles by selection and by example. To create a new custom style, you can select a paragraph with Normal formatting, choose Style, type a style name in the Style edit bar of the Style dialog box, and then choose menu commands or click ribbon and ruler buttons to specify the formatting characteristics for that style. Word records your format selections as instructions for the style.

You can also define a new style by first applying the formatting you want to a paragraph and then assigning a style name to that formatting sample. One major advantage to defining a style this way is that you can see the effects of your formatting instructions before you add them to your style sheet. This preview is especially helpful when you're designing a new style. You can use a formatted paragraph to define a new style and use the Apply button in the Style dialog box to copy the format of your example paragraph to other text. You can also define new styles in this manner by using the Style drop-down list box on the ruler.

Defining by selection

You can define a custom style by using the Style dialog box. For example, you can create a new style named Figure Caption, with 10-point New York Bold type, centered alignment, and a 12-point line space both above and below the formatted text. First, choose Style from the Format menu (or press Command-T). Word displays the Style dialog box. If Show All Styles is activated, you'll see all 33 of Word's standard styles and the custom styles you've specified for your document. If Show Document Styles is selected, only the standard styles used in the document and any custom styles you created are shown. Word always highlights New Style at the top of the list of styles in the dialog box, ready to add a new style to the style sheet.

Whenever you define a new style, Word assumes that you want the style to be based on that of the paragraph in which the insertion point is located when you choose the Style command. In our example, the insertion point is located in a paragraph formatted with the Normal style, so Word will create a new style based on Normal.

To create the Figure Caption style, type *Figure Caption* in the Style edit bar. Next, choose 10 Point from the Font menu and Bold from the Format menu. Then choose Paragraph from the Format menu. In the Paragraph dialog box, type *12* in both the Before and After Spacing edit bars, and click OK to close the Paragraph dialog box. Click the Center Alignment button on the ruler. The Style dialog box now looks like the one in Figure 9-8 on the next page. Word has recorded all the format selections in the style's instructions.

The last step is to add the new style to the style sheet by clicking Define in the Style dialog box. Word then places Figure Caption in the list of styles and leaves the Style dialog box open. To apply the style to the current paragraph at the same time you define it, select either OK or Apply. The OK button applies the style and closes the dialog box. The Apply button applies the style without closing the dialog box.

FIGURE 9-8.
As you're creating a new style, Word records your format selections in the instructions for that style.

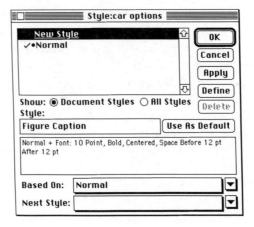

Defining by example

In most cases, you probably won't create a new style as quickly as the previous example suggests. The process of designing a format is a matter of trial and error. You might find it easier to experiment while you create the look you want and then use the final formatted text as an example for Word to follow in defining a new style.

Suppose that you have text you want to format for a figure caption. For example, Figure 9-9 shows an unformatted figure caption that's been selected.

FIGURE 9-9.
To define a new style by example, begin by entering and selecting the text you want to format.

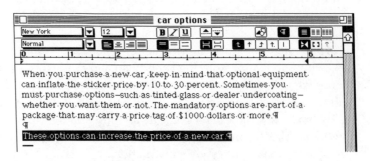

To format the figure caption, choose 10 Point from the Font menu and Bold from the Format menu. Next, enter 12 in both the Before and the After Spacing edit bars of the Paragraph dialog box, and click OK. Then click the Centered Alignment button on the ruler. The figure caption now looks like the one shown in Figure 9-10.

FIGURE 9-10.
*This screen shows the
formatted text that
serves as the example
for a new style.*

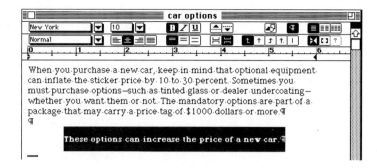

Save this style on the style sheet by positioning the insertion point anywhere in the formatted paragraph and choosing Style from the Format menu. Word highlights New Style at the top of the list of styles and also displays the formatting instructions for the current paragraph. Type *Figure Caption* in the Style edit bar, and then click either Define, OK, or Apply. The next time you open the Style dialog box you will see Figure Caption in the list of styles.

The Apply and Define buttons

The Apply button in the Style dialog box also lets you format by trial and error. For example, suppose you want to format a heading, but you're not sure how you want the heading text to look. Begin by placing the insertion point in the heading paragraph, and open the Style dialog box. Enter a name in the Style edit bar, and then define the format for the style. When you've completed the style instructions, click Apply. Word reformats the paragraph without closing the Style dialog box. You can revise the new style by selecting new formats and fonts and then clicking Apply again. Each time you click the Apply button, Word reformats your text to show any changes to the style instructions.

If the Style dialog box obstructs your view of the paragraph you're trying to format, you can easily drag the dialog box by its title bar until it is almost entirely off the screen. To display the dialog box again, simply drag it back to the middle of the screen.

The Define button lets you define a style without necessarily changing the format of the current paragraph. When you click the Define button, Word applies your changes to any paragraphs to which the style has been applied. If the insertion point is located within a paragraph formatted with a different style, Word doesn't change the format of the paragraph unless you click OK or Apply. Click the close box or the Cancel button to finish the style-definition procedure and close the Style dialog box.

Using the ruler

You can also define a new style by using the ruler. First apply the desired formatting to a paragraph, and then click the style name in the Style drop-down list box on the ruler. Next, type a new style name in the highlighted edit bar. When you press Return, Word displays the message shown in Figure 9-11. Click Define to define the new style using the format of the current paragraph.

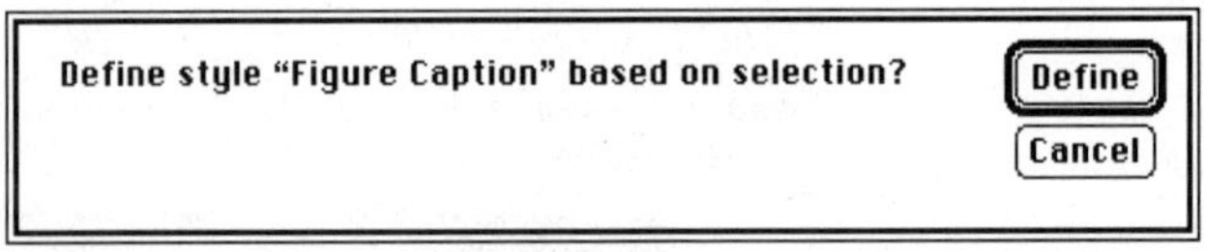

FIGURE 9-11.
When you type a new
style name and press
Return, Word displays
this message.

> Define style "Figure Caption" based on selection?   [**Define**]
>
> [Cancel]

Copying and pasting style instructions

Word allows you to create a new style by copying the instructions for an existing style and pasting them into a new style. Suppose you want to create a new style called Table Caption that is similar or identical to the existing Figure Caption style. First open the Style dialog box, select New Style, type *Table Caption*, and click Define. Then click the name of the style whose instructions you want to borrow—in this case, Figure Caption—and choose Copy from the Edit menu. (The keyboard shortcut won't work here.) Click the name of the new style—in this case, Table Caption—and choose Paste from the Edit menu. Word copies the formatting instructions for the Figure Caption style into the formatting instructions for the Table Caption style. If the style you're copying has a Based On style, Word also copies the name of the Based On style. (We discuss the Based On style in a few pages.)

You can use menu commands and ribbon and ruler buttons to revise the new style. Simply click Define to implement your changes.

Be sure to carry out the copy-and-paste procedure before you choose commands or ruler buttons. When you choose Paste, Word overwrites any existing style with the instructions of the style you've copied. As a result, you can't copy and paste the instructions for more than one style.

Style names

You should keep in mind the following rules regarding style names. Word accepts style names of up to 254 characters, but shorter names are generally easier to work with. One problem with extremely long names is that you might not be able to see the whole name in the Style dialog box. Word displays only about 26 characters of the name in the Style, Based On, and Next Style edit bars.

Word recognizes uppercase and lowercase letters in a style name. For example, a style sheet can include two completely different styles called Paragraph1 and paragraph1. If you assign an existing name to a new style, Word replaces the formatting instructions of the old style with the instructions you've entered for the new style.

You can assign more than one name to a style. As you're creating a new style, simply enter the different names in the Style edit bar, separating the names with commas. Because Word uses a comma to separate style names, you can't include a comma as part of a name, but you can use any other character in a style name, including characters created by Option-key combinations.

Word doesn't treat a style with two different names as two different styles. In fact, Word displays both names on the same line in the list of style names in the dialog box. Sometimes it is convenient to be able to assign two names to a style, one relatively long and descriptive and another with only one or two letters. As we'll explain later, the shorter style name can speed up the process of applying the style to your document.

Suppose, for example, that you assign the names Figure Caption and FC to a style. Figure 9-12 shows how Word displays those names in the Style dialog box. (Only the first name is displayed in the status box at the bottom of a window.)

FIGURE 9-12.
When you assign two or more names to a style, the names appear on the same line in the Style dialog box, separated by a comma.

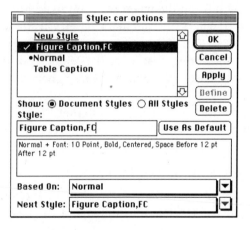

The Based On and Next Style options

Word automatically specifies links between each standard style and the Normal style, ensuring consistency in the appearance of document styles. You can create similar connections between any two styles by specifying the Based On and the Next Style options in the Style dialog box. If you use a style other than Normal as the basis for many styles in a document, these options will help you control the appearance of your document's text quickly and effectively.

The Based On option lets you base a style on an existing style so that you can change the format of many styles at once by redefining the single style on which they are based. The Next Style option lets you define the style that Word applies to the paragraph that follows the current paragraph. For example, you might use this option to specify that Word apply a body text style to every paragraph that immediately follows a heading.

The Based On option

Word allows you to link a style's formatting instructions to the instructions for another style by specifying the Based On style. Word automatically assigns a Based On style when you create a new style. You can make the new style totally independent by erasing the contents of the Based On edit bar. You can also change the Based On style at any time by entering a different style in the Based On edit bar.

When you define a new style, Word assumes the new style should be based on the style of the paragraph in which the insertion point is located. You can save time as you define the formatting instructions for the new style by moving the insertion point to a paragraph with a format that is similar to the style you want to create.

For example, to create Style1 with all the characteristics of the Normal style, except that the first line of each paragraph is indented half an inch, use Normal as the Based On style by placing the insertion point in a Normal paragraph. When you choose Style, Word enters Normal in the Based On edit bar and begins the instructions for the new style with Normal +. To complete the definition of Style1, simply drag the first-line indent marker to the 0.5-inch position on the ruler, and then click Define. Word bases all other formatting characteristics of Style1 on the Normal style.

You don't have to use the Based On style that Word suggests. Instead, you can select a new style name from the Based On list box. We describe this process in detail later in this chapter, in the section "Modifying Styles."

Creating an independent new style

To define a new style that is completely independent of other styles in your style sheet, simply highlight and delete the contents of the Based On edit bar in the Style dialog box.

For example, the Figure Caption style shown in Figure 9-12 is based on Normal. The style's instructions begin with Normal + and the word Normal appears in the Based On edit bar. If you want to make Figure Caption independent of Normal, highlight and delete the word Normal from the Based On edit bar, and then click Define. The Style dialog box now looks like the one in Figure 9-13.

The formatting instructions for the independent style differ from those in Figure 9-12 in two ways: They no longer begin with Normal +, and they now specify the New York font. When you eliminate the Based On style, the new style retains all the formats of the Based On style, expressing them in the form of explicit instructions. They must be spelled out because they no longer reference the instructions of another style.

FIGURE 9-13.
When you remove a style name from the Based On edit bar, the style becomes independent.

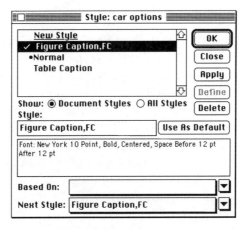

You'll want to avoid creating independent styles in most cases, as the following example indicates. Suppose you eliminate the link between the Figure Caption style and the Normal style. In this case, the left and right indents for Figure Caption are no longer tied to the indents for Normal. As long as you don't make any changes to Normal, the severed link should be of no consequence. But if you modify Normal by dragging the right indent marker to the 5-inch point on the ruler, the right margin of the main body text will change by 1 inch, and the right margin of any text formatted with the Figure Caption style will not change. All figure captions will then be off-center in relation to the main body text.

Notes on linked styles

One style can be indirectly linked to several styles. However, a style can be directly based on only one other style. For example, you might have a document in which Style3 is based on Style2, which is based on Style1, which is based on Normal. In this case, Style3 is indirectly linked to two styles, Style1 and Normal, but it is directly based on only one style, Style2.

Word doesn't allow you to create circular style references. For example, suppose Style3 is based on Style2, which is based on Style1. If you then try to make Style3 the Based On style for Style1, Word beeps and displays the message *Circular style reference.*

Word allows you no more than nine levels of linked styles, and you'll see an alert message if you try to create more than nine levels. For example, you can create a style sheet in which Style8 is based on Style7, which is based on Style6, which is based on Style5, and so on, through Style1, which is based on Normal. But if you try to create a Style9 based on Style8, Word displays the message *Too many levels of "Based on:" reference.* Of course, you can have more than nine styles indirectly linked to one another.

The Next Style option

You use the Next Style edit bar at the bottom of the Style dialog box to specify the style of the paragraphs that follow those to which you apply the style you're currently defining. To specify a Next Style, first click the arrow to the right of the Next Style edit bar. Select the name of the style from the list of styles currently specified for the document, and then click Define, Apply, or OK to implement the Next Style specification.

For example, if you are defining a Figure Caption style to format figure captions in your document, you can follow each caption with a paragraph that is formatted as Normal by specifying Normal in the Next Style list box. Word applies the Next Style only when you press Return to end a paragraph.

After a paragraph is formatted, if you place the insertion point in the middle of the paragraph and press Return, Word breaks the paragraph in two but does not apply the Next Style format to the second paragraph. Instead, Word formats the second paragraph with the same style as the first.

If you don't enter a style name in the Next Style edit bar, Word uses the style you are defining as the Next Style. For example, if you define the Figure Caption style without specifying a Next Style, the paragraph you type after a figure caption paragraph is also formatted with the Figure Caption style.

By carefully specifying the Next Style for each style on a style sheet, you can make one style automatically flow into another throughout a document. This technique can be especially helpful when you're creating a document in which you must frequently switch from one style to another.

Suppose you want to create a list of names and addresses. You can speed up the creation of this list by setting up a style sheet with four styles: Name, Address 1, Address2, and Phone. Name formats each person's name; Address1 formats the first line of each address; Address2 formats the second line of each address; and Phone formats each phone number. To help speed up text entry, define the Name style with Address1 as its Next Style, Address1 with Address2 as its Next Style, Address2 with Phone as its Next Style, and finally, to complete the loop, Phone with Name as its Next Style. After you've set up this style sheet, start with the Name style. As you press Return, Word automatically cycles through the Address1, Address2, and Phone styles, and then returns to the Name style.

Because you specify a Next Style by selecting an existing style name from the Next Style edit bar, it's actually easier to define new styles in reverse order. In the address list example, you might begin by defining the Phone style, then Address2, then Address1, and finally, Name.

Modifying styles

As you work with styles, you'll occasionally need to change their formatting instructions or names, or specify a different Based On style or Next Style. We look at these modifications in this section.

Modifying formatting instructions

To modify a style's instructions, choose Style from the Format menu, and click the style you want to change. Then choose the appropriate formatting commands and ribbon and ruler buttons to alter the style. After you've completed your changes, implement them by clicking Define.

Suppose you've used the standard heading 1 style to format some of the headings in a document, and you decide to change the appearance of those headings. The default instructions for heading 1 specify Normal plus the Helvetica font in bold, with underlining and a 12-point line space above the heading. Now you want first-level headings to appear in 14-point Helvetica Bold, with centered alignment, a 10-point line space above, and a 6-point line space below. You also want to remove the underlining.

To make these changes, first choose Style, and then click heading 1 to display this style's instructions in the dialog box, as shown in Figure 9-14.

FIGURE 9-14.
To modify a style,
begin by opening the
Style dialog box and
clicking the style's
name.

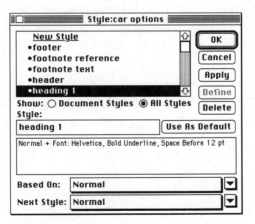

To change the instructions, leave the Style dialog box open, open the Character dialog box, and select None from the Underline drop-down list box. Then type 14 in the Size list box or select 14 from the drop-down list box of sizes. Click OK to close the Character dialog box. Next, change the line spacing above and below the heading by opening the Paragraph dialog box and replacing 12 points in the Before Spacing edit bar with 10. Then enter 6 in the After Spacing edit bar. Click

OK to close the Paragraph dialog box, and then click the Center Alignment button
on the ruler. Figure 9-15 shows the Style dialog box with the modified instructions for heading 1.

FIGURE 9-15.
As you choose
commands and
manipulate ruler
buttons, Word
modifies the style
instructions to reflect
your changes.

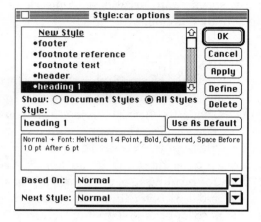

To complete the style change, click OK, Apply, or Define. If you click OK,
Word redefines heading 1, applies it to the current paragraph, and closes the dialog box. Word also reformats all paragraphs formatted with heading 1. Clicking
the Apply button has the same effect except that Word does not close the dialog
box. Clicking the Define button redefines the heading 1 style and applies its new
formatting instructions only to paragraphs that have been assigned that style.
The current paragraph is not affected unless it has already been formatted with
the heading 1 style.

Formatting instruction shortcuts

Word offers keyboard shortcuts to help you modify styles. For example, to delete
all the instructions for a style except the names of the Based On style and the Next
Style, click the style name in the Style dialog box, and press Command-Shift-P.

A similar shortcut deletes only the character formatting instructions for a
style. First select the style name in the Style dialog box, and press Command-
Shift-Spacebar. Word deletes such characteristics as underlining, italic, and bold
from the style instructions. Paragraph formatting instructions and the Based On
and Next Style settings are not changed when you use this shortcut.

You can use all the paragraph and character formatting shortcuts described
in Chapter 4, "Formatting Characters," and Chapter 5, "Formatting Documents
and Paragraphs," to define or change a style. (Appendix A, "Keyboard and
Mouse Techniques," includes a summary of these shortcuts.) For example, select
centered alignment by pressing Command-Shift-C. To specify bold character formatting, press Command-Shift-B.

Changing a style's name

To change the name of a style in your document, open the Style dialog box, click the Show Document Styles option, and then click the name you want to change. Word places the name in the Style edit bar. Use the Delete key to delete the name, and then type a new name and click Define. (Be sure to type a name that is not already in use.) Word displays an alert box like the one shown in Figure 9-16. If you click OK in this alert box, the new name replaces the old name. All references to the former style name—in the Based On or Next Style edit bars, for example—are changed so that they refer to the new name.

FIGURE 9-16.
Word displays this alert box to verify that you want to change the style name.

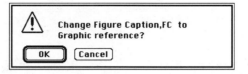

Change Figure Caption,FC to
Graphic reference?

OK   Cancel

Changing the Based On style

As we've explained, any changes to a Based On style are also made to the instructions for any dependent styles. To change the Based On style, open the Style dialog box, and then click the name of the style whose Based On style you want to change. Next, click the arrow to the right of the Based On edit bar to display the names of the styles currently specified for your document. Select a new style name, and click the Define button to implement the change. Specifying a new Based On style in no way changes the attributes of the current style.

For example, suppose your style sheet contains three styles: Normal, Style1, and Style2. The Normal style specifies 12-point New York with flush-left alignment and no indents. Style1 is based on Normal, and its instructions read

Normal + Bold Italic, Indent: Left 0.5 in Right 0.5 in, Justified

Style2 is identical to Style1, except that it specifies 10-point type. Figure 9-17 on the next page shows the formatting instructions for Style2.

To change the Based On style for Style2 to Normal, open the Style dialog box, and click Style2. Then select Normal as the name of your new Based On style, and click Define. Figure 9-18, also on the next page, shows the results.

Notice that the new instructions for Style2 include Normal as the Based On style and that the instructions for Style2 are now considerably longer. Because Style2 is now based on Normal, its formatting instructions must spell out all the differences between Style2 and Normal. Style2 doesn't take on any of the formatting characteristics of the Normal style.

FIGURE 9-17.
The only difference between Style2 and its Based On style, Style1, is the font size.

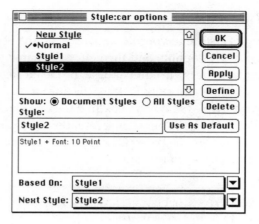

FIGURE 9-18.
After you change the Based On style, Word alters the instructions for the dependent style.

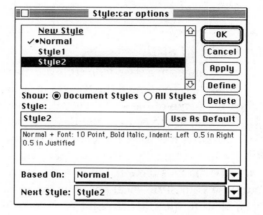

In general, a style should be based on another style. However, if you change a style that serves as the Based On style for other styles, your changes might also affect those other styles. To insulate certain styles from change, you can delete the Based On style by highlighting the name in the Based On edit bar and then pressing Delete to remove it. Click Define to implement the change.

Remember that the instructions for a dependent style spell out the differences between that style and its Based On style. If the change you make to a Based On style affects an area in which the dependent style is different, then the dependent style does not change. On the other hand, if the change involves a shared characteristic, then the dependent style's instructions do change.

Changing the Next Style option

To change the Next Style, select another style from the Next Style list box, and then click Define. When you change the Next Style option, Word doesn't reformat existing text. The new Next Style affects only text entered after the change. If you erase the contents of the Next Style edit bar without typing a replacement, Word beeps and displays the message *Valid style name is required.*

Using the ribbon to change a style

You can change a style without opening the Style dialog box by using the drop-down list of styles on the ribbon. (You can't alter a style's name, its Based On style, or its Next Style from the ribbon.) To change a style, first click anywhere in a paragraph that's formatted with that style. Then choose the formatting commands, ribbon buttons, and ruler buttons to format the paragraph in the same way that you'd define a new style by example. Next, select the style name from the Style drop-down list box on the ribbon. Word displays a dialog box like the one shown in Figure 9-19. Select Redefine The Style Based On Selection, and click OK.

FIGURE 9-19.
Select the Redefine option to redefine a style outside the Style dialog box.

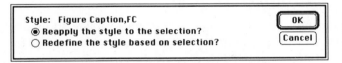

The effects of modifying a style

When you change a style, the change affects any text already formatted with that style, even if that text isn't selected at the time. For example, if you've used the standard heading 1 style to format several headings and you specify a different font for that style, all the heading 1 paragraphs are displayed in the new font.

Because Word saves the style sheet with the document, you save the changes you make to a document's style sheet each time you save the document text. Both standard and custom styles are saved. If you modify a standard style, your modifications don't affect the default instructions for that style in other documents, and any new document that uses the standard style will have default instructions for that style. You can, however, change the default instructions for a standard style, as we'll explain in the section called "Changing Defaults."

Deleting styles

You can delete any style on the style sheet except Word's standard styles. To delete a style from a style sheet, first open the Style dialog box, and then select the style you want to delete. Click the Delete button in the Style dialog box. Word then displays an alert box that asks you to confirm the deletion. If you click OK, Word eliminates the style from the style sheet.

When you delete a style, any text formatted with that style loses its special formatting and is reformatted in the Normal style.

If you delete a Based On style, the dependent style doesn't change. Instead, the deleted Based On formats become specifically stated style instructions. Normal takes the place of the style that was deleted and becomes the Based On style.

If you delete a style specified as the Next Style option, Word uses Normal as the Next Style in place of the style you deleted.

Using style sheets

Now that we've covered creating and modifying styles, we come to the heart of our subject: using a style sheet to format a document. In this section, we show you how to apply existing styles, make global changes with a style sheet, and copy styles from one document to another.

Applying styles

Word offers an efficient and easy way to apply a style in a document. First position the insertion point in the paragraph you want to format, and display the ruler (if it's not already displayed). Then select the name of the style you want to apply from the Style drop-down list box. Word immediately formats the paragraph with the style you've selected.

You can also use the Style dialog box to apply a style. Again, begin by positioning the insertion point in the paragraph you want to format. Then choose Style from the Format menu. In the Style dialog box, click the style, and then click OK or Apply. (You can also press Return.)

To apply a style to more than one paragraph in a single step, simply select some text from all the paragraphs. You can also select a style before you begin typing to apply that style to the text you type.

Applying styles from the keyboard

If you know the exact name of the style, you can use a keyboard shortcut to apply the style. First place the insertion point in the paragraph, and press Command-Shift-S. Word displays a Style prompt in the status box, as shown in Figure 9-20. Next, type the name of the style you want to use, and press Return.

FIGURE 9-20.
Pressing Command-
Shift-S displays the
Style prompt.

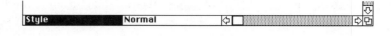

With this shortcut, you don't need to type the full name of the style as long as you type enough letters from the style's name to distinguish it from other style names. You also don't have to use the correct case, unless you've created two styles with names that are identical except for capitalization.

Assigning a second, abbreviated name to a style, as we explained earlier, makes this keyboard shortcut even faster.

Additional methods for applying styles

In Chapter 18, "Customizing Word," we introduce two additional techniques for quickly and easily applying styles to a document. Both require that you customize Word. You can assign a keystroke series to any style name so that you can apply a style simply by pressing the assigned keys. You can also create a Work menu containing style names. In Chapter 18, we give details about how to create custom key assignments and custom menus.

Manual formatting vs. style sheet formatting

You can combine manual formatting changes with style sheet formatting—Word simply adds the manual changes to the formatting features specified by the styles. For example, suppose your document's style sheet includes Style 1 with 12-point Courier Bold. Figure 9-21 shows some text with this style.

FIGURE 9-21.
This screen shows
some text that has
been formatted with
Style 1.

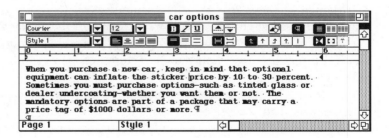

If you select a paragraph with this style and then choose Italic from the Format menu, the paragraph displays italic formatting in addition to the bold formatting and other features specified by Style 1. In addition, you can change the indentations, margins, and other paragraph formatting features of this paragraph. Figure 9-22 on the next page shows a paragraph formatted with both Style 1 and italics. We've also changed the first-line indent of this paragraph from the 0 position on the ruler to the 0.5-inch position. When you change paragraph formatting, Word adds a plus and ellipsis to the style name in the status box at the bottom of the window. However, Word doesn't add these elements to the status box if you make only character formatting changes.

FIGURE 9-22.
This text has been formatted with Style 1 and italics, which we've added manually.

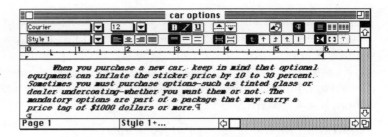

Manual formatting changes usually take precedence over style sheet formatting. When you manually assign a format that conflicts with the style of the text, the manual formatting overrides the style. As a result, when you apply a character format that can be toggled on and off (such as Italic or Bold), the manual formatting change can produce unexpected results. For example, if you've applied an italic style to a paragraph and you later select a word in that paragraph and then choose Italic from the Format menu, Word removes the italics from the selected word.

Applying a style after making manual formatting changes

If you format text manually and then apply a style to that text, the result depends on the manual formatting. If you first manually specify paragraph formatting and then assign a style to that text, the new style takes precedence.

Manual changes to character formats work differently, however. If your manual formatting changes affect more than half the characters in a paragraph, Word overrides those changes when you apply a style. If your manual formatting changes affect less than half the characters in a paragraph, Word doesn't override the formatting.

For example, suppose you've created a paragraph with 200 characters in the Normal style, and you select one word in that paragraph and apply bold formatting. If you reapply the Normal style, Word doesn't remove the bold formatting from the word. If you had applied bold formatting to most of the words in the paragraph, however, Word would remove all the bold formatting when you reapplied the Normal style.

This rule also affects how Word toggles formats on and off. If your manual formatting affects less than half of the paragraph and you later format the whole paragraph with a style that specifies that same format, Word toggles off the manual formatting—in effect undoing the formatting. However, if your manual formatting affects the majority of the characters in the paragraph, Word applies the style's formatting to the entire paragraph.

The Plain Text and Revert To Style commands

You can choose the Plain Text and the Revert To Style commands to remove character formatting that you've previously added to selected text. If you highlight the text and choose Plain Text from the Format menu, Word removes all character formatting from the selected text except the font, point size, position (superscripting or subscripting), and spacing (condensed or expanded) attributes. Features such as italics, underlining, and color are stripped away, even if they are part of the style definition for that text.

For example, suppose Style 1 specifies 14-point Times Italic. If you select a paragraph formatted with Style 1 and choose the Plain Text command, Word removes the italic formatting so that the paragraph appears in plain 14-point Times. Word doesn't alter the definition of Style 1 on the style sheet.

The Revert To Style command on the Format menu also removes manual character formatting but does not affect formatting that has been applied by a style. Suppose, for example, that you format a paragraph with Style 1 and then select the paragraph and choose 12 Point from the Font menu and Bold from the Format menu. The paragraph now appears in 12-point Times Bold Italic. If you later select the paragraph again and choose Revert To Style, Word removes the manually applied bold formatting and returns the text to the 14-point size that the Style 1 definition calls for. Word doesn't remove the italic formatting, however, because this formatting is part of the Style 1 formatting instructions.

Making global changes with a style sheet

After you've applied styles throughout your document, you can make significant format changes to the document merely by changing the instructions of one or more styles.

Figure 9-23 on the next page shows part of a document to which three styles have been applied. The title is formatted with a Title style that specifies 14-point New York Bold, flush-left alignment, and a 10-point space after the text. The heading is formatted with a Subheading style that uses Title as its Based On style but specifies 12-point size, a 4-point line space above the heading, and a 2-point line space below it. The body text is formatted with Normal, which specifies 12-point New York, a half-inch first-line indent, and justified alignment. We'll use these paragraphs to show how you can make extensive formatting changes by modifying several styles.

Suppose you want to change the title and heading shown in Figure 9-23 to Times with centered alignment. The Times font is smaller than the New York font, so you can increase the title size to 18 points and the heading size to 14 points. You also want to change the main body text to 12-point Helvetica. In just a few easy steps, you can apply these formatting changes throughout the entire document.

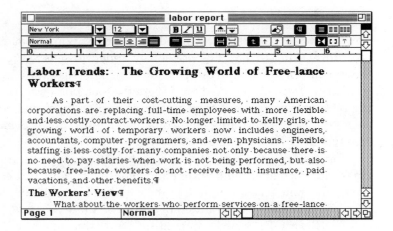

First, open the Style dialog box, and click Normal. Change this style by choosing Helvetica from the Font menu or the ribbon. Word adds these formats to the formatting instructions in the dialog box. Click Define to implement the changes.

Now change the Title and Subheading styles. Select Title in the Style dialog box, choose Times and 18 Point from the Font menu or the ribbon, and then click the Center Alignment button on the ruler. Again, click Define to implement the changes. Because Subheading is based on the Title style, the changes you made to the Title style carry over into the instructions for the Subheading style. The only formatting change you need to make to this style is to choose 14 Point from the Font menu or the ribbon.

After altering each style's instructions, click OK to apply the styles and close the Style dialog box. Word automatically changes the format of the paragraphs to which the modified styles are applied. Figure 9-24 shows the result. This technique lets you change the appearance of a document quickly and consistently.

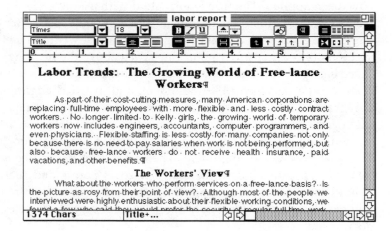

Importing styles from another document

Word allows you to copy styles from other documents and import them into your current document. You can borrow styles one at a time, or import all the styles from another document's style sheet. You save time because you don't have to redefine styles for each new document.

Copying styles one by one

To copy a style from one document to another, simply copy some text that has been formatted with that style. When you paste the text, Word adds the new style name and style instructions to the style sheet of the current document. If you copy the entire document, Word adds all the styles in that document's style sheet to the style sheet of the document into which you paste the text.

When you use this technique, you must be sure to copy the paragraph symbol (¶) at the end of the paragraph. Without a paragraph symbol, Word doesn't transfer the text formatting or the style name to the other document. Instead, the text you paste is formatted according to the destination document's Normal style. For example, suppose a document called Intro contains a First ¶ style, which you want to use in a document called Summary. In the Intro document, select some text formatted with the First ¶ style. Then choose Copy from the Edit menu. Next, open the Summary document, and choose Paste from the Edit menu. Word copies the text and its style into the Summary document. When you choose Style from the Format menu, you'll see that the First ¶ style is now part of the Summary style sheet.

When copying styles, Word handles duplicate style names by giving precedence to the style in the destination document. Going back to our example, suppose the style sheet for the Summary document already contains a First ¶ style. When you paste text to which First ¶ has been applied from Intro into Summary, Word uses the First ¶ style instructions in the Summary document to format the text, rather than importing the new style instructions from the Intro file. Avoid problems when copying formatted text from one document to another by making sure you don't have duplicate style names.

If the style you are copying includes a Based On style, Word might alter the Based On style when you paste the text into the destination document. If the paragraph you copy is based on a style that is not defined in the destination document, Word substitutes Normal as the Based On style. However, Word retains all the character and paragraph formats you assigned to that paragraph in the source document, by creating an explicit set of instructions for that style.

For example, suppose you are working on a document that contains Sub1 and Sub2 styles. Sub1 specifies 18-point Helvetica Bold. Sub2, which is based on Sub1, specifies 14-point Helvetica Bold. The formatting instructions for Sub2 are

Sub1 + Font: 14 Point

Now, suppose you copy a Sub2 paragraph into a new document window, which has only Normal in its style sheet. After pasting the Sub2 text into this document, Word adds Sub2 to the style sheet. Sub2's Based On style—Sub1—hasn't been used in this new document, so the formatting instructions for Sub2 will be

Normal + Font: Helvetica 14 Point, Bold

If the Based On style is defined in the destination document's style sheet, Word continues to use that Based On style. Word does not change the formatting characteristics of the copied style in any way.

In other words, Sub1 is still the Based On style for Sub2 in the new document, but Word has changed the formatting instructions for Sub2 so that they spell out all the differences between Sub2 and Sub1.

Importing a complete style sheet

Sometimes it's more efficient to import an entire style sheet from another document than to copy individual styles. Word makes it easy for you to reuse a style sheet in other documents.

To import a style sheet from another document, first choose Style from the Format menu. Then with the Style dialog box open, choose Open from the File menu. Word presents a list of all the available Word document files, as shown in Figure 9-25.

FIGURE 9-25.
*To import a style sheet
from another
document, first open
the Style dialog box,
and then choose Open
from the File menu.*

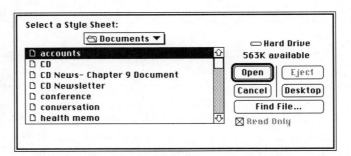

If the file containing the style sheet you want to use is not on the current disk, you can click the Desktop (Drive in System 6) button to access another disk drive, or you can click Eject and insert a different disk. When you see the name of the document that contains the style sheet you want to import, click the name to select it, and then click Open (or double-click the name). After a moment, Word adds the styles from that document to the current style sheet, which then contains both its original styles and all the styles from the style sheet of the other document.

If the imported style sheet contains styles with the same names as styles in the current document, the imported style overwrites the current style. As you might expect, any text in your document that is formatted with that style is then reformatted according to the instructions of the imported style.

For example, every document's style sheet contains the Normal style, but the formatting instructions for Normal can vary from document to document. If you're working with a document for which the Normal style specifies 12-point New York and you import a style sheet for which the Normal style specifies 10-point Courier, Word replaces the Normal style on your style sheet with the imported Normal instructions, and the main body text in your current document is then reformatted as 10-point Courier.

If many of the style names on your current style sheet are identical to the imported style names, your document may be radically reformatted. However, reformatting might be exactly what you want. Borrowing another style sheet is an excellent way to reformat an entire document rapidly.

Creating style sheet stationery

If you plan to use similar formats in several documents, you can increase efficiency by storing the formats in an empty Word stationery file. Such a template typically requires only about 2 KB of disk space—small enough to store easily. When you want to create a new document that uses the same style sheet template, simply open the stationery file to display a new, untitled document that contains the style sheet you've saved.

For example, suppose you write a weekly report using three styles: Title (for the report title), Normal (for the body text), and List (for the list of goals). By storing these styles in a stationery file, you can speed up the process of formatting your report each week. When you begin a new report, simply double-click the stationery file to open a new document that contains the styles you need. For more information about saving a Word file as a stationery file, see Chapter 16, "Finding and Sharing Files."

Instead of creating a separate style sheet template, you could copy the styles directly from the previous report, or you could open and save the previous report with a new name and then delete the old text. However, the stationery file is small enough that you can store copies of it in several folders, and you don't need to worry about retaining documents just so that you can reuse their styles.

Printing a style sheet

You can print a list of the styles and the corresponding formatting instructions in a style sheet. First, choose Style from the Format menu, and click either Show Document Styles to print only the styles used in the document or Show All Styles to print all custom and standard styles. Then choose Print from the File menu.

Figure 9-26 shows the first page of a style sheet printed with the Show All Styles option selected. As you can see, Word produces an alphabetical listing with the style names in bold and the formatting instructions indented and in plain type. (For more information on printing, see Chapter 8, ''Printing.'')

FIGURE 9-26.
You can print a list of all the styles on the current style sheet, together with their formatting instructions.

footer
> Normal + Tab stops: 3 in Centered; 6 in Right Flush

footnote reference
> Normal + Font: 9 Point, Superscript 3 Point

footnote text
> Normal + Font: 10 Point

heading 1,h1,Heading 1,Head1
> Font: Times 36 Point, Indent: Left 1.5in Flush left, Space Before 120 pt After 36 pt, Page Break Before, Keep With Next, Keep Lines Together Border: Bottom (Dotted)

heading 2,h2,Heading 2,Head2
> Font: Helvetica 14 Point, Bold Italic Caps, Subscript 3 Point, Flush left, Line Spacing: At Least 24 pt, Space Before 16 pt After 8 pt, Side-by-Side, Keep With Next

heading 3
> Font: Helvetica 14 Point, Bold Italic, Subscript 4 Point, Flush left, Space Before 12 pt After 8 pt, Keep With Next, Tab stops: 4.375in

heading 4
> Font: Helvetica 12 Point, Bold Italic, Flush left, Space Before 24 pt After 8 pt, Keep With Next

heading 5
> Normal + Bold, Subscript 4 Point, Space Before 12 pt After 8 pt, Keep With Next, Tab stops: 4.375in

Changing defaults

You can change the default style sheet so that your preferred styles are automatically available with each new document. You can also change the default characteristics of some of Word's standard styles, such as the Normal style. In this section, we explain how to change Word's defaults and how to return to the original default settings.

Modifying the default style sheet

Initially, the only document style on the default style sheet is the Normal style. To add a style to the default style sheet, first open the Style dialog box, and select the style name you want to add. Then click the Use As Default button. Word displays the alert box shown in Figure 9-27. Click Yes in the alert box to add the selected style to the default style sheet. Thereafter, when you open a new Word document, the style will be available on the style sheet.

FIGURE 9-27.
Word displays this
alert box when you
add a style to the
default style sheet.

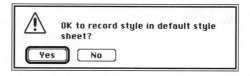

Modifying the Normal style

As we've explained, the Normal style is linked to all standard styles and most of the custom styles that you add to your document. You can easily change the default font and point size that Word assigns to Normal by choosing Default Font from the Font menu. Selecting a new default font or point size can dramatically change a document's appearance, and one of your first steps in setting up a new document should be to alter the Normal style to suit that particular document.

Modifying the Normal style's default font or point size offers many advantages over modifying text on a paragraph-by-paragraph basis. Changing the style ensures consistency between the main body text and the other text in the document. If you change the Normal style first, you might not have to change other standard styles. If you manually format the main body text, however, you'll probably have to reformat other document elements as well.

To change the font and point size, choose Default Font from the Font menu. Word displays the Default Font section of the Preferences dialog box. You can also display this dialog box by choosing Preferences from the Tools menu and selecting Default Font on the left side of the Preferences dialog box.

To specify a new default font or point size, select the options you want from the corresponding drop-down list box shown in Figure 9-28 on the next page. When you close the Preferences dialog box, Word applies your defaults to the current document and to all new documents you create. The format of the Normal style in existing documents is not changed.

FIGURE 9-28.
To change the default font and point size of the Normal style for current and future documents, choose Default Font to display the Default Font section of the Preferences dialog box.

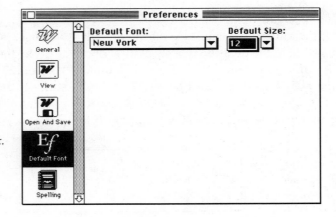

Modifying the default characteristics of standard styles

You can make permanent changes to a standard style by changing the instructions for the style and then specifying the changed format as the default. Then, when you use that style in any document, the modified instructions are used.

To change a standard style, choose Style from the Format menu, and click the desired style name. Then reformat the style. After you've made the necessary changes, click Use As Default in the Style dialog box. Word displays the alert box shown earlier in Figure 9-27. If you click Yes in the alert box, Word alters the style in the style sheet of your current document and of any new documents you create. Word also reformats any text in the current document to which the style has been applied. Any other standard styles based on the style, and any text to which those styles have been applied, might also be reformatted. Documents formatted and saved in the old default style retain their original formatting.

Returning to the original defaults

Word stores the default style sheet and standard styles in the Word Settings (5) file. To restore the default style sheet and return the standard styles to their original formats, choose Commands from the Tools menu, and click the Reset button at the bottom of the dialog box. Select the Reset To Microsoft Standard Settings option, and click OK. Then click the Close button in the Commands dialog box. (Chapter 18, "Customizing Word," explains the Commands command in detail.)

You can also return to the default style sheet by deleting or renaming the Word Settings (5) file. Then, the next time you load Word, it recreates the Word Settings (5) file using the original defaults.

If you delete or rename the Word Settings (5) file, or if you click Reset in the Commands dialog box, you'll affect more than just style sheets. You'll also return all menus, keystroke series, and dialog boxes to their original configurations. (For more information, see Chapter 18, "Customizing Word.")

10

Creating Professional Documents

*I*n Chapter 4, "Formatting Characters," and Chapter 5, "Formatting Documents and Paragraphs," we explained basic document formatting in Word, including page layout and paragraph and character formatting. In this chapter, we describe more advanced formatting features for creating professional-looking documents, such as creating individual document sections; creating headers and footers; numbering pages, lines, and paragraphs; linking documents in a series; handling left and right page formats; and positioning framed objects on the page.

Most of the features introduced in this chapter are specified in the Section dialog box, including header and footer placement, format and location of page numbers, and the appearance of columns in your document. You can also display the Line Number dialog box directly from the Section dialog box. If you divide your document into separate sections, you can control these features in each section individually. If your document contains only one section, the Section dialog box settings apply to your entire document.

In the first half of this chapter, we describe each of the Section dialog box settings in turn. Then we show you how to number document paragraphs using the Renumber command on the Tools menu, how to establish different right and left page layouts, and how to link documents together using the File Series dialog box. At the end of the chapter, we describe the Frame command, which enables you to place a block of text or a graphic anywhere on the page and flow other text around it.

Using the Section dialog box

Every new Word document consists of only one section. You can easily add sections throughout your document by defining them in the Section dialog box.

As you work in Word, you'll find creating sections gives you more control over headers and footers, page numbers, and columns. In a multisection document, you can create a separate header and footer for each section. You can also number the pages in each section independently, and you can vary the number of columns. If you're working with a long document, you'll also find that breaking it into smaller sections allows you to work more efficiently.

To create a new section, place the insertion point where you want that section to begin, and then choose Section Break from the Insert menu to mark the new section. You can also press Command-Enter to insert a section break. Word marks the section break on your screen with a double dotted line, as shown in Figure 10-1. Like page-break markers, section-break markers do not appear in a printed document.

FIGURE 10-1.
A section break
appears on your screen
as a double dotted line.

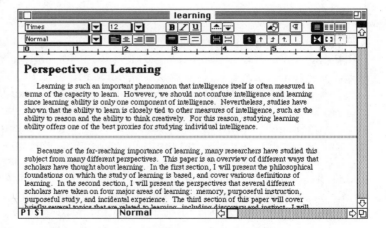

As Figure 10-1 shows, when you insert a section break, Word assigns each section a number that indicates its place in the current document. The status box in the lower-left corner of the screen displays the page and section number of the text at the top of the screen. Word adds a section and renumbers existing sections in your document each time you insert a section break. The first time you insert a section break, the text before the section break becomes part of Section 1 and the text after the section break becomes Section 2.

To merge adjacent document sections, delete the section break between them by clicking once in the selection bar to highlight the section-break marker and then pressing the Delete key. Word renumbers the sections in sequence. If the merged sections have different Section dialog box settings, the settings of the second section are used.

To specify characteristics for the pages within a section, first place the insertion point anywhere within the section. Next, choose the Section command from the Format menu to display the Section dialog box. As you can see in Figure 10-2, this dialog box is divided into four categories: Start, Columns, Header/Footer, and Page Numbers. Figure 10-2 displays the initial default settings for each category. You can specify new default settings by selecting the appropriate options and then clicking the Use As Default button on the right side of the Settings dialog box.

FIGURE 10-2.
The Section dialog box enables you to vary document characteristics from one section to another.

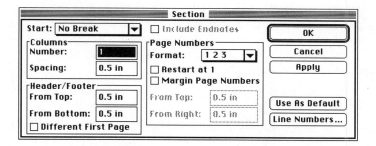

The Section dialog box displays the settings for the current section only. If you select text in more than one section before opening the Section dialog box, the edit bars appear blank and the check box options are dimmed. If you select a section-break marker, the settings apply to text in the section above the section-break marker. If you haven't inserted any section breaks in your document, Word treats the entire document as one section, and the settings displayed apply to the entire text.

In this chapter, we discuss the Start drop-down list box, and show you how to create headers and footers, page numbers, and snaking columns. We also show you how to use the Line Numbers button in the lower-right corner of the Section dialog box to number the lines of a document. (We explain the Include Endnotes check box option that appears at the top of the Section dialog box in Chapter 11, "Adding a Table of Contents, an Index, and Footnotes," when we discuss creating footnotes in Word.)

Specifying the section start

The drop-down list box of Start options in the Section dialog box lets you specify how to begin the current section when you print your document. As Figure 10-3 shows, Word's default Start option is No Break, which begins a new section without changing the layout of your document.

FIGURE 10-3.
Word offers five Start
options in the Section
dialog box.

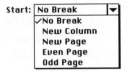

To place the paragraph following the section-break marker at the top of the next page, perhaps leaving part of the previous page blank when you print your document, select the New Page option. (These options have no effect on single-section documents.)

The New Column option starts a section at the top of a column. You'll use this option only when your document has a multicolumn layout.

Use the Even Page and Odd Page options in conjunction with the Mirror Even/Odd margins and gutter settings in the Document dialog box. These two options instruct Word to begin a section on the next even-numbered or odd-numbered page, sometimes forcing a blank page to appear in your document. You'll often find these options useful in a document with different left and right page layouts. (We discuss left and right page layouts later in this chapter.)

Numbering pages

In Chapter 8, "Printing," we showed you how to add page numbers to a document by using Print Preview's Page Number icon. You can also include page numbers within any section, either by using the Section dialog box or by placing page numbers within section headers or footers. To avoid page numbers in two locations on each page, use only one of these techniques. We'll discuss defining page numbers in the Section dialog box now. Later in this chapter, we'll show you how to add page numbers to headers and footers.

Defining page numbers in the Section dialog box

To add page numbers to your printed document from the Section dialog box, first choose Section from the Format menu. At the top of the Page Numbers section, the Format drop-down list box appears, as shown in Figure 10-4.

FIGURE 10-4.
*You can select from
five Page Numbers
formats.*

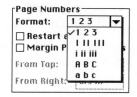

You use the Page Numbers options to add page numbers to your document. First select the page number format from the Format list box: Arabic numerals, uppercase Roman numerals, lowercase Roman numerals, uppercase letters, or lowercase letters. Word's default numbering scheme uses Arabic numerals. If you select a numeric format, Word numbers each page of your section in sequence. If you select the uppercase alphabetic format, Word combines letters for documents of more than 26 pages, using the characters AA, BB, CC, and so on for pages 27 through 52; AAA, BBB, CCC, and so on for pages 53 through 78; and so forth.

To position the page numbers on your printed page, select the Margin Page Numbers option. Notice that the From Top and From Right edit bars become active. Word's initial default settings of 0.5 inch mean that the page numbers will be printed a half inch from the top and right edges of the page—or in the upper-right corner, as shown in Figure 10-5. To change these settings so that your page numbers appear a half inch from the bottom of an 8-½-by-11-inch page, for example, change the From Top setting to 10.5 in. To center page numbers, enter a From Right setting of 4.25 in. If you have selected the Even/Odd Headers option in the Document dialog box, Word adjusts the position of your page numbers on odd and even pages. We'll discuss left and right pagination in detail later in this chapter.

FIGURE 10-5.
*Word's default
placement for
automatic page
numbers is a half inch
from the upper-right
corner of the page.*

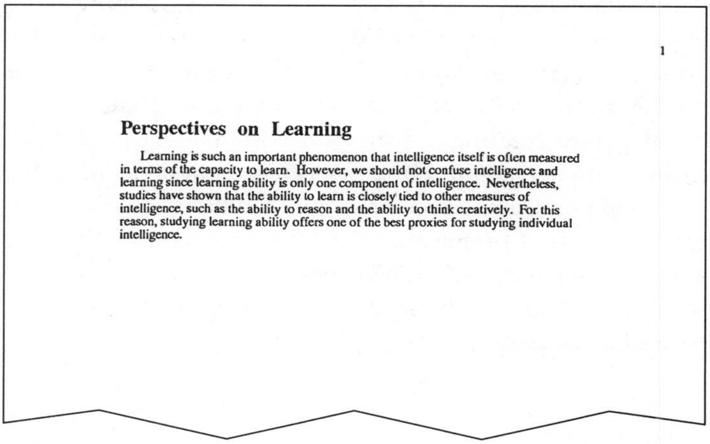

1

Perspectives on Learning

Learning is such an important phenomenon that intelligence itself is often measured in terms of the capacity to learn. However, we should not confuse intelligence and learning since learning ability is only one component of intelligence. Nevertheless, studies have shown that the ability to learn is closely tied to other measures of intelligence, such as the ability to reason and the ability to think creatively. For this reason, studying learning ability offers one of the best proxies for studying individual intelligence.

As we explained in Chapter 8, "Printing," you can also change a page number's position by moving the Page Number icon in Print Preview. With the Section dialog box, you can make this change with greater precision. You might want to display your document in Print Preview to verify changes you make in the Section dialog box.

Formatting page numbers

The format that Word applies to page numbers depends on how you've created them. Word uses a style called *page number* to format page numbers you specify in the Section dialog box. This style is based on your document's Normal style. To change the character format of your page numbers, redefine the page number style. Chapter 9, "Creating Style Sheets," describes this process.

As we'll explain in a few pages, if you've created page numbers in a header or footer window, Word uses the header or footer style to determine their formats. To alter the character format of page numbers in a header or footer, simply change the definition of the header or footer style, or manually change the format of the text in the header or footer window.

Eliminating numbers on the first page

When you add page numbers to a section, Word numbers each page within the section in sequence. If the first page of your document is a title page, you probably won't want a page number to appear on this page. You can either count this page but begin displaying page numbers on page 2, or you can insert a section break between the first and second pages of your document and start numbering the second section with page 1.

To omit a page number on page 1 and begin numbering the second page with page 2, select the Different First Page option in the Header/Footer portion of the Section dialog box. Word still begins numbering with page 1, but begins printing page numbers on the second page of the document.

If you're creating a document with a cover page, you can exclude this page from your page count. First, insert a section break after the cover page. Place the insertion point in the second section, and then open the Section dialog box. Select the Restart At 1 option and the New Page option from the Start drop-down list box, and then click OK. Then remove any page number you may have added to the first section. When you print your document, the first page of the first section won't have a page number, and the second section will begin with page 1.

Specifying section page numbers

In documents without sections, the page number position and format you specify in the Section dialog box are applied to page numbers throughout your document. You can easily change the page number format from one section to another. In a long publication, for example, lowercase Roman numerals are generally used on the pages that contain a preface or table of contents, and Arabic numerals are used on the pages of the main body of the document. To change numbering schemes within your document, place the insertion point in each section in turn, open the Section dialog box, and then select the numbering format you want to use from the Format drop-down list box.

Suppose you are working with a 20-page document that you have divided into two sections. The first section is the document front matter and occupies pages 1 through 3. The second section is the main body and occupies pages 4 through 20. To begin the second section with page 1, use the Restart At 1 option. Word renumbers the main-body pages 1 through 16. (As you scroll through this part of the document, the status box displays P1 S2, P2 S2, and so on.)

When you change page number formats, you'll almost certainly want to apply the Restart At 1 option. For example, suppose you have used the lowercase Roman setting to number the front-matter pages of the document from i to iii. When you reach the main body of the document on page 4, you start a new section and apply the Arabic numbering option (1, 2, 3). If you don't select the Restart At 1 option for this new section, your page numbers will start at 4 rather than at 1.

Specifying section and page numbers for printing

When we introduced the Print dialog box in Chapter 8, "Printing," we explained how to use the Pages From and To settings to print a specified range of pages. Word also offers Section Range From and To edit bars in the LaserWriter and ImageWriter Print dialog boxes. When you choose the Print command with a document that contains two or more sections, the dialog boxes shown in Figures 10-6 below and 10-7 on the next page appear. If your document contains only one section, you don't see Section Range From and To edit bars; instead, Word displays the number 1 as both the From and To setting in the Print dialog box.

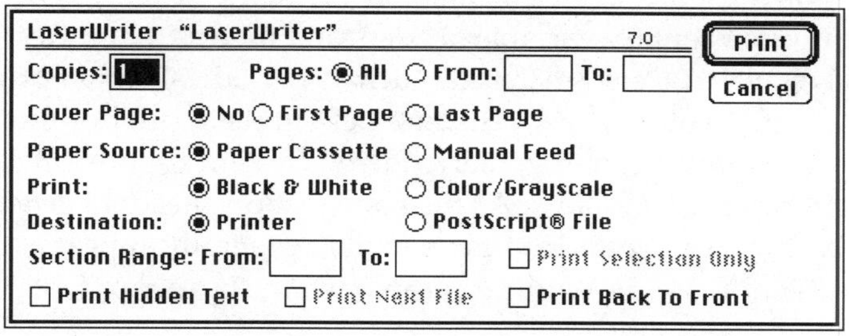

FIGURE 10-6.
You can print a range of sections by entering section numbers in the Section Range From and To edit bars of the LaserWriter Print dialog box.

```
LaserWriter  "LaserWriter"                        7.0    [ Print  ]
Copies:[1]              Pages: ● All  ○ From:[   ] To:[   ]   [ Cancel ]
Cover Page:    ● No ○ First Page ○ Last Page
Paper Source: ● Paper Cassette ○ Manual Feed
Print:         ● Black & White  ○ Color/Grayscale
Destination:   ● Printer        ○ PostScript® File
Section Range: From:[   ]  To:[   ]   □ Print Selection Only
□ Print Hidden Text   □ Print Next File   □ Print Back To Front
```

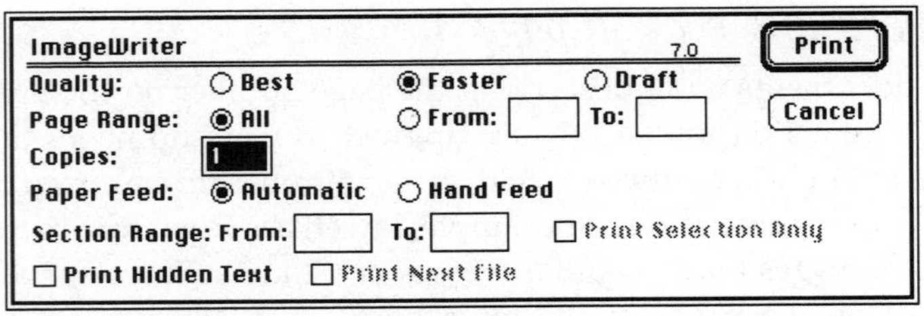

FIGURE 10-7.
*The Print dialog box
for the ImageWriter
printer also contains
Section Range
settings.*

```
┌──────────────────────────────────────────────────────────────────────┐
│ ImageWriter                                       7.0      [  Print  ] │
│ Quality:        ○ Best        ● Faster    ○ Draft                      │
│ Page Range:     ● All         ○ From: [      ] To: [      ] [ Cancel ] │
│ Copies:         [ 1 ]                                                  │
│ Paper Feed:     ● Automatic   ○ Hand Feed                             │
│ Section Range: From: [      ]  To: [      ]  ☐ Print Selection Only    │
│ ☐ Print Hidden Text    ☐ Print Next File                              │
└──────────────────────────────────────────────────────────────────────┘
```

To print a multisection document whose pages are numbered sequentially, you can specify the appropriate pages in the Pages From and To edit bars; you don't need to specify Section Range settings. To print a range of sections, specify the appropriate Section Range numbers and leave the Pages From and To edit bars blank. To print one section, enter the same section number in both the Section Range From and Section Range To edit bars, and leave the Pages From and To edit bars blank.

If you've numbered the pages of each section separately, specify both the section and page range to print part of a single section. To print pages from different sections, specify the range of page numbers in the Pages From and To edit bars, and then type the appropriate section numbers in the Section Range From and Section Range To edit bars. For example, if the pages of section 1 are numbered 1 through 12 and the pages of section 2 are numbered 1 through 8, you can print the last four pages of section 1 and the first two pages of section 2. Simply enter *9* in the Pages From edit bar and *2* in the Pages To edit bar. Then enter *1* in the Section Range From edit bar and *2* in the Section Range To edit bar.

If the section and page ranges you specify aren't compatible—for example, if you specify page numbers found only in section 1 but type *2* in the Section From and To edit bars—Word doesn't print any pages when you click the Print button in the Print dialog box.

Adding headers and footers

You see headers and footers in just about every book, magazine, and publication. Generally, headers and footers serve as guideposts for the reader, carrying information such as page numbers and the name of the publication. Longer publications often contain variable headers and footers that reflect the names of sections and chapters. Dated materials such as periodicals often present the date of publication and volume and issue numbers in the header or footer.

Word offers an extremely flexible system for creating, formatting, and editing headers and footers. As the names imply, headers generally appear at the top of each page in your document; footers generally appear at the bottom. To create a header or footer in Word, you can open the header or footer window and type the text you want. You can even paste in a graphic to use as a header or footer. Word automatically replicates the header or footer on every document page.

You can easily create a different header or footer for each section in your document, change the position of headers and footers, and apply character and paragraph formats to a header or footer. In addition, you can vary the appearance and content of headers and footers for odd and even pages and for the first page of a document or section.

While you're using Normal or Outline view, the headers and footers you create are tucked out of sight in separate windows but are stored with your document when you save it to disk. You display the header or footer window by choosing one of the header or footer commands from the View menu. To see how the header or footer appears on each document page, you must switch to Page Layout view or use the Print Preview window.

As we explained in Chapter 8, "Printing," you can specify the content and placement of headers and footers in the Page Layout and Print Preview windows. However, you can specify header and footer placement with more precision in the Section dialog box. The header and footer windows let you create, format, and edit document headers and footers more easily than you can in the Page Layout and Print Preview windows.

In this section, our examples focus mainly on headers, but creating footers is almost identical to creating headers. We'll address minor differences relating to footers as they arise, but when you've learned how to work with headers, you'll be able to work with footers as well.

Displaying the header window

To add a header or footer to a document, begin by choosing the Header or Footer command from the View menu. A small window appears at the bottom of your screen. The title bar indicates the document name. At the top of the window, Word displays three icons, as shown in Figure 10-8. You use the Page Number, Date, and Time icons to add dynamic page numbers, dates, and times to your

FIGURE 10-8.
Choose the Header command from the View menu to display the header window.

Page Number icon   *Date icon*   *Time icon*

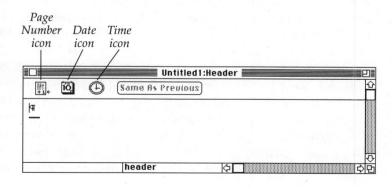

headers and footers. The Same As Previous button lets you link headers or footers in one section with those in the previous section in the document.

In most ways, the header and footer windows function like standard document windows. The insertion point initially appears at the first character space and a horizontal bar appears just below the insertion point to serve as an end mark. You can use the Show ¶ command or display the ribbon and the ruler in this window, just as you can in a standard document window. The header window also contains a close box, a zoom box, scroll bars, and a size box. Although you won't see page numbers in the status box, you can use the status bar to make glossary entries, apply styles, and perform other actions from the keyboard. The current style name is also displayed in the status bar. In a header window, for example, you'll initially see the header style name in the status bar.

To help you identify the contents of the window, the title bar in the header window displays the word *Header* and information that indicates the header's position within the document. As we'll demonstrate later in this chapter, Word allows you to create a separate header and footer on the first page of a document. When you open the header or footer window for this page, you'll see *First Header* or *First Footer* at the top of the window. If your document is divided into sections, you'll also see notations such as *(S1)* and *(S2)*, which tell you which section's header you're working with. If you're using different headers or footers on left and right pages, Word displays *Even Header*, *Odd Header*, *Even Footer*, or *Odd Footer* at the top of the window.

A new footer window differs from the header window shown in Figure 10-8 in two minor details: the word *Footer* appears in the window's title bar, and the footer style name appears in the status bar at the bottom of the window. As we explained in Chapter 9, "Creating Style Sheets," Word automatically formats headers and footers with the standard header and footer styles.

Creating a header

You can enter, format, and position header text just as you do main-body text in a standard document window. Suppose, for example, that you want the title of a project proposal called *Managing Computer Documentation Projects* to appear at the top of each page. Begin by typing the title in the empty header window, as shown in Figure 10-9.

Header text initially appears in the default header style. We have displayed the ruler in the header window by choosing Ruler from the View menu. You can see that the header's paragraph formats are initially flush-left, with a centered tab at 3 inches and a right-aligned tab at 6 inches. Our right indent marker falls at the 6-inch mark because we're using Word's default Document and Page Setup dialog box settings. (See Chapter 5, "Formatting Documents and Paragraphs," for more information on the relationship between margin settings and the ruler.)

FIGURE 10-9.
To create a header,
type the text you want
to use in the header
window.

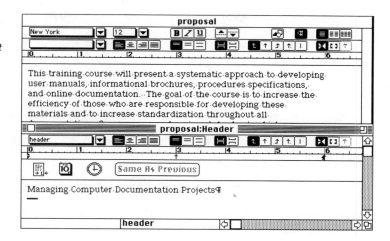

Although we'll want to do some more work on this sample header, let's see what happens when we print the document. To lock in your new header text, click the close box in the header window's title bar. Word removes the header window from the screen and reactivates the document window.

You specify in the Section dialog box how far from the top of the page you want to display the header. We haven't changed the header's default settings. As a result, when we print the document, the header appears a half inch from the top of the page, as shown in Figure 10-10. Notice also that the body of our document begins a half inch below the header and that the header begins 1.25 inches from the left side of the page, in alignment with the body text.

FIGURE 10-10.
The header initially
appears a half inch
from the top of the
page, left-aligned with
the body text.

Managing Computer Documentation Projects

This training course will present a systematic approach to developing user manuals, informational brochures, procedures specifications, and online documentation. The goal of the course is to increase the efficiency of those who are responsible for developing these materials and to increase standardization throughout all documentation. Our new comprehensive style sheet, which covers general corporate standards as well as project-specific standards, will be distributed to each unit manager at the first training session. After reviewing these standards, we will walk through a series of sample documentation projects and teach managers how to implement the new corporate documentation procedures. Managers will also be provided with material to help train junior personnel in our new documentation procedures.

Creating sectional headers and footers

If you haven't inserted a section break in your document, Word places the header or footer you create on every page. (If you have specified Even/Odd headers in the Document dialog box, Word places the header or footer on all odd or on all even pages, as appropriate.)

When you separate a document into sections, you can create different headers and footers for each section as long as the sections appear on different pages. When you insert a section break, the new section initially carries a header, a footer, and Section dialog box settings identical to those of the preceding section. The header or footer is linked to the preceding header or footer, and any change you make to the header or footer of the preceding section applies to the header or footer in the new section. However, if you add a new header to the new section, the header exists only in that section and any following sections, not in the preceding section.

To change a particular section's header or footer, place the insertion point anywhere in the section, and then choose Header or Footer from the View menu. Word displays the section number in the window's title bar to indicate the section to which your changes will apply. The header window in Figure 10-11, for example, carries the notation (S4), indicating that it is the header for the fourth section of a document.

FiGURE 10-11.
The title bar of the
header window
displays the number
of that section.

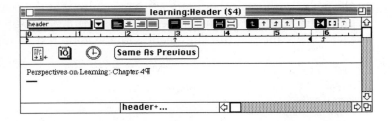

After opening a header or footer window, modify its contents as needed, and then close the window to change the text in the specified section. When you change a section's header or footer, Word applies the changes to the headers or footers in all the following sections of the document. Headers or footers that occur before the current section are unaffected. If you select two or more sections of a document and choose Header or Footer, the window displays the header or footer for the first section only.

To make global formatting changes to headers and footers, you can alter the definition of the header and footer styles in the Style dialog box. (See Chapter 9, "Creating Style Sheets," for more information about styles.)

Using the Same As Previous button

If you want a header or footer to contain the same text and formats as the header or footer in the previous section, click the Same As Previous button that appears at the top of the header or footer window. If the contents of the header or footer window are already identical to the previous section's header or footer, the Same As Previous button appears dimmed.

The Same As Previous button copies the header or footer text and formats from the previous section into the current window, establishing a link between the current header or footer and the previous section's header or footer. If the previous section contains no header or footer, Word searches toward the beginning of the document until it finds a header or footer. After this link is established, changing the contents of the first header or footer window updates the second header or footer window automatically.

Creating different first-page headers and footers

Often you'll want the first page of a document to display a different header or footer than the rest of the document or to display no header or footer at all. To change the header or footer on the first page, choose Section from the Format menu, and in the Header/Footer portion of the Section dialog box, select the Different First Page option. If your document contains more than one section, you can activate this option for any or all of the sections.

After you select the Different First Page option, two new commands appear on the View menu when you close the Section dialog box: First Header and First Footer. When you choose one of these commands, Word opens a new header or footer window with the words *First Header* or *First Footer* in the title bar. Figure 10-12 shows a sample first-page header window.

Initially, the first-page header and footer windows are blank and linked. To eliminate the header or footer on just the first page of each section, simply activate the Different First Page option. To create a new header or footer on the first page of each section, choose First Header or First Footer, and enter the new text in the header or footer window.

FIGURE 10-12.
When you select the Different First Page option in the Section dialog box, Word creates new header and footer windows for the first page.

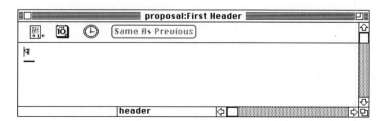

As with regular headers and footers, if you change the text or formatting in one of the first-page header or footer windows, you break the link between it and the first-page headers or footers for previous sections in the document. You also change the following section's first-page headers or footers. You can reestablish the link by clicking the Same As Previous button.

Formatting headers and footers

Because the header and footer styles are based on the Normal style, the text in a header or footer window contains the character formatting defined in the Normal style. As we explained in Chapter 9, "Creating Style Sheets," changing the definition of the Normal style automatically changes the header and footer styles. You can also format the header or footer text by altering the definition of the style named header or footer in your document's style sheet.

Even if you create different headers and footers for different sections of a document (we show you how to do this in a few pages), the header and footer styles apply to all sections of your document. Word doesn't create a separate style to format the header and footer of each new section. In some cases, this feature is an advantage. When you want sections with headers and footers with different text but the same appearance, for example, you can format them all consistently by changing the header or footer style instructions. When you want the headers and footers of each section to have different formats, however, you must use manual formatting techniques or define new styles, such as header2, header3, and so on, in your style sheet.

You can select and reformat header or footer text as you would any document text. For example, first click in the selection bar on the left side of the header window to select the entire line. Next, choose font and formatting commands from the Font and Format menus. Figure 10-13 displays the sample document with new header formatting.

You can add borders and shading, change alignment, and insert graphics to jazz up your headers and footers and help separate them from your body text. (Chapter 5, "Formatting Documents and Paragraphs," discusses adding borders and shading to selected paragraphs. Chapter 6, "Creating Graphics," describes how to create and add graphics to your document.)

FIGURE 10-13.
The header text is centered between the left and right margins.

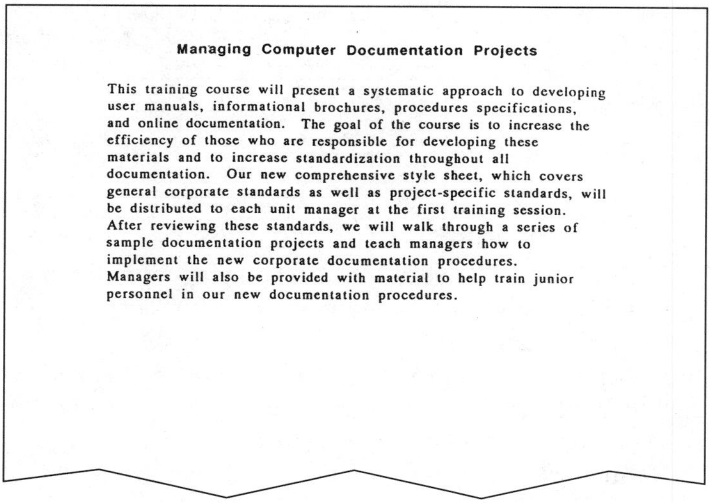

Managing Computer Documentation Projects

This training course will present a systematic approach to developing user manuals, informational brochures, procedures specifications, and online documentation. The goal of the course is to increase the efficiency of those who are responsible for developing these materials and to increase standardization throughout all documentation. Our new comprehensive style sheet, which covers general corporate standards as well as project-specific standards, will be distributed to each unit manager at the first training session. After reviewing these standards, we will walk through a series of sample documentation projects and teach managers how to implement the new corporate documentation procedures. Managers will also be provided with material to help train junior personnel in our new documentation procedures.

Positioning headers and footers

To distinguish the header or footer from document text, you can change the position of the header or footer text. In fact, Word lets you place headers and footers in the left and right margins, create multiline headers and footers, and position them anywhere on the page.

Placing headers and footers in the left and right margins

When you need the header or footer text to appear in the document margin instead of aligned with the main document text, you can use a negative indent. For example, in Figure 10-14, we've placed the header in the left margin of the page. To create this header, we used a left indent of –1.25 inches, as shown in the header window in Figure 10-15 on the next page.

FIGURE 10-14.
We placed this two-line header in the left margin.

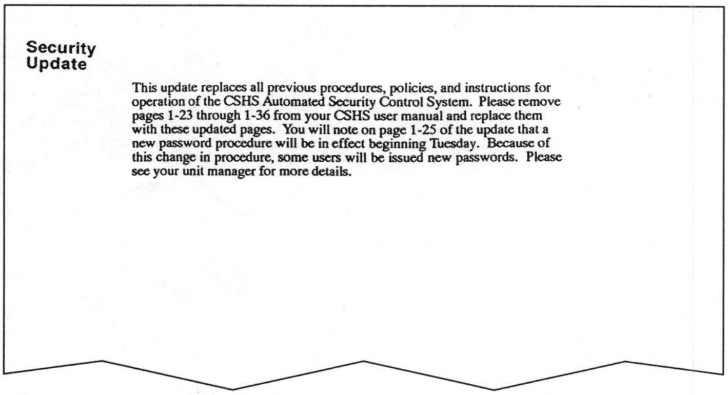

Security Update

This update replaces all previous procedures, policies, and instructions for operation of the CSHS Automated Security Control System. Please remove pages 1-23 through 1-36 from your CSHS user manual and replace them with these updated pages. You will note on page 1-25 of the update that a new password procedure will be in effect beginning Tuesday. Because of this change in procedure, some users will be issued new passwords. Please see your unit manager for more details.

FIGURE 10-15.
*We used a negative
indent to format
this header.*

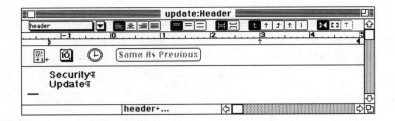

To create a negative indent, first display the ruler in the header or footer window by choosing Ruler from the View menu. Then scroll to the left, beyond the 0 mark on the ruler, and drag the first-line and left indent markers to –1.25. To place the header or footer in the right margin of the printed page, similarly drag the right indent marker to the right, and then move the first-line and left indent markers past the dotted line that marks your right margin. (For more information on changing a paragraph's left and right indents, see Chapter 5, "Formatting Documents and Paragraphs.")

Accommodating multiline headers and footers

Like any paragraph, headers and footers can contain as many lines of text as you like. In fact, if you haven't changed the default Top and Bottom Margins spacing option from At Least, Word automatically expands the top or bottom margin of a document to make room for a multiline header or footer.

In Figure 10-16, for example, the sample header contains five lines that serve as a company's letterhead. To accommodate these extra header lines, the first line of text in the document—which normally starts 1 inch from the top of the page— now appears about 1.75 inches from the top. Word maintains the default Top margin setting of At Least 1 inch in the Document dialog box to avoid overlapping the header text and the main body of the document. If you create a multiline footer using the At Least margin spacing option, Word expands the bottom margin without changing the Bottom margin setting in the Document dialog box.

FIGURE 10-16.
*Word expands the top
margin to make room
for a multiline header.*

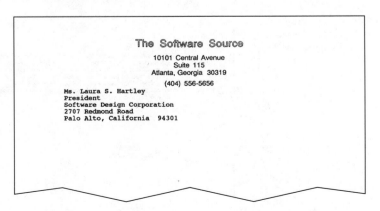

Changing the margin settings

Notice that in Figure 10-16 Word doesn't add an extra blank line between the header and the first line of the document text. You can add blank lines to a header or footer by pressing Return after the last line of header or footer text. You can add space more precisely, however, by changing the Top and Bottom margin settings in the Document dialog box.

To move the header or footer vertically on the page, change the settings in the From Top and From Bottom edit bars in the Header/Footer portion of the Section dialog box. The distance between the top of the page and the first line of a header is determined by the From Top setting, and the distance between the bottom of the page and the last line of a footer is determined by the From Bottom setting. The default value for both settings is 0.5 inch. To move the vertical location of the header or footer, simply change this value.

As the header's or footer's distance from the edge of the page increases, Word must begin or end the body text of your document closer to the middle of the page. If you change the vertical position of the header or footer, you might need to adjust the Top margin or Bottom margin settings in the Document dialog box as well. For example, specifying that the header begin 2 inches from the top of the page causes the first line of body text to appear 3 inches from the top of the page, if you don't change the default Top margin setting of 1 inch in the Document dialog box.

To add extra blank space between the last line of a header and the first line of text or between the last line of text and the first line of a footer, you can reduce the space between the header or footer and the top or bottom of the page. For example, if you change the From Top setting to 0.25, Word prints the first line of the body text 1.25 inches from the top of the page.

Although Word automatically adjusts the top or bottom margin to make room for long headers or footers, occasionally you might want to place a header or footer in the text area. To override Word's automatic top margin adjustment, simply select the Exactly spacing option next to the Top margin setting in the Document dialog box to fix the top margin. Then specify the appropriate From Top entry in the Header/Footer portion or the Section dialog box.

For example, refer to the sample header shown earlier in Figure 10-14. We assigned a –1.25-inch left indent to this header so that we could print it in the left margin of the page. To print this header in the left margin and align it with the first line of the body text, both the header and first line of text must begin 1 inch from the top of the page. To override Word's automatic top margin adjustment, first choose Document from the Format menu, and in the Document dialog box, specify a Top margin setting of 1 inch. Then select Exactly from the drop-down list box to the right of the Top margin edit bar, to prevent Word from adjusting the top margin to accommodate the header. Next, choose Section from the Format menu, and type *1* in the From Top edit bar in the Header/Footer portion of the dialog box to place the header 1 inch from the top of the page. Figure 10-17 shows the resulting printed page. As you can see, the header and body text are evenly aligned 1 inch from the top of the page.

FIGURE 10-17.
Both the header and
the main body text
now appear 1 inch
from the top of
the page.

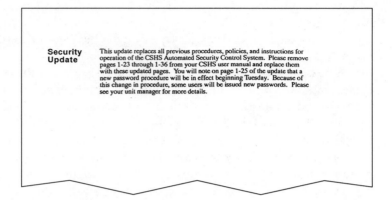

Security Update This update replaces all previous procedures, policies, and instructions for operation of the CSHS Automated Security Control System. Please remove pages 1-23 through 1-36 from your CSHS user manual and replace them with these updated pages. You will note on page 1-25 of the update that a new password procedure will be in effect beginning Tuesday. Because of this change in procedure, some users will be issued new passwords. Please see your unit manager for more details.

To change the From Top and From Bottom settings in two or more sections, simply select text in those sections, open the Section dialog box, and change the values in the From Top and From Bottom edit bars. If you change the setting without first selecting text, your changes apply only to the headers and footers of the current section, even if the headers and footers in subsequent sections are linked to this section. To be consistent from one section to the next, you might find it most efficient to select your entire document before you change the From Top and From Bottom settings.

Another way to place a header or footer in the margin is to use the Frame command. As we explain in detail at the end of this chapter, the Frame command lets you place selected text in a fixed position on the page and flows adjacent text around it.

Adding page numbers, dates, and times

The icons at the top of the header and footer windows let you insert the current page number, date, and time into header and footer text. These three elements are dynamic; whenever you open the header or footer window or print your document, Word updates the date and time from your system clock. The page number in the header or footer window reflects the number of the current page in your document window. When you print the document, each page in the document is numbered sequentially.

To insert a dynamic date, time, or page number entry into the header or footer text, place the insertion point where you want the entry to appear, and then click the corresponding icon. Figure 10-18 shows a sample header in which we've entered the time, date, and page number. When the Show ¶ command is in effect, Word displays dotted borders around the time, date, and page number to indicate they are dynamic entries. These borders don't appear when you print the document, nor do they appear if you choose Hide ¶.

FIGURE 10-18.
You can enter dynamic page numbers, dates, and times into the header or footer.

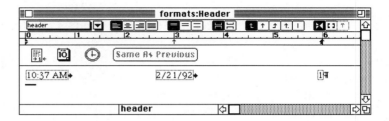

Formatting dynamic dates and times

Dynamic dates always appear in the form M/D/YY, and dynamic times always appear in the form HH:MM AM/PM. You can't change the content of dynamic date and time entries from within Word. (You can change the date and time settings in your system clock by using the General Controls control panel.)

Word treats a dynamic date or time entry as a single character and applies character formats to the entire entry. For example, you can't assign a character style, such as Bold, to only the month portion of a date.

Formatting page numbers

When you add a dynamic page number entry to the header or footer text, Word uses the numbering scheme you specified in the Section dialog box to format the numbers. For example, Figure 10-18 shows the default format. If you want uppercase Roman numerals instead, open the Section dialog box, and select the I II III option from the drop-down list box in the Page Numbers portion of the Section dialog box.

The page numbering format you select applies to the current section only. You can apply the same page numbering format to multiple sections by selecting text in each section, opening the Section dialog box, and then selecting the format you want to use.

Editing headers and footers

In general, you edit headers and footers as you would any other text in your document. The techniques for selecting, inserting, deleting, and overwriting text (introduced in Chapter 3, "Working in Word,") apply to header and footer windows as well. You can use the Cut, Copy, and Paste commands in the header and footer windows, and you can copy and move text between the header, footer, and document windows. You can also use Word's Find, Replace, Spelling, Thesaurus, and Hyphenation tools.

Copying and moving header and footer text

If you need to copy several items between your document and header or footer windows, keep in mind that the header and footer windows remain open when you click another window.

You can open only one header or footer window at a time, however. For example, if you are using odd and even headers (discussed later in this chapter) and you want to copy an item from the even header window to the odd header window, you must first open the even header window, select the text you want, and choose Copy. Then open the odd header window, and choose Paste. Similarly, if you've created a multisection document and you want to copy text from one section header to another, you must open the header windows for each section individually.

Other header and footer editing techniques

To perform a search or replace operation or to use the Hyphenation command in a header or footer window, treat the header or footer window as you would a document window. Because Word applies these commands to active windows only, be sure to open the header or footer window before you choose the command. If you are using different odd, even, or first-page headers and footers, remember to open each header or footer window in turn and perform separate find-and-replace and hyphenating procedures. In a multisection document, you'll have to click in the appropriate section of your document and then open the header or footer window for that section.

When you use the Spelling command (discussed in Chapter 7, "Editing and Proofing"), Word searches from the insertion point to the end of the main document and then checks each header and footer window, starting at the beginning of the document. Any misspelled words are displayed in the Spelling dialog box, indicating in which header or footer the unrecognized word was found. If your document contains multiple headers, the notation in the Spelling dialog box identifies the header or footer that contains the error.

Deleting headers and footers

To delete a header or footer, open its window, highlight all the text, and then press the Delete key. (You can also choose Cut from the Edit menu to delete the text.) After you've deleted the text, close the header or footer window to lock in the change you've made. Unless you change the specifications in the Section dialog box, Word retains the space for a header.

Creating columns

The Columns portion of the Section dialog box enables you to create documents with two or more columns of text on each page. This type of format, referred to as *snaking columns*, is shown in Figure 10-19. As you can see, the text in snaking columns automatically wraps, or "snakes," from the bottom of one column to the top of the next.

FIGURE 10-19.
The text in snaking columns wraps, or "snakes," from the bottom of one column to the top of the next column.

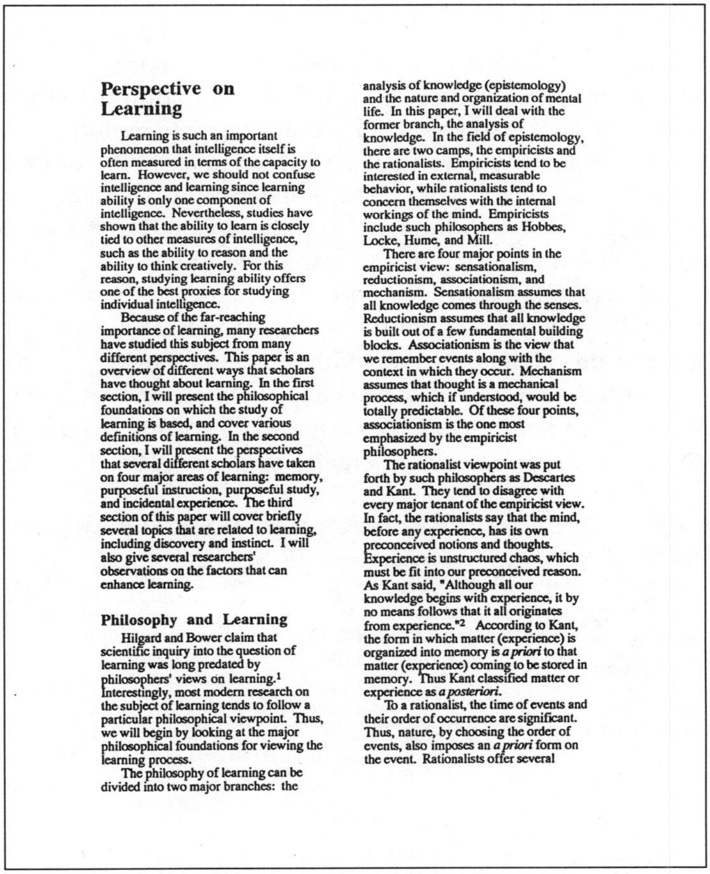

Perspective on Learning

Learning is such an important phenomenon that intelligence itself is often measured in terms of the capacity to learn. However, we should not confuse intelligence and learning since learning ability is only one component of intelligence. Nevertheless, studies have shown that the ability to learn is closely tied to other measures of intelligence, such as the ability to reason and the ability to think creatively. For this reason, studying learning ability offers one of the best proxies for studying individual intelligence.

Because of the far-reaching importance of learning, many researchers have studied this subject from many different perspectives. This paper is an overview of different ways that scholars have thought about learning. In the first section, I will present the philosophical foundations on which the study of learning is based, and cover various definitions of learning. In the second section, I will present the perspectives that several different scholars have taken on four major areas of learning: memory, purposeful instruction, purposeful study, and incidental experience. The third section of this paper will cover briefly several topics that are related to learning, including discovery and instinct. I will also give several researchers' observations on the factors that can enhance learning.

Philosophy and Learning

Hilgard and Bower claim that scientific inquiry into the question of learning was long predated by philosophers' views on learning.[1] Interestingly, most modern research on the subject of learning tends to follow a particular philosophical viewpoint. Thus, we will begin by looking at the major philosophical foundations for viewing the learning process.

The philosophy of learning can be divided into two major branches: the analysis of knowledge (epistemology) and the nature and organization of mental life. In this paper, I will deal with the former branch, the analysis of knowledge. In the field of epistemology, there are two camps, the empiricists and the rationalists. Empiricists tend to be interested in external, measurable behavior, while rationalists tend to concern themselves with the internal workings of the mind. Empiricists include such philosophers as Hobbes, Locke, Hume, and Mill.

There are four major points in the empiricist view: sensationalism, reductionism, associationism, and mechanism. Sensationalism assumes that all knowledge comes through the senses. Reductionism assumes that all knowledge is built out of a few fundamental building blocks. Associationism is the view that we remember events along with the context in which they occur. Mechanism assumes that thought is a mechanical process, which if understood, would be totally predictable. Of these four points, associationism is the one most emphasized by the empiricist philosophers.

The rationalist viewpoint was put forth by such philosophers as Descartes and Kant. They tend to disagree with every major tenant of the empiricist view. In fact, the rationalists say that the mind, before any experience, has its own preconceived notions and thoughts. Experience is unstructured chaos, which must be fit into our preconceived reason. As Kant said, "Although all our knowledge begins with experience, it by no means follows that it all originates from experience."[2] According to Kant, the form in which matter (experience) is organized into memory is *a priori* to that matter (experience) coming to be stored in memory. Thus Kant classified matter or experience as *a posteriori*.

To a rationalist, the time of events and their order of occurrence are significant. Thus, nature, by choosing the order of events, also imposes an *a priori* form on the event. Rationalists offer several

Word generally treats your document text as a single column whose boundaries are the left and right margins of the printed page. On the ribbon, the last set of buttons on the right allows you to create one, two, or three columns in a section. The Columns portion of the Section dialog box enables you to create as many as 100 columns on the pages in the current section. Because you can specify this formatting on a section-by-section basis, you can easily combine column formats within the same document—you can even combine column formats on the same page.

In this section, we show you how to create snaking columns using the column buttons on the ribbon and using the Section dialog box and how to modify the appearance of columns in your document. (You can place individual paragraphs side by side on the page by placing the text in tables or by using the Side By Side command. We discuss these options in Chapter 12, "Creating Tables.")

Using the ribbon's column buttons

The column buttons at the right end of the ribbon let you quickly format section text in one, two, or three columns. Place the insertion point in the section you want to format, and then click the appropriate button.

To create the page layout shown in Figure 10-19, for example, we used Word's default Document, Page Setup, and Section dialog box settings and simply clicked the Two-Column button on the ribbon. The default Section dialog box settings insert a half-inch space between columns.

Figure 10-20 shows how this document appears on the screen in the Normal view. As you can see, Word displays the text in a single column. This column's width is determined by the width of the document's text area, the number of columns on the page, and the distance between the columns. Word highlights the Two-Column button to indicate the active format. To see the columns as they will appear on the printed page, choose Page Layout or Print Preview.

FIGURE 10-20.
In Normal view,
the text in snaking
columns appears on
the screen as one
long column.

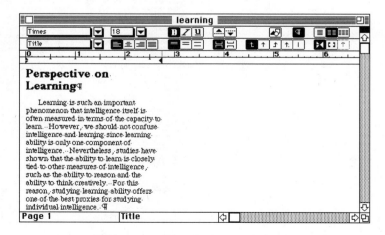

Notice that the right edge for the text column (indicated by the dotted vertical line on the ruler) now appears at the 2.75-inch position on the ruler, instead of at the 6-inch position. If you check the Document dialog box, however, you'll see that Word has not changed the default Right margin setting of 1.25. If you click the Margin Scale button on the ruler, you'll see brackets at the 1.25-inch and 4-inch positions, marking the boundaries of the first column, and at the 4.5-inch and 7.25-inch positions, marking the boundaries of the second column.

Using the Section dialog box

To create as many as 100 columns or to change the default spacing between columns, you can use the Columns portion of the Section dialog box. First place the insertion point in the appropriate section in your document, and then choose Section. In the Number edit bar of the Section dialog box, type the number of columns you want to create—up to 100. To change the default spacing between columns, enter a new value in the Spacing edit bar. To create the page shown in Figure 10-21, for example, we began with the text shown earlier in Figure 10-19. Then we chose Section, specified a Number setting of 4 and changed the Spacing setting to 0.25, as shown in Figure 10-22 on the next page.

FIGURE 10-21.
We've formatted the text in Figure 10-19 into four columns.

Perspective on Learning

Learning is such an important phenomenon that intelligence itself is often measured in terms of the capacity to learn. However, we should not confuse intelligence and learning since learning ability is only one component of intelligence. Nevertheless, studies have shown that the ability to learn is closely tied to other measures of intelligence, such as the ability to reason and the ability to think creatively. For this reason, studying learning ability offers one of the best proxies for studying individual intelligence.

Because of the far-reaching importance of learning, many researchers have studied this subject from many different perspectives. This paper is an overview of different ways that scholars have thought about learning. In the first section, I will present the philosophical foundations on which the study of learning is based, and cover various definitions of learning. In the second section, I will present the perspectives that several different scholars have taken on four major areas of learning: memory, purposeful instruction, purposeful study, and incidental experience. The third section of this paper will cover briefly several topics that are related to learning, including discovery and instinct. I will also give several researchers' observations on the factors that can enhance learning.

Philosophy and Learning

Hilgard and Bower claim that scientific inquiry into the question of learning was long predated by philosophers' views on learning.[1] Interestingly, most modern research on the subject of learning tends to follow a particular philosophical viewpoint. Thus, we will begin by looking at the major philosophical foundations for viewing the learning process.

The philosophy of learning can be divided into two major branches: the analysis of knowledge (epistemology) and the nature and organization of mental life. In this paper, I will deal with the former branch, the analysis of knowledge. In the field of epistemology, there are two camps, the empiricists and the rationalists. Empiricists tend to be interested in external, measurable behavior, while rationalists tend to concern themselves with the internal workings of the mind. Empiricists include such philosophers as Hobbes, Locke, Hume, and Mill.

There are four major points in the empiricist view: sensationalism, reductionism, associationism, and mechanism. Sensationalism assumes that all knowledge comes through the senses. Reductionism assumes that all knowledge is built out of a few fundamental building blocks.

Associationism is the view that we remember events along with the context in which they occur. Mechanism assumes that thought is a mechanical process, which if understood, would be totally predictable. Of these four points, associationism is the one most emphasized by the empiricist philosophers.

The rationalist viewpoint was put forth by such philosophers as Descartes and Kant. They tend to disagree with every major tenant of the empiricist view. In fact, the rationalists say that the mind, before any experience, has its own preconceived notions and thoughts. Experience is unstructured chaos, which must be fit into our preconceived reason. As Kant said, "Although all our knowledge begins with experience, it by no means follows that it all originates from experience."[2] According to Kant, the form in which matter (experience) is organized into

FIGURE 10-22.
Using the Number and
Spacing settings of the
Section dialog box is
one way to create
snaking columns.

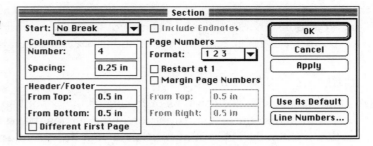

Figure 10-23 shows how this document appears on the screen in the Normal view. Notice that the default right edge of the single column displayed (indicated by the dotted vertical line on the ruler) now appears at the 1.25-inch mark, reflecting the new column size in the Section dialog box. If you click the Margin Scale button on the ruler, you'll now see four pairs of brackets, each pair marking the boundaries of one of the four columns.

FIGURE 10-23.
Word creates columns
based on the Number
and Spacing settings
in the Columns
portion of the Section
dialog box but displays
only one column in
Normal view.

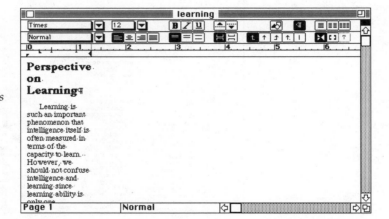

Modifying and formatting columns

With multiple columns, you can change the width of the columns in a section by adjusting the right indent marker on the ruler. By adding sections before and after the section that contains the columns, you can specify where a column ends on the page. This technique also enables you to combine column formats, create columns of equal length, and compose headings that extend across the width of the page.

Changing column width

When you create multiple columns, Word maintains the same column width for each column in the section. As a result, if you change the width of one column, Word changes the width of the other columns on the page to match. (To create columns of unequal width, use the Table command described in Chapter 12, "Creating Tables.")

To change the width of all the columns in a section, simply move the right indent marker on the ruler to the appropriate position. You cannot specify a column width that can't be accommodated within your current margin settings. Word maintains these settings and increases or decreases the space between the columns as necessary to format the columns in the new width. (You can also change column width by repositioning the brackets that mark the edges of columns on the ruler when the ruler is in margin scale.)

Controlling column breaks

Controlling column breaks is much like controlling page breaks. (For information about page breaks, see Chapter 5, "Formatting Documents and Paragraphs.") For example, the Widow Control option in the Document dialog box ensures that no single line from a paragraph appears alone at the top or bottom of a column. The Keep Lines Together option in the Paragraph dialog box prevents Word from splitting a paragraph between two columns. Similarly, the Keep With Next ¶ option in the Paragraph dialog box ensures that a paragraph appears in the same column as the paragraph that follows it. To display the correct column breaks, Word might need to repaginate your document.

When you're working with snaking columns, you can see column breaks in Page Layout view. In Normal view, Word displays only page breaks. In Page Layout view, Word also displays snaking columns side by side on the screen and shows the column boundaries with dotted lines. To see the column boundaries, choose Show ¶ from the View menu. Activating the Show Text Boundaries In Page Layout View option in the View portion of the Preferences dialog box displays column boundaries even when you've chosen Hide ¶.

Figure 10-24 on the next page shows the document from Figure 10-21 in Page Layout view. (Notice that Word has adjusted the location of the 0 mark on the ruler—in the indent scale—to show the width of the current column. The insertion point is in the second column, which causes the 0 mark to be shifted toward the right.)

FIGURE 10-24.
When you switch to
Page Layout view, you
can see columns of text
on the screen as well
as the dotted lines that
mark the column
boundaries.

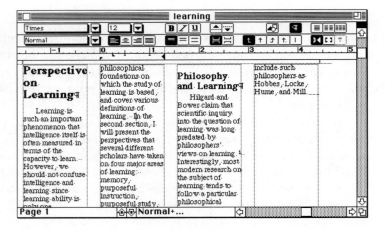

The column boundaries that you see in Page Layout view show how much space remains at the bottom of any column that does not quite fill a page. They also show you where Word has inserted blank lines in a column to control a widow, to keep two paragraphs together, or to keep all the lines of one paragraph in the same column.

Unfortunately, you can't simply insert a manual page break to move text to the next column. Word forces all the text after a manual page break to the top of the next page—not to the top of the next column. The only way to force a column break is to create a new section where you want the new column to start, open the Section dialog box, and then select New Column from the list of Start options.

For example, suppose you want the *Philosophy and Learning* heading shown earlier in Figure 10-21 to appear at the top of the third column. In the document window, first click in front of the heading, and then select Section Break from the Insert menu. Next, click below the section break marker, and choose the Section command. In the Section dialog box, select New Column from the Start drop-down list box. Figure 10-25 shows the result.

Combining column formats

Because snaking columns are controlled by the Section command, it's easy to specify several column formats on a single page. To specify a new column format, simply choose the Section Break command from the Insert menu, or press Command-Enter to create a new section. Then click in the new section, open the Section dialog box, specify the number of columns you want, and select No Break as your Start option.

FIGURE 10-25.
By creating a new section and using the New Column option, we forced a column break in this document.

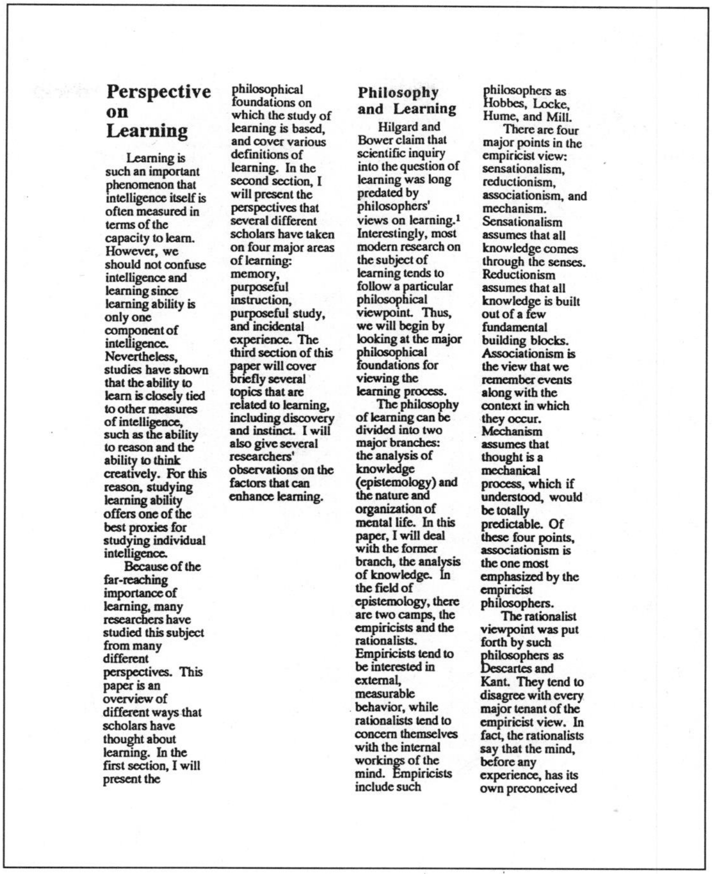

Perspective on Learning

Learning is such an important phenomenon that intelligence itself is often measured in terms of the capacity to learn. However, we should not confuse intelligence and learning since learning ability is only one component of intelligence. Nevertheless, studies have shown that the ability to learn is closely tied to other measures of intelligence, such as the ability to reason and the ability to think creatively. For this reason, studying learning ability offers one of the best proxies for studying individual intelligence.

Because of the far-reaching importance of learning, many researchers have studied this subject from many different perspectives. This paper is an overview of different ways that scholars have thought about learning. In the first section, I will present the philosophical foundations on which the study of learning is based, and cover various definitions of learning. In the second section, I will present the perspectives that several different scholars have taken on four major areas of learning: memory, purposeful instruction, purposeful study, and incidental experience. The third section of this paper will cover briefly several topics that are related to learning, including discovery and instinct. I will also give several researchers' observations on the factors that can enhance learning.

Philosophy and Learning

Hilgard and Bower claim that scientific inquiry into the question of learning was long predated by philosophers' views on learning.[1] Interestingly, most modern research on the subject of learning tends to follow a particular philosophical viewpoint. Thus, we will begin by looking at the major philosophical foundations for viewing the learning process.

The philosophy of learning can be divided into two major branches: the analysis of knowledge (epistemology) and the nature and organization of mental life. In this paper, I will deal with the former branch, the analysis of knowledge. In the field of epistemology, there are two camps, the empiricists and the rationalists. Empiricists tend to be interested in external, measurable behavior, while rationalists tend to concern themselves with the internal workings of the mind. Empiricists include such philosophers as Hobbes, Locke, Hume, and Mill.

There are four major points in the empiricist view: sensationalism, reductionism, associationism, and mechanism. Sensationalism assumes that all knowledge comes through the senses. Reductionism assumes that all knowledge is built out of a few fundamental building blocks. Associationism is the view that we remember events along with the context in which they occur. Mechanism assumes that thought is a mechanical process, which if understood, would be totally predictable. Of these four points, associationism is the one most emphasized by the empiricist philosophers.

The rationalist viewpoint was put forth by such philosophers as Descartes and Kant. They tend to disagree with every major tenet of the empiricist view. In fact, the rationalists say that the mind, before any experience, has its own preconceived

To create the sample page shown in Figure 10-26 on the next page, for example, we split a document into two sections, one section containing the introductory paragraph and the other containing the list of names, as shown in Figure 10-27, also on the next page. Then we clicked the second section, chose Section, and entered Number and Spacing settings of 2 and 0.5, respectively. We also selected No Break from the list of Start options.

FIGURE 10-26.
Word allows you to combine single-column and multicolumn layouts on the same page.

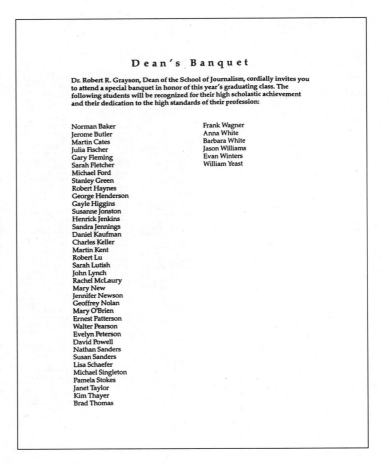

FIGURE 10-27.
To change column layouts, insert a section break, and select No Break as the section Start option.

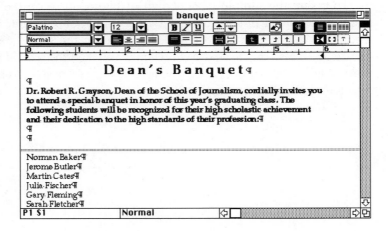

Creating columns of equal length

You can use section breaks and the No Break section Start option to align the length of columns. When a document contains multicolumn formatting and you select No Break as the Start option, Word breaks the columns at the section boundaries. As a result, the text from one section doesn't flow into the text of the next section. Word simply places the text from separate sections on the same page, wrapping the column text within each section separately from the text in other sections.

For example, in the document shown in Figure 10-26, the two columns are not balanced in length. To solve this problem, add another section break just below the last line of text in the two-column section, and select the No Break option for this third section. Word wraps the two-column text between the section breaks, as shown in Figure 10-28.

FIGURE 10-28.
We divided the document into three separate sections to create this layout.

Dean's Banquet

Dr. Robert R. Grayson, Dean of the School of Journalism, cordially invites you to attend a special banquet in honor of this year's graduating class. The following students will be recognized for their high scholastic achievement and their dedication to the high standards of their profession:

Norman Baker	Jennifer Newson
Jerome Butler	Geoffrey Nolan
Martin Cates	Mary O'Brien
Julia Fischer	Ernest Patterson
Gary Fleming	Walter Pearson
Sarah Fletcher	Evelyn Peterson
Michael Ford	David Powell
Stanley Green	Nathan Sanders
Robert Haynes	Susan Sanders
George Henderson	Lisa Schaefer
Gayle Higgins	Michael Singleton
Susanne Jonston	Pamela Stokes
Henrick Jenkins	Janet Taylor
Sandra Jennings	Kim Thayer
Daniel Kaufman	Brad Thomas
Charles Keller	Frank Wagner
Martin Kent	Anna White
Robert Lu	Barbara White
Sarah Lutish	Jason Williams
John Lynch	Evan Winters
Rachel McLaury	William Yeast
Mary New	

Creating long headings

In a newspaper-style layout, you might want to create headings that stretch across two or more columns. You might be tempted to click the heading text and drag the right indent marker to the right. If you use this method, however, the text in the second column overwrites the heading.

To get around this problem, place the heading in a separate section. First click the beginning of the first line after the heading, and insert a section break. Then click anywhere in the first section (the heading text), open the Section dialog box, and change the Number setting in the Columns portion of the dialog box to 1. Close the dialog box, and click the second section (the columns), choose Section, and select No Break in the list of Start options. When you print this document, the text in the second column starts on the same line as the text in the first column, rather than wrapping all the way back to the top of the page.

Numbering lines

Line numbers often appear in printed documents to make referencing specific items in the text easier. You can create line numbers in your printed documents by clicking the Line Numbers button in the Section dialog box. Word then displays the Line Numbers dialog box, shown in Figure 10-29, which allows you to indicate when Word should restart line numbering, the interval between printed numbers, and the distance that these numbers will appear from the text when the document is printed.

FIGURE 10-29.
Use the Line Numbers dialog box to specify line numbers in a printed document.

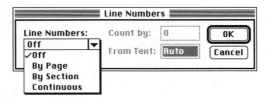

Word numbers every line of the main text, including titles, headings, and blank lines. If a paragraph's format specifies a space before or after it, however, Word doesn't assign a line number to that space. Word also doesn't number headers, footers, footnotes, tables, graphics, and side-by-side paragraphs. Line numbers appear on the screen only in Print Preview. Figure 10-30 shows part of a printed document with line numbers.

FIGURE 10-30.
Line numbers are present in the printed document but appear on the screen only in Print Preview.

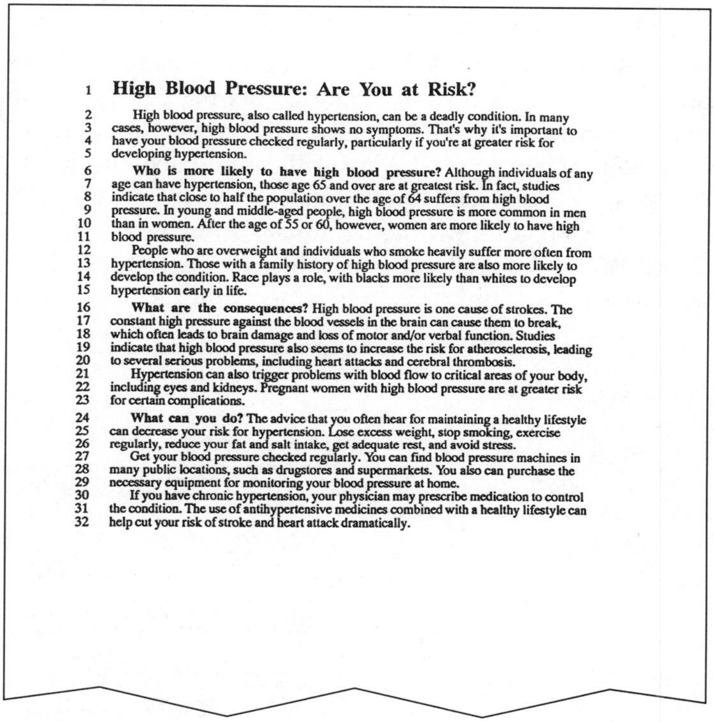

Restarting line numbers

You indicate how you want Word to number lines by selecting the appropriate option from the drop-down list box on the left side of the Line Numbers dialog box. Off is the default option; you can change the selection to By Page, By Section, or Continuous. These options apply only to the current section.

The By Page option numbers the lines on each page separately, beginning with the number 1. On a multicolumn page, Word numbers the lines in each column in sequence, and line numbering is continuous from the bottom of the first column to the top of the next column.

The By Section option numbers all the lines in each section without restarting the numbers on each new page. When you use this option, you can restart the line numbers anywhere you want simply by entering a section break. If your document contains only one section, the By Section option numbers all the lines in the document.

The Continuous option numbers lines continuously within more than one section without restarting the line count at page breaks or section breaks. For this option to work properly, however, be sure to select the Continuous option in every section of your document.

Specifying line number intervals

The Count By edit bar lets you control the line number intervals in your printed document. Word's default Count By setting of 1 prints a number next to every line, as shown in Figure 10-30. For larger intervals, enter a larger number. Whatever interval you specify, Word still counts each line; however, it prints line numbers only at the specified interval.

Figure 10-31 shows the document from Figure 10-30 after we changed the Count By value to 5. Notice that the first line number that appears in this document is 5.

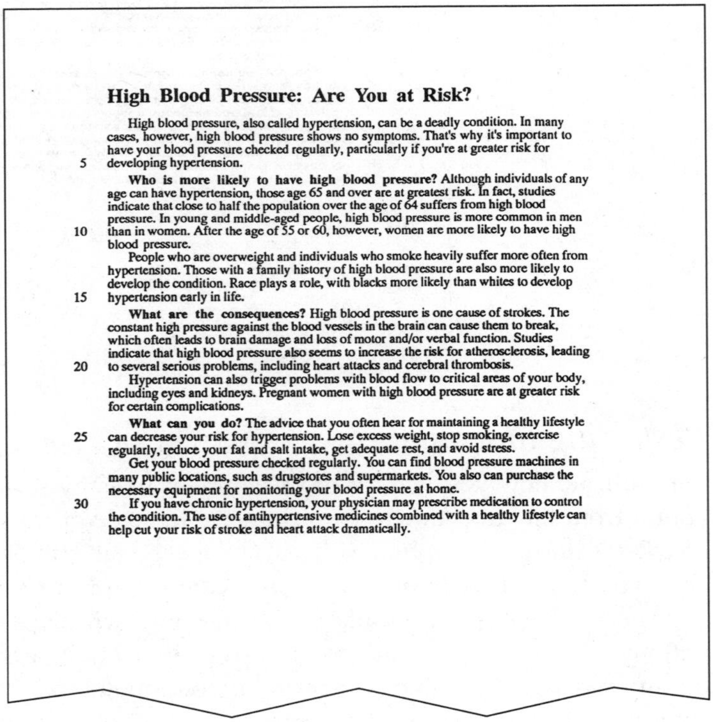

FIGURE 10-31.
By changing the Count By value to 5, you can print line numbers on every fifth line.

High Blood Pressure: Are You at Risk?

High blood pressure, also called hypertension, can be a deadly condition. In many cases, however, high blood pressure shows no symptoms. That's why it's important to have your blood pressure checked regularly, particularly if you're at greater risk for
5   developing hypertension.

Who is more likely to have high blood pressure? Although individuals of any age can have hypertension, those age 65 and over are at greatest risk. In fact, studies indicate that close to half the population over the age of 64 suffers from high blood pressure. In young and middle-aged people, high blood pressure is more common in men
10 than in women. After the age of 55 or 60, however, women are more likely to have high blood pressure.

People who are overweight and individuals who smoke heavily suffer more often from hypertension. Those with a family history of high blood pressure are also more likely to develop the condition. Race plays a role, with blacks more likely than whites to develop
15 hypertension early in life.

What are the consequences? High blood pressure is one cause of strokes. The constant high pressure against the blood vessels in the brain can cause them to break, which often leads to brain damage and loss of motor and/or verbal function. Studies indicate that high blood pressure also seems to increase the risk for atherosclerosis, leading
20 to several serious problems, including heart attacks and cerebral thrombosis.

Hypertension can also trigger problems with blood flow to critical areas of your body, including eyes and kidneys. Pregnant women with high blood pressure are at greater risk for certain complications.

What can you do? The advice that you often hear for maintaining a healthy lifestyle
25 can decrease your risk for hypertension. Lose excess weight, stop smoking, exercise regularly, reduce your fat and salt intake, get adequate rest, and avoid stress.

Get your blood pressure checked regularly. You can find blood pressure machines in many public locations, such as drugstores and supermarkets. You also can purchase the necessary equipment for monitoring your blood pressure at home.
30 If you have chronic hypertension, your physician may prescribe medication to control the condition. The use of antihypertensive medicines combined with a healthy lifestyle can help cut your risk of stroke and heart attack dramatically.

When you enter a Count By value other than 1, the results can be confusing. For example, if a document contains several sections and you select By Section, it may be hard to tell where one section ends and a new section and set of line numbers begins. In the document shown in Figure 10-32, a new section begins at the heading in the middle of the page (*Philosophy and Learning*). We've chosen to display every tenth line number, and a significant area of unnumbered lines exists around the section break. To make matters more difficult, two lines are numbered 10—one in the first section and one in the second section.

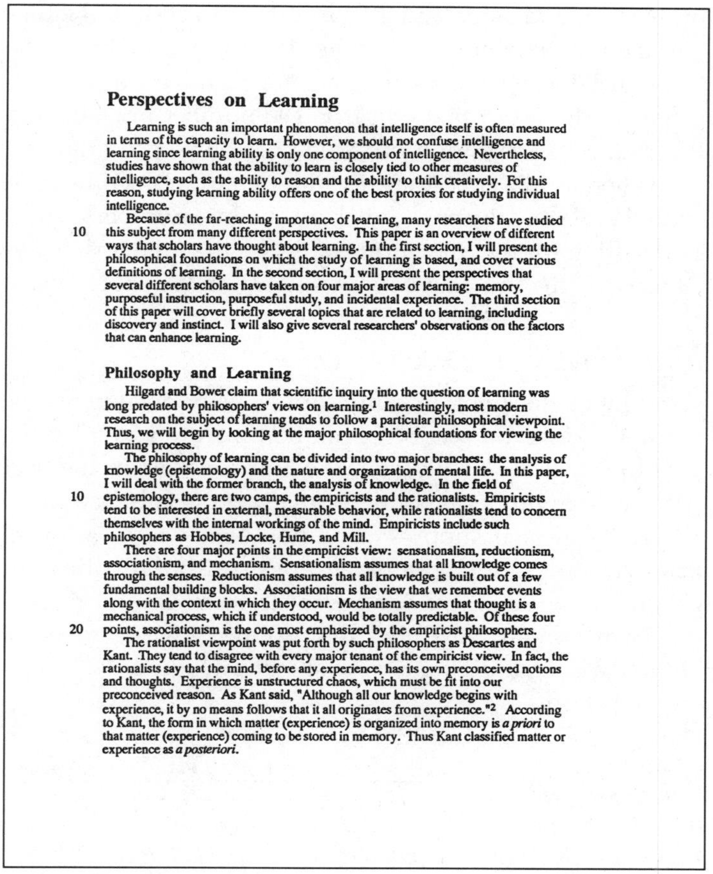

FIGURE 10-32.

If you choose not to number every line, you might find it difficult to determine whether a new set of line numbers begins at a section break.

Perspectives on Learning

Learning is such an important phenomenon that intelligence itself is often measured in terms of the capacity to learn. However, we should not confuse intelligence and learning since learning ability is only one component of intelligence. Nevertheless, studies have shown that the ability to learn is closely tied to other measures of intelligence, such as the ability to reason and the ability to think creatively. For this reason, studying learning ability offers one of the best proxies for studying individual intelligence.

10   Because of the far-reaching importance of learning, many researchers have studied this subject from many different perspectives. This paper is an overview of different ways that scholars have thought about learning. In the first section, I will present the philosophical foundations on which the study of learning is based, and cover various definitions of learning. In the second section, I will present the perspectives that several different scholars have taken on four major areas of learning: memory, purposeful instruction, purposeful study, and incidental experience. The third section of this paper will cover briefly several topics that are related to learning, including discovery and instinct. I will also give several researchers' observations on the factors that can enhance learning.

Philosophy and Learning

Hilgard and Bower claim that scientific inquiry into the question of learning was long predated by philosophers' views on learning.[1] Interestingly, most modern research on the subject of learning tends to follow a particular philosophical viewpoint. Thus, we will begin by looking at the major philosophical foundations for viewing the learning process.

The philosophy of learning can be divided into two major branches: the analysis of knowledge (epistemology) and the nature and organization of mental life. In this paper, I will deal with the former branch, the analysis of knowledge. In the field of

10   epistemology, there are two camps, the empiricists and the rationalists. Empiricists tend to be interested in external, measurable behavior, while rationalists tend to concern themselves with the internal workings of the mind. Empiricists include such philosophers as Hobbes, Locke, Hume, and Mill.

There are four major points in the empiricist view: sensationalism, reductionism, associationism, and mechanism. Sensationalism assumes that all knowledge comes through the senses. Reductionism assumes that all knowledge is built out of a few fundamental building blocks. Associationism is the view that we remember events along with the context in which they occur. Mechanism assumes that thought is a mechanical process, which if understood, would be totally predictable. Of these four

20   points, associationism is the one most emphasized by the empiricist philosophers.

The rationalist viewpoint was put forth by such philosophers as Descartes and Kant. They tend to disagree with every major tenant of the empiricist view. In fact, the rationalists say that the mind, before any experience, has its own preconceived notions and thoughts. Experience is unstructured chaos, which must be fit into our preconceived reason. As Kant said, "Although all our knowledge begins with experience, it by no means follows that it all originates from experience."[2] According to Kant, the form in which matter (experience) is organized into memory is *a priori* to that matter (experience) coming to be stored in memory. Thus Kant classified matter or experience as *a posteriori*.

Specifying line number position

Word's default position for line numbers is 0.25 inch to the left of single columns of text and 0.13 inch to the left of multiple columns. To change this position, enter a number in the From Text edit bar of the Line Numbers dialog box. For example, to position line numbers 0.5 inch from the left edge of your text, enter *.5* in the From Text edit bar.

When positioning line numbers, Word uses the Left margin setting in the Document dialog box. If you moved the indent markers on the ruler, Word doesn't recognize their settings when it positions line numbers. For example, suppose that your Left margin setting is 1.25 (Word's default) and that you've formatted every paragraph in your document by moving the first-line and left indent markers to the 1-inch position, for a total margin of 2.25 inches. If you activate line numbering and enter .5 in the From Text edit bar of the Line Numbers dialog box, the line numbers print 1.75 inches from the left edge of the page, not 2.75 inches.

Word doesn't allow you to enter a negative value or any value greater than 8.5 inches in the From Text edit bar. The number must be less than the width of the Left margin setting, or Word won't be able to print the line numbers on the page.

When numbering lines in a multicolumn document, be sure to allow enough space between columns to display the line numbers. Also be sure that the From Text setting for the line numbers is less than the Spacing setting for the columns. Otherwise, the line numbers will not fit in the space between the columns.

Numbering lines selectively

To number the lines in only part of your document—several paragraphs, for example—insert a section break both before and after the appropriate text. (Be sure to select No Break from the Start options in the Section dialog box.) Then specify line numbering only for the appropriate section.

You can also suppress line numbers within selected paragraphs, such as titles, headings, or empty paragraphs. To suppress line numbers, select the paragraph whose lines you don't want to number, and then choose Paragraph from the Format menu. Next, click the Suppress Line Numbers check box at the bottom of the Paragraph dialog box, as shown in Figure 10-33, and then click OK to close the dialog box.

FIGURE 10-33.
You can suppress line numbering in a selected paragraph by clicking the Suppress Line Numbers check box in the Paragraph dialog box.

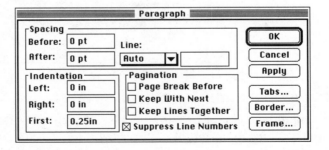

Numbering paragraphs

You can number paragraphs by choosing Renumber from the Tools menu. Word numbers only the paragraphs that contain text. When numbering paragraphs, Word doesn't recognize section breaks. If you choose the Renumber command without first selecting text, Word assigns a number to every paragraph in your document. If you select text from one or more paragraphs before you choose the Renumber command, Word assigns numbers only to the selected paragraphs.

Automatic paragraph numbering is particularly useful in documents with multiple levels of paragraphs, such as legal documents or outlines. Word lets you control the numbering format of each level. For example, first-level paragraphs might be numbered *1., 2., 3.*, and so on, while second-level paragraphs are numbered *1-A., 1-B., 1-C.*, and so on.

If you change your mind, you can click the Remove button in the Renumber dialog box to remove automatic or manual paragraph numbering.

Using the Renumber dialog box

To number the paragraphs in a document, choose Renumber from the Tools menu to display the Renumber dialog box, shown in Figure 10-34. To place an Arabic numeral beginning with 1 followed by a period (*1., 2., 3.*, and so on) at the beginning of each paragraph, simply click OK in this dialog box. Figure 10-35 shows the beginning of a document to which we've added default paragraph numbers.

FIGURE 10-34.
The Renumber dialog box lets you number paragraphs.

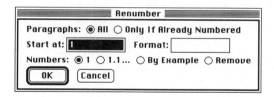

FIGURE 10-35.
Word's default numbering scheme places an Arabic numeral followed by a period at the beginning of each paragraph.

The Renumber command aligns each paragraph number with the first-line indent marker on the ruler. Word also inserts a tab character, moving the first character of text to the first tab stop after the first-line indent. In the current example, the first-line indent marker for each paragraph is located at the quarter-inch mark. Because we haven't changed Word's default tab stops, each paragraph's first character is aligned with the default tab stop that occurs at the ruler's half-inch mark. As a result, each paragraph is indented a quarter inch.

You can easily change the alignment of paragraph numbers and text in your document by changing the tab to a space and by manipulating the indent markers and tab stops.

Choosing a numbering scheme

Word's default numbering scheme for paragraphs uses Arabic numerals. To use Roman numerals or alphabetic characters instead, specify your preference in the Renumber dialog box. Simply enter the character type in the Format edit bar.

The first time you choose the Renumber command, the Format edit bar is blank. After you've numbered the first paragraph, however, the Format edit bar displays the numbering format of the first paragraph in your document or selection. To change the format, simply replace the characters in the Format edit bar. Type any Arabic numeral to specify an Arabic numbering scheme, and enter any letter (except *I*, *V*, or *X*) to indicate an alphabetic numbering scheme. Enter almost any Roman numeral to specify a Roman numeral numbering format. If you type a high Roman numeral that's only a single character, however—such as *L*, *C*, or *M*—Word interprets the entry as an alphabetic character. If you type a high Roman numeral that is made up of two or more characters—such as LIX or CM—Word interprets the entry as a Roman numeral. If you select an alphabetic or Roman numbering format, the case you use for the entry in the Format edit bar determines the case of the numbers in your document. For example, to use a lowercase alphabetic format, enter a lowercase letter—such as *c*—in the Format edit bar.

Choosing the separator characters

In addition to setting the paragraph number one tab space from the beginning of the paragraph, Word allows you to place a punctuation mark after a paragraph number. In Figure 10-35, you can see that Word has inserted its default separator character, a period, after each paragraph number. If you want to use a different separator character, enter that character following the number or letter in the Format edit bar.

You can enter any of the punctuation marks shown in Table 10-1 after a number in the Format edit bar. For example, to use a right parenthesis as the separator character and with lowercase Roman numerals as the format, enter *i)* in the Format edit bar.

You can also place a single separator character both before and after each paragraph number. For example, to enclose lowercase Roman numerals in parentheses, enter *(i)* in the Format edit bar.

Word won't accept a separator character before the number without a character after the number. For example, *-1-* and *(i)* are valid entries but *(1* is not. Word also doesn't allow more than one separator character on either side of the number.

Symbol	Name	Symbol	Name
,	Comma	-	Hyphen
:	Colon	;	Semicolon
/	Forward slash	()	Left and right parentheses
[]	Left and right brackets	{}	Left and right braces

TABLE 10-1.
You can specify any of these characters as separators in the Renumber dialog box.

If you type two separator characters before the number in the Format edit bar, such as *((1*, Word beeps and displays the message *Invalid number.* If you type two or more separator characters after the number, such as *1))*, Word ignores all separator characters after the first one.

When you're numbering multiple levels of paragraphs, Word also allows you to use a different separator character between each level number. We'll discuss the format of multiple-level paragraph numbers later in this chapter.

Specifying a start number

The Renumber command numbers each paragraph in sequence, starting with 1, A, or I, but you can use a different starting number. For example, if the first paragraph in the selection should be numbered 14, enter *14* in the Start At edit bar. Word then numbers the second paragraph 15, the third paragraph 16, and so on. If the first paragraph has already been assigned a number, Word displays that number in the Start At edit bar. Simply replace Word's suggestion if it's not correct.

You don't have to match a Start At edit bar entry to the format you've chosen for your numbering scheme. Suppose you want to use an alphabetic format beginning with the letter *d*. When you open the Renumber dialog box, type *a.* in the Format edit bar to specify an alphabetic numbering scheme, and enter either *d.* or *4.* in the Start At edit bar (because *d* is the fourth letter of the alphabet).

Formatting paragraph numbers

Word formats paragraph numbers to match the character formatting of the first character in each paragraph. This automatic formatting can be especially helpful in documents in which you've used character formatting to distinguish different kinds of topics. For example, Figure 10-36 on the next page shows a document after we've chosen the Renumber command. Notice that some of the numbers appear in New York Bold, and others appear in Helvetica Italic.

FIGURE 10-36.
*This document
contains paragraph
numbers with
different character
formatting.*

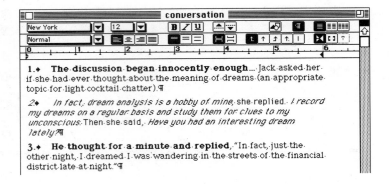

After you've numbered your paragraphs, you can change the format of the paragraph numbers. Word maintains the formatting changes you make, even if you reapply the Renumber command.

Aligning numbers and text

To change the amount of space between a paragraph number and the first character of paragraph text, simply place a tab at the appropriate place on the ruler. For example, Figure 10-37 shows some numbered paragraphs in which each number is aligned at the 0 position on the ruler, and the first character of text in each paragraph is aligned with the half-inch position on the ruler.

FIGURE 10-37.
*In these paragraphs,
the numbers are
aligned at the 0
position on the ruler,
and the first character
of text in each
paragraph is aligned at
the half-inch position.*

To indent the first character of text by an additional 0.25 inch, simply select the paragraphs, click the Left Tab button, and click the 0.75-inch position on the ruler. Figure 10-38 shows the result.

FIGURE 10-38.
*By inserting a tab,
you can change the
alignment of the first
line of paragraph text.*

By moving the left indent marker, you can change the alignment of subsequent lines in a paragraph in relation to the first line. Using this technique, you can "hang" paragraph numbers outside the paragraph text. Figure 10-39 shows the paragraphs from Figure 10-38 after we moved the left indent marker to the 0.5-inch position on the ruler.

FIGURE 10-39.
*By moving the left
indent marker, you
can create "hanging"
paragraph numbers.*

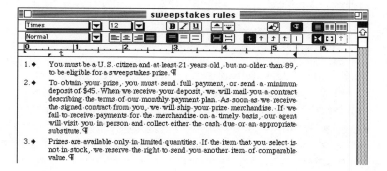

Notice in Figure 10-39 that the first line in each paragraph is aligned not with the tab stop at the 0.75-inch position, but with the left indent marker at the 0.5-inch position. In deciding where to align the first line of text, Word looks for the first "stopping place" on the ruler after the first-line indent. The first stopping place often occurs at a tab. However, you can create a stopping place before a tab, as we've done in Figure 10-39, by moving the left indent marker to the right of the first-line indent marker. In that case, Word aligns the first character of text with the left indent marker.

Moving the left indent marker to the left of the first-line indent marker indents the paragraph numbers. In Figure 10-40 on the next page, we've moved the left indent marker to the 0.5-inch position on the ruler.

FIGURE 10-40.
By moving the left indent marker to the left of the first-line indent marker, you can indent paragraph numbers.

To change the position of existing paragraph numbers, simply select paragraphs you want to adjust before you move the indent markers or insert tab stops. You can change the alignment of all the paragraphs in a document by selecting the entire document before you make your ruler changes, or you can alter the paragraph style in the document's style sheet. For information on how to use named styles to format paragraphs, see Chapter 9, "Creating Style Sheets."

Numbering selectively

When you number paragraphs, you might want to exclude certain paragraphs, such as the title, subheadings, figure captions, and so on. Although there's no automatic way to exclude selected paragraphs from the Renumber command, you can use the following techniques to achieve selective paragraph numbering.

One technique is to number a few paragraphs at a time, selecting only the paragraphs to which you want to assign numbers. As you number each subsequent group of paragraphs, be sure to enter the correct number in the Start At edit bar. Otherwise, the paragraph numbers won't appear in sequence.

Another technique is to number all the paragraphs in your document and then manually remove each unwanted number. Next, choose the Renumber command, and select the Only If Already Numbered option at the top of the Renumber dialog box. When you click OK, Word ignores paragraphs that don't already have numbers and places the remaining paragraph numbers in sequence.

Finally, you can assign the Hidden format to the paragraphs you don't want to number, hide these paragraphs, choose the Renumber command, and then redisplay the hidden paragraphs. When you assign the Hidden format to a paragraph and then deactivate the Show Hidden Text option in the View portion of the Preferences dialog box, the paragraph doesn't appear in the document window. As a result, Word doesn't number the paragraph when you choose Renumber. To display the hidden paragraph after numbering the visible paragraphs, reactivate the Show Hidden Text option in the Preferences dialog box. Then select the paragraphs again, and remove the Hidden format. (You can use the Replace command to find and replace this format quickly.)

Numbering blank paragraphs

When you number the paragraphs in a document, Word skips over any paragraph that doesn't contain text. To number these blank paragraphs in your document, use the Replace command to replace the paragraph symbol that defines the blank paragraph with a unique text string and paragraph symbol, and then choose the Renumber command. After Word has numbered each paragraph in sequence, simply use the Replace command again to replace the text string you used with a single paragraph symbol.

For example, to temporarily replace the empty paragraphs in a document with text, first choose Replace, and then type *^p^p* in the Find What edit bar, or select Paragraph twice from the Special drop-down list box. (Remember, paragraphs that contain text end with a paragraph symbol. To change only the empty paragraphs, you need to search for occurrences of two paragraph symbols in a row—^p^p.) Next, in the Replace With edit bar, type *^p@@^p* or something similar. When you choose Replace All, Word in effect "inserts" the text string you've specified between any occurrence of two paragraph symbols in your document.

After numbering the paragraphs in your document, reopen the Replace dialog box, and type @@*^p* in the Find What edit bar to identify the text in the paragraphs that you now want to delete. Then type *^p* in the Replace With edit bar, and click Replace All. Word deletes the specified text string, leaving only the paragraph number, a tab, and the paragraph symbol in the formerly blank paragraphs.

Removing paragraph numbers

Immediately after you choose the Renumber command and click OK, you can undo the numbering operation by choosing Undo Renumber from the Edit menu. If you choose Undo Renumber after renumbering a document for the first time, Word deletes all the paragraph numbers. If you used the Renumber command to update paragraph numbers, choosing Undo cancels only the latest changes.

You can remove paragraph numbers and the tab space that follows them by selecting the Remove option in the Renumber dialog box. If you don't select any text before selecting this option, Word removes every paragraph number in your document, even those you've created manually. If you want to remove the numbers from only some of the paragraphs, select those paragraphs before you choose Renumber and click the Remove option.

Numbering multiple levels of paragraphs

Paragraph numbering is particularly useful in documents that contain multiple levels of paragraphs, such as legal documents or teaching materials. Word can recognize different paragraph levels and assign a different numbering scheme—

and different separator characters—to each level. In Figure 10-41, we've specified two numbering schemes for the three levels of paragraphs. The first level uses Arabic numerals, the second level uses uppercase alphabetic characters, and the third level returns to Arabic numerals.

FIGURE 10-41.
Word can assign different numbering schemes to different paragraph levels.

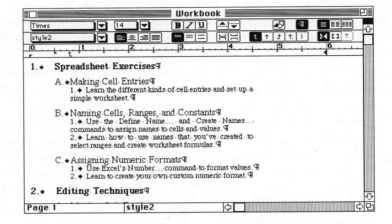

Word distinguishes the different levels of paragraphs in a document by noting the amount of indentation on the first line of each paragraph. The farther right a paragraph is indented, the more subordinate its level. As a result, the paragraph numbering assumes the look of outlining, as shown in Figure 10-41.

For example, suppose that the first lines of some paragraphs in a document are not indented. In other paragraphs, first lines are indented a quarter inch. When you choose the Renumber command, Word recognizes two levels of paragraphs in this document. All the paragraphs with no first-line indentation are considered first-level paragraphs and are numbered sequentially. The paragraphs with the quarter-inch first-line indentation are considered second-level paragraphs and are also numbered sequentially. When Word encounters a first-level paragraph, it knows to start the next set of second-level paragraphs with 1.

For Word to be able to differentiate paragraph levels, a paragraph's indentation must be created with the first-line indent marker on the ruler—not with tabs or spaces. Moving the first-line indent marker doesn't change the number applied to the corresponding paragraph until you choose the Renumber command again. Word then recognizes the new indentations and changes the paragraph numbering accordingly.

Because even a small difference in indentation (1/16 inch) can signal a new level, we recommend that you use the document's style sheet to format paragraph levels. That way, you can be sure that every paragraph at the same level has the same first-line indentation.

In addition to indentation, Word can use an outline created in Outline view to distinguish various paragraph levels. We discuss outlining in detail in Chapter 14, "Outlining."

Specifying a numbering scheme for each level

As shown in Figure 10-41, you can use a different numbering scheme for each paragraph level in a document. Simply enter the formats for each paragraph level in sequence in the Format edit bar. For example, suppose your document contains three levels of paragraphs for which you want to use a nonstandard outline numbering scheme. Figure 10-42 shows the entry you might make in the Format edit bar of the Renumber dialog box to specify this kind of paragraph numbering. Figure 10-43 shows the resulting document.

FIGURE 10-42.
In the Format edit bar, enter the format you want to use to number each paragraph level in your document.

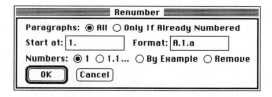

FIGURE 10-43.
This document shows the effects of the entries we made in the Format edit bar in Figure 10-42.

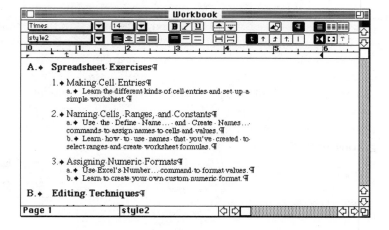

Word uses Arabic numerals to number the paragraph levels for which no format is specified. For example, suppose you're numbering a document with three paragraph levels, but you specify only one numbering format in the Format edit bar, a Roman numeral. Word uses Roman numerals to number the first-level paragraphs but uses the default Arabic numerals to number the second-level and third-level paragraphs.

If you've previously numbered the paragraphs at a subordinate level, you don't have to specify a numbering format when you next choose the Renumber command. The numbering format already applied to these paragraphs overrides Word's default; Word doesn't automatically convert the numbers of previously numbered paragraphs to the default Arabic numerals.

Using different separator characters at each level

When you type formats in the Format edit bar, you must use the same separator character for all paragraph levels. In other words, you must enter something like *I)A)1)a)* or *-I-A-1-a-*. If you specify different separator characters for different levels, the results are unpredictable. In most cases, Word selects one of the separator characters you enter and uses it for all paragraph levels, rather than using a different separator character for each level.

To use a different separator character for each paragraph level, you must first insert examples at the appropriate paragraph levels in your document. You then tell Word to renumber based on your example.

Suppose you want to number paragraphs using a standard outline numbering scheme (I., A., 1., a.) but with a variety of separator characters: a period after the first-level Roman numerals, a right parenthesis after the second-level uppercase alphabetic characters, a period after the third level of Arabic numerals, and another right parenthesis after the fourth level of lowercase alphabetic characters. First choose the Renumber command, enter *I.A.1.a.* in the Format edit bar, click the 1 Numbers option, and click OK. When Word has numbered your paragraphs, as shown in Figure 10-44, select the first "number" at each level, and insert the appropriate separator character. For example, select the first second-level *A.* in line 2 and, replace it with *A)*. Then select the first fourth-level *a.* in line 13, and replace it with *a)*. After you've created one "example" paragraph number at each level, your screen looks like Figure 10-45.

FIGURE 10-44.
We used the I.A.1.a. numbering scheme to number these paragraphs.

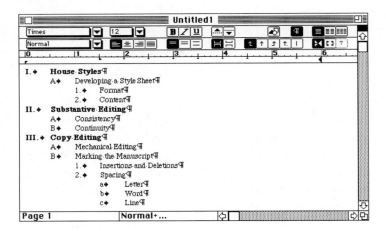

FIGURE 10-45.
We added our own separator characters to the first "number" at the second and fourth levels.

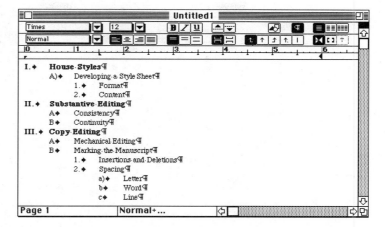

Next, choose the Renumber command, and delete the contents of the Format edit bar. Select the By Example option, and then click OK. The results look like Figure 10-46.

FIGURE 10-46.
Choosing the Renumber command and selecting the By Example option renumbers the paragraphs using the sample formats at each level.

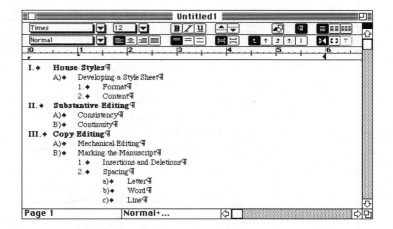

Displaying the number of superior levels

The 1.1 Numbers option in the Renumber dialog box allows you to include the numbers of all superior paragraph levels in your paragraph numbers. For example, going back to Figure 10-43, if you open the Renumber dialog box and click the 1.1. option, the result looks like Figure 10-47 on the next page. For each paragraph level, Word displays the number of all superior levels. When you display superior levels, you can use the method described earlier to specify a variety of separator characters between the level numbers—for example, *I.A)1.a)*.

FIGURE 10-47.
*When you click the
1.1 Numbers option in
the Renumber dialog
box, Word displays
the numbers of all
superior levels in each
paragraph's number.*

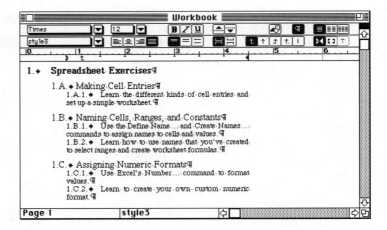

If you want the numbers for only some of the paragraphs to include their superior levels, use the By Example option in the Renumber dialog box to control the display of superior level numbers on a level-by-level basis.

For example, suppose you want to display the numbers of superior levels only for second-level paragraphs in the document shown in Figure 10-47. Begin by displaying the numbers of superior levels for all the paragraphs. Edit the numbers in the first paragraphs at all other levels so that they no longer display the superior levels. In the example, you must edit the number for the first third-level paragraph (which begins *Learn the different kinds*).

After editing the paragraph number, choose Renumber, and click By Example. When you click OK, Word changes the paragraph numbers to match the format of the first paragraph number at that level. Figure 10-48 shows the sample document with the numbers of superior levels displayed only for second-level paragraphs.

FIGURE 10-48.
*In this document,
only the second-level
paragraph numbers
display the numbers of
superior levels.*

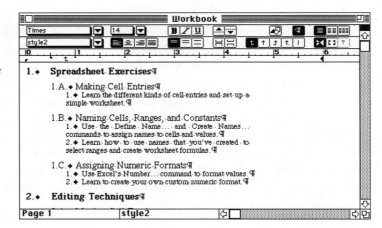

Specifying a Start At number

When you're working with a document that contains multiple paragraph levels, specifying a Start At number can be a bit tricky. The number you enter in the Start At edit bar must include the numbers of all superior paragraph levels, but it must not include the numbers of subordinate levels. For example, Figure 10-49 shows a document with three paragraph levels that are numbered with a standard outline numbering scheme. A new second-level topic (*Artificial Intelligence Issues*) and a couple of third-level topics have been inserted between second-level paragraphs A (*Software Issues*) and B (*Hardware Issues*).

FIGURE 10-49.
We inserted some new paragraphs in this three-level document.

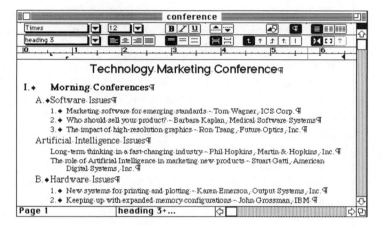

To renumber this document, first select all the text beginning with the new second-level paragraph. Then open the Renumber dialog box, and enter *I.A.1.* in the Format edit bar. In the Start At edit bar, enter *I.B* or *1.2*, and then click the 1 Numbers option. Also, be sure that the All option is activated at the top of the dialog box. Then click OK. Figure 10-50 shows the result.

FIGURE 10-50.
The document in Figure 10-49 has been renumbered.

Linking documents with the File Series command

With sufficient computer memory, you can create Word documents as long as 16 million characters (3,000 pages or more). However, you'll probably find that files longer than about 50 pages become slow to work with and difficult to handle, depending on your Macintosh configuration and the complexity of the document.

Word lets you divide long documents into several separate documents that can be linked through the Document dialog box. You can print the linked documents consecutively with a single index and table of contents, and even with consecutively numbered footnotes. (We show you how to link tables of contents, indexes, and footnotes in Chapter 11, "Adding a Table of Contents, an Index, and Footnotes.") Linking documents is also helpful when you want to mix a variety of document files for printing.

The File Series button in the Document dialog box makes it easy for you to link several documents into a larger, more complex document. Suppose, for example, that you've created a series of documents called Chapter 1, Chapter 2, and Chapter 3. Chapter 1 is 85 pages long, Chapter 2 is 97 pages long, and Chapter 3 is 68 pages long. To link these documents, first open the Chapter 1 document and choose Document from the Format menu. Next, click the File Series button in the Document dialog box. Word presents the File Series dialog box, shown in Figure 10-51, which lets you specify the page number and the line number with which the next file in the series begins.

FIGURE 10-51.
*In the File Series
dialog box, you can
specify both the
page number and the
line number with
which the next file in
the series begins.*

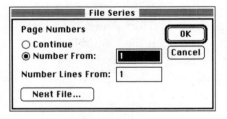

The default page number selection is Number From, which numbers pages in each file from 1, or any number you specify. Select Continue to consecutively number pages in a file series. To number the pages in Chapter 1 and Chapter 2 consecutively, for example, select Continue and click OK. Word automatically begins numbering pages in Chapter 2 with page 86. If you want to specify a beginning line number for the next document, complete the Number Lines From edit bar.

After you've defined the page and line numbers for the first file, click the Next File button. Word presents the Open dialog box. Select the name of the file you want to print after Chapter 1 (Chapter 2 in this example), and click Open. Word then displays that filename at the bottom of the File Series dialog box. Word also labels the Next File button Reset Next File; if you click this button again, Word resets the current Next File selection.

After choosing Chapter 2 as the Next File for Chapter 1, click OK, and then save and close the Chapter 1 file. Next, open the Chapter 2 file, choose Document, click the File Series button, and select the Continue option. Then click Next File, select Chapter 3 in the Open dialog box, and click the Open button. When the Chapter 3 filename appears at the bottom of the File Series dialog box, click OK to close the dialog box. Finally, click OK again to close the Document dialog box, and then save and close Chapter 2. You don't have to enter File Series settings for Chapter 3, because it is the last document in the series. Word numbers the pages in Chapter 3 beginning with 183, the number that immediately follows the last page in Chapter 2.

Now when you print Chapter 1, Word also prints Chapters 2 and 3. In fact, Chapters 2 and 3 don't even have to be open; Word automatically retrieves these files. Similarly, because Chapters 2 and 3 are now linked, Word automatically prints Chapter 3 if you choose Print from within Chapter 2.

Printing selected pages

When you link a series of documents for printing, you can use the Pages From and Pages To options in the Print dialog box to print any series of pages. If you've numbered the pages in each document sequentially, type the From and To values you want in the Print dialog box. In the previous example, if you choose Print from within Chapter 1 and enter a From setting of *80* and a To setting of *110*, Word prints the last six pages of Chapter 1 and the first 25 pages of Chapter 2—the pages that are numbered 80 through 110.

If you haven't chosen the Continue option in the File Series dialog box, you might get some unexpected results when you use the From and To settings to print linked documents. Word will keep printing linked documents until it finds a document that contains at least as many pages as you have specified in the To edit bar.

If the To setting that you specify is less than the number of pages in the first document in the series, Word prints pages from that document only. However, if the To setting is greater than the number of pages in the first document of the series, Word begins printing again with the second linked document. If the second document contains fewer pages than you've specified in the To edit bar, Word continues printing with the third document, and so on.

Using the same example, suppose that Chapters 1 and 2 contain 85 and 97 pages, respectively, but have not used sequential page numbering. When you choose Print from within Chapter 1 and type a From setting of *1* and a To setting of *90*, Word prints both pages 1 through 85 of Chapter 1, and pages 1 through 90 of Chapter 2.

Other Page Setup and Document options

When you print linked documents, Word remembers most of each document's Page Setup and Document dialog box options. As a result, you can specify different Paper and Margins settings for each document. Word also remembers each document's Orientation settings. You'll probably want these settings to be consistent from one document to the next, but the ability to use different formatting options for each document may come in handy on occasion.

If you're using headers, footers, or page numbers in your linked documents, keep in mind that you must create and format these items separately for each document in your linked series. In addition, you must specify all Section dialog box settings for every document in the series—even if you plan to use the same Section settings for all the documents.

Formatting left and right pages

If you plan to print on both sides of each sheet of paper and then bind your document, Word can create different left and right page layouts. This type of page layout is sometimes referred to as *facing pages* or *mirror margins* because the left and right margins of facing pages mirror each other. When you select left and right page layouts, Word follows publishing convention and automatically places even pages on the left and odd pages on the right.

You can create a document with different left and right page layouts in two ways. Instead of the conventional left and right margin measurements, you can specify an inside margin that appears on the binding edge of each sheet of paper, and an outside margin that appears opposite the binding edge. On every even-numbered page, the right side of the page is the binding edge and the inside margin. On every odd-numbered page, the left side of the page is the binding edge and the inside margin. Generally, you make the inside margin larger than the outside margin to allow room for binding.

A second approach to creating left and right page layouts uses standard left and right margin settings but adds a page gutter to allow room for binding. Word always adds the gutter to the binding edge of the page. On even-numbered pages, the gutter appears on the right edge, and on odd-numbered pages the gutter appears on the left edge.

You can also specify inside and outside margins and a page gutter, with the binding edge consisting of the inside margin measurement plus the page gutter measurement.

The key to setting up different left and right page layouts is the Document dialog box. When you choose Document from the Format menu, you'll see the Mirror Even/Odd check box in the Margins portion of the Document dialog box, the Even/Odd Headers check box, and the Gutter edit bar.

Use the Mirror Even/Odd option when you want to establish inside and outside margins on the pages of your document. After you select this option, Word changes the labels on the Left and Right margin edit bars to Inside and Outside.

For example, to create a document with margins that are 1.25 inches wide, with an additional 0.5 inch for binding, begin by activating the Mirror Even/Odd option in the Document dialog box. Then specify an Inside setting of 1.75 and an Outside setting of 1.25. Figure 10-52 shows a Document dialog box in which we've made these settings.

FIGURE 10-52.
When you select the Mirror Even/Odd option in the Document dialog box, the Left and Right margin edit bars change to Inside and Outside.

When you print this document, page 1 will have a left margin of 1.75 inches and a right margin of 1.25 inches. On page 2, these margins will be reversed: The left margin will be 1.25 inches, and the right margin will be 1.75 inches.

Another way to set up this same page layout is to use Word's default Left and Right margin settings of 1.25 and then enter .5 in the Gutter edit bar. The effect is the same: Word adds a half inch of gutter space to the right edge of all even-numbered pages and to the left edge of all odd-numbered pages. (You don't need to activate Mirror Even/Odd to specify a gutter.)

When you specify a Gutter setting, Word displays the gutter as a shaded area in the Print Preview window, as shown in Figure 10-53 on the next page. We've clicked the Margins icon to display the column boundaries. However, the gutter is not marked by a boundary, and you can't adjust the gutter width by dragging the boundary in the Print Preview window as you can the margins.

If you switch to the Page Layout view, you won't see the gutter as a shaded area. The gutter simply increases the amount of blank space between your text and the edge of the page.

FIGURE 10-53.
Word displays the gutter as a shaded area in the Print Preview window when you specify a Gutter setting.

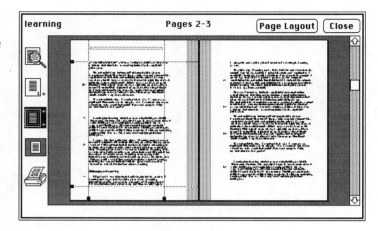

If you combine inside and outside margins with a page gutter, each page has blank space at the binding edge that is equal to the Inside margin setting plus the Gutter setting. For example, suppose you've activated the Mirror Even/Odd option in the Document dialog box, and you've specified an Inside margin setting of 1.25, an Outside margin setting of 1.5, and a Gutter setting of 0.75. When you print this document, Word creates a total of 2 inches of blank space on the binding edge of each page.

Using the ruler with left and right pages

When you use inside and outside margins or a page gutter, Word adjusts the ruler's appearance on your screen. As we explained in Chapter 5, "Formatting Documents and Paragraphs," to compute the width of the text area, Word subtracts the Left and Right margin settings from the width of your paper. When you activate the Mirror Even/Odd option, Word computes the width of the text area by subtracting the Inside and Outside margin settings from the width of your paper. If you've specified a gutter, Word also subtracts the Gutter setting.

For example, Word's default Left and Right margin settings of 1.25 create a text area that is 6 inches wide on standard 8.5-inch-wide paper. If you specify a Gutter setting of 0.5 inch, you decrease the width of your text area by half an inch. As a result, the dotted vertical line marking the right edge of your text moves to the 5.5-inch point on the ruler.

If you select Page Layout view and use the margin scale on the ruler, Word accounts for your Inside, Outside, and Gutter settings when placing the ruler's margin markers. As you scroll from an odd page to an even page, Word shifts the markers accordingly. Word does not adjust the margin markers if you're using Normal or Outline view to look at your document.

Formatting left and right headers and footers

In many books, the book title appears at the top of even pages and the chapter title at the top of odd pages. Even when the text of a header or footer is the same on left and right pages, you often see page numbers on the outside edge, the name of the publication in the center, and the date on the inside edge of each page.

The Even/Odd Headers check box in the Document dialog box allows you to vary the content and format of your headers (and footers) between left and right pages. This option also allows you to vary the position of automatic page numbers in left and right headers and footers. You can select the Even/Odd Headers option even if you are not using the Mirror Even/Odd option and the Gutter setting.

When you select the Even/Odd Headers option, Word replaces the Header and Footer commands on the View menu with four commands: Even Header, Odd Header, Even Footer, and Odd Footer. Use these commands and their corresponding windows to set up different headers and footers for left and right pages.

For example, Figures 10-54 and 10-55 show a pair of even and odd header windows that we used to create the headers for a book called *Latest Perspectives on Social Learning*. Notice that we placed a page number on the left side of the even header window and used a right-aligned tab at the 6-inch mark to align the book title with the right margin. In the odd header window, we placed the chapter title, *Perspectives on Learning*, on the left and used a right-aligned tab at the 6-inch mark to align the odd page numbers with the right margin. Figure 10-56 on the next page shows how these headers appear in the printed document.

FIGURE 10-54.
This header is designed for the even pages of a book.

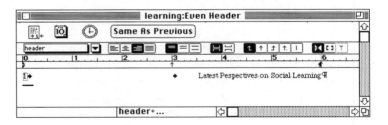

FIGURE 10-55.
This header is designed for the odd pages.

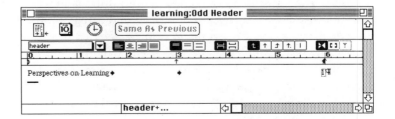

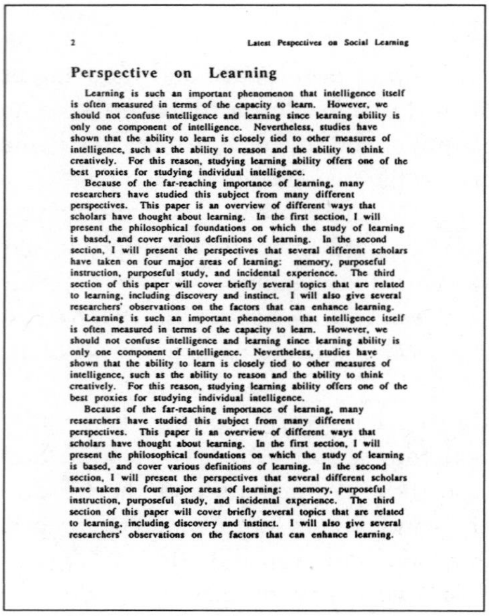

FIGURE 10-56.
In the printed document, the page numbers are aligned with the outside edge of each page, and the book and chapter titles are aligned with the inside margins.

Linking left and right headers and footers

If you're using Even/Odd Headers in a multisection document, the first section's headers and footers are linked to headers and footers in subsequent sections.

For example, suppose you have a single-section document with the Different First Page (in the Section dialog box) and Even/Odd Headers options deselected. You have chosen Header and entered the text *Title* in the header window. If you now open the Document dialog box and select the Even/Odd Headers option, the text *Title* appears in both the even and odd header windows. However, if you choose Section and select the Different First Page option, the header window for the first page is blank. (Word also adds the commands First Header and First Footer to the View menu.) If you split your document into three sections, the even and odd header windows in the second and third sections contain the same *Title* text that appears in the even and odd header windows for the first section. The first-page headers in these sections are blank.

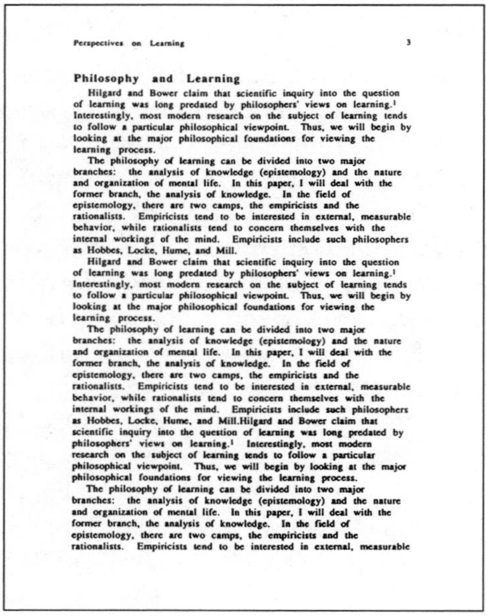

Suppose you now go back to the first section of your document, open the even header window, and change the existing text to *Chapter 1*. Next, you open the first-page header window and enter the text *First Page*. Because the second section's header windows "inherit" the contents of the first section's header windows, the even header window in the second section now contains the text *Chapter 1*, and the first-page header window contains the text *First Page*. If you click in the third section of the document and open the even and first-page header windows, you'll see that they also "inherit" the contents of the first section's header windows.

If you change the text in the even header window in the second section of your document to read *Chapter 2*, you break the link between that header and the even header of the first section. However, the even header of the third section remains linked to the even header of the second section and also reads *Chapter 2*. Any other changes you make to the text of the even header for the second section carry over to the even header for the third section.

To reestablish the link between the even headers of the second and first sections, click the Same As Previous button in the second section even header window. The text in this window then reads *Chapter 1* again, as does the text in the third section's even header window.

The rules are the same for first-page headers and footers. When you change a first-page header or footer in a section, that header or footer is no longer linked to the previous section's first-page header or footer. In addition, Word changes the first-page headers or footers in any subsequent sections so that they are identical to the header or footer you changed.

If you deselect the Even/Odd Headers option, Word uses the odd header and footer text in each section as the header and footer text for both the even and odd pages in that section. Similarly, if you deselect the Different First Page option, Word treats the first page of a section just like any other even or odd page. However, if you reselect the Different First Page or Even/Odd Headers options, Word remembers the original text and formats for those headers and footers.

Positioning page numbers

If you select the Even/Odd Headers option, Word positions each page number according to whether it appears on a left or right page. (You don't need to create a header or footer in order for Word to adjust the positions of the page numbers.) On right pages, the page number position is taken from the From Top and From Right edit bars of the Section dialog box. The page number is aligned flush-left at the From Right position. On left pages, the page number position is adjusted as though the From Right setting were now the From Left setting. The page number is aligned flush-right at this position. By making this kind of adjustment, Word ensures that the page numbers in your document always appear at the outside edge of the page.

Word adjusts the position of automatic page numbers only when you select the Even/Odd Headers option in the Document dialog box. If you don't activate this option but do activate Mirror Even/Odd or use a Gutter setting to create left and right page layouts, Word doesn't reverse the horizontal position of automatic page numbers on even and odd pages.

Positioning frames

Word's Frame command allows you to place a graphic, paragraph, or table any-where on a page and then automatically flow text around it. When we introduced the Picture command on the Insert menu in Chapter 6, "Creating Graphics," we explained that Word automatically places graphics in frames. To place a frame around a paragraph or one or more rows of a table so that you can position it on the page, you need to use the Frame command.

When you position an item with the Frame command, the item is called a *positioned object*. For example, Figure 10-57 shows a page of text with a table posi-tioned in the center. Word automatically reflows text around a positioned object.

FIGURE 10-57.

You can use the Frame command to place a paragraph, graphic, or table anywhere on a page.

Readers reveal their viewing habits in annual TV GORGE survey

Last fall, we surveyed 2,100 readers of TV GORGE magazine to ask them about their television viewing habits. Overall, there were few surprises in the survey results. Most of our readers consider television viewing to be one of the most important activities in their lives. In fact, 90% of the survey respondents watch 50 or more hours of TV each week. Often, they conduct and participate in social activities that revolve around TV viewing, such as Super Bowl parties or get-togethers with friends to view a movie or a mini-series.

Some respon-dents keep a TV set in every room of the house in order not to miss even a minute of a favorite program. In fact, one respondent has had a TV installed in the wall of his shower. Others told us that they have installed under-the-cabinet TV sets in the kitchen and keep a portable set at work.

As in past years, *Wheel of Fortune* topped the list of favorite shows. Sitcoms were also quite popular among many of the respondents. The *Cosby Show*, *Cheers*, and *Roseanne* were the most-watched shows in this category. Many TV GORGE readers also are faithful viewers of one or more of the "tabloid" talk shows. Oprah Winfrey's show was the hands-down favorite, followed by Geraldo Rivera, Phil Donahue, and Sally Jessy Raphael.

Finally, as in past years, our readers expressed a strong interest in Saturday morning children's shows. *Superman* and the *Bugs Bunny & Tweety Show* were the favorites in this category. Other respondents cited *Sesame Street*, and the *Smurfs* as their preferred child-ren's shows.

Many of our readers correspond regularly with one or more of their favorite TV stars. Some belong to celebrity fan clubs, such as the Vanna White Fan Club. Others seek to emulate their favorite stars in a variety of ways. For example, one woman told us about her *Rosanne* parties, where a group of friends gets together to dress up like the characters in the TV show.

Of course, the majority of our survey respondents consider a VCR to be an essential accessory for television viewing. As one person said, "With my VCR, I've been able to catch up on all the old reruns of *Mr. Ed* and *My Three Sons*. What a great invention!" Most respondents use their VCRs to tape cable movies and keep up with their favorite soaps.

Large-screen television sets are also increasing in popularity, as are the all-in-one home entertainment centers that incorporate a TV set, stereo, VCR, and other electronic equipment. The most common brands of televisions and related equipment cited by the respondents are Sony and Magnavox. Some readers expressed a strong preference for Japanese-made equipment. For example, one respondent said, "I love my Ford pickup, but when it comes to electronic equipment, you can't beat the Japanese!"

As usual, we asked our readers' opinions on the best food to munch on while watching TV. Most seemed to have no concern for calories when they plopped down in front of the tube. 55% of the

Fall Couch Potato Survey		
How many hours of TV do you watch each week?	10%	Less than 50
	25%	50 to 80
	30%	80 to 100
	35%	More than 100
How many television sets do you own?	20%	1
	20%	2
	40%	3
	20%	More than 3
If you could live the life of any character in a TV show, who would you choose?	35%	Rosanne
	25%	Big Bird
	18%	Vanna White
	12%	Beaver Cleaver
	10%	Bryant Gumbel
What is your favorite TV show?	44%	Wheel of Fortune
	24%	Oprah Winfrey
	22%	Cheers
	6%	Cosby Show
	4%	LA Law
What is your favorite snack while watching TV?	25%	Chips
	15%	Nachos
	15%	Ice cream
	45%	I do all my eating while watching TV

Word has two Frame commands. The Frame command on the Insert menu lets you apply a frame to a selected part of your document and then immediately position the framed element on the page in Print Preview. The Frame command on the Format menu also lets you apply a frame. However, choosing this command displays a dialog box in which you can specify precisely where you want to place the frame, as well as change the frame's width. After defining the frame, you can view the result in the Print Preview window or you can return directly to Normal view.

We explain how to use both commands in this section. Although Word's Frame commands let you create sophisticated desktop publishing layouts relatively easily, you'll find that some trial and error is often required to create an attractive page layout that includes positioned objects. We recommend that you have a good working knowledge of Word's character, document, and paragraph formatting features before using the Frame command.

Positioning a framed object in Print Preview

As we explained in Chapter 6, "Creating Graphics," when you insert a graphic into a Word document, Word automatically encloses the graphic within a frame. To place a frame around a paragraph or all or part of a table, first select the paragraph or table. (To select a paragraph, triple-click some text within it. To select a complete table, hold down the Option key and double-click anywhere within the table. To select part of a table, select the first cell in each row.) After making your selection, choose Frame from the Insert menu. Word then places a frame around the object and changes the screen display to Print Preview.

In Print Preview, Word displays boundary lines between the framed object and the document text that surrounds it. Moving the pointer within the framed object changes the pointer shape to a pair of cross hairs. Simply click anywhere within the frame, and then drag the cross-hair pointer to establish the frame's new location.

When you click the object, Word displays coordinates at the top of the Print Preview window that describe the position of the left and top boundaries of the framed object relative to the left and top edges of the page. For example, the coordinates 2.25, 2.75 tell you that the object's left boundary is 2.25 inches from the left edge of the page, and its top boundary is 2.75 inches from the top edge of the page. The coordinates change as you drag the object to a new position.

After you have repositioned the object, Word moves the boundary lines for the framed object and redraws the screen to show the document text flowing around it. For example, Figure 10-58 shows the page from Figure 10-57 after we chose the Frame command from the Insert menu and dragged the cross-hair pointer to the middle of the page. Figure 10-59 shows the Print Preview window after Word repositioned the table.

FIGURE 10-58.
After choosing Frame from the Insert menu, change the position of the framed object by dragging the frame in Print Preview.

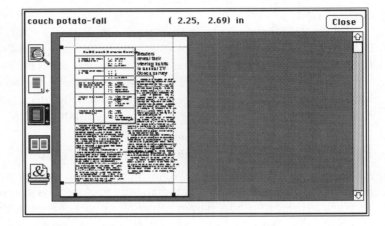

FIGURE 10-59.
After a moment, Word displays the positioned object's new location on the page.

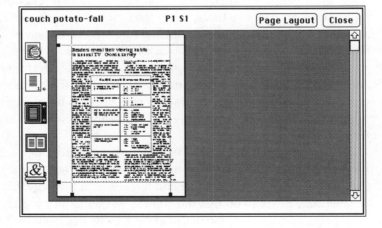

To see the page as it will appear when printed, you can also display the text in Page Layout view. Figure 10-60 shows the sample document from Figure 10-59 as it appears in Page Layout view.

FIGURE 10-60.
You can also view the position of an object on the page in Page Layout view.

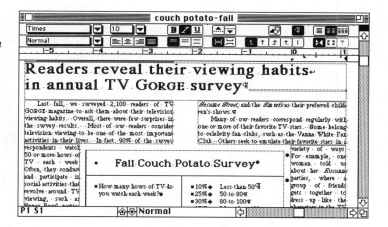

When you display the document again in Normal view, the positioned object appears to align with the left margin. The paragraph, graphic, or table to which you've assigned a special position appears in the same text column as the rest of your document. When the Show ¶ command is active, Word displays the paragraph properties mark (■) next to the framed object to indicate that it has been assigned a special format. Word doesn't print this mark.

Using the Frame dialog box

To reposition a framed object even more precisely, you can click anywhere within the frame and then choose the Frame command from the Format menu to display the Frame dialog box. For example, Figure 10-61 shows the Frame dialog box settings for Figure 10-60. You can also display the Frame dialog box by double-clicking the paragraph properties mark. The Frame dialog box enables you to define exactly where you want the framed object to appear on the page and lets you change the size of the frame.

FIGURE 10-61.
The Frame dialog box allows you to specify precisely where you want to place a framed object on a page.

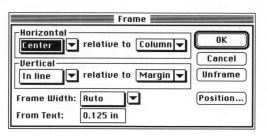

The alignment options

Two drop-down list boxes labeled Horizontal and Vertical enable you to specify the location of the framed object. To the right of each drop-down list box, you'll see the words *Relative To* followed by options in another drop-down list box. As these options suggest, positioning an object is simply a matter of specifying its horizontal and vertical position relative to a specific part of the page.

If you open the Frame dialog box without first selecting a framed object, you'll notice that Word's default horizontal alignment setting is Left Relative To Column. The default vertical alignment is In Line Relative To Margin. With these settings, the paragraph, graphic, or table appears with no special positioning. The first step in specifying an object's position is to select one of the Relative To options. These options define the part of the document page that you want to use as your point of reference when positioning the object. Next, specify how you want to align the object. Figure 10-62 shows the options available on the Horizontal and Vertical drop-down lists. For both the horizontal and vertical positions, you can either select an alignment option from the drop-down lists, or you can type a measurement in the edit bar at the top of the list.

FIGURE 10-62.
*Word offers several
standard options for
specifying the
horizontal and vertical
position of an object.*

After you've specified a position, click OK to apply it and return to your document. To see the reflowed text immediately, display the document in Print Preview by clicking the Position button on the right side of the Frame dialog box.

Horizontal options As you can see in Figure 10-62, the alignment options in the Horizontal drop-down list box are Left, Center, Right, Inside, and Outside. Left aligns the frame's left edge with the left margin, the left edge of the page, or the current column depending on which Relative To option you select: Margin, Page, or Column. Similarly, the Right option aligns the frame's right edge with the right margin, the right edge of the page, or the current column. When you select Center, Word centers the framed object between the left and right margins, between the left and right edges of the page, or between the boundaries of the current text column. Figures 10-63 and 10-64 illustrate these Left, Center, and Right Horizontal alignment options.

When you position an object near the edge of a page, keep in mind that a LaserWriter cannot print anything that falls less than a half inch from the edge of the paper.

FIGURE 10-63.
This layout sketch shows Horizontal alignment relative to the left and right margins and the left and right edges of the page.

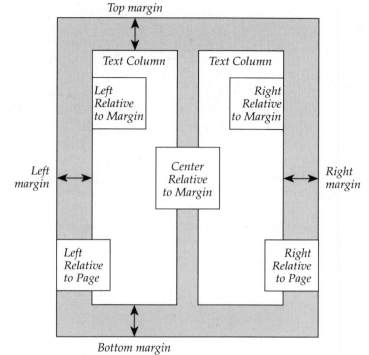

FIGURE 10-64.
This layout sketch shows Horizontal alignment relative to column boundaries.

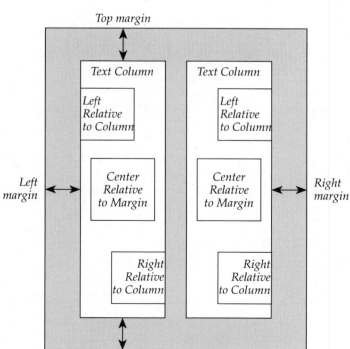

The Inside and Outside alignment options allow you to specify a position that depends on whether the positioned object falls on a left or right (even or odd) document page. You'll typically use these options when you've activated Mirror Even/Odd or specified a Gutter setting in the Document dialog box. However, they are available even if you haven't set up different left and right page layouts.

The Inside option aligns the edge of an object with the inside margin, the inside edge of a page, or the inside edge of a column. On even-numbered (left) pages, the right frame boundary is aligned with the right margin, the right edge of the page, or the right edge of the text column. On odd-numbered (right) pages, the left frame boundary is aligned with the left margin, the left edge of the page, or the left edge of the text column.

The Outside option aligns the frame boundary with the outside margin, the outside edge of a page, or the outside edge of a column. On even-numbered pages, the left boundary is aligned with the left margin, the left edge of the page, or the left column boundary. On odd-numbered pages, the right frame boundary is aligned with the right margin, the right edge of the page, or the right column boundary.

Figures 10-65 and 10-66 illustrate how the Inside and Outside options align a framed object.

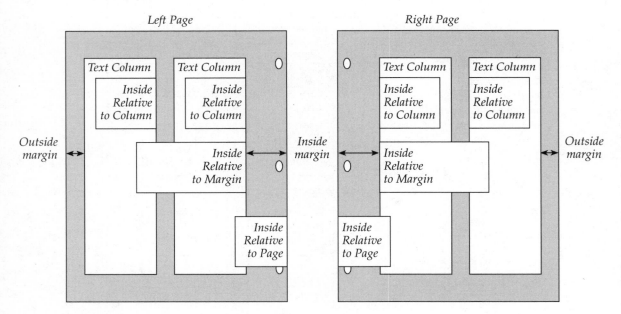

FIGURE 10-65.
This layout sketch shows how the Inside alignment option positions objects on facing pages.

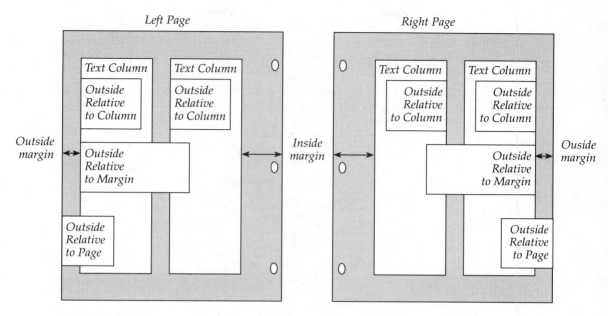

FIGURE 10-66.
This layout shows how the Outside alignment option positions objects on facing pages.

Vertical options The Vertical drop-down list box offers In Line, Top, Center, and Bottom options. Top aligns the top boundary of the framed object with the top of the page or with the top margin depending on whether you've selected Margin or Page as the Relative To option. Bottom aligns the frame's bottom boundary with the bottom of the page or with the bottom margin. Center centers the framed object either between the top and bottom margins or between the top and bottom edges of the page.

With the In Line option, the vertical alignment of a framed object changes relative to the surrounding document text, instead of being fixed on the page. If you insert a line of text above the positioned object, Word moves the vertical position of the framed object down one line. The Relative To options for the vertical position have no effect when you select the In Line option.

By combining the In Line option with a Horizontal option, you can change a framed object's horizontal position on a page without changing its alignment relative to preceding and subsequent text. This technique is similar to adjusting the left indent of a paragraph, with one important difference: When you specify a horizontal position and use the In Line Vertical option, Word flows text around the positioned object. In fact, if you select a horizontal alignment of Left Relative To Margin and a vertical alignment of In Line, Word positions the object just as it normally would, but flows text around the object (assuming that there's enough room for the text).

For example, Figure 10-67 shows some text that we've positioned using In Line as the vertical alignment and Left Relative To Margin as the horizontal alignment. Notice how the main body of the document flows around the specially positioned text. (To create this effect, we specified a Frame Width setting of 3.25 inches. We'll talk more about this setting in a moment. As you can see, we also created a border around the positioned paragraph.)

FIGURE 10-67.
When you use In Line
vertical alignment,
Word doesn't change
the vertical position of
an object but flows
text around it.

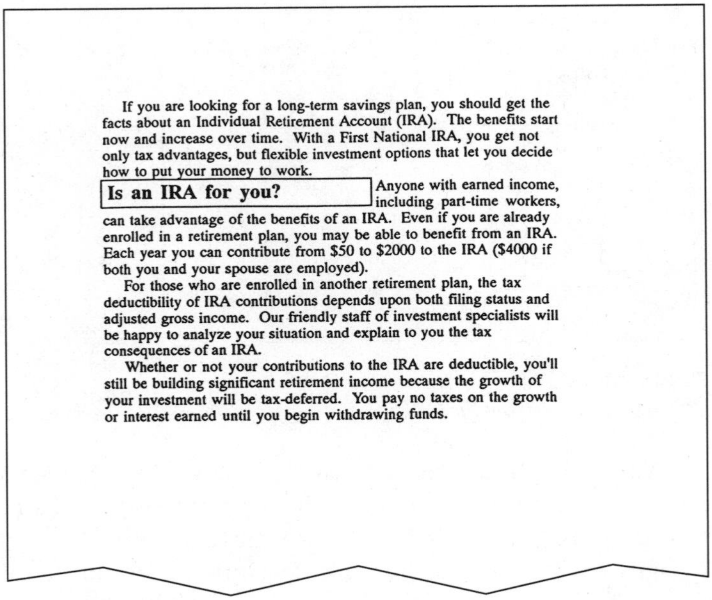

> If you are looking for a long-term savings plan, you should get the facts about an Individual Retirement Account (IRA). The benefits start now and increase over time. With a First National IRA, you get not only tax advantages, but flexible investment options that let you decide how to put your money to work.
>
> **Is an IRA for you?**   Anyone with earned income, including part-time workers, can take advantage of the benefits of an IRA. Even if you are already enrolled in a retirement plan, you may be able to benefit from an IRA. Each year you can contribute from $50 to $2000 to the IRA ($4000 if both you and your spouse are employed).
>
> For those who are enrolled in another retirement plan, the tax deductibility of IRA contributions depends upon both filing status and adjusted gross income. Our friendly staff of investment specialists will be happy to analyze your situation and explain to you the tax consequences of an IRA.
>
> Whether or not your contributions to the IRA are deductible, you'll still be building significant retirement income because the growth of your investment will be tax-deferred. You pay no taxes on the growth or interest earned until you begin withdrawing funds.

Specifying an alignment measurement

Instead of selecting an alignment option from the Horizontal or Vertical drop-down list box, you can use the Horizontal or Vertical edit bar to enter a positive number expressed in inches, centimeters, points, or picas (in, cm, pt, or pi). If you don't include a unit of measure, Word uses the default unit specified in the Preferences dialog box. Word also converts your entries in inches, centimeters, points, or picas to the default unit of measure.

When you use a measurement to specify an object's horizontal position, Word aligns the left boundary of the framed object depending on the Relative To option you select. For example, if you enter .5 in the Horizontal edit bar and select the Relative To Page option, Word positions the framed object 0.5 inch from the left edge of your paper.

When you use a measurement to specify an object's vertical position, Word similarly positions the object relative to the top edge of your paper or the top margin. Typing 3 in the Vertical edit bar and selecting the Margin option, for example, positions the selected object 3 inches from the top margin on the page.

Specifying a frame width

The Frame Width edit bar enables you to change the width of the frame area that surrounds the object.

If you display the Frame dialog box without first selecting a framed object, you'll see the word *Auto* in the Frame Width edit bar. The default width of a framed graphic is simply the width of the graphic (which you determined in your graphics window). Similarly, the default frame width of a framed table is the width of the table itself. However, framed paragraphs work a little differently.

Initially, Word matches the default width of a framed paragraph to the width of the text column in which the paragraph was created. For example, if you are using Word's default Page Setup and Document settings and have only one column of text, each paragraph—regardless of whether you assign a special position—is 6 inches wide. If you are using snaking columns, the width of each paragraph is equal to the width of a column.

When a framed paragraph is the same width as the text column, Word cannot flow text on the right or left side of the paragraph. Even if you move the indent markers on the ruler to make a framed paragraph narrower or wider, Word keeps the paragraph frame the same width as your text column. You can see the width of a positioned paragraph by displaying your document in Page Layout view and then choosing Show ¶ from the Edit menu. When you do this, Word marks the paragraph's boundaries on your screen with dotted lines.

For example, Figure 10-68 on the next page shows the document from Figure 10-67 in Page Layout view before we changed the Frame Width setting of the positioned paragraph. The dotted line at the top and bottom of the text marks the boundaries of the positioned paragraph. As you can see, with a Frame Width setting of Auto, the paragraph has the same width as the document's text area. Although the text of this framed paragraph is quite short, Word extends its frame boundaries to the full width of the text area and does not flow text to the right of the paragraph.

To reduce the frame's width so that text flows around the positioned paragraph, specify a Frame Width setting in the Frame dialog box. When you specify a Frame Width that is less than the width of the text area, Word rewraps the paragraph text within the frame to fit that setting, if necessary. Space permitting, Word also flows document text around the resized frame. For example, Figure 10-69 on the next page shows the sample paragraph from Figure 10-68 after we changed its Frame Width setting to 3.25 inches.

FIGURE 10-68.
With a Frame Width setting of Auto, the width of a framed paragraph is the same as that of the document's text column.

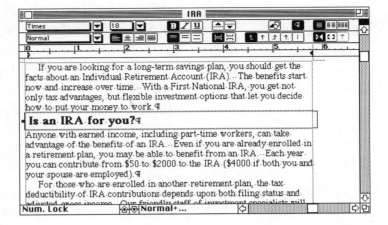

FIGURE 10-69.
After reducing the Frame Width setting, Word is able to flow text around the framed paragraph.

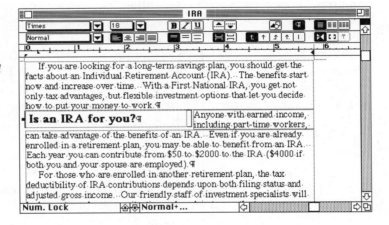

In addition, you can specify a Frame Width setting wider than the text column. The positioned paragraph then hangs outside the text column.

You can also change the Frame Width setting for a framed table or graphic, but you'll usually leave this setting on Auto. If you specify a setting that is greater than the initial width of the table or graphic, Word doesn't enlarge the table or graphic; it simply adds blank space to the right of the object. If you specify a Frame Width setting that is less than the initial width of a table or graphic, Word crops off part of the object's right edge.

Specifying the distance from text

You can control the space between a framed object and the text that surrounds it by using the From Text edit bar. When you position framed text or a graphic, Word normally allows 0.13 inch of blank space between the framed object and the text that flows around it. If you change the Auto setting in the Frame Width edit bar, you can add to the space between a positioned object and its surrounding text by entering a number in the From Text edit bar. The From Text setting can be as small as 0 or as large as 22 inches. Word adds the number you enter to its minimum spacing. Thus, if you specify 0 as your From Text setting, Word still allows 0.13 inch of space between the positioned object and its surrounding text.

Specifying a relatively large setting—a few inches or more—causes the positioned object to appear on a page by itself. When this happens, Word doesn't carry over any of the space specified in the From Text setting to previous or subsequent pages. Instead, Word places the positioned object on one page, with the text on the pages before and after the object appearing in the normal text area.

Although Word does a good job of controlling the horizontal distance between a framed object and its surrounding text, you might find that the vertical distance between document text and the top or bottom boundary of a framed object does not exactly match the From Text setting. The reason for this discrepancy is that Word adds the leading of the text that flows around the positioned object, plus any Space Above or Space Below settings, to the From Text setting.

Figure 10-70 shows a printed document in which one paragraph has been framed and positioned. The text flowing around the paragraph is 12 point. We've specified a From Text setting of 0.2 in the Frame dialog box.

FIGURE 10-70.
Word might not be able to create the specified amount of space between the top and bottom edges of a positioned object and the surrounding text.

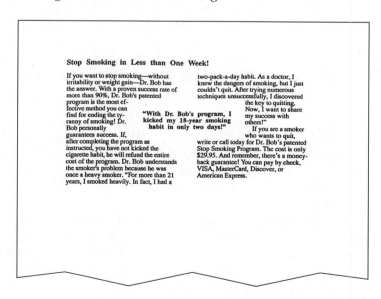

The From Text setting affects how Word flows text around the positioned object. To flow text beside an object, Word must have at least 1 inch of space between a framed boundary and the outer boundary of a text column. When determining whether there is 1 inch of available space, Word considers not only an object's horizontal position but also the From Text setting. If Word can't provide the specified distance between an object and its surrounding text and maintain at least 1 inch of space for text, it does not flow the document text around the frame.

For example, if you position a graphic 1 inch from the left margin and specify 0.1 as your From Text setting, Word can't flow text on the left side of the graphic. Only 0.77 inch remains after allowing for the 0.1-inch From Text setting, plus the minimum 0.13-inch space. To flow text on the left side of the graphic, you must be sure that the graphic is at least 1.23 inches from the left margin. In other words, you must specify a Horizontal setting of at least 1.23 inches.

If you position an object at the edge of a page, the From Text setting determines the space between that object and the edge of the page. For example, suppose you've positioned a graphic by selecting Right from the Horizontal drop-down list box and clicking the Relative To Page option. You've also changed the Auto setting in the Frame Width edit bar and specified 0.25 as the From Text setting. Word places the framed object 0.25 inch from the edge of the page.

A formatting tip

Usually you should avoid placing a framed object in the middle of a single text column, because Word splits each line of text at the edge of the framed object, making it difficult to read the document. In the sample documents we've shown in this section, we've used a two-column text layout when we've centered an object on a page, as shown earlier in Figure 10-57. This way, each text column flows around one side of the positioned object, and the lines of text in the document are not broken up by the object.

Changing the contents of a frame

In Chapter 6, "Creating Graphics," we explained that to modify a graphic, you double-click the graphic to display the Edit Picture window, where you can easily make changes. You can also crop and position a graphic within its frame by dragging its handles.

Because Word considers the text in a framed paragraph or table an independent object, you can edit and format the text directly, using standard formatting techniques. You can also place a border around the object. (For detailed information about using Word's Border command, see Chapter 5, "Formatting Documents and Paragraphs.")

Formatting framed paragraphs and tables

Use the ruler and the Paragraph dialog box to change the formatting characteristics of a framed paragraph or table. You can change the line spacing or add tab stops. When you click a framed paragraph, the ruler displays the width of the paragraph, with the 0 position on the ruler indicating the paragraph's left boundary and the dotted vertical line indicating its right boundary, as determined by the Frame Width setting.

Changing alignment and indents

If you change the alignment or indents of a framed paragraph, Word changes these settings relative to the paragraph's frame boundaries. For example, suppose you click the Right Alignment button to right align the sample paragraph shown earlier in Figure 10-69. As you can see in Figure 10-71, Word aligns the paragraph flush with the right frame boundary. If you then move the right indent marker for this paragraph, Word aligns the text with the indent marker rather than the right frame boundary.

FIGURE 10-71.
The paragraph shown earlier in Figure 10-69 is now right-aligned.

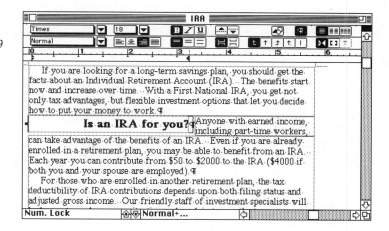

Because Word aligns the indent markers relative to a paragraph's boundaries, you should change the Frame Width setting before moving the indent markers. If you move the markers before you change the setting, you might get unexpected results.

For example, the text column in Figure 10-72 on the next page is 6 inches wide. We've moved the right indent marker for the framed paragraph 2 inches to the left, to the 4-inch position on the ruler. In the Frame dialog box, we've selected a horizontal alignment of Center Relative To Column and a vertical alignment of In Line. We used Word's default From Text setting of 0.13.

To flow text around the positioned paragraph, Word requires at least 0.13 inches of space on either side of the paragraph (1 inch for the text and 0.13 inch for the From Text setting). To create this space, we must change the Frame Width setting. Specifying a Frame Width setting of 3, for example, creates a framed paragraph 3 inches wide, centered on the 6-inch text column, with 1.5 inches of space on either side of the positioned paragraph.

FIGURE 10-72.
The right edge of the
second paragraph in
this document has
been indented 2 inches.

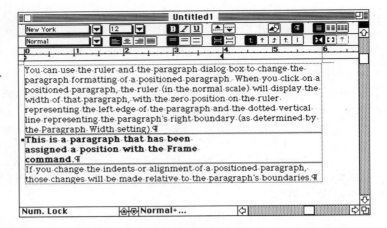

Figure 10-73 shows the positioned paragraph after we changed its Frame Width setting. Notice that Word has maintained the 2-inch right indent, so that the text is now wrapped within a 1-inch column.

FIGURE 10-73.
When we change the
Frame Width setting
to 3 inches, Word
maintains the 2-inch
right indent, wrapping
the text in a 1-inch
column.

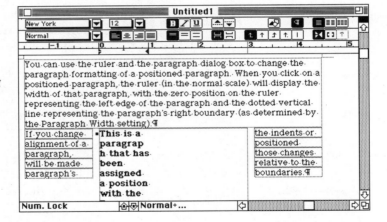

You can correct the problem shown in Figure 10-73 by moving the right indent marker on the ruler to the dotted vertical line that marks the right boundary of the paragraph. Figure 10-74 shows the document after we made this change.

To avoid problems like the one in Figure 10-73, always use the Frame Width setting—not the indent markers on the ruler—to adjust the width of a positioned paragraph. After setting the Frame Width, you might want to move the indent markers on the ruler to fine-tune the appearance of the positioned paragraph. Word allows you to move the indent markers beyond the left and right boundaries of the paragraph. Generally, however, you'll want to avoid doing this; when a framed object is pulled into surrounding text, Word truncates part of the object.

FIGURE 10-74.
We moved the right
indent marker to the
3-inch position on the
ruler to wrap the
framed paragraph
within its 3-inch
boundary.

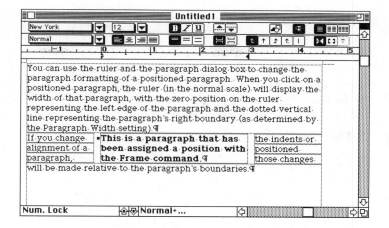

With the Before and After settings in the Paragraph dialog box or the Open Space button on the ruler, you can change the amount of space between the top and bottom edges of a framed paragraph and its surrounding text. When you insert space before or after a positioned paragraph, Word places that space within the paragraph's boundary.

Returning to normal positioning

If you decide that you do not want a paragraph, graphic, or table to have special positioning in your document, you can simply click the Unframe button in the Frame dialog box. Clicking this button returns the object to a normal position. The Horizontal setting is then Left Relative To Column, the Vertical setting is In Line, and the Frame Width setting is Auto.

Positioning tips

Keep in mind that the Frame command doesn't specify on which printed page a positioned object should appear. If you edit a document, or change the location of its page breaks, an object with fixed positioning might be moved to a different page. Whenever you use the Frame command to place a paragraph, table, or graphic in a specific position on a page, we strongly recommend that you first create and format your entire document without any framed objects. Then repaginate the document and position the objects, beginning at the top of the document and working your way to the end. After positioning each object, repaginate again.

In many other respects, applying special positioning to a paragraph is no different than applying more conventional paragraph formatting. In fact, you can use the settings in the Frame dialog box as part of a style definition. For example, suppose you want to place the illustrations throughout a document in one of four standard positions on a page. The easiest way to do this is to define four named styles whose definitions include the frame position settings. Simply choose Style from the Format menu or press Command-T to display the Style dialog box, and then select New Style from the list box. Next, type a name for the style—such as *position 1*—in the Style edit bar, and choose Frame from the Format menu. In the Frame dialog box, enter the desired position settings, and click OK. Finally, click the Define button in the Style dialog box to complete the style definition. Now you can position an illustration simply by clicking the illustration's frame and applying the position 1 style.

11

Adding a Table of Contents, an Index, and Footnotes

*B*usiness proposals, term papers, and other complex documents often use reference elements such as a table of contents, an index, and footnotes to help readers understand the material presented. Word's table of contents, index, and footnote features let you compose these elements quickly and easily.

The general steps for creating tables of contents and indexes in Word are quite similar. First you enter hidden codes to indicate the entries you want to include. After you've flagged each entry in your document, you choose Table Of Contents or Index from the Insert menu to compile the table of contents or index.

Word's Footnote command makes it just as easy to create footnotes. Word displays a dialog box that lets you create a footnote without losing your place in the document.

The table of contents is the simplest of the three reference elements to create, so we introduce it first in this chapter. Then we discuss Word's indexing and footnoting capabilities.

Creating a table of contents

Creating a table of contents is a two-step process: First, indicate the entries you want to appear, and then choose Table Of Contents from the Insert menu to compile the table.

The easiest way to indicate the table of contents entries is to apply one of Word's default heading styles to each heading, caption, or text selection you want to include in the table. You can also flag the entries with special codes. Then choose the Table Of Contents command. In the Table Of Contents dialog box, you can tell Word to compile your table of contents from either headings or codes. Word inserts the completed table in a new section at the beginning of your document, where you can format, edit, or copy it. Because you select the document text from which Word compiles the table, you can use the Table Of Contents command to compile figure and graphics listings as well.

Using heading styles

As we explained in Chapter 9, "Creating Style Sheets," Word provides a standard set of styles for documents you create, including nine levels of headings (heading 1 through heading 9). As long as you've used these style names to create your document's headings, you can compile a table of contents directly from the headings in your document simply by choosing the Table Of Contents command.

When you use heading styles to create a table of contents, Word searches your document for all the paragraphs formatted with the heading 1 through heading 9 styles. Heading 1 styles become first-level table of contents entries; heading 2 styles become second-level table of contents entries; and so on.

Using table of contents codes

If you want to create a table of contents for a document that has no headings or if you don't want to use heading styles, you can use a special code to flag text as table of contents entries. A complete table of contents entry contains three elements: a hidden start-of-entry marker, the entry text, and a hidden end-of-entry marker. You can flag text in your document as a table of contents entry by typing the start-of-entry and end-of-entry markers at the beginning and end of the text, respectively, or you can choose TOC Entry from the Insert menu.

To manually flag an entry, start the entry with a three-character code that contains a period, the letter c, and another period (.c.). Then assign the Hidden format to this code so that Word recognizes it as a table of contents marker. To end the entry, type a paragraph symbol (¶), an end-of-line symbol (↵), or a semicolon (;). Because you don't want this symbol to print, we recommend using a paragraph symbol or an end-of-line symbol.

If you use a semicolon, be sure to assign the Hidden format to that character to prevent it from appearing when you print. If you use a semicolon (or any other special character) as literal text in your table of contents entry, place single quotation marks around the entry text to prevent the semicolon from being treated as the end-of-entry marker. For example:

.c.'Division of Parts: Delineation of roles; Books II and III';

To use the TOC Entry command on the Insert menu to add these codes automatically, simply select the text you want to appear in the table of contents, and then choose TOC Entry. Word inserts a hidden .c. code in front of the selection and places a hidden semicolon after the selection. If the selection ends with a paragraph symbol or an end-of-line symbol, Word recognizes it as the end of the entry.

Generally, it's more efficient to apply start-of-entry and end-of-entry markers to existing document headings and subheadings, but you can also type text specifically for the table of contents.

To insert a set of table of contents codes for new text, place the insertion point where you want the entry to appear, and then choose TOC Entry. Word inserts the .c. and ; at the current insertion point and places the insertion point between the two codes so that you can type the entry text. Word applies the Hidden format to the text you type, but you can select and then reformat it as needed.

We have created three table of contents entries in the document shown in Figure 11-1. The first entry, in the title, takes advantage of an existing heading. Notice that the .c. code appears with a gray underline, indicating that it has the Hidden format. The paragraph symbol at the end of the heading serves as the end-of-entry marker.

FIGURE 11-1.
We created three table of contents entries in this sample document.

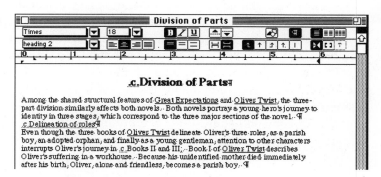

The second table of contents entry, *Delineation of roles*, appears just after the first paragraph of body text. This entry is not part of our document text, so we've assigned the Hidden format to the entire entry.

The third entry, *Books II and III*, takes advantage of existing body text. We assigned the Hidden format only to the .c. and ; portions of the entry to prevent them from appearing in our printed document.

Creating multilevel table of contents entries ·

You can create as many as nine levels of entries for a table of contents by including a numeric level argument in the *.c.* codes. When you compile the table of contents, Word indents the entries according to their levels. To assign a level to an entry, enter a value from 1 through 9 between the *c* character and the second period of the *.c.* code. The level code is optional for first-level entries.

In the screen shown in Figure 11-2, for example, we used a *.c1.* table of contents code to flag the heading at the top of the screen as level 1, a *.c2.* code to flag the entry *Delineation of roles* as level 2, and a *.c3.* code to define the entry *Books II and III* as level 3.

FIGURE 11-2.
We've created three levels of table of contents entries in this document.

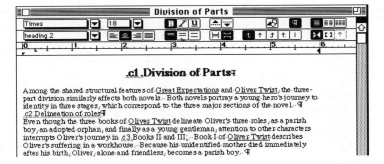

Creating subentries

Generally, a table of contents displays the page number on which each entry appears. However, you can create a table of contents that displays page numbers only after selected entries. For example, you might want headings of a particular level to serve as references to major sections without being followed by page numbers. You can create such a table of contents by designating subentry levels.

To create a subentry, you enter the heading levels in sequence, separating each level by a hidden colon and placing the end-of-entry marker only after the last entry—that is, after the entry whose page number you want to display in the table of contents. To include page numbers only after a level 3 entry, for example, you would create a table of contents code like this one:

.c.Division of Parts:Delineation of roles:Books II and III;

When you choose the Table Of Contents command, Word creates a level 1 entry from the text *Division of Parts*, a level 2 entry from *Delineation of roles*, and a level 3 entry from *Books II and III*, placing a page number only after the level 3 entry.

Compiling the table of contents

To create the table of contents from the entries you've flagged, choose Table Of Contents from the Insert menu to display the Table Of Contents dialog box, shown in Figure 11-3. The option you select in the Collect section of the Table Of Contents dialog box tells Word the type of table of contents entries you want to collect from your document. Select the Outline option to create a table of contents that outlines your document by compiling entries from heading styles only. Select the .C. Paragraphs option to use all entries to which you've applied a table of contents code.

FIGURE 11-3.
The Table Of Contents dialog box appears when you choose the Table Of Contents command.

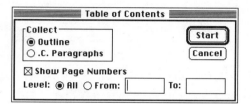

The edit bars at the bottom of the Table Of Contents dialog box let you specify the entry levels you want Word to include in the table of contents. Select All to include all the entry levels in your document, or specify a range of levels in the From and To edit bars. To include page numbers in the table of contents, select the Show Page Numbers option.

When you've specified the entries you want to collect, click the Start button to compile the table. Word repaginates the text, compiles the table of contents, and then inserts the table of contents in a new section at the beginning of the document. Press Command-period to cancel this procedure. If you've already compiled a table of contents, Word asks if you want to replace the existing table. If you click No, Word places the new table of contents in another new section at the beginning of the document, in front of the old one.

Figure 11-4 on the next page shows the first part of a sample table of contents compiled in Word. Each entry contains the table of contents text, followed by a tab marker, dot leaders, and the page number. A paragraph symbol ends each entry. Word inserts a section break at the end of the table of contents so that you can format it without affecting the rest of your document.

Remember, to ensure accurate page numbers, Word repaginates your document when you choose Table Of Contents. For this reason, the best time to compile the table of contents is immediately before you print the final version of your document. If the document contains hidden text that you don't want to print, be sure to deselect the Show Hidden Text option in the View portion of the Preferences dialog box to prevent Word from including this text as it repaginates.

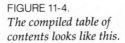

FIGURE 11-4.
The compiled table of contents looks like this.

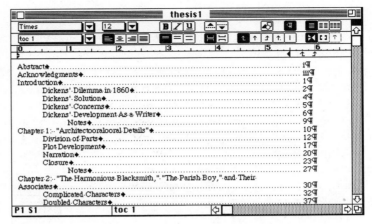

Formatting the table of contents

Word applies default styles to table of contents entries. However, you can change the character and paragraph formats of this text just as you would any text in your document, either by applying new formatting to selected text or by redefining the style definitions that Word has applied to the table. You can also add page numbers so that the table of contents is consistent with the rest of your printed document.

Table of contents styles

Word applies the character formatting of the document's Normal style to the table of contents. (See Chapter 9, "Creating Style Sheets," for more on style sheets and defining the Normal style.) Although Word doesn't assign special character formatting to a table of contents, it does assign paragraph formats to each table entry. This paragraph formatting determines the indentations, tab stops, and dot leaders used for each entry level.

For each entry level in the completed table of contents, Word adds a style name—toc 1, toc 2, and so on—to the document's style sheet. By default, toc 1 entries are not indented; they align with the default left margin of your body text. Word indents each successive toc style an additional half inch. All toc styles contain two tab stops: a left-aligned tab with dot leaders at the 5.75-inch mark and a right-aligned tab at the 6-inch mark. (You can see the right indent and tabs on the ruler in Figure 11-4.)

You can easily modify a toc style by highlighting a table of contents entry to which that style has been applied and then changing the style definition in the Style dialog box. (For more information about defining and changing paragraph styles, see Chapter 9, "Creating Style Sheets.")

Word spacing

You might find that some words are spaced too far apart in the table of contents. Irregular word spacing often occurs if you've manually numbered paragraphs in your document and used spaces to separate the numbers from the text. This spacing problem also results if you use a proportionally spaced font as part of a toc style.

If you manually number document paragraphs, using tabs instead of spaces to separate the numbers from the text smooths out irregular word spacing in a table of contents. If you're printing on a LaserWriter, you can correct irregular word spacing when you print by choosing the Fractional Widths option in the LaserWriter Page Setup dialog box. You can also smooth out irregular word spacing by using a monospaced font such as Courier, Monaco, or Dover for table of contents entries.

Spacing between dots

The spacing between the dots in the tab leaders in a table of contents can differ from line to line when the tab characters are formatted with a proportionally spaced font. To standardize this space, format the tab characters in the table with a monospaced font such as Courier. The space between dots might then be larger, but the distances between the dots will be the same.

Double-line spacing

If you use double-spacing in a table of contents, entries that wrap to a second line in the table will be double-spaced. To tighten this space and still maintain double-spacing between table entries, select the table of contents entry, and then adjust the Spacing setting in the Paragraph dialog box.

Paginating the table of contents

Because the table of contents is generally considered part of a document's front matter, you'll probably want to create a special numbering scheme for the table of contents pages, the title page, acknowledgments page, and so on.

To number your table of contents pages, click anywhere in the table of contents section, and then choose Section from the Format menu. Select the numbering format you want to use from the Format drop-down list box, then select the Margin Page Numbers option, and specify the position for your page numbers in the From Top and From Right edit bars. To use a different page numbering style for the body of your document, click in the first section of the main document and choose Section, select the numbering format you want to use, and then select the Restart At 1 option in the Section dialog box. (Chapter 10, "Creating Professional Documents," discusses page numbering in detail.)

If you want the table of contents pages to be numbered sequentially as the first pages of your document, reserve pages for them before you choose Table Of Contents by inserting manual page breaks or section breaks where the table will appear. When you choose Table Of Contents, Word includes the blank pages in its page count as it compiles the table of contents.

Creating other tables

You can create and compile special tables such as figure and graphics listings just as you do a table of contents: either apply Word's default heading styles or insert table of contents codes.

To create both a table of contents and a figure listing for the same document, apply one heading-level range to document headings and another heading-level range to figure titles. Alternatively, it may be easier to apply heading styles to headings in your document and table of contents codes to figure titles. When you've flagged entries for both tables, compile one table, and then complete the process again for the second table.

Working with multiple documents

If your document is composed of individual sections or chapters stored in separate Word files, you can create a table of contents by linking the files in series, using the File Series dialog box that you access from the Document dialog box. (Chapter 10, "Creating Professional Documents," discusses how to work with long documents.)

After you've linked the files and specified the table of contents entries in each file, place the insertion point within the first document, and choose Table Of Contents as you normally would. Word compiles the table of contents from each file in sequence and inserts the table of contents at the beginning of the first document in the file series.

Creating an index

Building an index is similar to building a table of contents. First you identify the entries you want to compile, and then you compile the index by choosing Index from the Insert menu, and finally you format the compiled index as you would any other text.

Defining index entries

To flag an entry for inclusion in an index, indicate the start of the entry with a three-character code that contains a period, the letter *i*, and another period (.*i*.). Then apply the Hidden format to this code so that Word will recognize the code as an index marker. Indicate the end of an index entry with a paragraph symbol (¶), an end-of-line symbol (↵), or a semicolon. Because you don't want the end-of-entry marker to print, we recommend using a paragraph symbol or an end-of-line symbol.

If you use a semicolon, be sure to assign the Hidden format to that character to prevent it from appearing when you print. If you use a semicolon (or any other special character) as literal text in your index entry, place single quotation marks around the entry text to prevent the semicolon from being treated as the end-of-entry marker. For example:

.i.'Division of Parts: Delineation of roles; Books II and III';

You can use the Index Entry command on the Insert menu to insert and format index codes automatically. To use this command to flag existing document text, simply select the text that you want to appear in the index, and then choose Index Entry from the Insert menu. Word inserts a hidden .i. code before and a hidden semicolon after the selection. If the selection ends with an end-of-entry marker, Word omits the trailing semicolon.

Generally, it's more efficient to apply the hidden start-of-entry and end-of-entry markers to existing document text, but you can also type text specifically for an index entry.

To insert a set of index entry codes for new text, place the insertion point where you want the entry to appear, and then choose the Index Entry command. Word inserts the .i. and ; at the current insertion point and places the insertion point between the two codes, so you can type the entry text. Word applies the Hidden format to the text you type, but you can select and then reformat the text as needed.

We have created three index entries in the sample document shown in Figure 11-5. The first entry at the top of the screen, *Division of Parts*, takes advantage of existing text. The .i. flag appears with a gray underline, indicating the Hidden format. The ¶ symbol after the heading serves as the end-of-entry marker.

FIGURE 11-5.
We created three index entries in this sample document.

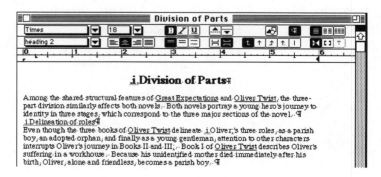

The second index entry, *Delineation of roles*, occurs just after the first paragraph of body text. Because it's not part of the document text, we have hidden the entire entry.

The third entry (*Oliver*), which appears in the second paragraph of body text, also takes advantage of existing text. We assigned the Hidden format to the *.i.* and *;* portions of the entry to prevent them from appearing in the printed document.

Creating subentries

You can create as many as seven index levels by creating subentries within an index entry. To specify subentries, type the index code, the main index entry, and a colon, and then add the subentry text and an end-of-entry marker. To specify additional subentry levels, separate each subentry by a colon. Word orders each subentry in the index alphabetically.

For example, to define the second and third index entries in the document shown in Figure 11-5 as subentries under the main heading *Division of Parts*, type

.i.Division of Parts:Delineation of roles;

to create first-level and second-level index entries, and

.i.Division of Parts:Delineation of roles:Oliver;

to specify *Oliver* as a third-level subentry.

Every time you type a subentry, you must also type its main entry. You must use a colon to introduce each subentry level and mark the end of the complete entry with an end-of-entry marker. (Remember to assign the Hidden format to this entire entry.) Figure 11-6 shows the sample document with the level 1, 2, and 3 index entries in place.

FIGURE 11-6.
We added level 2 and level 3 subentries under the main entry, Division of Parts.

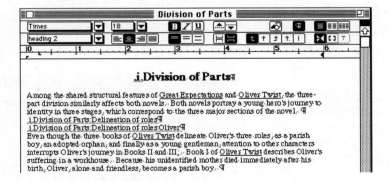

Compiling the index

To compile the index entries you've specified, choose Index from the Insert menu to display the Index dialog box shown in Figure 11-7. The Index dialog box lets you indicate how you want to display compiled index entries and the alphabetic range of entries you want to collect. After you've specified this information, you generate the index from this dialog box.

FIGURE 11-7.
Word presents the
Index dialog box when
you choose the Index
command.

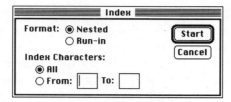

Before you display the Index dialog box, be sure that the Show Hidden Text option is not selected in the View portion of the Preferences dialog box. If your document contains hidden text that you don't want to print, this text might produce inaccurate page number references in the finished index.

Select Nested in the Index dialog box if you want Word to indent each index subentry on a new line under the main entry, as shown in Figure 11-8. Select Run-In to include each subentry in the same paragraph as its main entry. When you select the Run-In option, Word separates each subentry by a semicolon, as shown in Figure 11-9.

FIGURE 11-8.
When you select the
Nested option, Word
indents each subentry
on a new line.

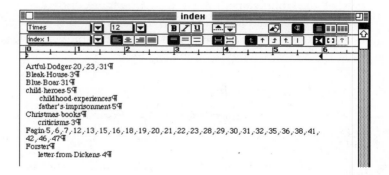

FIGURE 11-9.
When you select the
Run-In option, Word
includes subentries
in the same paragraph
as the main entry.

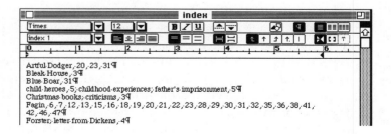

Leave the default All option in the Index Characters portion of the dialog box selected to compile a complete index. Select the radio button next to the From and To edit bars to compile a partial index by specifying a range of entries. For example, to index only those entries that start with the letters *a* through *m*, type the letter *a* in the From edit bar and the letter *m* in the To edit bar. This option is particularly helpful when you want to recompile a portion of an index to make corrections to a specific range of entries.

When you have specified how you want Word to select and format index entries, click the Start button in the upper-right corner of the Index dialog box. Word repaginates the document to ensure accurate page numbers. Then Word compiles and alphabetizes index entries in your document by merging duplicate entries, deleting duplicate page references, and inserting page numbers. You can cancel the indexing procedure by pressing Command-period.

When compilation is complete, Word adds the index to a new section at the end of your document so that you can format it separately from the rest of your text. You can use Cut and Paste to move the index (whole or in part) to another part of your document. If you've already compiled an index, Word asks if you want to replace the existing index. If you click No, Word adds the new index in a new section that follows the existing index.

If you're using the From and To edit bars to compile an index in stages, save yourself the trouble of cutting and pasting index entries by first compiling entries *a* through *g*, for example, and then *h* through *p*, and so on. You'll probably want to delete the section breaks that Word inserts at the end of each index when you bring the separate index sections together.

Formatting the index

After you've created an index, you can reformat characters and paragraphs. The easiest way to reformat index text is to redefine the style definitions Word applies to each entry level.

For each entry level in the completed index, Word adds a style name to the document's style sheet. If you use the Nested option to compile an index, Word adds index 1, index 2, and so on to the style sheet to correspond to the entry levels you've created for your index. The styles are based on the Normal style, with each subentry level indented a quarter inch from the previous level entry. If you used the Run-In option (as shown in Figure 11-9), Word creates only index 1.

You can easily modify an index style by highlighting an index entry to which that style has been applied and then changing the style's definition in the Style dialog box. Formatting changes you make to an index style affect the entire index entry—both the text and the page number reference. (For more information about defining and changing styles, see Chapter 9, "Creating Style Sheets.")

Special index arguments

Word lets you format specific index entries by adding hidden character codes to an entry's index code. As shown earlier in Figure 11-8, Word places a single space between the index entry and its page number in the compiled index. By adding character codes to index codes, you can format page numbers, add text references, and add spaces or other characters between index entries and their page numbers. You can also specify a character code to create page-range references for an index entry.

Formatting page numbers

You can add hidden characters to an index code to change the appearance of page numbers in the compiled index. To format the page number in bold, type the character *b* after the *i* but before the period in the index code. To format the page number in italic, type the letter *i* instead of the letter *b*. Format the page number in bold and italic by typing both characters.

For example, the arguments in the first column produce the index entry in the second column:

.ib.Division of Parts;   Division of Parts **1**

.ii.Division of Parts;   Division of Parts *1*

.iib.Division of Parts;   Division of Parts ***1***

Following an entry with text

You can add a hidden character to index-entry text to tell Word to replace the page number with a cross-reference that refers readers to another part of the index for further information. To add a text reference to an index entry, type and hide a # symbol after the entry, and then type the reference and hide it. For example:

.i.Delineation of roles#(see Division of Parts);

appears like this in the compiled index:

Delineation of roles (see Division of Parts)

You can also add hidden formatting characters to the index code to emphasize the cross-reference. Adding *i* or *b* to the code formats only the cross-reference portion of the entry—the text that appears after the # symbol. For example, add an italic code like this:

.ii.Delineation of roles#(see Division of Parts);

to create this index entry:

Delineation of roles *(see Division of Parts)*

Adding spaces or other characters to an entry

You can add spaces to the single space that Word inserts between an index entry and a page number or text reference by pressing the Spacebar to insert additional spaces between the entry text and the end-of-entry marker. To add a character— for example, a comma like those shown earlier in Figure 11-9—type the character immediately after the entry text and before the end-of-entry marker. Be sure to format these spaces or characters as hidden text so that they appear in the index, not in the document.

For example, if the entry *Delineation of roles* appears on page 12 of your document, typing the entry in the first column would result in the index entry in the second column:

.i.Delineation of roles ;   Delineation of roles 12
.i.Delineation of roles,;   Delineation of roles, 12

Indicating page ranges

If an indexed topic extends beyond a single page, you can create an index entry that lets the reader know that the topic is discussed on consecutive pages. To indicate a page range, first create an index entry on the page where the topic begins, and then type a left parenthesis between the *i* and the second period in the index code. Next, create exactly the same entry on the concluding page, and type a right parenthesis between the *i* and the second period in the index code.

For example, if the topic *Division of Parts* extends from page 5 to page 10, type

.i(.Division of Parts;

on page 5 of your document, and apply the Hidden text format. Then move to page 10 and type

.i).Division of Parts;

Word creates an index entry like this:

Division of Parts 5–10

Combining index and table of contents entries

Often, you want the same text to appear in both the table of contents and the index. If you're creating a level 1 index entry, you can combine the index and table of contents codes. For example, to include the heading *Division of Parts* in both the table of contents and the index, set the entry up like this:

.c..i.Division of Parts;

If you want to include a subentry in an index entry, you must type separate entries for the table of contents and the index. Otherwise, Word includes the subentry text in the table of contents as well as in the index. Remember to assign the Hidden format to the separate index entry so that the entry doesn't appear in your printed document.

Working with multiple documents

If your document is composed of individual sections or chapters stored in separate Word files, you can create a common index by linking the files in series using the File Series dialog box that you access from the Document dialog box. (Chapter 10, "Creating Professional Documents," discusses working with long documents in detail.)

After you've linked the documents and specified the index entries in each file, place the insertion point within the first document, and click Start in the Index dialog box. Word compiles index entries from each linked document and inserts the index at the end of the last document in the file series.

Creating footnotes

A footnote has two parts: a reference mark that appears within the document text and the footnote itself. The reference mark is usually a number that indicates the footnote's ordered place in the document, but it can also be a character (such as an asterisk) or even a word (such as *Note*). The footnote text provides more information about the topic flagged by the reference mark.

Word's default settings let you create and print footnotes almost effortlessly. You can type footnote text of any length and format footnote text just as you do document text. You can even add pictures or graphics to a footnote. In this section, we show you Word's default footnote settings and explain how to customize the way footnotes appear in your document. You can print footnotes at the bottom of the page, at the end of document sections, or at the end of the entire document. You can also format footnote text and customize the line that separates footnote text from document text.

Inserting footnotes

To insert a footnote, first place the insertion point where you want the reference mark to appear. For example, to add a footnote at the end of the first paragraph of body text in Figure 11-10 on the next page, place the insertion point at the end of that paragraph, between the period and the paragraph symbol.

FIGURE 11-10.
*We'll insert a sample
footnote in this
document.*

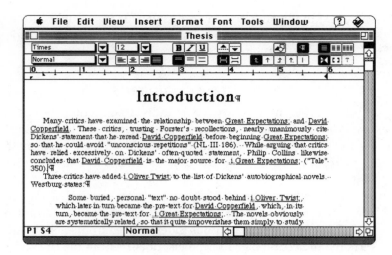

After you've indicated where you want to place the reference mark, choose Footnote from the Insert menu, or press Command-E. Word presents the Footnote dialog box shown in Figure 11-11. The top portion of this box lets you specify the reference mark you want to use to identify the footnote in your document. The bottom section lets you specify the line that separates footnote text from document text. (We'll discuss footnote separators in a few pages.)

FIGURE 11-11.
*The Footnote dialog
box lets you enter a
reference mark at the
insertion point.*

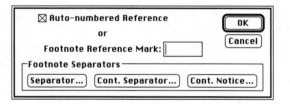

To use numbers to identify footnotes, select the Auto-Numbered Reference option in the Footnote dialog box. Word will then adjust the reference number whenever you insert or delete another automatically numbered footnote. If you prefer to use a different character as the reference mark, type the character in the Footnote Reference Mark edit bar.

After you specify the reference mark, click OK in the upper-right corner of the Footnote dialog box. Word inserts the reference mark in your document to the right of the insertion point. Word also splits the document window. The bottom window displays the text of all the footnotes you have created for your document. Word inserts the reference mark of the new footnote in the bottom window and then moves the insertion point after the mark. You type the text of the new footnote after the reference mark in the bottom window just as you would type text in your document. The footnote can be any length and can include multiple paragraphs. Word scrolls beyond the currently visible part of the footnote window to accommodate the text.

Figure 11-12 shows a sample footnote. The dotted border around the reference mark both in the document text and in the footnote window indicates that the Auto-Numbered Reference option is selected, and that the footnote reference is dynamic. This border appears only when the Show ¶ command is active.

FIGURE 11-12.
The Footnote command inserts a footnote reference mark and splits the document window. We entered footnote text in the footnote window at the bottom of the screen.

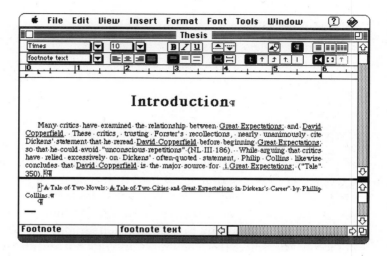

Repeat this procedure any time you want to insert a footnote in your document. When you select the Auto-Numbered Reference option, you don't need to change any Footnote dialog box settings. Simply press Command-E, and then press Return. Word automatically inserts the appropriate reference number in your document and in the footnote window. You need only type the footnote text.

After entering the footnote text, click anywhere in the window above the split bar to resume work in your document. Word continues to display the footnote window at the bottom of the screen. You can return to your previous place in the document window by pressing Command-Option-Z. If you have a numeric keypad, you can also press the 0 key to move back to the previous insertion point location.

The footnote window

The split-screen window created by Word when you choose the Footnote command differs from the split-screen window that appears when you drag the split bar down from the upper-right corner of the document window. You can move through the document and footnote windows simultaneously. When both windows are open, Word scrolls the footnote window to display the footnote text that corresponds to the reference mark on the screen. Similarly, when you scroll through footnotes in the footnote window, Word scrolls the corresponding part of your document into view in the document window.

To expand the document window when both windows are open, drag the split bar toward the bottom of the screen. To completely hide the footnote window, drag the split bar past the top or bottom of the document window, or press Command-Option-Shift-S to toggle the footnote window in and out of view.

Editing footnotes

You can insert, delete, cut, copy, and paste footnote text just as you do text in the document window. You can also use Word commands such as Find and Replace and tools such as Hyphenate and Spelling to edit footnote text. Word includes footnote text as part of the document text when you choose any of these commands.

Changing footnote text doesn't affect the reference mark to which the text is assigned in the document window. To change the reference mark, you must change the reference mark in your document. Simply select the mark in the document, open the Footnote dialog box, and then type the new reference mark in the Footnote Reference Mark edit bar. Word changes the mark in both the document and footnote windows and automatically adjusts numbered footnotes.

For example, if you want to change a bibliography-style reference mark from *Smith* to *Costello*, select the *Smith* mark in your document, choose Footnote, and then type *Costello* in the Footnote Reference Mark edit bar. When you click OK, Word changes the reference mark in the document and footnote windows.

Deleting the text of a footnote from the footnote window doesn't delete the footnote. Although the text disappears, the reference mark remains in your document. To delete a footnote, you must delete the reference mark in the document window. Word then deletes the corresponding footnote text and renumbers all subsequent footnote references.

Don't try to change a reference mark by highlighting and typing over it in the document window. Remember, deleting the reference mark in the document deletes both the mark and the footnote text. (If you accidentally delete a reference mark, immediately choose the Undo command from the Edit menu to undo the deletion.)

To copy a footnote, select only the reference mark whose footnote you want to copy, choose Copy from the Edit menu, and then paste the reference mark in the new location. Word copies the corresponding footnote text and places that text in the appropriate location in the footnote window. When you copy an automatically numbered reference mark, Word changes the number to reflect the footnote's new position and renumbers the other reference marks throughout your document.

Formatting footnotes

When you insert footnotes in a document, Word adds two new style names to the style sheet: footnote reference and footnote text. The footnote reference style formats footnote reference marks to appear in 9-point type, superscripted 3 points. The footnote text style formats footnote text to appear in 10-point type. Both styles appear in the font specified for the document's Normal style.

The easiest way to change the format of your footnote text or reference marks is to change its style definition in the Style dialog box. When you change a style, the format of all footnote text or reference marks in your document change. (Chapter 9, "Creating Style Sheets," discusses creating and modifying paragraph styles.) You can also reformat reference marks manually.

Positioning and numbering footnotes

The positioning and numbering of footnotes is controlled by settings in the Document dialog box shown in Figure 11-13. The Footnotes Position drop-down list box in the lower-left corner of the Document dialog box lets you select where footnotes will appear when you print your document: Bottom Of Page, Beneath Text, End Of Section, or End Of Document. The Document dialog box also lets you indicate whether you want to number automatically numbered footnotes consecutively throughout the document or separately on each page or in each section. You can also specify a starting footnote number other than Word's default of 1 in the Number from edit bar.

FIGURE 11-13.
*You can position
and number footnotes
from the Document
dialog box.*

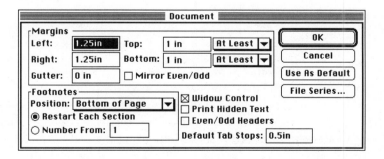

Select Bottom Of Page (the default) in the Footnotes Position drop-down list box to display each footnote at the bottom of the page on which its reference mark occurs, as shown in Figure 11-14 on the next page. The Beneath Text option places footnotes on the same page as their reference marks, but Word prints them directly below the last paragraph on the page, as shown in Figure 11-15. When you select Bottom Of Page or Beneath Text, Word numbers footnotes continuously from page to page. Select Restart Each Page/Section in the Document dialog box to renumber footnotes beginning with 1 on each document page.

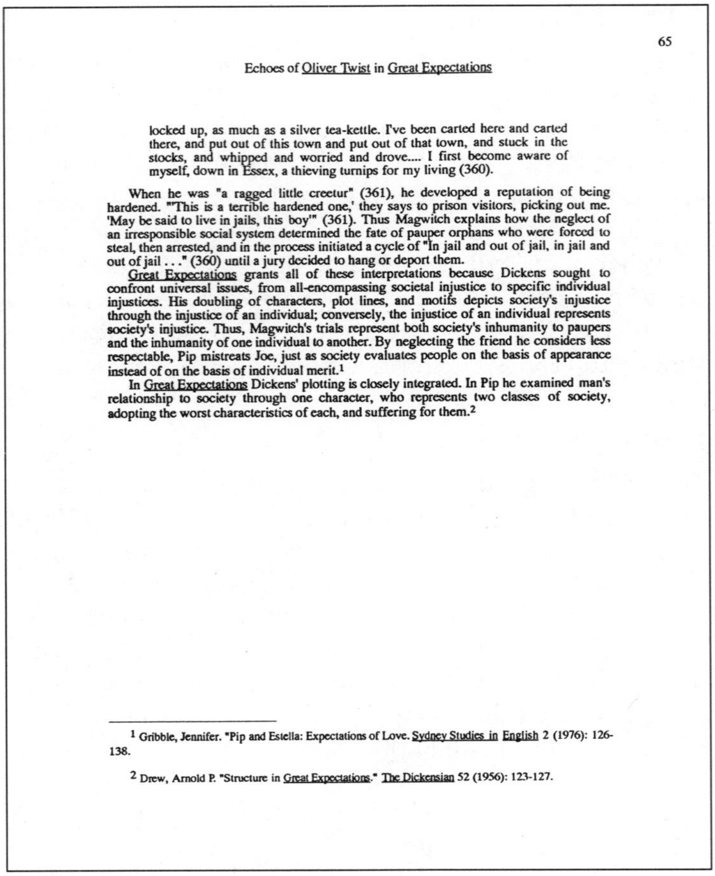

FIGURE 11-14.
When you select the Bottom Of Page option, the footnote text appears at the bottom of the page on which its reference mark appears.

65

Echoes of Oliver Twist in Great Expectations

locked up, as much as a silver tea-kettle. I've been carted here and carted there, and put out of this town and put out of that town, and stuck in the stocks, and whipped and worried and drove.... I first become aware of myself, down in Essex, a thieving turnips for my living (360).

When he was "a ragged little creetur" (361), he developed a reputation of being hardened. "'This is a terrible hardened one,' they says to prison visitors, picking out me. 'May be said to live in jails, this boy'" (361). Thus Magwitch explains how the neglect of an irresponsible social system determined the fate of pauper orphans who were forced to steal, then arrested, and in the process initiated a cycle of "In jail and out of jail, in jail and out of jail . . ." (360) until a jury decided to hang or deport them.

Great Expectations grants all of these interpretations because Dickens sought to confront universal issues, from all-encompassing societal injustice to specific individual injustices. His doubling of characters, plot lines, and motifs depicts society's injustice through the injustice of an individual; conversely, the injustice of an individual represents society's injustice. Thus, Magwitch's trials represent both society's inhumanity to paupers and the inhumanity of one individual to another. By neglecting the friend he considers less respectable, Pip mistreats Joe, just as society evaluates people on the basis of appearance instead of on the basis of individual merit.[1]

In Great Expectations Dickens' plotting is closely integrated. In Pip he examined man's relationship to society through one character, who represents two classes of society, adopting the worst characteristics of each, and suffering for them.[2]

---

[1] Gribble, Jennifer. "Pip and Estella: Expectations of Love. Sydney Studies in English 2 (1976): 126-138.

[2] Drew, Arnold P. "Structure in Great Expectations." The Dickensian 52 (1956): 123-127.

To group footnotes at the end of each document section, select the End Of Section option in the Footnotes Position drop-down list box. Footnotes printed with this option selected appear immediately after the section's last paragraph, not at the bottom of the last page or on a separate page. If your document contains only one section, Word places footnotes at the end of the document. If you select End Of Section, Word automatically activates the Include Endnotes option in the Section dialog box. Deselect this option for sections in which you don't want footnotes to print.

Footnotes grouped at the end of each section can be numbered sequentially throughout the entire document or by section. The Restart Each Section option in the Document dialog box numbers the footnotes in each section separately. Deselect this option to number all the footnotes in the document sequentially.

FIGURE 11-15.
When you select the Beneath Text option, the footnote text appears directly below the last paragraph on the page.

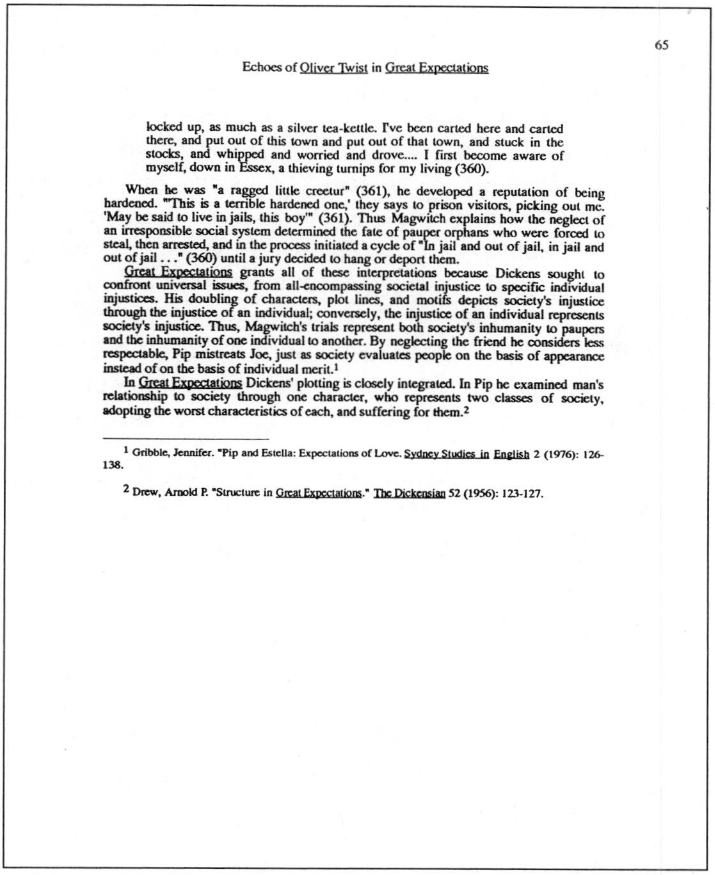

65

Echoes of Oliver Twist in Great Expectations

locked up, as much as a silver tea-kettle. I've been carted here and carted there, and put out of this town and put out of that town, and stuck in the stocks, and whipped and worried and drove.... I first become aware of myself, down in Essex, a thieving turnips for my living (360).

When he was "a ragged little creetur" (361), he developed a reputation of being hardened. "'This is a terrible hardened one,' they says to prison visitors, picking out me. 'May be said to live in jails, this boy'" (361). Thus Magwitch explains how the neglect of an irresponsible social system determined the fate of pauper orphans who were forced to steal, then arrested, and in the process initiated a cycle of "In jail and out of jail, in jail and out of jail . . ." (360) until a jury decided to hang or deport them.

Great Expectations grants all of these interpretations because Dickens sought to confront universal issues, from all-encompassing societal injustice to specific individual injustices. His doubling of characters, plot lines, and motifs depicts society's injustice through the injustice of an individual; conversely, the injustice of an individual represents society's injustice. Thus, Magwitch's trials represent both society's inhumanity to paupers and the inhumanity of one individual to another. By neglecting the friend he considers less respectable, Pip mistreats Joe, just as society evaluates people on the basis of appearance instead of on the basis of individual merit.[1]

In Great Expectations Dickens' plotting is closely integrated. In Pip he examined man's relationship to society through one character, who represents two classes of society, adopting the worst characteristics of each, and suffering for them.[2]

[1] Gribble, Jennifer. "Pip and Estella: Expectations of Love. Sydney Studies in English 2 (1976): 126-138.

[2] Drew, Arnold P. "Structure in Great Expectations." The Dickensian 52 (1956): 123-127.

To group all footnotes at the end of the document, select the End Of Document option in the Footnotes Position drop-down list box. Word saves footnotes until it reaches a section in which you've selected the Include Endnotes setting in the Section dialog box or until it reaches the end of your document. Word then prints the footnotes below the last paragraph in the document. When you specify that footnotes should appear at the end of the document, Word always numbers them sequentially.

Changing footnote separators

Word prints a short horizontal line like the one shown in Figure 11-14 to separate the document text and footnote text. If the footnote text extends beyond the bottom of the page, Word places the remaining text on the following page and extends a horizontal line from margin to margin. You can change the appearance of the separators by clicking the Separator or the Cont. Separator button in the Foot-note dialog box and then entering a new footnote separator.

Clicking the Separator button displays a Footnote Separator window, like the one shown in Figure 11-16, which displays the separator currently specified for your document. When you first open this window, Word displays the default separator, a horizontal line about 1.5 inches long that begins in the left margin. You can add text or graphics to the existing line, or you can highlight the line and overwrite it. You can use text characters, either by entering the characters directly or by cutting and pasting text into the window as needed. You can create a graphic to use in place of a separator by choosing the Picture command from the Insert menu. You can also distinguish footnotes with a shaded line or border. In addition, you can use the icons at the top of the Footnote Separator window to add a dynamic page number, date, and time to the separator.

FIGURE 11-16.
Use the Footnote Separator window to customize the separator line that divides your footnotes from your body text.

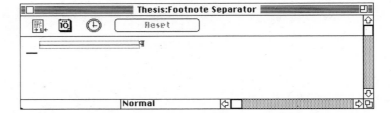

Clicking the Cont. Separator button in the Footnote dialog box displays the Footnote Cont. Separator window, shown in Figure 11-17. This window contains the margin-to-margin line that Word uses as the default separator between docu-ment and footnote text when footnotes continue from one page to another. This line is identical to the Footnote Separator line except for its length. You can add text or graphics or overwrite the separator line in this window.

FIGURE 11-17.
Use the Footnote Cont. Separator window to customize the line that indicates footnote text continues from the previous page.

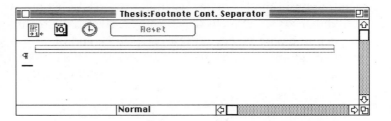

In addition to customizing separators in your document, Word lets you place a notice at the end of a footnote to let your reader know that the footnote text con-tinues on the next page. To create a continuation notice, select the Cont. Notice button in the Footnote dialog box. Word displays a Footnote Cont. Notice window, like the one shown in Figure 11-18. You can enter a phrase such as *(continued on*

next page) in this window, or you can click icons to insert the current page number, date, or time into the continuation notice. Word prints the contents of the Footnote Cont. Notice window only when footnote text flows from one page to the next.

FIGURE 11-18.
You can use the Footnote Cont. Notice window to create a message that indicates a footnote continues on the next page.

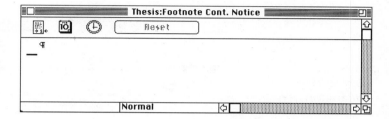

To demonstrate how you might use the Footnote Separator, Footnote Cont. Separator, and Footnote Cont. Notice windows, we have created the document pages shown in Figure 11-19. Figure 11-20 on the next page shows the footnote separator we created in the Footnote Separator window, and Figure 11-21 shows the new footnote continued separator in the Footnote Cont. Separator window. Figure 11-22 shows the Footnote Cont. Notice window.

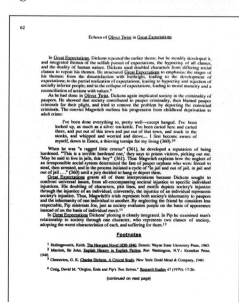
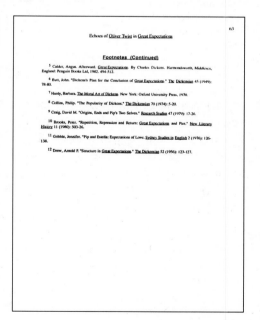

FIGURE 11-19.
These printed pages show the customized separators and continuation notice.

FIGURE 11-20.
*We replaced Word's
default line separator
with the word*
Footnotes.

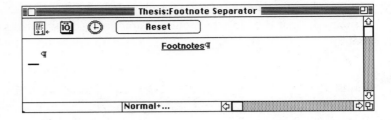

FIGURE 11-21.
*We modified the
continuation separator
to display the words*
Footnotes
(Continued).

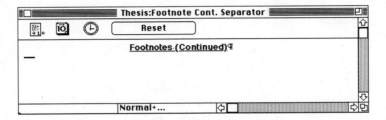

FIGURE 11-22.
We added a
(continued on next
page) *message in the
Footnote Cont. Notice
window.*

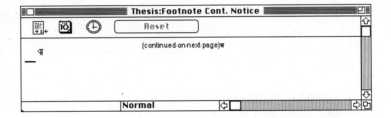

The separators and continuation notices you create in these windows apply to your entire document. If you want to reapply Word's default values, press the Reset button that appears in the Footnote Separator, Footnote Cont. Separator, and Footnote Cont. Notice windows to return the contents of the current window to the default setting.

12

Creating Tables

Word's Table feature lets you create columns of text, numbers, or graphics within your document. You can use the Table feature to create simple tabular layouts, such as a two-column list, or more complex page designs, such as side-by-side text or business forms.

In this chapter, we first show you how to make a simple table. Then we demonstrate the editing and formatting techniques you can use to alter a table and its contents, and explain how you can easily convert document text into a table. At the end of the chapter, we introduce ways to modify a table within your document, as well as some helpful shortcuts that will enable you to create and format tables quickly.

Creating simple tables

You create a new table in Word by choosing the Table command from the Insert menu. Word then displays the Insert Table dialog box, where you define the dimensions of your table. After you close the Insert Table dialog box and insert the table in your document, you can use the indent and table scales on the ruler to change the table's dimensions. You can navigate, type, and format text in the table much as you can elsewhere in a Word document.

Inserting a new table in a document

Let's begin by creating the two-column table shown in Figure 12-1. The text in the second column of this document wraps from one line to the next. You can create this same effect using tabs, but formatting this text in a table is much easier.

FIGURE 12-1.
The Table command makes it easy to create tables like this one.

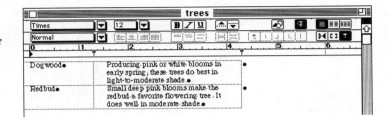

To create a new table, first place the insertion point where you want the table to appear, and then choose Table from the Insert menu. Word displays the Insert Table dialog box shown in Figure 12-2 and suggests a two-column-by-two-row table. You can easily change these dimensions after you create the table.

FIGURE 12-2.
When you choose the Table command, Word displays the Insert Table dialog box.

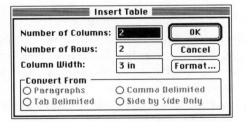

The Insert Table dialog box also lets you define column width. Word determines the suggested column width in the Column Width edit bar by dividing the width of the current text column by the number of columns in the table. When you use Word's default Page Setup and Document settings, your document's text column width is 6 inches. Word divides this area by 2, the number in the Number Of Columns edit bar, and suggests 3 inches as the width of each column in a two-column table.

To use the suggested column width, specify only the number of columns and rows for the table, and then click OK. Word inserts a blank table and places the insertion point in the first cell of the table. For example, to create the table shown in Figure 12-3, we accepted the default Number Of Columns setting and added a third row by entering 3 in the Number Of Rows edit bar.

FIGURE 12-3.
We used the Table
command to create
this blank table.

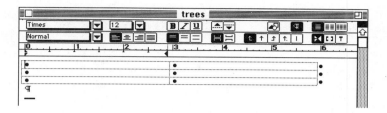

Getting your bearings

As Figure 12-3 shows, Word indicates the rows and columns of the table with gridlines. The area created by the intersection of rows and columns is called a *cell*. When Show ¶ is chosen, Word displays a bold black dot called an *end-of-cell marker* in each cell. The dot indicates the end of the last paragraph of text in that cell. Another black dot, the *end-of-row marker*, appears to the right of each row to mark the right edge of the table. (Word doesn't include the table gridlines and end-of-cell and end-of-row markers when you print the document.)

Word displays table gridlines on the screen by default. You can deselect the Table Gridlines option in the View portion of the Preferences dialog box, but you'll probably find it helpful to display gridlines while you're working with a table. Without them, you might have a hard time discerning table characteristics, such as column width, row depth, and alignment. (If you deselect the Table Grid-lines option, you can still display gridlines by clicking the ¶ button on the ribbon, or choosing the Show ¶ command from the View menu.)

Using the ruler with a table

As you work with tables, you'll use both the indent and table scales on the ruler. When you insert a table, the table scale is automatically activated. To switch to the indent scale, click the Indent Scale button, the third button from the right end of the ruler, as shown in Figure 12-3. The ruler in Figure 12-3 shows the indent scale. As this figure indicates, the left edge of the text area begins at the 0 point on the ruler, and the right edge is marked by a dotted vertical line. Each column is 3 inches wide. In Figure 12-3, the insertion point is in the first cell of the first column. The text area of this cell begins at the 0 point on the ruler and extends to the dotted line just beyond the 2⅞-inch point. (For reasons we will explain in a moment, Word doesn't extend the width all the way to the 3-inch point on the ruler.)

In Figure 12-4 on the next page, the insertion point is in the first cell of the second column, and the ruler's zero point now aligns with the left edge of this cell's text area. Similarly, the dotted vertical line at the 2⅞-inch position now marks the area's right edge.

FIGURE 12-4.
When we move the
insertion point to the
second column, Word
shifts the ruler
display.

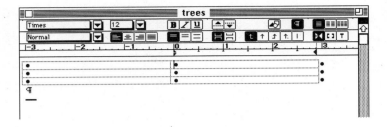

You use the table scale on the ruler to change the width of table columns. To switch to the table scale, click the Table Scale button at the far right end of the ruler. Figure 12-5 shows the document in Figure 12-4 with the table scale displayed.

FIGURE 12-5.
When we switch to the
table scale on the ruler,
Word marks the
position of our column
boundaries.

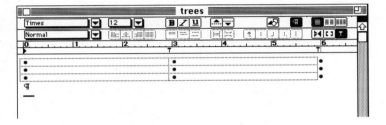

In the table scale, the 0 point on the ruler represents the left edge of your document's text column, while the dotted vertical line (at the 6-inch point in Figure 12-5) marks the column's right edge. (Note that, for reasons we'll explain later, the right edge of the document's text column actually extends slightly beyond the right edge of the text area in the last cell on each row.)

The position of the left edge of the table is denoted by an indent marker (▶), called the *row indent*. Don't confuse this indent marker with the left and first-line indent markers that appear on the ruler in the indent scale. The row indent marker is a solid arrowhead. The right edge of each cell in the current row is marked by a ⊤ symbol just below the ruler line. Notice in Figure 12-5 that each of these markers corresponds to a cell boundary, without taking into account the space between cells.

Navigating within a table

The easiest way to move around in a table is to click the spot where you want to work. You can also navigate a table using the keyboard, as follows:

■ Pressing the Tab key moves the insertion point forward from cell to cell, or from the end of one row to the beginning of the following row. Word moves the insertion point forward one cell and positions the insertion point in front of the first character space in that cell. If the insertion point is in the last cell of the last row of the table, pressing Tab adds a new row to the end of the table.

- Pressing Shift-Tab moves the insertion point backward from cell to cell or from the beginning of one row to the end of the preceding row.

- Pressing the Up direction key or the 8 key on the numeric keypad moves the insertion point to the cell immediately above.

- Pressing the Down direction key or the 2 key on the numeric keypad moves the insertion point to the cell immediately below.

- Pressing the Left direction key or the 4 key on the numeric keypad moves the insertion point one character to the left. If the insertion point is on the first character, pressing either of these keys moves the insertion point to the preceding cell.

- Pressing the Right direction key or the 6 key on the numeric keypad moves the insertion point one character to the right or to the next cell.

- Pressing Command-Option and either the 4 or 6 key on the numeric keypad moves the insertion point directly to an adjacent cell. For example, pressing Command-Option-4 moves the insertion point one cell to the left without stopping at each character in the current cell.

Entering text in a table

To enter text in a table, simply click the cell where you want the text to appear and begin typing. To create the table shown earlier in Figure 12-1, for example, click the first cell of the table, and type the word *Dogwood*. Then press the Tab key or click the cell at the top of the second column, and enter the descriptive text that begins *Producing pink or white blooms*. Figure 12-6 shows the result. You will notice that when the text you enter is longer than the width of the current cell, Word wraps the text within the cell and increases the depth of the other cells in the same row so that the rows in the table remain even.

FIGURE 12-6.
Word wraps text within each cell and readjusts the height of other cells in the row to match.

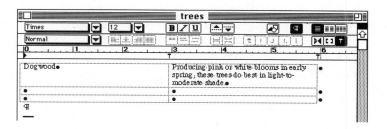

All the cells in a new table share either the Normal style for the current document or assume the formatting of the paragraph that contained the insertion point when you chose the Table command. (For the tables in this chapter, the Normal style font is 12-point Times. We changed the Normal style font from New York, which we specified when we installed Word, to display more text in each table cell. For more information about changing styles, see Chapter 9, "Creating Style Sheets.")

Selecting text in a table

After creating a table, you will often need to modify it. To make most types of modifications, you first need to select all or part of the table text. In many respects, selecting table text is no different than selecting text anywhere in a Word document. However, you can't select part of the text in several cells at the same time. When you select text in two or more cells in a table, Word highlights all the text in all the affected cells, because each cell and each column in a table has its own selection bar.

When you move the pointer to the left edge of a cell, the pointer changes to a right arrow to indicate that it's in the cell's selection bar. Clicking the selection bar quickly selects the entire contents of the cell. Double-clicking the selection bar of any cell selects the contents of every cell in that row. Word highlights the entire row, as shown in Figure 12-7.

FIGURE 12-7.
*Select a row in a table
by double-clicking the
selection bar for any
cell in that row.*

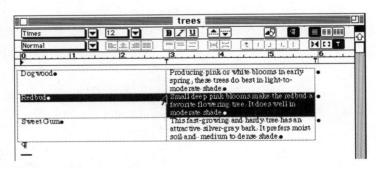

When you move the pointer to the top of a column, the pointer changes to a downward arrow to indicate that it's in the column's selection bar. To select an entire column of text, click the column's selection bar, or press the Option key and click anywhere in that column.

To quickly select an entire table, press the Option key, and double-click anywhere in the table.

Modifying parts of tables

After you create a table, you can modify it in various ways. You can change the width of cells and columns, the spacing between columns, and the height of rows. You can add and delete cells, columns, and rows, and you can merge and split cells. You can also edit and format the table's text. We explain how to make these modifications in this section.

Adjusting cell and column width

You can easily adjust the width of a cell or column by repositioning the end-of-cell marker on the ruler, or by specifying the cell or column width you want in the Table Cells dialog box.

Using the ruler

Unless your table requires extremely precise column dimensions, using the table scale on the ruler is the easiest way to change a cell's width. To adjust the width of a single cell, click the cell, and reposition its end-of-cell marker on the ruler where you want the cell's new right edge to be. As you drag the marker, Word displays the current width of the cell in the status box at the bottom of the document window, helping you to zero in on the exact width you want. To change the width of adjacent cells in a column, select each cell before you drag the marker.

When you use the ruler to change the width of a cell, Word maintains the size of the other cells in the same row, increasing or decreasing the total width of the row as necessary. To change the width of a cell without changing the total row width, press the Shift key as you drag the end-of-cell marker on the ruler. Then if you drag the marker to the right, Word increases the width of the current cell and decreases the width of the cell to the right. If you drag the marker to the left, Word decreases the width of the current cell and increases the width of the cell to the right.

To use the ruler to change the width of an entire column, select the column, click the Table Scale button on the ruler to display the table scale, and drag the marker that indicates the boundary of the column. Word then displays the width of the selected column in the status box. (If the column contains cells of different widths, Word dims the ruler and displays the width of the top cell only. The new width you specify will apply to all the cells in the selected column.) Word maintains the widths of the columns located to the right of the selected column and increases or decreases the total width of the table, as necessary. To change the width of a column without changing the total table width, press the Shift key as you drag the marker. Word then increases or decreases the width of the adjacent column as you drag to maintain the width.

For example, to reduce the width of the first column in the sample table, select the column by pressing the Option key and clicking the column. Click the marker that appears at the 3-inch position on the ruler, and drag it to the 1.5-inch position. The marker at the 6-inch position moves to the 4.5-inch position. Figure 12-8 shows the result.

FIGURE 12-8.
We dragged the marker on the ruler to decrease the width of the first column.

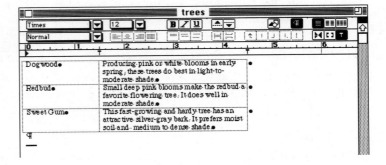

Using the Table Cells dialog box

To adjust the width of a cell or a column more precisely, you can use the Table Cells command. Click the cell or column, and then choose Table Cells from the Format menu. Word displays the dialog box shown in Figure 12-9. (You can also access the Table Cells dialog box by clicking the Format button in the Insert Table dialog box.)

FIGURE 12-9.
You can use the Table Cells dialog box to change the features of a table.

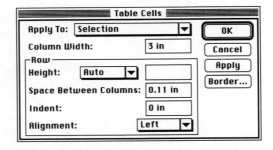

Initially, the formatting that you apply in the Table Cells dialog box affects only the selected cells. The Apply To drop-down list box at the top of the dialog box indicates the part of the table currently selected. You can easily extend the formatting to other parts of the table by selecting other options from the Apply To drop-down list box.

For example, to change the width of an entire column without selecting the column, click one of its cells, and then choose Table Cells. In the Table Cells dialog box, select the Entire Columns Selected option in the Apply To list box. Similarly, to change the width of two or more columns, select one or more cells in each column before you choose Table Cells, and then select the Entire Columns Selected option in the Apply To list box.

When the Apply To edit bar indicates the part of the table you want to modify, enter a measurement in the Column Width edit bar. If you don't specify a unit of measure (in, cm, pt, or pi), Word assumes inches (or the default unit of measurement you've specified in the Preferences dialog box). When you click OK or Apply, Word changes the width of the part of the table you've selected.

Adjusting the space between columns

When you enter text in a cell, some space remains between the cell's left edge and the first character in each line, and between the last character in each line and the cell's right edge. Word automatically reserves this space, which is not marked on your screen, to ensure that the text in adjacent cells doesn't overlap or become difficult to read.

Word's default spacing between columns is ⅑ inch. When you create a new table and open the Table Cells dialog box, the value *.11* is displayed in the Space Between Columns edit bar. This setting determines the maximum space between the text areas of adjacent columns, not between the columns themselves. If you change this setting, you won't see any change in the width of the table cells. Instead, you'll notice that Word rewraps the text in each cell to reflect the new spacing you've defined.

Word allocates half of the Space Between Columns setting to each edge of each cell in the selected row. For example, if you specify 0.5 inches as the Space Between Columns setting, Word maintains a quarter inch of space at the right and left edges of each cell. Unlike the Width setting, however, the Space Between Columns setting affects all the cells in the current row—including the first and last cells. The space doesn't fall only "between columns" as the name of the setting implies.

If you look again at Figure 12-7, for example, you'll notice that although each column is 3 inches wide, text in the table is formatted with Word's default Space Between Columns setting of .11. As a result, the width of the text area in the first cell is slightly less than 3 inches, extending from the 0 position on the ruler to the dotted line. In Figure 12-7, the left boundary line of the table falls just to the left of the 0 position, and the text in the first column of the table is aligned with the 0 position. The space between the table's left boundary line and the text in each cell in the first column is the "space between columns" that Word has allotted to the left edge of each cell.

Figure 12-10 on the next page shows the table after we entered 0.5 as the Space Between Columns setting for the entire table. As you can see, the left boundary of the table is no longer visible on the screen. Word now allots a quarter inch of space to each edge of each cell. To create this space, Word shifts the left edge of all the column boundaries to the left. Because the text area in the right column is now only 2.5 inches wide, Word wraps the text to a new line as needed.

FIGURE 12-10.
We've increased the
Space Between
Columns setting to
0.5 inch.

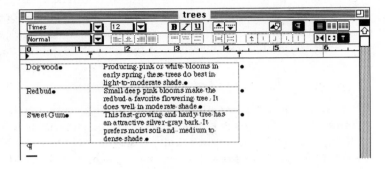

When increasing the space between columns, Word doesn't change the relative alignment of the text in the table. The left edge of all the text in all the columns retains its original alignment. As we explain later in this chapter, you can use paragraph formatting techniques to change the alignment of text within cells. By moving the indent markers on the ruler, you can actually "pull" text into the Space Between Columns area that Word allots to the edges of a cell. We also show you how to shift the entire table to the right or left.

Adjusting row height

As you enter text or graphics in a table, Word adjusts the height of each row to accommodate the content of the individual cells in that row. In Figure 12-8, for example, Word adjusted the height of all the cells in each row to accommodate the wrapping text lines in the second column. If we had increased the font size, Word would have increased the row height even further.

You can specify a minimum height for each row by completing the Height edit bar in the Table Cells dialog box. Word increases the height of a row by inserting space below the text. To insert space above the text instead, use the Open Space button on the ruler or the Before setting in the Paragraph dialog box. (We'll show you how to insert space above rows later in this chapter.)

To increase the height of the rows in the table shown in Figure 12-8, for example, select the entire table, and open the Table Cells dialog box. Then type *.65 in* in the Height edit bar, and click OK. Figure 12-11 shows the result.

FIGURE 12-11.
*We've slightly
increased the height
of all the rows in
the table.*

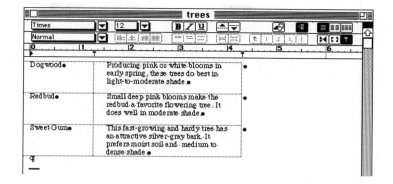

As Figure 12-11 indicates, the Height setting affects all the cells in a row. Word makes certain that the height of each cell is at least 0.65 inch, adding blank space below the text in the cells as necessary. Notice, however, that Word doesn't add space to cells whose height already exceeds this measurement. As a result, the spacing between the text in adjacent rows can appear irregular.

The drop-down list box options immediately to the left of the Height edit bar enable you to specify how Word is to consider the measurement. The default option, Auto, adjusts the row height to contain any text or graphics you insert in any cell in the row, up to the height of the page. When you type a value in the Height edit bar, Word changes the selected option to At Least, indicating that Word will maintain this minimum height and adjust the size of the table cells accordingly. If you select Exactly, Word maintains the exact measurement by cropping cell contents if they exceed the height you set for the row. Select Exactly if you want Word to maintain the row height specified in the Height edit bar, even if this height doesn't leave enough space to separate text in adjacent rows. Word will maintain the row height and overlap the text as necessary to fit within the cell.

To return a row to the default height, open the Table Cells dialog box, and select Auto from the Height drop-down list box.

Adding and deleting table elements

Word allows you to add rows, columns, and cells to an existing table. Adding rows to the end of a table is a simple keyboard procedure, whereas adding columns or cells and deleting any of these elements from a table involves use of the Table Layout command on the Format menu. We show you how to perform each operation in this section.

Adding rows

To add a new row to the end of a table, click an insertion point anywhere in the last cell of the last row, and then press the Tab key. A new blank row appears at the bottom of the table with the same format settings (alignment, indent, and row height) as the preceding row.

For example, to add another row to the sample table, simply click after the last character in the last cell of the table (where the description of the Sweet Gum tree appears), and then press the Tab key once. Figure 12-12 shows the result. Using this new row, we can add a new tree description, as shown in Figure 12-13.

FIGURE 12-12.
To add a new blank row to the end of a table, simply click the last cell of the table, and press the Tab key.

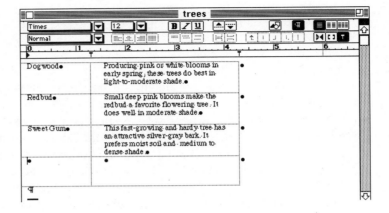

FIGURE 12-13.
We used the new row to add another tree description to the table.

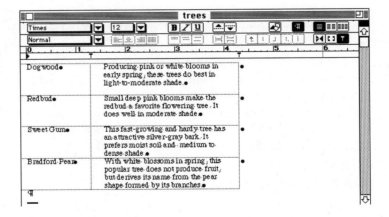

To add a row to any other part of a table, select the row above which you want to insert a new row, and choose Table Layout from the Format menu. To add a row to the top of the sample table, for example, first click any cell in the top row. Then choose Table Layout to display the dialog box shown in Figure 12-14.

FIGURE 12-14.
The Table Layout dialog box allows you to insert and delete rows and columns.

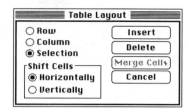

The radio buttons indicate the table elements that Word can insert: Row, Column, or Selection. If you select less than a full row or column, Word activates the Selection option. To add an entire row to the table, select Row, and then click Insert. Word inserts a new blank row, as shown in Figure 12-15, with the same format settings as those of the row immediately below it.

FIGURE 12-15.
Using the Row option in the Table Layout dialog box, we inserted a new row at the top of the sample table.

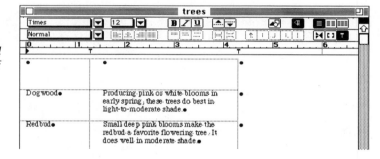

To insert more than one row in a table in a single step, indicate the number of rows you want to insert by selecting cells from that number of rows. For example, to insert three rows in a table, select cells in the three adjacent rows above which you want to make the insertion, and choose Table Layout. In the Table Layout dialog box, select Row, and then click Insert. Word adds three new rows above the rows you selected. The new rows share the formatting characteristics of the top row in your original selection.

Adding columns

You insert columns in a table in much the same way that you insert rows. Suppose you want to insert a new column in the sample table to add text about the mature height of each tree. Click anywhere in the second column, and then choose Table Layout from the Format menu. In the Table Layout dialog box, select the Column option, and then click Insert. Word inserts a new blank column, as shown in Figure 12-16 on the next page.

FIGURE 12-16.
Using the Column
option in the Table
Layout dialog box, we
inserted a new column
in the sample table.

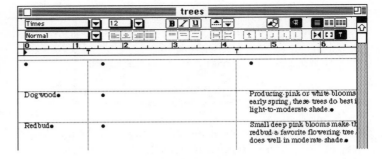

The cells in the new column have the same width as the first cell in the column immediately to the right (the column you selected before inserting the new column). You can easily change the width of the cells in the new column using either the ruler or the Table Cells dialog box. For example, after inserting the new column in the sample table, we reduced its width to 1.25 inches and entered text in that column. We also typed column headings in the blank row at the top of the table. Figure 12-17 shows the results. Later in this chapter, we'll change the text and paragraph settings of the headings.

FIGURE 12-17.
A new column in the
sample table displays
the mature height of
each tree.

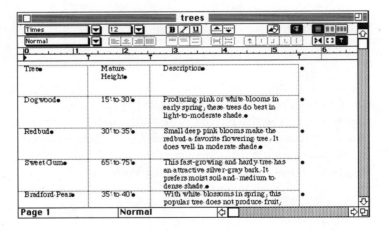

To add several adjacent columns with a single Table Layout command, select cells from adjacent columns in the table to indicate the number of columns you want to insert. For example, to insert two columns, select cells in two columns, open the Table Layout dialog box, select Column, and then click the Insert button. Word adds the new columns to the left of the columns you selected. The new columns have the same width as the top cell in the first column of the selection.

To add a column to the right side of a table, click the area beyond the right edge of the table. Word positions the insertion point between the edge of the table and the end-of-row marker. Next, open the Table Layout dialog box, select the

Column option, and click Insert. Word inserts a new blank column, as shown in Figure 12-18. (We have scrolled to the right in the document window to display the new column.) As you can see, the new column has the same width as the column immediately to the left.

FIGURE 12-18.
With the Table Layout dialog box, you can add a new blank column to the right side of a table.

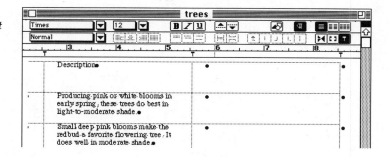

You can't append two or more columns to the right side of a table at the same time. You must add each column separately.

Deleting rows and columns

If you try to use normal editing commands—Cut or Clear—to delete a row or column, Word deletes only the text in the selected row, not the row itself. To delete a row or column, use the Delete button in the Table Layout dialog box.

To delete an entire row, select one or more cells in the row you want to delete, open the Table Layout dialog box, select Row, and then click Delete. Word removes the selected row and shifts up any rows from below so that no gap appears in the table.

To delete a column, select one or more cells in the column, open the Table Layout dialog box, select Column, and click Delete. For example, to delete the extra column at the right side of the sample table, click any cell in the column, choose Table Layout, select Column, and click Delete. The table now looks as it did in Figure 12-17.

If you accidentally delete a row or column, immediately choose the Undo command to recover the deleted element. Word doesn't place a deleted row or column on the Clipboard, so you can't recover it by pasting it back into your document.

Adding and deleting cells

The Table Layout dialog box includes two Shift Cells options: Horizontally and Vertically. These options insert or delete less than a full column or full row of cells by shifting the cells of the table in order to perform the insertion or deletion.

Word inserts a new cell at the current insertion point. If you select the Shift Cells Horizontally option, Word moves existing cells one column to the right to accommodate the new cell. If you select the Shift Cells Vertically option, Word moves existing cells down one row.

To insert two or more adjacent cells, select two or more cells in the table to indicate the number of cells you want to insert. Figure 12-19 shows a simple four-column-by-six-row table. We've selected two adjacent cells in the second row. To insert two cells to the left of the selected cells, open the Table Layout dialog box, select the Shift Cells Horizontally option, and then click Insert. Figure 12-20 shows the result.

FIGURE 12-19.
We'll use this simple table to illustrate the techniques for inserting and deleting table cells.

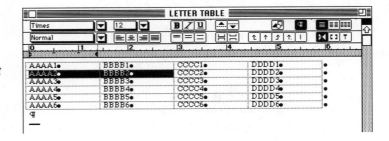

FIGURE 12-20.
The table in Figure 12-19 looks like this after you open the Table Layout dialog box, select Shift Cells Horizontally, and click Insert.

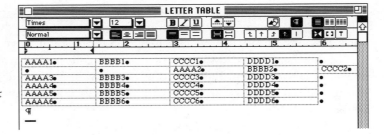

Figure 12-21 shows what happens if you select Shift Cells Vertically instead of Shift Cells Horizontally. Word inserts new cells above the selected cells and adds a new row to the bottom of the table to contain the shifted cells.

FIGURE 12-21.
The table in Figure 12-19 looks like this after you open the Table Layout dialog box, select Shift Cells Vertically, and click Insert.

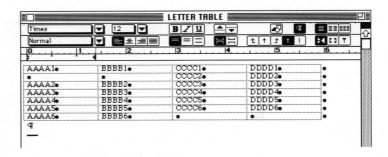

You also use the Table Layout command to delete the two cells selected in Figure 12-19. If you select the Shift Cells Horizontally option and click Delete, Word moves the cells on the right side of the deleted cells to the left, as shown in Figure 12-22. Figure 12-23 shows what happens when you select the Shift Cells Vertically option instead. Notice that the sixth row of the table now has two blank cells.

FIGURE 12-22.
When you select the Shift Cells Horizontally option and delete the cells selected in Figure 12-19, Word shifts the remaining cells in the row horizontally.

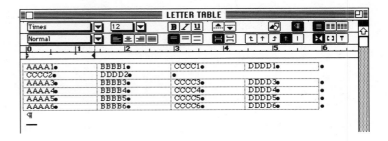

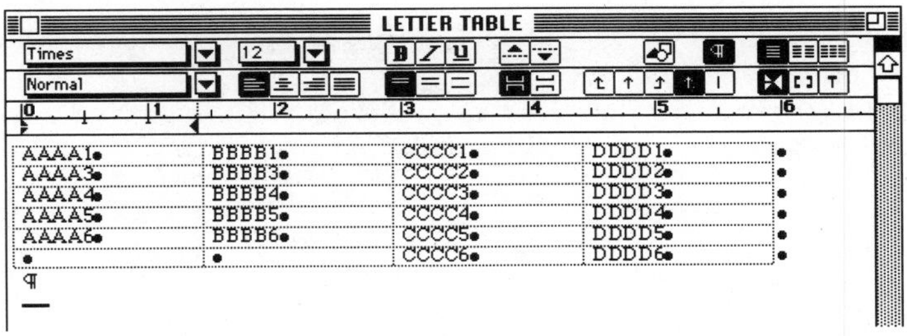

FIGURE 12-23.
When you select the Shift Cells Vertically option and delete the cells selected in Figure 12-19, Word shifts up cells from the rows below.

Merging and splitting cells

The Table Layout dialog box also enables you to merge adjacent cells in the same row. (You can't merge cells in the same column.) To merge cells, select the cells you want to combine, open the Table Layout dialog box, and then click the Merge Cells button. Word removes the boundaries between the selected cells and creates a single cell whose width is equal to the combined widths of the merged cells. Word places any text in the selected cells within the new cell, separating the text from previously separate cells with paragraph symbols so that each paragraph begins on a different line. The text in each paragraph retains its character and paragraph formatting.

One excellent use for cell merging is to create a title that stretches across two or more columns. For example, to add a title row to the table shown in Figure 12-17, first add a new row to the top of the table by selecting all the cells in the top row, opening the Table Layout dialog box, and clicking Insert. Next, merge the three cells in this new row into one cell by selecting the entire row (double-click the selection bar for any cell in the row), opening the Table Layout dialog box, and clicking Merge Cells. Figure 12-24 shows the result.

FIGURE 12-24.
We merged the three cells in the new row at the top of the table into a single cell.

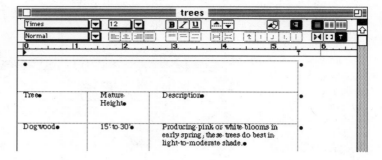

Figure 12-25 shows the table after we entered a table title in the new cell and then centered the title by clicking the Center Alignment button on the ruler.

FIGURE 12-25.
We entered a table title in the top row and then centered it.

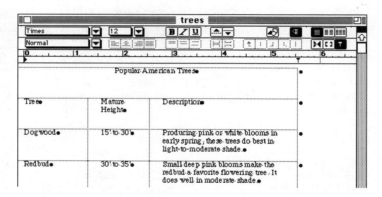

To cancel the merging of two or more cells, you can immediately use the Undo command. You can also click the Split Cell button in the Table Layout dialog box. (When you click a cell that you created by merging two or more cells, Word replaces the Merge Cells button with the Split Cell button.) When you click the Split Cell button, Word breaks the merged cell into the number of cells you originally merged. However, the orginal cell-width formatting is lost, and the split cells are all the same width.

Editing table text

You can easily edit the text within table cells. When you press the Return key in a cell, Word begins a new paragraph within that cell; it doesn't move the insertion point to the next row of the table. In most other respects, you change table text in the same way you change text located anywhere in your document, using all the basic editing techniques we described in Chapter 3, "Working in Word." However, if you want to delete text from a group of selected cells, be sure to choose Cut from the Edit menu or press Command-X. Pressing the Delete key removes the contents of only the first cell in the selection.

You can move and copy table text to locations inside and outside the current table. When you copy or cut and then paste table text, the results of your paste vary, depending on whether you copied or cut an end-of-cell marker. If the selection you paste into a cell contains an end-of-cell marker, Word replaces the entire contents of that cell with the pasted selection. (Word changes the Paste command on the Edit menu to Paste Cells, to alert you that you've selected the entire cell.)

For example, Figure 12-26 shows a table in which we've selected text and an end-of-cell marker. If we choose Copy, click an insertion point in the last cell in the fourth column of the table, and choose Paste Cells, the result is as shown in Figure 12-27. As you can see, the text we copied, AAAA2, replaces the text DDDD6 that formerly appeared in the last cell of the table.

FIGURE 12-26.
*We've selected both the
text and the end-of-cell
marker in a cell.*

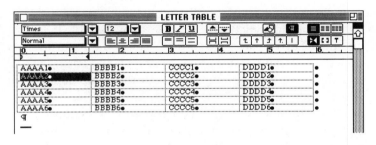

FIGURE 12-27.
*Because we copied the
end-of-cell marker,
Word replaces the
contents of the last
cell in the last row of
the table with the
copied text.*

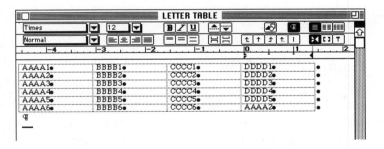

If the selection you paste into a cell doesn't include an end-of-cell marker, Word simply adds that text to the existing cell contents. For example, if the selection in Figure 12-26 included only the text AAAA2 and not the end-of-cell marker, the result of the paste operation would be as shown in Figure 12-28 on the next page. (We inserted a paragraph symbol between the original and copied text to make the result more obvious.)

FIGURE 12-28.
*When the selected text
does not include an
end-of-cell marker,
Word adds the text to
the contents of the
existing cell when
you paste.*

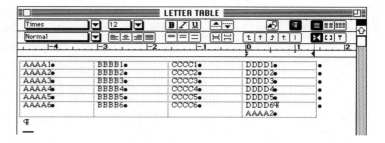

Because you can't select text from two or more cells without also selecting the end-of-cell markers, you must copy or cut the text from each cell individually. Similarly, you can drag and drop text from one part of the table to another. However, you can use this technique to select text in a single cell only; you can't drag and drop a selection that includes an end-of-cell marker.

Selecting a paste area within a table

To paste a group of cells in a table, place the insertion point in the first cell that you want to contain part of the pasted text, and then choose the Paste command. For example, to copy the first two rows of the table in Figure 12-26 and paste them into the last two rows of that table, select the two rows, and choose Copy. Then click the cell that contains AAAA5, and choose Paste Cells. Word pastes the entire selection, overwriting any entries in the paste area beginning with the cell in which the insertion point is located.

You can also highlight the paste area and choose Paste Cells. However, the highlighted paste area must then correspond in both size and shape to the area that you copied or cut. If you select a paste area that is either larger or smaller than the copied or cut area, Word displays the message *Copy and Paste areas are different shapes.*

To paste cells into blank rows, you must first insert new cells.

Pasting text outside a table

You can also paste a group of cells outside a table. If you select text without an end-of-cell marker and then paste or drop the text in a new location outside the table, Word pastes the text without any table formatting. If the selected text includes an end-of-cell marker, Word pastes the text in a new table by creating new table cells to contain the pasted text. The new cells maintain the same dimensions and alignment as the cells you cut or copied from the original table.

For example, in Figure 12-29 a three-column-by-three-row block of cells has been selected. If you copy the block of cells to an area immediately outside the table, Word attaches the new table cells to the existing table. Figure 12-30 shows the table from Figure 12-29 after we inserted a blank paragraph between the original table and the copied cells. As you can see, because we also copied the end-of-cell markers, Word creates a completely new table with cells that are identical to the corresponding cells in the original table.

FIGURE 12-29.
We'll copy this block of cells to an area outside the table.

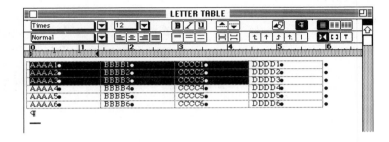

FIGURE 12-30.
When we pasted the block of cells outside the table, Word created a new table.

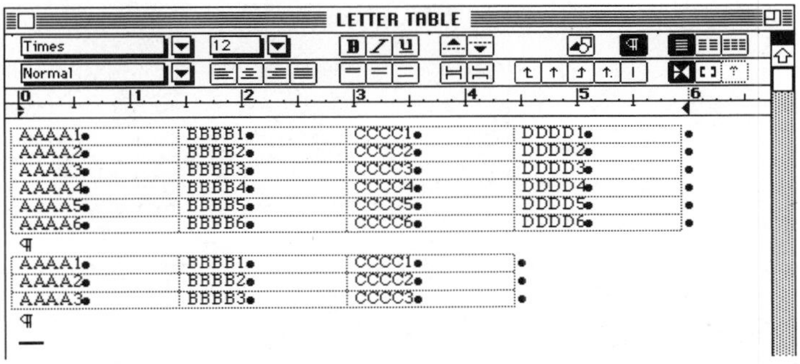

Formatting table text

You can apply any combination of character and paragraph formatting to the text of a table. To make formatting faster and easier, you can also define and apply styles to table text.

Each paragraph in a table can be formatted independently of other paragraphs, displaying different indents, alignment, line spacing, and tabs. Word imposes only a few restrictions: You can't force table text to flow across a cell boundary; you can't create a table within a table; and a table must always be contained within a single document section.

To demonstrate table text formatting, let's return to the sample table we constructed earlier in the chapter. To format the title in Figure 12-25 in 18-point bold type, first select the title, *Popular American Trees*, and then choose Bold from the Format menu and 18 Point from the Font menu. Finally, open the Paragraph dialog box, and add 8 points of Before and After spacing to the title. (We've already formatted this title with centered alignment.)

Follow these same steps to add bold formatting, centered alignment, and Before and After spacing to the column headings (*Tree*, *Mature Height*, and *Description*) and to change the size of these headings to 14 point. Select the entire row, and then choose Bold from the Format menu and 14 Point from the Font menu. Next, open the Paragraph dialog box, and enter 2 in both the Before and After edit bars. Finally, click the Center Alignment button on the ruler's indent scale. Figure 12-31 shows the result of these formatting changes.

FIGURE 12-31.
We formatted the title and column headings in the sample table.

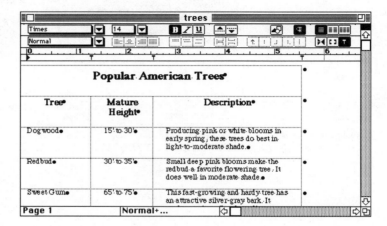

Using paragraph styles in a table

When you create a table, Word assigns to the table text the style of the paragraph in which the insertion point was positioned when you chose the Table command. If you create a table in a new blank document, every cell is formatted with the Normal style. Applying other paragraph styles to table text allows you to format the contents of different cells quickly and consistently.

For example, you can easily define a style named *trees* and apply it to the tree names in the first column of the table. To determine the characteristics of the trees style, format the first tree name, Dogwood, as the "example" for a new style. Select the cell that contains Dogwood, click the Center Alignment button on the ruler, and then click the Open Space button. To define these characteristics as a new style, click the style name that appears in the Styles drop-down list box on the ruler, type the new style name *trees*, and press Return. When the message *Define style "trees" based on selection?* is displayed, click Define. To apply this new style to the other tree names, select the cells containing the names, and then select the trees style from the Styles drop-down list box on the ruler.

Figure 12-32 shows the table after we applied the trees style to the first column. Because we wanted to format the text in the second column in the same way, we also applied the trees style to it. We followed a similar procedure to define the *description* style used to format the third column. The description style calls for 6 points of space before each paragraph.

FIGURE 12-32.
We used styles to format the columns of the sample table.

If you press Return to start a new paragraph in the same cell, Word applies the style used for the previous paragraph to the new paragraph, unless the style specifies a different Next Style. However, the styles don't "carry over" from one cell to the next as you enter text.

For example, suppose you've applied a style named *cells* to the first cell in a table, typed some text in this cell, and pressed the Tab key to move to the adjacent cell. When you begin typing, Word uses the Normal style (or the style that has been applied to that particular cell) to format the text. If you want the adjacent cell to also have the correct cell's style, you must apply it to the cell.

Indenting table text

Using the indent scale on the ruler, you can change table text alignment by moving the indent markers. Changing indents has an effect similar to changing the Space Between Columns setting—Word moves the text closer to or farther from the left and right cell boundaries. Unlike the Space Between Columns setting, however, text alignment can be adjusted selectively, on a cell-by-cell basis.

To indent table text, first be sure the ruler appears in the indent scale. Then select the text you want to indent, and drag the indent markers on the ruler. You can change the indents for a single paragraph using this technique. Any other paragraphs in the same cell remain unaffected.

To change the indents for paragraphs in two or more adjacent cells in the same column, first select the cells, and then drag the indent markers on the ruler. (If the paragraphs in the selection have different indent settings, Word dims the ruler and displays the indent markers for the top paragraph in the selection.) You can't simultaneously change the indent settings for more than one cell in the same row. If you select two or more adjacent cells in a row, the ruler displays indent markers for only the leftmost cell.

Moving the indent markers on the ruler overrides the Space Between Columns setting. As you know, Word divides the Space Between Columns setting between the left and right edges of each cell. If you specify a Space Between Columns setting of 0.5 for one row of a table, Word inserts a quarter inch of space at both edges of each cell in that row. To push the text closer to the cell boundaries, select the cells you want to adjust, and move the indent markers on the ruler.

For example, Figure 12-33 shows a table that has 2-inch wide columns and a Space Between Columns setting of 0.5 inch. Suppose you want to move the text in the first column closer to the left table boundary and the text in the second column closer to the right table boundary. Begin by selecting the first column, and then with the ruler in the indent scale, drag the left and first-line indent markers a quarter inch to the left. Next, select the second column, and drag the right indent marker a quarter inch to the right. Figure 12-34 shows the result.

FIGURE 12-33.
This table has a Space Between Columns setting of 0.5 inch, which creates extra space between the table boundaries and the table text.

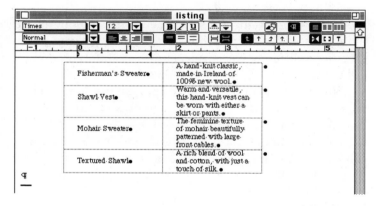

FIGURE 12-34.
By moving the indent markers on the ruler, we moved the text closer to the table boundaries.

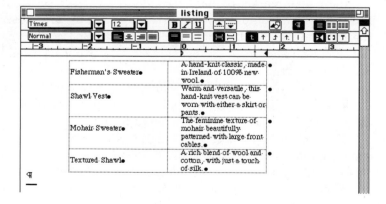

Applying Before and After spacing to table text

The Before and After settings in the Paragraph dialog box (and the Open Space button on the ruler) offer ways to create space between table text and the top and bottom boundaries of each cell. When you apply Before spacing, After spacing, or both to paragraphs in a cell, Word increases the height of that cell and other cells in the same row. Word does not apply the Before and After spacing to the text in all the cells in the row, however. If you want the spacing between all the cells in a row and the cells immediately above to be uniform, you must select all the cells in the row before adjusting the spacing.

Using tab stops in a table

You can use tab stops to align the text in one or more cells or to split a cell into two or more "columns" without having to insert a new cell. Splitting a cell with tabs is especially convenient when only a few cells need columnar formatting. You can also use tab stops to decimal-align a column of numbers.

Pressing the Tab key in a table moves the insertion point to the next cell in the same row. To move to the next tab stop in a table, press Option-Tab. (For more information on setting and using tab stops, see Chapter 5, "Formatting Documents and Paragraphs.")

Figure 12-35 shows an example of a table that includes tab stops. As you can see on the ruler, we used a decimal tab to align the numbers in the third column.

FIGURE 12-35.
You can use tab stops in a table to align text and numbers.

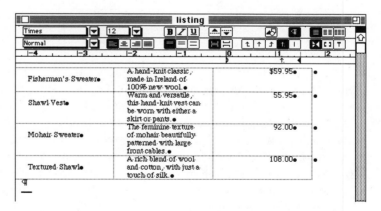

Modifying tables in relation to their documents

When a table and the text within it appear the way you want, you can use options in the Table Layout dialog box to align the table within the margins of the document page or to indent selected rows. You can also split the table into two or more separate tables and apply borders and shading to an entire table or to selected table cells. We discuss these options in this section.

(The Frame command on the Format menu enables you to position a table on a page. Use this command, for example, to position a table in the middle of a page with text surrounding it. We discuss the Frame command in detail in Chapter 10, "Creating Professional Documents.")

Changing table and row alignment

Occasionally you'll want to specify a different alignment for an entire table or for selected rows. After you select cells in the rows whose alignment you want to change, use the Alignment drop-down list box in the Table Cells dialog box, shown in Figure 12-36, to change either the alignment of the entire table or of the individual rows.

FIGURE 12-36.
Use the Alignment drop-down list box in the Table Cells dialog box to change the position of a table.

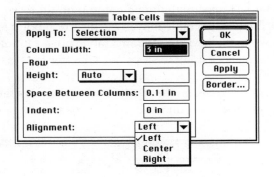

The options in the Alignment drop-down list box change the position of a table relative to the document's text area. The default Left option aligns the left boundary of the table with the left edge of the text area. (The table boundary actually appears slightly to the left of the edge of the text area because of the Space Between Columns setting.) The tables shown up to this point all have left alignment. Select the Center option to center the table on your document's text area. Select Right alignment to align the right boundary of the table with the right edge of the text area. (Again, because of the Space Between Columns setting, the right edge of the table text will not be aligned exactly with the right edge of your document's text area.)

You can apply an Alignment option to individual rows in a table or to the entire table. If you select one or more cells in every row of the table, Word applies the alignment to the entire table. You can also select any cell or cells in the table and then select Each Cell In Table from the Apply To drop-down list box to achieve the same effect. If you want to apply an Alignment option to certain rows in a table, select a cell or group of cells from the rows, and then select Entire

Rows Selected from the Apply To drop-down list box. The alignment of a table or
a row has nothing to do with the alignment of the text within individual cells of
that table.

For example, suppose you want to center the table shown earlier in Figure
12-19. After clicking a cell, open the Table Cells dialog box, select the Center option, and then select the Each Cell In Table option from the Apply To drop-down
list box. Figure 12-37 shows the result. (We've reduced the size of the cells in this
table and added some text using Word's default margin settings to better illustrate the result.)

FIGURE 12-37.
*We used the Center
alignment option to
center the table on
the page.*

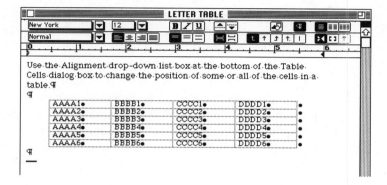

Figure 12-38 shows the same table after we applied left alignment to the first
two rows, center alignment to the middle two rows, and right alignment to the
last two rows.

FIGURE 12-38.
*We applied the Left,
Center, and Right
alignment options to
the rows in this table.*

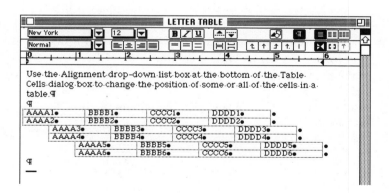

The Indent setting in the Table Cells dialog box allows you to shift one or
more rows to the right or left in relation to the document's text area. For example,
suppose you're using the default Left alignment and you want to shift the entire
table half an inch to the right. Enter .5 in the Indent edit bar, and then select the

Each Cell In Table option from the Apply To drop-down list box. When you click OK or Apply, Word shifts all the rows of the table half an inch to the right.

Because Word allows you to place a row in the margin area of your page, you can cause part of a table to "hang" outside the margin by adjusting the indentation of one or more rows. For example, suppose you want to create a hanging row in a table that has the default Left alignment. Click one cell in that row, open the Table Cells dialog box, and enter an Indent setting of –.5. Select the Selection option in the Apply To drop-down list box, and click OK or Apply. Word shifts the row half an inch to the left.

An Indent setting other than the default of 0 affects the table's alignment. For example, suppose you specify an Indent setting of 0.5, and then you select Center as the Alignment option and Each Cell In Table as the Apply To option. Word centers the table between the half-inch indent that you've specified and the right edge of the text area.

You can also use the ruler's table scale to indent one or more rows of a table. As we've pointed out, in the table scale the ruler displays a row indent marker (▶) at the 0 position. By dragging this marker, you can change the indentation of selected rows. To indent the entire table by half an inch, select any column in the table, and drag the row indent marker half an inch to the right.

Splitting a table

To split a table horizontally, you insert a paragraph symbol between the two rows where you want the table to split. Simply click anywhere on the row below which you want the split to occur. Then press Command-Option-Spacebar.

For example, to split the six-row table shown in Figure 12-37 into two three-row tables, first click anywhere on the fourth row of the table, and then press Command-Option-Spacebar. Word inserts a paragraph symbol before row four, as shown in Figure 12-39. You can then enter text or graphics or even another table in the blank area between the two smaller tables.

FIGURE 12-39.
You can split a table by pressing Command-Option-Spacebar.

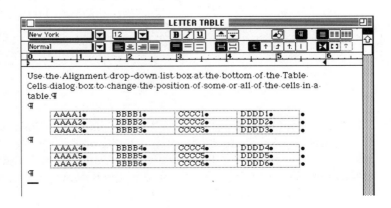

If you open a new document, create a table, and then want to add some text before the table, click anywhere in the table's first row, and press Command-Option-Spacebar. Word shifts the table down and inserts a paragraph symbol above the table. Simply place the insertion point before the paragraph symbol, and begin typing.

Another way to split a table horizontally is to convert one or more rows in the table to text by selecting those rows and choosing the Table To Text command from the Insert menu. (This command replaces the Table command when you select any part of a table.) Word then displays the Table To Text dialog box shown in Figure 12-40.

FIGURE 12-40.
The Table To Text dialog box lets you convert the text in selected rows to normal document text.

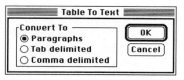

Select one of the three Convert To options (Paragraphs, Tab Delimited, or Comma Delimited), and click OK. Word converts the selected rows to the specified type of document text. If you select blank rows in the table, Word creates blank paragraphs to divide the table. We'll talk more about the Table To Text command later in this chapter.

Word doesn't provide a method for splitting a table vertically between columns. However, you can simulate a vertical split by inserting one or more blank columns in the middle of a table. Simply select the Insert button in the Table dialog box to insert a blank column where you want the vertical "split" to occur.

Adding borders, shading, and gridlines to a table

As we've explained, the lines that define a table's row and column boundaries on the screen don't appear when you print the table. But you can easily add borders and gridlines to the table by clicking the Border button in the Table Cells dialog box. Word then displays the Border dialog box, which you can use to apply borders or shading to an entire table, to selected rows and columns, or to individual cells. You can also add gridlines to the entire table.

To apply a border or shading, either select the part of the table you want to format, or select a cell or group of cells in the table. Next, choose Table Cells from the Format menu. If you selected the entire table, the Apply To drop-down list box is not available because Word assumes you want to format all the cells in the table. If you selected only part of the table, you can use the Apply To options to apply borders or shading to the selected cells, rows, or columns, or to the entire table. When you've selected the Apply To option you want, click the Border button. When only one cell is selected, Word displays the Border dialog box shown in Figure 12-41.

FIGURE 12-41.
Use the Border dialog box to apply borders to selected parts of a table or an entire table.

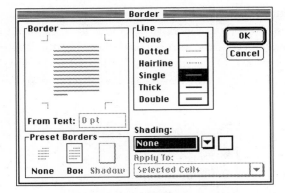

The Border dialog box includes five Line options: Dotted, Hairline, Single, Thick, and Double. In the upper-left corner is a diagram you can use to "draw" the type of border you want to create. After you select a Line option, click different parts of the border diagram to add and remove borderlines. For example, to add a thick borderline to the right side of a selected cell or group of cells, click the Thick Line option, and then click the right side of the diagram.

You can also select the Box option from the Preset Borders area at the bottom of the dialog box to put a box around the selection. (The Shadow option isn't available for tables.) For example, to put a thick box around the sample table shown earlier in Figure 12-32, first select the entire table by pressing the Option key and then double-clicking the table. Next, open the Table Cells dialog box, click Border to open the Border dialog box, and select Thick. Then click the Preset Borders Box option at the bottom of the Border dialog box. Figure 12-42 shows the Border dialog box at this point.

FIGURE 12-42.
You can use these settings in the Border dialog box to put a border around an entire table.

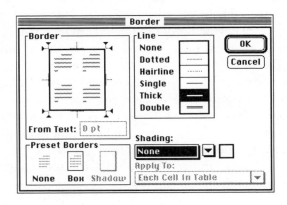

To add the border, click OK in the Border dialog box and in the Table Cells dialog box. Figure 12-43 shows the printed table.

FIGURE 12-43.
*We put a border
around the sample
table.*

Popular American Trees

Tree	Mature Height	Description
Dogwood	15' to 30'	Producing pink or white blooms in early spring, these trees do best in light to moderate shade.
Redbud	30' to 35'	Small deep pink blooms make the redbud a favorite flowering tree. It does well in moderate shade.
Sweet Gum	65' to 75'	This fast-growing and hardy tree has an attractive silver-gray bark. It prefers moist soil and medium to dense shade.
Bradford Pear	35' to 40'	With white blossoms in spring, this popular tree does not produce fruit, but derives its name from the pear shape formed by its branches.

To apply shading to the part of the table identified in the Apply To edit bar in the Table Cells dialog box, simply select a shading percentage from the Shading drop-down list box in the Border dialog box. Word fills the box next to the list box to indicate the result.

Figure 12-44 on the next page shows the sample table after we removed the border and selected the 10% option in the Shading list box.

To add gridlines to a table, first select the entire table, or select part of the table and then select the Each Cell In Table option in the Apply To drop-down list box. Then open the Border dialog box, and click in the middle of the diagram to "draw" lines between the cells, as shown in the dialog box in Figure 12-45 on the next page.

FIGURE 12-44.
We applied a 10%
shade to the sample
table.

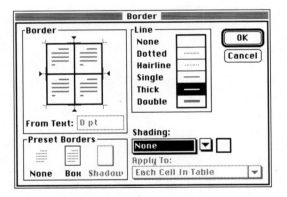

Popular American Trees

Tree	Mature Height	Description
Dogwood	15' to 30'	Producing pink or white blooms in early spring, these trees do best in light to moderate shade.
Redbud	30' to 35'	Small deep pink blooms make the redbud a favorite flowering tree. It does well in moderate shade.
Sweet Gum	65' to 75'	This fast-growing and hardy tree has an attractive silver-gray bark. It prefers moist soil and medium to dense shade.
Bradford Pear	35' to 40'	With white blossoms in spring, this popular tree does not produce fruit, but derives its name from the pear shape formed by its branches.

FIGURE 12-45.
These dialog box
settings will create
gridlines in the
sample table.

Using different line styles

You can enhance the appearance of your borders by mixing borderline styles. For example, you could define the cells in Figure 12-43 by using thick lines for the outline border and thinner lines for the gridlines between rows and columns.

Put a thick box around the table by clicking the Thick Line option in the Border dialog box and then clicking the Preset Borders Box option. Next, click the middle of the diagram to add gridlines, and click the Single Line option to make these lines thinner. Click OK in the Border dialog box, and then click OK in the Table Cells dialog box. Figure 12-46 shows the printed result.

FIGURE 12-46.
You can use different line styles for different parts of the table.

Popular American Trees		
Tree	Mature Height	Description
Dogwood	15' to 30'	Producing pink or white blooms in early spring, these trees do best in light to moderate shade.
Redbud	30' to 35'	Small deep pink blooms make the redbud a favorite flowering tree. It does well in moderate shade.
Sweet Gum	65' to 75'	This fast-growing and hardy tree has an attractive silver-gray bark. It prefers moist soil and medium to dense shade.
Bradford Pear	35' to 40'	With white blossoms in spring, this popular tree does not produce fruit, but derives its name from the pear shape formed by its branches.

You might also want to use different Line options for different sections of an individual cell's border. To do this, select each cell individually, and then apply the borders you want in the Border dialog box.

Deleting borders and shading

To delete all or part of a border, select the cells with borders you want to remove, and open the Border dialog box. To delete all the borders from the selected cells, select None in the Preset Borders section. To remove only selected parts of the border, select None as the Line option, and then click the individual borderlines in the diagram. To remove shading, select the None option at the top of the Shading drop-down list box. Click OK to close the Border dialog box, and then click OK to close the Table Cells dialog box and implement the changes.

Deleting tables

As we've explained, Word doesn't allow you to delete table cells by selecting them and pressing Delete on the keyboard. However, you can delete an entire table from your document in a number of ways. First, you can select the table, choose the Table Layout command from the Format menu, and then click Delete in the Table Layout dialog box. You can also select all the cells in one column of the table, open the Table Layout dialog box, click the Row option, and then click Delete. Word then deletes all the rows in which you've selected a cell—or the entire table. Finally, you can select an entire row of the table, open the Table Layout dialog box, click the Column option, and then click Delete.

You can use the Undo command to recover a deleted table. However, because Word doesn't place a deleted table on the Clipboard, you can't recover a table by pasting it back into your document.

Converting document text to table text and vice versa

You can convert existing document text to a table by using the Text To Table command, which replaces the Table command on the Insert menu when you select text in your document. You can similarly convert text in a table to document text by using the Table To Text command, which replaces the Table command on the Insert menu when you select table text.

Converting document text into a table

One of Word's most convenient features is its ability to convert existing document text into a table. You can easily convert text whose elements are separated by tabs or commas—such as a database imported from another program. These elements are said to be *delimited* by the punctuation mark that separates them. You can also convert plain paragraphs that have no tabs, commas, or special formatting into a table.

To convert existing text into a table, first select the text, and choose Text To Table from the Insert menu. When the Insert Table dialog box appears, the Convert From options are available at the bottom of the dialog box, as shown in Figure 12-47. (Normally, these options are dimmed.)

FIGURE 12-47.
If you select text before choosing the Text To Table command, the Convert From options in the Insert Table dialog box are available.

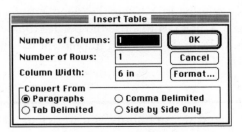

Word usually selects the Convert From option that best describes the type of text you're converting. If the selected text contains a mixture of delimited types, however, Word might select the wrong option. For example, if you select one line of text that contains words separated by tabs and another line that contains words separated by commas and then choose the Text To Table command, Word selects the Tab Delimited option. When you click OK to create the table, Word places the text in the comma-delimited line in a single cell. If you change the option to Comma Delimited, Word places the text in the tab-delimited line in a single cell.

The Side By Side Only option converts any side-by-side paragraphs in your text selection into table format, ignoring the rest of the paragraphs in the selection. We discuss the Side By Side command later in this chapter. To convert the other paragraphs into a table format, you must select them, choose the Text To Table command, and then select the Paragraphs option.

When you convert existing text into a table, Word suggests Number Of Columns and Column Width settings based on the text selection. If you select the Tab Delimited option, the paragraph with the most tabs determines the suggested Number Of Columns setting. Similarly, if you select the Comma Delimited option, the paragraph with the most commas determines the suggested Number Of Columns setting. The width of the current text column is then divided by the number of columns to determine the Column Width setting.

When you convert plain or side-by-side paragraphs, Word suggests 1 as the Number Of Columns setting. Enter a 2 into the Number Of Columns edit bar to convert side-by-side paragraphs into a two-column table. You'll probably need to adjust the paragraph margins settings for each column after conversion.

When you select tab-delimited or comma-delimited text, the Number Of Rows setting in the Insert Table dialog box is dimmed. Word sets the number of rows in the new table based on the number of text lines you are converting to table format.

Let's look at a quick example of how you might convert existing text to table format. Figure 12-48 shows a document that lists names and addresses. You might have created this list as the data document in a print merge procedure, separating the fields (FirstName, LastName, Address, and so on) by tabs.

FIGURE 12-48.
You can convert tab-delimited text like these names and addresses to table format.

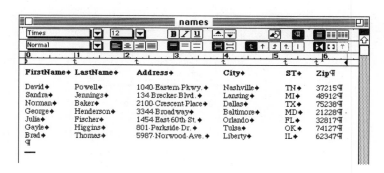

To convert this text to a table, select all the rows, and then choose Text To Table from the Insert menu. Because Word suggests the correct settings for the table in the Insert Table dialog box, you can simply click OK to complete the procedure. Figure 12-49 shows the result.

names
Times
12
Normal
FirstName• LastName• Address• City• ST• Zip•
David• Powell• 1040 Eastern Pkwy.• Nashville• TN• 37215•
Sandra• Jennings• 134 Brecker Blvd.• Lansing• MI• 48912•
Norman• Baker• 2100 Crescent Place• Dallas• TX• 75238•
George• Henderson• 3344 Broadway• Baltimore• MD• 21228•
Julia• Fischer• 1454 East 60th St.• Orlando• FL• 32817•
Gayle• Higgins• 801 Parkside Dr.• Tulsa• OK• 74127•
Brad• Thomas• 5987 Norwood Ave.• Liberty• IL• 62347•
Page 1
Normal

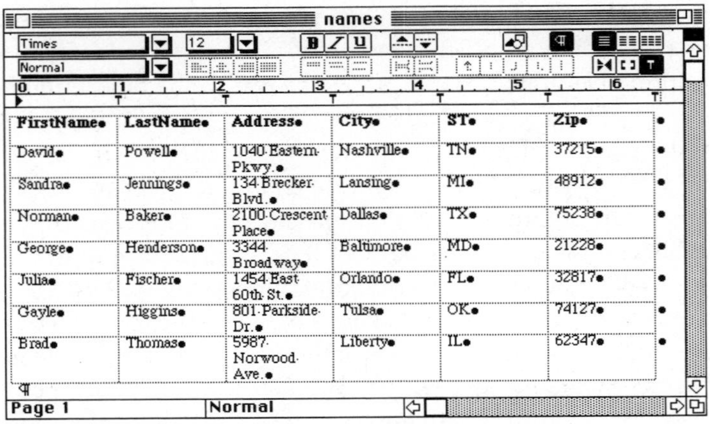

FIGURE 12-49.
Word created this table from the document shown in Figure 12-48.

In the third column of Figure 12-49, notice that Word wraps the address on two lines to fit it within the cell boundaries. If you wanted to print this table, you could widen this column and adjust adjacent columns to ensure that each address appears on a single line. However, Word has no trouble interpreting the wrapped information in a print merge procedure.

Converting a table to text

Word makes it easy for you to convert selected rows of a table, or an entire table, to document text. To convert table text, first select the row or rows you want to convert. You must select entire rows; otherwise, Word won't be able to complete the conversion. Next, choose the Table To Text command from the Insert menu to display the dialog box shown in Figure 12-50. Select one of the Convert To options, and click OK.

Table To Text
Convert To
Paragraphs
Tab delimited
Comma delimited
OK
Cancel

FIGURE 12-50.
Word displays this dialog box when you choose the Table To Text command.

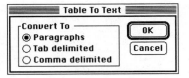

If you select the Paragraphs option, Word places the text in each table cell in a separate paragraph. If a cell contains multiple paragraphs, the paragraphs remain separate after the conversion. Any paragraph formatting applied to the table text, such as indentation or line spacing, is preserved.

If you select the Tab Delimited or Comma Delimited option, Word separates the text of each cell in a row with tabs or commas. Each row of the table is converted into a single paragraph. If a cell contains multiple paragraphs, the paragraphs remain separate after the conversion.

Sorting tables

In Chapter 13, ''Using Word Tools,'' we explain the Sort command on Word's Tools menu. In addition to sorting document text, you can sort all or part of a table. When sorting a table, Word follows most of the rules for sorting explained in Chapter 13. For example, Word uses ASCII codes to determine how to sort the table, and the default sort order is ascending. To sort a table in descending order, press the Shift key as you choose the Sort command.

Word always sorts a table by rows; you can't use the Sort command to rearrange the cells in a row by columns. To sort a table, Word looks at the first character (or first few characters) in each cell. The order of paragraphs within cells is not affected by sorting.

For example, to sort the information in the trees table we created earlier in this chapter into alphabetical order by tree name, select the tree names in the first column. (Do not select the *Tree* column heading, and don't select all the rows. When Word sorts the table, it will keep the rows intact.) Then choose Sort from the Tools menu. Figure 12-51 shows the result.

FIGURE 12-51.
Using the Sort command, we arranged this table in alphabetical order by tree name.

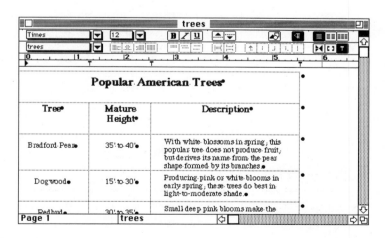

The column you select serves as the key to the sort procedure. As Figure 12-51 indicates, Word sorts the text in all the rows of a table—based on the names in the selected column. To sort the sample table by tree height, for example, begin by selecting the second column of the table, as shown in Figure 12-52. (If you select more than one column, Word uses the leftmost column in the selection as the key to the sort procedure.) Then choose Sort from the Tools menu. Figure 12-53 shows the result.

FIGURE 12-52.
The column you select before choosing the Sort command serves as the key for the sort.

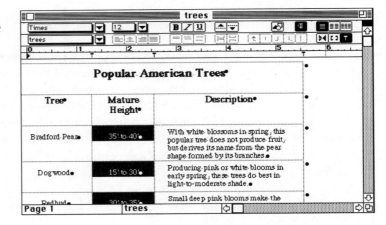

FIGURE 12-53.
The table is now arranged in ascending order by height.

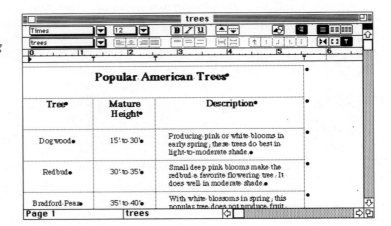

Table shortcuts

If you often work with tables in Word, you'll soon discover ways to expedite table formatting. Three shortcuts in particular are certain to help you. Displaying a table in Outline view enables you to drag and drop entire rows quickly. Saving formatted tables as glossary entries lets you insert the table as a template without having to create and format it every time you want to use it. Finally, adding many of the options available in the Table Layout dialog box directly to a Word menu, or establishing keystroke combinations for these options, enables you to bypass dialog boxes and apply options quickly.

You might consider using the Side By Side command to format paragraphs instead of creating a table. Adding this command to a menu (using the Commands dialog box) enables you to place paragraphs side by side in your document without creating a table.

Moving rows quickly in Outline view

The fastest way to reposition table rows uses Word's outline feature. Chapter 14, "Outlining," describes this feature in detail. Even if you're not familiar with Outline view, you can easily use the outline feature to reposition a selected row quickly. You can even move a row to a location outside the table.

To move a row quickly, first choose Outline from the View menu. Word replaces the ruler at the top of your screen with a row of outline icons and displays a □ symbol next to each row in the table. Simply select the row you want to move, and drag the symbol beside the row up or down to specify a new location. As you drag, Word displays an arrow to the left of the table to indicate the row's new position on the page. For example, in Figure 12-54 we selected the fifth row of the table and moved the symbol between the second and third rows. When we released the mouse button, Word moved the row as shown in Figure 12-55.

FIGURE 12-54.
Move an entire row quickly by dragging and dropping the row in Outline view.

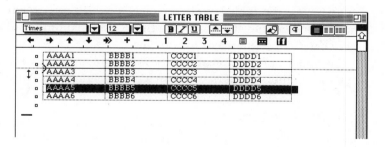

FIGURE 12-55.
When you release the mouse button, Word moves the selected row to its new location.

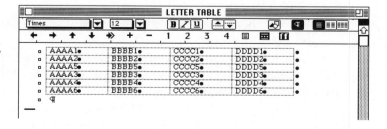

After you've repositioned table rows as you want, choose Normal from the View menu to return to the normal document window.

Saving tables as glossary entries

If you plan to use a table's layout again and again, you can store the table as a glossary entry. As we explain in Chapter 13, "Using Word Tools," the glossary enables you to preserve text or graphics that you use often as templates so that you can insert them as needed into Word documents.

To create a table template, first set up the table the way you want it to be each time you use it. For example, format the first row to contain column headings. If the heading text will be the same every time you use the template, include the text in the first row. If the remaining rows will all have the same formatting, you need to store only a few rows of the table in the glossary. When you insert the template in a document, you can add rows as needed by moving to the last cell and pressing the Tab key.

For more information about Word's glossary feature, see Chapter 13, "Using Word Tools."

Adding Table Layout dialog box options to a menu

In addition to saving table layouts as glossary entries, you can speed up table formatting by adding the Table Layout dialog box options to a Word menu or assigning a keystroke combination to each option. Creating these shortcuts allows you to bypass the Table Layout dialog box, which can expedite your work considerably. For example, if you add the Insert Rows command to a menu, you can directly choose the command to add rows.

For more information about adding commands to Word menus and defining keystroke combinations, see Chapter 18, "Customizing Word."

Side-by-side paragraphs

Tables can slow down both scrolling and screen refreshing. Sometimes you might prefer to use the Side By Side command to format text in adjacent columns, instead of creating a table.

To apply side-by-side formatting, first create and format the text that you want to appear in adjacent columns. Type each entry in a separate paragraph, and format each paragraph by specifying nonoverlapping left and right margins that define where you want the text to appear on the page. Then select the paragraphs, and choose the Side By Side command. (The Side By Side command does not initially appear on a Word menu. However, you can use the Commands dialog box to add this command to a menu, or you can access the command from the

Commands dialog box. For more information about customizing menus and using the Commands command, see Chapter 18, "Customizing Word.")

For example, you can use the Side By Side command to format the tree names and descriptions shown earlier in Figure 12-1 in adjacent columns, instead of creating a table. First type each tree name, followed by its description, in separate paragraphs. Next format each paragraph as necessary, and specify nonoverlapping left and right margins. Then select each set of paragraphs that you want to appear in adjoining columns, and choose Side By Side.

Figure 12-56 shows the text for the first two side-by-side entries. Notice that the left margin of the description begins at the 2-inch mark on the ruler. Although you can't see it, the right margin of the corresponding tree name ends at 1.5 inches. Also notice that Word places a paragraph formatting mark next to each paragraph to which the side-by-side format is applied.

FIGURE 12-56.
We applied the side-by-side format to these paragraphs.

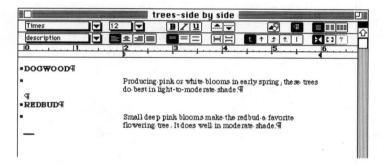

Choose the Page Layout or Print Preview command to see the paragraphs as they will appear when you print. For example, Figure 12-57 shows the text in Figure 12-56 as it appears in Page Layout view. As you can see, Word aligns the first lines of text in each set of paragraphs.

FIGURE 12-57.
Choose the Page Layout or Print Preview command to see the side-by-side paragraphs as they will appear when you print.

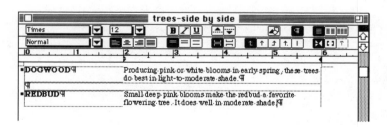

You can make changes to the second paragraph in each side-by-side set of paragraphs in Page Layout view. To make changes to the first paragraph, return to Normal view.

Word-Processing Utilities

13

Using Word Tools

*I*n previous chapters, we've looked at a number of commands and special features that enable you to work in Word quickly and easily. In this chapter, we show you how to take advantage of additional features and tools, such as the glossary (which enables you to save Word text and graphics that you use frequently), the Date command (which lets you insert the current date at the insertion point), and the Symbol command (which lets you view the characters and symbols included in the current font and insert them directly into your document at the insertion point). We look at each of these features in turn in this chapter. Then we look at the Sort, Word Count, and Calculate commands on the Tools menu. As its name suggests, the Sort command sorts document paragraphs and table columns alphabetically or numerically. The Word Count command counts the number of characters, words, lines, and paragraphs in a document. The Calculate command performs simple calculations within Word.

At the end of this chapter, we show you how to format mathematical formulas and symbols within your document by specifying character formulas.

Using the glossary

The glossary is a Word file in which you can store text and graphics that you reproduce often, such as text with unusual formatting, frequently used mailing addresses, a company name or logo, or a common closing to a letter. You can then insert the stored text or graphic into a document without retyping or importing it.

The default glossary is called the Standard Glossary. Word stores this glossary as a separate file, independent of any document files. Initially the Standard Glossary file contains a set of stored entries called *standard* entries. These standard entries include dynamic date and time entries that enable you to insert the current date or time into your document in a variety of formats. In addition to Word's Standard Glossary, you can use any of the three supplemental glossary files—the Date and Time, Formula, and Page Layout glossaries—that come with the Word program. You can add to the contents of the Standard Glossary file by creating your own entries. You can also create separate glossary files, each containing unique sets of entries, and you can open and merge the contents of glossary files. We discuss each of these options in this section.

Glossary basics

A glossary entry can be a single character, a single graphic, or several pages of text and graphics. To create a glossary entry, select the text or graphic you want to store, display the Glossary dialog box, and give the selection a descriptive name. Word saves the selection in the Standard Glossary file. To insert the glossary entry into a Word document, open the Glossary dialog box, select the entry's name, and click Insert. Word inserts the entry at the insertion point.

Displaying the Glossary dialog box

When you open Word, you automatically load the Standard Glossary file. To use the Standard Glossary, choose Glossary from the Edit menu, or press Command-K. Word displays the Glossary dialog box, which lists the standard and user entries currently stored in the file, as shown in Figure 13-1.

FIGURE 13-1.
When you choose the Glossary command from the Edit menu, Word displays the Glossary dialog box.

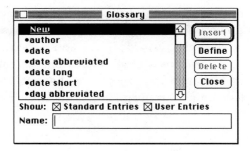

When you choose Glossary from the Edit menu, both the Show Standard Entries and the Show User Entries check boxes are activated. To view only user entries, deselect the Show Standard Entries check box. To view only standard entries, deselect the Show User Entries check box.

No matter which check box option you select, the first entry in the Glossary list box is always New, which you use to define a new entry. After New, the list box displays the glossary entries in alphabetical order. Click the scroll bar or scroll arrows to view all available glossary entries.

When you select a glossary entry from the list box, Word displays the first few characters of the stored text at the bottom of the dialog box. The entry you select appears in the Name edit bar. If you select the Standard Glossary entry *print time with seconds*, for example, the dialog box looks like Figure 13-2.

FIGURE 13-2.
*When you click an
entry in the Glossary
dialog box, Word
displays the first few
characters of the
corresponding text at
the bottom of the
dialog box.*

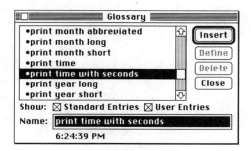

If the stored text for a glossary item is too long to be displayed completely in the dialog box, Word displays as much of the text as will fit, followed by an ellipsis. If you store a graphic in the glossary, Word represents the graphic with a small box at the bottom of the Glossary dialog box.

Using Standard Glossary entries

Word's Standard Glossary file contains 38 standard entries. These entries enable you to insert information from the current document's Summary Info dialog box; information about the current file, page, or section; the date and time specified in various formats; and a print merge entry. Table 13-1 lists the name and corresponding content of each entry. You can't delete these entries from the Standard Glossary file, and any glossary file you create contains them.

Standard Glossary entry	Content or sample content
author	Name of author from Summary Info dialog box
date	February 1, 1993

TABLE 13-1.   *(continued)*
*Selecting a Standard Glossary entry from the first column inserts
the type of entry displayed in the second column.*

TABLE 13-1. *Continued*

Standard Glossary entry	Content or sample content
date abbreviated	Mon, Feb 1, 1993
date long	Monday, February 1, 1993
date short	2/1/93
day abbreviated	Mon
day long	Monday
day of month	1
file name only	Name of current file
file name with path	Volume, folder, and filename
keywords	Keywords from Summary Info dialog box
month abbreviated	Feb
month long	February
month short	2
page number	Current page number
print date	February 1, 1993
print date abbreviated	Mon, Feb 1, 1993
print date long	Monday, February 1, 1993
print date short	2/1/93
print day abbreviated	Mon
print day long	Monday
print day of month	1
print merge	« »
print month abbreviated	Feb
print month long	February
print month short	2
print time	3:00 PM
print time with seconds	3:00:32 PM
print year long	1993
print year short	93
section	Current section number
subject	Subject from Summary Info dialog box
time	3:00 PM
time with seconds	3:00:32 PM
title	Title from Summary Info dialog box
version	Document version from Summary Info dialog box
year long	1993
year short	93

When inserting dates and times in your documents, Word uses the date and time information that you set using the General Controls control panel. Notice that the Glossary list box includes two sets of date and time entries. Entries that are not preceded by the word *print* are static. Selecting a static entry inserts the current date or time in your document as simple characters, like those you type from the keyboard. After insertion, you can edit these entries as you would any other text. Entries preceded by the word *print* are dynamic. When you insert a dynamic date or time into your document, Word automatically updates the date or time each time you print the document. Word also draws a dotted box around the date or time, as shown in Figure 13-3. (This dotted box appears only when Show ¶ is active.)

FIGURE 13-3.
*When you insert a
dynamic date or time
in a document, Word
draws a dotted box
around it.*

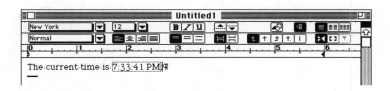

Word treats dynamic date and time entries as single characters, and you can't edit them. You can cut, copy, and paste the entire date or time, but not a portion of it, and you can format only the entire date or time.

When you use the glossary to insert a standard entry in a document, Word formats the entry to match the character formatting of the surrounding text. For example, if you insert the current date between two words with bold formatting, the date also appears in bold.

Defining user entries

Although Standard Glossary entries can save you time, you'll also want to define and save your own text or graphic entries. Suppose you often type documents that include the name of your company. If you add the name to the glossary, you need only to open the glossary and select the name, rather than typing it repeatedly. At first this technique might seem to require additional steps, but after the entry is defined you can add it to your document with just a few keystrokes. You can also add glossary entries to Word's menus or assign keystroke shortcuts to them. (We discuss adding commands to menus in more detail in Chapter 18, "Customizing Word.")

Defining a glossary entry

To define a glossary entry, first type anywhere in your document the full text you want to add to the glossary. Let's use a fictitious company name, *International Consolidated Systems, Inc.,* as an example. After typing the text, drag through it to select it. Be sure to select the single space at the end of the phrase so that you won't have to add a space after you insert the glossary entry in your document. Then choose Glossary from the Edit menu to open the Glossary dialog box. With New highlighted in the list box, type a short identifying name in the Name edit bar—for example, type the abbreviation *ICS*—and then click Define. At this point, the dialog box looks like Figure 13-4. (We've selected only the Show User Entries option to make this example clearer.) To return to your document, click Close, the close box, or anywhere in the document window.

FIGURE 13-4.

After you define a new glossary entry, Word displays the entry name in the Name edit bar and in the list of glossary entries.

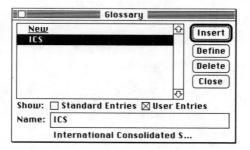

Naming a glossary entry

A glossary name can consist of several words, but can't exceed 31 characters. If you keep each glossary entry as short as possible, you can type it in the Name edit bar quickly and remember it easily.

You can use any characters to specify the glossary entry name, including punctuation marks and special characters produced with Option-key combinations. Word places names that begin with special characters at the end of the list of names in the Glossary dialog box.

If you type a name that has already been defined and then click Define, Word displays the message *That name is already defined*. Word doesn't recognize the case of the text you enter in the Name edit bar. For example, Word considers a lower-case *g* to be the same as an uppercase *G* and the name *go* to be the same as the name *Go*. As a result, you'll find the glossary easier to use.

If you don't enter a name in the Name edit bar, but simply click Define, Word supplies a name like *Unnamed1*. To use a different name, replace *Unnamed1* with the name you want, and then click Define again.

Formatting a glossary entry

Word stores paragraph formatting in the paragraph symbol at the end of a paragraph or a graphic. If the glossary text includes a paragraph symbol, the text retains its paragraph formatting when you insert it in a document. If the glossary text doesn't include a paragraph symbol, the text assumes the formatting of the paragraph into which you insert it.

Although Word stores the formatting for glossary text, you don't see any of the formatting when you view the glossary text in the Glossary dialog box. Word displays all text in the dialog box in 12-point Chicago.

Adding a glossary entry to the Work menu

If you use a glossary entry often, you might want to add the entry to a Word menu so that you can insert it in your document in a single step. As we explain in Chapter 18, "Customizing Word," you can easily add any glossary entry to Word's Work menu. (This menu appears only after you've added an option or command to it.) When you select a glossary entry from the Work menu, Word inserts the text associated with that entry at the insertion point, as if you had selected the entry from the Glossary dialog box.

To add a glossary entry to the Work menu, first press Command-Option-=. The pointer changes to a bold plus sign, indicating that Word will add the next option or entry you select to a menu. Next, choose Glossary from the Edit menu, and select the entry you want to add. To add additional entries, you can press Command-Option-= and select them one by one. To close the Glossary dialog box, click the Close button or the close box. (For more information, see Chapter 18, "Customizing Word.")

Storing graphics as glossary entries

If you'll later want to reproduce a graphic that you've created in Word or imported from another program, you can easily store the graphic as a glossary entry. Word considers each graphic to be a single character, and you can cut, copy, or paste it just as you would a text character.

You add a graphic to the glossary the same way you add any other glossary entry. First, click the graphic to select it. You'll know the graphic is selected by the small black boxes, or handles, that appear on its frame. (Handles are explained in Chapter 6, "Creating Graphics.") If you want to store the formatting applied to the frame that contains the graphic, be sure to select the paragraph symbol that immediately follows the graphic.

With the graphic selected, choose Glossary from the Edit menu, and type a name for the glossary entry in the Name edit bar. Then click Define, and close the Glossary dialog box.

Storing the Clipboard contents as a glossary entry

If you have cut or copied selected text or a graphic, Word stores the selection on the Clipboard. To use the Clipboard contents as a glossary entry, first open the Glossary dialog box, and specify a name in the Name edit bar. Next, choose Paste from the Edit menu to paste the Clipboard contents into the glossary file. Word displays the text or the graphic box at the bottom of the dialog box.

Inserting a glossary entry

Selecting a glossary entry in the Glossary dialog box and clicking Insert is one way to insert the entry in a document, but other ways are also available. Word offers a keystroke shortcut that enables you to insert glossary entries quickly. You can also insert glossary entries from the Work menu. If you want to insert the same glossary entry repeatedly in the same document, you can use the Repeat command.

Inserting entries from the Glossary dialog box

To insert a glossary entry in a Word document, first position the insertion point, and then open the Glossary dialog box. Select Show User Entries, Show Standard Entries, or both, and then type or select the name of the entry you want. Click Insert or press Return to insert the entry at the insertion point.

For example, the next time you need to use the company name we created in Figure 13-4, insert it with the Glossary command. When the Glossary dialog box opens, select *ICS* in the list box, and then click Insert. Word inserts the full text— *International Consolidated Systems, Inc.*—in your document at the current insertion point and automatically closes the Glossary dialog box.

Inserting entries from the keyboard

To insert a glossary entry using the keyboard, press Command-Delete after positioning the insertion point. Instead of the Glossary dialog box, you'll see a *Name* prompt in the status box, as shown in Figure 13-5. Type either the complete glossary entry name or enough of the name to distinguish the entry you want, and then press Return. Word inserts the entry in your document.

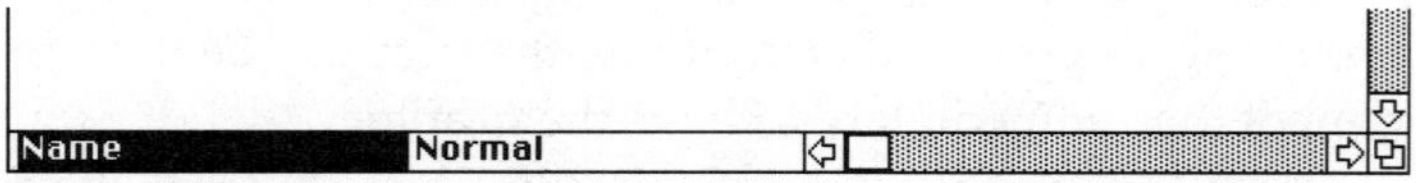

FIGURE 13-5.
Pressing Command-
Delete displays a
Name prompt in the
status box.

| Name | Normal | | |

Inserting entries from the Work menu

Using Command-Delete is an efficient way to insert a glossary entry, but the fastest way is to place the entry on the Work menu. As we've already mentioned, the Work menu does not appear on the menu bar unless you've created at least one custom menu item. After you add a glossary entry to the Work menu, all you have to do to insert one of the entries is choose it from the menu. You don't need to open the Glossary dialog box or type the glossary entry.

You can also add complete glossary files to the Work menu. After adding a file to the menu, choosing it causes Word to open the file and merge it with the current glossary file. Chapter 18, "Customizing Word," discusses the Work menu in detail and explains how to add glossary entries, glossary files, and other commands to that menu.

Using the Repeat command for repeated insertions

After you insert a glossary entry either by using the Glossary command or by pressing Command-Delete, you can insert the entry elsewhere in your document by using the Repeat command on the Edit menu. Simply click the next spot where you want to insert that same entry, and either choose Repeat Insert Glossary Entry or press Command-Y.

Choosing the Repeat command reproduces the last command you chose, so you can use this technique only as long as you don't choose another command or make any other editing or formatting changes to your document.

Undoing an insertion

If you press Command-Delete to display the Name prompt in the status box, you can cancel this procedure before you actually insert the glossary entry in your document simply by pressing Command-period, or by clicking anywhere on your screen. To delete a glossary entry that you've just inserted, immediately choose Undo Insert Glossary Entry from the Edit menu, or press Command-Z.

Modifying glossary entries

Occasionally you might need to change a glossary entry. You can change the glossary entry name and edit the corresponding entry. You can also delete individual glossary entries.

Changing an entry name

To change a glossary entry name, first choose Glossary from the Edit menu. In the list box, select the name you want to change so that it's displayed in the Name edit bar. Type the new name in the Name edit bar, and then click Define to lock in your change. Word places the new name in the list box and removes the original name. To return to your document, click Close, the close box, or anywhere in the document window.

Changing entry text

Changing glossary text is much like creating a new glossary entry. First insert the glossary entry you want to change in your document, and make the desired changes to this entry. Next, select the new version, and choose Glossary from the Edit menu. In the Glossary dialog box, click the name of the glossary entry you want to replace. Word displays that name in the Name edit bar and all or part of the corresponding entry text at the bottom of the dialog box. When you click Define, Word replaces the old glossary entry with the currently selected text. Return to your document by clicking Close, the close box, or the document window.

Deleting a glossary entry

To delete a user-defined entry, open the Glossary dialog box, select the glossary entry you want to delete, and then click Delete. Word asks you to verify that you want to delete the selected glossary entry. Click Yes to remove the selected entry from the glossary. The Glossary dialog box remains open on your screen so that you can insert or delete more entries if necessary. You can also delete a user-defined entry by selecting it and choosing Cut from the Edit menu.

You can't delete a Standard Glossary entry, however. Selecting a Standard Glossary entry and then clicking Delete or choosing Cut displays the message *Can't cut a Standard Glossary entry*.

Deleting all user entries

Occasionally you might want to remove all existing entries from a glossary—for example, before you load another glossary file. With one command, you can delete all entries except the standard entries. Simply open the Glossary dialog box, and choose New from the File menu. Word displays a dialog box that asks, *Delete all nonstandard glossary entries?* If you click Yes, Word deletes every user-defined glossary entry.

Saving glossary files

Unless you save the current glossary file, the changes you make remain in effect only until you quit Word. To make a permanent change—for example, to create a new glossary entry that you can use in later Word sessions—you must save the revised glossary file.

Because glossary files are independent Word files, saving changes to them is much like saving Word document files. You can save the current collection of glossary entries in a new glossary file or in the Standard Glossary file. When you quit Word after making changes to a glossary file, Word asks whether you want to save the glossary changes. If you click Yes, Word displays the Save Glossary As dialog box shown in Figure 13-6. You can also display the Save Glossary As dialog box during a Word session by choosing Glossary from the Edit menu to open the Glossary dialog box and then choosing Save or Save As from the File menu.

FIGURE 13-6.
*When you save
glossary files,
Word displays this
dialog box.*

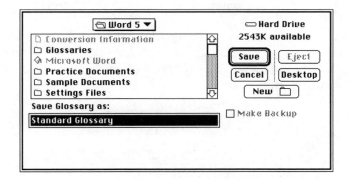

Creating a new glossary file

To create a new glossary file in which to store new entries, type a name for the file in the Save Glossary As edit bar, and then click Save. (The Fast Save and Make Backup options are not available when saving a glossary file.)

Updating an existing glossary file

To save new glossary entries in an existing glossary file, accept the proposed glossary filename—you'll see the name Standard Glossary if you haven't created additional glossaries—or type the name of another existing glossary file in the Save Glossary As edit bar. (Word dims the names of all files on the current disk in the Save As dialog box.) After you type the name and press Return, you see a message asking whether you want to replace the existing glossary file on disk. Click Yes to overwrite that file with your current glossary.

Opening, merging, and creating glossary files

When you install Word, you store the Date and Time, Formula, and Page Layout glossaries in the Glossaries folder. You can open any of these glossaries, or any glossary that you've created, from the Finder. You can also merge the contents of two or more glossaries and delete glossary files you no longer need.

Opening a glossary file from the Finder

When you open Word, you also automatically load the Standard Glossary file. To open Word and a different existing glossary file in one step, simply double-click the icon for the glossary file at the Finder level.

When you open a glossary file, you don't see the glossary file on your screen. However, the glossary entries from that file appear in the list in the Glossary dialog box. If you open the Formulas glossary file, for example, you'll see an alphabetical list of the contents of that glossary in the list box.

Merging glossary entries

To add the contents of a glossary file to the current glossary file, first open the Glossary dialog box, and then choose Open from the File menu. Word displays the dialog box shown in Figure 13-7 so that you can locate all the glossary files on the current disk.

FIGURE 13-7.
When you open the
Glossary dialog box
and then choose Open
from the File menu,
Word displays this
dialog box.

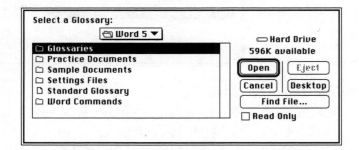

You can open a glossary file by clicking the filename and then clicking Open, or by double-clicking the filename. Opening a glossary file adds the user entries in that file to the current glossary file; it doesn't replace the contents of one glossary with the contents of another. To merge several glossary files, simply load each file into the current glossary file. Word expands the glossary to accommodate the entries from all the glossary files that you open (your computer's memory permitting).

For example, suppose you create a glossary file named Contracts. To merge the entries from this file with another glossary file named Legal, open the Legal file to load its glossary entries. Then merge the entries from the Contracts glossary file simply by opening that file using the procedure we just described.

If an entry exists in both glossaries, Word overwrites the entry in the current glossary file with the entry from the new file. For example, suppose you've created a glossary entry named *mw*, which represents the text *Microsoft Word*. If you open a second glossary file that also contains an entry named *mw*, which represents the text *Michael Williams*, the *mw* entry in the combined glossary represents *Michael Williams*. *Microsoft Word* is no longer in the glossary.

You can also load the entries from several glossary files at the same time and then open Word. At the Finder level, press the Shift key, and click the icon for each glossary file you want to use. Next choose Open from the File menu to load Word. You'll see a new blank document window. When you check the glossary in the Glossary dialog box, you'll find that it contains all the entries from the files you selected at the Finder level.

Deleting glossary files

You can delete a glossary file at the Finder level by dragging the icon for that file into the Trash. A word of warning: Don't delete the Standard Glossary file or move the Standard Glossary file from the folder that contains the Word program to another folder on the desktop. If you delete or move this file, Word will be unable to find and open the Standard Glossary when you start a new Word session.

Printing the glossary file

To view a printed copy of the complete glossary contents, open the Glossary dialog box, and then choose Print from the File menu. Word prints an alphabetical listing of glossary entries along with the corresponding text or graphic as each would appear when inserted into a document.

Using the Date command

The Date command is an alternative to the Print Date in the glossary. You can insert the current date directly into your document by choosing the Date command from the Insert menu. Word takes the date information that you set using the General Controls control panel in Month/Day/Year format—February 1, 1993, for example—and inserts the current date at this location each time you open or print the document.

Using the Symbol command

In addition to the text characters and punctuation marks that appear on the keyboard, most fonts include symbols—such as ™, ¶, ¬, and §—which you can insert in your document by pressing specific keys together with the Option key.

Much like Key Caps on the Apple menu, the Symbol command on Word's Insert menu lets you view the characters and the symbols available in the currently selected font in the Symbol window and lets you insert a selected character or symbol in your document at the insertion point. You can also display the Symbol window by pressing Command-Option-Q. Figure 13-8 on the next page, for example, shows the characters and symbols available for the New York font. To see all the symbols, use the scroll bars to scroll other parts of the window into view. To close the Symbol window, click the close box, choose Close from the File menu, or press Command-W.

Not all symbols or special characters are available in every font. To view the characters included in a different font, simply choose the new font from the Font menu while the Symbol window is open. Word changes the font applied to the insertion point in the document only if you insert a character from a different font.

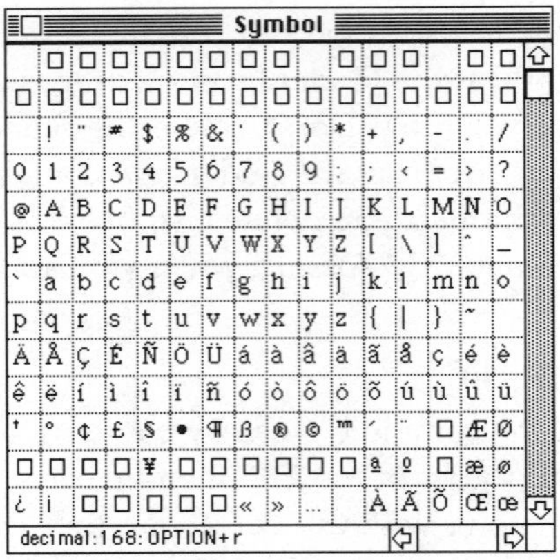

FIGURE 13-8.
*Choose the Symbol
command to view
the characters and
symbols available
for the currently
selected font.*

If you change fonts in the Symbol window and then insert a character, remember to reselect the original font after closing the window.

To insert a special character using the Symbol command, first position the insertion point where you want the character to appear. Then choose Symbol, and use the scroll arrows to view all the available symbols. When you locate the character or symbol you want, click the character in the Symbol window to select it. At the bottom of the Symbol window, Word displays the character's ASCII code and the keystroke combination you can use to insert the character in your document. Figure 13-8, for example, shows the ASCII code (*decimal: 168*) and keystroke combination (*OPTION+r*) for the character ®. You can use the keystroke combination directly to insert a character in your document, instead of opening the Symbol window and selecting the character.

The Symbol command must be installed in the Word Commands file in order to display the Symbol window. If you didn't install the Symbol command, you can insert a symbol or character at the insertion point by pressing Command-Option-Q, specifying the character's ASCII code, and pressing Return. For more information, see Appendix B, "ASCII Codes," which lists the Macintosh character set and each character's ASCII code.

Using the Sort command

Word's Sort command alphabetically or numerically rearranges paragraphs and lists. Word sorts text in ascending or descending order according to the first character or first few characters in each paragraph or table entry. To sort only a portion of the document, select the text you want to sort, and then choose Sort from the Tools menu.

Sorting paragraphs

Word sorts selected text by arranging paragraphs or table columns based on the leftmost character. Word's default sort order is ascending (A to Z, 1 and up). To sort in descending order, press the Shift key as you choose the Sort command from the Tools menu.

To sort the list of names in Figure 13-9 in ascending alphabetical order (from A to Z), for example, select the names, and then choose Sort. After a moment, Word displays the list, sorted as shown in Figure 13-10. To sort the names in descending alphabetical order (from Z to A), select the text, hold down the Shift key, and then choose the Sort Descending command.

FIGURE 13-9.

To sort a portion of a document, select the text before choosing the Sort command.

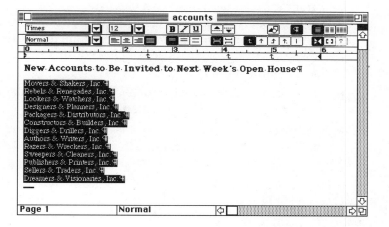

FIGURE 13-10.

When you choose Sort from the Tools menu, Word sorts the highlighted text in ascending order.

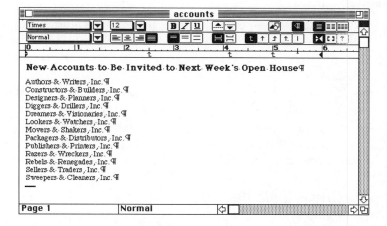

You can also use Word's Sort command to arrange paragraphs by the first word or number in each paragraph. You might, for example, sort a list of items in alphabetic or numeric order, a document whose paragraphs you've previously numbered out of order, or the contents of data documents before using the Print Merge command.

Word uses a character's ASCII code to determine its sort priority. If your document or text selection contains letters, numbers, and special characters, Word sorts according to these rules:

- Word ignores an indentation, tab, or blank space that appears before the first text character in a paragraph or line.

- Word ignores paragraphs or lines that contain only a paragraph mark with no text.

- Paragraphs or lines whose first character is a punctuation mark or another nonalphanumeric character precede numbers; numbers precede letters. (If a paragraph begins with a straight quotation mark ("), however, Word sorts that paragraph according to the first character after the quotation mark.)

- Word ignores diacritical marks like accents and umlauts. International characters sort as they appear in the alphabet.

- Uppercase letters precede lowercase letters. For example, a paragraph that begins with *G* precedes one that begins with *g*. Both paragraphs precede one that begins with *H*.

- If two or more paragraphs begin identically, Word scans the characters in each paragraph until it finds one that differs and sorts on that basis.

Sorting numbers

Word sorts Roman numerals alphabetically as strings of normal characters—I, II, III, IV, IX, VI, and so on. Use Arabic numerals or alphabetic characters to number paragraphs you might want to sort. Also be cautious about sorting documents with multiple levels of numbered paragraphs. For example, if the first level is numbered with Roman numerals (I, II, III, and so on) and the second level is numbered with capital letters (A, B, C, and so on), you'll find that Word sorts all the paragraphs alphabetically, placing I, II, and III in sequence after H and before J. In a case like this one, use the Renumber command instead of the Sort command. (For more information on the Renumber command, see Chapter 10, "Creating Professional Documents.")

Sorting a table by key column

In addition to sorting the alphabetic characters and numbers at the beginning of paragraphs, you can sort the entries in one column of a table and rearrange the table rows according to the sorted column. In Chapter 12, "Creating Tables," we explained how to sort the elements of a table created with the Table command.

You can also sort the rows of a table created with tabs based on the contents of one column, several columns, or all the columns in the table.

The column you use to determine how rows of related information are sorted is called the *sort key*. To sort a list by its first column, select all the paragraphs you want to sort. To sort a list based on the contents of a column other than the first column or a group of columns, hold down the Option key, and then drag across the column or columns. You can sort on more than one column of data if the columns are adjacent in the table and prioritized, left to right. Word evaluates the leftmost column first and then uses the contents of succeeding adjacent columns to determine the final sort order.

For example, suppose you want to sort the table of data shown in Figure 13-11 into ascending order using *Sales Rep* as the sort key. Begin by pressing the Option key and dragging down through the second column. Select only the names in the second column, not the column head, as shown in Figure 13-12. After you've

FIGURE 13-11.
You can use Word's Sort command to sort a table like this one.

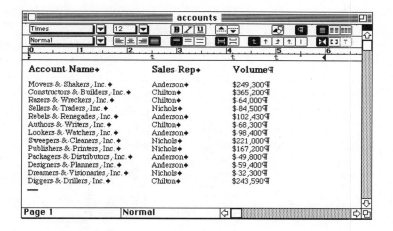

FIGURE 13-12.
The first step in sorting the table is to select the column you want to use as your sort key.

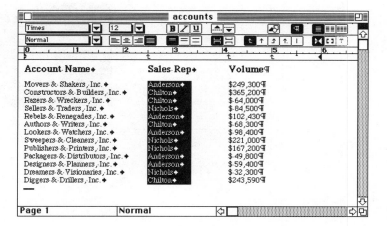

selected the sort key, simply choose Sort from the Tools menu. Figure 13-13 shows the result.

FIGURE 13-13.
When you choose Sort from the Tools menu, Word sorts the table according to the column you selected.

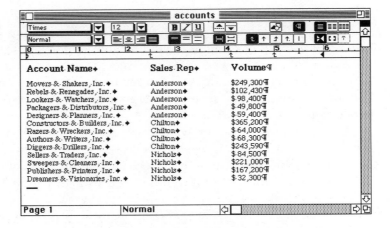

You can also sort the table in Figure 13-11 on the basis of both sales representative and volume. To define the keys for this sort, select both columns before choosing the Sort command, as in Figure 13-14. In this case, Word treats the leftmost selected column, the Sales Rep column, as the primary sort key and the Volume column as the secondary sort key. Figure 13-15 shows the table from Figure 13-14 after you choose Sort. Notice that the information is grouped by sales representatives, in ascending order by volume of sales.

FIGURE 13-14.
To sort two columns, select both columns before you choose Sort from the Tools menu.

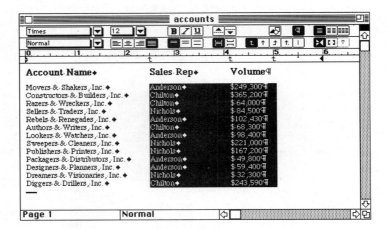

FIGURE 13-15.
Here, Word has sorted the table on the basis of both the sales representatives' names and account volume.

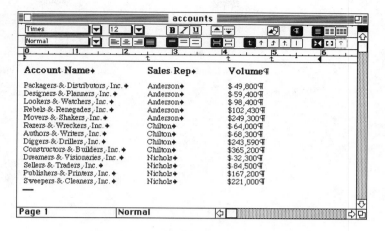

When you use two or more sort keys, Word applies the same sort order—either ascending or descending—to each of the sort keys. You can get around this limitation by performing separate Sort procedures. To sort the table in Figure 13-11 according to the sales representatives' names and account volume, but with the accounts listed in descending order, first sort by sales representative so that your table looks like Figure 13-13. Then select the volume numbers for one sales representative and sort in descending order by pressing the Shift key when you choose Sort. For example, Figure 13-16 shows the result of sorting by sales representative and then selecting and sorting all the volume numbers for Anderson. When you've repeated this procedure for each of the three sales representative groupings, the table looks like Figure 13-17 on the next page.

FIGURE 13-16.
To sort the accounts into descending order by volume, select the information in the third column for one sales representative, and press the Shift key when you choose Sort.

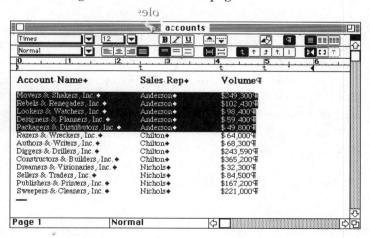

FIGURE 13-17.
The information in
this table has been
sorted in alphabetical
order by sales
representative and,
within each sales
representative's
grouping, in
descending order by
volume.

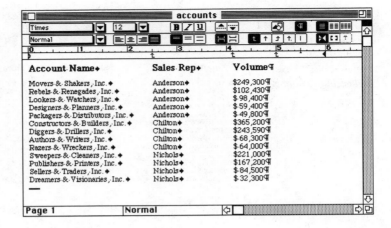

Undoing a sort

Because the Sort command can dramatically change the appearance of document text, always save your document before choosing this command. If the sort produces unexpected results, you can close the document without saving the changes and then simply reopen the document.

You can also immediately choose the Undo Sort command from the Edit menu to undo a sort.

Using the Word Count command

The Word Count command enables you to count the number of characters, words, lines, and paragraphs in the currently active document. The Word Count command examines the main text of a document and its footnotes, but not its headers and footers.

Choose Word Count from the Tools menu to display the Word Count dialog box shown in Figure 13-18. The first time you open this dialog box, three of the four options are activated. (Only the Lines option is deactivated.) Click the Count button to begin counting. As Word counts the text, you'll see in the lower-right corner of the dialog box the percentage of the document that Word has examined. When the count is complete, Word provides a total for each requested element in the right column of the dialog box.

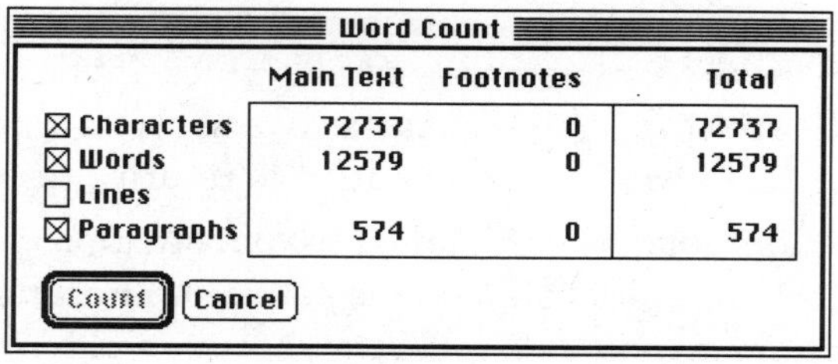

FIGURE 13-18.
The Word Count command allows you to keep track of the text elements in a document.

Word Count	Main Text	Footnotes	Total
☒ Characters	72737	0	72737
☒ Words	12579	0	12579
☐ Lines			
☒ Paragraphs	574	0	574

[Count] [Cancel]

To cancel the Word Count procedure, click Stop. (Word changes the Count button to Stop when it begins counting.) Click the Cancel button when Word finishes the Word Count procedure to return to your document.

Using the Calculate command

Word's Calculate command enables you to perform basic mathematical calculations. You can calculate percentages and add, subtract, divide, and multiply values. Word displays the result of each calculation in the status box at the bottom of the document window and also places the result in the Clipboard so that you can easily paste it into your document.

Performing mathematical calculations

The +, −, *, /, and % characters serve as mathematical operators when you perform calculations in Word. The + character tells Word to add a series of values; the − character tells Word to subtract. The * and / characters perform multiplication and division, respectively. And the % character tells Word to calculate a percentage. Unless you specify another mathematical operator, Word's Calculate command automatically adds selected numbers.

Word uses these guidelines when performing calculations:

- Word calculates from left to right within a line and line by line from the top to the bottom of a selection.

- Word recognizes the use of parentheses to group the values and operators contained within them. Word performs calculations on expressions in parentheses separately. For example, selecting *3 + 6 * 4* and choosing Calculate results in the value 36. However, *3 + (6 * 4)* results in the value 27.

- Word considers a single number in parentheses to be a negative number. For example, selecting *3 + 6 (4)* and choosing the Calculate command results in the value 5.

- Word ignores alphabetic characters and treats numbers on either side of the alphabetic characters as separate values. If you select *10 × 9*, for example, Word treats this string as two separate values, 10 and 9, and uses the default addition calculation to return a result of 19.

- Word ignores blank spaces and most punctuation and special characters. If you include a period or comma between numbers, Word considers the punctuation mark to be a separator. For example, Word considers the period in 100.25 to be a decimal point. If a space appears before or after a period or comma, however, Word treats numbers on either side of the punctuation mark as two separate values.

- Word extends the results of a calculation to the same number of decimal places as the number with the most decimal places in the selection.

- Word displays an alert box and the message *Math Overflow* when you divide by zero or when the result of any calculation exceeds 99,999,999,999,999.

Adding numbers

To add a series of numbers, simply select the values and then choose the Calculate command. For example, suppose you've created a table of cash receipts, like the one in Figure 13-19, and you want to compute your total receipts for the week and insert that total value in the table. Begin by highlighting the cells of the table that contain the numbers to be added, and then press Command-=, or choose Calculate from the Tools menu. Word adds the selected figures and displays the total value in the status box in the lower-left corner of the screen, as shown in Figure 13-20.

FIGURE 13-19.
Word totals a column of numbers, like the cash receipts shown in this table, when you choose Calculate from the Tools menu.

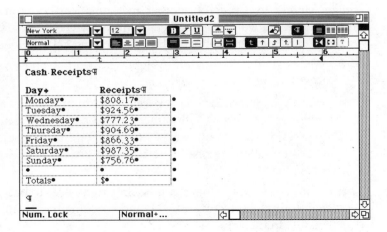

FIGURE 13-20.
*Word displays the
result of its calculation
in the status box in the
lower-left corner of
the screen.*

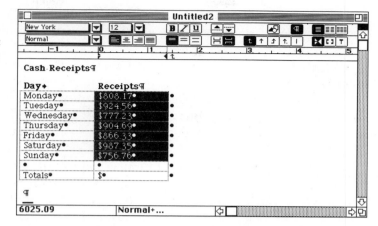

Because Word places the result on the Clipboard, you can paste the total into your document. For example, to paste the sample total from the status box, click to the right of the dollar sign in the Totals line, and choose Paste from the Edit menu. Figure 13-21 shows the table after you paste this value into the Totals line.

FIGURE 13-21.
*You can paste the
result of a calculation
anywhere in your
document.*

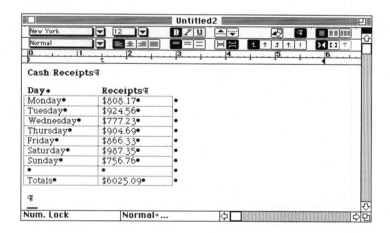

Because Word ignores alphabetic characters, you could select entire rows in the table shown in Figure 13-19 before choosing the Calculate command. Of course, when a table contains more than one column of numbers, you must be sure to select only the numbers that you want to include in the calculation.

Other calculations

To perform calculations other than addition, you must enter mathematical operators. For example, to multiply 10 times 2, type:

10 * 2

in your document, select those characters, and then choose Calculate from the Tools menu. Word displays the result, *20*, in the status box and places the result on the Clipboard.

If you don't want Word to perform the indicated mathematical operations in order from left to right, include parentheses to control the order of operations. For example, if you choose Calculate to determine the result of *10 − 8 * 2 + 15*, Word performs the operations in the order of their appearance—in this case returning the value *19*. However, selecting *10 − (8 * 2) + 15* and choosing Calculate results in the value *9*.

Table 13-2 shows some sample formulas and their results. Notice that you enter the +, −, * and / operators before the number you want to add, subtract, multiply, or divide by, and that you enter the % sign after the number to which you want it to apply. Thus, you would use the formula *18% * 70* to determine that 18 percent of the value 70 is equal to 12.6. Similarly, the formula *20% + 5* is equal to .2 + 5, or 5.2.

Formula	Result	Formula	Result
5 * 4 + 3	23	10 − 9	1
4 + 3 * 5	35	10/9	1
3 + 4 * 5	35	10/9.000	1.111
10 * (9)	-90	10% * 6	0.6
10 * 9	90	10% + 6	6.1
10 + (9)	1	10% + 10%	0.2

TABLE 13-2.
This table lists sample formulas and their results.

Specifying character formulas

You can use Word's Equation Editor program to create scientific and mathematical formulas, which you can then easily add to your documents. The Equation Editor, which is described in Appendix D, "Using the Equation Editor Program," lets you create a formula and insert it as a picture into a Word document. If you want to be able to change the individual components of a formula, you can use Word's character formula commands to create formulas within a Word document. Word's character formulas can also be used in other ways. With a little imagination, you can use character formulas to create a variety of special symbols and to present ordinary text in unusual ways.

Word has ten commands that you can use to build character formulas. In general, you specify each command by typing its first letter after the \ symbol, which looks like a period followed by a backslash. Although you often need only a single command to achieve a particular result, you can combine different commands in a single formula and embed one command as the argument of another command.

In this section, we discuss each of Word's ten character formula commands:

- Array (\A) draws a two-dimensional array.
- Box (\X) draws a box around specified characters.
- Bracket (\B) inserts a bracket or similar character next to specified text.
- Displace (\D) moves characters forward or backward a specified number of points.
- Fraction (\F) creates a fraction.
- Integral (\I) creates an integral or similar character.
- List (\L) creates a list of values separated by commas, which you can then place within another character formula.
- Overstrike (\O) places two or more characters in the same space.
- Radical (\R) creates a radical sign (a square root symbol).
- Superscript/Subscript (\S) positions characters above or below the current baseline.

The general form of character formulas

The basic form of a character formula is

$$\backslash C \backslash On(a1, a2, \ldots an)$$

where \ is a special formula symbol; C is the formula command; O is a command option that defines the result of the formula more clearly; n is the option's argument; and $a1$, $a2$, and so on are the command's arguments. These variables might seem daunting at first, but if you take the formula elements in sequence, you'll see that it's easy to specify a formula in Word.

The special symbol, \, tells Word that the next few characters should be interpreted as a formula instead of as literal characters. You create the symbol by pressing Command-Option-\. The formula symbol is followed by one or more commands, each of which requires one or more arguments. The commands refer to the action you want to perform, and the command arguments indicate the character or characters you want to be affected. A command's argument(s) must always be enclosed in parentheses.

For example, the Box command draws a box around each character that you specify in the command's argument. You specify this command by pressing Command-Option-\ to insert the formula symbol (choose Show ¶ to display the period that precedes the backslash), and then typing the letter X followed by the argument in parentheses. For example, specify

> \X(4)

to place the character 4 in a box. When you choose Hide ¶ or print the document, Word formats the character like this:

> 4

Some commands have options that affect how Word executes the command. The Box command, for example, includes options that draw only the top, bottom, right, or left edge of the box. You can combine these options to draw parts of the box, such as the top and right edges. When you specify an option with a command, you must remember to enter the option after the command name and before the command argument. You must also precede the option with the \ symbol formula. If you use more than one option, precede each option with the \ symbol. In a few cases, an option requires its own argument—a character that precisely defines how that option should affect the formula.

You can enter a character formula anywhere in a document. Begin by creating the special \ symbol using Command-Option-\, and then enter the formula's components. You can use either uppercase or lowercase letters when you specify formula commands and options, but for characters that are to appear in your document, be sure to use the appropriate capitalization and formatting. For example, if you want your formula result to display a bold superscripted character, apply the Bold format to that character as you create the formula.

Viewing character formulas and their results

When specifying a formula, use the Show ¶ command on the View menu or the ¶ button on the ribbon to display the formula's commands. As long as Show ¶ is active, you see only character formulas, not their results. When you finish specifying the formula, choose the Hide ¶ command to see the result of the formula as it will appear when you print. If you enter a formula incorrectly, Word will not display or print the formula results. Choose the Show ¶ command again if you need to edit or format the individual components of a formula.

Word requires that a formula's displayed result fit on a single line. (The formula itself can be as long as you want; Word wraps the formula from one line to the next as necessary.) You might break up a long formula into two or more separate formulas so that each formula's result occupies no more than one line.

The Array command

The Array command, \A, creates a two-dimensional array using the arguments you specify. The simplest form of the array command is

> \A(a1,a2,a3,...an)

The arguments specify the elements of the array. The simplest form of the Array command creates a one-column array with the elements centered one on top of the other. For example, specify

.\A(10,20,30,40,50)

to create this array in your printed document:

10
20
30
40
50

The Array command has several options. The HS*n* option controls horizontal spacing, and the VS*n* option controls vertical spacing. In both cases, *n* is a whole number that indicates the amount of space, in points, that you want to add to the normal space between the rows or columns of the array. For example, if you use the HS1 option, Word adds one additional point of space between the rows of the array. If you use the VS1 option, Word adds one additional point of space between the columns. Normally, Word doesn't place any additional space between the columns of an array. The default amount of space between the rows in an array is equal to the leading of normal lines of text.

The AL, AR, and AC options—which stand for align left, align right, and align center, respectively—enable you to align the characters within the columns of the array. If you don't specify an alignment option, Word creates an array with left alignment.

You can also control the number of columns in an array. To create a multi-column array, use the CO*n* option, where *n* is a number that indicates how many columns you want to include in the array.

The Box command

As we've already mentioned, the Box command, .\X, draws a border around text. Unlike the options in the Border dialog box, you can apply the Box command to single characters. The Box command has the form

.\X(a1)

where *a1* is the character(s) you want to be boxed. For example, if you want the name of your company, *National Systems Corporation*, to appear with a border around it, type:

.\X(National Systems Corporation)

This text appears in your printed document like this:

> National Systems Corporation

The Box command can accept only one argument. If the argument includes a comma, precede that comma with the \ symbol. Otherwise, Word tries to read more than one argument and cannot evaluate the formula. (If the argument contains many commas, consider using the List command, \L, covered later in this chapter, rather than inserting a separate \ for each comma.)

The Box command has four options: TO, BO, LE, and RI. These options stand for top, bottom, left, and right border, respectively. Combine these options in any way to draw a partial border around the characters specified in the argument.

The Bracket command

The Bracket command, \B, encloses its argument in the bracketing character you specify. In its simplest form, the Bracket command looks like this:

   \B(a1)

This command places parentheses around the argument *a1*. The command \B(ABC) encloses the string ABC in parentheses, like this: *(ABC)*.

The Bracket command is essential when you are building a formula and you want an argument to appear in parentheses in the formula result. If you simply type the parentheses, you could confuse another command in the formula. For example, suppose you want to create the fraction $\frac{3}{4}$ surrounded by parentheses. If you type the parentheses as part of the argument for the Fraction (\F) command, which we describe shortly, you'll create an invalid formula. To specify this argument without creating this problem, enter

   \B(\F(3,4))

to create this bracketed fraction in your printed document:

   $\left(\frac{3}{4}\right)$

Word alters the size of the parentheses to be compatible with the height of the fraction.

You can use the BC option to specify bracketing characters other than parentheses. You must always follow the BC option by \ and the character that you want to use for bracketing. Specify only the opening (or left bracket) character— such as { or [. Word supplies the closing bracket character automatically.

You can use the LC and RC options to place a bracket character only to the left or right of the argument, respectively. As with the BC option, follow each option by \ and the character you want to use.

The Displace command

The Displace command, \D, moves characters forward or backward by a specified number of points. The Displace command does not accept any arguments but displaces the characters that immediately follow the command. Nevertheless, you must place a pair of parentheses after the command.

The Displace command requires one of three options: FO*n*, BA*n*, or LI. The FO*n* option moves all characters that follow the Displace command in the current paragraph forward *n* points. If the *n* value for the FO option is large enough, some characters on the current line might wrap to the next line.

For example, to create exactly 18 points of space between two words in the same line, specify

Jack and Jill\D\FO18()went up the hill.

to make the sentence print this way:

Jack and Jill   went up the hill.

The BA*n* option moves all characters that follow the Displace command in the same paragraph backward *n* points. Because the Displace command does not affect the characters that come before the command, the displaced characters can overwrite other characters in the same line. If the *n* value that you specify is large enough, the displaced characters might be placed to the left of the beginning of the line beyond the left margin, but they won't "wrap up" to the previous line. To view the displaced characters, you must press Shift and click the left arrow in the horizontal scroll bar so that the characters come into view.

The LI option simply draws a line in the space you create with the Displace command. The LI option must always be used with either the FO*n* or BA*n* option. When you use the LI option with the FO*n* option, Word underlines the space created by the FO*n* option. If you use the LI option with the BA*n* option, Word draws the line under the characters that have been displaced by the BA*n* option.

The Fraction command

As you saw earlier in the discussion on the Bracket command, the Fraction command creates a fraction using the arguments as numerator and denominator. The form of the Fraction command is

\F(a1,a2)

where *a1* is the numerator and *a2* is the denominator. For example, specify this formula:

\F(231,1441)

to create this fraction in your printed document:

$\frac{231}{1441}$

The Fraction character formula command does not have any options. The numerator and denominator arguments can be whole numbers, formulas, such as $4x^2 + 12y - 23$, or even text.

The Integral command

The Integral command, \I, draws integrals, summations, products, and any other formulas that take a similar form. The simplest form of this command is

    \I(a1,a2,a3)

where *a1* is the lower limit, *a2* is the upper limit, and *a3* is the integral character. For example, specify this formula:

    \I(4,0,x^{2}dx)

to create this integral in your printed document:

$$\int_{4}^{0} x^2 dx$$

To enhance the appearance of the resulting integral formula, we assigned a smaller point size to the first two arguments of the command.

The Integral command offers the option of displaying a summation symbol, Σ, or a product symbol, π, instead of the integral symbol, $\int$. To create a summation formula, use the SU option in your integral formula, and to create a product formula, use the PR option.

You are not limited to the $\int$, Σ, and π symbols when you use the Integral command. By adding the FC or VC option to your formula, you can use any character on the keyboard in place of the default $\int$ symbol. The FC option uses your choice of a character of fixed height. The VC option indicates a character of variable height. Word changes the size of the character to correspond with the size of the third argument. This option is particularly appropriate in cases where the third argument of the \I command is a fraction. To use the FC or VC option, insert a \ symbol before the option and another \ symbol before the character you want to substitute for the $\int$ symbol.

You can use one other option with the \I command: IN. This option changes the placement of the first two arguments in the formula result, causing them to appear to the right of the integral symbol in "inline" format.

The List command

Like the Bracket command, the List command, \L, is designed to be used with other commands. This command creates a list, separated by commas, of the arguments you specify. In its simplest form, the List command looks like this:

    \L(a1,a2,...an)

Because Word normally interprets a comma as an argument separator, the List command comes in handy whenever you want to use a list of items as a single argument. For example, suppose you want to create a list of numbers with a box drawn around the entire list. Because the Box command (\X) can accept only one argument, the formula *\X(10,20,30,40,50)* is invalid. To overcome this limitation, use the List command and specify

> \X(\L(10, 20, 30, 40, 50))

to create this boxed list in your printed document:

> 10, 20, 30, 40, 50

The Overstrike command

The Overstrike command, \O, causes two or more characters to appear in the same space. The form of this command is

> \O(a1,a2,...an)

where *a1*, *a2*, and so on are the characters that are to appear "on top of" one another. Each argument can be as short as one character or as long as several words.

If you want to represent the "short" *e* sound, as in the word *pet*, for example, you need to print a lowercase *e* with a breve symbol (˘) over it. To achieve the desired result, type the letter *p*, specify the character formula and the text you want to be affected, and then type the letter *t*:

> p\O(e,˘)t

This text appears in your printed document like this:

> pĕt

The Overstrike command has three options: AR, AL, and AC. These options, which stand for align right, align left, and align center, determine the placement of the character in the second argument relative to the character in the first argument. If you don't specify an option, however, Word assumes that you want centered alignment (AC).

The Radical command

The Radical command, \R, draws a radical, or square root symbol. The form of the command is

> \R(a1,a2)

If you specify only one argument, Word places that argument inside the radical to create a square root. If you specify two arguments, Word places the second argument (*a2*) inside the radical and places the first argument (*a1*) above the radical to indicate the root being computed.

When you use the second argument with the Radical command, you can format the characters in the first argument so that the exponent outside the radical symbol is smaller than the number inside the radical. For example, to create a formula that displays the cube root of 100, specify:

\R(3,100)

Word then displays this formula in the printed document:

$$\sqrt[3]{100}$$

The Superscript/Subscript command

The simplest form of the Superscript/Subscript command (\S) is:

\S(a1)

This command positions its single argument as a superscript. In the sample formula below, for example, we've created a superscripted 2. (We've reduced the point size of the 2 to enhance the appearance of the formula result.) Specify

10\S(2)

to create this superscript in your printed document:

10^2

When you use the \S command with no options, Word superscripts the argument by three points. To superscript the argument by a different number of points, specify the option UPn in the formula, where n is the number of points by which to superscript the argument.

The DOn option lets you create a subscript instead of a superscript. Again, n specifies the number of points by which to subscript the argument.

With the UPn or the DOn option, you must specify an n value; otherwise Word cannot superscript or subscript your argument.

You can specify multiple arguments with the Superscript/Subscript command. However, when you specify multiple arguments, Word doesn't recognize the UPn and DOn options.

14

Outlining

*W*hen you create a document, you often know exactly what you want to say and how you want to say it. But if you can't seem to get started, or if you have so much information that structuring your ideas seems overwhelming, Word's Outline view can help you organize your thoughts and build a document from the ground up.

Outline view simply offers another view of your document. You can create, edit, and organize text just as if you were working in Normal or Page Layout view. Outline view offers additional advantages: Because Word automatically assigns default paragraph styles to outline headings, you can easily distinguish different heading levels and automatically create a table of contents for your document. You can also rearrange the headings—and the text under them—with just a few keystrokes.

In this chapter, we show you how to create a document in Outline view. We also show you how to edit and reposition document headings and text, and how to number outline headings. As you'll see, you aren't confined to using the Outline view to create new documents; you can use Outline view to reformat any document text quickly and easily.

Displaying a document in Outline view

To access Word's Outline view, choose Outline from the View menu. (You can also display the Outline view by pressing Command-Option-O.) In the space where the ruler appears in Normal view, Word then displays the icon selection bar shown in Figure 14-1. As we walk through the process of creating and editing text in the Outline view, we'll show you how to use these icons to organize and assign priorities to information in your document and to expand and collapse your view of the document.

FIGURE 14-1.
When you choose Outline, this set of icons appears at the top of your screen.

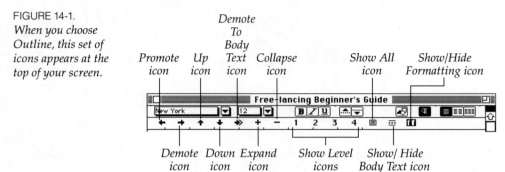

Outline view and Normal view divide your document text into two categories: headings and body text. Generally, you enter document headings in Outline view and then return to Normal view to enter body text. Word assigns each heading a level, labeled *heading 1* through *heading 9*. Heading 1 entries represent your broadest, or most important, ideas. Headings 2 through 9 represent headings that are subordinate to the main headings. You can use any of these entries as headings in your finished document, or you can hide them from view after you've completed your outline.

Word helps you visualize the relationships between outline topics by indenting different levels in the outline window. Main topics labeled heading 1 start at the left margin. Heading 2 entries are indented half an inch, heading 3 entries are indented 1 inch, and so on. Word indents body text in the outline window one tab stop to the right of where the preceding heading begins.

Building an outline

The easiest way to learn how to use Outline view is to create a sample document. To illustrate, we'll create an article entitled *Free-lancing Beginner's Guide*, using the Outline view to organize our ideas and then building on this outline to create a finished document. If you'd like to follow along with our example, open a new document, and then choose Outline from the View menu.

Figure 14-2 shows a new document in Outline view after we typed the first heading, *Cutting Loose*, and pressed Return. When you begin a new outline, Word assumes that your first paragraph is a heading 1 entry. Word formats the text in this paragraph in underlined 12-point Helvetica Bold—heading 1's default style. A minus sign appears next to the entry to indicate that this heading has no subordinate text. When you press the Return key at the end of the paragraph, Word assumes that the subsequent paragraph should be at the same level—in this case, heading 1—and displays a minus sign at the beginning of the next line, as shown in Figure 14-2.

FIGURE 14-2.
In Outline view, Word assumes that the first paragraph you type is a heading 1 entry.

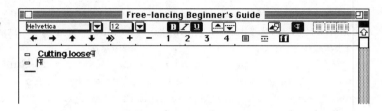

To create the rest of the sample outline shown in Figure 14-3, type the appropriate heading on each line, and click the Demote and Promote icons at the top of the window to specify the paragraph's heading level. (You can type the heading and then specify the heading level, or vice versa.)

FIGURE 14-3.
Start by entering topics in the outline window and assigning heading levels to each topic.

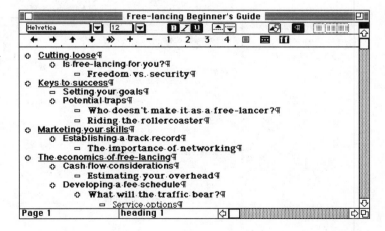

To create the subordinate heading in the second line of the sample outline, for example, click the Demote icon, and then type the phrase *Is free-lancing for you?* Word demotes the second paragraph to the heading 2 level and indents the paragraph half an inch from the left margin to indicate that this heading is subordinate to the first heading. Word changes the minus sign next to the first entry to a plus sign to indicate that it has subordinate text. When you press Return at the end of this second-level heading, Word assumes that you want the next level to appear as a heading 2 entry as well. Click the Demote icon to demote the third paragraph to a heading 3 entry.

Complete the outline shown in Figure 14-3, clicking the Demote and Promote icons as needed to demote and promote each heading. This outline uses only four heading levels, but Word allows you to create as many as nine. Generally, the more detailed your outline, the greater the number of heading levels you use.

As Figure 14-3 indicates, to the left of the headings in the outline window, Word displays a set of selection icons that identify the paragraph as body or heading text. A small square, which you'll see later, indicates a paragraph of body text. The minus sign indicates a heading without subordinate text. The plus sign indicates that all the headings and body text between the current heading and the next heading are of an equal or higher level.

In addition to indenting heading levels, Word also assigns different character formats to the heading levels in the outline window. As we'll explain in a few pages, these heading formats are controlled by your document's style sheet. If you think an unformatted display will be easier to interpret, you can click the Show/Hide Formatting icon to display all the text in the default Normal style, as shown in Figure 14-4. To redisplay character formatting, click the Show/Hide Formatting icon again.

FIGURE 14-4.
You can click the
Show/Hide Formatting
icon to suppress
character formatting
in Outline view.

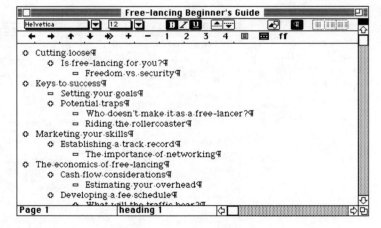

Viewing an outline in Normal view

As we explained in Chapter 9, "Creating Style Sheets," the heading styles that appear in Outline view are defined by the current document's style sheet. When you choose Normal from the View menu or press Command-Option-N to return to the normal document window after typing text in Outline view, Word formats the text according to the styles you've established for the headings.

For example, if you return to Normal view after typing the text shown in Figure 14-3, your screen looks like the one shown in Figure 14-5. Each heading level carries different character or paragraph formats. The status box at the bottom of the screen indicates the heading level assigned to each paragraph. (For more information about Word's default standard styles, see Chapter 9, "Creating Style Sheets.")

FIGURE 14-5.
When you display the document in Normal view, the outline text looks like this.

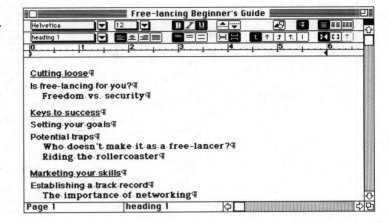

Adding body text

After you've entered your topics as document headings, you can fill in the document by adding body text. In the Normal view, click at the end of the first paragraph, and then press Return to begin a new paragraph. As you type, Word formats the body text in the Normal style, as shown in Figure 14-6.

FIGURE 14-6.
When you click at the end of a heading paragraph and press Return, Word assigns the Normal style to the body text paragraph you enter.

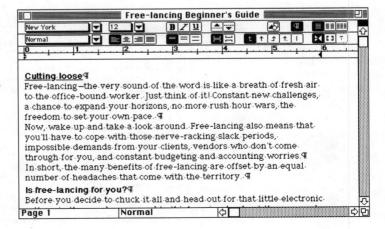

Figure 14-7 shows what happens when you return to Outline view. (As you can see, we've added more text to the document in Figure 14-6.) In Outline view, indentations reappear to give you a clear view of the relationship between each heading in the document. Word indents each body text paragraph a quarter inch to the right of the heading under which it falls, and selection icons (the small squares) appear to the left of the text.

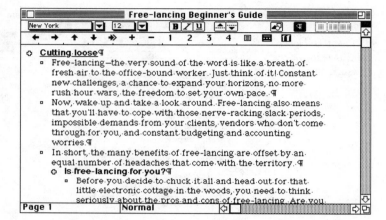

To save space in the outline window and to provide a better view of the document's structure, you can click the Show/Hide Body Text icon. When you hide the body text, Word condenses each paragraph of body text to only one line, and displays an ellipsis at the end of the line to indicate that additional text is hidden, as shown in Figure 14-8. To display the full text again, click the Show/Hide Body Text icon a second time.

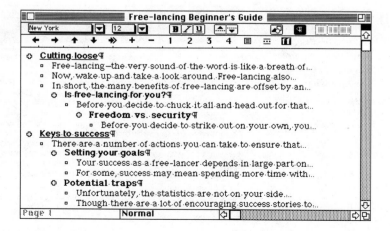

Selection techniques

Word offers many shortcuts for editing your document in Outline view. You can use the selection techniques we introduced in Chapter 3, "Working in Word," to select text. For example, to select an entire word, double-click that word. To select an entire sentence, press the Command key, and then click that sentence. You can also drag and drop selected text in Outline view.

In Normal view, you select an entire paragraph by double-clicking in the selection bar next to that paragraph or by triple-clicking anywhere in the paragraph. In Outline view, select an entire heading by clicking only once in the selection bar or by pressing the Option key and clicking the selection icon.

When you double-click in the selection bar or click the selection icon for a heading, Word highlights that heading and all the subordinate text under it. For example, click once in the selection bar to the left of the heading 1 entry *Cutting loose* in Figure 14-8 to highlight the entire paragraph, including the ¶ symbol. Now double-click in the selection bar next to this heading. Word highlights the *Cutting loose* paragraph and its subordinate text, as shown in Figure 14-9.

FIGURE 14-9.
To highlight a heading and its subordinate text, double-click in the selection bar next to the heading, or click the selection icon for that heading.

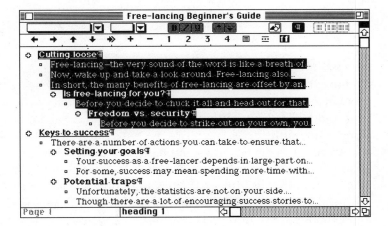

Collapsing and expanding the outline

The Expand and Collapse icons let you display and hide selected outline text. Your outline can get pretty lengthy after you've created several levels of headings and inserted body text under each one. You can keep track of all these levels by using the number icons at the top of the outline window to hide headings and body text from view. These techniques enable you to move through a large document quickly.

Using the Show Level and Show All icons

Suppose you want to see only the heading 1 entries in your outline. To collapse the outline so that only first-level headings are visible, click the Show Level 1 icon at the top of the outline window. As Figure 14-10 shows, Word displays a gray line under each heading 1 entry to indicate the existence of hidden body text and subheadings.

To expand the outline again, click another Show Level icon. For example, click the Show Level 3 icon to display heading 1, heading 2, and heading 3 entries. The body text remains hidden from view. To bring all your headings and the body text back into view, click the Show All icon. You can also press the asterisk key on the numeric keypad to display all headings and body text.

FIGURE 14-10.
When you click the Show Level 1 icon, Word collapses your outline to show only heading 1 entries.

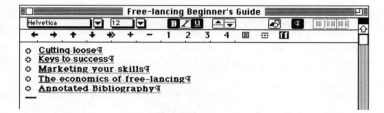

Using the Expand and Collapse icons

Whereas the Show Level icons affect the display of your entire outline, the Expand and Collapse icons affect only selected portions of it. You can also use the plus and minus keys on the numeric keypad to expand or collapse selected portions of an outline.

To collapse the headings and body text that appear under the second level 1 heading in the example shown in Figure 14-9, for example, simply place the insertion point in that heading, and click the Collapse icon or press the minus key on the numeric keypad. Word collapses all the body text under that heading, as shown in Figure 14-11. If you click the Collapse icon or press the minus key again, Word collapses all the heading 3 entries that appear under that heading and then all the heading 2 entries. To reverse this process, click the heading, and then click the Expand icon or press the plus key on the numeric keypad.

These expand and collapse techniques change the appearance of only the text that falls between the current heading and the next heading at an equal or higher level, not of all the text in your outline. In Figure 14-11, for example, only the text between the second and third heading 1 entries is affected.

To expand or collapse all the subordinate text under a heading in a single step, double-click the selection icon next to that heading. For example, to collapse all the subheadings and body text under *Keys to success* in our sample outline, double-click the icon next to that heading. Figure 14-12 shows the results.

FIGURE 14-11.
*Use the Collapse icon
or the minus key on
the numeric keypad to
collapse portions of the
outline.*

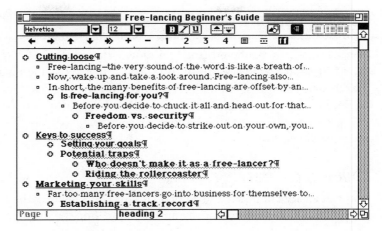

FIGURE 14-12.
*To collapse all
subordinate text
under a heading,
simply double-click
the heading's
selection icon.*

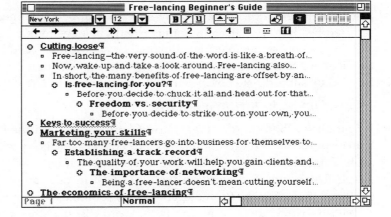

To expand the outline, double-click the selection icon once more. Or you can reselect the entire paragraph containing the heading *Keys to success* and click the Expand icon.

A navigation tip

Collapsing subheadings and body text in the outline window makes it easy to navigate quickly through a long document. To move to another area in your document, first display the document in Outline view, and then collapse the outline by clicking one of the Show Level icons. Next, highlight the heading or body text that represents the section you want to work with. Finally, scroll the highlighted text to the top of your screen. When you choose Normal from the View menu or press Command-Option-N to display the text in Normal view, Word displays the highlighted text at the top of the document window.

Editing the outline

You can use any of the editing techniques described in Chapter 3, "Working in Word," to edit text in a Word outline. You can also use the Find and Replace commands described in Chapter 7, "Editing and Proofing." (When you choose a Find or Replace command in Outline view, Word operates only on the text that is not collapsed under a heading.) Word also enables you to change and reposition heading levels easily.

Changing a heading level

You can easily change the level of a heading by selecting the heading or the paragraph that contains the heading and then clicking the Promote or Demote icon, or by pressing the Left and Right direction keys to promote or demote the heading. Word changes the indentation of that paragraph to reflect its new level and adjusts the indentation of any body text that appears immediately under the selected heading to indicate that the text still belongs to that heading.

To promote or demote a heading and its subordinate text, first click the selection icon for that heading, or double-click in the selection bar to select the heading and its subordinate text. Then click the Promote or Demote icon.

Promoting body text to a heading

If you click a body text paragraph in Outline view and then click the Promote icon or press the Left direction key, Word converts the body text to the same level as its immediately superior heading. For example, if you click the body text paragraph that begins *Free-lancing—the very sound* in our sample outline in Figure 14-12 and then click the Promote icon, Word promotes the paragraph to a heading 1 level. As you can see in Figure 14-13, Word displays the entire contents of the heading, not just the first line.

FIGURE 14-13.
We used the Promote icon to convert the first paragraph of body text to a heading 1 entry.

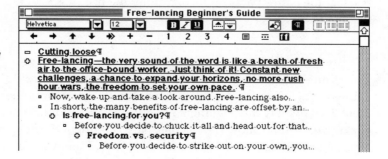

If you click the body text paragraph and then click the Demote icon or press the Right direction key, Word converts the selected body text to the next subordinate heading level—in this case, heading 2. Again, Word displays the entire contents of the body text paragraph and indents the heading half an inch to the right of the preceding heading 1 entry.

Demoting a heading to body text

To convert a heading to body text, click the heading and then click the Demote To Body Text icon. When you demote a heading to body text, the heading and its body text become part of the subordinate body text for the preceding heading.

For example, if you select the heading 2 entry *Is free-lancing for you?* in the sample outline and then click the Demote To Body Text icon, the outline looks like the one in Figure 14-14. The body text formerly attached to the heading 2 entry now carries the same indentation as the rest of the body text for the heading 1 entry *Cutting loose*. Word also assigns the Normal style to the text and displays *Normal* in the status box at the bottom of the screen. Notice that Word did not change the heading 3 entry *Freedom vs. security* that appears below the demoted heading 2 entry.

FIGURE 14-14.
You can use the Demote To Body Text icon to convert any heading in your outline to standard body text.

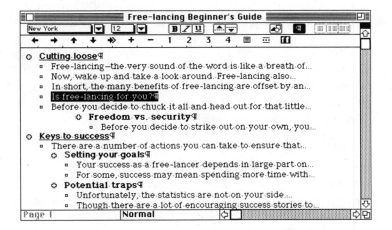

Dragging text

Perhaps the simplest way to promote and demote text is to drag it. Click one of the selection icons, and drag the entire heading left to promote the heading or right to demote it. As you drag, notice that Word displays different heading levels in the status box. If you drag far enough right (past heading 9), the text becomes body text, and the status box indicates that its assigned style is Normal.

Deleting a heading

As you know, selecting a heading in a collapsed outline also selects all the subordinate text for that heading. Before you delete a heading, be sure that you won't inadvertently delete the subordinate text for that heading as well. Expand the outline, and then press the Option key and click the selection icon to select headings without selecting subordinate text.

After you've expanded the outline and selected the heading or body text paragraph you want to delete, simply press the Delete key or choose the Cut command to remove the heading or text.

Moving a heading

You can move blocks of text in Outline view in three ways. You can use regular cut-and-paste techniques, or you can use the Up and Down icons to move text, or you can click a selection icon and drag the text.

Cutting and pasting text

To use cut-and-paste techniques to rearrange your outline, select the heading plus any subordinate text that you want to move, choose Cut, click where you want to place the text, and then choose Paste. You can also drag and drop selected text in Outline view.

When cutting and pasting text, your changes can affect more than the text visible on your screen. If you want to include the subordinate text in your selection, you might find it easier to collapse the outline before you begin the cut-and-paste or the drag-and-drop procedure. Otherwise, expand the outline before selecting the heading and choosing the Cut command.

Using the Up and Down icons

In addition to the standard editing techniques available in Normal view, you can use the Up and Down icons to rearrange blocks of text. Suppose you want to move the heading 2 entry *Setting your goals* and its subordinate text to a position just below the body text paragraph that begins *Before you decide to chuck it all*. Simply click the heading's selection icon to select it and all of its subordinate text. Now, click the Up icon to move the selected block toward the beginning of the document. Each time you click Up, Word moves the selected block up through the outline window one heading at a time. Word skips past any body text paragraphs, however. Continue clicking the Up icon until the block is in the desired position. Figure 14-15 shows the results.

FIGURE 14-15.
To reposition a selection in Outline view, click the Up and Down icons.

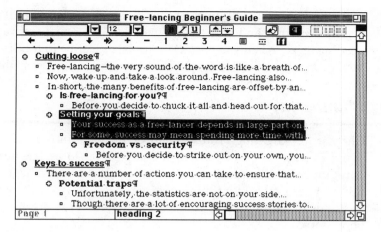

Dragging a selection icon

Just as you can drag text left and right to change its level, you can click a selection icon and drag a heading and its subordinate text up or down in your document. Moving a block of text in the outline window changes only the sequence of the affected paragraphs; heading levels or the relationship between your headings and subordinate body text don't change.

Outline headings and style sheets

When you begin a document in Outline view, Word assumes you will want to use each topic in the outline as a text heading within your document and automatically assigns a different paragraph style to each outline level. (We explained working with paragraph styles and style sheets in Chapter 9, "Creating Style Sheets.")

The heading styles that Word assigns to outline levels are handled just like any other styles. In fact, Word uses these heading styles to create a Table of Contents (see Chapter 11, "Adding a Table of Contents, an Index, and Footnotes"), which is another good reason for planning a document in Outline view.

If you switch from Outline view to Normal view and then place the insertion point on any line, you'll see the name assigned to that level in the status box at the bottom of the document window. Each level has a corresponding style name in the document's style sheet. If, for example, you display the Style dialog box by choosing Style from the Format menu or by pressing Command-T, you'll see that the style sheet for the sample document includes the style names heading 1, heading 2, heading 3, and heading 4, each based on the Normal style.

To modify a style, follow the procedure described in Chapter 9, "Creating Style Sheets." Click a heading at the level you want to format, and choose Style from the Format menu. In the Style dialog box, click the name of the style you want to modify, and then select the character and paragraph formats for this heading level. When you click OK, Apply, or Define in the Style dialog box, Word applies the specified formats to all the headings that carry that level style.

Numbering an outline

Chapter 10, "Creating Professional Documents," introduced the Renumber command on the Tools menu, which enables you to assign numbers to document paragraphs. Word uses the relative indentation of document paragraphs to determine and assign paragraph numbering. Because Word automatically indents the headings in Outline view, you can use Renumber to create an outline with numbered topics.

It's much easier to enter the text in Outline view and then use the Renumber command to number the levels than it is to manually type a number for each topic. With the Renumber command, you can add letters and numbers to your outline automatically, while you're still planning your document. Later, you can remove the numbers by using the Remove option in the Renumber dialog box.

For example, to number the outline shown earlier in Figure 14-9, first choose the Renumber command from the Tools menu. In the Format edit bar of the Renumber dialog box, enter the numbering scheme you want to use. For standard outline numbering, enter *I.A.1.a.i.* to specify the scheme for five levels. (For fewer than five levels, enter as many characters in the Format edit bar as you have levels.) Leave the other options as they are. When you click OK, Word numbers each outline level, as shown in Figure 14-16. Word does not number body text paragraphs, however.

FIGURE 14-16.
*You can use the
Renumber command
to number the outline.*

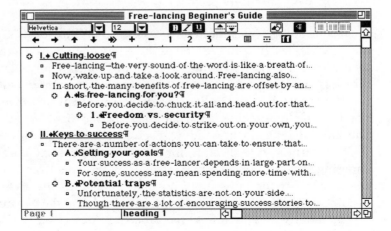

In this example, Word numbered all the outline text because we didn't collapse any part of the outline first. If you collapse the outline before you number it, Word assigns numbers only to the visible headings. For example, if you had collapsed the outline so that all text below level 2 was hidden, Word would have numbered only the level 1 and level 2 text.

Collapsing the outline and choosing Renumber doesn't remove existing numbers from lower levels in the outline. For example, suppose that after numbering an entire outline, you click the Show Level 2 icon so that all level 3 and level 4 text collapses out of view. If you then choose Renumber, Word updates the visible numbers. However, when you expand the outline to show level 3 and level 4, those entries retain the numbers assigned by the first Renumber command.

You can switch to Normal view before choosing the Renumber command. Although the text doesn't display different amounts of indentation in Normal view, Word still recognizes the outline levels and numbers the paragraphs appropriately. Choosing the Renumber command in Normal view also has the advantage of numbering body text paragraphs. (For more information about the Renumber command, see Chapter 10, "Creating Professional Documents.")

Printing an outline

To print an outline, choose the Print command from Outline view just as you would from Normal view. You can print the entire outline or collapse it to print only specific levels. Word prints the outline exactly as it appears in Outline view, with one exception: If the first line of any body text paragraphs is visible in your outline window, Word prints the paragraph in its entirety.

Word ignores character or paragraph formats you assigned to text in your document window, but recognizes Document and Section dialog box settings when you print the outline. Any headers, footers, section breaks, or manual page breaks you've created for the document also appear in the printed outline.

15

Merging Documents

Word's Print Merge command takes the time and tedium out of repetitive tasks—for example, sending out billing notices to clients or churning out dozens of personal invitations to the grand opening of your company's new production facility. Print Merge lets you combine data from two or more files to create customized documents. When you choose the Print Merge command, Word produces multiple versions of a document, automatically customizing each version with information—for example, a name, address, and account balance—from a second document.

To create grand opening invitations, for example, you might enter the text of the invitation in one document and the names and addresses of each guest in another. When you merge the two files, Word creates a personal letter of invitation for each guest. Similarly, you can store the text of a billing notice in one document and the name, address, and balance due for each client in a second document. Then you can merge the information in these two files, creating all your billing statements with just a few keystrokes.

In the first half of this chapter, we describe Word's Print Merge command in detail. First we show you how to use Print Merge Helper to set up and merge files. Next we review the guidelines for creating merge documents and show you how to convert data from other applications for use in merged documents. The second half of this chapter describes special instructions that let you do such things as create conditional statements, insert other documents into a merge file, and perform calculations using merged data.

Creating merge documents

To generate a series of merge documents you need at least two files: a data document and a main document. The data document contains the text that varies for each merge document. The main document contains the standard text that remains constant for each merge document. Word combines the information from the data document and the main document to create a series of customized merge documents.

To illustrate Word's Print Merge command, we'll create a series of letters that offer personalized horoscopes, using a data document containing information such as name, address, and horoscope sign, and the main document shown in Figure 15-1. The words set off by print merge characters (« ») in this figure refer to the general categories of variable data that we'll merge with this main document.

FIGURE 15-1.
We'll use this main document to create a personalized horoscope.

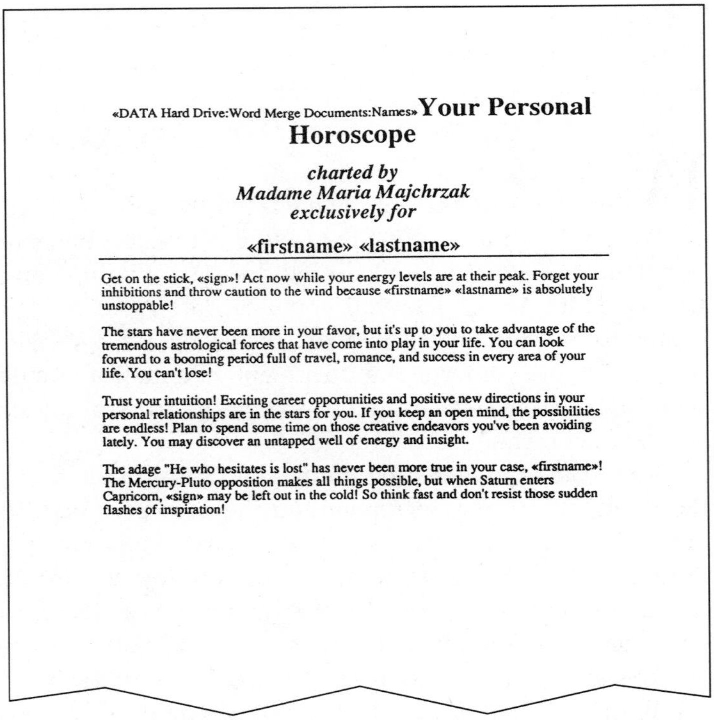

«DATA Hard Drive:Word Merge Documents:Names»**Your Personal Horoscope**

charted by
Madame Maria Majchrzak
exclusively for

«firstname» «lastname»

Get on the stick, «sign»! Act now while your energy levels are at their peak. Forget your inhibitions and throw caution to the wind because «firstname» «lastname» is absolutely unstoppable!

The stars have never been more in your favor, but it's up to you to take advantage of the tremendous astrological forces that have come into play in your life. You can look forward to a booming period full of travel, romance, and success in every area of your life. You can't lose!

Trust your intuition! Exciting career opportunities and positive new directions in your personal relationships are in the stars for you. If you keep an open mind, the possibilities are endless! Plan to spend some time on those creative endeavors you've been avoiding lately. You may discover an untapped well of energy and insight.

The adage "He who hesitates is lost" has never been more true in your case, «firstname»! The Mercury-Pluto opposition makes all things possible, but when Saturn enters Capricorn, «sign» may be left out in the cold! So think fast and don't resist those sudden flashes of inspiration!

Generally, creating merge documents is easiest if you develop the data document first. In fact, if you know the categories of information that will vary within your main document, you can use the Print Merge Helper command to do much of the work required to merge your documents.

Although a data document and a main document take a little time and planning to develop, you can use these files again and again. You can also mix and match information: You can merge a data document with any number of main documents, and you can draw information from any number of data documents into a main document by directing Word to the files you want to use.

Creating the data document

A data document is a structured collection of table entries, stored in a standard Word file. This file can contain any kind of information—for example, inventory numbers and prices; or names, addresses, and telephone numbers.

Every data document consists of a table composed of three elements: records, fields, and field name headers. Each line in the table is a record, and each column is a field. When you merge this data with the main document, each record provides the variable data needed to create a new merged document. The field name headers, which appear at the top of the data document, identify the information stored in each field. These field names are the key link between your data document and main document.

Figure 15-2 shows a sample data document. The first line in this table contains the field name headers: lastname, firstname, address1, address2, city, st, zip, and sign. Each row below this first row of field names is a separate record, containing the information needed for one merged document. As you can see, Word wraps this information to fit the width of the field as necessary.

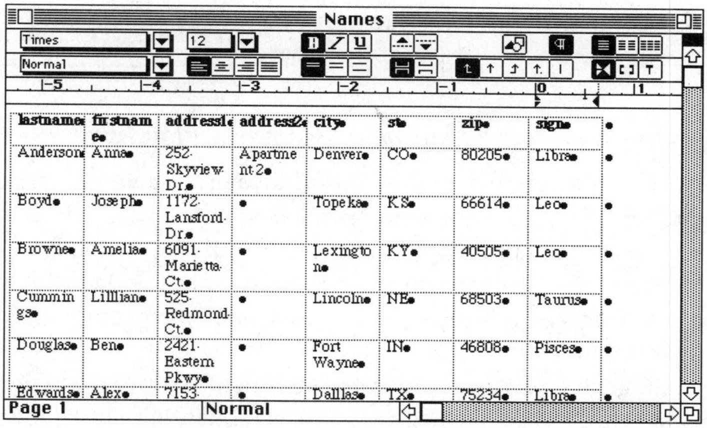

FIGURE 15-2.
We'll use this data document to create some sample merged documents.

Although you can use the Table command on the Insert menu to create a table like the one in Figure 15-2, we strongly recommend that you use Word's Print Merge Helper to create a data document. As you'll see, choosing the Print Merge

Helper command from the View menu displays a dialog box, which enables you to define field headers and create a table automatically.

We'll walk through creating a data document with the Print Merge Helper. At the end of this section, we'll review the rules you must follow to create a data document without choosing this command. (Creating a data document involves inserting and formatting a table. If you're unfamiliar with the procedures for creating and modifying tables in Word, be sure to review Chapter 12, "Creating Tables," before working with the Print Merge command.)

Using the Print Merge Helper

To create the main document and the data document shown in Figures 15-1 and 15-2, respectively, first open a new Word document by choosing New from the File menu. As you'll see in a few moments, Word considers this new document to be the main document. To create the data document quickly and easily, next choose Print Merge Helper from the View menu. Word displays the dialog box shown in Figure 15-3.

FIGURE 15-3.
When you choose
Print Merge Helper,
Word displays this
dialog box so that you
can open or create a
data document.

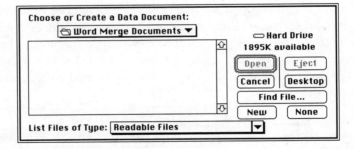

Using the Data Document Builder dialog box

As the title of this dialog box indicates, when you first choose Print Merge Helper, Word allows you to open a new or existing data document. Click the New button to display the Data Document Builder dialog box, and then specify each category of data that you want to include in the data document. As you'll see in a moment, Word inserts the category names you enter as column headings in the data document.

Figure 15-4 shows the Data Document Builder dialog box after we entered the name and address categories. To establish a field name that you'll specify in the main document, simply type the name in the Field Name edit bar, and then click the Add button. Word adds each name, in sequence, to the list box in the dialog box.

FIGURE 15-4.
Type the names of the fields you want to include in the data document in the Data Document Builder dialog box.

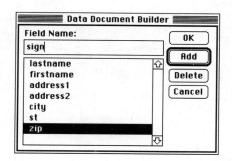

A field name can contain any character except a comma and can have up to 253 characters, including spaces. Word disregards any capital letters. You can specify field names in any order in the Data Document Builder dialog box. This order doesn't affect the order in which you can insert individual entries in the main document.

Each data record can contain as many as 31 fields. As you set up your fields, think about how you will use the information when you create merged documents. Try to design fields that facilitate access to the information. For example, you might be tempted to type your clients' names in a single field. Instead, consider using three separate fields to hold each person's first name, middle initial, and last name. You might also want to create additional fields for titles like Dr., Mr., and Ms. and for professional designations like C.P.A. and Vice President. If creating a separate field for every piece of information in a data document seems like a lot of trouble, keep in mind that this technique will allow you to sort and select records on the basis of key information, such as the state and zip code.

If you want to insert a new field at a specific place in the list box, begin by typing the field name in the Field Name edit bar. Next, in the list box, select the field name after which the new field name is to appear. Finally, click Add to insert the new field name. To delete a field, simply select the field name, and then click Delete.

Click the OK button when the list box contains all the field names you want to define in the data document. Word opens a new document window and displays the Save As dialog box. Select the folder where you want the data document to be stored, and then type the data document name in the Save Current Document As edit bar. Don't use commas in the data document name; if you do, Word won't be able to merge the file.

When you have saved the new document, Word inserts a table, as shown in Figure 15-5 on the next page. (We've called our data document *Names*.) The table contains a column for each field name you specified in the Data Document Builder dialog box. The field names appear in the table's first row, which is the field header for the entries that will appear beneath it.

FIGURE 15-5.
*After you name the
data document, Word
automatically creates a
table whose first row
contains the field
names specified in the
Data Document
Builder dialog box.*

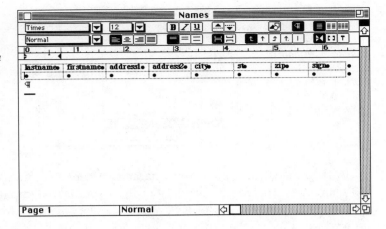

Creating the main document

After inserting the table in the data document, Word activates the main document (the document from which you selected the Print Merge Helper command) and inserts information about the data document's location, as shown in Figure 15-6. When you choose the Print Merge Command, Word uses this information, called a *DATA instruction,* to find the data document you want to merge with the main document. Word doesn't print this instruction.

FIGURE 15-6.
*After creating a table
in the data document,
Word next inserts a
DATA instruction in
the main document.*

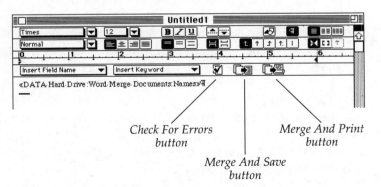

Check For Errors
button

Merge And Save
button

Merge And Print
button

Word inserts the DATA instruction at the insertion-point position, which should be at the beginning of the main document. The instruction must appear at this location for the merge procedure to work correctly. Unfortunately, Word doesn't automatically apply the hidden format to the paragraph mark at the end of the DATA instruction line. You will probably want to assign hidden text to this paragraph symbol to prevent it from affecting your document layout.

You can shorten the DATA instruction so that only the filename is specified. Shortening the instruction raises the possibility that you will have to help Word locate the data document when you choose Print Merge. Occasionally, however, shortening the instruction makes it possible to include the DATA instruction on the same line as the first line of text.

As you can see in Figure 15-6, Word also displays the Print Merge Helper bar at the top of the main document window. This bar contains two drop-down list boxes that allow you to insert elements into a main document. We'll discuss the Insert Field Name list and the Insert Keyword list later in this chapter. The Check For Errors, Merge And Save, and Merge And Print buttons activate Print Merge dialog box options directly from the main document window. We describe these options in just a few pages.

Completing the data document

If you're sure that the correct field names are at the top of the data document table, you'll probably want to finish the data document before preparing the main document. To return to the data document, select its name from the Window menu. With the insertion point in the first cell of the table's second row, use Figure 15-7 as a guide and type the information for each field in the first record, pressing the Tab key to move to the next cell. After typing the appropriate data in the last cell of the second row, press Tab again to add a new row of cells to the table. The table can contain as many as 31 records. After completing the first three rows of data, the data document should look like Figure 15-7.

FIGURE 15-7.
*We entered data
in the first three rows
of the data document.*

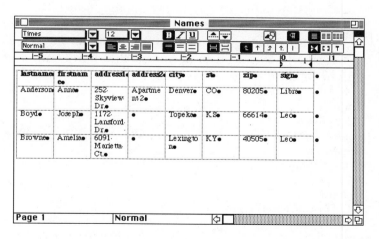

Later, when you merge the data document with the main document, the information in each cell automatically takes on the formatting characteristics of the paragraph text into which it is inserted. As a result, you don't need to be concerned with the way data wraps within a particular table cell. Type the data exactly as you want it to appear; press Return to break the line, or press Tab to leave the cell blank. Type spaces in empty cells only if you want Word to merge these spaces with the main document.

If, after creating a substantial portion of the table, you want to add a new field, you can add a column using the techniques described in Chapter 12, "Creating Tables." Remember, however, that the order in which the data fields appear in the data document is not important.

To add a column to the end of the table, place the insertion point at the end of the first row of cells, between the end-of-cell marker and the table's dotted gridline. To add a column to the left of an existing column, select the column to the right of where you want to add the new field, by clicking at the top of the column. Then choose Table Layout from the Format menu, select the Column option, and click Insert. Word adds a new column to the end of the table or to the left of the selected column, as appropriate.

Completing the main document

You create, edit, and format the main document exactly as you would any Word document, except that you add placeholders to indicate where you want Word to fill in the variable information specified by field names in the data document.

If you've used the Print Merge Helper to create the data document, Word lists the field names in the Insert Field Name drop-down list box on the Print Merge Helper bar located at the top of the main document. To insert a field name at the insertion point in the main document, simply select the name from the list. Word automatically encloses the field name within a special set of characters (« »). Figure 15-8 shows the Insert Field Name drop-down list box containing the field names specified in the data document shown in Figure 15-7. (The last three entries in the list box are always present.)

FIGURE 15-8.
The Insert Field Name drop-down list box contains the field names specified in the data document identified by the DATA instruction at the top of the main document window.

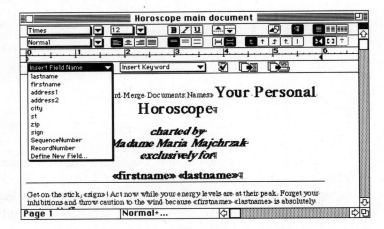

Figure 15-8 also shows the opening paragraphs of the main document shown earlier in Figure 15-1. The DATA instruction at the top of the document window does not appear when you print your merge documents, nor does it affect the line or character spacing for the first line of the document. However, you must be sure not to insert any blank lines, text, or spaces before the DATA instruction. This instruction must be the first element in the main document.

You can insert a field name as often as you like in the main document. Word adds the field name you select from the Insert Field Name drop-down list box at the insertion point, enclosing it within print merge characters. For example, in the first line of body text, we inserted the «sign» field name to extract the addressee's astrological sign from the data document. Above the body of text and in the second line of text, we inserted the «firstname» and «lastname» field names, which tell Word to extract the entries from the firstname and lastname fields of the data document and place them in the main document.

When Word prints the first merged document, it extracts *Libra*, *Anna*, and *Anderson* from the first record in the corresponding data document. When printing the second merged document, Word plugs *Leo* into the sign location, *Joseph* into the firstname location, and *Boyd* into the lastname location. Unless we specify otherwise, Word creates a new merged document for each record in the data document.

Formatting the merged data

You can control the character formats of the variable text as it is inserted into the main document, by applying the desired formats to the field names. Word uses the character formats of the first character in the field name to format the complete text that replaces the field name in the merge documents.

For example, if you want the addressee's astrological sign to appear in Helvetica Italic, you can assign those formats to the letter *s* in the field name, like this: «sign». (For readability, however, you might prefer to italicize the entire field name, like this: «*sign*».)

Word uses the Page Setup, Document, Section, and Paragraph settings from your main document to format your merged documents.

Adding a new field name

If you decide, while creating the main document, to insert a category of information not represented by a field name in the data document, you can easily define the new field name in the main document. Of course, you must still add the field and the data records to the table in the data document if you want Word to insert corresponding field entries.

To add a new field name, first select the Define New Field option from the Insert Field Name drop-down list box. Word displays the Insert New Field dialog box shown in Figure 15-9 on the next page. Type the new field name in the text box, and then click OK. Word adds the name to the Insert Field Name list and also inserts the name at the insertion point in your document.

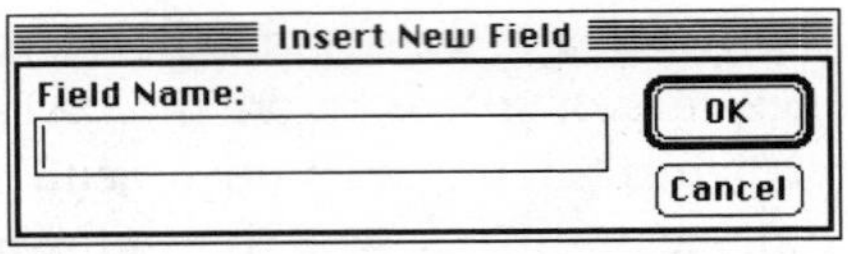

FIGURE 15-9.
Use the Insert New Field dialog box to add a new field name to your main document.

Inserting a SequenceNumber or RecordNumber field name

In addition to data field names, you can insert two additional fields in the main document: SequenceNumber and RecordNumber. Select SequenceNumber from the Insert Field Name drop-down list box to insert the current record's position within the sequence of records merged with the main document, and select RecordNumber to insert the record's absolute position in the data document within a merged document.

SequenceNumber specifies the position that the current record occupies within the merged documents created during the merge procedure. If you merge a data document that contains ten records, for example, Word inserts the number 1 in the SequenceNumber field of the first document, 2 in the second document, and so on. If you merge only the last five of these records, Word inserts the number 1 in the first merged document it creates—the document that corresponds to the sixth record in the data table.

RecordNumber specifies a record's absolute position in the data table. If you merge the last five records from a ten-record data document, for example, Word inserts the numbers 6, 7, 8, and so on in the RecordNumber fields of the respective merged documents.

You'll find these options helpful when you want to establish the terms under which the conditions specified in an IF instruction are met. We show examples of these instructions when we discuss the IF instruction later in this chapter.

Merging the documents

After you save the data and main documents, you're ready to create your merged documents. Select the main document to be sure that it's active, and then choose Print Merge from the File menu.

As long as the main document's DATA instruction identifies the data document, the data document doesn't have to be open. If Print Merge can't find the data document, it presents an Open File dialog box and asks you to locate the file. You must locate the data document before continuing with the merge procedure.

When you choose the Print Merge command, Word displays the Print Merge dialog box shown in Figure 15-10. The Records section at the top of this dialog box and the three Merge Results buttons offer further options for merging these documents. You can easily cancel a merge procedure by pressing Command-period or the Escape key.

FIGURE 15-10.

Choose the Print Merge command to display the Print Merge dialog box.

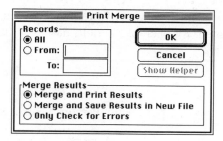

Specifying data records

To create merged documents for every record in your data document, leave the default All option selected. To print a selected range of records, use the From and To edit bars. For example, to merge the data from the fourth, fifth, and sixth data records, type 4 in the From edit bar and 6 in the To edit bar.

You'll find that the From and To edit bars come in handy if your printer jams or an error interrupts document merging. If you know which data record number is next, you can type this number in the From edit bar, rather than starting over.

Merging and printing results

Click the Merge And Print Results button to merge and print a document for each record specified in the Records section of the dialog box. Then click OK, select the print options that you want, and click OK to print the merged files. You can also merge and print directly from the main document window by clicking the Merge And Print icon at the far right end of the Print Merge Helper bar.

See Chapter 8, "Printing," for a complete description of the Print dialog box. If you plan to specify printing options, keep in mind that the Pages options in the Print dialog box refer to the number of document pages you want to print, not to the number of data document records. If you specify From and To values in the Print dialog box, Word prints that range of pages once for each record in your data document. If you have a four-page document and you use From and To values of 2 and 3, for example, Word prints only pages 2 and 3 of the merged document for every specified data document record. Similarly, the Copies option refers to the number of copies of each merged document you want to print, not the total number of documents you want to print.

After you click OK in the Print dialog box, Word displays the alert message *Unknown field name* if it doesn't recognize one of the field names in your main document. If you continue, Word inserts this error message at each field location each time it prints a merged document.

Figure 15-11 shows the first merged document that Word creates when we merge the Names data document with the Horoscope main document shown earlier in Figures 15-2 and 15-8. As you can see, Word prints the Horoscope file, substituting the text from the firstname, lastname, and sign fields of the first record in the data document for each of the field names in the main document.

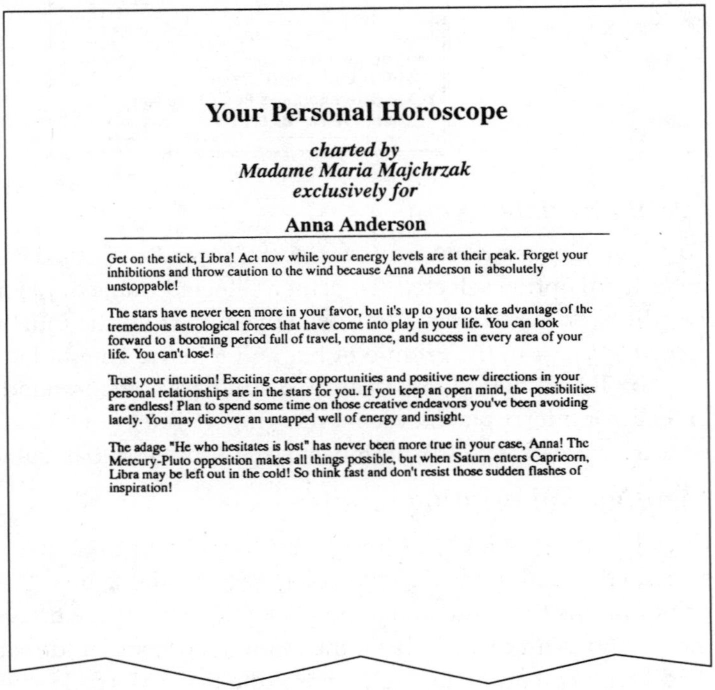

FIGURE 15-11.
To create this merged document, Word extracted information from the first record in the data document.

Your Personal Horoscope

charted by
Madame Maria Majchrzak
exclusively for

Anna Anderson

Get on the stick, Libra! Act now while your energy levels are at their peak. Forget your inhibitions and throw caution to the wind because Anna Anderson is absolutely unstoppable!

The stars have never been more in your favor, but it's up to you to take advantage of the tremendous astrological forces that have come into play in your life. You can look forward to a booming period full of travel, romance, and success in every area of your life. You can't lose!

Trust your intuition! Exciting career opportunities and positive new directions in your personal relationships are in the stars for you. If you keep an open mind, the possibilities are endless! Plan to spend some time on those creative endeavors you've been avoiding lately. You may discover an untapped well of energy and insight.

The adage "He who hesitates is lost" has never been more true in your case, Anna! The Mercury-Pluto opposition makes all things possible, but when Saturn enters Capricorn, Libra may be left out in the cold! So think fast and don't resist those sudden flashes of inspiration!

Merging and saving the results in a new file

Rather than route the merged document directly to a printer, you can select the Merge And Save Results In New File option to place all the merged documents in one Word file. When you select this option and press OK, Word merges the documents and places them in a new Word document called Merge1. Word sequentially numbers each successive file that you create in this manner—Merge2, Merge3, and so on. You can also merge and save directly from the document window by clicking the Merge And Save icon on the Print Merge Helper bar.

To separate the merged documents, Word inserts a section break between them. For example, if we select the Merge And Save Results In New File option to merge the files in our example, Word creates the document shown in Figure 15-12

FIGURE 15-12.
You can save your merged text in a file rather than print it.

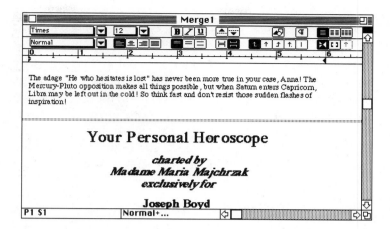

by first creating the merged document for Anna Anderson, inserting a section-break marker, and then creating the merged document for Joseph Boyd.

By viewing the Merge1 document, you can see the results of your merge instructions before you print. This spot-checking technique can save a lot of time, frustration, and paper. If your data document contains many records, you may want to use the From and To options in the Print Merge dialog box to create a merge file from only a few records as a way of previewing your merged documents. To print the Merge1 document, choose the Print command from the File menu to display the Print dialog box.

The Merge1 document is not linked in any way to either the main document or data document used to create it. If you change the information in either of those files, be sure to choose the Print Merge command again to create a new, updated merge file.

Checking for errors

Select the Only Check For Errors option if, instead of merging the main document and the data document, you want Word to check the contents of both these documents and alert you to errors that might prevent you from merging them successfully. You can also check for errors directly from the document window by clicking the Check For Errors icon on the Print Merge Helper bar.

You should always select this option if you create a data document and a main document without using Print Merge Helper. Word flags errors such as occurrences of field names in the main document that don't match the field names in the data document, or occurrences of field names that are missing a « or » character.

Creating merge documents without using the Print Merge Helper

Although you can create a data document and a main document most easily by using the Print Merge Helper as we've described, you can also create these documents without the help of this command. You might find this necessary, for example, if you import text for a main document or data document from another application into Word. If you create these documents without the Print Merge Helper, be sure to define the field names in the data document and the DATA instruction and the field name instructions in the main document carefully and consistently.

Using data from other applications

If you want to create a data document that uses data from an application like Microsoft Excel or a similar spreadsheet or database program, you can convert the data file to Word format or copy the text into a Word document. If you're using System 7, you can even subscribe to an edition file that contains the most up-to-date information for your merge documents.

Copying text Data from Microsoft Excel or from a similar spreadsheet program can be copied easily to the data document table. As we explain in Chapter 17, "Importing and Exporting Text and Graphics," when you paste spreadsheet information from Microsoft Excel into Word, Word automatically places the information in a table. Word also preserves any character formatting you've applied to the selection.

After pasting the data into Word, you can use the Table Layout command on the Format menu to insert a row at the top of the new table and then add field name headings, as necessary. (For more information about working with tables, see Chapter 12, "Creating Tables.")

Converting text Generally, to convert text from another application into Word, save the file in Text (ASCII) format. Next, open the Text file as a Word document. In most cases, you'll find each record converted to a paragraph, and each field within the record separated by tabs or by commas. When you insert the tab-delimited text into a Word table that is large enough to accommodate each record, Word uses the tabs to separate each record in the table. (For more information about importing files created in other applications into Word, see Chapter 17, "Importing and Exporting Text and Graphics.")

Subscribing to text If you plan to use data that constantly changes—for example, if you plan to send letters to people using a mailing list that is updated weekly—you can take advantage of Word's ability to share information with other files and other programs by connecting the information in another file to the Word data document.

If you're using System 7, you can use the Create Publisher and Subscribe To commands to link data within different files or applications. If you're using System 6, you can use Word's Paste Link commands. Chapter 16, "Finding and Sharing Files," describes how you can use these commands to share data with Word documents.

Creating data documents

If you use the Table command on the Insert menu to create the table in the data document, be sure that no text, spaces, or blank lines appear above the table in the data document. Each record should occupy a separate table row, and each field should occupy a separate column. Your records can contain as many as 31 fields, but every record must contain the same number of fields. To leave a field blank, you must enter a tab as a placeholder in that field.

Field headers must occupy the very first row of the data document table. Each field name can contain as many as 253 characters. However, if you plan to type each field name in the main document, we suggest that you use short, easy-to-remember field names and that you avoid using blank spaces; these considerations make setting up the document easier and less prone to error.

Although the field names in the data document must appear exactly as you type them in the main document, the formats of the individual table records in the data document are ignored when Word creates your merged documents, so you can use Character, Paragraph, Document, and Section formats in a data document to make the records easy to read and edit.

If you plan to use as field entries text that is delimited by commas, paragraph symbols, or spaces, first use the Replace command to replace the delimiters with tabs, and then paste the newly formatted text into the data document table.

For example, to change records whose field entries are separated by commas, choose Replace from the Edit menu, type a comma in the Find What edit bar and ^t in the Replace With edit bar, and then click the Replace All button. After you close the Replace dialog box, be sure that the table in the data document contains enough rows and columns to accommodate the tab-delimited text. Next select the text, choose the Cut or Copy command, and place the insertion point in the table cell for the first record. When you choose Paste, Word pastes the text into the table, placing text that appears after each tab in the next cell in the row for each record selected. For detailed information about importing text into tables, see Chapter 12, "Creating Tables."

Creating main documents

The sample main document shown earlier in Figure 15-8 uses the two most common merge instructions—the DATA instruction and the field name instruction. Although you'll find it easier to use the Print Merge Helper to create these instructions in new documents, you can also type these instructions in the main document.

To separate these instructions from standard text in the main document, use a pair of print merge characters (« and »). To enter the opening « character, press Option-\. To enter the closing » character, press Shift-Option-\.

You can also enter these characters from the Glossary. Choose Glossary from the Edit menu, select the Show Standard Entries option, and then highlight Print Merge in the Glossary list box. When you click the Insert button, Word places the print merge characters in your document around the insertion point. All you need to do is type the field name. (Chapter 13, "Using Word Tools," describes the Glossary command in detail.)

The DATA instruction As we've explained, the main document must begin with the DATA instruction, which takes the form:

«DATA document»

For example, the DATA instruction *«DATA Hard Drive:Word Merge Documents: Names»* tells Word the drive and folder in which the Names data document can be found.

You can shorten the DATA instruction to include only the filename. For example, you can type *«DATA Names»* to reduce the effect the instruction has on the main document's format. However, Word might not be able to locate the data document automatically as a result.

Word does not distinguish between uppercase and lowercase letters in a DATA instruction. You can enter the first word of a DATA instruction as *data*, *DATA*, or *Data*. Similarly, the document name in the DATA instruction can be in either uppercase or lowercase letters.

When you type a DATA instruction, be sure to enter a blank space between the word *DATA* and the beginning of the data document name. If the filename contains blank characters, include them in your argument as well.

Field name instructions As we've said, the field names at the top of a data document provide the link between the main document and the information stored in the data document. To plug in text from a field in the data document, you simply type the field name, enclosed in print merge characters, in the main document.

You can use the same field as many times as you like in a main document, and you can enter the field names in any order. As long as the field names in your main document exactly match the field headers in the data document, Word can extract the needed information from the appropriate field in each record.

If you use blank spaces in a field header of a data document, be sure to enter these spaces correctly when you type the field name in the main document. It's best to avoid blank spaces, however. You'll run into fewer errors if you develop some rules for consistent field name references.

Using merge instructions

In addition to the DATA and field name instructions, Word offers instructions that let you vary the contents of your merged documents. Each of the following instructions tells Word how you want to merge a main document with a data document:

- The IF, ENDIF, and ELSE instructions specify conditions that must be met before Word prints the variable text in a merged document or carries out another merge instruction.

- The SET and ASK instructions let you manually update selected information each time you choose the Print Merge command. SET updates information within a set of merged documents that might vary from printing to printing. ASK lets you specify new information in each merged document you create.

- The INCLUDE instruction inserts the contents of a separate document into the main document at the location of this instruction.

- The NEXT instruction lets you insert data from two or more records in the same merged document.

- The CALCULATIONS instruction lets you perform simple mathematical calculations using numeric values or parts of a data record.

To define any of these instructions within a main document, you must enclose the correct form of the instruction in print merge characters. (As we've explained, you specify these characters by typing Option-\ and Shift-Option-\ or by choosing the Print Merge entry from the Glossary dialog box.) You need not merge the main document with a data document to use these special instructions, but you must always use the Print Merge command to execute them.

As Figure 15-13 on the next page illustrates, you can also select merge instructions from the Insert Keyword drop-down list box located on the Print Merge Helper bar. You'll probably find it much easier to add an instruction to the main document using this list box. When selected, most of these options display a dialog box to help you construct the instruction without creating a syntax error. (If the Print Merge Helper bar doesn't appear at the top of the main document window, display it by choosing Print Merge Helper from the View menu.)

FIGURE 15-13.
*The Insert Keyword
drop-down list box lets
you insert a selected
option at the insertion
point automatically.*

The IF and ENDIF instructions

Word's IF and ENDIF instructions let you insert special text into a merged document that depends on information in one of the fields in your data document, by setting up conditional tests in the main document. The simplest form of the IF instruction is:

«IF field name, operator, value»text«ENDIF»

where *field name* is a field name specified in the data document, *operator* is a relationship like = or >, *value* is a text string that you specify, and *text* is the text that Word inserts at the location of the instruction if the condition specified in the rest of the instruction is true. (As we explain in a few pages, if you specify a text string that you want Word to compare with a field name, you must enclose this text in quotation marks.) Instead of text, you can also insert another command at this location in the instruction. If the specified condition is true, Word then executes the nested instruction. ENDIF, which concludes the instruction, both indicates the end of the conditional text and the end of the IF instruction. (Each IF instruction must have its own concluding ENDIF instruction.)

You can use the IF and ENDIF instructions to check for the presence of an entry in a specified field, to compare text and numbers, and to construct more elaborate logical combinations. If the conditional test is true, Word prints the text that appears between the IF and ENDIF instructions. If the conditional test is false, Word omits the text from the current merged document.

Suppose, for example, that you want to further personalize the horoscope reading whose main document appears earlier in Figure 15-8. You can easily use the IF and ENDIF instructions to evaluate the state name of the letter's addressee and then insert a message in your document based on this information. For example, this instruction

«IF st = "New York"»Madame Majchrzak knows that the fast-paced life in
New York can be confusing. «ENDIF»

inserts the customized text that begins *Madame Majchrzak* in the merged document of each data record whose st field contains the text *New York*. (You must place quotation marks around *New York* in the IF instruction to identify it as a text string.)

Similarly, if you want to reply to the first 20 customers who responded to a new promotional ad, you can create an IF instruction that evaluates the data record's RecordNumber. For example,

«IF RecordNumber<21»Congratulations! Your entry was among the first twenty to reach our offices. «ENDIF»

automatically inserts the text beginning *Congratulations* in each of the merged documents created for the first 20 records. If the RecordNumber is not less than 21, Word doesn't insert this text.

To insert an IF instruction, first position the insertion point. Then select IF... ENDIF... from the Insert Keyword drop-down list box on the Print Merge Helper bar. Word displays the Insert IF dialog box shown in Figure 15-14, which allows you to specify the instruction by letting Word enter it for you. Selecting IF... ENDIF... ensures that the ENDIF part of the instruction is not forgotten. (Selecting IF from the Insert Keyword drop-down list box inserts only the IF part of the instruction, and selecting ENDIF inserts only the ENDIF part of the instruction.)

FIGURE 15-14.
Select IF... ENDIF...
from the Insert
Keyword drop-down
list box to display the
Insert IF dialog box.

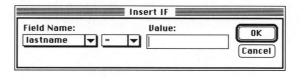

The Field Name drop-down list box in the Insert IF dialog box includes the names of all the fields specified in the data document. To define the instruction, first select the field name from this list. Next, select a mathematical operator to indicate how you want the field information to be evaluated. Finally, indicate the comparison value in the Value edit bar. The value can be either a number or text, and you can specify uppercase and lowercase letters as appropriate. If you specify in the Value edit bar a text string that you want Word to compare with a field name, Word encloses the text string in quotation marks so that it stands out in the instruction.

When you click OK, Word inserts the IF instruction into your document in the following form:

«IF field name, operator, value»text or instruction«ENDIF»

Word places the insertion point before the «ENDIF» instruction so that you can type the conditional text or instruction. Anything you type between IF and ENDIF is conditional, based on the result of the IF comparison. The text between the IF and ENDIF instructions can be any length and can contain page-break and section-break markers and other print merge instructions, such as the SET, ASK, and INCLUDE instructions.

Checking for the presence of an entry in a field

Suppose you've created an invitation that contains only the first paragraph and the opening and closing shown in Figure 15-15, and you want to include a note to your married clients, inviting their spouses to the grand opening celebration. You can include a field in your data document that contains the name of each married client's spouse. For those clients who are not married, this field in the data document is blank. You can easily set up a conditional instruction, like the one shown in the second text paragraph in Figure 15-15, to test for the presence of an entry in the spouse field of your data document.

FIGURE 15-15.
The second paragraph of this letter appears only if the record contains an entry in the spouse field.

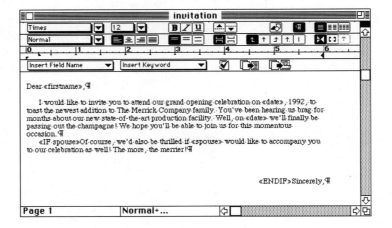

To insert the IF instruction, first position the insertion point where you want the conditional text printed—in this case, at the beginning of the paragraph that follows the first text paragraph. Then select IF... ENDIF... from the Insert Keyword drop-down list box in the Print Merge Helper bar.

Word displays the Insert IF dialog box shown earlier in Figure 15-14. To create the instruction shown in Figure 15-15, select spouse from the Field Name drop-down list box, and then select Field Not Empty in the operator drop-down list box in the middle of the dialog box. In this case, you want Word to check only whether the spouse field is empty, so leave the Value edit bar blank, and then click OK. Word inserts the following instruction at the insertion point in the document:

«IF spouse»«ENDIF»

and places the insertion point just before the «ENDIF» instruction. To complete the instruction, type the conditional text that you want to print when the conditions specified in the instruction are met. Be sure to enclose any field name references in the conditional text in print merge characters.

For example, type: *Of course, we'd also be thrilled if «spouse» would like to accompany you to our celebration as well! The more, the merrier!* When printing this text, Word will substitute the name from the spouse field for the «spouse» field instruction. If the spouse field is empty, Word will omit this paragraph.

Notice that in Figure 15-15 we placed the ENDIF instruction after the ¶ symbol at the end of the conditional text—just in front of the word *Sincerely* in the closing of the invitation letter. By doing so, we avoid any unwanted blank lines in our merged documents. Remember, when you enter conditional text in your main document, Word considers everything between the IF and ENDIF instructions—including paragraph symbols—to be conditional. Thus, placing the ENDIF instruction at the beginning of the next paragraph—after the ¶ symbol—ensures that no blank lines appear in your merged documents when the IF condition is false. To move the ENDIF statement from the end of a line, simply select the text without selecting the adjacent paragraph symbol, choose Cut from the Edit menu, and then paste the text at the beginning of the next paragraph.

Comparing text and numbers

Rather than simply testing for the presence of an entry in a field, you can use an IF instruction to compare the contents of a field to a string or value that you specify. Word lets you compare text entries as well as numeric values with these two forms of the IF instruction:

«IF field name, operator, "comparison text"»text or instruction«ENDIF»

«IF field name, operator, comparison value»text or instruction«ENDIF»

Returning to the sample horoscope document, suppose you want to include a birthday greeting to those people on your mailing list whose birthdays are approaching. Let's assume you'll be mailing the letters in mid-September, so the Libras are the next group of clients with birthdays on their astral horizons. You can create an IF instruction like the one in Figure 15-16 on the next page to include a birthday greeting for clients with Libra as their sign field entry.

To define this instruction, place the insertion point before the paragraph symbol on the line that contains the «firstname» and «lastname» field name instructions, and then press Return to create a new line with the same paragraph formatting. Next, select IF... ENDIF... from the Insert Keyword drop-down list box to display the Insert IF dialog box, and then select sign from the Field Name drop-down list box and = from the operator drop-down list box. Finally, type *Libra* in the Value list edit bar, and press OK. Word adds the instruction to the document and places the insertion point within the instruction so that you can type *Happy Birthday*. Notice in Figure 15-16 that we moved the «ENDIF» instruction to the beginning of the next paragraph so that the formatting of documents that don't include the birthday salutation won't be affected.

FIGURE 15-16.
*This IF instruction
tells Word to print a
birthday greeting for
all the Libras on the
mailing list.*

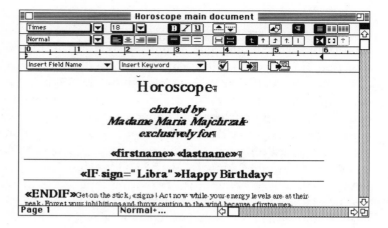

Alternatively, suppose you need to send a series of billing notices and that the data document includes an od field that lists the number of days that each payment is overdue. To include a special message to people whose payments are more than 15 days late, use the Insert IF dialog box to create an IF instruction like the one shown in Figure 15-17 to determine whether the value in the od field is greater than 15. If the logical test *od>15* is true, Word includes the sentence *Your bill is seriously past due!* in the billing notice for that client. If payment is 15 days overdue or less, this sentence doesn't appear in the merged document.

FIGURE 15-17.
*We used a comparison
value in an IF
instruction to
determine whether
each client's payment
is more than 15 days
overdue.*

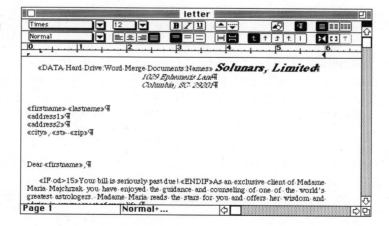

If you specify text in the Value edit bar, Word encloses the text in quotation marks to indicate that the value is a sequence of characters rather than a number. These quotation marks are also required when specifying comparison text. If you decide to add a comparison text value to the instruction yourself, be sure to use straight quotation marks (" "), not smart quotation marks (" "). You might need to deselect the "Smart" Quotes option in the Preferences dialog box in order to enter straight quotation marks. If you place quotation marks around numeric values, Word treats the values as text rather than as numbers. (As we'll explain, there's an exception to this rule.)

When you're using the IF instruction to compare field entries, you can use any one of the comparison operators summarized in Table 15-1 with both text and numeric fields. When a field contains text, Word uses the ASCII value of that text to perform the conditional test.

Operator	Meaning
=	Equal to
>	Greater than
<	Less than
>=	Greater than or equal to
<=	Less than or equal to
<>	Not equal to

TABLE 15-1.
You can use these conditional operators to specify an IF condition.

Word can also create IF instructions to compare the contents of one field with another field in the same record. The form of this instruction is:

«IF field name1, operator,"«field name2»"»text or instruction«ENDIF»

Again, be sure you use straight quotation marks to surround the «field name2» portion of the instruction.

«IF amount paid="amount due"»Thank you for your complete
    payment«ENDIF»

This instruction inserts the text beginning *Thank you* only if the text in the amount paid field exactly matches the text in the amount due field.

Using the ELSE instruction to print alternative text

So far, all our conditional tests have been instructions to insert text in a merged document only if a given condition is true. Occasionally, you will want to insert alternative text when the condition is false. Word's ELSE instruction works hand-in-hand with the IF instruction to let you accomplish this task.

The ELSE instruction, which takes no arguments of its own, is designed to be nested within the IF instruction, like this:

«IF field name, operator, value»conditional text or instruction
    «ELSE»alternative text or instruction«ENDIF»

For example, Figure 15-18 shows the letter shown earlier in Figure 15-15 with an ELSE instruction that adds an alternative line of text inviting those with no entry in the spouse field to bring a guest. To create the alternative text, we added the nested instruction:

«ELSE»Please feel free to invite a guest to help us celebrate this momentous occasion!

to the IF instruction.

FIGURE 15-18.
We used an ELSE instruction to add alternative text for unmarried clients.

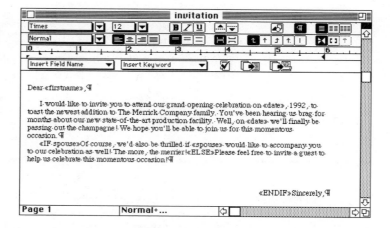

To add the ELSE instruction to the IF instruction, insert the IF... ENDIF... instruction using the Insert IF dialog box as you normally would. Next, with the insertion point just before «ENDIF» in the IF instruction, type the text you want to print or the action you want Word to perform if the condition is true. Then select ELSE from the Insert Keyword drop-down list box. Word simply inserts «ELSE» into the instruction. With the insertion point between «ELSE» and «ENDIF», type the text you want to print or the instruction you want Word to perform if the condition is false.

Nesting IF instructions

You can nest two or more IF instructions in a main document to test for a number of possible conditions. In fact, Word allows you to create logical AND, OR, and NOT combinations. When the IF instructions must all be true in order for Word to print the conditional text, think of the IF instructions as being tied together with logical ANDs. When only one of the IF instructions must be true for Word to print the conditional text, think of the IF instructions as being combined with logical ORs. If none of the IF instructions must be true, think of the IF instructions as being combined with logical NOTs.

Logical AND combinations To combine IF instructions with a logical AND, string the instructions together, enclosing the contents of both the IF and the AND statements inside parentheses for clarity, like this:

«IF (field name1, operator, "comparison text") AND (IF field name2, operator, "comparison text")»text or instruction«ENDIF»

or

«IF (field name1, operator, comparison value) AND (IF field name2, operator, comparison value)»text«ENDIF»

For example, let's return to the horoscope document. You can increase the effectiveness of the overdue notice by including this instruction:

«IF (od>15) AND (IF sign="Scorpio")» This is not the time for a «sign» to risk bad credit! «END IF»

The conditional text prints only if both conditions are met. Notice that all the IF instructions are displayed before the conditional text and that a single ENDIF instruction follows the conditional text.

Unfortunately, you cannot use an ELSE instruction when you string together two or more IF instructions in a logical AND combination. If you do include an ELSE instruction, Word executes it only when all the IF conditions are false. If even one of the IF conditions is true, Word ignores the ELSE instruction.

Logical OR combinations In a logical OR combination, only one IF instruction must be true for the conditional result to occur. You set up a logical OR combination like this:

«IF (field name, operator, "comparison text") OR (field name, operator, "comparison text")»text or instruction«ENDIF»

or

«IF (field name, operator, comparison value) OR (field name, operator, comparison value)»text or instruction«ENDIF»

As with AND, you can use either the same or different field names in each IF instruction.

For example, suppose you want to add a sentence that introduces a special birthday rate to repeat clients. You can create an instruction like the one below, which evaluates the contents of the sign field to determine whether to print a special birthday announcement at the place of the instruction in the main document. The instruction

«IF (sign="Aries") OR (sign="Taurus")»Visit in the next three weeks and take 20% off the charge for a detailed reading in honor of your birthday. «ENDIF» inserts the text that begins *Visit in the next three weeks* in each merged document created for records that contain *Aries* or *Taurus* in the sign field. If a record contains neither entry, Word doesn't print the conditional text.

Logical NOT combinations In a logical NOT combination, the IF instruction must be false, or not true, for the conditional result to occur. You set up a logical NOT combination like this:

«IF (field name, operator, "comparison text") AND NOT (field name, operator, "comparison text")»text or instruction«ENDIF»

or

«IF (field name, operator, comparison value) AND NOT (field name, operator, comparison value)»text or instruction«ENDIF»

Again, you can use either the same or different field names in each IF instruction.

For example, suppose you add a field called notice in which you record whether overdue notices have been sent to customers with delinquent accounts. You can use the instruction below to insert a message that thanks a customer whose bill is paid on time:

«IF (amount paid="amount due") AND NOT (notice)»Thank you for your timely payment. «ENDIF»

This instruction first verifies that the text in the amount paid field matches the text in the amount due field. If this text matches—that is, if the account has been paid in full—and if no entry has been made in the record's notice field—that is, if no notice has been sent—Word inserts the text specified in the instruction at the current insertion point.

The SET instruction

Use the SET instruction to print variable information that isn't defined in a data document. For example, this command is particularly helpful if you want to insert a reply date that varies depending on when the merged document is printed. You can specify the reply date within a SET instruction and then change this data as necessary in the main document before you choose the Print Merge command.

To insert the SET instruction in the main document, select SET from the Insert Keyword drop-down list box on the Print Merge Helper bar. Word displays the Insert SET dialog box shown in Figure 15-19, which allows you to define a new field and to specify the text that you want to appear in this field.

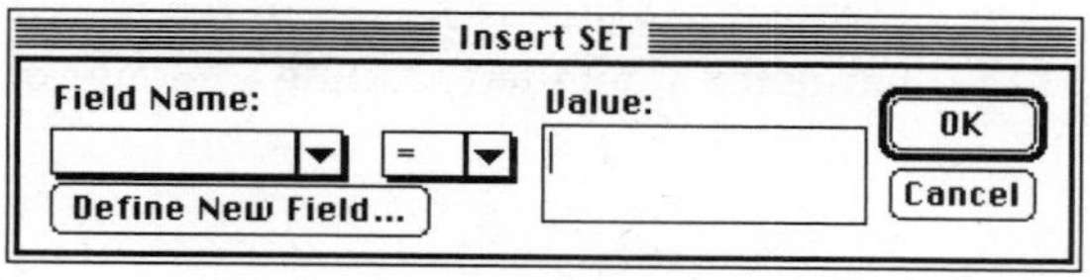

FIGURE 15-19.
Select SET from the Insert Keyword list to display the Insert SET dialog box.

The Field Name drop-down list box displays only the names of fields you've established for use in the Insert SET dialog box. You must define a field to be used within a SET instruction by clicking Define New Field. Word then displays a dialog box that lets you enter a name for the new field. When you click OK, Word adds the field name to both the Insert Field Name drop-down list box on the Print Merge Helper bar and the Field Name list in the Insert SET dialog box.

After specifying the field name in the Field Name list box, you can select two different operators from the operator drop-down list box. Select = from the operator drop-down list box, and then type the number or the text for the SET instruction in the Value edit box. You can use as many as 253 characters in a SET instruction, including the SET keyword, the field name and operator, and the value. When you click OK after completing the edit box, Word inserts the instruction at the insertion point in this form:

«SET field name=value»

This instruction is complete; click OK to place it at the insertion point in the main document where you want the field name to occur.

You can insert a SET instruction anywhere in your document, with two exceptions: You can't insert the SET instruction before the DATA instruction if you're also merging data from a data document; and the SET instruction must precede any field names in the text that refer to the instruction. Generally, it's a good idea to place the SET instruction immediately after the DATA instruction (or as close to it as possible, if you're also specifying other instructions). Placing the SET instruction between the DATA instruction and the paragraph symbol on that line ensures that you don't add a blank line to your document.

After defining the SET instruction, you must also place the field name specified in the SET instruction within your document. To insert the field name, place the insertion point where you want the text to appear, and then select the field name from the Insert Field Name drop-down list box. When you merge the main document, Word replaces this field name with the value in the Insert SET dialog box.

Using the text option

If you select = as an operator and then type text in the Value edit box, you can change this value in your main document before you choose the Print Merge command. For example, suppose you're using the Print Merge command to create a series of personalized invitations to your company's grand opening and that the party is going to be so big that you must spread it over three days in order to accommodate all your guests. To create three sets of form letters that carry different invitation dates, you could define a SET instruction with a field name called date, like this:

«SET date=March 1»

Then, to vary the definition of the date field, edit this SET instruction each time you chose the Print Merge command so that it specifies a different date.

For example, Figure 15-20 shows an invitation letter in which the SET instruction appears immediately after the DATA instruction. After defining the new date field in the Insert SET dialog box, we selected = from the operator drop-down list box, and then typed *March 1* in the Value edit box. After we clicked OK to insert this SET instruction into the main document, we used the In-sert Field Name drop-down list box to insert the «date» instruction in the first line of the body text of the letter.

FIGURE 15-20.
We used the SET instruction to vary the invitation dates in this form letter.

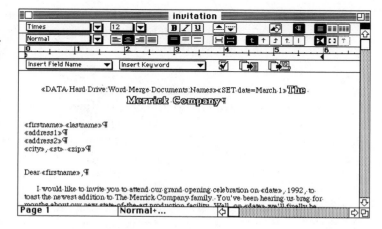

To divide the invitations into three groups, each with a different invitation date, we can use three Print Merge commands. Using the From and To options in the Print Merge dialog box, we can specify a range of data records for each merge procedure. For example, suppose the data document contains 30 records. We might use From and To arguments of 1 and 10 to print the first batch of invita-tions, 11 and 20 to print the second batch, and 21 and 30 to print the last batch.

To vary the invitation date for each group of letters, we can simply change the text in the SET instruction before choosing the Print Merge command. For the second batch of invitations, for example, the SET instruction might be

«SET date=March 2»

whereas the value for the third batch might be *March 3*.

Using the SET prompt

You can choose whether to have Word prompt you for the value each time you perform a merge procedure. To specify the prompt, select =? from the operator drop-down list box, and then type a short prompt that Word will display in a dialog box each time you merge the main document. When you click OK, Word inserts the SET instruction at the insertion point in this form:

«SET field name=?prompt»

For example, Word presents the dialog box shown in Figure 15-21 if you specify the text *Enter the Invitation Date* in the Insert SET dialog box.

FIGURE 15-21.
*You can create your
own prompts for the
SET dialog box.*

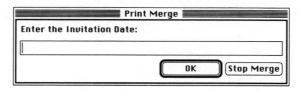

To create the three sets of party invitations, you specify the first From and To settings in the Print Merge dialog box, and click OK. When Word displays the dialog box shown in Figure 15-21, type *March 1*, and then click OK. After Word prints the first set of invitations, specify new From and To settings in the Print Merge dialog box, and then type a new date in the dialog box for the second set of invitations. If you need to stop the merge procedure, press the Stop Merge button.

You can also choose to specify no text with the prompt. In this case, when you click OK, Word inserts this instruction at the insertion point:

«SET field name=?»

and doesn't display any identifying text when it prompts you for the value.

We recommend that you always specify a prompt. Otherwise, you might have difficulty knowing exactly what information to enter.

The ASK instruction

The ASK instruction is similar to the SET instruction, except that it can vary a field value for each merged document in a set. Instead of varying a field for each Print Merge command, the ASK instruction varies the content of the field for each merged document created using only one Print Merge command. You supply the values as Word merges the documents. You can't specify a value when you define an ASK instruction. Unlike the SET instruction, the ASK instruction requires that Word prompt you for the variable information.

To insert the ASK instruction at the insertion point in the main document, select ASK from the Insert Keyword drop-down list box on the Print Merge Helper bar. Word displays the Insert ASK dialog box shown in Figure 15-22 on the next page, which, like the Insert SET dialog box, allows you to define a new field to insert in the main document. This dialog box also lets you specify the prompt Word displays each time it creates a new merged document.

FIGURE 15-22.
Select ASK from the
Insert Keyword list to
display the Insert ASK
dialog box.

The Field Name drop-down list box in the Insert ASK dialog box displays the names of the fields you've established to use with the SET or ASK command. Select a field name from this list, or click the Define New Field button to define a new field to be used within an ASK instruction. Word doesn't allow you to select the name of a field defined in the data document for an ASK instruction. (You can, however, use a field defined in the Insert SET dialog box.)

If you click the Define New Field button, Word displays a dialog box that lets you define a name for the new field. Click OK to close this dialog box, and type the prompt that you want Word to display in the Prompt edit box. You can use up to 253 characters in an ASK instruction, including the ASK keyword, the field name, and the prompt. When you click OK after completing the Prompt edit box, Word adds the field to the Insert Field Name list box on the Print Merge Helper bar and inserts the instruction at the insertion point in this form:

«ASK field name=?prompt»

You can also leave the Prompt edit box blank. Then, when you click OK, Word inserts this instruction at the insertion point:

«ASK field name=?»

and displays no identifying text when it prompts you for the variable value.

When the ASK instruction is complete, press OK to insert it at the insertion point in the main document. You can insert an ASK instruction anywhere in your document, with two exceptions: You can't insert the ASK instruction before the DATA instruction if you're also merging data from a data document; and the ASK instruction must precede any field names in the text that refer to the instruction. Generally, it's a good idea to place the ASK instruction immediately after the DATA instruction, or as close after it as possible, if you're also specifying other instructions. Placing the ASK instruction between the DATA instruction and the paragraph symbol on the same line ensures that you don't add a blank line to your document.

After defining the ASK instruction, you must also place the field name within your document. To insert the field name, place the insertion point where you want the text to appear, and then select the field name from the Insert Field Name drop-down list box. When you merge the main document, Word replaces this field name with the value you enter at the prompt.

For example, suppose you decide to create a personalized greeting for each invitation. You might set up a form letter like the one in Figure 15-23. The ASK instruction in the letter's salutation causes Word to prompt you for a greeting for each letter.

FIGURE 15-23.
You can use the ASK instruction to vary a field entry for each merged document.

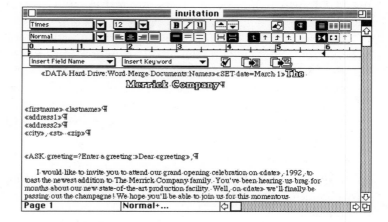

Unfortunately, depending on how you've set up your main document—how long it is, where you have embedded field names, and so on—you might not be able to tell which record is being processed when you see the ASK prompt. To get around this problem easily, you can nest one or more field name instructions in the ASK prompt to identify the current record. For example, rather than using the instruction

    «ASK greeting=?Enter a greeting:»

in Figure 15-23, you can use an instruction like

    «ASK greeting=?HOW DO YOU WANT TO GREET «firstname» «lastname»?»

When you choose the Print Merge command, Word presents a dialog box like the one in Figure 15-24 as it creates a merged document for each record in your data document.

FIGURE 15-24.
You can embed field name instructions in your ASK messages to keep track of which record is being processed.

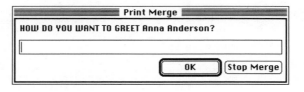

If you need to stop the merge procedure, you can click the Stop Merge button in the ASK Prompt dialog box.

The INCLUDE instruction

The INCLUDE instruction lets you insert the contents of another file into the main document. You can insert the contents of another Word file or any file with a format that Word recognizes. If any additional main document text appears after the INCLUDE instruction, Word prints that text immediately after the text that has been "included."

To insert the INCLUDE instruction at the insertion point in the main document, select INCLUDE from the Insert Keyword drop-down list box on the Print Merge Helper bar. Word displays a dialog box to let you select the document to be included when you merge the main document. Unless you move the file identified in this dialog box's list box, Word finds this file and automatically inserts its contents. After you identify the file, Word inserts this INCLUDE instruction at the insertion point:

«INCLUDE document»

After specifying an include document, you can make changes to it as needed. Any changes you make to the include document are incorporated into the main document text.

Section breaks or manual page breaks in the include document can affect the appearance of the text included in the main document. You might need to remove characters like section and paragraph symbols before choosing the Print Merge command.

Suppose you want to include a "sun sign profile" after the text in the sample horoscope document, using a file called Profile, which is shown in Figure 15-25.

FIGURE 15-25.
This file contains the sun sign profile text.

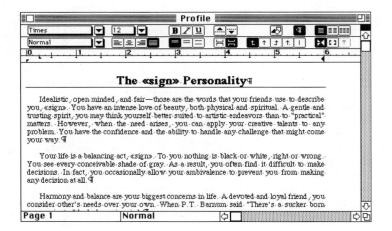

To include this document, select INCLUDE from the Insert Keyword drop-down list box, and then locate the Profile document in the Open File dialog box. After you click Open, Word inserts the instruction

«INCLUDE Hard Disk:Word Files:Profile»

at the insertion point, as shown in Figure 15-26. When you merge the main, data, and include documents, Word creates a series of merged documents like the one shown in Figure 15-27 on the next page.

FIGURE 15-26.
Insert the INCLUDE instruction where you want the additional text to appear.

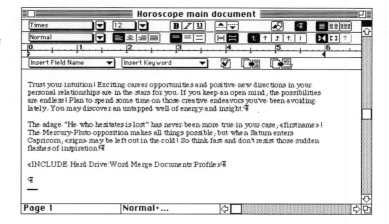

In Figure 15-25, notice that the Profile document contains field name instructions to fill in the client's sign. An include document can contain any of the special instructions you use in a main document, except for the DATA instruction.

You can use the IF instruction, for example, to extract data from different include documents, depending on the results of certain conditional instructions. If the main document and the include document contain field names, be sure that all fields are defined either in the data document specified by the DATA instruction or in a SET or ASK instruction in the appropriate include document.

A document specified in an INCLUDE instruction can also contain INCLUDE instructions. You can create a chain of as many as 55 documents by nesting an INCLUDE instruction in a document specified within an INCLUDE instruction. An INCLUDE instruction cannot specify the name of the document in which it resides, however. For example, Word won't let you merge a document named Invitation Update that contains the instruction «INCLUDE Invitation Update».

FIGURE 15-27.
*When you choose
the Print Merge
command, Word
combines the text from
all three documents.*

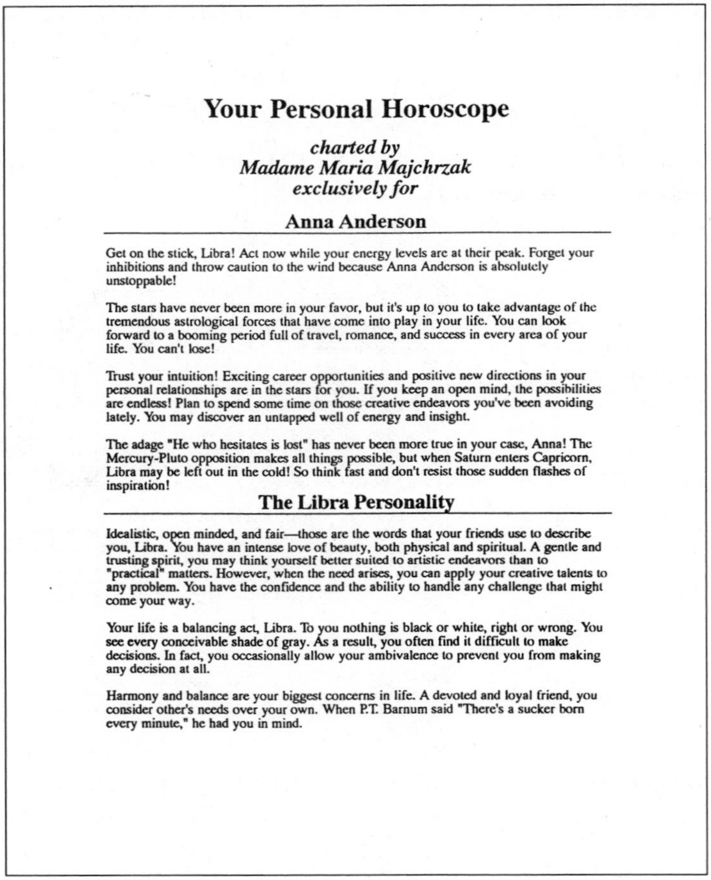

> **Your Personal Horoscope**
>
> *charted by*
> *Madame Maria Majchrzak*
> *exclusively for*
>
> **Anna Anderson**
>
> Get on the stick, Libra! Act now while your energy levels are at their peak. Forget your inhibitions and throw caution to the wind because Anna Anderson is absolutely unstoppable!
>
> The stars have never been more in your favor, but it's up to you to take advantage of the tremendous astrological forces that have come into play in your life. You can look forward to a booming period full of travel, romance, and success in every area of your life. You can't lose!
>
> Trust your intuition! Exciting career opportunities and positive new directions in your personal relationships are in the stars for you. If you keep an open mind, the possibilities are endless! Plan to spend some time on those creative endeavors you've been avoiding lately. You may discover an untapped well of energy and insight.
>
> The adage "He who hesitates is lost" has never been more true in your case, Anna! The Mercury-Pluto opposition makes all things possible, but when Saturn enters Capricorn, Libra may be left out in the cold! So think fast and don't resist those sudden flashes of inspiration!
>
> **The Libra Personality**
>
> Idealistic, open minded, and fair—those are the words that your friends use to describe you, Libra. You have an intense love of beauty, both physical and spiritual. A gentle and trusting spirit, you may think yourself better suited to artistic endeavors than to "practical" matters. However, when the need arises, you can apply your creative talents to any problem. You have the confidence and the ability to handle any challenge that might come your way.
>
> Your life is a balancing act, Libra. To you nothing is black or white, right or wrong. You see every conceivable shade of gray. As a result, you often find it difficult to make decisions. In fact, you occasionally allow your ambivalence to prevent you from making any decision at all.
>
> Harmony and balance are your biggest concerns in life. A devoted and loyal friend, you consider other's needs over your own. When P.T. Barnum said "There's a sucker born every minute," he had you in mind.

The NEXT instruction

The NEXT instruction tells Word to print information from the next data record without starting a new merged document. You can use this instruction to insert information from different records within a single merged document. The NEXT instruction takes no arguments of its own; you simply insert it within another merge instruction or in the main document where you want the next data record to begin printing.

For example, suppose you want to create a list of your clients' names with ten names printed on a page. If you create a main document containing only the field name instructions

«firstname» «lastname»

Word prints only one client name on a page. To print ten names on a page, set up the main document so that it repeats these field name instructions nine times. Include a NEXT instruction in each instruction after the first, like this:

«NEXT»«firstname» «lastname»

Each time Word encounters a NEXT instruction, Word extracts the first and last name information from another record in the data document and merges it into the main document, where the next «firstname» «lastname» sequence appears—without creating a new document.

Using calculations in merge instructions

In addition to the merge instructions we've discussed so far, Word also lets you perform calculations in the main document using numbers and field names. If you enclose a calculation within print merge characters, Word computes the calculation in the order in which the operators appear in the instruction, using the value specified in the data document record to determine the result for each merged document. When you choose the Print Merge command, Word calculates the expressions in parentheses first and then inserts the result in the merged document at the place of the instruction.

You can insert a calculation within a main document or within another merge instruction. Simply position the insertion point where you want the calculation result to appear, and select Calculations from the Insert Keyword drop-down list box. Word displays the Insert Calculation dialog box, shown in Figure 15-28.

FIGURE 15-28.
Select Calculations
from the Insert
Keyword list to
display this dialog box.

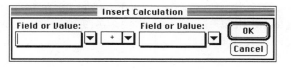

In each Field Or Value edit bar, type either the numeric value that you want to include in the calculation or the field name whose contents will be a numeric value when you merge the main document. In addition to the fields specified in the data document, you can select field names specified in the SET or ASK dialog box, and you can select a record's SequenceNumber or RecordNumber for use in a calculation. In the operator drop-down list box, specify a mathematical operator to add, subtract, multiply, or divide the values specified in the Field Or Value edit bars. When you click OK, Word inserts the calculation at the insertion point in the form

«Field or Value, operator, Field or Value»

Notice that Word doesn't insert the word *CALCULATION* in the instruction.

You might use this instruction, for example, to include a statement in the letter shown earlier in Figure 15-17 that identifies the amount due after a penalty of 10 percent is added. To create such a calculation, first specify a new field called balance in the data document identified in the DATA instruction at the top of the main document. Next, use the Insert Calculation dialog box to create the calculation instructions shown in Figure 15-29. Notice that the first instruction determines the penalty amount by multiplying the balance by 10 percent. The second instruction adds this penalty to the balance.

FIGURE 15-29.
You can use a
calculation instruction
to perform calcula-
tions in a merged
document or in
another instruction.

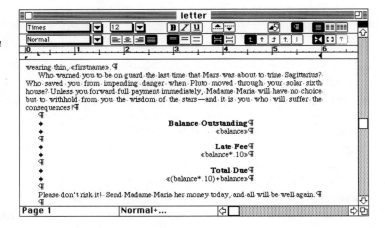

If you want to perform a calculation within another merge instruction, first specify the other instruction. After Word inserts the other instruction in the main document, select Calculations from the Insert Keyword drop-down list box, and proceed as just described.

16

Finding and Sharing Files

*T*his chapter introduces the Word commands you use to find and share information created in Word and in other Macintosh programs. First we show you how to use the Find File command, and then we describe other Word commands and features that make it easy to share information with other users.

With the Find File command, you can locate any file stored on any disk that can be accessed by your Macintosh—not just those files you've created in Word. Word locates the files that match selection criteria you specify and even lets you view the contents of a selected file. When you find the file you want, you can open it, delete it, or print it directly from the Find File dialog box.

Word's Create Publisher and Subscribe To commands let you link a Word document with other Word documents or with documents created in other applications. With linked information in two documents, changes you make to one document also appear in the other so that the most up-to-date information is shared between documents.

You can also use the Paste Link and Paste Special commands on the Edit menu to ensure that changes you make to an original selection appear immediately in the pasted copy. Paste Special also lets you specify a new format for the pasted copy. With the Paste Link and Paste Special commands, you can embed within a Word document the information used to create a text or a graphic in another application. Then double-clicking the text or graphic lets you access the original application without closing Word. You can change or edit the text or graphic in the original application and then return directly to the Word document.

If you're using System 7, you can use the Create Publisher and Subscribe To commands to share information between files created in any application that supports System 7. You can also use the Paste Link and Paste Special commands to link files created in any application that supports both System 7 and linking. And you can embed information from another application if that application supports both System 7 and information embedding.

If you're using System 6, you can use the Paste Link and Paste Special commands together with QuickSwitch to link files.

In addition to making selected information available to other users, you can also share a Word document by saving it as a stationery file. Saving a document as stationery in the Save As dialog box creates a document template you can use to reproduce a complete file automatically.

If you want to add a message to a file you're sharing with other users, the Voice Annotation command on the Insert menu lets you add brief audio recordings to a Word document. Although your Macintosh must be equipped with a microphone in order to create a voice annotation, you can listen to a voice annotation on any Macintosh by choosing Voice Annotations from the View menu.

We discuss creating stationery at the end of this chapter. Word's Voice Annotation command is discussed in Appendix E, "Voice Annotation."

Finding files

The Find File command on the File menu enables you to locate all the files on a specified disk that match the search criteria you define. When you first choose Find File from the File menu, Word displays the Search dialog box, where you specify information about the file you want to locate. If you know the filename, you can enter the name in the Search dialog box. If you know the file's creation date, you can enter the date. If you remember only part of the filename or who created the file, or if you know that the file was created sometime during the month of March, Word can search for the file based on the partial information.

In addition to finding a file by its name or date, you can search by any entry in the Summary Info dialog box or by comments in the file's Get Info dialog box. Word can also locate a file by using text within the file as the search criteria. You can, for example, look for all letters addressed to a business associate by searching for the phrase *Dear Ms. Johnson*. You can also limit the search to a particular type of file or extend the search to all files on your disk.

When you click OK in the Search dialog box, Word searches your drive for files that match the search criteria. After a moment, Word lists the matching files in the Find File dialog box. You can sort this list or search again using different search criteria. When you find the file you want, you can select its name to learn its location, or you can open, save, or print the file directly from the Find File dialog box.

Defining the search

When you choose Find File, Word first displays the Search dialog box shown in Figure 16-1, where you specify search criteria to narrow the list of files displayed in the Find File dialog box.

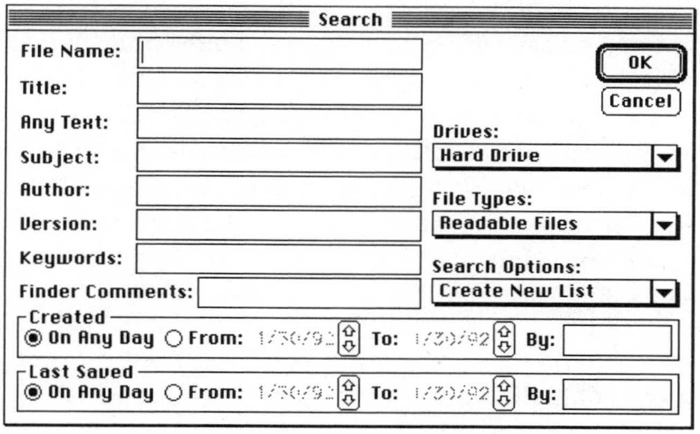

FIGURE 16-1.
The Search dialog box allows you to narrow the list of files that appear in the Find File dialog box.

By default, all search criteria edit bars are blank, and Word finds all readable files when you click OK. (These files vary depending on the conversion files currently installed in the Word Commands folder. For information about installing these files, see the Introduction.) The more information you provide about the file, the smaller the list of files that match the criteria will be. If you're searching a very large hard drive, specifying search criteria speeds up the search by significantly narrowing the list of files that Word must consider.

You can enter up to 255 characters in any Search dialog box edit bar. Word matches only characters, not case. As a result, you can use either uppercase or lowercase text in the edit bars. You must manually type each edit bar entry, however; Word doesn't allow you to use the Paste command to paste entries in the Search dialog box.

Specifying a filename or document text

If you know the exact name or part of the name of the file you want to find, enter this information in the File Name edit bar. For example, you can type a particular filename, such as *Monthly Report-September*, to locate that file, or you can type *Monthly Report* to find every file with these words in its name.

Word can also search for documents that contain the text you enter in the Any Text edit bar, by scanning all the characters in all the stored documents. You can use wildcards and special formatting symbols to represent variable text in the Any Text edit bar. (These wildcard characters and formatting symbols are the same as those used in the Find dialog box. For more information about them, see Chapter 7, "Editing and Proofing.")

Specifying summary information

The Summary Info dialog box contains fields you can use as search criteria. We first introduced the Summary Info dialog box in Chapter 2, "Handling Files." Choose the Summary Info command from the File menu to open the dialog box so that you can record information you can use later to identify the contents of the file. The Summary Info dialog box contains five edit bars—Title, Subject, Author, Version, and Keywords. You can enter criteria to match this information in the Search dialog box.

Specifying finder comments

The Finder Comments edit bar lets you find specific text in a document's Get Info dialog box. This dialog box is displayed when you select a document from the Finder and choose Get Info from the File menu. As your Macintosh system documentation explains, the Get Info dialog box contains a Comments field that provides another way to identify a selected file. For example, you can enter information in the Comments edit bar about the contents of a graphic or spreadsheet file. You can then use that information as a search criterion in the Finder Comments edit bar.

Specifying created and last saved information

The Created and Last Saved sections at the bottom of the Search dialog box let you narrow the search to files created or last modified during a specific time period or by a specific person. The default option, On Any Day, instructs Word to search for files that match the search criteria specified in the other edit bars. Clicking the From button places the current date in both the From and To date fields. To change either date, click the month, day, or year, and then press the Up or Down direction key to specify the date you want. In the From field, specify the earliest creation or modification date you want Word to search for. In the To field, specify the latest creation or modification date.

For example, changing the From date to 01/01/92 and the To date to 01/31/92 in the Created section tells Word to display all files that both meet all the other search criteria specified in the dialog box and were created during January, 1992. Changing the From date to 01/01/92 and the To date to 01/01/92 in the Last Saved section instructs Word to Find only those files that were last modified on January 1, 1992.

The By edit bar in the Created and Last Saved sections lets you specify the author who created or modified the file during the time period defined by the From and To dates. If you complete either field, Word searches for a matching entry in the Author field of the Summary Info dialog box for files created or modified during the date range specified. If you work on a network or share files among many users, you can use this field to narrow the search to those files created by a particular author.

Specifying a drive and file type

You can also narrow the places that Word searches for a file. The Drives drop-down list box on the right side of the Search dialog box lets you specify the drive on which you want the search performed. All mounted hard drives and floppy disk drives appear in the list. The File Types drop-down list box lets you select a particular file format or a group of file formats to be considered in the search. The exact content of this list varies, depending on the file converters currently installed.

Figure 16-2 displays the available File Types options. The default option, Readable Files, instructs Word to search all the files whose contents it can read. Selecting another option, such as Excel Files, instructs Word to search only Excel files that match the search criteria. Selecting All Files instructs Word to consider every file on the specified drive.

FIGURE 16-2.
The File Types drop-down list box lets you select the type of file you want Word to consider during the search.

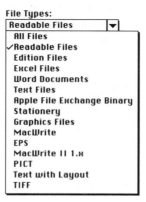

Specifying search options

You view the results of a search in the Find File dialog box. The Search Options drop-down list box lets you define how you want to display the files Word finds using the specified criteria. Later, we'll explain each option in detail.

Using the Find File dialog box

Clicking OK in the Search dialog box displays the Find File dialog box. When this dialog box first appears, Word reports in the upper-right corner the percentage of documents it has finished scanning. After completing its scan of the drive, Word lists the names of the matching files in the drop-down list box on the left side of the dialog box. Word then selects the first file and displays its contents, as shown in Figure 16-3.

FIGURE 16-3.
*Click OK to display
the Find File dialog
box, which lists the
files that meet the
search criteria.*

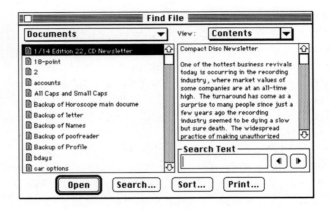

To the left of each filename in the drop-down list box, Word displays a small icon that indicates the contents of each file. An icon that looks like a page of text appears beside Word files and other files created in text programs. Files created in graphics programs display a graphic within the icon frame. Files created by other applications display a blank file icon.

After selecting a filename from the list of files, you can use the other dialog box elements to view the file's location, display different parts of the document, move forward and backward through the document text, and search for a particular text string within the selected document. Buttons at the bottom of the Find File dialog box enable you to sort the list of files, open or print a selected file, or return to the Search dialog box.

Viewing document information

The View drop-down list box in the upper-right corner of the Find File dialog box lets you display information that helps identify the currently selected file. The type of information selected from this list appears immediately below, in the box that occupies most of the dialog box's right side. As Figure 16-3 indicates, the default selection in the View drop-down list box is Contents, and—if the file was created in a text program—the first several lines of text in the first found file are displayed. Word shows the text without formatting, representing special elements such as dynamic glossary entries as small rectangles, and graphics as rectangles containing graphic symbols. If the file was created in a graphics program, Word displays a preview of the stored graphic in the Find File dialog box.

If you specified search criterion in the Any Text edit bar in the Search dialog box, Word also displays this criterion in the Search Text edit bar. You can enter new search text in the Search Text edit bar, including the wildcards and special formatting characters introduced in Chapter 7, "Editing and Proofing." Click the direction arrows on the right side of the Search Text edit bar to highlight the next or previous occurrence of the search text in the selected file.

You can also select Statistics, Comments, or Summary Info from the View drop-down list box. Statistics lets you view author, version, file type, and file size information, as well as the date and time that the file was created and last saved. Comments displays any information specified in the Get Info dialog box from the Finder. Summary Info displays any information specified for the selected file in its Summary Info dialog box.

Finding the file's storage location

To discover where a selected file is located on your disk, simply click the name of the folder or drive that appears above the Files list box, and hold down the mouse button. Word displays the complete file hierarchy for the file, first listing the folder in which the file is stored and then the location of the file on the drive. If the file isn't stored in a folder, Word displays only the drive name.

For example, Figure 16-3 indicates that the newsletter is stored in a folder called Documents. Clicking this name and then holding down the mouse button displays the hierarchy shown in Figure 16-4 on the next page. As you can see, the Documents folder is in another folder called Documents For Word 5, which is stored on the hard drive.

FIGURE 16-4.
*To find out where a
file is stored, click the
name that appears
above the list of files to
view the directory
hierarchy for the file.*

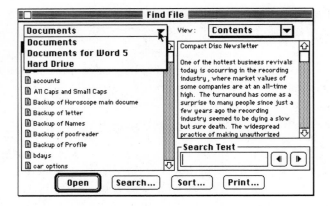

Sorting the displayed files

To change the way that the list of files is organized—for example, to view the
files in chronological order—you can use the Sort button located at the bottom of
the Find File dialog box. Clicking Sort displays the Sort dialog box shown in
Figure 16-5. The Sort dialog box contains two sections: the Sort By drop-down list
box, which lets you indicate how you want Word to organize the files, and the
Sort Order buttons, which specify the order of the listed files. Together, these options let you organize the file display to suit your needs.

FIGURE 16-5.
*Click the Sort button
at the bottom of the
Find File dialog box to
display this Sort
dialog box.*

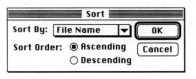

To sort the list of files, first select an option from the Sort By drop-down list
box. You can display files by File Size, File Type, Date Created, or Date Last
Saved, in addition to the default option, File Name. Then, change the Sort Order
option, if necessary. The default Sort Order option, Ascending, sorts the filenames in alphabetic, numeric, or chronologic order, depending on the Sort By option you specified. Select Descending to display files from Z to A when you have
also selected the File Name or File Type option; from largest to smallest when
you have also selected the File Size option; and from most to least recently created when you have also selected the Date Created or Date Last Saved option.

If you change your mind and no longer want to sort the files, click Cancel to
return to the Find File dialog box. Click OK to close the Sort dialog box and sort
the list of files according to your specifications. This process can take a few seconds if many files are listed.

Figure 16-6, for example, shows the files originally displayed in Figure 16-3 after we selected Date Last Saved and changed the Sort Order option to Descending. Sorting in this way can help you locate a file you've just created, even if you can't remember its name.

FIGURE 16-6.
We've sorted the files displayed in Figure 16-3 so that the most recently saved file appears at the top of the list.

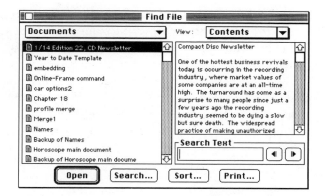

Managing a selected file

You'll often use the Find File command to locate a file that you want to open, print, rename, or delete immediately. You can open or print a selected file by clicking the appropriate button at the bottom of the Find File dialog box or by choosing the corresponding command from Word's File menu. You can also rename a selected file directly from the Find File dialog box. To delete a selected file, you simply choose Delete from the File menu.

To open, print, rename, or delete several of the files in the list at once, simply hold down the Shift key as you select each filename, and then click the appropriate dialog box button or choose the appropriate command. When you select several files, the action you choose affects them in the order that they appear in the list of files.

Opening a file

To open one of the files in the list, select the file, and then click the Open button or choose Open from the File menu. Word immediately opens the selected document and closes the Find File dialog box.

If you open a file created in another application from the Find File dialog box, keep in mind that you're in Word, and that choosing the Open command opens the file as a Word document—no matter what its originating application. Selecting a graphics file created in MacPaint and clicking Open, for example, opens the graphic in a new Word document. To save the document as a Word file, choose Save As from the File menu. (For more information about opening and saving files in Word, see Chapter 2, "Handling Files." Chapter 17, "Importing and Exporting Text and Graphics," discusses opening files created in other applications.)

Printing a file

To print one of the files in the list of files as a Word document, select the file, and then click the Print button or choose Print from the File menu. Word closes the Find File dialog box and opens the document in Word, making the document active. Word then displays the Print dialog box for the active document. Specify printing options, as necessary, and then click OK in the Print dialog box to print the document. Word then closes both the Print dialog box and the document you've just printed, making the document from which you originally chose the Find File command active again. (For detailed information about printing files in Word, see Chapter 8, "Printing.")

Renaming a file

To store a copy of a selected file as a Word file with a different name, choose Save As from the File menu. Word opens the file and displays the Save As dialog box. Type a new name in the Save Current Document As edit bar, and click Save. Word saves the selected file under the new name, closes the file, and reactivates the document from which you chose the Find File command.

Deleting a file

As you know, you can delete a file to increase the available disk space, by dragging the file's icon to the Trash icon in the Finder. The file is stored in the Trash and remains on your disk until you choose the Empty Trash command from the Finder's Special menu. In Apple System 6, the Trash is emptied automatically when you shut down your computer.

You can also delete files while working in Word by using Word's Delete command. This command does not initially appear on a Word menu. If you want to be able to delete documents from within Word, you must assign the Delete command to a menu or shortcut key using the Commands command on the Tools menu. (We show you how to add commands to Word menus in Chapter 18, "Customizing Word.") After you add the Delete command to a menu, you can use it to remove a selected file from the Find File dialog box.

To delete one of the files in the list, select the file, and then choose the Delete command. Word displays an alert box asking you to confirm that you want to delete the file. When you click OK, Word removes the file from the disk.

If you choose Delete from the menu without first using the Find File command, Word displays a dialog box similar to the one that is displayed when you choose the Open or Save As command. As with those dialog boxes, you can use the Desktop (or Drive) button to see the contents of any disk and navigate through the folders until you locate the file you want to delete.

Word's Delete dialog box displays all files—not just the Word documents— on the active disk. The only filenames that don't appear in the list box are those of files that are currently open in Word and of files such as the System, Finder, and Word applications, which are protected.

When you select a file in the Delete dialog box and click OK, Word displays an alert box to safeguard against mistakes. If you're certain you want to delete the file, click Yes. Otherwise, click the No or Cancel button. If you click Yes, Word deletes the file and redisplays the Delete dialog box. At that point, you can select another file to delete, or click the Cancel button to remove the dialog box from your screen. Click No to redisplay the Delete dialog box so that you can select another file. Clicking Cancel returns you to the document you were working on when you chose the command.

You can't recover a file after you've deleted it from within Word. If you're uncertain about the contents of a file you're considering deleting, open the document and take a look at the file before you use the Delete command.

Performing another search

If your search doesn't produce the file you're looking for, you can click the Search button at the bottom of the Find File dialog box to redisplay the Search dialog box with the original search criteria. Try making the search slightly more specific or less specific, depending on the results you achieved the first time. The Search Options drop-down list box shown in Figure 16-7 lets you choose whether to create a completely new list of files or revise the existing list.

FIGURE 16-7.
The Search Options list lets you specify how you want Word to display the results of a new search.

The Search Options default, Create New List, replaces the list of found files in the Find File dialog box with the new list that results from the search criteria currently specified in the Search dialog box.

The Add Matches To List option adds any filenames found using the current search criteria to the list of files displayed previously in the Find File dialog box. You might use this option when you're searching the contents of different drives. First you list the files that match the search criteria on one drive. Then you click the Search button in the Find File dialog box to redisplay the Search dialog box, respecify the search criteria, change the selection in the Drives drop-down list box, and select Add Matches To List. When you click OK, Word displays the contents of both drives in the Find File dialog box.

To narrow the search performed with new search criteria to the files currently displayed in the Find File dialog box, select the Search Only In List option. When you click OK, Word applies the new search criteria only to the listed files.

Publishing and subscribing

If you work on a network, or if you often update the same text in different documents or different applications, you'll find that System 7's publishing and subscribing features make sharing and updating information almost effortless. Word's Create Publisher and Subscribe To commands let you create links between sets of Word documents and between a Word document and information created in other applications. After you create this link, Word automatically updates the information in the linked file whenever you make changes to the original.

Suppose, for example, that each Friday afternoon you create a report that details the progress of a large project. Along with your own summary of the week's activities, this report also includes summaries from each member of your work group. Instead of collecting each coworker's status reports and reproducing each report in your document, you can link each person's status report to your document and let Word collect them for you.

As Figure 16-8 suggests, each worker can publish a summary that indicates the current project status. Anyone who wants this information can subscribe to it, assigning to Word the job of updating the most recent versions of the required information.

Publishing and subscribing features aren't available in programs created before the release of System 7. Although publishing and subscribing are standard features in applications designed to work with System 7, you must be using System 7 with these programs to use this feature.

If you're unsure whether an application contains the Create Publisher and Subscribe To commands, check the application's Edit menu, and review the documentation that came with the software. For more information about using the publishing and subscribing features with different kinds of applications, see your System 7 documentation. If you're using Word with an earlier system version, you can still link information using QuickSwitch. (For more information, see "Linking information between applications using System 6" later in this chapter.)

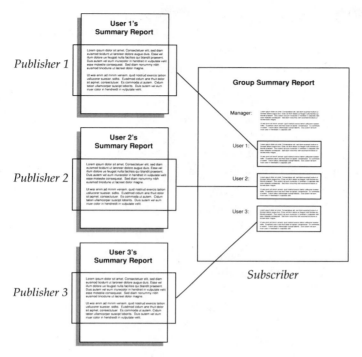

FIGURE 16-8.
Publishing and subscribing enable you to automatically share information between users.

Publishing and subscribing basics

Publishing and subscribing don't require you to prepare the information that you want to share in a special way. The selection that you make available for use with other applications or for other users on your network is called a *publisher*. If you're using System 7, you can designate any part of a Word document as a publisher by first highlighting a selection and then choosing the Create Publisher command. Word identifies publishers in your document by enclosing them in brackets. Show ¶ must be turned on to view the brackets. Otherwise, the publisher text is not different from any other part of your Word document—you can edit and reformat it as you want, and you can cut, copy, and paste the selection.

Creating a publisher automatically produces a copy of the selected information, called an *edition*, as a separate file that you can save on your hard drive, network, or floppy disk. Whenever you change information in the publisher, your Macintosh system automatically makes these changes in the edition. Using the Publisher Options dialog box, you can specify how often you want Word to update the edition.

To obtain the contents of the publisher, other users can subscribe to this edition. The text that appears in the receiving file is called a *subscriber*. You can choose to update the subscriber automatically each time the edition changes or only when an update is requested. No matter which option you select, the received update replaces the previous subscriber text, ensuring that the subscriber is up to date—even if the document containing the subscriber isn't open.

Figure 16-9 illustrates the relationship between publisher, edition, and subscriber. A document can contain any number and any combination of publishers and subscribers. You can create these elements from any application that supports System 7 and that offers the Create Publisher and Subscribe To commands on its Edit menu.

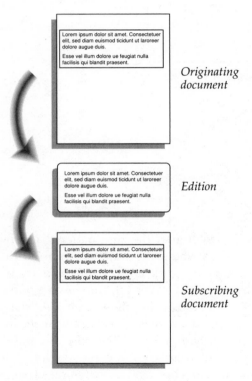

Originating document

Edition

Subscribing document

FIGURE 16-9.
This figure illustrates the relationship between publisher, edition, and subscriber.

In this section, we show you how to create a publisher and a subscriber in a Word document. In our examples, we share information between files stored on the same hard drive. You can also use publishing and subscribing to share information across a network. You can publish a selection in one Word document and then subscribe to it in another Word document. You can even subscribe to published information that originates in the same Word document.

If you're planning to share the publisher with a larger Word document—for example, if the publisher is going to be part of a report created by subscribing to parts of several other documents—you'll find the process works best if the publisher's paragraph and character styles match those in the subscriber file. As we explain later in this chapter, you can easily reformat or edit the contents of a subscriber. However, taking the time to coordinate format and style decisions before you begin publishing and subscribing can save you time later.

Publishing parts of a Word document

You can use the Create Publisher command on the Edit menu to share a selected part of a Word document with other users. Then you can specify how often to update the edition in the Publisher Options dialog box. If you no longer want to use the publisher, you can simply cancel it. Although canceling a publisher breaks its link to the edition, the contents of the publisher remain within the originating document.

Creating a publisher

To create a publisher, select any combination of text or graphics that you want to publish, and then choose Create Publisher from the Edit menu. If you select the entire document, be sure to highlight the final paragraph symbol; otherwise, information you later add to the end of the document won't be included in the publisher.

For example, to publish the selected paragraph in Figure 16-10 on the next page, first choose the Create Publisher command. Word displays the Create Publisher dialog box shown in Figure 16-11 also on the next page. This dialog box displays the selected text as a preview of the publisher. If you select only a single graphic or table, you'll also see a preview of the graphic or table. However, if any part of the selected publisher includes text, you'll see only text in the Preview box.

Enter the name you'll use to identify the new edition in the Name Of New Edition edit bar, and then use the Eject, Desktop, and New Folder buttons, as necessary, to indicate where to store the edition. If you're working on a network, be sure you place the edition within a folder or disk that other users can access.

FIGURE 16-10.
We're going to publish the selected paragraph, making it available to other users.

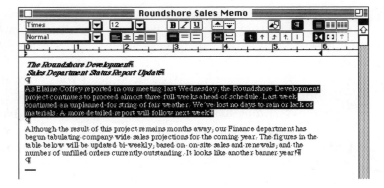

FIGURE 16-11.
In the Create Publisher dialog box, you name the edition that will contain the selected text, and you indicate where to store the edition.

If you decide not to publish the selection, you can click Cancel to return to your document.

To create the edition and return to your document, click Publish. Word encloses the publisher in gray brackets, as shown in Figure 16-12. Word does not print these brackets, which appear only when the Show ¶ command is active.

FIGURE 16-12.
Word encloses the publisher in gray brackets to distinguish it in the document.

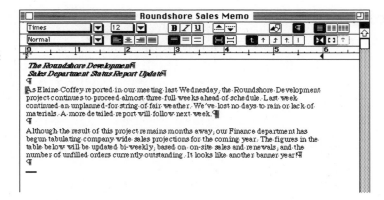

Specifying edition updates

After you define a publisher and create its corresponding edition, you can specify the conditions for sending a revised publisher to the edition. By default, Word updates the edition each time you save the document containing the publisher. Instead, you can update a publisher's edition only when you manually request the update, or you can update the edition immediately, as you edit the publisher.

Word displays all three Edition Update options in the Publisher Options dialog box. To display this dialog box, first place the insertion point anywhere between the brackets that define the publisher in the originating text. Then choose the Publisher Options command from the Edit menu to display a Publisher Options dialog box like the one shown in Figure 16-13. The Publisher To drop-down list box indicates the name of the publisher edition specified in the Create Publisher dialog box and the edition's current location.

FIGURE 16-13.
*Choose Publisher
Options from the Edit
menu to display the
Publisher Options
dialog box.*

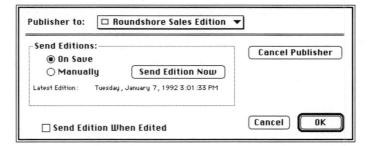

Select the On Save option to update the edition each time you save the originating document. The Manually option gives you control over when the edition is updated. When you select this option, Word updates the edition only if you open the Publisher Options dialog box and click Send Edition Now. Use this option, for example, if the publisher contains many elements that you want to change before sharing the publisher with other users.

Select the Send Edition When Edited option to send changes immediately to the edition. Keep in mind that selecting this option determines how often the edition receives updates, but not how frequently subscribers receive new editions. This option can result in the sharing of unfinished versions of the publisher. Word might also operate a little more slowly than it does when you select either of the other two options, because it must continually update the edition.

To specify when you want a publisher's edition updated, select the option you want, and then click OK. Word records the selection and closes the dialog box. Clicking the Cancel button at the bottom of the Publisher Options dialog box closes the dialog box without making any changes. (As we explain in a few pages, the Cancel Publisher button cancels the publisher in which the insertion point was located when you chose the Publisher Options command.)

Editing the publisher

Specifying part of your document as a publisher does not change the selection itself. The publisher selection remains part of the Word document. You can add or delete text, specify new character and paragraph formatting, and change the names and definitions of the paragraph styles applied to text.

Keep in mind that if you've selected the Send Edition When Edited option in the Publisher Options dialog box, Word immediately sends any changes you make to the publisher to the edition. However, Word saves changes to the publisher in the originating document itself only when you save the file to disk.

Deleting and canceling the publisher

If you no longer want to publish information, you can either delete the information from the originating document or cancel the publisher. The option you select depends, in part, on whether you want subscribers to retain the latest edition of the published information.

Removing all the text from between publisher brackets doesn't cancel the publisher—instead it creates a publisher that is currently empty. The brackets remain in your document, and the next time the corresponding edition is updated, the new edition and subscribers are empty.

Although you might want to delete the contents of a publisher—for example, if you publish questions or ideas to create the agenda for a weekly meeting, you might find yourself with nothing to contribute for a particular week—usually you'll want to cancel the publisher itself. Although subscribers no longer receive updated versions of the edition, the last version received before cancellation remains in the subscriber documents. Word removes the brackets from the publisher in the originating document, but the information itself remains unchanged.

To cancel a publisher, place the insertion point anywhere between the brackets that surround the publisher in the originating text. Choose Publisher Options from the Edit menu to display the Publisher Options dialog box, shown in Figure 16-13. Then click Cancel Publisher. Word displays the alert box shown in Figure 16-14 to verify the cancellation. Clicking Yes in this alert box cancels the publisher, closes the Publisher Options dialog box, and reactivates the document window; you don't need to save the document to secure the cancellation.

FIGURE 16-14.
Clicking Yes in this alert box cancels the publisher in which the insertion point is located.

Subscribing to an edition in Word

To access an edition, use the Subscribe To command to locate the edition and add its contents to your document. The selection inserted in your document is called the subscriber; any updates sent to the edition are automatically shared with your subscriber. In fact, Word updates the subscriber as long as the edition and the file that contains the subscriber remain on the same hard drive or server volume— even if you change the names of these files.

After you create a subscriber in a Word document, you can specify when you want to receive updates in the Subscriber Options dialog box. The update option you select determines how you're able to edit or format the subscriber's contents. You can also access the publisher directly from the subscriber in your Word document. You can cancel the subscriber by clicking the Cancel Subscriber button in the Subscriber Options dialog box.

Creating a subscriber

To insert the contents of an edition in a Word document, first place the insertion point where you want the edition's text or graphics to appear. Next, choose Subscribe To from the Edit menu to display the Subscribe To dialog box, which enables you to locate editions stored on the desktop, on a network server, or on another drive.

Figure 16-15, for example, shows a publisher that we defined in a Microsoft Excel document. Using procedures much like the ones we outlined in this chapter, we created a publisher in the Excel document and named the corresponding edition Chart3 Edition #1. By subscribing to this edition, we will always have the latest sales figures in a summary report created in Word. (Notice that Excel doesn't enclose the publisher in brackets the way that Word does.)

FIGURE 16-15.
*We want to sub-
scribe to the edition
published by this Excel
document.*

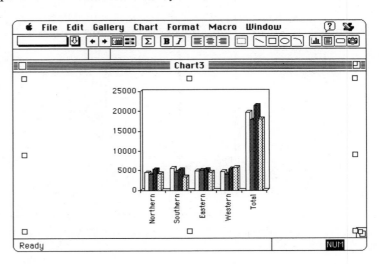

Figure 16-16 shows the Subscribe To dialog box that appeared when we chose Subscribe To from the summary report we created in Word. As you can see, small boxes appear to the left of edition names in the list box. We located Chart3 Edition #1 and then selected it. Selecting an edition displays a preview of its contents on the left side of the dialog box. If the edition contains only a single graphic or table, you'll see a preview of the graphic or table. If any part of the selected publisher includes text, however, you'll see only text in this box.

FIGURE 16-16.
The Subscribe To dialog box enables you to subscribe to a selected edition.

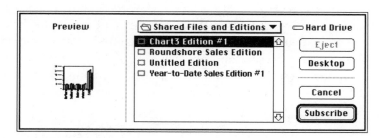

If you click Cancel, Word closes the Subscribe To dialog box without inserting a subscriber at the insertion point. To insert the contents of the selected edition, click Subscribe. Word places the subscriber in your document, enclosing it in brackets that are a darker gray than those of a publisher. Figure 16-17 shows the subscriber in our summary report. Although we cropped and then centered the graphic in Word, Word still encloses the subscriber in identifying brackets.

FIGURE 16-17.
When you insert a subscriber in your document, Word encloses the selection in dark gray brackets.

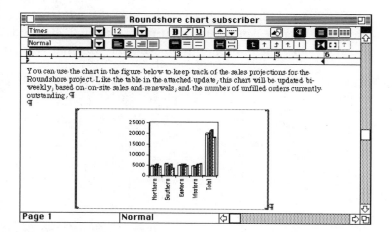

Updating a subscriber

By default, Word updates the subscriber each time the corresponding edition receives new information from the publisher. If you don't change this default and the On Save option has been selected in the Publisher Options dialog box, Word updates the subscriber each time the file that contains the publisher is saved—even if no changes have been made to the publisher itself.

You can tell Word when you want to update the subscriber. To change the update option, first click part of the subscriber to select it. Then choose Subscriber Options from the Edit menu to display a Subscriber Options dialog box like the one shown in Figure 16-18.

FIGURE 16-18.
Choose Subscriber Options from the Edit menu to display the Subscriber Options dialog box.

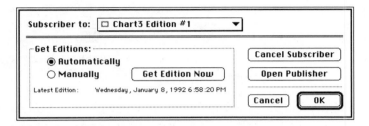

The top of the Subscriber Options dialog box displays a drop-down list box that shows the name of the edition linked to the subscriber and the edition's current location. The date and time that the edition was last updated is displayed in the middle of the dialog box.

To determine when the subscriber receives an edition update, select the appropriate option from the Get Editions section of the dialog box. The Manually option updates the subscriber only when you open the Subscriber Options dialog box and click Get Edition Now. When you select this option, Word displays the date and time that the subscriber was last updated in the middle of the dialog box as a reference.

Clicking Cancel in the Subscriber Options dialog box closes the dialog box without making any changes. (The Cancel Subscriber button cancels the selected subscriber.) Clicking OK activates the update option and then closes the dialog box. Keep in mind, however, that changing the subscriber edition update options doesn't affect how often the publisher sends updates to the edition.

Formatting a subscriber

In addition to specifying update processes, the Automatically and Manually options in the Subscriber Options dialog box determine whether or not you can edit the contents of subscriber text. (You cannot edit a subscriber graphic.)

If you select Automatically, you cannot edit the selection. Instead, Word preserves the update exactly as it appears in the publisher and treats the contents of the subscriber as a single block. You can change the paragraph styles or the font or size applied to this block, but you can't select individual words, characters, or graphics in the subscriber.

If you select Manually, you can select, edit, and format any part of the subscriber text.

No matter which option you select, the next time the subscriber is updated, its contents—including your changes—are overwritten.

Displaying a subscriber's publisher

If you want to make permanent changes to the contents of a subscriber, you should change the publisher itself. To access the publisher's originating document, select the subscriber, and then choose Subscriber Options from the Edit menu. When Word displays the Subscriber Options dialog box (shown earlier in Figure 16-18), click Open Publisher. Word immediately opens the document that contains the publisher (in its originating application, if necessary) scrolls the publisher into view, and selects it.

For example, to open the Excel document shown in Figure 16-15 from the Word document shown in Figure 16-17, select the subscriber, and then choose Subscriber Options. Then click Open Publisher. Word loads Microsoft Excel if it's not currently open, and opens the document that contains the publisher. (You must have enough memory available to open both applications; otherwise, Word displays an alert box telling you that the new application can't be opened.)

After you display the publisher, you can change its contents, save and close the document in which it's located, and then quit the application. The publisher updates the corresponding edition, and the edition updates its subscribers, according to the update options specified for the publisher and subscriber.

Canceling a subscriber

You can easily cancel a subscriber without affecting the contents of the corresponding edition or the originating publisher.

To cancel a subscriber, place the insertion point anywhere between the brackets of the subscriber, and then choose Subscriber Options from the Edit menu to display the Subscriber Options dialog box shown earlier in Figure 16-18. Next click the Cancel Subscriber button. Word displays the alert box shown in Figure 16-19, asking you to verify the cancellation.

FIGURE 16-19.
Clicking Yes in this
alert box cancels the
subscriber in which
the insertion point is
located.

Clicking Yes in this alert box cancels the subscriber, closes the Subscriber Options dialog box, and then reactivates the document window. The current contents of the subscriber remain in your document, but Word removes the brackets. You can then edit or delete this text as you would any regular text.

Linking in Word

As we've explained, with the publishing and subscribing features you can share and update information between any applications specifically designed for use with System 7—even across a network. To share information between two Word documents or between Word and Microsoft Excel on the same Macintosh, you can also use the Link commands on the Edit menu. In fact, you'll probably find that this feature enables you to link dynamic information in Word documents more effectively than using the publishing and subscribing features.

By pasting a link in Word, you can share information directly between two documents—without an intermediary edition file that takes up disk space. You can create links between parts of a single Word document, between two Word documents, or between Word files and files of other applications that support both System 7 and dynamic data exchange. You can share information between Word files without leaving the Word program. If you're working with many files and many links, this direct connection speeds up processing time considerably. (As we explain at the end of this section, you can also link documents if you're using QuickSwitch and Multifinder with System 6.)

Figure 16-20 shows the relationship between the selection in the originating file, called the *source*, and the selection in the receiving file, called the *destination*.

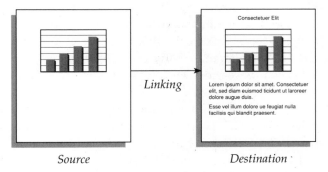

Source   *Destination*

FIGURE 16-20.
Linking enables you to share information without creating an intermediary file.

Creating a link

To link a selection in Word, highlight the selection in the source file, and copy it to the Clipboard. After placing the insertion point in the destination file, hold down the Shift key, and choose the Paste Link command from the Edit menu. The Paste Link command inserts the selection together with a link that connects the selection to the originating document. If you want the selection in the destination to be formatted differently from the source, choose the Paste Special command instead of Paste Link to display the Paste Special dialog box. You can then specify a format for the contents of the Clipboard.

Inserting a link

Suppose you want to share the information in the Excel worksheet shown in Figure 16-21 with a Word document. If this worksheet changes frequently, you can let Word automatically update the information.

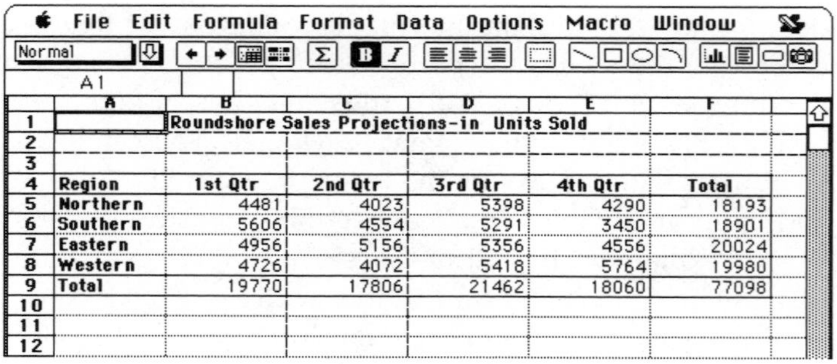

	A	B	C	D	E	F
1		Roundshore Sales Projections-in Units Sold				
2						
3						
4	Region	1st Qtr	2nd Qtr	3rd Qtr	4th Qtr	Total
5	Northern	4481	4023	5398	4290	18193
6	Southern	5606	4554	5291	3450	18901
7	Eastern	4956	5156	5356	4556	20024
8	Western	4726	4072	5418	5764	19980
9	Total	19770	17806	21462	18060	77098
10						
11						
12						

FIGURE 16-21.
We want to link the information in this Excel worksheet to a Word document.

To link the selection in both documents, first copy the source selection. In this case, select the cells you want to reproduce in the Word document, and then choose Copy from Excel's Edit menu. Next, activate the Word document in which you want to paste the selection. If Word isn't currently open, open it and then open the appropriate document. Then place the insertion point where you want the linked text to appear.

If you press the Shift key as you open the Edit menu, the Paste Link command replaces the Paste Special command. You can also press Option-F4 to choose Paste Link from the keyboard. Choosing Paste Link inserts the contents of the Clipboard, automatically linking it to the source selection. As you can see in Figure 16-22, if you copy a selection of cells from an Excel document, Word places a dark gray bracket immediately before the first cell that contains text and places a small marker at the end of the imported information. If you link text or graphics created in Word, Word encloses this information in dark gray brackets to distinguish it in the destination document. These brackets, which display only when Show ¶ is activated, don't appear in the printed document. Similar brackets distinguish the information in the source file.

Region	1st Qtr	2nd Qtr	3rd Qtr	4th Qtr	Total
Northern	4481	4023	5398	4290	18193
Southern	5606	4554	5291	3450	18901
Eastern	4956	5156	5356	4556	20024
Western	4726	4072	5418	5764	19980
Total	19770	17806	21462	18060	77098

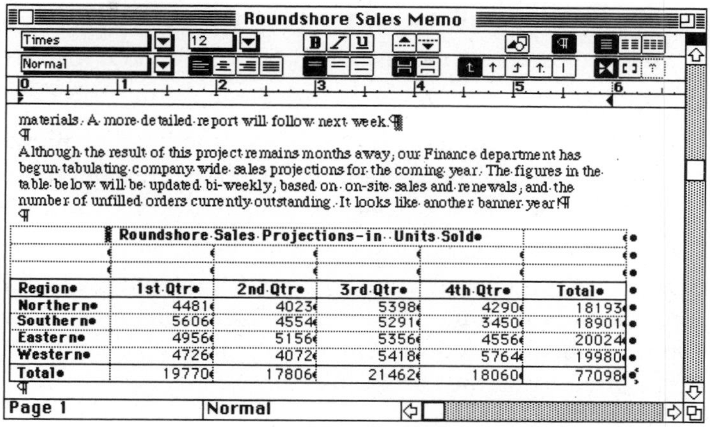

FIGURE 16-22.
When you choose Paste Link, Word pastes the contents of the Clipboard at the insertion point, enclosing the linked information in brackets.

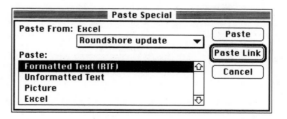

Saving the Word document ensures that changes you make to the source selection will appear automatically in this destination file.

Inserting a link format

If you want to specify the format of the selection in the destination document, first copy the text, and then place the insertion point where the pasted selection is to appear. Next, choose Paste Special from the Edit menu. Word displays a Paste Special dialog box like the one shown in Figure 16-23.

FIGURE 16-23.
Choose Paste Special from the Edit menu to display the Paste Special dialog box.

At the top of the Paste Special dialog box, the Paste From drop-down list box displays the name of the originating application and shows the name and location of the source document when you click on the arrow. In the Paste list box at the bottom of the dialog box, you can select the format in which you want the information to appear. Clicking the Paste Link button inserts the selection from the Clipboard in the format indicated and links the selection to the originating document.

Suppose, for example, that you want to reproduce the Excel data from Figures 16-21 and 16-22, which we pasted without specifying a format. Figure 16-23 shows the Paste Special dialog box that appears when you copy the Excel text selected in Figure 16-21 to the Clipboard. The options in the Paste list box indicate the formats available for the selection:

- You can paste the text either with or without formatting information.

- You can paste the complete contents of the selection as a single picture.

- You can embed the text with information that allows you to access the originating application. (We'll talk more about this option later in the chapter, when we describe embedding objects in Word.)

To insert the Excel data as a single picture that maintains the formatting applied to the original selection, choose Picture and then click Paste Link. Word inserts the data within a frame in the Word document, as shown in Figure 16-24. Although the data appears as a picture, this selection functions just like the data we inserted using the Paste Link command.

FIGURE 16-24.
We chose Picture in the Paste Special dialog box to insert this Excel data as a picture in our Word document.

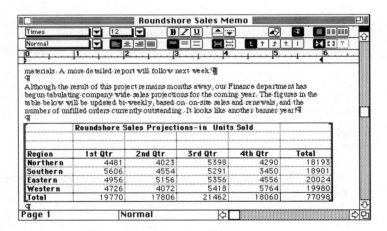

You can also specify any of the other options in the Link Options dialog box for the selection. Selecting Formatted Text (RTF) inserts the text as it appears on the Clipboard, just as if you had chosen Paste Link. Selecting Unformatted Text inserts only the text, without formatting. Selecting the option that contains the name of the originating application—selecting Excel in Figure 16-23, for example—enables you to embed information about the originating application itself, in addition to the selection. (We discuss embedding in detail later in this chapter.)

Updating a link

By default, Word updates the information in the destination file as you change the source file. If you reformat or edit the source file, you'll see this change immediately in each linked destination file. You can change the conditions under which the destination is updated, however. You can update the destination file only when you request it, or you can instruct Word not to permit updates to the destination file.

To select a link update option, first select all or part of the linked selection in your Word document, and then choose Link Options from the Edit menu. Word displays a Link Options dialog box like the one shown in Figure 16-25. The top section of the Link Options dialog box identifies the source and indicates its location on the disk. The middle section of the dialog box specifies how you want the destination updated. The Format drop-down list box at the bottom of the dialog box recreates the format options for the specified link.

FIGURE 16-25.
Choose Link Options
from the Edit menu to
display the Link
Options dialog box.

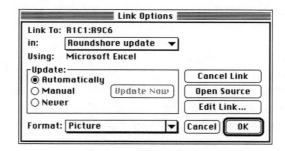

To change the Update option from Automatically to Manual or Never, click the appropriate button. Manual updates only when you select the destination, open the Link Options dialog box, and then click the Update Now option. With the Never option, the destination is not updated until you select another update option. Selecting this option enables you to sever the connection between the source and destination without canceling the link.

Clicking Cancel in the Link Options dialog box closes the dialog box without making any changes. (The Cancel Link button cancels the link selected when you chose the Link Options command. We'll discuss this procedure in a moment.) To specify when you want a link updated, select the option, and then click OK. Word records the selection and then closes the dialog box.

Formatting a link

In addition to specifying the update process, the Automatically and Manual options in the Link Options dialog box determine how the destination file considers the contents of the destination.

If you select Automatically, you cannot edit the selection. Word preserves the update exactly as it appears in the source and treats the contents of the link as a single block. You can change the paragraph styles, font, or size applied to this block, but you can't select individual words, characters, or graphics in the destination.

If you select the Manual update option, you can select, edit, and format any part of the link. Keep in mind that the next time the destination is updated, its contents—including your changes—will be overwritten. You cannot edit linked pictures no matter which update you select.

Displaying a link's source

To make permanent changes to the contents of a destination, you should change the source that contains the original selection. To access the file in which the source resides, you can select the information to be changed in the destination, and then choose Link Options from the Edit menu. When Word displays the Link Options dialog box shown in Figure 16-25, click Open Source. Word immediately opens the document that contains the source, loading the originating application if necessary.

For example, to open the original Excel document shown earlier in Figure 16-21 from the Word document shown in Figure 16-24, select the linked information, and then choose Link Options. Next, click Open Source. Word loads Microsoft Excel if it's not currently open and then opens the document that contains the source. (You must have enough memory available to open both applications.) Make changes in the source as necessary, save and close the source file, and then quit the application. The source updates the destination, according to the update options specified in the Link Options dialog box.

Canceling a link

As we've explained, if you want to preserve a link created for a destination in your document but want to temporarily prevent Word from updating the destination, you can select the Never option in the Link Options dialog box. If you're certain that you no longer want the destination to receive updates from the source, however, you can easily cancel the link. Canceling a link in no way affects the source itself.

To cancel a link, place the insertion point anywhere between the brackets that enclose the linked information, and then choose Link Options from the Edit menu to display the Link Options dialog box shown in Figure 16-25. Next click Cancel Link. Word cancels the link, closes the Link Options dialog box, and reactivates the document window. The previously linked information remains in your document as normal text, without the brackets that enclosed it.

Linking information between applications using System 6

If you're not using System 7, you can still share information created by other applications with Word documents. Using System 6 and the QuickSwitch feature, you can easily copy a selection from a source document and link the selection to a destination document. To use QuickSwitch, your Macintosh must have enough memory to load MultiFinder, Word, and any other application with which you want to share information.

Unfortunately, updating the selections that you link using the QuickSwitch feature is not a completely automatic process. If you're using the Paste Link and Paste Special commands with System 6, you must request updated information from the source document each time you want to update the destination document. In addition, you cannot link parts of the same Word document or two different Word documents using QuickSwitch.

Creating a link

To link a selection from an application such as Excel or SuperPaint, copy the selection to the Clipboard, and then activate the Word document in which you want to paste the selection. Position the insertion point, hold down the Shift key, and choose Paste Link from the Edit menu, or press Option-F4 to insert the contents of the Clipboard and create the link. Alternatively, choose Paste Special from the Edit menu to display the Paste Special dialog box. Next, select the format in which to insert the selection, and then click Paste Link. Word inserts the information in the specified format. (You can't embed objects if you're using System 6. As a result, in the Paste list box you won't see the formatting option that displays the name of the application used to create the selection.)

Modifying a link

The default update option for a link that uses QuickSwitch is Manually. Word updates the link only when you choose Link Options from the Edit menu and then click Update Now. If you click Never, the link will not be updated until you select another update option.

A note of warning: If you link a graphic created in a program like SuperPaint, the link connects only the portion of that application's document window in which you originally selected the graphic. If you move or resize the graphic in the originating application, you might find parts missing when you update a Word file. If you need to make substantial changes to a graphic, cancel the link and then recreate it when the graphic is in its final form.

Displaying a link's source

If you want to extensively change linked information, make the changes in the source document. Generally, accessing a source document using QuickSwitch is no different from performing this operation using System 7. You can display the source document directly from the destination selection by selecting the linked information that you want to edit and then choosing Link Options from the Edit menu. When Word displays the Link Options dialog box, click the Open Source button. Word opens the originating application when needed and then displays the source document. (You must have sufficient memory available to open both applications. Otherwise, Word displays an alert box to inform you that the new application can't be opened.)

After you make changes to the source document, you must press Command-comma to switch back to the destination document and update the linked information. If you simply close the document, you must open the Link Options dialog box and click Update Now to update the destination.

Canceling a link

To preserve a link while temporarily preventing an update, select the Never option in the Link Options dialog box. To restore the link, simply select another update option.

If you're certain that you no longer want the destination to receive updates from the source, you can easily cancel the link. Canceling a link in no way affects the source itself. To cancel a link, place the insertion point anywhere between the brackets that enclose the link, and then choose Link Options from the Edit menu to display a Link Options dialog box. Then click the Cancel Link button. Word cancels the link, closes the Link Options dialog box, and then reactivates the document window. The previously linked information remains in your document as normal text after Word removes the brackets that enclosed it.

Embedding objects in Word

In addition to sharing text or graphics, you can use the Copy and Paste Special commands on the Edit menu to embed information from another application in a Word document. You must be using System 7 for embedding to work. Embedding lets you use the commands of the originating application from within Word. For example, if you copy a formula created in the Equation Editor program that comes with Word or a spreadsheet from Excel, you can simply double-click the pasted selection to open a window containing the formatting and instruction commands you need to edit the selection. After you make the changes, closing this window automatically returns you to your Word document.

Pasting a selection in this way is called *embedding*. The selection, together with its supporting information, is referred to as a single *object*. You can embed a selection already created in another application together with its supporting information, or you can embed only the application information itself. Embedding an Excel graphic or chart, for example, enables you to access the Excel application and make changes to the graphic or chart without closing Word. Embedding only the application information enables you to access a new untitled Excel document and insert the information you add to that document immediately in your Word document.

Embedding an object in a Word document doesn't affect the text or graphic in the originating file. Any changes you make to the embedded object affect only the selection in the Word document.

Embedding an existing object

To embed information created in another application, first open the document in the other application. Select the information you want to embed, and then choose Copy from the Edit menu to store the selection on the Clipboard. Next, activate the Word document in which you want to paste the selection, opening Word if necessary.

To paste the selection and its supporting information, hold down the Shift key, and choose Paste Object from the Edit menu. (This command replaces Paste when the Shift key is held down.) Word inserts the embedded object at the insertion point.

Alternatively, you can choose Paste Special from the Edit menu to display the Paste Special dialog box shown earlier in Figure 16-23. From the formatting options in the Paste list box, select the name of the application in which the object was created. Then click the Paste button at the top of the Paste Special dialog box to insert the embedded object at the insertion point. Word deactivates the Paste Link button when you select the application name option.

Embedding a new object

You can create a new object in Word by embedding information from any application on your Macintosh that supports embedding. Simply position the insertion point in your document where you want the new object to appear, and then choose Object from the Insert menu. Word displays an Insert New Object dialog box like the one shown in Figure 16-26 on the next page, listing the types of objects you can embed.

Only those objects whose corresponding applications support embedding can appear in the Object Type list box. In addition, for Word to be able to retrieve this information from the Embedding Preferences file in the Preferences folder in the System Folder, you must have previously run the application.

FIGURE 16-26.
Choose Object from the Insert menu to display the Insert New Object dialog box.

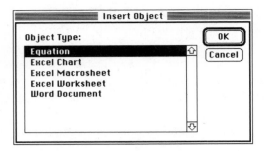

Select the object type from the Object Type list box, and then click OK. Word opens the application and displays an empty object window in which you can create the object you specified—just as if you had quit Word and opened the corresponding application. After creating the object, choose Close from the File menu to close the object window and insert the new object in your document.

Editing an object

After you insert an object, you can edit it by choosing Edit Object from the Edit menu or by double-clicking it and making changes in the object window. For example, Figure 16-27 shows a Word document in which we embedded a selection from the Excel worksheet shown earlier in Figure 16-15. After double-clicking this selection, the window shown in Figure 16-28 is displayed. Notice that the embedded selection now appears in an Excel worksheet and that the Excel menu bar now appears at the top of the screen. The Word document remains open, however. (You can see the left edge of the document beneath the Excel information.) You can edit the worksheet using Excel commands. Changes you make in this window do not affect the Excel document in which the object originated.

FIGURE 16-27.
We embedded an object created in Excel in this Word document.

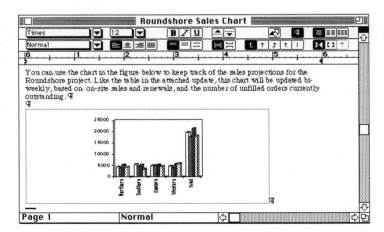

FIGURE 16-28.
Double-clicking an embedded object displays an object window, where you can make changes to the selection without leaving Word.

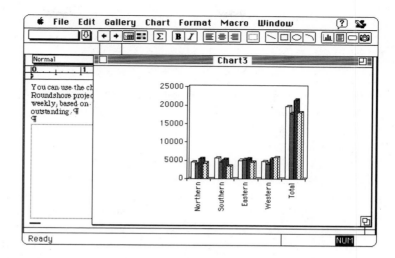

After editing the object, choose Update from Excel's File menu to close the object window and update the Word document. (Update replaces Quit on the File menu when the Excel window appears.) If you want to save the updated information in Excel, choose Save or Save Copy As, and then choose Update after specifying the filename.

Canceling embedding

As you might expect, including the information used to create an object in another application can substantially increase the size of your Word documents. After you've finished working with an embedded object, you can choose the Object Options command and click the Freeze Picture button in the Object Options dialog box to remove the supporting information without removing the object from your document. As the name of this button suggests, after you cancel an embedded object, Word treats its contents as a single imported graphic. You can use Word commands to reposition this graphic as you would any imported graphic.

To display the Object Options dialog box, select the object whose embedding you want to cancel, and then choose Object Options from the Edit menu. Word displays a dialog box like the one shown in Figure 16-29.

FIGURE 16-29.
Choose Object Options from the Edit menu to display the Object Options dialog box.

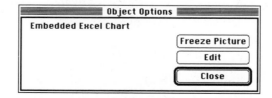

To cancel the embedding, select the Freeze Picture button. Word cancels the embedding automatically and closes the Object Options dialog box.

Creating stationery

Word's stationery feature enables you to save a document as a template that can be reproduced in another file. If you create documents that often share a common design or formatting—for example, if you often write letters or memos with company letterhead—saving a document as stationery enables you to reproduce this information quickly and accurately. Instead of recreating text, graphics, styles, or the layout and formatting common to a group of documents, you need only open a copy of a template file that contains this standard information and then add any unique information required.

Word comes with sample stationery documents whose format and content you can easily modify for your own use. These files include business memo and letter stationery, as well as newsletter and brochure stationery. You can open these templates and incorporate some or all of their contents into your own Word files. You can also create and save your own stationery files just as you would any other Word file.

Opening and using stationery files

To open a stationery file from the Finder, double-click the stationery file icon, which looks like a pad of paper beneath the Word document logo. If you're viewing documents by name on the Finder desktop, stationery files are shown with *Microsoft Word st...* in the Kind column.

To open a stationery file from within Word, choose Open from the File menu to display the Open dialog box. You can display only stationery files in the Open dialog box by selecting Stationery from the List Files Of Type drop-down list box. After you locate the file you want, click Open to display a copy of the stationery in a new untitled document.

In the new document, enter the elements that are unique to the document you want to create, and then save this copy as you would any other document. If you choose Save to save the new file, Word displays the Save As dialog box and sets the Save File As Type option to Normal. Save the file in any format you want. The original stationery file remains unaffected.

Saving documents as stationery files

The steps you follow to save a file as stationery are the same as those outlined for saving a file in Chapter 2, "Handling Files." After incorporating as many recurring elements as you can in the document, choose Save As from the File menu to display the Save As dialog box, and select Stationery in the Save File As Type drop-down list box. Next, type a name for the stationery in the Save Current Document As edit box, and then click Save to display the Summary Info dialog box. Record information that further describes the stationery file, and then click the OK button. Word saves the file and displays a copy of the stationery in a new document window.

Although you can delete a stationery file, Word doesn't allow you to make changes to the file itself. To edit or revise stationery, open a copy as an untitled Word document, and then make the necessary changes. When you finish editing the document, choose Save As from the File menu to display the Save As dialog box. In the Save Current Document As edit box, type the name of the stationery file exactly as it appears in the list box, select Stationery in the Save File As Type drop-down list box, and click Save. Word displays an alert box asking you to confirm that you want to replace the previous version of the document with the new document. Click Replace to save the new stationery document.

Combining stationery with other Word features

In most respects, stationery files function like any other Word document. You can use the Find File command to locate stationery, and because Word opens a copy of the stationery as a normal Word document, you can also use all of Word's editing commands.

You can combine stationery with other Word features to significantly expedite your work. For example, if you are working on a project with other writers, you can create stationery that contains the paragraph styles established for the project. Even if no text will be shared between the documents each writer creates, creating a common style sheet ensures standardized styles. We discuss creating style sheet templates in Chapter 9, "Creating Style Sheets."

If you create memo or report stationery, you can insert a dynamic date or time entry from the glossary in the stationery file. Then each time Word creates a copy of this stationery, it inserts the current date in the new document. For detailed information about using Word's glossary feature, see Chapter 13, "Using Word Tools."

Similarly, you can use Word's publishing and subscribing or linking features to automatically insert up-to-date information in memo or report stationery. (We introduced these features earlier in this chapter.)

17

Importing and Exporting Text and Graphics

If you're like most Word users, you rely on your Mac for more than word processing. For example, you might use a program such as Microsoft Excel to create detailed spreadsheets, a graphics package such as SuperPaint to create illustrations and charts, or a page-layout application such as PageMaker to create documents that require extensive desktop publishing. In Chapter 16, "Finding and Sharing Files," we showed you how Word's publishing and subscribing and linking features create interactive links between Word and other Macintosh applications.

At the beginning of this chapter, we show you how to import and export text in Word. Then we discuss exchanging graphics and graphics files. At the end of the chapter, we explain how to share data with three programs that you're likely to use often: Microsoft Excel, Aldus PageMaker, and Microsoft Mail. As you'll see, it's easy to exchange data between Word and other applications.

Using the Clipboard and the Scrapbook

As we explained in Chapter 3, "Working in Word," you can exchange information between files, or between other programs and Word, by copying the information to, and pasting it from, the Clipboard or the Scrapbook. (The easiest way to transfer data is to open both the file that contains the original text and the file in which you want to paste the text.

To import a text selection or a graphic into Word using the Clipboard, first open the file containing the information to copy. Next, select the information and copy the selection to the Clipboard. (The selection remains on the Clipboard until you cut or copy again or shut down your computer.) Then return to your Word document, click where you want to place the information, and choose Paste from the Edit menu. Word pastes the information from the Clipboard into your Word document at the insertion point.

If you plan to use a selection often, you can transfer it to the Scrapbook. The Scrapbook stores information in a file called Scrapbook File, rather than in memory. Anything you paste in the Scrapbook remains there until you remove it. It isn't lost when you cut or copy another selection or shut down your computer.

For more information about the Clipboard and the Scrapbook, see Chapter 3, "Working in Word."

Importing and exporting text files

Word allows you to view and use documents created in several different applications. Use the Open command on the File menu to open text documents that were created by another word-processing application. If you installed the text conversion files that came with the Word program, Word automatically recognizes and converts the file formats of many word-processing applications. You can also save a Word file in a format that allows it to be easily opened by a specific application, or as an ASCII or RTF file, which can be opened by many different applications.

If you haven't installed the text conversion file for a particular format, you won't be able to convert the files in that format. To install the converter files, quit Word, and then use the Installer to copy the files from your program disks into the folder on your hard drive that contains the Word program. (For more information about installing Word, see the Introduction.)

Opening text files created in other applications

To open a file created in another application, simply select the file's name in the Open dialog box. Word can convert the following file formats:

- Microsoft Word for the Macintosh, versions 1.0, 3.0, and 4.0
- Microsoft Word for DOS, versions 1.0, 2.0, 3.0, 4.0, 5.0, and 5.5
- Microsoft Word for Windows, versions 1.0 and 2.0
- Microsoft Works for the Macintosh, version 2.0
- MacWrite, versions 4.5 and 5.0
- MacWrite II I.x
- WordPerfect for the Macintosh, version 2.0
- WordPerfect for DOS, versions 5.0, and 5.1
- Interchange Format (RTF)
- Revisable Form Text (RFT-DCA)
- Text Only
- Text Only With Line Breaks
- Text With Layout
- Stationery
- Apple File Exchange binary
- Graphics Files
- EPS (Encapsulated PostScript)
- PICT
- TIFF

To display the Open dialog box, choose Open from the File menu or press Command-O. You can view all the files available in a folder or on a disk by holding down the Shift key as you choose Open, which then changes the selection in the List Files Of Type drop-down list box to All Files. To find a particular file type, use the List Files Of Type drop-down list at the bottom of the Open dialog box to specify the file type, as shown in Figure 17-1.

FIGURE 17-1.
Use the List Files Of Type drop-down list box at the bottom of the Open dialog box to specify the type of file that you want to appear in the Open dialog box.

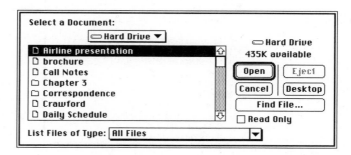

Click the Find File button to display the Find File dialog box if you need help in locating the file. When you find the file you want to open, double-click the file-name, or select the filename and then click Open. Word converts the file and displays it in a new Word document. (For detailed information about the Open dialog box, see Chapter 2, "Handling Files." Chapter 16, "Finding and Sharing Files," describes the Find File command.)

The converted text document displays all the paragraph and character formatting assigned to it in the originating word-processing program. However, as you review the file, you might find that some formatting has been lost during conversion. If this occurs, review the information about converting that particular file format in the Conversion Information file that comes with Word. Choose Save or Save As from the File menu to save the converted document as a Word file.

Saving Word documents in other file formats

Word makes it easy for you to share data with other word-processing programs. Use the Save File As Type drop-down list box in the Save As dialog box to save a Word document in one of several file formats that can be loaded by another program. You can also save a document as an ASCII text file that can be opened by many different applications.

To save a file in another format, choose Save As from the File menu. Next, in the Save Current Document As edit bar, enter a different name for the file. Then access the list of file format options shown in Figure 17-2 by clicking the arrow to the right of Save File As Type.

FIGURE 17-2.
To save a Word
document in a
different file format,
choose Save As from
the File menu, and
then click the arrow to
the right of Save File
As Type to see the list
of format options.

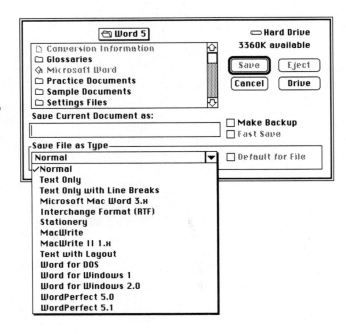

Saving a document in another application's format

To save the current document in a format that can be opened by another application, select the corresponding file format from the Save File As Type drop-down list box. (If the file format you want doesn't appear on the list, you probably need to close Word and then install the appropriate converter in the Word Commands folder.) Next, type a new name for the document in the Save Current Document As edit bar. When you click Save, you'll see the current document in the file format you've selected.

After you close the new document, in most cases you'll be able to load that document directly into another word-processing program. Character and paragraph formats are generally converted, but special features available only in Word do not transfer to the new format.

If the word processor with which you're exchanging files runs on a computer that is not a Macintosh, you might need to transfer the files via modem or special cable, because other computers format disks differently than the Mac does. If your Macintosh is equipped with a SuperDrive, you can use the Apple File Exchange program to copy the files to an IBM PC disk in your computer's disk drive. Your computer dealer or consultant can help you with this process.

Saving a document in ASCII format

The ASCII format uses a three-digit code to represent each number, letter, and symbol on the keyboard. For example, your computer knows the character *e* as 101. Most word-processing programs, including Word, can save documents in the ASCII file format. In addition, nearly every word-processing, spreadsheet, and database program reads ASCII files.

Think of the ASCII file format as the "lowest common denominator" format. When you save a Word file in this format, you create a text file without any special character or paragraph formatting. When you load an ASCII file into Word, you see plain text on your screen. This plain nature of ASCII files makes them useful for moving documents from one program to another.

To save a Word document as an ASCII file, choose Save As from the File menu, and then display the Save File As Type drop-down list box to view the list of format options, as shown in Figure 17-2. Select the Text Only option to save the text without formatting. This option converts end-of-line markers, section breaks, and page breaks to paragraph symbols. Selecting the Text Only With Line Breaks option saves text without formatting and places a paragraph symbol at the end of each line of document text. The Text Only With Line Breaks option is designed primarily for transferring information from Word to spreadsheet and database programs. Use the Text Only option to save your document in an ASCII format suitable for loading into another word-processing program.

After selecting the appropriate option, enter a new filename in the Save Current Document As edit bar, and then click Save. Word then displays the ASCII version of the document. All character, paragraph, and section formatting except paragraph breaks are removed. If you selected the Text Only With Line Breaks option, you'll see additional paragraph breaks at the end of every line.

Opening an ASCII file in Word

To open an ASCII file in Word, choose Open from the File menu. Next, open the ASCII file. You can edit and format this text just as you would any other document. (You can easily delete any stray coding characters you see.) After you've edited and formatted the text, save the document in Word format by choosing the Save or Save As command.

Importing and exporting graphics

Chapter 6, "Creating Graphics," explains how to create simple graphics using the Picture command on the Insert menu. Word treats each graphic as a single character, which can be cut, copied, and pasted just like a text element. You can size and crop graphics to fit your layout needs, and you can use the Frame command to place a graphic at any absolute position on a page and flow text around it.

You can import an image from graphics programs such as SuperPaint or MacDraw simply by copying the graphic to the Clipboard, switching to Word, and pasting the graphic into your document.

You can also import a complete graphics file using the Picture command. When you open files in the following formats, Word places the contents of these files in a Word document:

- PICT/PICT2
- TIFF
- Encapsulated PostScript (EPS)
- Bitmap

You can also open files with any of these graphics formats in a new Word document by using the Open command on the File menu.

After you import a graphic or graphics file into your Word document, you can resize the elements contained in the graphics file by repositioning the boundary lines around the image. However, Word treats the contents of the frame as a single object, so you must make other changes in the graphics application.

Although you can add elements to an imported graphic by displaying the graphic in Word's Edit Picture window, you can't, for example, delete parts of the graphic or change the position of the drawing layers in Word. And, although you can import and display a graphics file that includes many different colors, editing a color graphic in Word's Picture window changes it to an 8-color graphic and sometimes dramatically changes its appearance.

Importing a graphic image using the Clipboard

Bitmap graphics are created in paint programs such as MacPaint and SuperPaint. PICT and PICT2 graphics are created by drawing programs such as MacDraw and Cricket Draw. TIFF graphics are created by many scanning programs. You can easily import bitmap, PICT, PICT2, and TIFF graphics into Word by selecting the graphic in the originating paint or drawing program, copying the graphic to the Clipboard, and then pasting the graphic into your Word document. You can also use this technique to import encapsulated PostScript (EPS) graphics and PostScript codes.

Importing bitmap, PICT, or TIFF graphics

Suppose, for example, that you want to import the graphic shown in Figure 17-3, which was created in SuperPaint, into a Word document. First use the Selection tool on the SuperPaint Tool palette to select the graphic, and then choose the Copy command to place the selection on the Clipboard. Next, switch to your Word document, click the spot where you want the graphic to appear, and then choose Paste. Word pastes the graphic from the Clipboard and frames it in the document window, as shown in Figure 17-4 on the next page.

Although the frame shows the area that the graphic and its surrounding blank space occupy in your document, the frame does not appear in your printed document.

FIGURE 17-3.
*We created this
graphic in SuperPaint.*

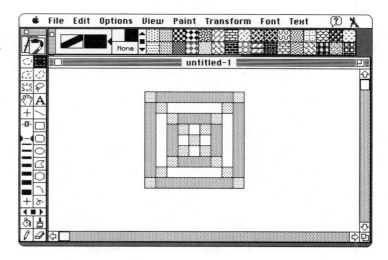

FIGURE 17-4.
*We pasted the graphic
into a Word document.*

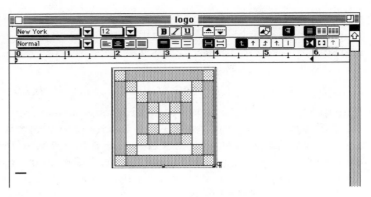

Importing EPS graphics

Some illustration programs, such as Adobe Illustrator and Aldus FreeHand, produce two versions of a graphic: a screen version and a print version that contains PostScript code. This format, encapsulated PostScript (EPS), prints in the highest possible resolution—even in Word. You can import both the screen version of the graphic and its PostScript printing code into Word. If you don't need to view the graphic in Word, you can import only the PostScript code.

Importing an EPS graphic and its PostScript code To import an EPS graphic, first select the graphic in the graphics program, and then hold down the Option key as you choose the program's Copy command to copy both the screen version and the PostScript code to the Clipboard. Next, simply paste the graphic and the embedded PostScript code at the insertion point in your Word document. You'll see the screen version of the graphic in your document. When you print the document on a PostScript printer, the resolution of the printed version will be of much higher quality than the screen version.

Importing only an EPS graphic's PostScript code It's generally a good idea to import both versions of a graphic so that you can display it on the screen. Sometimes, however, you might want to import only the PostScript version of the graphic. When you paste the PostScript code into your Word document, you won't see the graphic on the screen, but Word will print the graphic correctly on a PostScript printer.

To import only the PostScript code, first choose Open from Word's File menu. Then, find the file that contains the PostScript code, and click Open. Word places the PostScript code in a new window. Next, select the PostScript code, and in the Style list box of the Style dialog box, click the All Styles button. Select the Post-Script style from the Style list box, and then click OK. Word applies the PostScript style to the PostScript code. The PostScript style formats the code as hidden text. With the code still selected, choose Copy from the Edit menu to copy the code to the Clipboard. Then position the insertion point at the place in your document where you want the graphic to appear, and choose Paste from the Edit menu. Word pastes the PostScript code at the insertion point. Although you can't see the graphic when you view the document in the document window, the graphic will appear when you print.

Importing a graphics file using the Picture command

To import a complete graphics file, first place the insertion point where you want the graphics file to appear. Next, choose the Picture command from the Insert menu. Word displays the dialog box shown in Figure 17-5, which enables you to locate and select the file you want to import.

FIGURE 17-5.
To import a graphics file, choose the Picture command from the Insert menu to display this dialog box.

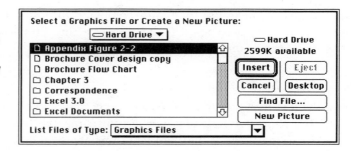

After locating the graphics file in this dialog box, double-click the filename, or select the name and then click Insert, to insert the graphic in your document. Word treats the complete contents of the file as a single graphic, enclosing the file in a frame.

Because Word treats the contents of the imported file as a single graphic, you can't change individual components of the graphic in Word the way you can in the original graphics application. For this reason, be sure that the graphic appears exactly as you want it before you import it into Word.

For example, if you import a MacDraw file that contains several pages, Word inserts the complete graphics file in the Word document. If the page size of the graphics file is larger than the Word document's page size, part of the graphic might be cropped. For more information on resizing graphics, see Chapter 6, "Creating Graphics."

Importing a graphic using the Open command

You can open bitmap graphics files directly from within Word. Simply choose Open from Word's File menu or press Command-O to display the Open dialog box. Next, locate and select the file, and then click Open. Word places the graphics file in a new untitled Word document.

Resizing and formatting graphic frames

After you import a graphic into Word, simply click the graphic to display its frame and its handles. Then you can apply any of the techniques described in Chapter 6, "Creating Graphics," to resize or format the graphic frame.

After placing a graphic in your document, you can use the Border command described in Chapter 5, "Formatting Documents and Paragraphs," to apply a border to all or some of the frame's sides. You can also select the frame and apply styles from the Character dialog box to it.

In addition, you can use the Frame command to position the graphic at any absolute position on the page. Chapter 10, "Creating Professional Documents," describes the Frame command in detail.

Converting text to a graphic

Some of the text that you create in Word cannot be read by other programs. For example, the character formulas you create using the technique described in Chapter 13, "Using Word Tools," will not translate to other word processors or to desktop publishing programs such as PageMaker.

To get around this problem, convert the text into a graphic. First highlight the text, and then press Command-Option-D. Word places a copy of the selection on the Clipboard in graphic form. You can then paste this text picture back into your document or in a document in another program.

Exporting Word graphics

You can export a Word graphic to another program by copying the graphic to the Clipboard and then pasting it in a new location. When you select the graphic in Word, keep in mind that you won't be able to adjust the size of its frame or change the appearance of its components after you export it to another document. Be sure the graphic appears within its frame exactly as you want it before selecting it in Word.

After copying the graphic to the Clipboard, simply place the insertion point in the document window where you want the graphic to appear, and choose Paste. (If you're exporting the graphic to a drawing program, you'll probably need to paste the graphic first and then reposition it as necessary.) Then save the graphic in the new file.

When you copy a Word graphic to paste it into another application, you copy only as much of the graphic as appears within the graphic frame when you select it. Because the program into which you paste the Word graphic treats the contents of the frame as a single element, you will not be able to change the elements you created in Word. If you reselect the graphic and then paste it back into Word, Word will treat it as an imported graphic, and you won't be able to make any changes to it.

Exchanging data with spreadsheet programs

You can follow a set of general procedures to import and export data between Word and most spreadsheet programs. This section describes the techniques for exchanging data between Word and Microsoft Excel. You can use similar techniques to transfer data between Word and other Macintosh spreadsheet and database programs, including Microsoft Multiplan, Microsoft File, and the Microsoft Works spreadsheet and database.

Exchanging data with Excel

You can import data from almost any Macintosh spreadsheet program into your Word documents either by copying via the Clipboard or the Scrapbook, or by saving the data in a text format that Word can read. You can also paste text from a Word document into Excel. If the Word text appears in a tabular format, it is automatically divided among cells in an Excel worksheet.

Importing spreadsheet data

When you want to import data from an Excel spreadsheet or chart into a Word document, you can usually copy it from the Excel worksheet to the Clipboard and then paste it into your Word document.

For example, suppose you've created an Excel sales projections worksheet like the one in Figure 17-6 on the next page and you want to import the data from cells A4:F9 into a Word document. Begin by loading Excel and Word, and then open both the Word document and the Excel spreadsheet. In the Excel worksheet, highlight the range of cells to copy, and then choose Copy from Excel's Edit menu. Next, click Word's document window, and place the insertion point where you want to insert the Excel data. Choose Paste to place a copy of the data in your document. Figure 17-7 on the next page shows the results.

When you paste the contents of an Excel worksheet into a Word document, Word automatically places the data in the selected cells in a Word table. Word also preserves any character formatting you applied to the selection in the originating spreadsheet program. For example, the currency format assigned to the values in Excel is transferred to the Word document, as well as the bold formatting. Notice in Figure 17-7 that Word places end-of-row markers at the end of each row and displays the table gridlines.

FIGURE 17-6.
*We want to copy the
data from cells A4:F9
of this Excel worksheet
into a Word document.*

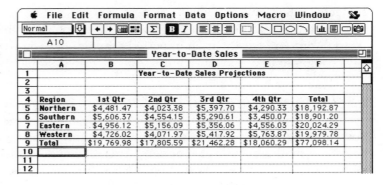

FIGURE 17-7.
*We pasted the Excel
data into a Word
document.*

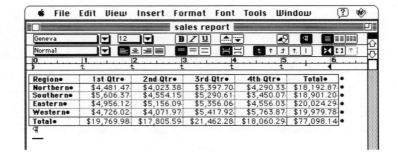

If you don't want the worksheet data to appear in a table, you can select the table and use the Table To Text command on the Insert menu. (For more information about the Table To Text command and creating tables, see Chapter 12, "Creating Tables," which describes the Table command in detail.)

Using Excel databases with Word

The structure of an Excel database is similar to that of a Word print merge data document. As a result, you can use Excel database files as data documents for Word print merge operations, making it easy to create mailing labels, form letters, and so on, with the data from an Excel database.

To use your Excel database as a data document that is readable by Word, save the database worksheet as a text file by choosing the Save As command from Excel's File menu. Then click the Options button to display the Options dialog box, and select the Text option in the File Format drop-down list box. Click OK to record your selection.

You open the Excel database text file in Word as you would any other document. When the database text file is open, you'll see that each database record occupies one paragraph and that the fields are separated by tab markers. Field names above the database text serve as the field header row. You can reformat the database text by selecting it and moving the tab markers on the ruler. You can also select the text and then use the Text To Table command to convert it into table format.

Importing images of Excel worksheets and charts

If you want to import the image of an Excel worksheet as a graphic, or if you want to import an Excel chart, use Excel's Copy Picture command to first copy the graphic to the Clipboard. Then paste the graphic into your Word document.

To use Excel's Copy Picture command, first select the cells or the chart you want to copy. Next, hold down the Shift key, and select the Copy Picture command from the Edit menu. Excel displays the Copy Picture dialog box, in which you specify how you want the selected elements to be copied to the Clipboard. Click OK to apply the default option, As Shown When Printed, to reproduce the selection reflecting the settings in Excel's Page Setup dialog box. Select the As Shown On Screen option to reproduce the selection as it appears on the screen, including row and column headings.

After you've copied the selection to the Clipboard, simply return to your Word document, place the insertion point where you want the graphic to appear, and then choose the Paste command from the Edit menu. Word pastes the selection as a single element, enclosing it in a graphic frame. You can use any of the techniques we've described for sizing, formatting, and positioning graphics to change the appearance of the selection.

Exporting Word text to Excel

You can transfer data from Word to Excel simply by copying the information from the Word document and pasting it into an Excel worksheet.

Use tabs to separate the data you want to place in separate worksheet columns, or format the text as a Word table. When you export a Word table into Excel, the information in each table cell appears in a separate cell of the Excel worksheet. If you don't use tabs or a table to format your Word document, the information isn't divided correctly among the columns of the Excel worksheet. You cannot use commas instead of tabs.

Exchanging data with PC-based spreadsheets

Exchanging data with a PC-based spreadsheet or database application is a little more complicated than exchanging with Macintosh-based programs. The key to this kind of data exchange is the ASCII file format. Before you save a Word document in ASCII format, however, check the manual for your PC application to see what special characters the program uses as field delimiters. Some PC applications do not recognize tabs as field delimiters. For example, Lotus 1-2-3 requires that fields be separated by commas, and that the contents of each text field be enclosed in quotation marks. To convert a table so that Lotus 1-2-3 can read it, select the table, and then select the Comma Delimited option in the Table To Text dialog box.

After you set up your Word document with the correct field delimiters, save the document in the Text Only or Text Only With Line Breaks format. If you pressed Return to insert a paragraph symbol at the end of each line in your document (or if your paragraphs are all quite short), then you can safely use the Text Only option. The paragraph symbols will separate your document into discrete lines in the ASCII file so that when you load this file into the PC program, each line appears in a separate row. On the other hand, if you are transferring a block of text from Word that does not include paragraph symbols at the end of each line, you should save the file using the Text Only With Line Breaks option.

After saving your document as an ASCII text file, you need to transfer the file to an IBM PC disk. Connect your Mac to the PC using a specially configured cable or a modem, and then use communications software to transfer the file. If your Mac is equipped with a SuperDrive, you can copy the file directly to a 3.5-inch IBM PC disk using Apple File Exchange software.

Because Word can read ASCII files, you can import data from a PC-based spreadsheet into Word by saving the data in ASCII format. You need to transfer the ASCII file onto a Macintosh-readable disk before you can load the file in Word. When you open the file, you'll see that Word automatically inserts tabs between the information in each column to reproduce the layout of the original spreadsheet. You can easily format this information as a Word table by selecting the text and choosing Text To Table from the Insert menu. (For detailed information about converting existing document text to a table in Word, see Chapter 12, "Creating Tables.")

Removing extraneous characters from an imported file

If you import a spreadsheet or database program file that contains extended ASCII characters (ASCII codes 127 and higher), formatting instructions (ASCII codes 0 through 31), or graphics characters, Word might display those characters as rectangular boxes. Even if the imported file contains a lot of these boxes, they probably represent only a few different characters. Although you can delete the boxes manually, you'll find it much faster to delete them using the Replace command.

To replace the boxes, simply select one, and copy it. Then choose Replace from the Edit menu. In the Find What edit bar, paste the copied box. Word pastes in the character as it appears in the original document. Next, be sure that the Replace With edit bar is empty and that the Search option is set to All. When you click the Change All button, Word deletes each box. You can repeat this procedure to delete other extraneous characters from the file. (For detailed information about the Replace command, see Chapter 7, "Editing and Proofing.")

Exchanging data with desktop publishing programs

If you create a lot of publications, you might want to take advantage of one of the many desktop publishing packages available for the Macintosh. Most of these programs can read Word files directly from disk, with no copying or pasting between applications.

In this section, we look briefly at Aldus PageMaker, the most popular desktop publishing package on the market. PageMaker enables you to control the layout and format of your documents. You can use this program to save PageMaker text files as Word files and to place Word documents in predefined master page templates that you design with PageMaker's special tools.

Importing PageMaker files into Word

PageMaker has an export feature that saves PageMaker files in a Word format. The Export command removes any special PageMaker features not supported by Word and saves the PageMaker document as a Word file.

If you use this command to export from PageMaker text that you originally created in Word, PageMaker resets a few Word features that were removed from the document when it was first imported into PageMaker. For example, if you used Word's Border command to draw a box or border around a paragraph, PageMaker ignored this formatting when it imported the Word document. However, when you export the document from PageMaker back to Word, the border reappears.

PageMaker strips hidden characters from Word files and removes codes or hidden text used to create an index, footnotes, or table of contents. These characters and codes are not restored when you convert a PageMaker document back into Word format. However, the text portions of the index, table of contents, and so on, are still a part of the file.

Exporting Word files to PageMaker

To transfer a Word document into PageMaker, first save the document as a Word file, and then open it in PageMaker. PageMaker recognizes most character and paragraph formatting, but it doesn't retain Document or Section dialog box settings—PageMaker handles these page layout tasks differently from Word. Table 17-1 on the next page shows the formatting characteristics that PageMaker retains when you load a Word file.

Format	Effect in PageMaker
Fonts	PageMaker uses its default Times font if Word's font is not installed in the PageMaker System file.
Sizes	PageMaker accepts Word's point sizes.
Character formats	PageMaker converts Double and Dotted Underline formats to standard, unbroken underlines. Hidden text is deleted. All other character formats are retained.
Page and section breaks	Manual page breaks and section breaks, and the Page Break Before, Keep Lines Together, and Keep With Next ¶ paragraph formats are removed.
Paragraph and line breaks	All paragraph and line breaks carry over.
Line and paragraph spacing	Line spacing and Space Before and Space After formats are retained.
Line numbers	Numbered lines are not retained.
Paragraph numbers	Numbered and lettered paragraphs are retained.
Tabs	All tab formats carry over except the vertical bars created with the Vertical Line button.
Borders	All borders and shading are removed.
Indents	First-line, left, and right indents are retained, but PageMaker uses the margins settings specified for the PageMaker document. As a result, line width can vary from Word to PageMaker.
Alignment	Left, right, centered, and justified alignment settings are retained.
Multicolumn format	Multicolumn formats are not retained. Text appears as a single column.
Headers, footers, and page numbers	These are removed.
Tables of contents, indexes, and footnotes	The compiled table of contents and index are retained, but the hidden codes used to define table of contents and index entries are removed. Footnotes carry over, but are grouped at the end of the document.
Styles and outlines	Style names and formatting descriptions are retained.
Graphics	Any graphics in the Word document appear in PageMaker; however, the results of the Frame command are not carried over.
Tables	These do not carry over.

TABLE 17-1.
This table shows the formatting characteristics that are retained or removed when you open a Word file in PageMaker.

Using Microsoft Mail in Word

If your AppleTalk network is equipped with the Microsoft Mail electronic mail program, you can use the Open Mail and Send Mail commands on the File menu to take advantage of Microsoft Mail's capabilities from within Word. Choose Open Mail to display your Mailbox window. You can view selected messages, and read, edit, and print files enclosed with a Mail message. When you're through reading an enclosed file, you can easily save it as a Word document. Choose Send Mail to send a file created in Word to other users on your network. (You can't use this method to send a message without sending the currently active file, however. If you want to send a message without sending the active Word file, open the Microsoft Mail desk accessory from the Apple menu.)

The Open Mail and Send Mail commands work only if your Macintosh is connected to a Microsoft Mail server on an AppleTalk network and if you are signed into your mailbox. (For information on installing and signing into the Microsoft Mail system and for detailed instructions on using Mail, refer to the manual that came with your Microsoft Mail software.)

Opening messages in Word

To open messages that reside in your mailbox from within Word, choose Open Mail from the File menu. Word activates the Microsoft Mail program and presents a Mailbox window like the one shown in Figure 17-8. (This figure shows the window that appears if you're using Microsoft Mail 3.0. Other versions of Microsoft Mail work with Word; however, the appearance and operation of Mail dialog boxes varies slightly with each version.)

FIGURE 17-8.
Choose Open Mail from the File menu to view and open messages that reside in your Microsoft Mail mailbox.

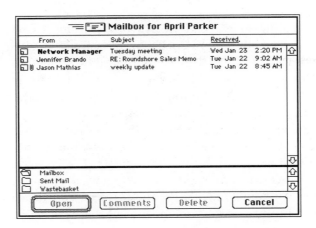

The list box that occupies the majority of the screen lists the messages currently in your mailbox that contain files in a format that Word can read or convert. Messages you have not yet read appear in bold type in the list box. Select the messages you want to open just as you would if you had opened Microsoft Mail from the Apple menu. To open more than one message, hold down the Shift key as you click each one, and then click the Open button to open all the selected messages at once. Word opens each message in its own window.

To view the Comments window for a selected message, click the Comments button. After reviewing the message, click Close to close the message window and return to the Mailbox window.

An Enclosure icon shaped like a paper clip next to a sender's name in the Mailbox window indicates that a file was sent along with the message. To open an enclosed file as a Word document, double-click the message in the list box, or click the message and then click Open. Word displays an Enclosures dialog box like the one shown in Figure 17-9 so that you can indicate the enclosed files you want to open. Select the filename and click Open to open the file as a Word document. If more than one filename appears, hold down the Shift key and select them in turn to open each enclosure in its own Word document window.

FIGURE 17-9.
Use the Enclosures dialog box to open an enclosed file as a Word document.

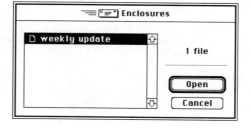

After opening an enclosed file in Word, you can edit or print a copy of it just as you would any other Word document. When you finish reviewing the file, you can close the document and save it as a Word document.

To delete a message from your mailbox, highlight the message in the list box, and then click the Delete button. To delete multiple messages, hold down the Shift key as you click each one, and then click Delete.

You can also view the contents of the Sent Mail and Wastebasket folders displayed at the bottom of the Mailbox window. Simply click the folder, and then click the Open button to display its contents. The Wastebasket folder holds any mail you've deleted from the Mailbox window.

To close the Mailbox window, click Cancel. Word closes the Microsoft Mail program and returns you to the document that was active when you chose the Open Mail command.

Sending mail in Word

The Send Mail command on the File menu enables you to send the currently active Word document to another user on your network. Word sends the file in Word format, just as it appears in the document window. (To send the file in a format other than a Word format, hold down Shift as you choose Send Mail from the File menu. Word then displays a dialog box that enables you to specify the format in which you want to send the file. The format of the original file remains unchanged.)

To use Microsoft Mail to send a file you've created in Word, choose Send Mail from the File menu. Word displays an Address Mail dialog box like the one shown in Figure 17-10.

FIGURE 17-10.
Choose Send Mail from the File menu to send an active Word document using Microsoft Mail.

You use the Address Mail dialog box to specify the recipient of a message. Indicate this information just as if you had displayed the dialog box by choosing Microsoft Mail from the Apple menu. You can type the names of the recipients in the Type Names edit bar, or you can select each name you want from a list of user names that appears in the Choose Names list box. Icons on the left side of the Address Mail window let you specify which addresses should appear in the Choose Names list box. Select a name, or hold down the Shift key and select more than one name. Click Cc or Bcc before selecting a name from the list to send a copy or a blind copy of the message to the selected user. Then click Add to add the names to the Message Recipients list box.

After specifying the message's recipient, click Close to display a Send Document dialog box like the one shown in Figure 17-11 on the next page. By default, Word places in the Subject edit bar the name of the Word document that was active when you first chose the Send Mail command. Change this entry if you want the recipients to see another subject name when they open their mail. (Changes you make in this edit bar don't affect the name of the Word file.)

FIGURE 17-11.
*Clicking Close in the
Address Mail window
displays the Send
Document dialog box,
where you can specify
options, enclose
additional files, and
type a comment to
accompany the file.*

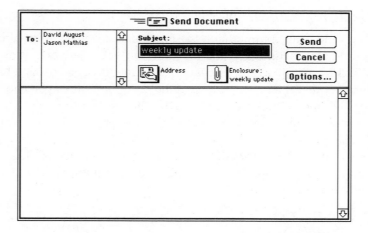

Use the other icons and buttons in the Send Document dialog box to complete
your message. You can display the Send Mail Options dialog box by clicking Options. The options in this dialog box let you mark your mail as urgent, request a
return receipt, retain a copy in your Sent Mail folder, and add the mail's recipient
to your Address Book. You can also enclose additional files with your message by
clicking the Enclosure button in the Send Document dialog box. You can even add
a comment to the file that you're sending by typing a message in the lower part of
the Send Document dialog box.

When you're satisfied with all the Send Document settings, click the Send
button to send your message to each recipient's mailbox. When the send procedure is completed, the Send Document dialog box disappears, and Word again
displays the document that was active when you chose the Send Mail command.

Customizing Word

18

Customizing Word

*E*ven if you've used the Preferences dialog box only to specify a default font or select the Show Hidden Text option, you know that you can tailor Word to fit your needs. This chapter describes in detail the options available in the Preferences dialog box. It also introduces another of Word's most useful features: customizing menus and keystroke shortcuts.

Creating custom menus and keystroke combinations speeds up tasks that you regularly perform. You can add almost all of the check box, radio button, or drop-down list box options in Word's dialog boxes to a menu, as well as the options represented by ruler buttons and outline window icons. You can also add file-names, glossary entries, and paragraph styles to a special menu called the Work menu. The Work menu does not appear on the menu bar until you have placed at least one item on it. Word also makes it easy to define keystroke shortcuts for any of these options so that you can use features directly from the keyboard.

The Commands command on the Tools menu is even more powerful than the Preferences command. With the Command dialog box, you can place any command, feature, or option on any Word menu and can alter the keystroke shortcut assigned to any command. You can even use the Command dialog box to modify or delete Word's preset menu positions and keystroke shortcuts.

Changes to the Preferences dialog box and to Word commands are stored in Word's configuration file when you quit the Word program. At the end of this chapter, we discuss the Word Settings (5) file, which stores most of Word's default settings, and we describe how you can create other configuration files to store additional sets of defaults.

Setting preferences

With the Preferences command on the Tools menu, you can tailor Word's operations. Choosing Preferences displays the Preferences dialog box. Selecting one of eight icons displays the options and default settings for the corresponding category. For example, clicking the Default Font icon lets you specify default font preferences, and clicking the Spelling icon displays the options that determine how Word conducts spelling checks. Settings you specify in the Preferences dialog box take effect as soon as you click the close box and close the dialog box. Word saves your preferences in the current Word Settings (5) file.

In this section, we review the Preferences dialog box options. Use the information in this chapter as a reference. For detailed information about how the options affect your work in Word, see the related discussions of each option earlier in this book.

General preferences

The General section of the Preferences dialog box, shown in Figure 18-1, enables you to specify your user name and initials, a custom paper size, and the unit of measure that appears on the ruler. In addition, this section contains four check boxes that let you activate or deactivate options that affect Word's general operation. This section appears when you first choose the Preferences command from the Tools menu. You can switch to this section from another Preferences dialog section by clicking the General icon on the left side of the Preferences dialog box.

FIGURE 18-1.
*This is the General
section of the
Preferences dialog box.*

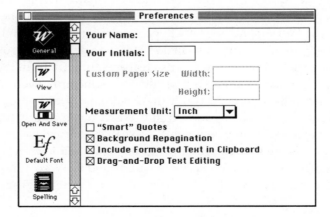

Your Name

Use this edit bar to specify the name that will appear in the Author edit bar of the Summary Info dialog box. By default, the name used is the one you supplied when you installed Word.

Your Initials

Use this edit bar to specify the name or initials you want to use to identify yourself as the creator of voice annotations you insert in your documents. Word displays the text you type in this edit bar in the Voice Annotations dialog box when you select the voice annotation and then choose the Voice Annotations command from the View menu.

Custom Paper Size (Width and Height)

Use these edit bars to specify a custom paper size for nonstandard-size documents. The width and height appear as an option in the Page Setup dialog box when you use an Apple ImageWriter or ImageWriter LQ printer.

Measurement Unit

Use this drop-down list box to select the unit of measure that appears on the ruler and in dialog boxes. Word uses this unit for elements such as margins, indentations, and tab settings. You can select Inch, Cm (centimeter), Points, or Picas from the drop-down list box.

For greater precision, Word uses picas and points as the unit for character measurements such as superscript and subscript, line spacing, and expanded and condensed spacing. However, you can specify a different unit of measure when you enter these settings in the Character dialog box.

"Smart" Quotes

Activate this option to substitute typeset-quality, curly quotation marks (' ' and " ") when you type ' or " on the keyboard. When this option is selected, Word uses "smart" quotes but does not substitute smart quotes for straight quotation marks you have already typed in the document.

Background Repagination

Activate this option if you want Word to automatically repaginate documents. Word stops repaginating when you start typing and resumes repaginating when you pause.

If background repagination slows Word's operation, deactivate this option, and choose Repaginate Now from the Tools menu when you want to repaginate your document.

Include Formatted Text In Clipboard

When active, this option ensures that text copied from Word to the Clipboard and pasted into a different document retains its original formatting. Deactivate this option if you want to insert plain, unformatted text from the Clipboard into a new document.

Drag-and-drop text editing

When active, this option enables you to select and drag a highlighted block of text or graphic to another location in your document. Selecting and dragging text, for example, moves the text to the place where the insertion point is located when you release the mouse button. Pressing the Command key and then selecting and dragging copies the selection at the insertion point. Word does not place the selected text or graphic on the Clipboard when you use this technique.

View preferences

Click the View icon on the left side of the Preferences dialog box to configure the elements that Word displays in document windows and on menus, using the options shown in Figure 18-2. (Chapter 1, "Touring Microsoft Word," describes Word document windows and menus in detail.)

FIGURE 18-2.
*This is the View
section of the
Preferences dialog box.*

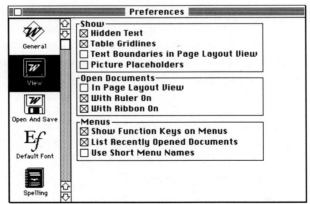

Show

The Show options in the Preferences dialog box determine which document elements display by default in Word documents.

Hidden Text Activate this option to show hidden text in an open document. Word distinguishes hidden text in the document window with a dotted underline. Word ignores hidden text when compiling a table of contents or an index.

Displaying hidden text affects the layout and page breaks in Normal and Page Layout view, but not when printing or viewing the document in Print Preview. To print hidden text, select the Print Hidden Text option in either the Print or the Document dialog box.

Table Gridlines Activate this option to display dotted lines that define rows and columns in tables. Word does not print table gridlines.

Text Boundaries In Page Layout View Activate this option to display dotted rectangles that help delineate text elements such as headers, footers, and framed objects in Page Layout view.

Picture Placeholders Activate this option to display gray rectangles in place of graphics in a document. You will find this option handy when working on documents with many graphics, because Word scrolls slowly when it has to redraw each graphic on the screen. Graphics still print correctly when you select this option.

Open Documents

The Open Documents options specify the elements that appear in the document window each time you open a new or existing document in Word. Use these options to open documents in Page Layout view or to display the ruler or ribbon in Normal view.

In Page Layout View By default, Word opens a new or existing document in Normal view. If you often open existing documents to make slight formatting changes, you might want to activate this option to open documents in Page Layout view rather than Normal view.

With Ruler On If you often make paragraph formatting changes, activate this option to automatically display the ruler at the top of the document window each time you open a document.

With Ribbon On If you often make character formatting changes, activate this option to automatically display the ribbon at the top of the document window each time you open a document.

Menus

Two Menu options specify the items that appear on Word menus. An additional option lets you change the appearance of menu names.

Show Function Keys On Menus Activate this option to display the keystroke equivalents of commands on the menu beside the command names. If you deactivate this option, you can still use these keyboard shortcuts.

List Recently Opened Documents Activate this option to list on the File menu the last four documents opened or saved. You can open a listed document by selecting its name directly from the File menu.

If you delete a document or move it to another folder, its name still appears on the list. When you select the filename, Word displays a message asking you to locate the file.

Use Short Menu Names Activate this option to shorten the names that appear in the Word menu bar. Deactivate this option to display complete names of the Word menus.

Open And Save preferences

The Open And Save section of the Preferences dialog box contains options that determine how Word opens and saves documents. Click the Open And Save icon to display the options shown in Figure 18-3. (Chapter 2, "Handling Files," describes in detail the procedures for opening and saving Word files.)

FIGURE 18-3.
This is the Open And Save section of the Preferences dialog box.

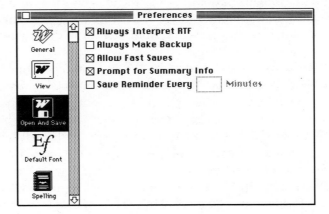

Always Interpret RTF

Activate this option if you want Word to always translate documents saved in Rich Text Format (RTF) or Interchange Format. Rich Text Format is a format used to preserve document formatting. Selecting this option tells Word to interpret information that determines the document's formatting in its original application and to use this information when a file is opened in Word.

Always Make Backup

Activate this option to automatically create a backup copy each time you save a document in Word. The backup copy is then stored under the name "Backup of *document name*."

Selecting this option automatically selects the Make Backup option in the Save As dialog box and prevents you from using the Fast Save option.

Allow Fast Saves

Activate this option to reduce the time required to save a document. When you select Allow Fast Saves, Word attaches your changes to the end of the document file, rather than updating the entire file as it normally would. Word occasionally performs a normal save to consolidate the file. Selecting this option automatically selects the Fast Save option in the Save As dialog box and prevents you from using the Make Backup option.

Prompt For Summary Info

Activate this option to display the Summary Info dialog box each time you save a new document. The Summary Info dialog box allows you to attach identifying information that is useful for locating the file with the Find File command.

If you deactivate this option, you can still choose Summary Info from the File menu to display the Summary Info dialog box for the active document.

Save Reminder Every ☐ *Minutes*

Activate this option if you want Word to remind you to save your document at the interval you specify in the edit bar. By default, Word suggests that it display a reminder every 15 minutes. However, an entry of any number from 1 to 120 is valid. If you type 10 in the edit bar, for example, Word displays a dialog box every ten minutes to prompt you to save the active document. Word doesn't display the dialog box if you have saved the document and have made no further changes to it.

Default Font preferences

The Default Font section of the Preferences dialog box, shown in Figure 18-4 on the next page, specifies the font and point size for a new document. You can make these settings by clicking the Default Font icon or choosing the Default Font command from the Font menu. (Chapter 4, "Formatting Characters," explains how to specify fonts and point sizes.)

FIGURE 18-4.
*This is the Default
Font section of the
Preferences dialog box.*

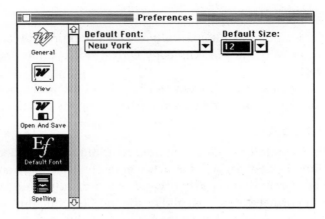

Default Font

Use this edit bar to specify the default font for the Normal style, or select a font from the drop-down list box that is displayed when you click the arrow.

Default Size

Use this edit bar to specify the default point size for the Normal style, or select a point size from the drop-down list box that is displayed when you click the arrow.

Spelling preferences

The Spelling section of the Preferences dialog box, shown in Figure 18-5, contains options for specifying the main dictionary used during a spelling check, for creating and editing custom dictionaries, and for spelling-check rules. Click the Spelling icon on the left side of the Preferences dialog box, or select Options in the Spelling dialog box to display this section. (Chapter 7, "Editing and Proofing," discusses the Spelling command in detail.)

FIGURE 18-5.
*This is the Spelling
section of the
Preferences dialog box.*

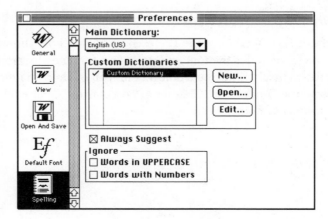

Main Dictionary

Use this drop-down list box to specify the main dictionary Word should use when performing a spelling check. Only the dictionaries located in the Word Commands folder appear on this list.

Custom Dictionaries

Use this section of the dialog box to specify custom dictionaries Word should use during a spelling check. Word displays the name of each custom dictionary in the list box. Specify a dictionary by clicking to the left of the dictionary name. The resulting check mark indicates that the dictionary is open and that its name appears in the Add Words To drop-down list box in the Spelling dialog box. Close an open dictionary by clicking the check mark. Word removes the dictionary name from the Add Words To drop-down list box in the Spelling dialog box.

The New button to the right of the Custom Dictionaries list box lets you create a new custom dictionary. The Open button lets you open an existing dictionary. The Edit button lets you view and delete entries from a selected dictionary.

Always Suggest

Activate this option if you want Word to suggest an alternative spelling when an unfamiliar word is found. If you deactivate this option, you can still use the Suggest button in the Spelling dialog box to request suggested spellings.

Ignore

The Ignore options instruct Word to ignore particular types of words during a spelling check.

Words In UPPERCASE Activate this option to ignore any words typed in all uppercase letters during a spelling check. When you select this option, Word continues to check the spelling of words to which the All Caps or Small Caps character formats have been applied.

Words With Numbers Activate this option to ignore words composed of character and number combinations during a spelling check.

Grammar preferences

The Grammar section of the Preferences dialog box, shown in Figure 18-6 on the next page, contains the style and grammar rules of the Grammar command on the Tools menu. Click the Grammar icon on the left side of the Preferences dialog box, or select Options in the Grammar dialog box to display this section. (Chapter 7, "Editing and Proofing," discusses the Grammar command in detail.)

FIGURE 18-6.
*This is the Grammar
section of the
Preferences dialog box.*

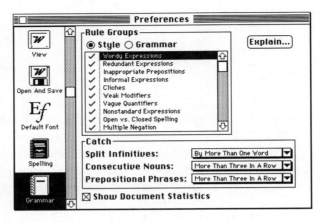

Rule Groups

The Rule Groups options control the style and grammar rule groups that Word considers during a grammar check. Clicking Style displays the style rule groups in the list box. Clicking Grammar displays the grammar rule groups.

Style rules Click Style to display a list of style rule groups. To view an explanation of a rule group, select the group from the list, and click Explain. During the grammar check, Word observes the rule groups that appear with a check mark. Click the check mark column to the left of the rule group name to activate or deactivate the rule.

Grammar rules Click Grammar to display a list of grammar rule groups. To view an explanation of a rule group, select the group from the list, and click Explain. During a grammar check, Word observes the rule groups that appear with a check mark. Click the check mark column to the left of the rule group name to activate or deactivate the rule.

Catch

The Catch options specify the conditions under which Word flags a potentially confusing or stylistically incorrect sentence. Word displays guidelines for each construction in the drop-down list box that appears to the right of the construction name. To change the number of occurrences of a particular construction you will permit, select another option from the corresponding drop-down list box.

Split Infinitives An infinitive is a verb form in which the verb is preceded by the word *to*—*to swim, to feel, to eat,* for example. To split an infinitive is to insert a word or words between the *to* and the verb—*to quickly swim, to sometimes feel, to happily and greedily eat,* for example. In some circles, splitting an infinitive is considered a hallmark of poor writing. Select an option from this list box to specify the number of words that can fall between the word *to* and the verb before Word flags the sentence.

Consecutive Nouns Generally, too many consecutive nouns make a sentence difficult to understand. Select an option from this list box to specify the number of consecutive nouns that can appear in a sentence before Word flags the sentence during a grammar check. For example, selecting More Than Two In A Row allows no more than one noun to modify another noun and causes Word to question *Action Item Committee* but not *Action Committee*.

Prepositional Phrases Like too many nouns, too many prepositional phrases can make a sentence difficult to understand. Select an option from this list box to specify the permissible number of prepositional phrases.

Show Document Statistics

Activate this option to display a statistical count of the words, characters, sentences, and paragraphs in a document after a grammar check. Word also displays several statistical indexes that indicate your writing's level of difficulty.

Thesaurus preferences

The Thesaurus section of the Preferences dialog box, shown in Figure 18-7, contains a drop-down list box that enables you to specify the dictionary that Word uses when you choose Thesaurus from the Tools menu. Click the Thesaurus icon to display this section. (Chapter 7, "Editing and Proofing," discusses the Thesaurus command in detail.)

FIGURE 18-7.
This is the Thesaurus section of the Preferences dialog box.

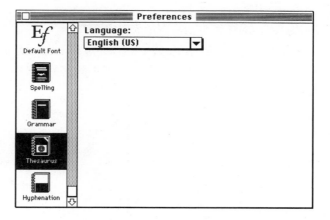

Hyphenation preferences

The Hyphenation section of the Preferences dialog box, shown in Figure 18-8 on the next page, contains a drop-down list box which enables you to specify the dictionary that Word uses when you choose the Hyphenation command from the Tools menu. Click the Hyphenation icon to display this section. (Chapter 7, "Editing and Proofing," discusses the Hyphenation command in detail.)

FIGURE 18-8.
This is the
Hyphenation section
of the Preferences
dialog box.

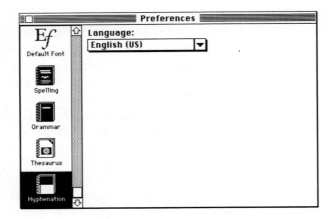

Customizing Word from the keyboard

In addition to specifying preferences that define how Word operates, you can customize Word by modifying the contents of Word menus and by defining keystroke shortcuts. These techniques enable you to add commands not initially found on Word menus and delete commands you seldom or never use. You can customize Word from the keyboard or by using the Commands command. We look at keyboard methods in this section.

Customizing menus from the keyboard

Adding and deleting items from Word menus is remarkably easy. Figure 18-9, for example, shows the Format menu before and after we added and deleted menu items.

FIGURE 18-9.
We customized the
Format menu by
adding and deleting
menu items.

Format	
Character...	⌘D
Paragraph...	⌘M
Section...	⌥F14
Document...	⌘F14
Border...	
Table Cells...	
Table Layout...	
Frame...	
Style...	⌘T
✓Revert To Style	⌘⇧_
Change Case...	
✓Plain Text	⌘⇧Z
Bold	⌘⇧B
Italic	⌘⇧I
Underline	⌘⇧U

Format	
Character...	⌘D
Paragraph...	⌘M
Section...	⌥F14
Document...	⌘F14
Border...	
Frame...	
Style...	⌘T
Change Case...	
Plain Text	⌘⇧Z
✓**Bold**	⌘⇧B
Italic	⌘⇧I
Underline	⌘⇧U
✓Flush Left	⌘⇧L
Centered	⌘⇧C
Flush Right	⌘⇧R

In this section, we discuss the procedures for adding dialog box options to Word menus and show you how to delete items. When you add a dialog box option to a menu from the keyboard, Word decides on which menu to place the option. Use the Commands dialog box to add an item to a menu that you specify.

Adding menu items .

To add an item to a menu, press Command-Option-= in Word's document window. This keystroke shortcut temporarily changes the I-beam pointer to a bold plus sign, and Word will add the next option you select to the appropriate Word menu. After you select the option, Word flashes the destination menu name to verify that the option has been added successfully. The pointer then resumes its normal shape.

To add several options from the same dialog box to a menu, you don't need to close and reopen a dialog box for each item. After you've added one option, simply press Command-Option-= while the dialog box is still open. When the pointer assumes the plus shape, click the next option to add. To add several options at one time, hold down the Shift key as you click each option. Word then adds each option to the appropriate menu.

If you add more options to a menu than can be shown at one time, an arrow at the bottom of the menu indicates that more items are available. View the items by dragging the pointer beyond the menu's lower edge.

To add an option, you can also press its keystroke shortcut instead of selecting it with the mouse. For example, to add the All Caps format to the Format menu, press Command-Option-=, and then immediately press Command-Shift-K.

If, after pressing Command-Option-=, you decide not to add a menu item, press Command-period or the Esc key to cancel the procedure.

Adding character formatting options

You can add any of the options in the Character dialog box to the Format menu. For example, if you often use the All Caps option and apply underlining to text, adding these options to the Format menu allows you to use the mouse to choose them without first opening the Character dialog box.

For example, suppose you want to add an option that superscripts text by 3 points to a menu. Simply press Command-Option-=, open the Character dialog box, and then click the Superscript option. Word automatically enters *3 pt* in the By edit bar next to the Superscript option. The menu bar flashes to acknowledge that the option and its default numeric argument have been added to the Format menu, and the pointer resumes its normal shape. The Format menu now includes the item *Superscript 3 pt*.

You can also press Command-Option-= and then click the Superscript button on the ribbon to add this option to the Format menu. When you select a ribbon button, Word adds the option specified by the button, not the button itself. (Word does not apply the option to the insertion point when you use a ribbon button as it does when you select the option from a dialog box.)

To add an option with a numeric setting other than Word's default, you must specify the setting in the appropriate Character dialog box edit bar before you press Command-Option-=. For example, to add an option that superscripts text by 4 points, first choose Character from the Format menu, and in the Character dialog box, click the Superscript option, and type 4 in the By edit bar. Next, press Command-Option-=, and use the plus pointer to click the Superscript option again. The Format menu flashes, and the pointer resumes its normal shape. When you pull down the Format menu, you'll see that it includes *Superscript 4 pt*.

If you press Command-Option-= and select a font name or size in the Character dialog box, Word adds the option to the Font menu. You can add a nonstandard font size to the font menu by opening the Character dialog box, typing that size in the Size edit bar, and then pressing Command-Option-=. Use the plus pointer to click the new size and add it to the menu.

Adding paragraph formatting options

Because Spacing and Indentation settings often vary within a document, you can't create menu items from Spacing or Indentation options in the Paragraph dialog box. In addition, you can't add the Suppress Line Numbers option to a menu. However, you can add any of the other three options in the Paragraph dialog box—Page Break Before, Keep With Next ¶, and Keep Lines Together—to the Format menu. You can also create a menu item that opens the Tabs dialog box, by pressing Command-Option-= and then clicking the Tabs button. (Unlike the commands that display the Border and Frame dialog boxes, the Tabs command does not appear by default on the Format menu.)

You can add many of the formatting options controlled by ruler buttons to the Format menu. Simply press Command-Option-=, and click the button. You cannot create a menu item to control tab placement or placement of the vertical line, however.

Adding Border dialog box options

Although Word doesn't allow you to add Tabs dialog box or Frame dialog box options to a menu, you can add a border specified in the Border dialog box to the Format menu. First choose the Border command from the Format menu, or press the Border button in the Paragraph dialog box, to display the Border dialog box.

In the Border dialog box, click the type of borderline you want to use (Dotted, Hairline, Single, Thick, or Double). Next, specify the placement of the border by clicking to add each borderline to the sample diagram on the left side of the dialog box or by selecting either the Box or Shadow option. Finally, enter a number in the From Text edit bar if you want to insert extra space between the border and the paragraph text.

After specifying the border you want to add, press Command-Option-=, and use the plus pointer to click the sample diagram. Word adds the border specifications as an item on the Format menu and then returns the pointer to its normal arrow shape.

After adding a border, you'll see a new item, such as *TLBRM Thick Paragraph Border*, on the Format menu. The capital letters indicate where the borderlines appear relative to your text. *T* indicates a line at the top of the paragraph(s); *L* indicates a line to the left; *B* indicates a line below the paragraph(s); *R* indicates a line to the right; and *M* indicates a line between selected paragraphs.

The menu item also indicates the type of borderline (Dotted, Hairline, Single, Thick, or Double). If you specified a custom border with two or more line styles, Word places a plus sign next to the first line style and then the second line style (for example, *TLBRM Single + Paragraph Border*). Any From Text settings do not appear as part of the new menu item, but Word does apply the spacing when you choose the item.

Adding section formatting options

Word allows you to add most of the options in the Section dialog box to the Format menu. You can add any of the Start, Columns Number, and Different First Page options. You can also add any of the page number options. However, Word doesn't allow you to add the Columns Spacing or the Header/Footer From Top and From Bottom options to the Format menu.

Adding most of these options to the Format menu is simply a matter of pressing Command-Option-= and selecting the option in the Section dialog box. For example, to add a page numbering format to the Format menu, press Command-Option-=, and then use the plus pointer to open the Section dialog box. Select the option you want from the Format drop-down list box. If you select the default format (1 2 3), for example, you'll see the item *Arabic Page Numbers* the next time you pull down the Format menu.

To add a Columns Number option to the Format menu, first enter a Number setting in the edit bar. Then press Command-Option-=, and click the setting using the plus pointer. When you choose this item from the menu, however, remember that you still must specify the amount of space between columns by entering a Spacing setting in the Section dialog box.

Adding Preferences dialog box options

You can add most of the check box options in the General, View, and Open And Save sections of the Preferences dialog box to a menu. Word adds Preference dialog box options to the Tools and Edit menus, as appropriate. You cannot add options that appear in a drop-down list box—such as the Measurement Unit options displayed in the General section of the Preferences dialog box. Nor can you add the options that appear in the Default Font, Spelling, Grammar, Thesaurus, or Hyphenation sections of the Preferences dialog box.

For example, to create a menu item that activates "smart" quotes, first press Command-Option-=. Next, use the plus pointer to choose the Preferences command from the Tools menu. In the General section of the Preferences dialog box, select the "Smart" Quotes option. When the pointer returns to its normal arrow shape, click OK or Cancel to close the dialog box.

Adding outline options

To add an outline option to the Edit menu, first choose Outline from the View menu. Then press Command-Option-=, and use the plus pointer to click the appropriate icon at the top of the document window. (For a detailed description of these options, see Chapter 14, "Outlining.")

Adding header and footer window elements

If you press Command-Option-= and click a dynamic option in the header or footer window, Word adds only the Same As Previous option to the View menu. If you frequently change the arrangement of sections within your document, adding this item to the View menu enables you to standardize the content of headers and footers in each document section without having to open each section's header and footer window.

Although you can't add the dynamic date, time, and page number options that appear at the top of the header and footer windows to a Word menu, you can easily add their corresponding entries from Word's Standard Glossary to the Work menu, as we explain in a moment.

Adding options to the Work menu

Word adds filenames, names of glossaries, individual glossary entries, and paragraph styles to the Work menu, which doesn't appear on the menu bar until you add one of these items. Adding entries and names to the Work menu is much like adding options to other Word menus. You simply press Command-Option-= and then select the item. Figure 18-10 shows a Work menu that includes two filenames, a glossary entry, and a style name. The Work menu displays filenames first, then glossary entries, and then style names. A line separates the sections, and menu items appear alphabetically within each section.

FIGURE 18-10.
Word separates the items on the Work menu into three sections, placing filenames first, then glossary entries, and then style names.

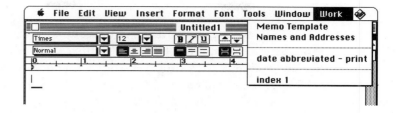

Adding filenames To add a filename to the Work menu, press Command-Option-=, and when the pointer changes to a plus sign, choose Open from the File menu. After you locate the file you want to add to the menu, select the filename, and click Open. The pointer returns to its normal shape, and Word closes the Open dialog box.

You can add any Word file to the Work menu from the Open dialog box—including glossary files. Word doesn't allow you to add one of the four most recently opened files by choosing it from the bottom of the File menu. You can add non-Word files to the Work menu, but the file is opened in Word, not in its original application. For example, if you add a SuperPaint file to the Work menu, Word displays the contents of the file within a frame in a new Word document.

When you choose a filename from the Work menu, Word opens the file. If Word can't find the file on your current disk, it displays a dialog box that enables you to locate the file. Choosing the name of a document that is already open displays the document in a new window.

Adding glossary entries To add a glossary entry to the Work menu, press Command-Option-=, and choose Glossary from the Edit menu. Then click the entry you want to add to the Work menu. The Glossary dialog box remains open, so you can press Command-Option-= again and add other entries as necessary. To close the Glossary dialog box, click Close or click the close box.

When you choose a glossary entry from the Work menu, Word inserts the text designated by that entry at the current insertion point, as if you had selected the entry from the Glossary dialog box.

Adding paragraph styles To add a paragraph style to the Work menu, press Command-Option-=, and then select the style from the Style drop-down list box on the ruler. Word adds the name of the style to the Work menu, and the pointer resumes its normal shape. You can also press Command-Option-=, open the Style dialog box, and click a style name. The pointer returns to its normal arrow shape, but the dialog box remains open, so you can press Command-Option-= and select another style name to add to the Work menu. Close the Style dialog box when you finish adding styles.

Choosing a style from the Work menu applies the style to the current paragraph, just as if you had opened the Style dialog box, selected the style name, and clicked OK, or selected the style from the drop-down list box on the ruler.

Work menu tips

As we explain in a few pages, Word stores the commands and options available on each Word menu in the Word Settings (5) file. As a result, the items on the Work menu are available each time you use Word. If you choose an item that Word is unable to use—such as a glossary entry that's not in the current glossary—Word beeps to indicate that the item is unavailable.

If you use identical glossary entry names and style names in different documents, the glossary entries and styles on your Work menu will have different effects, depending on which document you're working in and which glossary file(s) you open. This approach gets more mileage out of fewer menu items.

For example, suppose several documents include a *Title* style, which you've added to the Work menu. When you choose Title from the Work menu, Word looks at the style's definition on the current style sheet. Although different documents might assign a different set of formatting instructions to the *Title* style, you can use the same style name on the Work menu.

Deleting menu items

To delete an item from a Word menu, first press Command-Option-minus. This keystroke shortcut temporarily changes the I-beam pointer to a bold minus sign, and Word will remove the next menu item you choose from the appropriate menu. To delete several menu items at one time, hold down the Shift key as you choose each item. After you choose an item, Word flashes the menu name to verify the deletion. The pointer then resumes its normal shape.

If after pressing Command-Option-minus you no longer want to delete a menu item, press Command-period or the Esc key to cancel the procedure.

Deleting commands You can press Command-Option-minus to remove any menu item, including the commands that appear by default on Word menus. You can, for example, remove one of Word's default character formats, such as Bold, from the Format menu.

Removing a menu item does not remove the command or option from Word, however, and you can still choose the command by using its assigned keystroke shortcut. If you remove Bold from the Format menu, for example, you can still select Bold in the Character dialog box, or you can press Command-B. If you delete a command that is not available in a dialog box—for example, if you delete the Sort command from the Tools menu—you can choose Commands from the Tools menu to restore the command to a menu. (We discuss the Commands command later in this chapter.)

To delete a command, you can also press its keystroke shortcut. For example, to delete the Underline command from the Format menu, press Command-Option-minus, and then press Command-U.

Deleting separator lines You can't remove the preset separator lines from Word menus by pressing Command-Option-minus and selecting them, but Word removes a separator line automatically if you delete the commands that the line separates.

To remove a separator line that is a result of your menu item additions, press Command-Option-minus, and then select the separator line. Word deletes the separator line and returns the pointer to its normal shape.

Customizing keystrokes from the keyboard

Word also lets you create your own keystroke shortcuts easily. You can assign a keystroke shortcut to Word's default menu commands and to any items that you add to a menu. If you want, you can even assign a second or third set of keystrokes to a command that already has a keystroke shortcut. If you assign more than one keystroke shortcut, Word displays only one shortcut next to the item name on the menu.

To assign a keystroke shortcut using the keyboard, press Command-Option-plus, using the plus key on the numeric keypad. (Num Lock must be turned off.) The pointer assumes the shape of the Command symbol. Using this pointer, choose the item. Word then asks you to type the keystrokes you want to use as the shortcut.

For example, suppose that you want to assign a keystroke shortcut to the Table command on the Insert menu. You can easily designate your own keystroke shortcut, such as Command-\, for this command. Begin by pressing Command-Option-plus (using the plus key on the numeric keypad). Then choose Table from the Insert menu. Press Command-\ when Word displays the dialog box shown in Figure 18-11. Word records the new keystroke shortcut and displays it next to the command name on the menu, as shown in Figure 18-12 on the next page. Table 18-1, also on the next page, shows the different symbols used to indicate keystrokes on Word menus.

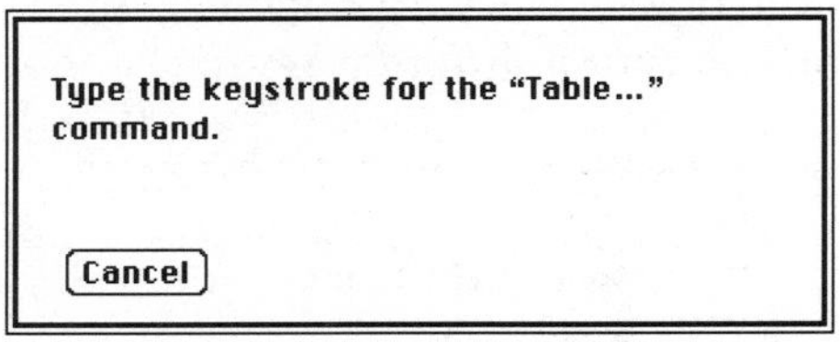

FIGURE 18-11.
Word presents a dialog box like this one so that you can assign a keystroke shortcut to the specified command.

> Type the keystroke for the "Table..."
> command.
>
> [Cancel]

FIGURE 18-12.
The Insert menu now
shows a keystroke
shortcut for the Table
command.

Symbol	Key	Symbol	Key
⌘	COMMAND	→|	TAB
⬎	OPTION	⌫	DELETE or (BACKSPACE)
⇧	SHIFT	▦	Key following symbol is on the numeric keypad
^	CONTROL		
↵	RETURN	⌧	ESC
⤨	ENTER	← →	Arrow keys
␣	SPACEBAR	↑ ↓	

TABLE 18-1.
Word uses these symbols on Word menus to indicate keystrokes.

If you type a keystroke shortcut that has already been assigned, Word displays an alert box like the one shown in Figure 18-13, which gives you the choice of removing the keystroke shortcut from the command to which it is currently assigned or clicking Cancel. If you click Cancel, you again see the dialog box shown in Figure 18-11, and you can type a different keystroke shortcut.

FIGURE 18-13.
Typing a keystroke
shortcut that has
already been assigned
displays this alert box.

A keystroke shortcut that you assign to an item can use as many as four keys. In addition, you must use the Command key in most combinations. If you have an extended keyboard, you can use the function keys in your keystroke shortcuts. You can also create keystroke shortcuts that use the Command key and a character key together with the Shift key, the Option key, or the Control key. Word won't let you use the Control key in a keystroke shortcut unless you also include the Command key. You don't need the Command key with function keys or with keys on the numeric keypad. (Num Lock must be turned off in order to choose an item using a key on the numeric keypad.)

Customizing Word from the Commands dialog box

The Commands dialog box allows you to add and delete commands from menus and lets you link any command, feature, or action that Word can perform to any valid keystroke shortcut. Using this command, you can also alter Word's preset menu selections and keystroke shortcuts.

In the Commands dialog box, you can set up customized configurations of menus, keystroke shortcuts, and defaults, and you can save them in configuration files that you use for special purposes. You can then access one of these new configuration files or return to Word's default configuration. (We discuss configuration files later in this chapter.)

To display the Commands dialog box, choose Commands from the Tools menu. You can also display the Commands dialog box by pressing Command-Shift-Option-C. As you can see in Figure 18-14, a list box dominates the left side of the dialog box. Here, you'll find all the Word features, commands, and actions that you can assign to menus or keystroke shortcuts.

FIGURE 18-14.
*Choose Commands
from the Tools menu
to display the
Commands dialog box.*

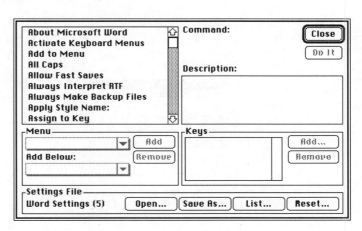

You can move through the Commands list by using the scroll arrows. You can also press an alphabet key to move immediately to that section of the list. For example, press *d* to view the commands beginning with the letter *d*.

Customizing menus from the Commands dialog box

Using the Commands dialog box, you can add, remove, and move items from one menu to another. Let's look first at the technique you use to add items to a menu.

Adding menu items

To add an item to a menu, first choose that item from the list box on the left side of the Commands dialog box. Word displays the item and a brief description in the upper-right section of the Commands dialog box.

The Menu drop-down list box in the left corner of the Commands dialog box suggests a menu to which you can add the chosen item. If the item already appears on a Word menu, the menu name is dimmed, and Word highlights the Remove button. If the item does not currently appear on a menu, the menu name is not dimmed, and Word highlights the Add button. When you select an item, Word also displays any keystroke shortcuts currently assigned to that item in the Keys list box and highlights the Add button next to this list.

To place the selected item on the suggested menu, simply click Add in the Menu section of the dialog box. To place the item on a different menu, click the arrow next to the Menu drop-down list box, and select another menu.

For example, to add the Dotted Underline option to a menu, select Dotted Underline from the list of items. Word displays Format as the suggested menu in the Menu drop-down list, as shown in Figure 18-15. To place this option on the Format menu, click Add.

FIGURE 18-15.
When you select an item from the list box, Word suggests a menu for that item.

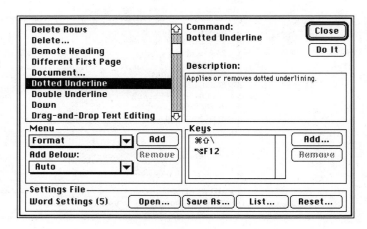

The Add Below drop-down list box beneath the Menu drop-down list box specifies the location where the item should appear on the selected menu. Click the arrow to the right of this drop-down list box to display the current contents of the menu selected in the Menu drop-down list box. To place the item on the menu in the recommended position, leave Auto—the default setting—unchanged. To place the item at the top or bottom of the menu, select the At Top or At Bottom option. To place the item below a particular item, select the existing item from the Add Below drop-down list box.

For example, Figure 18-16 shows the Format menu after we added the Dotted Underline option selected in Figure 18-15 to the bottom of the menu.

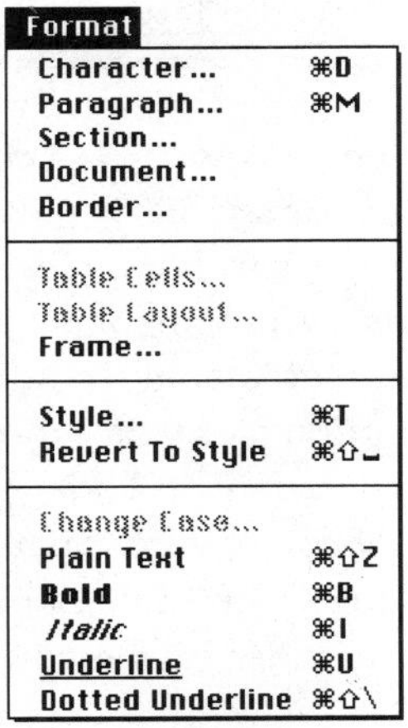

FIGURE 18-16.
We selected the At Bottom option in the Add Below drop-down list box to insert the Dotted Underline option at the bottom of the Format menu.

Format	
Character...	⌘D
Paragraph...	⌘M
Section...	
Document...	
Border...	
Table Cells...	
Table Layout...	
Frame...	
Style...	⌘T
Revert To Style	⌘⇧⌐
Change Case...	
Plain Text	⌘⇧Z
Bold	⌘B
Italic	⌘I
Underline	⌘U
Dotted Underline	⌘⇧\

Items displayed with a colon A colon appears after some items on the list in the Commands dialog box, indicating that you'll need to supply additional information in order to place that item on a menu. Word prompts you for the information when you select such an item. For example, if you select Apply Style Name:, shown in Figure 18-14, you must specify the style name. Figure 18-17 on the next page shows the Commands dialog box after you select Apply Style Name:.

In the upper-right section of the Commands dialog box, Word displays the name of the selected item (Apply Style Name:) and a drop-down list box containing the names of all the styles in the current document. Simply select the style from the drop-down list box. In this case, Word suggests the Work menu as the location for the new style. You can select a different menu and change the location of the style on whatever menu you select. If the style already appears on the selected menu, a diamond symbol appears next to the style name in the list.

FIGURE 18-17.
*When you select an
item that's followed by
a colon, Word prompts
you for more
information.*

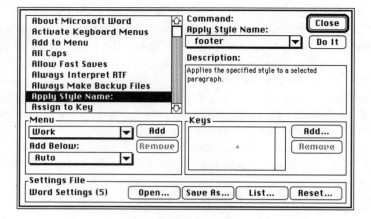

In some cases, when you select an item followed by a colon, Word displays a combination drop-down list box and edit bar so that you can select an item from the list or enter your own setting in the edit bar. For example, if you select Paragraph Shading: from the Commands list, Word displays a drop-down list box containing shading options in 10 percent increments. To add an item that applies a 20% shade to a paragraph, select that option from the drop-down list box. Word adds this item to the selected menu when you click Add.

Similarly, if you select Open File Name:, Word displays a button labeled Open File. When you click this button, the Open dialog box appears so that you can select the name of the file you want to place on a menu.

Creating separator lines on menus

You can add separator lines to divide different categories of menu items, like the line that appears between Help and Show Clipboard on the Window menu. The list of items in the Commands dialog box includes an item called *Separator*. When you select this item, you must select the menu on which to place the separator line from the Menu drop-down list box. Then use the options in the Add Below drop-down list box to specify the exact location of the separator on the menu.

Adding all items to menus

Word can add all the items listed in the Commands dialog box to menus. First, open the Commands dialog box, and click the Reset button in the lower-right corner. Word displays the dialog box shown in Figure 18-18. Select the bottom option, and then click OK. Word then adds all the items to their default menus. You can select this option and then remove selected items to pare menus down to a more manageable size. (When we discuss Word's settings files later in this chapter, we discuss the other options available in this dialog box.)

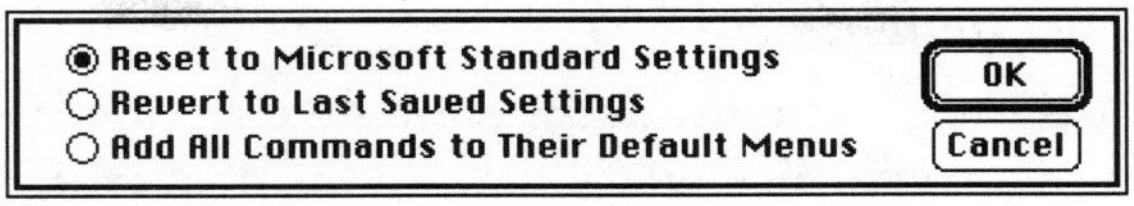

FIGURE 18-18.
Click Reset in the
Commands dialog box
to display these options.

⦿ **Reset to Microsoft Standard Settings**
◯ **Revert to Last Saved Settings**
◯ **Add All Commands to Their Default Menus**

[OK]
[Cancel]

The Close and Do It buttons

After using the Commands dialog box, close it by clicking either the Close or Do It button. Clicking Close closes the dialog box without undoing any of the changes made to menus or keystroke shortcuts.

Clicking Do It closes the dialog box and carries out the currently selected item. For example, after selecting the Show Hidden Text command and clicking Add, you can click Do It to close the Commands dialog box and display hidden text in the document window.

You can use the Do It button to carry out any item in the Commands list. Suppose you've opened the Commands dialog box and made several changes to your menus. To return to your document and save it in one step, for example, click Save in the Commands list, and then click Do It.

Deleting menu items

After you become familiar with Word's commands and keystroke shortcuts, you might want to simplify your menus by removing items you rarely access from a menu. The procedure for removing an item from a menu is similar to that for adding items. Open the Commands dialog box, scroll down the list, and choose the item you want to remove. If you select an item that appears on a menu, Word dims the Add button and highlights the Remove button. Click Remove to delete the menu item. If you select an item that's followed by a colon, you must also supply additional information so that Word knows exactly which menu item you want to delete.

For example, if you've added Columns 3 to the Format menu and want to remove it, first select Columns: in the Commands list. When Word displays the combination drop-down list box and edit bar that contains the various Columns options, select the Columns 3 option from the drop-down list box, and then click Remove.

If you remove an item from a menu, you can still access that item from the keyboard if it has a keystroke shortcut, and you can open the Commands dialog box to access the item. For example, suppose you remove the Paragraph command from the Format menu but don't alter Word's default keystroke shortcuts for that command (Command-M and Shift-F14). You can still open the Paragraph dialog box with either keystroke shortcut. You can also access the Paragraph dialog box by opening the Commands dialog box, selecting Paragraph in the Commands list, and then clicking Do It.

Moving menu items

Word doesn't allow an item to appear on more than one menu at a time. To move an item from one menu to another, remove the item from its current menu, and then add it to another.

For example, you can move the Page Layout command from the View menu to the File menu by opening the Commands dialog box and selecting Page Layout from the Commands list. Word displays View in the Menu drop-down list box, and activates the Remove button. Click Remove to delete the command from the View menu. Next, select File from the Menu drop-down list box. If you want to specify the location of the command on the File menu, select an option in the Add Below drop-down list box before you click the Add button.

Customizing keystrokes from the Commands dialog box

As we've said, creating your own keystroke shortcuts is an excellent way to streamline procedures that you use frequently. The Commands dialog box lets you assign keystroke shortcuts to Word's commands, options, and features. You can also alter and remove Word's preset keystroke shortcuts.

Any item that can be placed on a menu can also be assigned a keystroke shortcut. However, you don't need to place an item on a menu in order to assign it a keystroke shortcut. For example, Word lets you assign keystroke shortcuts to filenames, glossary entries, style names, font names, font sizes, and window names without placing them on a menu.

Assigning keystroke shortcuts

To assign a keystroke shortcut to an item, first select the item from the list in the Commands dialog box. Word displays the keystroke shortcut currently assigned to that item in the Keys list box; if no shortcut is assigned, the Keys list box is blank. When you click the Add button next to the Keys list box, Word displays a message asking you to type the keystroke shortcut you want to assign to the selected item. Word then displays the symbols for the keys you pressed.

For example, suppose you want to assign a keystroke shortcut to the Show Hidden Text option in the Preferences dialog box. To begin, open the Commands dialog box, and select Show Hidden Text from the list of items. As shown in Figure 18-19, the Keys list box is initially blank. When you click the Add button to the right of the Keys list box, Word displays a message similar to the one shown in Figure 18-11. Type the keystroke shortcut. If you type Command-8, for example, Word displays those key symbols in the Keys list box, as shown in Figure 18-20.

FIGURE 18-19.
*By default, no
keystroke shortcut is
assigned to the Show
Hidden Text
command.*

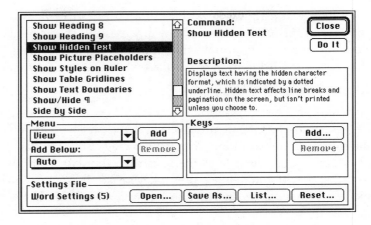

FIGURE 18-20.
*Word displays the new
keystroke shortcut in
the Keys list box.*

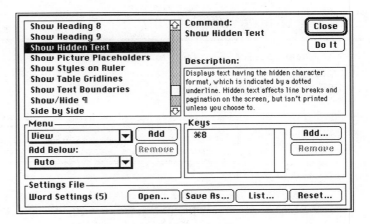

A keystroke shortcut that you assign to an item can use as many as four keys. In addition, you must use the Command key in most combinations. If you have an extended keyboard, you can use the function keys in your keystroke shortcuts. You can also create keystroke shortcuts that use the Command key and a character key together with the Shift key, the Option key, or the Control key. Word won't let you use the Control key in a keystroke shortcut unless you also include the Command key. You don't need the Command key with function keys or with keys on the numeric keypad. (Num Lock must be turned off in order to choose an item using a key on the numeric keypad.)

When you assign a keystroke shortcut to an item, Word displays the new shortcut in the Keys list box below any existing shortcuts. When you add more than one shortcut to an item that appears on a Word menu, only the first keystroke shortcut listed in the Keys list box appears on the menu.

Removing keystroke shortcuts

To remove a keystroke shortcut from any item, simply open the Commands dialog box, and select the item whose keystroke shortcut you want to remove. When the shortcuts appear in the Keys list box, select the one you want to remove, and click Remove. Word deletes the keystroke shortcut from the item and from the Keys list box. If you delete a preset keystroke shortcut assigned to one of Word's menu commands, the shortcut no longer appears next to the command name on the menu.

Creating a table of commands

To help you keep track of your menu configurations and keystroke shortcuts, you can create a table of commands and shortcuts. Clicking the List button at the bottom of the Commands dialog box displays the dialog box shown in Figure 18-21.

FIGURE 18-21.
Click the List button
in the Commands
dialog box to display
this dialog box.

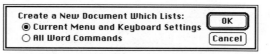

To create a list that displays the current menus and keystroke shortcuts, select the Current Menu And Keyboard Settings option. To create a list that displays all the items listed in the Commands dialog box—even those not currently assigned to menus or keys—select the All Word Commands option.

When you select one of these options, Word closes the dialog box and creates a new document containing a table of the requested items and their corresponding keystroke shortcuts. It might take Word several minutes to compile the table. Figure 18-22 shows how this table looks on the screen. Because Word creates this list as a new document, you can save the information and use the Print command to print a copy of it.

FIGURE 18-22.
Use the List button in the Commands dialog box to create a table of Word's commands.

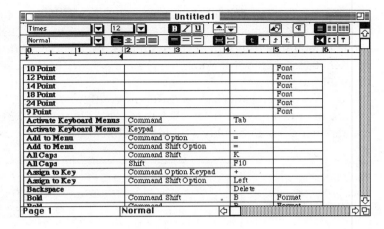

10 Point			Font
12 Point			Font
14 Point			Font
18 Point			Font
24 Point			Font
9 Point			Font
Activate Keyboard Menus	Command	Tab	
Activate Keyboard Menus	Keypad	.	
Add to Menu	Command Option	=	
Add to Menu	Command Shift Option	=	
All Caps	Command Shift	K	
All Caps	Shift	F10	
Assign to Key	Command Option Keypad	+	
Assign to Key	Command Shift Option	Left	
Backspace		Delete	
Bold	Command Shift	B	Format

Using Word's configuration files

Word saves menus and keystroke shortcuts in a special configuration file. Word's default configuration file is called Word Settings (5). This file also stores other program defaults, including settings in the Page Setup, Preferences, Print, Style, Document, Section, Spelling, and Glossary dialog boxes.

You'll find the Word Settings (5) file stored in the Preferences folder located in the System Folder on your hard drive. You don't need to open this file. Word automatically stores all relevant information each time you quit Word and return to the Finder.

If you discard or rename this file, or remove it from the System Folder on your hard drive, Word creates a new Word Settings (5) file with all settings returned to their defaults.

Creating a new configuration file

Word allows you to create new configuration files to store different default settings. Using different configuration files is useful when you repeatedly create different kinds of documents. You can create one configuration file with default settings, menus, and shortcuts for technical manuals; another for newsletters; and so on. Only one configuration file can be open at a time. Word displays the name of the current configuration file at the bottom of the Commands dialog box.

To create a new configuration file, first specify the new defaults. For example, if you want to specify a new set of Page Setup, Document, and Section setting defaults, open each dialog box in turn, and then specify the new default by clicking the Use As Default button. To change the default menus or keystroke shortcuts, use the techniques we described earlier in this chapter. You can also change default settings in the Preferences dialog box. After you've made all your changes, quit Word. Your changes are automatically saved in the Word Settings (5) file.

To save your changes in a different configuration file, choose Commands instead of quitting Word. Then click the Save As button at the bottom of the Commands dialog box to display a dialog box like the one in Figure 18-23.

FIGURE 18-23.
*Word automatically
saves a configuration
file in the Preferences
folder.*

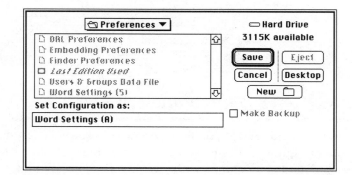

Enter a name for the new configuration file. (As you can see, Word automatically opens the Preferences folder in the System Folder when saving a configuration file but you can store a configuration file anywhere on your hard disk.) Use a distinctive group of names for your configuration files to make it easier to identify those files later. For example, in Figure 18-23, we chose the filename *Word Settings (A)* to store our new default settings. Then click Save.

When you save a new configuration file, Word treats that file as the current configuration file. Its name appears in the lower-left corner of the Commands dialog box, and changes to Word's menus and other default settings are saved in this file when you quit Word and return to the Finder.

Opening a configuration file

At startup, Word uses the settings in the Word Settings (5) file. If you want to use another configuration file, load Word, open the Commands dialog box, and then click the Open button at the bottom of the dialog box. Word presents a dialog box much like the standard Open dialog box and displays the message *Select a Configuration File*. Click the name of the configuration file you want to use, and then click Open.

You can also open a configuration file by double-clicking its icon at the Finder level. Opening the file in this way also loads Word.

When you open a new configuration file, all the settings stored in that file, including menus and keystroke shortcuts, replace the settings currently in effect, and Word displays the name of the new configuration file at the bottom of the Commands dialog box. Any additional changes you make to Word's menus and other default settings are saved in this file when you quit Word and return to the Finder.

Recovering previous defaults

You can preserve a current configuration file without saving any changes made to Word's menus and default settings during the current session. To revert to the last saved settings, open the Commands dialog box, and click the Reset button before you quit Word and return to the Finder. Word displays the dialog box shown earlier in Figure 18-18. Selecting the Revert To Last Saved Settings option and then clicking OK cancels any changes you've made since loading the current configuration file.

If you don't quit Word and return to the Finder at the end of a Word session—in other words, if you simply turn off your computer or if your computer crashes—Word doesn't record any changes to menus or other default settings in the current configuration file. When you next load Word, the menus and other settings will be the same as they were at the beginning of the previous session.

Returning to Word's preset defaults

To return to Word's original default settings, open the Commands dialog box, and select the Reset button. When Word displays the dialog box shown earlier in Figure 18-18, select the Revert To Microsoft Standard Settings option, and click OK. Then close the Commands dialog box.

Appendixes

A

Keyboard and Mouse Techniques

*A*s you know, most of Word's menu commands also have keystroke shortcuts. This appendix summarizes these keystroke shortcuts, along with additional keyboard and mouse techniques that you can use to make working in Word faster and easier. (You must turn on Num Lock to use all shortcuts in the following table that involve keys on the numeric keypad.)

Each command in this appendix is described in detail earlier in this book. For information about changing Word's preset keystroke shortcuts, or about defining your own shortcuts, see Chapter 18, "Customizing Word."

Selection commands

Select word	Double-click word
Select sentence	Press Command, and click sentence
Select line	Click next to line in selection bar
Select paragraph	Double-click next to paragraph in selection bar, or triple-click paragraph

(continued)

Selection commands, continued

Select column	Press Option key, click next to first character in column, and then drag down
Select document	Press Command-A or Command-Option-M, or press Command and then click in selection bar
Select frame	Click inside frame
Extend selection	Click at beginning of block, press Shift, and then click at end of block
Extend selection to character	Press minus on keypad, and then type character

Navigation commands

In Normal view

Move up one line	Press Up direction key or 8 on keypad
Move down one line	Press Down direction key or 2 on keypad
Move left one character	Press Left direction key or 4 on keypad
Move right one character	Press Right direction key or 6 on keypad
Move left one word	Press Command-Left direction key or Command-4 on keypad
Move right one word	Press Command-Right direction key or Command-6 on keypad
Move to beginning of line	Press 7 on keypad
Move to end of line	Press 1 on keypad
Move to beginning of previous sentence	Press Command-7 on keypad
Move to beginning of next sentence	Press Command-1 on keypad
Move to beginning of previous paragraph	Press Command-Up direction key or Command-8 on keypad
Move to beginning of next paragraph	Press Command-Down direction key or Command-2 on keypad
Move to top of window	Press Command-5 on keypad
Move to bottom of window	Press End
Move to beginning of document	Press Command-Home or Command-9 on keypad
Move to end of document	Press Command-End or Command-3 on keypad
Scroll up one screen	Press Page Up or 9 on keypad
Scroll down one screen	Press Page Down or 3 on keypad

In Page Layout view

Move to first text area	Press Command-Option-7 on keypad
Move to last text area	Press Command-Option-1 on keypad
Move to next text area	Press Command-Option-3 on keypad
Move to previous text area	Press Command-Option-9 on keypad
Move up one text area	Press Command-Option-8 on keypad
Move down one text area	Press Command-Option-2 on keypad
Move left one text area	Press Command-Option-4 on keypad
Move right one text area	Press Command-Option-6 on keypad

In a table

Move to next cell in table	Press Tab or Command-Option-3 on keypad
Move to previous cell in table	Press Shift-Tab or Command-Option-9 on keypad

Windowing and scrolling commands

Activate another window	Press Command-Option-W
Zoom window	Press Command-Option-]
Open or close split window	Press Command-Option-S
Scroll up one screen	Press 9 on keypad or Page Up
Scroll down one screen	Press 3 on keypad or Page Down
Scroll up one line	Press asterisk on keypad
Scroll down one line	Press plus on keypad
Move to bottom of window	Press End
Move to top of window	Press Home

Editing commands

Insert nonbreaking hyphen	Press Command-~
Insert optional hyphen	Press Command-hyphen
Insert ellipsis	Press Option-semicolon
Insert long hyphen (em-dash)	Press Shift-Option-hyphen
Insert space	Press Spacebar
Insert nonbreaking space	Press Option-Spacebar
Insert tab	Press Tab
Insert new line	Press Shift-Return
Insert new paragraph	Press Return

(continued)

Editing commands, continued

Insert new paragraph with same formatting	Press Command-Return
Insert new paragraph after insertion point	Press Command-Option-Return
Insert new paragraph above table row	Press Command-Option-Spacebar
Insert hard page break	Press Shift-Enter on keypad
Insert section break	Press Command-Enter on keypad
Delete character to left	Press Delete
Delete character to right	Press Command-Option-F
Delete previous word	Press Command-Option-Delete
Delete next word	Press Command-Option-G
Delete a selection	Press Delete
Copy as text	Press Command-Option-C
Copy as picture	Press Command-Option-D
Copy formats	Press Command-Option-V
Move text	Press Command-Option-X
Insert symbol or special character	Press Command-Option-Q, and then select symbol or type decimal code for character
Insert glossary text	Press Command-Delete, type name of glossary entry, and then press Return
Extend to	Press Command-Option-H
Insert formula	Press Command-Option-\

Menu commands

Bold	Press Command-B
Calculate	Press Command-=
Character	Press Command-D
Close	Press Command-W
Copy	Press Command-C
Cut	Press Command-X
Find	Press Command-F
Font Size Up (1 point)	Press Command-]
Font Size Down (1 point)	Press Command-[
Footnote	Press Command-E
Footnotes	Press Command-Option-Shift-S
Glossary	Press Command-K

Go To	Press Command-G
Italic	Press Command-I
New	Press Command-N
Normal	Press Command-Option-N
Open	Press Command-O
Outline	Press Command-Option-O
Page Break	Press Shift-Enter
Page Layout	Press Command-Option-P
Paragraph	Press Command-M
Paste	Press Command-V
Plain Text	Press Command-Shift-Z
Print	Press Command-P
Print Preview	Press Command-Option-I
Quit	Press Command-Q
Repeat	Press Command-Y
Replace	Press Command-H
Revert To Style	Press Command-Shift-Spacebar
Ribbon	Press Command-Option-R
Ruler	Press Command-R
Save	Press Command-S
Section Break	Press Command-Enter
Select All	Press Command-A
Show or Hide ¶	Press Command-J
Spelling	Press Command-L
Style	Press Command-T
Underline	Press Command-U
Undo	Press Command-Z
Open menu	Press decimal point on numeric keypad, and then type first letter or number of menu; press Left or Right direction key to move to adjacent menu after desired menu has been opened
Select item from open menu	Press Down direction key or Up direction key
Add dialog box option to menu	Press Command-Option-=, and then select desired option
Remove item from menu	Press Command-Option-minus, and then select desired menu item
List all files on disk	Press Shift, and choose Open
Repaginate entire document	Press Shift, and choose Full Repaginate Now
Perform descending sort	Press Shift, and choose Sort

Function-key commands

File commands

New	Press F5
Open	Press F6
Save	Press F7
Save As	Press Shift-F7
Print Preview	Press Option-F13
Page Setup	Press Shift-F8
Print	Press F8

Edit commands

Undo	Press F1
Cut	Press F2
Copy	Press F3
Paste	Press F4
Paste Link	Press Option-F4
Copy character or paragraph formats	Press Shift-F4
Copy text	Press Shift-F3
Move text	Press Shift-F2

View commands

Outline	Press Shift-F13
Page Layout	Press F13

Insert commands

None

Format commands

Character	Press F14
Paragraph	Press Shift-F14
Section	Press Option-F14
Document	Press Command-F14
Revert To Style	Press F9
Plain Text	Press Shift-F9
Bold	Press F10
Italic	Press F11
Underline	Press F12

Word Underline	Press Command-F12
Double Underline	Press Shift-F12
Dotted Underline	Press Option-F12
Outline (Format menu)	Press Shift-F11
Shadow	Press Option-F11
All Caps	Press Shift-F10
Small Caps	Press Option-F10
Hidden Text	Press Option-F9

Font commands

None

Tools commands

Spelling	Press F15
Hyphenate	Press Shift-F15
Word Count	Press Option-F15
Renumber	Press Command-F15

Window commands

New Window	Press Shift-F5

Character formatting commands

All Caps	Press Command-Shift-K
Bold	Press Command-B
Dotted Underline	Press Command-Shift-\
Double Underline	Press Command-Shift-[
Hidden Text	Press Command-Shift-X
Italic	Press Command-I
Outline (Format menu)	Press Command-Shift-D
Plain Style	Press Command-Shift-Z
Revert To Style	Press Command-Shift-Spacebar
Shadow	Press Command-Shift-W
Small Caps	Press Command-Shift-H
Strikethru	Press Command-Shift-/
Subscript	Press Command-Shift-minus
Underline	Press Command-U
Word Underline	Press Command-Shift-]
Font	Press Command-Shift-E, type font name, and then press Return

(continued)

Character formatting commands, continued

Font Size Up (1 point)	Press Command-]
Font Size Up (next largest standard size)	Press Command-Shift->
Font Size Down (1 point)	Press Command-[
Font Size Down (next smallest standard size)	Press Command-Shift-<
Symbol Font	Press Command-Shift-Q

Paragraph formatting commands

Normal	Press Command-Shift-P
Left-Aligned	Press Command-Shift-L
Right-Aligned	Press Command-Shift-R
Centered	Press Command-Shift-C
Justified	Press Command-Shift-J
Nest Paragraphs	Press Command-Shift-N
Unnest Paragraphs	Press Command-Shift-M
Hanging Indentation	Press Command-Shift-T
Double-Space	Press Command-Shift-Y
Open Space	Press Command-Shift-O
Apply Style	Press Command-Shift-S, type style name, and then press Return

Outline commands

Display in Outline view	Press Command-Option-O
Promote selection	Press Option-Left direction key
Demote selection	Press Option-Right direction key
Move selection up	Press Option-Up direction key
Move selection down	Press Option-Down direction key
Demote heading to body text	Press Command-Right direction key
Expand current heading	Press Option-Shift-Left direction key or plus on keypad
Collapse current heading and all subtext	Press Option-Shift-Right direction key or minus on keypad
Display all text	Press Option-Shift-Left direction key or asterisk on keypad
Display either first line only or all text	Press Option-Shift-Down direction key or equal sign on keypad
Display or hide character formatting	Press Option-Shift-Up direction key or equal sign on keypad

Dialog box commands

Choose current item	Press 0 on keypad
Cancel command	Press Esc or Command-period
Move to next option	Press Command-Tab or decimal point on keypad
Move to previous option	Press Command-Shift-Tab
Move to next edit bar	Press Tab
Move to previous edit bar	Press Shift-Tab
Move left or right in edit box	Press Left or Right direction key
Move up in list box	Press Up direction key
Move down in list box	Press Down direction key
Choose item directly	Press Command and first letter of option
Move up in folder hierarchy	Press Command-Up direction key
Move down in folder hierarchy	Press Command-Down direction key

Mouse shortcuts

Open Character dialog box	Double-click beside any button on ribbon
Open Paragraph dialog box	Double-click anywhere above scale line on ruler
Open Section dialog box	Double-click section mark in document
Open Document dialog box	Double-click any page corner in Page Layout view
Open Style dialog box	Double-click style name displayed at bottom of document window
Open Tabs dialog box	Double-click tab-stop marker on ruler
Open Go To dialog box	Double-click page number displayed in status bar at bottom of document window
Open Voice Annotation dialog box	Double-click voice annotation symbol
Open application in which embedded object was created	Double-click embedded object in Word document
Zoom or return window to original size	Double-click title bar
Split document window in half	Double-click split box at top of vertical scroll bar
Open Footnote window	Double-click automatically numbered footnote reference mark

B

ASCII Codes

Chapter 13, "Using Word Tools," describes Word's Symbol font and the Symbol command. Chapter 13 also shows you how to insert characters specified by a particular ASCII decimal code by selecting them in the Symbol window. This appendix presents the characters in the standard Macintosh fonts that correspond to each ASCII code. If you haven't installed the Symbol command that came with your Word software, you can add a letter or special character at the insertion point by pressing Command-Option-Q, typing the corresponding decimal code, and then pressing Return.

ASCII codes above 217 display the characters shown in this appendix only in Courier, Helvetica, and Times fonts. You can't reproduce any ASCII character codes above 217 in Chicago, New York, Monaco, or Geneva fonts.

ASCII Code	Character		ASCII Code	Character
6	\		73	I
9	✦	(Tab)	74	J
10		(Line feed)	75	K
11	↵	(End-of-line mark)	76	L
12		(Page-break mark)	77	M
13	¶	(Paragraph symbol)	78	N
30	≃	(Nonbreaking hyphen)	79	O
31	÷	(Optional hyphen)	80	P
32		(Blank space)	81	Q
33	!		82	R
34	"		83	S
35	#		84	T
36	$		85	U
37	%		86	V
38	&		87	W
39	'		88	X
40	(		89	Y
41	)		90	Z
42	*		91	[
43	+		92	\
44	,		93	]
45	-		94	^
46	.		95	_
47	/		96	'
48	0		97	a
49	1		98	b
50	2		99	c
51	3		100	d
52	4		101	e
53	5		102	f
54	6		103	g
55	7		104	h
56	8		105	i
57	9		106	j
58	:		107	k
59	;		108	l
60	<		109	m
61	=		110	n
62	>		111	o
63	?		112	p
64	@		113	q
65	A		114	r
66	B		115	s
67	C		116	t
68	D		117	u
69	E		118	v
70	F		119	w
71	G		120	x
72	H		121	y

(continued)

ASCII Code	Character	ASCII Code	Character
122	z	172	..
123	{	173	≠
124	|	174	Æ
125	}	175	Ø
126	~	176	∞
128	Ä	177	±
129	Å	178	≤
130	Ç	179	≥
131	É	180	¥
132	Ñ	181	µ
133	Ö	182	∂
134	Ü	183	Σ
135	á	184	Π
136	à	185	π
137	â	186	∫
138	ä	187	ª
139	ã	188	º
140	å	189	Ω
141	ç	190	æ
142	é	191	ø
143	è	192	¿
144	ê	193	¡
145	ë	194	¬
146	í	195	√
147	ì	196	ƒ
148	î	197	≈
149	ï	198	Δ
150	ñ	199	«
151	ó	200	»
152	ò	201	…
153	ô	202	(Hard space)
154	ö	203	Á
155	õ	204	Ã
156	ú	205	Õ
157	ù	206	Œ
158	û	207	œ
159	ü	208	–
160	†	209	—
161	°	210	"
162	¢	211	"
163	£	212	'
164	§	213	'
165	•	214	÷
166	¶	215	◊
167	ß	216	ÿ
168	®	217	Ÿ
169	©	218	/
170	™	219	¤
171	´	220	‹

(continued)

ASCII Code	Character	ASCII Code	Character
221	›	239	Ô
222	fi	240	
223	fl	241	Ò
224	‡	242	Ú
225	·	243	Û
226	‚	244	Ù
227	„	245	ı
228	‰	246	ˆ
229	Â	247	˜
230	Ê	248	¯
231	Á	249	˘
232	Ë	250	˙
233	È	251	˚
234	Í	252	
235	Î	253	˝
236	Ï	254	
237	Ì	255	ˇ
238	Ó		

C

Using PostScript Commands in Word

*P*ostScript is a powerful, flexible page-description language that tells PostScript printers how text, images, and graphics should appear on a printed page. First popularized by Apple's LaserWriter printer family, PostScript is now the computer industry's standard page-description language for desktop publishing.

Most applications that run on the Macintosh, including Microsoft Word, generate PostScript commands for your printer when you choose the Print command. These commands tell the printer how to form the characters and symbols that make up your document. If you want, however, you can embed PostScript commands in a document to control how printed text appears when you print the page on a PostScript printer.

This appendix shows you how to embed and format PostScript commands in a Word document and introduces the PostScript command groups and variables. This appendix does not explain the details of the PostScript programming language, however. It is intended as a reference for knowledgeable PostScript users who want to select PostScript commands from within Word.

PostScript basics

To embed a PostScript command in a Word document, first type the command text itself, and then apply the PostScript paragraph style to the command text to identify it as a command.

After you've entered all the necessary PostScript commands, choose Print to send the document to the printer. When the printer receives the document, it executes the PostScript commands, rather than printing the words that make up these commands.

You can print the results of the embedded PostScript commands on all Laser-Writer printers. Printing a document that contains PostScript commands on a non-PostScript printer generally prints only the document text; any PostScript commands defined in the document are ignored. In some cases, however, the printer produces several pages of gibberish.

An example

Suppose you want to embed the PostScript commands shown in Figure C-1, which print an outline of the word *Microsoft* at several rotations around a single point. First choose New from the File menu to open a new document, and then type the commands shown in Figure C-1. Note that the first line is the word *para* surrounded by two periods, not blank spaces. On the ninth line, the number 5 is also preceded by a period, not a blank space.

After entering the PostScript commands in the document, you assign the PostScript style to the commands. To do this, highlight the entire block of text that contains the commands, and choose Style from the Format menu to display the Style dialog box. If it's not currently selected, click the All Styles option in this dialog box, and then select the PostScript style. The formats for the PostScript style appear in the Style dialog box, as shown in Figure C-2.

The format for the PostScript style is *Normal + Font: 10 Point, Bold Hidden.* You can change the formatting instructions defined by this style, but the style must include hidden text. If you remove the Hidden format from the PostScript style definition, the LaserWriter prints your instructions instead of carrying them out.

FIGURE C-1.
We'll use the commands in this sample document to demonstrate the process of formatting and sending PostScript commands to a PostScript printer.

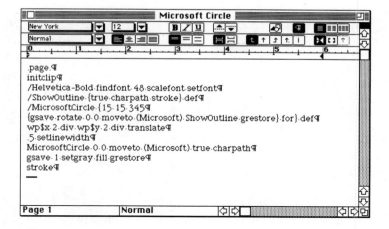

FIGURE C-2.
Select the PostScript style in the Style dialog box, and then click Apply to apply the style to the PostScript commands.

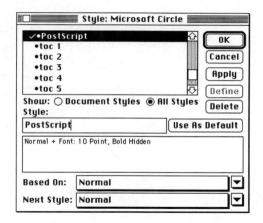

After you've selected the PostScript style, as we've done in Figure C-2, click Apply to apply the style to the currently selected text, and then click OK. Next, choose Print from the File menu, and click the Print button. Figure C-3 on the next page shows how the sample document appears when printed on an Apple Laser-Writer printer.

FIGURE C-3.
We created this page
by applying the
PostScript style to the
text in Figure C-1 and
then printing the
document on an Apple
LaserWriter printer.

PostScript coordinates

All PostScript printers draw within the bounds of an area called the *clipping path,* or the *clipping rectangle.* The lower-left corner of the clipping rectangle is called the *graphics origin.*

The coordinate system used by the PostScript language is different from Word's coordinate system. PostScript's graphics origin (0,0) initially lies in the lower-left corner of the page, and positive directions are to the right and up. Word's origin lies in the upper-left corner of the page, and positive directions are to the right and down. Always specify coordinates consistent with PostScript's coordinate system when you enter PostScript commands into a Word document.

Although the graphics origin is initially located in the lower-left corner of the page, you can change its position by specifying PostScript's translate command.

You can also change the size and shape of the clipping rectangle by using Post-Script's clip or initclip commands.

PostScript command groups

The PostScript commands you enter in Word are organized into groups. A group is made up of sequential paragraphs to which the PostScript style is assigned. Each time your PostScript printer encounters a group of PostScript commands, it saves and restores the state of the PostScript printer's virtual memory. For this reason, one group of PostScript commands cannot use the procedures or variables that have been defined by another group.

Each command group operates on its own clipping rectangle, and all the commands within a group operate on the same clipping rectangle. Five types of clipping rectangles are available: page, paragraph, picture, cell, and row. You can also define a dictionary group. You specify a clipping rectangle by typing a group command at the beginning of a paragraph and then applying the Post-Script style to the entire paragraph. Table C-1 indicates how each command defines the text that follows it.

Command	Defines
.page.	The clipping rectangle extends to the boundaries of the page that contains the first line of the next non-PostScript paragraph.
.para.	The clipping rectangle is the portion of the next non-PostScript paragraph that fits on the same page containing the first line of that paragraph. If the next non-PostScript paragraph doesn't fit on the current page, the clipping rectangle is bounded by the portion that lies on the current page.
.pic.	The clipping rectangle is the enclosing frame of the graphic (picture) in the next non-PostScript paragraph. If the next non-PostScript paragraph contains many graphic images, you can enter several .pic. commands. Each command applies to the corresponding graphic in the following paragraph.
.cell.	The clipping rectangle is the table cell that contains the PostScript command. You can use this command only in tables created with the Table commands on the Insert menu.
.row.	The clipping rectangle is the table row that contains the PostScript command. You can use this command only in tables created with the Table commands on the Insert menu.
.dict.	Use this command to create a PostScript group that contains definitions and procedures for a single page.

TABLE C-1.
These command groups define the clipping rectangle upon which the current group of commands operates.

A group command stays in effect until another group command or a non-PostScript paragraph appears in the document. If you don't specify a group command at the beginning of a PostScript group, the printer uses the entire page as the clipping rectangle (just as if you'd typed the .page. command).

Group variables

Word provides variables you can use in PostScript commands. Variables are values describing the current page or paragraph. Table C-2 lists the variables you can use in the .page., .para., and .pic. command groups. Table C-3 lists the variables you can use only in .page. command groups, and Table C-4 lists the variables you can use only in .para. command groups. Values returned by these variables

Variable	Defines
wp$box	Path containing the clipping rectangle
wp$x	Clipping rectangle width
wp$y	Clipping rectangle height
wp$xorig	Left edge of the clipping rectangle
wp$yorig	Bottom edge of the clipping rectangle
wp$fpage	String representing the current page number in the appropriate format (Arabic, Roman, or alphabetic)
wp$page	Current page number
wp$date	Current date string
wp$time	Current time string

TABLE C-2.
You can use these variables in either the .page., .para., or .pic. command groups.

Variable	Defines
wp$top	Top margin
wp$bottom	Bottom margin
wp$left	Left margin, including the gutter margin on facing pages
wp$right	Right margin, including the gutter margin on facing pages
wp$col	Number of columns (in the page's first paragraph)
wp$xcol	Width of each column (in the page's first paragraph)
wp$xcolb	Space between columns (in the page's first paragraph)

TABLE C-3.
You can use these variables in .page. command groups.

Variable	Defines
wp$top	Space before the paragraph (same as the Before setting in the Paragraph dialog box)
wp$bottom	Space after the paragraph (same as the After setting in the Paragraph dialog box)
wp$left	Amount of indentation from the left margin to the left indent
wp$right	Amount of indentation from the right margin to the right indent
wp$first	Amount of indentation from the right margin to the first indent
wp$style	Name of the style for the paragraph to which the PostScript style applies

TABLE C-4.
You can use these variables in .para. command groups.

are measured in points (the standard PostScript unit), except the variables returning the current page number, current date string, and current time string.

Commands to avoid

Because your PostScript printer prints the text and graphics in your Word document on the same page as the text and graphics generated by the document's PostScript commands, you shouldn't use any of the PostScript commands that reset the printer or the printer's PostScript environment. Avoid using these PostScript commands in your Word documents:

banddevice	initmatrix
copypage	nulldevice
framedevice	renderbands
grestoreall	showpage
initgraphics	

Additional information

Chapter 13, "Using Word Tools," introduces the Page Layout glossary, with which you can insert ready-to-use PostScript commands in a Word document to create graphics. Chapter 17, "Importing and Exporting Text and Graphics," shows you how to import encapsulated PostScript (EPS) graphics into Word.

For detailed information on PostScript programming, see the *PostScript Language Tutorial and Cookbook*, the *PostScript Language Program Design*, and the *PostScript Language Reference Manual*, all published by Addison-Wesley Publishing Company.

D

Using the Equation
Editor Program

*I*f you think all radicals are political activists, then you will probably never have occasion to use the Equation Editor program that comes with Word. However, if your line of work involves equations, you'll probably find the Equation Editor helpful (even if those equations don't include radicals). Chapter 13, "Using Word Tools," discusses the typesetting commands you use to create formulas and equations within a Word document. In addition to these commands, you can use the Equation Editor program to create equations and formulas that might otherwise require specialized typesetting. Although the Equation Editor is an independent program, if you are running System 7, you can use the Object command on the Insert menu to access this application directly from Word. After opening the Equation Editor, you create the equation in a window using a series of icon palettes. Embedding the completed equation in your Word document is as simple as closing this window.

Chapter 16, "Finding and Sharing Files," discusses object embedding in detail. In this appendix, we show you how to access the Equation Editor program from Word, how to create a simple equation in this program and then insert it in your document, and how to access the Equation Editor's detailed online help.

When you're familiar with these basics, you'll find it easy to use the Equation Editor to add equations to Word documents.

Accessing the Equation Editor

You can open the Equation Editor independently of Word and copy and paste elements you create in this program in your Word document. In fact, System 6 users must use this method. If you're running System 7, you'll probably find it even easier to access the program directly from Word, as long as you have enough memory to open both applications. (The Equation Editor requires at least 512 KB of RAM.)

You must have installed the Equation Editor on your hard drive to be able to access it from Word. (The Introduction shows you how to install the Word program and commands.)

To open the Equation Editor without closing Word, simply position the insertion point in your Word document where you want the equation to appear, and then choose Object from the Insert menu. Word displays the Insert Object dialog box shown in Figure D-1, which enables you to select the type of object you want to embed. (For more information about object embedding, see Chapter 16, "Finding and Sharing Files," which describes this dialog box and object embedding in detail.) Simply select Equation in the list box, and click OK.

FIGURE D-1.
Select Equation in the
Insert Object dialog
box, and click OK to
open the Equation
Editor from Word.

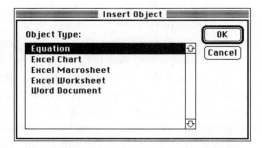

When you select Equation, the Equation Editor window appears over your Word document. The name *Word Object* and an identifying number appear in the window's title bar, as shown in Figure D-2.

FIGURE D-2.
The name Word
Object *and an*
identifying number
appear in the title bar
of the Equation Editor
window.

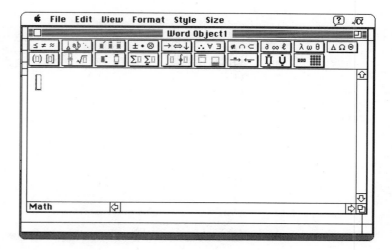

Creating and inserting an equation

As Figure D-2 indicates, the Equation Editor's own menu bar appears at the top of the Equation Editor window. The window itself has two sections. Icons at the top of the window enable you to select a formula template or a special character. The Equation Editor inserts your selection at the insertion point that appears immediately beneath these icons.

To select a formula template or character, first click the appropriate icon to display a drop-down palette of related choices. Hold down the mouse button, drag to highlight the template or character you want to insert, and then release the mouse button.

For example, clicking the second icon in the second row allows you to choose one of nine templates for creating a fraction or radical in the Equation Editor window. Selecting the template highlighted in Figure D-3 on the next page inserts the template for the equation at the insertion point and positions the cursor in one of the text fields indicated by a dimmed rectangle, as shown in Figure D-4, also on the next page.

You can combine formulas and symbols as necessary to create the equation you want. To enter keyboard characters in the fields in the template, simply select the field and type the text you want. To insert a mathematical character from a drop-down palette or another formula template, click the appropriate icon to display the palette, and then highlight the selection you want. Move from one field to another within an inserted template by clicking the field or by pressing the Tab key.

FIGURE D-3.
Display equation templates or characters by clicking the corresponding icon at the top of the Equation Editor window.

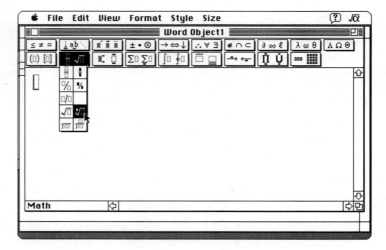

FIGURE D-4.
After you select a template or character, Word inserts it in the Equation Editor window.

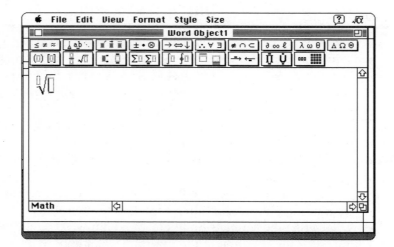

When you've finished the equation, choose Update from the File menu to insert the formula at the insertion point in your Word document without closing the Equation Editor window. Click the close box or choose Close from the File menu to insert the formula, close the Equation Editor window, and return to your Word document. (You cannot save an equation in an Equation Editor file.) System 6 users should first copy the equation, and then paste it in their Word document.

Figure D-5 shows a Word document into which we've inserted the equation whose template we selected in Figure D-3. After typing text to complete the equation, we clicked Update to insert it. By default, the Equation Editor sizes the new equation to match 12-point type. Word treats the equation—no matter what its contents—as a single graphic and places it in a frame at the insertion point.

FIGURE D-5.
Choosing Update,
Close, or Quit inserts
the equation in the
Word document.

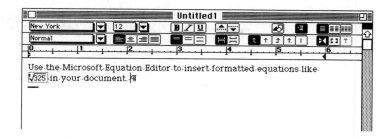

Modifying the equation

After you've inserted the equation in the Word document, you can modify the equation just as you would any information within a Word frame. You can, for example, crop the equation by clicking the frame to display its handles and then dragging the handles to their new positions. You can similarly change the size of the equation by holding down the Shift key as you drag the frame's handles to their new positions. You can also reposition the frame on the page by choosing the Frame command. (Chapter 6, "Creating Graphics," explains how to crop and scale the contents of a frame. Chapter 10, "Creating Professional Documents," describes the Frame command in detail.)

To change the formula itself, you have to return to the Equation Editor. System 7 users can simply double-click anywhere within the frame. Because you've embedded information about the Equation Editor program with the equation, Word opens the program and automatically inserts the framed formula in the Equation Editor window. After making the necessary changes, choose Update, Close, or Quit from the File menu to insert the updated equation in your Word document. System 6 users must first copy the equation in Word and then paste it back in the Equation Editor. After changes have been made, the equation can be copied and pasted back in the Word document.

Getting additional information

In addition to using the icons at the top of the Equation Editor window, you can also use keyboard shortcuts to insert templates for many formulas directly from the keyboard. Commands on the Equation Editor menus let you magnify the view of characters and symbols in the Equation Editor window, align equation elements precisely, and change the default font and point sizes applied to equation text. The Equation Editor comes with its own online help file, which explains the features in detail.

To display the Equation Editor's Help dialog box, choose Equation Editor Help from the Help menu at the far right of the screen. You'll see the initial Help dialog box shown in Figure D-6. Click a topic at the bottom of the Help dialog box to view additional information, and use the buttons on the right side of the dialog box to navigate through the Help file. Click Done to close the Help dialog box and return to the Equation Editor window.

FIGURE D-6.
*Choose Equation
Editor Help from the
Help menu to display
this Help dialog box.*

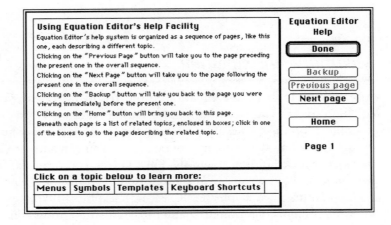

E

Voice Annotation

*I*f your Macintosh is equipped with a microphone, you can use the Voice Annotation command on the Insert menu to insert a recorded message anywhere in a document. If you're sharing information with another user, you can use this command to add a comment without typing a message or changing the current document layout. To record a voice annotation, you simply speak into the microphone attached to your Macintosh. When you've finished recording, Word inserts a speaker symbol in a frame at the insertion point to mark the annotation in the document.

Although you need a microphone to create a voice annotation, you can play back an annotation on any Macintosh that runs Word, by selecting the annotation's marker. You can also locate and listen to all the annotations in the current document by choosing Voice Annotations from the View menu.

Creating an annotation

To record an annotation, first highlight the text or position the insertion point at the place in your document where you want the annotation to appear. Next, choose Voice Annotation from the Insert menu to display the Voice Record dialog box shown in Figure E-1 on the next page. Use the Record, Stop, Pause, and Play buttons to record and play a voice annotation. As you record, the pie chart in the middle of the dialog box indicates the available time remaining. The Level meter in the lower-left corner indicates the recording volume. A menu bar at the top of the Voice Record dialog box enables you to get information about the annotation, save and edit the annotation, adjust sound quality and recording time, and specify recording preferences.

FIGURE E-1.
Choose Voice
Annotation from the
Insert menu to display
the Voice Record
dialog box.

Recording an annotation

The four buttons on the left side of the Voice Record dialog box function just like the corresponding buttons on a tape recorder: You click Record to begin recording, Stop to complete recording, Pause to temporarily halt recording, and Play to listen to the recording.

To record an annotation, click Record, and then speak into the microphone in a normal voice. As you speak, Word indicates the percentage of available recording time you have used by shading the circle in the middle of the dialog box. Immediately to the right of this circle, Word displays the total available recording time and the amount of disk space the recording requires.

The Level meter indicates the relative sound level. Annotations recorded at a level between 0.5 and 0.75 on the Level meter work best. If your recording level measures at the far right end of the meter, speak softer or move farther away from the microphone. If your recording level measures at the far left end of the meter, speak louder or move closer to the microphone. If the microphone you're using comes with its own volume control, adjust these controls as necessary.

To pause while you're recording, click Pause. Then click Pause again to resume recording. When you've finished your message, click Stop. Click Play to listen to the message, and click Stop to halt the playback. You can rerecord the message as often as you want.

Click Cancel to close the dialog box without inserting the current recording. Click OK to close the Voice Record dialog box and return to your document.

After you record an annotation, Word inserts a symbol like the one shown in Figure E-2 in a frame at the insertion point, formatting the symbol as hidden text so that it doesn't appear when you print. If you highlighted text before recording your annotation, brackets appear around the text to indicate that it is the annotated text. When you save your document, Word automatically saves the annotation as well.

FIGURE E-2.
Word marks the voice annotation in your document with a speaker symbol and formats the symbol as hidden text.

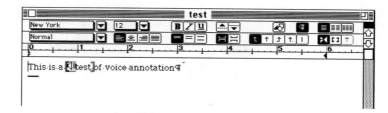

In addition to the annotation marker and brackets, Word records identifying information about the annotation to make it easy to locate later. Word assigns each annotation a number that indicates its current position in the sequence of annotations in the current document and uses the entry in the Your Initials edit bar of the General section of the Preferences dialog box to identify the person who created the annotation. Users can view this information by choosing Voice Annotations from the View menu. (For detailed information about the Preferences dialog box, see Chapter 18, "Customizing Word.")

Displaying device and sound information

If you want to find out more about the recording device currently in use on your Macintosh or about the current sound, you can display this information by selecting options from the ? menu in the Voice Record dialog box.

Display information about the recording device you're using by choosing Device Info from the ? menu. Word displays a dialog box like the one shown in Figure E-3 on the next page, which identifies the recording device and indicates the sample kilohertz rate and the compression ratio that corresponds to each of Word's three recording Quality options. The sample kilohertz rate measures the detail at which sounds are recorded. A higher rate produces better sound and requires more memory. The compression ratio measures the bytes of sound compressed to form a single byte of recording memory. A higher ratio increases available recording time and decreases recording quality. After viewing this information, click OK to close the dialog box.

If you've just recorded a message, you can display information about it by choosing Current Sound Info from the ? menu. Word displays a dialog box like the one shown in Figure E-4 on the next page, which identifies the current sound, indicates the kilohertz rate and the compression ratio at which the sound was recorded, and indicates its exact size and length. After viewing this information, click OK to close the dialog box.

FIGURE E-3.
Choose Device Info
from the ? menu to
display information
about the recording
device currently in use
on your Macintosh.

FIGURE E-4.
Choose Current Sound
Info from the ? menu
to display information
about the current
annotation.

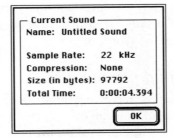

Specifying recording quality

As we explain more fully in a moment, when you choose Voice Annotations from the View menu, Word automatically tries to create a recording at the time and quality level specified in the Voice Record Preferences dialog box. Unless you change the default values in this dialog box, Word attempts to create a 10-second recording that uses the best possible sound. However, the actual amount of available recording time depends on how much random access memory (RAM) is available when you record. If you're using the Best quality option with 4 MB of RAM, you will often be able to create a recording that lasts only a few seconds. To increase the time available for the recording, choose an option from the Quality menu to decrease the quality of the sound. As you can see in Figure E-5, Word offers three Quality options: Best, Better, and Good. Although the recording Quality options are constant, the time available for the current annotation when you choose each option varies, depending on the RAM currently available. In Figure E-5, for example, choosing Best results in an annotation of up to 10 seconds; choosing Better results in an annotation of up to 30 seconds; and choosing Good results in an annotation of up to 60 seconds. After you choose the Quality option, Word confirms your selection by displaying the time available in the Voice Record dialog box.

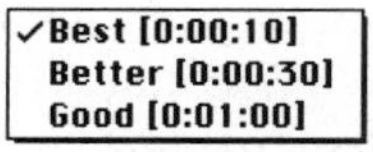

FIGURE E-5.
*Use these Quality
options to increase
your recording time.*

> ✓ **Best [0:00:10]**
> **Better [0:00:30]**
> **Good [0:01:00]**

Specifying recording preferences

The Preferences command on the Voice Record dialog box's Options menu enables you to specify the recording level and time you prefer. When Word opens the Voice Record dialog box, it tries to accommodate your specifications. If the amount of available memory is insufficient to create a recording at these levels, Word approaches them as best it can.

Figure E-6 shows the default Voice Record Preferences dialog box settings. To change the amount of time you want Word to try to provide, type a new value in the time edit bar. To change the recording level, click the current option, and select a new one from the drop-down list box of Quality options. Click the Longer Recordings check box to request longer recordings.

FIGURE E-6.
*The Voice Record
Preferences dialog box
lets you specify the
time and sound
quality you prefer.*

Saving sound files

As we've explained, when you click OK in the Voice Record dialog box, Word inserts the recording at the insertion point in the document. To save the annotation in the document, choose Save from Word's File menu or press Command-S.

Word also allows you to save annotations as individual sound files. If you frequently use the same annotation—for example, if you often insert a standard greeting or announcement at the beginning of an interoffice memo—saving an annotation as an independent sound file enables you to preserve and reproduce the annotation in different documents. You can also save sounds you create in Word for use in other applications. And you can open sound files created in other programs in Word and add the sounds to your Word documents.

You can save a new annotation or an annotation already inserted in your Word document as a separate sound file by choosing Save As from the Voice Record dialog box's File menu. Word then displays the Save Sound As dialog box shown in Figure E-7, which functions just like the dialog box that appears when you choose this command from Word's File menu.

FIGURE E-7.
Choose Save As from the Voice Record dialog box's File menu to display the Save Sound As dialog box.

Indicate where you want the file to be stored on disk, and type a name for the file in the Save Sound As edit bar. Leave the default Format option, Audio IFF, to save the sound file in Macintosh's standard Audio Interchange File Format. If you want to specify another file format, simply click the format name currently displayed to view the Format drop-down list box. Table E-1 presents the four formats in which you can save the sound file. After selecting the format you want, click the Save button.

Format	Result
SoundWave	Saves the sound in a format compatible with the Macintosh sound applications SoundWave and SoundEdit (FSSD file)
Audio IFF	Saves the sound in the Macintosh standard Audio Interchange File Format
Audio IFF-C	Saves the sound in a compressed Macintosh sound file in the Audio Interchange File Format
Resource	Saves the sound as an SND resource for storing sounds inside an application. If you select this format, also specify the application in the Save Sound As edit bar.

TABLE E-1.
You can save a voice annotation as a sound file in any of these formats.

Recording annotations without displaying the Voice Record dialog box

While you are familiarizing yourself with voice annotations, we recommend that you use the Voice Record dialog box to create annotations. As you become comfortable with the annotation recording process, you might prefer to record and insert messages in your document without displaying the Voice Record dialog box. Although this method allows you to record an annotation quickly, you lose the advantage of being able to select options from the dialog box.

To create a voice annotation without displaying the Voice Record dialog box, press the Option key as you choose Voice Annotation from the Insert menu. Word begins recording immediately and displays the message *Recording Voice* in the status box at the bottom of the document window. As you record, Word periodically displays the percentage of elapsed recording time in the status box.

Pressing Command-period stops recording and deactivates the Voice Annotation command. Word then inserts an annotation marker at the insertion point in your document.

You can also choose the Quick Record Voice Annotation command to record a voice annotation without displaying the Voice Record dialog box. Although Quick Record Voice Annotation doesn't appear on a Word menu, you can easily install it on the View menu by using the Commands dialog box. (For more information, see Chapter 18, "Customizing Word.")

Playing back annotations

You can play back any voice annotation in your Word document, even if your Macintosh isn't equipped with a microphone. To listen to a voice annotation, hold down the Option key, and double-click the annotation symbol in your document. Word highlights any text that was highlighted when the annotation was recorded, and plays the annotation.

(If the Show Hidden Text option in the View section of the Preferences dialog box is currently deactivated, you won't be able to see any annotation markers in your document. To activate the Show Hidden Text option, choose Preferences from the Tools menu, click the View icon on the left side of the dialog box, and then click the check box immediately to the left of this option. For more information, see Chapter 18, "Customizing Word.")

If you want to play back an annotation located in another part of the document, you can choose Voice Annotations from the View menu to display the Voice Annotations dialog box shown in Figure E-8 on the next page. This dialog box displays the size and length of the first annotation after the insertion point and identifies the annotation's creator. The bottom of the dialog box indicates the number

FIGURE E-8.
The Voice Annotations
dialog box displays
identifying
information about the
currently selected
annotation.

of the selected annotation and the total number of annotations in the current document. (Word takes the Annotator information from the Your Initials edit bar in the General section of the Preferences dialog box. For more information, see Chapter 18, "Customizing Word.") You can specify the number of the annotation you want to locate in the number edit bar, or use this dialog box to locate annotations as they appear in turn. Each time Word locates a voice annotation, it scrolls to the annotated text, highlights it, and then displays information about the current recording. Word locates annotation markers in your document even if the Show Hidden Text option in the Preferences dialog box is currently deactivated.

Specifying an annotation number

If you know the number of the annotation you want, choose Voice Annotations from the View menu, type the annotation number in the Number edit bar, and click Find. For example, to play back the second recording in your document, type 2 in the Number edit bar, and click Find. After Word locates the recording, click Play to play back the annotation.

Playing back voice annotations in sequence

To listen to voice annotations in sequence, beginning with the first annotation after the insertion point, click Play in the Voice Annotations dialog box to play back the first recording. When you're through listening to this annotation, click Next to move to the next annotation and display information about the recording in the dialog box. Click Play to play back the current annotation. If you don't want to listen to the current annotation, click Next to proceed to the next marker or Previous to go back to the previous marker. Click Cancel to close the Voice Annotations dialog box and return to your document.

Modifying annotations

After you add an annotation to your document, Word treats the annotation marker and its recorded message as a single element. To delete a recording, delete its marker by choosing Cut from Word's Edit menu or by pressing the Delete key. To copy or move a recording within the current document, simply select its annotation marker, and either choose the appropriate command or drag-and-drop the marker in its new location. You can also copy annotations to other Word documents. Copying annotations to a document created in applications other than Word reproduces the symbol without the Word frame.

To replace an annotation with a new recording, first select the annotation marker. Next, choose Edit Voice Annotation from the bottom of the Edit menu to display the Voice Record dialog box shown earlier in Figure E-1. (Edit Voice Annotation appears on the Edit menu only when an annotation marker is selected.) Choose Cut or Clear from the Edit menu in the Voice Record dialog box to delete the existing message. To create a new message, click Record to begin recording. To append a recording to the end of an existing one, click Record without choosing Cut or Clear.

Deleting and merging sound files

Use the Delete command on the Voice Record dialog box's File menu to delete previously saved sound files.

Use the Merge command to join sound files. Begin by opening the Voice Record dialog box for the sound to which you want to append another sound. Then choose Merge from the File menu, locate the sound file, and click Open. Word appends that sound file to the end of the current sound file.

Index

U–V

About the Author

Mark Nieker operates a technical writing business in Seattle, Washington, which specializes in Macintosh applications. He has taught at the University of Illinois and at the University of Washington. *Word 5 Companion* is his first book for Microsoft Press.

The manuscript for this book was prepared and submitted to Microsoft Press in electronic form. Text files were processed and formatted using Microsoft Word.

Principal word processor: Christina Smith
Principal proofreader: Polly Fox Urban
Principal typographer: Ruth Pettis
Interior text designer: Darcie Furlan
Principal illustrator: Lisa Sandburg
Cover color separator: Wescan Color Corporation

Text composition by Microsoft Press in Palatino with display type in Palatino Italic, using the Magna composition system and a Linotronic 300 laser imagesetter.

Printed on recycled paper stock.

Outstanding Resources on Microsoft® Excel

MICROSOFT® EXCEL FOR THE
APPLE® MACINTOSH® STEP BY STEP, 2nd ed.
Version 4
Microsoft Corporation

If you prefer the timesaving step-by-step approach to learning, MICROSOFT
EXCEL STEP BY STEP is the book-and-software package you need to get up and running
with Microsoft Excel 4. Learn to create useful, error-free spreadsheets the most effective
way—by combining self-paced lessons, disk-based practice files, and real-world
business examples. Become a spreadsheet expert the easy way!
325 pages, softcover with one 3¹/₂-inch disk $29.95 ($39.95 Canada)

COMPLETE GUIDE TO
MICROSOFT® EXCEL MACROS
Charles W. Kyd and Chris Kinata

This valuable and timesaving resource—for beginning to advanced users—is your
guide to unleashing the power of Microsoft Excel macros. Includes dozens of shortcuts,
tips, and case studies to make your work with macros easier and more productive. Learn
how to create simple function and command macros; debug, edit, and speed up your macros;
develop interactive macros; and more. A handy appendix includes listings of Microsoft
Excel's worksheet and macro functions by category and alphabetically.
Covers Microsoft Excel 3 for Windows and the Apple Macintosh.
480 pages, softcover $29.95 ($36.95 Canada)

MICROSOFT® EXCEL 4 COMPANION
The Cobb Group: Douglas Cobb and Judy Mynhier with
Craig Stinson, Mark Dodge, and Chris Kinata

Today's bestselling book on Microsoft Excel for the Macintosh is now updated to cover the
exciting new features of version 4. This is the most comprehensive tutorial and reference book
available for users of all levels—from novice spreadsheet users and Lotus 1-2-3 converts to
power spreadsheet users. Written in the friendly, easy-to-read style that is The Cobb Group's
hallmark, this book is packed with in-depth explanations, great examples, and expert advice.
950 pages, softcover $29.95 ($39.95 Canada)
Available June 1992

Microsoft Press books are available wherever quality computer books are sold.
*Or call **1-800-MSPRESS** for ordering information or placing credit card orders.**
*Please refer to **BBK** when placing your order. Prices subject to change.*

* In Canada, contact Macmillan Canada, Attn: Microsoft Press Dept., 164 Commander Blvd., Agincourt, Ontario, Canada M1S 3C7, or call (416) 293-8141.
In the U.K., contact Microsoft Press, 27 Wrights Lane, London W8 5TZ.

Make the Most of Your Macintosh®